D1393378

500 DELICIOUS DESSERTS

500 DELICIOUS DESSERTS

An incredible collection of tempting hot and cold ways to end
the meal, from simple classics to wickedly indulgent sweet treats

edited by ann kay

LORENZ BOOKS

This edition is published by Lorenz Books, an imprint of Anness Publishing Ltd,
Blaby Road, Wigston, Leicestershire LE18 4SE

www.lorenzbooks.com; www.annesspublishing.com

If you like the images in this book and would like to investigate using them for publishing, promotions or advertising,
please visit our website www.practicalpictures.com for more information.

Publisher: Joanna Lorenz
Editorial Director: Helen Sudell
Project Editor: Ann Kay
Copy Editor: Julia Canning
Design: Diane Pullen and Design Principals
Production Controller: Wendy Lawson

ETHICAL TRADING POLICY

Because of our ongoing ecological investment programme, you, as our customer, can have the pleasure and reassurance
of knowing that a tree is being cultivated on your behalf to naturally replace the materials used to make the book you
are holding. For further information about this scheme, go to www.annesspublishing.com/trees

© Anness Publishing Ltd 2005, 2011

All rights reserved. No part of this publication may be reproduced, stored in a retrieval system,
or transmitted in any way or by any means, electronic, mechanical, photocopying, recording or otherwise,
without the prior written permission of the copyright holder.

A CIP catalogue record for this book is available from the British Library.

Previously published as *500 Desserts*

NOTES
Bracketed terms are intended for American readers.
For all recipes, quantities are given in both metric and imperial measures and, where appropriate, in standard cups
and spoons. Follow one set of measures, but not a mixture, because they are not interchangeable.
Standard spoon and cup measures are level. 1 tsp = 5ml, 1 tbsp = 15ml, 1 cup = 250ml/8fl oz.
Australian standard tablespoons are 20ml. Australian readers should use 3 tsp in place of 1 tbsp for
measuring small quantities.
American pints are 16fl oz/2 cups. American readers should use 20fl oz/2.5 cups in place of 1 pint when
measuring liquids.
Electric oven temperatures in this book are for conventional ovens. When using a fan oven, the temperature will
probably need to be reduced by about 10–20°C/20–40°F. Since ovens vary, you should check with your manufacturer's
instruction book for guidance.
The nutritional analysis given for each recipe is calculated per portion (i.e. serving or item), unless otherwise stated. If the
recipe gives a range, such as Serves 4–6, then the nutritional analysis will be for the smaller portion size, i.e. 6 servings.
The analysis does not include optional ingredients, such as salt added to taste.
Medium (US large) eggs are used unless otherwise stated.
Pregnant women, the elderly, the ill and very young children should avoid recipes using raw or lightly cooked eggs.

Main front cover image shows Summer Berry Frozen Yogurt – for recipe, see page 48.

PUBLISHER'S NOTE
Although the advice and information in this book are believed to be accurate and true at the time of going to press,
neither the authors nor the publisher can accept any legal responsibility or liability for any errors or omissions that may
have been made nor for any inaccuracies nor for any loss, harm or injury that comes about from following instructions
or advice in this book.

Contents

Introduction

Desserts are always popular, whether they are sumptuous creations or the simplest of dishes. Indeed, a well-chosen dessert is guaranteed to round off a meal on a high note and can turn

even the most ordinary meal into a memorable occasion. As a finale, a mouthwatering fruit tart, a delicately flavoured ice cream or a luxurious chocolate treat will delight guests and give you, the cook, great satisfaction.

Whether you are planning an elaborate dinner party or an everyday family meal, the key to success is to make sure that the dessert you select balances perfectly with the main course. If you are serving a filling or rich main course you will need to choose a delicate or fruity option to follow, while you can afford to indulge in a rich, creamy dessert if you opt for a light main dish. With the fantastic selection of recipes featured in this book, you will never be at a loss for ideas to create a perfectly balanced menu.

The other factors that might affect your choice of dessert, such as seasonal availability and the amount of time you have for preparation, are also catered for in this collection. Many of the desserts can be made a day or two in advance, others can be started early in the day and finished off just before you eat, while frozen desserts and ice creams can be made weeks in advance, ready to serve whenever you need them. When entertaining, the more preparation

you can do ahead, the better, as this means that you will have time to enjoy the meal as much as your guests. However, there's also a wide choice of quick-to-make recipes that can be rustled up in a matter of minutes. In addition, whatever the season, you'll find a recipe to suit the time of year, and with the wide variety of tropical ingredients now available in the stores, there's a range of exciting dishes that will add an exotic flavour to your meals.

As a back-up to the recipes in this book, the introductory pages provide helpful information on preparing and baking pastry for pies and tarts, plus an invaluable guide to preparing fruit, from making perfect orange segments to creating delicate decorations. There are also ideas for easy dessert sauces to help you whip up instant desserts, plus clever presentation methods that will help you to achieve professional finishing touches. All the recipes in this book have clear, step-by-step instructions, so that even dishes that are commonly regarded as tricky, such as soufflés

and roulades, are easy to make and will look and taste delicious. The important thing is to read the whole recipe through before you start, so that you understand all the steps involved and can plan the preparation properly. A large number of recipes have helpful Cook's Tips and Variations boxes, offering advice on specific aspects of a dish or interesting alternatives to get your imagination going or to help out when you don't necessarily have all the specified ingredients to hand.

The recipe chapters feature over 500 tempting dishes, grouped under helpful categories such as Hot Desserts, Cold Desserts and International Flavours, as well as desserts reflecting our modern lives: Healthy Options and Quick & Easy. Popular classics feature alongside more unusual recipes that are destined to become new favourites. Most of the recipes have a full-colour photograph, showing clearly the kind of end result that you are aiming to achieve.

Have fun leafing through these pages at any time of year and for any occasion. For summer days you can't go wrong with a cooling Ginger and Kiwi Sorbet, while Sticky Toffee Pudding or exotic Fragrant Rice with Dates are warming choices for winter. Instant entertaining is provided by Passion Fruit Soufflés or Pistachio and Coffee Mascarpone Creams, but to pull out all the stops, impress guests with the unusual Luxury Dark Chocolate Ravioli. International classics range from Austrian Apple Strudel to Indian ice cream, and baked delights from Strawberry Roulade to Plum Crumble Pie. Whether you are a novice or an experienced chef, are in a hurry, on a budget, preparing a mid-week family meal or catering for a lavish or important event, this ultimate dessert collection will provide all the answers, and indulge every taste.

Working with Pastry

Making your own pastry may seem daunting at first, but if you follow a few basic rules and stick to the right quantities, you will soon find the technique easy. The key is not to hurry and to keep your hands cool when handling the dough. The crisp, light results are always worth the effort and the popularity of your home-made tarts and pies will be truly satisfying.

SHORTCRUST PASTRY

With shortcrust pastry and its variations, once the dough has been formed into a ball, it is usually chilled for about 20 minutes to make handling easier. After the pastry has been rolled out and used to line a tin (pan), it should be chilled again to minimize shrinkage during baking. A filled tart or pie needs only about 30 minutes otherwise the pastry will turn soggy. An empty shell, prior to blind baking, can be chilled for longer.

Heating the Oven

Whatever type of pastry you are baking, always allow time to preheat the oven; it will take about 15 minutes to reach the required temperature (fan ovens may heat more quickly). If you are baking blind or cooking a double-crust pie, it's a good idea to put a heavy baking sheet in the oven to heat up. The hot baking sheet will give the base of the pie an initial blast of heat to help keep the base crisp. It will also make it easier to slide the dish in and out of the oven.

Baking Shortcrust Pastry

Shortcrust pastries are usually baked at 200°C/400°F/Gas 6, but the temperature is often reduced part-way through baking to allow the filling to cook sufficiently. As a general rule, bake pastry in the middle of the oven, or just above the middle, unless the recipe tells you otherwise. Take care with pastries that contain added sugar; they should be removed from the oven as soon as they are golden, because they can burn quickly at this stage.

Baking Rules

When following a recipe, baking times may vary slightly depending on your oven and how chilled the pie was before cooking. Always check the pie at least 5 minutes before the end of the suggested cooking time. Don't keep opening the oven door though, or the temperature will drop and the pastry will not be as crisp. Avoid cooking the pastry with other foods that release a lot of steam as this also prevents a crisp result.

Baking Blind

This process is used for a number of reasons. It is used to partly cook an empty pastry case so that it does not become soggy when the filling is added and the final baking is done. It is also used to completely bake a pastry case when the filling cooks in a relatively short time and you need to ensure that the pastry is fully cooked through. The process is also required when the pastry case is to contain a precooked mixture or an uncooked filling. Lining the pastry case with baking parchment or foil and filling it with baking beans stops the pastry from rising up during cooking.

1 Cut out a round of baking parchment or foil about 7.5cm/3in larger than the flan tin (tart pan). Prick the base of the pastry all over with a fork.

2 Lay the baking parchment or foil in the pastry case and press it smoothly over the base and up the side.

3 Put either the commercially made ceramic baking beans, or dried beans or peas, in the case, spreading them out evenly to cover the base. Whichever kind you choose, they can be used over and over again.

4 To partially bake the pastry, bake in an oven preheated to 200°C/400°F/Gas 6 for 15 minutes, or until the pastry is set and the rim is dry and golden. Remove and lift out the paper and beans. Return the case to the oven for a further 5 minutes. The pastry case can now be filled and the baking completed.

5 For fully baked pastry, bake the case at 200°C/400°F/Gas 6 for 15 minutes, then remove the paper and beans and return to the oven. Bake for a further 5–10 minutes, or until golden brown. Cool completely before filling.

6 To bake tartlets, bake blind in the same way as flans, but allow only 6–8 minutes for partial baking, and 12–15 minutes for fully baked pastry.

Cook's Tip

Fully baked pastry cases, both large and small, may be baked up to two days ahead if carefully stored in airtight containers. Interleave them with greaseproof (waxed) paper, or use baking parchment, if you are keeping several, and always make sure that they are cooled before storing.

Cook's Tips

• When moving rolled-out pastry dough to line a tin (pan) or dish or top a pie, roll the dough loosely around the rolling pin, lift up, then carefully unroll it on top of the container. Press gently in place.

• If you find any small holes in a cooked pastry case, repair them by brushing with a little beaten egg, then return the case to the oven for 2–3 minutes to seal. Any larger holes or tears that appear during baking should be repaired by pressing a little raw pastry in the gap, brushing with beaten egg, and then returning to the oven.
• If the pastry starts to bubble up during baking, remove from the oven, prick again with a fork to allow the trapped air to escape and return to the oven. If it has bubbled up when you take it out after cooking, don't try to press it flat, or you will crack the pastry. Make a very small slit in the case with a knife and leave it to shrink back on its own.

• If the pastry becomes fully browned before the filling has cooked through completely, then you should protect it by covering with foil. Cover single- or double-crust pies completely, but make a hole in the top of the foil to allow the steam to escape. When baking open flans, cover the pastry edge only – by using strips of foil.

PUFF PASTRY

The baking method for puff, rough puff and flaky pastry has much in common with that used for shortcrust. Chilling the pastry before baking is essential, and shaped puff pastries should be chilled for at least an hour to prevent the pastry becoming mis-shapen during baking. Take great care when brushing the pastry with egg glaze; any that runs down the sides of the pastry will make the layers stick together and prevent the pastry from rising well and evenly.

Oven Temperature

This type of pastry must be cooked in a preheated hot oven, so that the air trapped within the layers expands and lifts up the pastry. If the oven is too cool, the butter will melt before the dough has a chance to cook, and the pastry will not rise well. The oven temperature is usually 230°C/450°F/Gas 8, but small pastries are sometimes cooked at 220°C/425°F/Gas 7. Reduce the temperature after about 15 minutes, to give the filling time to cook through.

Releasing Steam

When baking puff pastry pies, up to three slits or holes (depending how moist the filling is) should be made in the pastry top to allow the steam from the filling to escape. Don't make too many steam holes though, or too much air will be lost and the pastry won't rise well. After baking, cover steam holes with cooked pastry decorations.

Unlike shortcrust pastries, a steamy atmosphere helps the puff pastry to rise. Put a dish of hot water on the lowest shelf when preheating the oven. Remove it for the last few minutes of cooking. If the pastry starts to sink after cooking, it hasn't cooked sufficiently and should be returned to the oven for a little longer.

FILO PASTRY

Unlike shortcrust and puff pastries, filo pastry does not require chilling before baking. The most important point to remember is that filo must never dry out, or it will become brittle and hard to fold and shape. Keep the sheets you are not working with covered with a damp dish towel. It may also crumble if it is too cold so, before using, remove the unopened packet from the refrigerator and allow to stand for 1 hour.

Filo must always be lightly brushed with melted butter before baking to give it a shiny glaze; unsalted (sweet) butter is ideal because it has a lower water content than ordinary butter, or oil can also be used. Choose a mild-flavoured oil when making sweet pastries as you do not want the flavour of the oil to overpower delicate tastes. Be careful not to overdo the melted fat; it should be brushed as thinly and evenly as possible to create light crisp layers. Never brush filo with egg or milk as this would make it soggy.

Oven Temperature

The usual temperature for baking filo pastry is 200°C/400°F/Gas 6, although it can be cooked at a slightly lower temperature without its crisp texture being affected. Filo pastry colours very quickly, so always check frequently towards the end of the cooking time. If the pastry has browned sufficiently before the filling is cooked, cover it loosely with foil, then remove again for the last few minutes to make sure the top of the pie is dry and crisp.

Leftover Filo Pastry

Wrap any unused filo in clear film (plastic wrap) and return it to the refrigerator. It will keep for seven to ten days. It is possible to re-freeze filo, but don't do this more than once.

Preparing Fruit

Fresh fruit provides the perfect base for all manner of delicious and healthy desserts. To make the most of the different types of fruit, there are certain preparation techniques that will always be useful, whether you are making a fresh fruit salad or creating a more elaborate dessert. For professional results, just follow the step instructions below.

BUYING FRUIT

Obviously, the best time to buy fruit is when it is fully ripe and at its peak. The exceptions are fruits such as bananas and pears, which ripen quickly and can therefore be bought in an under-ripe condition and allowed to ripen fully at home. You are most likely to find top-quality fruits in markets and shops that have a quick turnover of fresh produce, preferably with a daily delivery. Although most fruits are now available almost all the year round, they are nearly always best and cheapest when in season in the country of origin. Only buy as much fruit as you need at one time so that it remains fresh and appetizing.

PREPARING FRUIT

For some fruits, the only preparation needed is washing or wiping with a damp cloth; others must be peeled, cored, stoned (pitted) or seeded. Wash fruit only just before using. If necessary, cut away any bruised or damaged parts.

Peeling Firm Fruit

Some firm fruits, such as eating apples and pears, can be served raw without peeling. For cooking, peeling is often necessary. Pare off the skin as thinly as possible to avoid losing the valuable nutrients under the skin.

I To peel fruit, first wash it and then pat it dry by using kitchen paper. Use a small, sharp paring knife or a vegetable peeler to pare off the skin in long, thin vertical strips all round the fruit, making sure that you cut into the fruit as thinly as possible. Pears in particular are best peeled by this method.

2 Alternatively, for apples, thinly peel all round the fruit in a spiral.

Coring Firm Fruit

I To core whole apples and pears, place the sharp edge of a corer over the stem end of the fruit.

2 Press the corer down firmly into the fruit, and then twist it slightly; the core, complete with all of the pips (seeds), should come away in the centre of the corer. Now push out the corer from the handle end to remove the complete core cleanly.

Cook's Tips

Storage methods depend on the type of fruit, but there are some basic guidelines:
• Do not wash fruit before storing, but only when ready to use.
• Store fruit at the bottom of the refrigerator or in the salad crisper.
• Do not refrigerate unripe fruit; keep it at room temperature or in a cool, dark place, depending on the variety.
• Fragile fruits such as summer berries are easily squashed during storage, so spread them out in a single layer on a tray lined with kitchen paper.

Segmenting Firm Fruit

I Halve the fruit lengthways, then cut into quarters or segments.

2 Now cut out the central core and pips using a small, sharp knife, taking care not to cut yourself as you work the knife towards you.

Cook's Tip

Some fruits, such as apples, pears and bananas, quickly oxidize and turn brown when exposed to the air. To prevent discoloration, brush cut fruits with lemon juice. Alternatively, acidulate a bowl of cold water by stirring in the juice of half a lemon. Drop the cut fruits into the bowl immediately after preparing.

Peeling Citrus Fruit

It is very important to remove all of the bitter white pith that lies just beneath the rind of citrus fruits.

1 To peel firm-skinned fruits, hold the fruit over a bowl to catch the juice and use a sharp knife to cut off the rind.

2 Alternatively, cut a slice off the top and bottom of the fruit, place on a board and, cutting downwards, slice off the rind in strips.

3 For loose-skinned fruit, such as tangerines, pierce the skin with your forefinger at the stalk end and peel off the rind. Pull off all the white shreds adhering to the fruit.

Segmenting Citrus Fruit

1 Using a small serrated knife, cut down between the membranes enclosing the segments; ease out the flesh.

Grating Citrus Fruit

1 For finely grated rind, grate the fruit against the fine face of a grater. Remove only the coloured rind; if you grate too deeply into the peel, you will be in danger of including the bitter white pith.

2 For thinly pared strips of rind, use a cannelle knife (zester) or vegetable peeler, then cut into shreds if necessary.

Decorating with Citrus Fruit

1 To make thick julienne strips of rind, cut lengthways, using a cannelle knife.

2 To make twists, slice the fruits thinly, cut to the centre, then twist the ends in opposite directions to make an S-shape.

Peeling Soft Fruit

Fruits such as peaches, nectarines and apricots can be peeled with a sharp paring knife, but this may waste some of the delicious flesh. It is better to loosen the skins by dipping them briefly in boiling water.

1 To remove the skins quickly and cleanly from peaches, nectarines and apricots, start by making a tiny nick in the skin, using the point of a sharp knife. This is done in order to help the skins spring off the flesh when the fruits are immersed in water. Take care when you are handling the soft fruit as the flesh can be easily damaged by clutching the fruit too firmly.

2 Cover with boiling water and leave for 15–30 seconds, depending on the ripeness of the fruit. Remove the fruit with a slotted spoon and peel off the skin, which should come away easily.

Removing Stones (Pits) and Seeds

1 Cut all round the fruit through the seam. Twist the halves in opposite directions, then lever out the stone (pit).

2 To pit cherries, simply place a cherry in a cherry stoner and then push the bar firmly into the fruit. The pit will be neatly ejected.

3 To remove the seeds from grapes, first cut the grapes in half, and then pick out the tiny pips using the tip of a small sharp knife.

4 To remove either papaya or melon seeds, you should first cut the fruit in half using a sharp knife, and then neatly scoop out all of the seeds with a spoon.

Dessert Sauces

Fresh custards and flavoured sweet white sauces are classic dessert sauces, but quick and easy dessert toppings can be made almost instantly from ready-made ingredients. These are ideal to serve over scoops of ice cream or with crêpes to create no-fuss desserts. Simple sauces can also be used imaginatively to create special finishing touches to desserts.

USING VANILLA PODS (BEANS)

Vanilla pods are often used in sweet dessert sauces – most commonly to flavour milk, cream or sugar.

Vanilla Infusions

1 To infuse (steep) vanilla flavour into milk or cream for a sauce, put the milk or cream in a pan, add the whole vanilla pod and heat gently over a low heat until almost boiling. Remove from the heat, cover and leave to stand for 10 minutes. Remove the pod, rinse and dry; it may be re-used several times.

2 To get maximum flavour, use a sharp knife to slit the pod lengthways, then open it out. Use the tip of the knife to scrape out the sticky black seeds inside: add to the hot sauce.

Vanilla Sugar

Many dessert sauces benefit from the delicate flavour of vanilla-flavoured sugar. This is available ready-made from shops but it is easy to make your own version.

1 To make vanilla sugar, simply bury a vanilla pod in a jar of white sugar. Cover tightly for a few weeks until the sugar takes on the vanilla flavour. Shake the jar occasionally.

SPEEDY SAUCES FOR TOPPING ICE CREAM

Store-cupboard (pantry) ingredients can often be transformed into irresistible sauces to spoon on top of ice cream.

Marshmallow Melt

1 Melt 90g/3½oz marshmallows with 30ml/2 tbsp milk or cream in a small pan. Add a little grated nutmeg and stir until smooth. Serve immediately.

Black Forest Sauce

1 Drain a can of black cherries, reserving the juice. Blend a little of the juice with a little arrowroot or cornflour (cornstarch).

2 Add the cornflour mixture to the rest of the juice in a pan. Stir until boiling and lightly thickened, then add the cherries and a dash of kirsch and heat through.

Raspberry Coulis

1 Purée some thawed frozen raspberries, with icing (confectioners') sugar to taste, then press through a sieve (strainer).

2 Blend a little cornflour (cornstarch) with some orange juice, and stir into the purée; cook for 2 minutes until thick. Cool.

Chocolate-Toffee Sauce

1 Chop a Mars bar and heat very gently in a pan, stirring until just melted. Spoon over scoops of vanilla ice cream and sprinkle with chopped nuts.

Marmalade Whisky Sauce

1 Heat 60ml/4 tbsp chunky marmalade in a pan with 30ml/2 tbsp whisky, until just melted. Allow to bubble for a few seconds then spoon over ice cream.

Nutty Butterscotch Sauce

1 Melt 75g/3oz/6 tbsp butter and 175g/6oz/¾ cup soft dark brown sugar in a heavy pan, then bring to the boil and boil for 2 minutes. Cool the mixture for 5 minutes.

2 Heat 175ml/6fl oz/¾ cup evaporated (unsweetened condensed) milk to just below boiling point, then gradually stir into the sugar mixture. Cook over a low heat for 2 minutes, stirring frequently.

3 Spread 50g/2oz/½ cup hazelnuts on a baking sheet and toast under a hot grill (broiler). Turn them on to a clean dish towel and rub off the skins. Chop the nuts roughly and stir into the sauce.

PRESENTATION IDEAS

When you've made a delicious sauce for a special dessert, why not make more of it by using it for decoration on the plate, too? Try one of the following simple ideas to make your sauce into a talking point. Individual slices of desserts, cakes or tarts, or a stuffed baked peach, look especially good served with sauce presented in this way.

Marbling

Use this technique when you have two contrasting sauces of a similar thickness, such as a fruit purée with cream or thin fresh custard.

I Spoon alternate spoonfuls of the two sauces on to a serving plate or shallow dish. Using a spoon, stir the sauces lightly together, gently swirling to create a marbled effect.

Yin-Yang Sauces

This oriental pattern is ideal for two contrasting colours of purée or coulis, such as a raspberry and a mango fruit coulis. It is important to make sure that the flavours of the sauce complement one another.

I Spoon a sauce on one side of a serving plate or shallow bowl. Add the second sauce to the other side, then gently push the two sauces together with the spoon, swirling one around the other, to make a yin-yang shape.

Drizzling

I Pour a smooth sauce or coulis into a container or tube with a fine pouring lip.

2 Drizzle the sauce in droplets or fine wavy lines on to the plate around the area where the dessert will sit.

Piping Outlines

I Spoon a small amount of fruit coulis or chocolate sauce into a piping (pastry) bag fitted with a plain writing nozzle.

2 Carefully pipe the outline of a simple shape on to a serving plate, then spoon in the same sauce to fill the space within the outline.

Feathering Hearts

I Flood the plate with a smooth sauce such as chocolate sauce or fruit purée. Add small droplets of pouring cream into it at intervals.

2 Draw the tip of a small knife through the droplets of cream, to drag each drop into a heart.

QUICK SAUCES FOR CRÊPES

Give crêpes and pancakes a lift with these three easy ideas.

Rich Butterscotch Sauce

I Heat 75g/3oz/6 tbsp butter, I75g/6oz/¾ cup soft light brown sugar and 30ml/2 tbsp golden (light corn) syrup in a pan over a low heat until melted.

2 Remove from the heat and add 75ml/5 tbsp double (heavy) cream, stirring constantly, until smooth.

Orange Caramel Sauce

I Melt 25g/1oz/2 tbsp unsalted (sweet) butter in a heavy pan. Stir in 50g/2oz/¼ cup caster (superfine) sugar and cook until golden brown.

2 Add the juice of 2 oranges and ½ lemon; stir until the caramel has dissolved.

Summer Berry Sauce

I Melt 25g/1oz/2 tbsp butter in a frying pan. Add 50g/2oz/¼ cup caster (superfine) sugar and cook until golden.

2 Add the juice of 2 oranges and the rind of ½ orange and cook until syrupy. Add 350g/12oz/3 cups mixed summer berries and warm through.

3 Add 45ml/3 tbsp orange-flavoured liqueur and set alight. Serve immediately.

Hot Ice Cream Fritters

Deep-fried ice cream may seem a contradiction in terms, but once you've made these crisp fritters, you'll be converted! The secret is to encase the ice cream thoroughly in two layers of sweet cookie crumbs. This will turn crisp and golden during frying, and the ice cream inside will melt only slightly.

Serves 4

750ml/1¼ pints/3 cups firm
  vanilla ice cream
115g/4oz amaretti
115g/4oz/2 cups fresh brown
  breadcrumbs
1 egg
45g/1¾oz/3 tbsp plain
  (all-purpose) flour
oil, for deep frying

For the caramel sauce
115g/4oz/generous ½ cup
  caster (superfine) sugar
150ml/¼ pint/⅔ cup water
150ml/¼ pint/⅔ cup double
  (heavy) cream

1 Line a baking sheet with baking parchment and put it in the freezer for 15 minutes, at the same time removing the ice cream from the freezer to soften slightly. Scoop about 12 balls of ice cream, making them as round as possible, and place them on the lined baking sheet. Freeze for at least 1 hour, until firm.

2 Meanwhile, put the amaretti in a strong plastic bag and crush with a rolling pin. Turn into a bowl and add the breadcrumbs. Mix well, and then transfer half the mixture to a plate. Beat the egg in a shallow dish. Sprinkle the flour on to a second plate.

3 Using cool hands, and working very quickly, roll each ice cream ball in the flour, then dip in the beaten egg until coated. Roll the balls in the mixed crumbs until completely covered. Return the coated ice cream balls to the baking sheet and freeze for at least 1 hour more.

4 Repeat the process, using the remaining flour, egg and mixed crumbs so that each ball has an additional coating. Return the ice cream balls to the freezer for at least 4 hours, preferably overnight, to firm up.

5 Make the sauce. Heat the sugar and water in a small, heavy pan, stirring occasionally, until the sugar has dissolved. Bring to the boil and boil the syrup for about 10 minutes without stirring until deep golden. Immediately immerse the base of the pan in a bowl of cold water to prevent the syrup from cooking any more.

6 Pour the cream into the syrup and return the pan to the heat. Stir until the sauce is smooth. Set aside while you fry the ice cream balls.

7 Pour oil into a heavy pan to a depth of 7.5cm/3in. Heat to 185°C/365°F or until a cube of bread added to the oil browns in 30 seconds. Add several of the ice cream balls and fry for about 1 minute until the coating on each is golden. Drain on kitchen paper and quickly cook the remainder in the same way. Serve the fritters with the caramel sauce.

Toasted Marzipan Parcels with Plums

Melting ice cream, encased in lightly toasted marzipan, makes an irresistible dessert for anyone who likes the flavour of almonds. Lightly poached apricots, cherries, apples or pears can be used instead of the plums.

Serves 4

400g/14oz golden marzipan
icing (confectioners') sugar, for
  dusting
250ml/8fl oz/1 cup almond,
  ginger or vanilla ice cream

For the plum compote
3 red plums, about 250g/9oz
25g/1oz/2 tbsp caster (superfine)
  sugar
75ml/5 tbsp water

1 Roll out the marzipan on a surface lightly dusted with sifted icing sugar to a 45 × 23cm/18 × 9in rectangle. Stamp out eight rounds using a plain 12cm/4½in cookie cutter.

2 Place a spoonful of the ice cream in the centre of one of the circles. Bring the marzipan up over the ice cream and press the edges together to completely encase it.

3 Crimp the edges with your fingers. Transfer to a small baking sheet and freeze. Fill and shape the remaining parcels in the same way and freeze overnight.

4 Make the plum compote. Cut the plums in half, remove the stones (pits), then cut each half into two wedges. Heat the sugar and water in a heavy pan, stirring occasionally, until the sugar has completely dissolved.

5 Add the plums and cook very gently for 5 minutes or until they have softened but retain their shape. Test with the tip of a sharp knife – the flesh of the plums should be just tender.

6 Preheat the grill (broiler) to high. Place the marzipan parcels on the grill rack and cook for 1–2 minutes, watching closely, until the crimped edge of the marzipan is lightly browned. Transfer the parcels to serving plates and serve with the warm plum compote.

Fritters Energy 1064Kcal/4453kJ; Protein 15.1g; Carbohydrate 121.6g, of which sugars 77g; Fat 58.6g, of which saturates 28.1g; Cholesterol 145mg; Calcium 319mg; Fibre 1.4g; Sodium 454mg.
Marzipan Parcels Energy 547Kcal/2307kJ; Protein 8g; Carbohydrate 92g, of which sugars 91.3g; Fat 18.1g, of which saturates 4.9g; Cholesterol 15mg; Calcium 140mg; Fibre 2.9g; Sodium 59mg.

Ice Cream with Hot Cherry Sauce

Hot cherry sauce transforms ice cream into a delicious dessert for any occasion. Serve immediately to ensure that the sauce is still warm to the taste.

Serves 4

425g/15oz can pitted black cherries in juice
10ml/2 tsp cornflour (cornstarch)
finely grated rind of 1 lemon, plus 10ml/2 tsp juice
15ml/1 tbsp caster (superfine) sugar
2.5ml/½ tsp ground cinnamon
30ml/2 tbsp brandy or kirsch (optional)
400ml/14fl oz/1⅔ cups dark (bittersweet) chocolate ice cream
400ml/14fl oz/1⅔ cups classic vanilla ice cream
drinking chocolate powder, for dusting

1 Drain the cherries, reserving the canned juice. Spoon the cornflour into a small pan and blend to a paste with a little of the reserved juice.

2 Stir in the remaining canned juice with the lemon rind and juice, sugar and cinnamon. Bring to the boil, stirring, until smooth and glossy.

3 Add the cherries, with the brandy or kirsch, if using. Stir gently, then cook for 1 minute.

4 Scoop the chocolate and vanilla ice cream into shallow dishes. Spoon the sauce around, dust with drinking chocolate powder and serve.

Variation
The hot cherry sauce also makes a delicious filling for pancakes. For a speedy dessert, use heated, ready-made sweet pancakes – just spread a little sauce in the centre of each pancake and fold into a triangle shape or roll up. Then arrange in a serving dish and spoon the rest of the sauce over the top. Finish with spoonfuls of thick yogurt or whipped cream.

Prune Beignets in Chocolate Sauce

Combining soft-textured prunes with a crisp batter coating works brilliantly! The rich chocolate sauce is the perfect finishing touch.

Serves 4

75g/3oz/⅔ cup plain (all-purpose) flour
45ml/3 tbsp ground almonds
45ml/3 tbsp oil or melted butter
1 egg white
60ml/4 tbsp water

oil, for deep frying
175g/6oz/1 cup ready-to-eat pitted prunes
45ml/3 tbsp vanilla sugar
15ml/1 tbsp cocoa powder (unsweetened)

For the sauce
200g/7oz milk chocolate, chopped into small pieces
120ml/4fl oz/½ cup crème fraîche
30ml/2 tbsp Armagnac or brandy

1 Make the sauce. Melt the chocolate in a bowl over a pan of hot water. Remove from the heat, stir in the crème fraîche until smooth, then add the Armagnac or brandy. Replace the bowl over the water, off the heat, so that the sauce stays warm.

2 Beat the flour, almonds, oil or butter and egg white in a bowl, then beat in enough of the water to make a thick batter.

3 Heat the oil for deep frying to 180°C/350°F or until a cube of dried bread browns in 30–45 seconds. Dip the prunes into the batter and fry a few at a time until the beignets rise to the surface and are golden brown. Remove each batch of beignets with a slotted spoon, drain on kitchen paper and keep hot.

4 Mix the vanilla sugar and cocoa in a bowl or stout paper bag, add the drained beignets and toss well to coat. Serve in individual bowls, with the chocolate sauce poured over the top.

Cook's Tip
Vanilla sugar is available from good food stores, but it's easy to make your own: simply store a vanilla pod in a jar of sugar for a few weeks until the sugar has taken on the vanilla flavour.

Ice Cream Energy 529Kcal/2213kJ; Protein 8.4g; Carbohydrate 59.5g, of which sugars 57g; Fat 30.2g, of which saturates 18.1g; Cholesterol 0mg; Calcium 218mg; Fibre 0.7g; Sodium 130mg.
Beignets Energy 727Kcal/3039kJ; Protein 11.3g; Carbohydrate 71.7g, of which sugars 56.5g; Fat 44.1g, of which saturates 24.2g; Cholesterol 69mg; Calcium 209mg; Fibre 4.8g; Sodium 176mg.

Ice Cream Bombes with Hot Sauce

These individual ice cream
bombes, with a surprise
vanilla and chocolate-chip
centre, are served with a
hot toffee cream sauce to
make a truly indulgent
dessert.

Serves 6
*1 litre/1¾ pints/4 cups soft-scoop
   chocolate ice cream*
*475ml/16fl oz/2 cups soft-scoop
   vanilla ice cream*
*50g/2oz/¹/₃ cup plain (semisweet)
   chocolate chips*
115g/4oz toffees
*75ml/5 tbsp double (heavy)
   cream*

1 Divide the chocolate ice cream equally among six small cups.
Push it roughly to the base and up the sides, leaving a small
cup-shaped dip in the middle. Put them in the freezer and leave
for 45 minutes. Take the cups out again and smooth the ice
cream in each to make cup shapes with hollow centres. Return
to the freezer.

2 Put the vanilla ice cream in a small bowl and break it up
slightly with a spoon. Stir in the chocolate chips and use this
mixture to fill the hollows in the cups of chocolate ice cream.
Smooth the tops, then cover the cups with clear film (plastic
wrap), return to the freezer and leave overnight.

3 Melt the toffees with the cream in a small pan over a very
low heat, stirring constantly until smooth, warm and creamy.

4 Turn out the bombes on to individual plates and pour the
toffee sauce over the top. Serve immediately.

> **Cook's Tips**
> • *To make it easier to unmould the bombes, dip them briefly in
> hot water, then turn out immediately on to serving plates. If you
> wish, you can return the unmoulded bombes to the freezer for
> about 10 minutes to firm up.*
> • *Serve with crisp little biscuits (cookies) for a crunchy contrast.*

Summer Berries in Warm Sabayon Glaze

This luxurious combination
of summer berries under a
light and fluffy alcoholic
sauce is lightly cooked to
form a crisp, caramelized
topping.

Serves 4
*450g/1lb/4 cups mixed summer
   berries, or soft fruit*
4 egg yolks
*50g/2oz/¹/₄ cup vanilla sugar or
   caster (superfine) sugar*
*120ml/4fl oz/¹/₂ cup orange
   liqueur, or a white dessert
   wine*
*a little icing (confectioners')
   sugar, sifted, and mint leaves,
   to decorate (optional)*

1 Arrange the fruit in four individual heatproof dishes. Preheat
the grill (broiler).

2 Whisk the egg yolks in a large heatproof bowl with the sugar
and liqueur or wine.

3 Place the bowl containing the egg yolks, sugar and liqueur or
wine over a pan of hot water and whisk constantly until the
mixture is thick, fluffy and pale.

4 Pour equal quantities of the sauce over the fruit in each
individual dish. Place under the grill for 1–2 minutes until just
turning brown.

5 Sprinkle the fruit with the icing sugar and scatter with mint
leaves just before serving, if using. Add an extra splash of
liqueur, if you wish.

> **Cook's Tip**
> *If you want to omit the alcohol, use a pure juice substitute such
> as grape, mango or apricot.*

Hot Mocha Rum Soufflés

These light-as-air individual soufflés, flavoured with cocoa and coffee, are ideal for serving after a fairly substantial main course.

Serves 6
25g/1oz/2 tbsp unsalted (sweet) butter, melted
65g/2½oz/9 tbsp cocoa powder (unsweetened)
75g/3oz/6 tbsp caster (superfine) sugar
60ml/4 tbsp made-up strong black coffee
30ml/2 tbsp dark rum
6 egg whites
icing (confectioners') sugar, for dusting

1 Preheat the oven to 190°C/375°F/Gas 5. Grease six 250ml/8fl oz/1 cup soufflé dishes with melted butter.

2 Mix 15ml/1 tbsp of the cocoa with 15ml/1 tbsp of the caster sugar in a bowl. Sprinkle the mixture into each of the dishes in turn, rotating them so that they are evenly coated.

3 Mix the remaining cocoa with the coffee and rum in a medium bowl.

4 Whisk the egg whites in a clean, grease-free bowl until they form firm peaks. Whisk in the remaining sugar. Stir a generous spoonful of the egg whites into the cocoa mixture to lighten it, then fold in the remaining whites.

5 Spoon the mixture into the prepared dishes, smoothing the tops. Place on a hot baking sheet, and bake for 12–15 minutes or until well risen. Serve immediately, dusted with icing sugar.

> **Cook's Tip**
> You can use either a hand whisk or an electric version to beat the egg whites, but take care not to overbeat with the electric beaters. The whites should stand in soft peaks, with the tips gently flopping over. Overbeaten eggs will look dry.

Chocolate & Orange Soufflé

The base in this hot soufflé is an easy-to-make semolina mixture, rather than the thick white sauce that many soufflés call for.

Serves 4
butter, for greasing
600ml/1 pint/2½ cups milk
50g/2oz/generous ⅓ cup semolina
50g/2oz/scant ¼ cup soft light brown sugar
grated rind of 1 orange
90ml/6 tbsp fresh orange juice
3 eggs, separated
75g/3oz plain (semisweet) chocolate, grated
icing (confectioners') sugar, for sprinkling
single (light) cream, to serve

1 Preheat the oven to 200°C/400°F/Gas 6. Butter a shallow 1.75 litre/3 pint/7½ cup ovenproof dish.

2 Pour the milk into a heavy pan, sprinkle over the semolina and sugar, then heat, stirring the mixture constantly, until boiling and thickened.

3 Remove the pan from the heat, beat in the orange rind and juice, egg yolks and all but 15ml/1 tbsp of the grated chocolate.

4 Whisk the egg whites until stiff, then lightly fold one-third into the semolina mixture. Fold in another third, followed by the remaining egg white. Spoon into the buttered dish and bake for about 30 minutes, until just set in the centre.

5 Sprinkle the soufflé with the reserved grated chocolate and the icing sugar, then serve immediately, with the cream handed around separately.

> **Variation**
> For a sophisticated touch, replace 30ml/2 tbsp of the orange juice with the same amount of orange-flavoured liqueur, such as Cointreau or Grand Marnier.

Rum Soufflés Energy 148Kcal/619kJ; Protein 5g; Carbohydrate 14.3g, of which sugars 13.1g; Fat 5.8g, of which saturates 3.6g; Cholesterol 9mg; Calcium 23mg; Fibre 1.3g; Sodium 190mg. **Choc. & Orange Soufflé** Energy 321Kcal/1353kJ; Protein 12.2g; Carbohydrate 43.7g, of which sugars 33.8g; Fat 12.2g, of which saturates 5.9g; Cholesterol 153mg; Calcium 219mg; Fibre 0.8g; Sodium 123mg.

Hot Chocolate Soufflés

These rich, individual chocolate soufflés have the merest hint of orange in them, and are divine with the white chocolate sauce poured into the middle.

Serves 6

butter, for greasing
45ml/3 tbsp caster (superfine) sugar, plus extra for dusting
175g/6oz plain (semisweet) chocolate, chopped
150g/5oz/10 tbsp unsalted (sweet) butter, cut into small pieces
4 large eggs, separated
30ml/2 tbsp orange liqueur (optional)
1.5ml/¼ tsp cream of tartar
icing sugar, for dusting

For the chocolate sauce
75g/3oz white chocolate, chopped
90ml/6 tbsp whipping cream
15–30ml/1–2 tbsp orange liqueur
grated rind of ½ orange

1 Generously butter six 150ml/¼ pint/⅔ cup ramekins. Sprinkle each with a little caster sugar and tap out any excess. Place the ramekins on a baking sheet.

2 Melt the chocolate and butter in a bowl placed over a pan of simmering water, stirring constantly. Remove from the heat and cool slightly, then beat in the egg yolks and orange liqueur, if using. Set aside, stirring occasionally.

3 Preheat the oven to 220°C/425°F/Gas 7. In a large, grease-free bowl, whisk the egg whites slowly until frothy. Add the cream of tartar, increase the speed and whisk until the whites form soft peaks. Gradually sprinkle over the caster sugar, 15ml/1 tbsp at a time, whisking until the whites become stiff and glossy.

4 Stir a third of the whites into the cooled chocolate mixture to lighten it, then pour the mixture over the remaining whites.

5 Gently fold the sauce into the whites, cutting down to the bottom, then along the sides and up to the top in a semicircular motion until the chocolate mixture and egg whites are just combined; don't worry about a few white streaks. Spoon the combined mixture into the prepared dishes.

6 Make the white chocolate sauce. Put the chopped white chocolate and the cream into a small pan. Place over a very low heat and warm, stirring constantly, until melted and smooth. Remove from the heat and stir in the liqueur and orange rind, then pour into a serving jug (pitcher) and keep warm.

7 Bake the soufflés in the preheated oven for 10–12 minutes until risen and set, but still slightly wobbly in the centre. Dust with icing sugar and serve immediately with the warm sauce.

> **Cook's Tip**
> These soufflés are ideal for serving at a dinner party because they can be prepared in advance, ready for baking at the last minute. Follow steps 1–5 above, then tightly cover the uncooked soufflés with clear film (plastic wrap). Set aside in a cool, but not cold, place until ready to cook.

Hot Blackberry & Apple Soufflés

The deliciously tart flavours of blackberry and apple complement each other perfectly to make a surprisingly low-fat dessert.

Serves 6

butter, for greasing
150g/5oz/¾ cup caster (superfine) sugar, plus extra for dusting
350g/12oz/3 cups fresh blackberries
1 large cooking apple, peeled and finely diced
grated rind and juice of 1 orange
3 egg whites
icing (confectioners') sugar, for dusting

1 Preheat the oven to 200°C/400°F/Gas 6. Generously grease six 150ml/¼ pint/⅔ cup individual soufflé dishes with butter and dust with sugar, shaking out the excess sugar.

2 Put a baking sheet in the oven to heat. Cook the blackberries, diced apple and orange rind and juice in a pan for 10 minutes or until the apple has pulped down well. Press through a sieve (strainer) into a bowl. Stir in 50g/2oz/¼ cup of the sugar. Cool.

3 Put a spoonful of the fruit purée into each prepared dish and smooth the surface. Set the dishes aside.

4 Whisk the egg whites in a large grease-free bowl until they form stiff peaks. Very gradually whisk in the remaining sugar to make a stiff, glossy meringue mixture. Fold in the remaining fruit purée and spoon into the prepared dishes. Level the tops.

5 Place the dishes on the hot baking sheet and bake for 10–15 minutes until the soufflés have risen well and are lightly browned. Dust the tops with icing sugar and serve immediately.

> **Cook's Tip**
> Run a table knife around the inside edge of the soufflé dishes before baking to help the soufflés rise evenly without sticking to the rim of the dish.

Blackberry & Apple Soufflés Energy 123Kcal/522kJ; Protein 2.1g; Carbohydrate 30.1g, of which sugars 30.1g; Fat 0.1g, of which saturates 0g; Cholesterol 0mg; Calcium 38mg; Fibre 2g; Sodium 33mg.
Chocolate Soufflés Energy 543Kcal/2257kJ; Protein 7.1g; Carbohydrate 35g, of which sugars 34.8g; Fat 42.3g, of which saturates 25g; Cholesterol 198mg; Calcium 80mg; Fibre 0.7g; Sodium 218mg.

Amaretto Soufflé

A mouthwatering soufflé
with more than a hint of
Amaretto liqueur.

Serves 6
butter, for greasing
90g/3½oz/½ cup caster
  (superfine) sugar
6 amaretti, coarsely crushed, plus
  extra for dusting

90ml/6 tbsp Amaretto liqueur
4 eggs, separated, plus 1 egg white
30ml/2 tbsp plain (all-purpose)
  flour
250ml/8fl oz/1 cup milk
pinch of cream of tartar
icing (confectioners') sugar, for
  dusting

1 Preheat the oven to 200°C/400°F/Gas 6. Butter a 1.5 litre/
2½ pint/6¼ cup soufflé dish and sprinkle it with a little sugar.

2 Put the amaretti in a bowl. Sprinkle them with 30ml/2 tbsp of
the Amaretto liqueur and set aside. In another bowl, carefully
mix together the 4 egg yolks, 30ml/2 tbsp of the sugar and all
of the flour.

3 Heat the milk just to the boil in a heavy pan. Gradually add
the hot milk to the egg mixture, stirring. Pour the mixture
back into the pan. Set over a low heat and simmer gently for
3–4 minutes or until thickened, stirring occasionally. Add the
remaining Amaretto liqueur. Remove from the heat.

4 In a clean, grease-free bowl, whisk the 5 egg whites until they
will hold soft peaks. Add the cream of tartar as soon as the
whites are frothy. Add the remaining sugar and continue
whisking until stiff.

5 Add about one-quarter of the whites to the liqueur mixture
and stir in. Add the remaining whites and fold in gently. Spoon
half of the mixture into the prepared soufflé dish. Cover with a
layer of the moistened amaretti, then spoon the remaining
soufflé mixture on top.

6 Bake for 20 minutes or until the soufflé is risen and lightly
browned. Sprinkle with sifted icing sugar and serve immediately.

Pears in Chocolate Fudge Blankets

Warm poached pears coated
in a rich chocolate fudge
sauce – who could resist?

Serves 6
6 ripe eating pears
30ml/2 tbsp fresh lemon juice
75g/3oz/6 tbsp caster
  (superfine) sugar
300ml/½ pint/1¼ cups water
1 cinnamon stick

For the sauce
200ml/7fl oz/scant 1 cup double
  (heavy) cream
150g/5oz/scant 1 cup light
  muscovado (brown) sugar
25g/1oz/2 tbsp unsalted (sweet)
  butter
60ml/4 tbsp golden (light corn)
  syrup
120ml/4fl oz/½ cup milk
200g/7oz plain (semisweet)
  chocolate, broken into squares

1 Peel the pears thinly, leaving the stalks on. Scoop out the
cores from the base. Brush the cut surfaces with lemon juice to
prevent browning.

2 Place the sugar and water in a large pan. Heat gently until the
sugar dissolves. Add the pears and cinnamon stick with any
remaining lemon juice, and, if necessary, a little more water, so
that the pears are almost covered.

3 Bring to the boil, then lower the heat, cover the pan and
simmer the pears gently for 15–20 minutes.

4 Meanwhile, make the sauce. Place the cream, sugar, butter,
golden syrup and milk in a heavy pan. Heat gently until the
sugar has dissolved and the butter and syrup have melted, then
bring to the boil. Boil, stirring constantly, for about 5 minutes or
until thick and smooth.

5 Remove the pan from the heat and stir in the chocolate, a
few squares at a time, stirring until it has all melted.

6 Using a slotted spoon, transfer the poached pears to a dish.
Keep hot. Boil the syrup rapidly to reduce to 45–60ml/3–4 tbsp.
Remove the cinnamon stick and gently stir the syrup into the
chocolate sauce. Serve the pears with the sauce spooned over.

Amaretto Soufflé Energy 222Kcal/936kJ; Protein 7.1g; Carbohydrate 33g, of which sugars 25.6g; Fat 5.6g, of which saturates 2g; Cholesterol 129mg; Calcium 96mg; Fibre 0.3g; Sodium 105mg.
Pears in Blankets Energy 613Kcal/2570kJ; Protein 3.6g; Carbohydrate 84.8g, of which sugars 84.5g; Fat 31.2g, of which saturates 19.1g; Cholesterol 58mg; Calcium 90mg; Fibre 4.1g; Sodium 77mg.

Citrus & Caramel Custards

These are wonderfully smooth and delicious custards – delicately scented and enhanced with aromatic cinnamon and tangy citrus flavours.

Serves 4
450ml/¾ pint/scant 2 cups milk
150ml/¼ pint/⅔ cup single (light) cream

1 cinnamon stick, broken in half
thinly pared rind of ½ lemon
thinly pared rind of ½ orange
4 egg yolks
5ml/1 tsp cornflour (cornstarch)
40g/1½oz/3 tbsp caster (superfine) sugar
grated rind of ½ lemon
grated rind of ½ orange
icing (confectioners') sugar, to dust

1 Place the milk and cream in a heavy pan. Add the cinnamon stick halves and the strips of pared lemon and orange rind.

2 Bring this milk to the boil, then reduce the heat and simmer for 10 minutes. Preheat the oven to 160°C/325°F/Gas 3.

3 Whisk the egg yolks, cornflour and sugar together. Remove the citrus fruit rinds and cinnamon from the hot milk and cream and discard. Whisk the hot milk and cream into the egg yolk mixture.

4 Add the grated citrus rind to the custard mixture and stir through. Pour into four individual dishes, each measuring 13cm/5in in diameter.

5 Place in a roasting pan and pour warm water into the pan to reach three-quarters of the way up the sides.

6 Bake for about 25 minutes, or until the caramel custards are just set. Remove all of the dishes from the pan of water and set them aside to cool thoroughly. Once cool, chill the custards in the refrigerator.

7 Preheat the grill (broiler) to high. Sprinkle the custards liberally with icing sugar and place under the grill until the tops turn golden brown and caramelize.

Coconut Pancakes

These light and sweet pancakes are often served in the streets of Bangkok and they make a delightful dessert.

Makes 8
75g/3oz/⅔ cup plain (all-purpose) flour, sifted
50g/2oz/¼ cup rice flour

40g/1½oz caster (superfine) sugar
50g/2oz/⅔ cup desiccated (dry unsweetened shredded) coconut
1 egg
275ml/9fl oz/generous 1 cup coconut milk
vegetable oil, for frying
lime wedges and maple syrup, to serve

1 Place the plain flour, rice flour, sugar and coconut in a bowl, stir to mix and then make a small well in the centre. Break the egg into the well and pour in the coconut milk.

2 With a whisk or fork, beat the egg into the coconut milk and then gradually incorporate the surrounding dry ingredients, whisking constantly until the mixture forms a batter. The mixture will not be entirely smooth, because of the coconut, but there shouldn't be any large lumps.

3 Heat a little oil in a 13cm/5in non-stick frying pan. Pour in about 45ml/3 tbsp of the mixture and quickly spread to a thin layer with the back of a spoon. Cook over a high heat for about 30–60 seconds, until bubbles appear on the surface of the pancake, then turn it over with a spatula and cook the other side until golden.

4 Slide the pancake on to a plate and keep warm in a very low oven. Make more pancakes in the same way. Serve warm with lime wedges for squeezing and maple syrup for drizzling.

Cook's Tip
Although maple syrup is not a typical Thai ingredient, it is an international favourite for serving with pancakes and tastes very good with these ones. Buy the pure syrup for the best flavour.

Citrus Custards Energy 229Kcal/958kJ; Protein 8g; Carbohydrate 17.7g, of which sugars 16.6g; Fat 14.6g, of which saturates 7.3g; Cholesterol 229mg; Calcium 197mg; Fibre 0g; Sodium 70mg.
Coconut Pancakes Energy 136Kcal/572kJ; Protein 2.6g; Carbohydrate 21.3g, of which sugars 8.1g; Fat 4.9g, of which saturates 3.6g; Cholesterol 24mg; Calcium 33mg; Fibre 1.3g; Sodium 49mg.

Chocolate & Orange Scotch Pancakes

Fabulous mini pancakes in a rich orange liqueur sauce.

Serves 4

115g/4oz/1 cup self-raising (self-rising) flour
30ml/2 tbsp cocoa powder (unsweetened)
2 eggs
50g/2oz plain (semisweet) chocolate, broken into squares
200ml/7fl oz/scant 1 cup milk
finely grated rind of 1 orange
30ml/2 tbsp orange juice
butter or oil, for frying
60ml/4 tbsp chocolate curls, to decorate

For the sauce

2 large oranges
25g/1oz/2 tbsp unsalted (sweet) butter
40g/1½oz/3 tbsp light muscovado (brown) sugar
250ml/8fl oz/1 cup crème fraîche
30ml/2 tbsp orange liqueur

1 Sift the flour and cocoa into a bowl and make a well in the centre. Add the eggs and beat well, gradually incorporating the surrounding dry ingredients to make a smooth batter.

2 Mix the chocolate and milk in a heavy pan. Heat gently until the chocolate has melted, then beat into the batter until smooth and bubbly. Stir in the grated orange rind and juice.

3 Heat a large heavy frying pan or griddle. Grease with a little butter or oil. Drop large spoonfuls of batter on to the hot surface. Cook over a moderate heat. When the pancakes are lightly browned underneath and bubbling on top, flip them over to cook the other side. Slide on to a plate and keep hot, then make more in the same way.

4 Make the sauce. Grate the rind of 1 of the oranges into a bowl and set aside. Peel both oranges, taking care to remove all the pith, then slice the flesh fairly thinly. Heat the butter and sugar in a wide, shallow pan over a low heat, stirring until the sugar dissolves. Stir in the crème fraîche and heat gently.

5 Add the pancakes and orange slices to the sauce, heat gently for 1–2 minutes, then spoon on the liqueur. Sprinkle with the reserved orange rind. Scatter over chocolate curls and serve.

Chocolate Crêpes with Plums & Port

The crêpes, filling and sauce can be made in advance and assembled at the last minute.

Serves 6

50g/2oz plain (semisweet) chocolate, broken into squares
200ml/7fl oz/scant 1 cup milk
120ml/4fl oz/½ cup single (light) cream
30ml/2 tbsp cocoa powder (unsweetened)
115g/4oz/1 cup plain (all-purpose) flour
2 eggs

For the filling

500g/1¼lb red or golden plums
50g/2oz/¼ cup caster (superfine) sugar
30ml/2 tbsp water
30ml/2 tbsp port
oil, for frying
175g/6oz/¾ cup crème fraîche

For the sauce

150g/5oz plain (semisweet) chocolate, broken into squares
175ml/6fl oz/¾ cup double (heavy) cream
30ml/2 tbsp port

1 Place the chocolate and milk in a heavy pan. Heat gently until the chocolate dissolves. Pour into a blender or food processor and add the cream, cocoa, flour and eggs. Process until smooth. Turn into a jug (pitcher) and chill for 30 minutes.

2 Meanwhile, make the filling. Halve and stone (pit) the plums. Place in a pan with the sugar and water. Bring to the boil, then lower the heat, cover and simmer for about 10 minutes or until the plums are tender. Stir in the port and simmer for a further 30 seconds. Remove from the heat and keep warm.

3 Have ready a sheet of baking parchment. Heat a crêpe pan, grease lightly with a little oil, then pour in just enough batter to cover the base of the pan, swirling to coat it evenly. Cook until the crêpe has set, then flip it over to cook the other side. Slide on to the paper, then cook 9–11 more crêpes in the same way.

4 Make the sauce. Put the chocolate and cream in a pan. Heat gently, stirring until smooth. Add the port and stir for 1 minute.

5 Divide the plums between the crêpes, add a dollop of crème fraîche to each and roll up. Serve with the sauce spooned over.

Choc. Pancakes Energy 752Kcal/3131kJ; Protein 12.1g; Carbohydrate 58.1g, of which sugars 35.5g; Fat 53.2g, of which saturates 27g; Cholesterol 185mg; Calcium 282mg; Fibre 3.9g; Sodium 304mg.
Choc. Crêpes Energy 867Kcal/3604kJ; Protein 10.6g; Carbohydrate 57.4g, of which sugars 41.7g; Fat 67g, of which saturates 36.7g; Cholesterol 184mg; Calcium 175mg; Fibre 3.4g; Sodium 115mg.

Chocolate Chip Banana Pancakes

These tasty little morsels will go down well with both adults and children alike.

Makes 16
2 ripe bananas
2 eggs
200ml/7fl oz/scant 1 cup milk
150g/5oz/1¼ cups self-raising
 (self-rising) flour, sifted
25g/1oz/⅓ cup ground almonds
15g/½oz/1 tbsp caster
 (superfine) sugar

pinch of salt
15ml/1 tbsp plain (semisweet)
 chocolate chips
butter, for frying
50g/2oz/½ cup toasted flaked
 (sliced) almonds

For the topping
150ml/¼ pint/⅔ cup double
 (heavy) cream
15g/½oz/1 tbsp icing
 (confectioners') sugar

1 Mash the bananas in a bowl. Beat in the eggs and half the milk. Mix in the flour, ground almonds, sugar and salt. Add the remaining milk and the chocolate chips.

2 Stir the mixture well until it makes a thick batter. Heat a knob (pat) of butter in a non-stick frying pan. Spoon the pancake mixture into the pan in heaps, allowing room for them to spread. When the pancakes are lightly browned underneath and bubbling on top, flip them over to cook the other side. Slide on to a plate and keep hot. Make more pancakes in the same way.

3 Make the topping. Pour the cream into a bowl. Add the icing sugar to sweeten it slightly, and whip to soft peaks. Spoon the cream on to the pancakes and decorate with flaked almonds. Serve immediately.

Cook's Tips
• To toast flaked (sliced) almonds, simply put under the grill (broiler) for a few minutes, shaking the pan, until lightly golden.
• You could add sliced banana, tossed in lemon juice, to the topping to enhance the banana flavour of the pancakes. If you prefer, use yogurt as a low-fat alternative to cream.

Chocolate Amaretti Peaches

A delicious dish of peaches stuffed with chocolate. This is a simple dessert but nonetheless one that is simply bursting with Italian style and flavour.

Serves 4
115g/4oz amaretti, crushed
50g/2oz plain (semisweet)
 chocolate, chopped

finely grated rind of ½ orange
15ml/1 tbsp clear honey
1.5ml/¼ tsp ground cinnamon
1 egg white, lightly beaten
4 firm ripe peaches
150ml/¼ pint/⅔ cup white
 wine
15g/½oz/1 tbsp caster
 (superfine) sugar
whipped cream, to serve

1 Preheat the oven to 190°C/375°F/Gas 5. Mix together the crushed amaretti, chopped chocolate, orange rind, honey and cinnamon in a bowl. Add the beaten egg white and mix to bind the mixture.

2 Halve the peaches, remove the stones (pits) and fill the cavities with the chocolate mixture, mounding it up slightly.

3 Arrange the stuffed peaches in a lightly buttered, shallow ovenproof dish that will just hold the peaches comfortably.

4 Mix the wine and sugar in a jug (pitcher). Pour the wine mixture around the peaches.

5 Bake the peaches for 30–40 minutes, or until the peaches are tender when tested with a metal skewer and the filling has turned a golden colour.

6 Serve immediately with a little cooking juice spooned over. Accompany with cream.

Cook's Tip
• To stone (pit) peaches, halve them and twist the two halves apart, then lever out the stone (pit) with the point of a knife.

Choc. Pancakes Energy 192Kcal/798kJ; Protein 3.4g; Carbohydrate 13.7g, of which sugars 6.3g; Fat 14.1g, of which saturates 7.1g; Cholesterol 51mg; Calcium 70mg; Fibre 0.8g; Sodium 89mg.
Choc. Amar. Peaches Energy 282Kcal/1190kJ; Protein 4.1g; Carbohydrate 47g, of which sugars 34.4g; Fat 7.4g, of which saturates 3.8g; Cholesterol 1mg; Calcium 56mg; Fibre 2.4g; Sodium 117mg.

Baked Apples with Apricot Filling

Baked apples of all kinds have long been a top favourite. Here, this popular classic has been given a new twist with a refreshing apricot-flavoured filling.

Serves 6

75g/3oz/scant ½ cup chopped, ready-to-eat dried apricots

50g/2oz/½ cup chopped walnuts
5ml/1 tsp finely grated lemon rind
2.5ml/½ tsp ground cinnamon
90g/3½oz/½ cup soft light brown sugar
25g/1oz/2 tbsp butter, at room temperature
6 large eating apples
15ml/1 tbsp melted butter
natural (plain) yogurt, to serve

1 Preheat the oven to 190°C/375°F/Gas 5. Place the apricots, walnuts, lemon rind and cinnamon in a bowl. Add the sugar and butter and stir until thoroughly mixed.

2 Core the apples, without cutting all the way through to the base. Peel the top of each apple and then slightly widen the top of each opening to make room for the filling.

3 Spoon the filling into the apples, packing it down lightly.

4 Place the stuffed apples in an ovenproof dish large enough to hold them all comfortably side by side.

5 Brush the apples with the melted butter, then bake for 45–50 minutes, until they are tender. Serve hot, topped with spoonfuls of yogurt.

Cook's Tips

• You can also use traditionally dried apricots for the filling, but they should be rehydrated first. Leave them to soak in warm water for 30 minutes or, for extra flavour, in dry white wine for 2 hours. Drain, squeeze out gently and chop.
• The easiest way to chop nuts is in a food processor or blender. Add 5ml/1 tsp of the sugar to stop them from sticking.

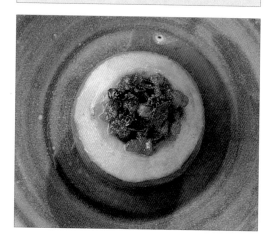

Baked Apples with Caramel Sauce

A creamy caramel sauce transforms an old favourite.

Serves 6

3 green dessert apples, cored but not peeled
3 red dessert apples, cored but not peeled
175ml/6fl oz/¾ cup water
150g/5oz/¾ cup light brown sugar
2.5ml/½ tsp grated nutmeg

1.5ml/¼ tsp ground black pepper
40g/1½oz/¼ cup walnut pieces
40g/1½oz/scant ¼ cup sultanas (golden raisins)
50g/2oz/¼ cup butter, diced, plus extra for greasing

For the caramel sauce

15g/½oz/1 tbsp butter
120ml/4fl oz/½ cup whipping cream

1 Preheat the oven to 190°C/375°F/Gas 5. Grease an ovenproof dish just large enough to hold the apples.

2 With a small knife, cut at an angle to enlarge the core opening at the stem-end of each apple to about 2.5cm/1 in in diameter. (The opening should resemble a funnel in shape.) Arrange the apples in the prepared dish, stem-end up.

3 In a small pan, combine the water with the brown sugar, nutmeg and pepper. Bring the mixture to the boil, stirring. Boil for 6 minutes.

4 Mix together the walnuts and sultanas. Spoon some of the walnut-sultana mixture into the opening in each apple. Top each apple with some of the diced butter or margarine.

5 Spoon the brown sugar sauce over and around the apples. Bake for 45–50 minutes, basting occasionally with the sauce, until the apples are just tender. Transfer the apples to a serving dish, reserving the sauce in the dish. Keep the apples warm.

6 For the caramel sauce, mix the butter, cream and reserved brown sugar sauce in a pan. Bring to the boil, stirring occasionally, and simmer for about 2 minutes until thickened. Leave the sauce to cool slightly before serving.

Baked Apples/Apricot Energy 239Kcal/1008kJ; Protein 2.3g; Carbohydrate 34.2g, of which sugars 34.1g; Fat 11.4g, of which saturates 3.9g; Cholesterol 14mg; Calcium 32mg; Fibre 3.5g; Sodium 47mg.
Baked Apples/Caramel Energy 430Kcal/1778kJ; Protein 2g; Carbohydrate 11.5g, of which sugars 11.5g; Fat 42.2g, of which saturates 24.1g; Cholesterol 97mg; Calcium 31mg; Fibre 1.4g; Sodium 225mg.

Peach Cobbler

A satisfying pudding in which fresh peaches are topped with a hearty almond-flavoured pastry.

Serves 6
about 1.5kg/3lb peaches,
   peeled and sliced
45ml/3 tbsp caster
   (superfine) sugar
30ml/2 tbsp peach brandy
15ml/1 tbsp freshly squeezed
   lemon juice
15ml/1 tbsp cornflour
   (cornstarch)
ice cream or crème fraîche,
   to serve

For the topping
115g/4oz/1 cup plain
   (all-purpose) flour
7.5ml/1½ tsp baking powder
1.5ml/¼ tsp salt
40g/1½oz/¼ cup finely ground
   almonds
50g/2oz/¼ cup caster
   (superfine) sugar
50g/2oz/¼ cup butter or
   margarine
85ml/3fl oz/⅓ cup milk
1.5ml/¼ tsp almond extract

1 Preheat the oven to 220°C/425°F/Gas 7. Place the peaches in a bowl and add the sugar, peach brandy, lemon juice and cornflour. Toss together, then spoon the peach mixture into a 2 litre/3½ pint/8 cup baking dish.

2 Now make the topping. Sift the flour, baking powder and salt into a mixing bowl. Stir in the ground almonds and all but 15ml/1 tbsp of the sugar. With two knives, or a pastry blender, cut in the butter or margarine until the mixture resembles coarse breadcrumbs.

3 Add the milk and almond extract and stir until the topping mixture is just combined.

4 Carefully drop the topping in spoonfuls on to the peaches in the baking dish. Sprinkle the top with the remaining tablespoon of caster sugar.

5 Bake for 30–35 minutes until the cobbler topping is browned. Serve hot with ice cream or crème fraîche, if you prefer.

Peachy Chocolate Bake

A sublime combination of peaches and chocolate, this lightweight baked dessert is guaranteed to be popular with everyone – and it has the added bonus of being easy to make. For smart presentation, drizzle cream or yogurt over each serving and sprinkle lightly with chocolate powder.

Serves 6
200g/7oz dark (bittersweet)
   chocolate, chopped into small
   pieces
115g/4oz/½ cup unsalted (sweet)
   butter, plus extra for greasing
4 eggs, separated
115g/4oz/generous ½ cup caster
   (superfine) sugar
425g/15oz can peach slices,
   drained
whipped cream or Greek (US
   strained plain) yogurt, to serve

1 Preheat the oven to 160°C/325°F/Gas 3. Butter a wide ovenproof dish. Melt the chocolate with the butter in a heatproof bowl over barely simmering water, then remove from the heat.

2 Whisk the egg yolks with the sugar until thick and pale. In a clean, grease-free bowl, whisk the whites until stiff.

3 Beat the melted chocolate into the egg yolk mixture. Stir in a large spoonful of the egg whites, then gently fold in the remaining whites.

4 Fold the peach slices into the mixture, then turn into the prepared dish. Bake for 35–40 minutes or until risen and just firm. Serve hot, with cream or yogurt.

Variations
Pears also taste delicious with chocolate, and canned pears can be used very successfully in this recipe, instead of the peaches. During the summer months, try using very ripe peaches or a mix of soft berries instead of the canned fruit.

Peachy Bake Energy 465Kcal/1942kJ; Protein 6.5g; Carbohydrate 48.2g, of which sugars 47.9g; Fat 28.8g, of which saturates 16.6g; Cholesterol 170mg; Calcium 47mg; Fibre 1.4g; Sodium 175mg.
Peach Cobbler Energy 299Kcal/1265kJ; Protein 4.9g; Carbohydrate 53.5g, of which sugars 36.6g; Fat 7.6g, of which saturates 4.5g; Cholesterol 19mg; Calcium 72mg; Fibre 4.4g; Sodium 62mg.

Apple Couscous Pudding

This unusual couscous mixture makes a delicious family pudding with a rich fruity flavour, but virtually no fat content. Serve with low-fat yogurt as a healthy finale to a meal.

Serves 4
600ml/1 pint/2½ cups apple juice
115g/4oz/⅔ cup couscous
40g/1½oz/scant ¼ cup sultanas (golden raisins)
2.5ml/½ tsp mixed spice
1 large cooking apple, peeled, cored and sliced
25g/1oz/2 tbsp demerara (raw) sugar
natural low-fat yogurt, to serve

1 Preheat the oven to 200°C/400°F/Gas 6. Place the apple juice, couscous, sultanas and spice in a pan and bring to the boil, stirring. Cover and simmer for 10–12 minutes, until all the free liquid is absorbed.

2 Spoon half the couscous mixture into a 1.2 litre/2 pint/5 cup ovenproof dish and top with half the apple slices. Top with the remaining couscous.

3 Arrange the remaining apple slices overlapping over the top and sprinkle with demerara sugar. Bake for 25–30 minutes, or until the apples are golden brown. Serve hot with yogurt.

> **Cook's Tip**
> Couscous is a grain product made from semolina. Normally, it is used in savoury dishes, but it makes a tasty, healthy addition to this sweet dish. The grains soften and swell on cooking.

> **Variation**
> To ring the changes, substitute other dried fruits for the sultanas in this recipe – try chopped dates or ready-to-eat apricots.

Lemon Surprise Pudding

This is a much-loved dessert many of us remember from childhood. The surprise is the unexpected sauce concealed beneath the delectable sponge.

Serves 4
50g/2oz/¼ cup butter, plus extra for greasing
grated rind and juice of 2 lemons
115g/4oz/generous ½ cup caster (superfine) sugar
2 eggs, separated
50g/2oz/½ cup self-raising (self-rising) flour
300ml/½ pint/1¼ cups milk

1 Preheat the oven to 190°C/375°F/Gas 5. Use a little butter to grease a 1.2 litre/2 pint/5 cup baking dish.

2 Beat the lemon rind, remaining butter and caster sugar in a bowl until pale and fluffy. Add the egg yolks and flour and beat together well. Gradually whisk in the lemon juice and milk (don't be alarmed if the mixture curdles horribly!).

3 In a grease-free bowl, whisk the egg whites until they form stiff peaks. Fold the egg whites lightly into the lemon mixture, then pour into the prepared baking dish.

4 Place the dish in a roasting tin (pan) and pour in hot water to come halfway up the side of the dish. Bake for about 45 minutes until golden. Serve immediately.

> **Cook's Tips**
> • The uncooked mixture may look like a curdled disaster, but as the dessert cooks it separates into a top layer of firm sponge, with a luscious lemony sauce beneath.
> • Standing the dish in a layer of water in the pan creates a gentle method of cooking – this "bain-marie" method is often used for custards and other delicate egg dishes.
> • For a slightly different accompaniment, whip thick cream with a little vanilla extract and icing (confectioners') sugar.

Apple Couscous Pudding Energy 187Kcal/797kJ; Protein 2.2g; Carbohydrate 46.4g, of which sugars 31.7g; Fat 0.5g, of which saturates 0g; Cholesterol 0mg; Calcium 26mg; Fibre 0.8g; Sodium 10mg.
Lemon Pudding Energy 319Kcal/1341kJ; Protein 7g; Carbohydrate 43.1g, of which sugars 33.8g; Fat 14.5g, of which saturates 8.1g; Cholesterol 126mg; Calcium 166mg; Fibre 0.4g; Sodium 190mg.

Steamed Chocolate & Fruit Puddings

Some things always turn out well, just like these wonderful little puddings. Dark, fluffy chocolate sponge with tangy cranberries and apple is served with a honeyed chocolate syrup.

Serves 4

butter or oil, for greasing
115g/4oz/1/2 cup muscovado (molasses) sugar
1 eating apple, peeled and cored
75g/3oz/3/4 cup cranberries, thawed if frozen
115g/4oz/1/2 cup soft margarine
2 eggs
75g/3oz/2/3 cup plain (all-purpose) flour
2.5ml/1/2 tsp baking powder
45ml/3 tbsp cocoa powder (unsweetened)

For the chocolate syrup
115g/4oz plain (semisweet) chocolate, broken into squares
30ml/2 tbsp clear honey
15ml/1 tbsp unsalted (sweet) butter
2.5ml/1/2 tsp vanilla extract

1 Prepare a steamer or half fill a pan with water and bring it to the boil. Grease four individual heatproof bowls and sprinkle each one with a little of the muscovado sugar to coat all over.

2 Dice the apple into a bowl. Add the cranberries and mix well. Divide the mixture equally among the prepared bowls.

3 Put the remaining sugar in a mixing bowl. Add the margarine, eggs, flour, baking powder and cocoa. Beat well until smooth.

4 Spoon the mixture into the bowls, on top of the fruit, and cover each with a double thickness of foil. Steam for about 45 minutes, topping up the boiling water as required, until the puddings are well risen and firm.

5 Make the syrup. Mix together the chocolate, honey, butter and vanilla in a small pan. Heat gently, stirring, until smooth.

6 Run a knife around the edge of each pudding to loosen it, then turn out on to individual plates. Serve immediately, with the chocolate syrup poured over the top.

Chocolate Chip & Banana Pudding

Hot and steamy, this superb light pudding tastes extra special when served with ready-made fresh chocolate sauce or custard.

Serves 4

200g/7oz/1¾ cups self-raising (self-rising) flour
75g/3oz/6 tbsp unsalted (sweet) butter or margarine
2 ripe bananas
75g/3oz/6 tbsp caster (superfine) sugar
60ml/4 tbsp milk
1 egg, beaten
60ml/4 tbsp plain (bittersweet) chocolate chips or chopped chocolate
whipped cream, to serve

1 Prepare a steamer or half fill a pan with water and bring to the boil. Grease a 1 litre/1¾ pint/4 cup ovenproof bowl.

2 Sift the flour into a mixing bowl and rub in the butter or margarine until the mixture resembles breadcrumbs. Mash the bananas in a bowl. Stir them into the creamed mixture, with the caster sugar.

3 Whisk the milk with the egg in a bowl, then beat into the pudding mixture. Stir in the chocolate.

4 Spoon the mixture into the prepared bowl, cover closely with a double thickness of foil, and steam for 2 hours, topping up the water as required during cooking.

5 Run a knife around the top edge of the pudding to loosen it, then turn it out on to a warm serving dish. Serve hot, with a spoonful of whipped cream.

Cook's Tip
If you have a food processor, make a quick-mix version by processing all the ingredients, except the chocolate, until smooth. Then stir in the chocolate, spoon into the prepared bowl and finish as described in the recipe.

Choc/Fruit Puddings Energy 672Kcal/2811kJ; Protein 8.7g; Carbohydrate 73.1g, of which sugars 57.3g; Fat 40.4g, of which saturates 13.9g; Cholesterol 105mg; Calcium 84mg; Fibre 3.2g; Sodium 366mg.
Choc/Ban. Pudding Energy 528Kcal/2220kJ; Protein 8.1g; Carbohydrate 79.3g, of which sugars 40.9g; Fat 22g, of which saturates 13g; Cholesterol 89mg; Calcium 222mg; Fibre 2.5g; Sodium 320mg.

Maple & Pecan Croissant Pudding

This variation of the classic English bread and butter pudding uses rich, flaky croissants, topped with a delicious mixture of fruit and nuts. Custard flavoured with maple syrup completes this mouthwatering dessert.

Serves 4

75g/3oz/scant ½ cup sultanas (golden raisins)
45ml/3 tbsp brandy
4 large croissants

50g/2oz/¼ cup butter or margarine, plus extra for greasing
40g/1½oz/⅓ cup pecan nuts, roughly chopped
3 eggs, lightly beaten
300ml/½ pint/1¼ cups milk
150ml/¼ pint/⅔ cup single (light) cream
120ml/4fl oz/½ cup maple syrup
25g/1oz/2 tbsp demerara (raw) sugar
maple syrup and pouring (half-and-half) cream, to serve

1 Lightly grease the base and sides of a small, shallow ovenproof dish. Place the sultanas and brandy in a small pan and heat gently, until warm. Leave to stand for 1 hour.

2 Cut the croissants into thick slices and spread with butter on one side. Arrange the slices, buttered side uppermost and slightly overlapping, in the greased dish. Sprinkle the brandy-soaked sultanas and the pecan nuts evenly over the croissant slices.

3 In a large bowl, beat the eggs and milk together, then gradually beat in the single cream and maple syrup. Pour the egg custard through a sieve (strainer), over the croissants, fruit and nuts in the dish. Leave the pudding to stand for 30 minutes so that some of the custard is absorbed by the croissants. Meanwhile, preheat the oven to 180°F/350°C/Gas 4.

4 Sprinkle the demerara sugar evenly over the top, then cover the dish with foil. Bake the pudding for 30 minutes, then remove the foil and continue to cook for about 20 minutes, or until the custard is set and the top is golden brown.

5 Leave the pudding to cool for about 15 minutes before serving warm with extra maple syrup and pouring cream.

Fresh Currant Bread & Butter Pudding

Fresh mixed currants add a tart touch to this scrumptious hot pudding.

Serves 6

8 medium-thick slices day-old bread, crusts removed
50g/2oz/¼ cup butter, softened
115g/4oz/1 cup redcurrants
115g/4oz/1 cup blackcurrants

4 eggs, beaten
75g/3oz/6 tbsp caster (superfine) sugar
475ml/16fl oz/2 cups creamy milk
5ml/1 tsp pure vanilla extract
freshly grated nutmeg
30ml/2 tbsp demerara (raw) sugar
single (light) cream, to serve

1 Preheat the oven to 160°C/325°F/Gas 3. Generously butter a 1.2 litre/2 pint/5 cup oval baking dish.

2 Spread the slices of bread generously with the butter, then cut them in half diagonally. Layer the slices in the dish, buttered side up, sprinkling the currants between the layers.

3 Beat the eggs and caster sugar lightly together in a large mixing bowl, then gradually whisk in the milk, vanilla extract and a large pinch of freshly grated nutmeg. Pour the milk mixture over the bread, pushing the slices down. Sprinkle the demerara sugar and a little nutmeg over the top.

4 Place the dish in a roasting pan and then add hot water so that the water reaches halfway up the sides of the dish. Bake for 40 minutes, then increase the oven temperature to 180°C/350°F/Gas 4 and bake for 20–25 minutes until golden. Serve with single cream.

> **Variation**
> A mixture of blueberries and raspberries would work very successfully instead of the currants.

Croissant Pudding Energy 738Kcal/3088kJ; Protein 15.1g; Carbohydrate 74.2g, of which sugars 51.3g; Fat 45.6g, of which saturates 19.5g; Cholesterol 226mg; Calcium 218mg; Fibre 1.8g; Sodium 508mg.
Bread & But. Pudding Energy 328Kcal/1377kJ; Protein 10.3g; Carbohydrate 42.2g, of which sugars 25.4g; Fat 14.3g, of which saturates 7.4g; Cholesterol 156mg; Calcium 186mg; Fibre 1.9g; Sodium 321mg.

Chocolate, Date & Walnut Pudding

This tempting pudding is not steamed in the traditional way, but baked in the oven. The result is still completely irresistible.

Serves 4
25g/1oz/1¼ cup chopped walnuts
25g/1oz/2 tbsp chopped dates

2 eggs, separated
5ml/1 tsp vanilla extract
30ml/2 tbsp golden caster (superfine) sugar
45ml/3 tbsp plain wholemeal (all-purpose whole-wheat) flour
15ml/1 tbsp cocoa powder (unsweetened)
30ml/2 tbsp skimmed milk

1 Preheat the oven to 180°C/350°F/Gas 4. Grease and base-line with baking parchment a 1.2 litre/2 pint/5 cup ovenproof bowl. Spoon in the walnuts and dates.

2 Combine the egg yolks, vanilla extract and sugar in a heatproof bowl. Place over a pan of hot water.

3 Whisk the egg whites to soft peaks. Whisk the egg yolk mixture until it is thick and pale, then remove the bowl from the heat. Sift the flour and cocoa over the mixture and fold them in with a metal spoon. Stir in the milk, to soften the mixture, then fold in the egg whites.

4 Spoon the mixture over the walnuts and dates in the prepared bowl and bake for 40–45 minutes or until the pudding is well risen and firm to the touch. Run a knife around the pudding to loosen it from the bowl, and then turn it out on to a plate and serve immediately.

Cook's Tips
• Pudding fans won't be satisfied without custard to accompany this dessert. Why not serve a real custard, Crème Anglaise, made using cream, egg yolks, caster (superfine) sugar and a few drops of vanilla extract?
• If you wish, the cocoa can be omitted and the sponge mix flavoured with grated orange rind instead.

Cabinet Pudding

This rich custard is baked with dried fruit and sponge cake to make a delightful old-fashioned dessert. You can leave out the brandy if you wish, but it definitely adds a touch of something special to the dish.

Serves 4
25g/1oz/2½ tbsp chopped raisins
30ml/2 tbsp brandy (optional)
butter, for greasing

25g/1oz/2½ tbsp glacé (candied) fruit
25g/1oz/2½ tbsp angelica, chopped
2 trifle sponge cakes, diced
50g/2oz ratafia biscuits (almond macaroons)
2 eggs
2 egg yolks
30ml/2 tbsp sugar
450ml/¾ pint/scant 2 cups single (light) cream or milk
a few drops of vanilla extract

1 Place the raisins in a bowl with the brandy, if using, and leave to soak for several hours.

2 Grease a 750ml/1¼ pint/3 cup charlotte mould or round ovenproof dish with butter and arrange some of the cherries and angelica in the base.

3 Mix the remaining cherries and angelica with the sponge cakes, ratafias and raisins. Mix in the brandy, if using, and spoon into the mould or dish.

4 Lightly whisk together the eggs, egg yolks and sugar. Bring the cream or milk just to the boil in a pan, then stir into the egg mixture with the vanilla extract.

5 Strain the egg mixture into the mould or dish, then leave to stand for 15–30 minutes.

6 Preheat the oven to 160°C/325°F/Gas 3. Place the mould in a roasting pan, cover with baking parchment and pour in boiling water so that it comes halfway up the side of the mould or dish. Bake for 1 hour, or until the custard is set. Leave to stand for 2–3 minutes, then loosen the edge with a knife and turn out on to a warm plate, to serve.

Cab. Pudding Energy 436Kcal/1818kJ; Protein 11.5g; Carbohydrate 34.2g, of which sugars 27.6g; Fat 29.2g, of which saturates 15.8g; Cholesterol 326mg; Calcium 164mg; Fibre 0.7g; Sodium 119mg.
Choc., Date & Wal. Energy 171Kcal/716kJ; Protein 6.2g; Carbohydrate 19.5g, of which sugars 10.5g; Fat 8.2g, of which saturates 1.7g; Cholesterol 96mg; Calcium 55mg; Fibre 1.1g; Sodium 76mg.

Rich Chocolate Brioche Bake

This dessert is amazingly easy to make and doesn't require many ingredients. Richly flavoured and quite delicious, it's the perfect dish for mid-week entertaining, when you are pushed for time. Serve with a platter of sliced tropical fruit as a foil to the richness of the dish.

Serves 4
40g/1½oz/3 tbsp unsalted
  (sweet) butter, plus extra
  for greasing
200g/7oz plain (semisweet)
  chocolate, chopped into
  small pieces
60ml/4 tbsp bitter marmalade
4 individual brioches, cut into
  halves, or 1 large brioche
  loaf, cut into thick slices
3 eggs
300ml/½ pint/1¼ cups milk
300ml/½ pint/1¼ cups single
  (light) cream
30ml/2 tbsp demerara
  (raw) sugar
crème fraîche, to serve

1 Preheat the oven to 180°C/350°F/Gas 4. Using the extra butter, lightly grease a shallow ovenproof dish.

2 Melt the chocolate with the marmalade and butter in a heatproof bowl over just simmering water, stirring the mixture occasionally, until smooth.

3 Spread the melted chocolate mixture over the brioche slices, then carefully arrange them in the dish so that the slices overlap in neat rows.

4 Beat the eggs in a large bowl, then add the milk and cream and mix well. Transfer to a jug (pitcher) and pour evenly over the slices.

5 Sprinkle the mixture with the demerara sugar and bake for 40–50 minutes, until the custard has set lightly and the brioche slices are golden brown. Serve immediately, topped with dollops of crème fraîche.

Sticky Toffee Pudding

Filling and warming, this tasty variation on a classic pudding will soon become a firm family favourite.

Serves 6
115g/4oz/1 cup toasted
  walnuts, chopped
175g/6oz/¾ cup butter
175g/6oz/scant 1 cup soft
  brown sugar
60ml/4 tbsp single (light) cream
30ml/2 tbsp freshly squeezed
  lemon juice
2 eggs, beaten
115g/4oz/1 cup self-raising
  (self-rising) flour

1 Prepare a steamer or half fill a pan with water and bring it to the boil. Grease a 900ml/1½ pint/3¾ cup heatproof bowl and add half the walnuts.

2 Heat 50g/2oz/4 tbsp of the butter with 50g/2oz/4 tbsp of the sugar, the cream and 15ml/1 tbsp of the lemon juice in a small pan, stirring until smooth. Pour half the sauce into the greased bowl, then swirl to coat it a little way up the sides. Reserve the remaining sauce.

3 Beat the remaining butter and sugar until light and fluffy, then gradually beat in the eggs. Fold in the flour and the remaining nuts and lemon juice and spoon into the bowl.

4 Cover the bowl with baking parchment with a pleat folded in the centre, then tie securely with string. Steam the pudding for about 1¼ hours, topping up the boiling water as required, until it is set in the centre.

5 Just before serving, gently warm the remaining sauce. To serve, run a knife around the edge of the pudding to loosen it, then turn out on to a warm plate and pour over the sauce.

Cook's Tip
Putting a pleat in the paper cover allows room for the pudding to rise. Secure tightly to prevent water or steam entering.

Sticky Toffee Pudding Energy 571Kcal/2378kJ; Protein 7.3g; Carbohydrate 46g, of which sugars 31.6g; Fat 41.1g, of which saturates 18g; Cholesterol 131mg; Calcium 124mg; Fibre 1.3g; Sodium 275mg.
Brioche Bake Energy 987Kcal/4143kJ; Protein 25.9g; Carbohydrate 127.8g, of which sugars 59.1g; Fat 45g, of which saturates 25.4g; Cholesterol 213mg; Calcium 460mg; Fibre 4.4g; Sodium 1060mg.

Moroccan Rice Pudding

A simple and delicious alternative to a traditional British rice pudding. The rice is cooked in almond-flavoured milk and delicately highlighted with cinnamon and orange flower water.

Serves 6

25g/1oz/¼ cup almonds, chopped
450g/1lb/2¼ cups pudding (short grain) rice
25g/1oz/¼ cup icing (confectioners') sugar
1 cinnamon stick
50g/2oz/¼ cup butter or margarine
1.5ml/¼ tsp almond extract
175ml/6fl oz/¾ cup milk
175ml/6fl oz/¾ cup single (light) cream
30ml/2 tbsp orange flower water
toasted flaked (sliced) almonds and ground cinnamon, to decorate

1 Put the almonds in a food processor or blender with 60ml/ 4 tbsp very hot water. Process until the almonds are finely chopped, then push through a sieve (strainer) into a bowl. Return the almond mixture to the food processor or blender; add a further 60ml/4 tbsp very hot water, and process again. Push the almond mixture through the sieve into a pan.

2 Add 300ml/½ pint/1¼ cups water and bring the mixture to the boil. Add the rice, icing sugar, cinnamon stick, half the butter, the almond extract, half the milk and half the cream.

3 Bring to the boil, then simmer, covered, for about 30 minutes, adding more milk and cream as the rice mixture thickens. Continue to cook the rice, stirring and adding the remaining milk and cream, until the pudding becomes thick and creamy.

4 Stir in the orange flower water, then taste the rice pudding for sweetness, adding a little extra sugar, if necessary.

5 Pour the rice pudding into a serving bowl and sprinkle with the toasted flaked almonds. Dot with the remaining butter and dust with a little ground cinnamon. Serve the pudding hot.

Baked Rice Pudding, Thai-style

Black glutinous rice, also known as black sticky rice, has long dark grains and a nutty taste reminiscent of wild rice. This baked pudding has a distinct character and flavour all of its own, as well as an intriguing appearance.

Serves 4–6

175g/6oz/1 cup white or black glutinous rice
30ml/2 tbsp soft light brown sugar
475ml/16fl oz/2 cups coconut milk
250ml/8fl oz/1 cup water
3 eggs
30ml/2 tbsp granulated sugar

1 Combine the glutinous rice and brown sugar in a pan. Pour in half the coconut milk and the water.

2 Bring to the boil, reduce the heat to low and simmer, stirring occasionally, for 15–20 minutes, or until the rice has absorbed most of the liquid. Preheat the oven to 150°C/300°F/Gas 2.

3 Spoon the rice mixture into a single large ovenproof dish or divide it among individual ramekins. Beat the eggs with the remaining coconut milk and sugar in a bowl.

4 Strain the egg mixture into a jug (pitcher), then pour it evenly over the par-cooked rice in the dish or ramekins.

5 Place the dish or ramekins in a roasting pan. Carefully pour in enough hot water to come halfway up the sides of the dish or ramekins.

6 Cover with foil and bake for about 35–60 minutes, or until the custard has set. Serve warm.

Cook's Tip
Throughout South-east Asia, black glutinous rice is usually used to make sweet dishes, while its white counterpart is more often used in savoury recipes.

Moroccan Rice Pudding Energy 443Kcal/1847kJ; Protein 8.5g; Carbohydrate 66.6g, of which sugars 6.6g; Fat 15.6g, of which saturates 8.4g; Cholesterol 36mg; Calcium 89mg; Fibre 0.3g; Sodium 72mg.
Baked Rice Pudding Energy 198Kcal/834kJ; Protein 5.9g; Carbohydrate 36.2g, of which sugars 14.3g; Fat 3.5g, of which saturates 0.9g; Cholesterol 95mg; Calcium 47mg; Fibre 0g; Sodium 124mg.

Exotic Tapioca Pudding

This pudding, made from large pearl tapioca and coconut milk and served warm, is much lighter than the traditional Western-style version. You can adjust the sweetness to your taste. Serve with lychees or the smaller, similar-tasting longans – also known as "dragon's eyes".

Serves 4
115g/4oz/⅔ cup tapioca
475ml/16fl oz/2 cups water
175g/6oz/¾ cup granulated
 sugar
pinch of salt
250ml/8fl oz/1 cup coconut milk
250g/9oz prepared tropical fruits
finely shredded lime rind and
 shaved fresh coconut (optional),
 to decorate

1 Put the tapioca in a bowl and pour over enough warm water to cover completely. Leave to soak for 1 hour so the grains swell. Drain well.

2 Pour the measured water in a large pan and bring to the boil over a medium heat. Add the sugar and salt and stir until completely dissolved.

3 Add the tapioca and coconut milk, reduce the heat to low and simmer gently for 10 minutes, or until the tapioca becomes tender and transparent.

4 Spoon into one large or four individual bowls and serve warm with the tropical fruits. Decorate with the lime rind and coconut shavings, if using.

Cook's Tip
• *Tapioca pearls are a product of cassava, which is a tropical root plant, originating in America. Cassava flour is processed to form the pearls. In the past, tapioca milk pudding was a popular British dessert.*
• *For a tropical fruit accompaniment, arrange sliced and peeled pineapple, ripe mango and papaya on a platter with chunks of oranges for added juiciness. Sprinkle with finely grated lime rind.*

Fragrant Rice with Dates

The rice puddings that are popular all over Morocco are served liberally sprinkled with either nuts and honey or wrapped in pastry. This is a low-fat version.

Serves 4
75g/3oz/½ cup pudding (short
 grain) rice
about 900ml/1½ pints/3¾ cups
 skimmed milk
30ml/2 tbsp ground rice
50g/2oz/¼ cup caster (superfine)
 sugar
15g/½oz/2 tbsp ground almonds
5ml/1 tsp vanilla extract
2.5ml/½ tsp almond extract
a little orange flower water
 (optional)
30ml/2 tbsp chopped dates
30ml/2 tbsp unsalted pistachio
 nuts, finely chopped

1 Place the rice in a pan with 750ml/1¼ pints/3 cups of the milk and gradually heat until simmering. Cook, uncovered, over a very low heat for 30–40 minutes, until the rice is completely tender, stirring frequently.

2 Blend the ground rice with the remaining milk and add to the pan, stirring. Slowly bring back to the boil and continue to cook for 1 minute.

3 Stir in the sugar, ground almonds, vanilla and almond extracts and orange flower water, if using. Cook, stirring frequently, until the pudding is thick and creamy.

4 Pour into serving bowls and sprinkle with the chopped dates and pistachios. Allow to cool slightly before serving.

Cook's Tip
• *Orange flower water, made from the flowers of the bitter orange, is a traditional ingredient of the Middle East, where it is used to add delicate fragrance to all manner of desserts.*
• *Chopped ready-to-eat dried apricots and toasted flaked (sliced) almonds also make a good topping for the dish, complementing the flavours of the rice.*

Tapioca Pudding Energy 325Kcal/1388kJ; Protein 1g; Carbohydrate 84.9g, of which sugars 57.4g; Fat 0.4g, of which saturates 0.2g; Cholesterol 0mg; Calcium 51mg; Fibre 1.8g; Sodium 74mg.
Fragrant Rice Energy 302Kcal/1272kJ; Protein 11.2g; Carbohydrate 46.7g, of which sugars 26.4g; Fat 8.4g, of which saturates 3g; Cholesterol 13mg; Calcium 292mg; Fibre 0.8g; Sodium 139mg.

Eve's Pudding

The tempting apples beneath the sponge topping are the reason for the pudding's name.

Serves 4–6
115g/4oz/½ cup butter
115g/4oz/generous ½ cup caster (superfine) sugar
2 eggs, beaten
grated rind and juice of 1 lemon
90g/3½oz/¾ cup self-raising (self-rising) flour
40g/1½oz/⅓ cup ground almonds
115g/4oz/scant ½ cup soft brown sugar
675g/1½lb cooking apples, cored and thinly sliced
25g/1oz/¼ cup flaked (sliced) almonds
bought fresh custard or single (light) cream, to serve

1 Beat together the butter and caster sugar in a large mixing bowl until the mixture is very light and fluffy.

2 Gradually beat the eggs into the butter mixture, beating well after each addition, then fold in the lemon rind, flour and ground almonds.

3 Mix the brown sugar with the apples and lemon juice in a bowl, then turn into an ovenproof dish. Spoon the sponge mixture on top of the apples, levelling the surface, then sprinkle with the almonds.

4 Bake for 40–45 minutes, until golden. Serve immediately with fresh custard or cream.

Variations
• To ring the changes, replace half the apples with fresh blackberries. Halved apricots and sliced peaches can also be used instead of the apples as they go well with the topping.
• To vary the sponge topping, leave out the ground and flaked almonds and use demerara (raw) sugar instead of the caster sugar, then serve sprinkled with icing (confectioners') sugar.

Chocolate Cinnamon Cake with Banana Sauce

This mouthwatering cake, bursting with lovely flavours, is brilliantly complemented by the tasty banana sauce.

Serves 6
25g/1oz plain (semisweet) chocolate, chopped into small pieces
115g/4oz/½ cup unsalted (sweet) butter, at room temperature
15ml/1 tbsp instant coffee powder
5 eggs, separated
225g/8oz/1 cup granulated sugar
115g/4oz/1 cup plain (all-purpose) flour
10ml/2 tsp ground cinnamon

For the sauce
4 ripe bananas
45ml/3 tbsp soft light brown sugar
15ml/1 tbsp fresh lemon juice
175ml/6fl oz/¾ cup whipping cream
15ml/1 tbsp rum (optional)

1 Preheat the oven to 180°C/350°F/Gas 4. Grease a 20cm/8in round cake tin (pan).

2 Place the chocolate and butter in the top of a double boiler or in a heatproof bowl set over a pan of simmering water. Stir until the chocolate and butter have melted. Remove from the heat and stir in the coffee. Set aside.

3 Beat the egg yolks with the granulated sugar until thick and lemon-coloured. Add the chocolate mixture and beat on low speed until just blended.

4 Stir the flour and cinnamon together in a bowl. In another bowl, beat the egg whites until they hold stiff peaks.

5 Fold a dollop of whites into the chocolate mixture to lighten it. Fold in the remaining whites in three batches, alternating with the sifted flour mixture.

6 Pour the mixture into the prepared tin. Bake for 40–50 minutes or until a skewer inserted in the centre comes out clean. Remove from the oven and turn the cake out on to a wire rack. Preheat the grill (broiler).

7 Make the sauce. Slice the bananas into a shallow, flameproof dish. Stir in the brown sugar and lemon juice. Place under the grill for 8 minutes, stirring occasionally, until caramelized.

8 Mash the banana mixture until almost smooth. Tip into a bowl and stir in the cream and rum, if using. Slice the cake and serve with the sauce.

Cook's Tip
Take care when folding the egg white and flour into the chocolate mixture – do not be tempted to stir, otherwise you will break down the air bubbles in the mixture and the cake will not rise well.

Eve's Pudding Energy 473Kcal/1988kJ; Protein 6.4g; Carbohydrate 62.3g, of which sugars 50.8g; Fat 24g, of which saturates 11g; Cholesterol 104mg; Calcium 116mg; Fibre 3.1g; Sodium 200mg.
Choc. Cake Energy 642Kcal/2691kJ; Protein 8.9g; Carbohydrate 80.9g, of which sugars 64.8g; Fat 33.8g, of which saturates 19.4g; Cholesterol 230mg; Calcium 100mg; Fibre 1.4g; Sodium 186mg.

Hot Chocolate Cake

This is wonderfully wicked served as a dessert with a white chocolate sauce. The basic cake freezes well – thaw, then warm in the microwave before serving.

Makes 10–12 slices
200g/7oz/1¾ cups self-raising wholemeal (self-rising whole-wheat) flour
25g/1oz/¼ cup cocoa powder (unsweetened)
pinch of salt
175g/6oz/¾ cup soft margarine
175g/6oz/¾ cup soft light brown sugar
few drops vanilla extract
4 eggs
75g/3oz white chocolate, roughly chopped
chocolate leaves and curls, to decorate

For the chocolate sauce
75g/3oz white chocolate
150ml/¼ pint/⅔ cup single (light) cream
30–45ml/2–3 tbsp milk

1 Preheat the oven to 160°C/325°F/Gas 3. Sift the flour, cocoa and salt into a bowl, adding in the whole wheat flakes from the sieve (strainer).

2 Cream the margarine, sugar and vanilla extract together until light and fluffy, then gently beat in one egg.

3 Gradually stir in the remaining eggs, one at a time, alternately folding in some of the flour mixture, until the eggs and flour have been used up and the mixture is blended in.

4 Stir in the white chocolate and spoon into a 675–900g/ 1½–2lb loaf tin (pan) or an 18cm/7in greased cake tin (pan). Bake for 30–40 minutes, or until just firm to the touch and shrinking away from the sides of the tin.

5 Meanwhile, make the sauce. Heat the white chocolate and cream very gently in a pan until the chocolate is melted. Add the milk and stir until cool.

6 Serve the cake sliced, in a pool of sauce and decorated with chocolate leaves and curls.

Magic Chocolate Mud Cake

Guaranteed to be a big hit, this scrumptious dessert can be put together in no time at all.

Serves 4
50g/2oz/¼ cup butter, plus extra for greasing
90g/3½oz/¾ cup self-raising (self-rising) flour
5ml/1 tsp ground cinnamon
75ml/5 tbsp cocoa powder (unsweetened)
200g/7oz/1 cup light muscovado (brown) or demerara (raw) sugar
475ml/16fl oz/2 cups milk
crème fraîche, Greek (US strained plain) yogurt or vanilla ice cream, to serve

1 Preheat the oven to 180°C/350°F/Gas 4. Grease a 1.5 litre/ 2½ pint/6¼ cup ovenproof dish with butter. Place the dish on a baking sheet and set aside.

2 Sift the flour and ground cinnamon into a bowl. Sift in 15ml/ 1 tbsp of the cocoa and mix well.

3 Place the butter in a pan. Add 115g/4oz/½ cup of the sugar and 150ml/¼ pint/⅔ cup of the milk. Heat gently without boiling, stirring from time to time, until the butter has melted and all the sugar has dissolved. Remove the pan from the heat.

4 Stir in the flour mixture, mixing evenly. Pour the mixture into the prepared dish and level the surface.

5 Mix the remaining sugar and cocoa in a bowl, then sprinkle over the pudding mixture. Pour the remaining milk evenly over the pudding.

6 Bake for 45–50 minutes or until the sponge has risen to the top and is firm to the touch. Serve hot, with the crème fraîche, yogurt or ice cream.

> **Cook's Tip**
> A delicious sauce "magically" appears beneath the sponge.

Hot Choc. Cake Energy 343Kcal/1432kJ; Protein 5.4g; Carbohydrate 35.7g, of which sugars 23.1g; Fat 20.8g, of which saturates 7.1g; Cholesterol 71mg; Calcium 124mg; Fibre 0.8g; Sodium 221mg.
Mud Cake Energy 480Kcal/2025kJ; Protein 10g; Carbohydrate 77.6g, of which sugars 58.3g; Fat 16.7g, of which saturates 10.2g; Cholesterol 34mg; Calcium 227mg; Fibre 3g; Sodium 309mg.

Warm Lemon & Syrup Cake

The combination of pears, sticky syrup and lemon makes this a real winner. Drizzle with thin cream for extra luxury.

Serves 8

3 eggs
175g/6oz/³⁄₄ cup butter, softened
175g/6oz/³⁄₄ cup caster
  (superfine) sugar
175g/6oz/1½ cups self-raising
  (self-rising) flour
50g/2oz/½ cup ground almonds

1.5ml/¼ tsp freshly grated
  nutmeg
50g/2oz/5 tbsp candied lemon
  peel, finely chopped
grated rind of 1 lemon
30ml/2 tbsp lemon juice
poached pears, to serve

For the syrup

175g/6oz/³⁄₄ cup caster
  (superfine) sugar
juice of 3 lemons
75ml/3 tbsp water

1 Preheat the oven to 180°C/350°F/Gas 4. Grease and base-line a deep, round 20cm/8in cake tin (pan).

2 Place all the cake ingredients in a large bowl and beat well for 2–3 minutes, until the mixture is light and fluffy.

3 Transfer the mixture to the prepared tin, spread level and bake for 1 hour, or until golden and firm to the touch.

4 Meanwhile, make the syrup. Put the sugar, lemon juice and water in a pan. Heat gently, stirring until the sugar has dissolved, then boil, without stirring, for 1–2 minutes.

5 Turn the cake out on to a plate with a rim. Prick the surface of the cake all over with a fork, then pour over the hot syrup. Leave to soak for about 30 minutes. Serve the cake warm with thin wedges of poached pears.

Cook's Tip
To speed up the preparation, mix the ingredients together in a food processor, but take care not to overbeat.

Gingerbread Upside-Down Pudding

A proper pudding goes down well on a cold winter's day. This one is quite quick and easy to make and looks very impressive.

Serves 4–6

sunflower oil, for brushing
15ml/1 tbsp soft brown sugar
4 medium peaches, halved and
  stoned (pitted), or canned
  peach halves
8 walnut halves

For the base

130g/4½oz/generous 1 cup
  wholemeal (whole-wheat) flour
2.5ml/½ tsp bicarbonate of soda
  (baking soda)
7.5ml/1½ tsp ground ginger
5ml/1 tsp ground cinnamon
115g/4oz/scant ½ cup
  muscovado (molasses) sugar
1 egg
120ml/4fl oz/½ cup skimmed
  milk
50ml/2fl oz/¼ cup sunflower oil

1 Preheat the oven to 180°C/350°F/Gas 4. For the topping, brush the base and sides of a 23cm/9in round springform cake tin (pan) with oil. Sprinkle the sugar over the base.

2 Arrange the peaches, cut side down, in the tin, placing a walnut half in each.

3 Sift together the flour, bicarbonate of soda, ginger and cinnamon, then stir in the sugar. Beat together the egg, milk and oil, then mix into the dry ingredients.

4 Pour the mixture evenly over the peaches and bake for 35–40 minutes, until firm to the touch. Turn out and serve hot.

Cook's Tips
• To turn out successfully, run the point of a sharp knife round the edge of the pudding, then place a serving plate upside-down on top. Holding the plate and tin (pan) firmly, invert. Release the sides of the tin and remove.
• To accentuate the ginger flavour, finely chop 15ml/1 tbsp drained stem ginger in syrup and add at the end of step 3.

Lemon Cake Energy 488Kcal/2047kJ; Protein 6g; Carbohydrate 66.5g, of which sugars 50.1g; Fat 23.9g, of which saturates 12.3g; Cholesterol 118mg; Calcium 138mg; Fibre 1.4g; Sodium 259mg.
Gingerbread Pud. Energy 272Kcal/1145kJ; Protein 4.8g; Carbohydrate 44.1g, of which sugars 27.5g; Fat 9.7g, of which saturates 1.4g; Cholesterol 33mg; Calcium 77mg; Fibre 1.5g; Sodium 23mg.

Hot Plum Batter Pudding

Other fruits can be used in place of plums, depending on the season. Canned black cherries are a convenient substitute to keep in the store cupboard.

Serves 4
450g/1lb ripe red plums, quartered and stoned (pitted)
200ml/7fl oz/scant 1 cup skimmed milk
60ml/4 tbsp skimmed milk powder
15ml/1 tbsp light muscovado (brown) sugar
5ml/1 tsp vanilla extract
75g/3oz/²⁄₃ cup self-raising (self-rising) flour
2 egg whites
icing (confectioners') sugar, to sprinkle
natural (plain) yogurt or crème fraîche, to serve

1 Preheat the oven to 220°C/425°F/Gas 7. Lightly oil a wide, shallow ovenproof dish and add the plums.

2 Pour the milk, milk powder, sugar, vanilla extract, flour and egg whites into a blender or food processor. Process the mixture to form a smooth batter.

3 Pour the batter over the plums in the dish. Bake for 25–30 minutes, or until the top is puffed and golden. Sprinkle with icing sugar and serve immediately with yogurt or crème fraîche.

> **Cook's Tips**
> • If you don't have a food processor, then place the dry ingredients for the batter in a large bowl and gradually whisk in the milk and egg whites.
> • Flavoured cream would be delicious served with this dessert. Lightly whip double (heavy) cream, stir in a spoonful or two of your favourite liqueur and sweeten to taste.

> **Variation**
> Halved fresh or canned apricots are tasty instead of the plums, or try cherries, pre-soaked in a little kirsch for an added kick.

Glazed Apricot Sponge

Proper puddings can be extremely high in saturated fat, but this particular version uses the minimum of oil and no eggs. Fat-free natural or apricot yogurt would make a suitably healthy and tasty accompaniment to this delicious dessert.

Serves 4
10ml/2 tsp golden (light corn) syrup
411g/14½oz can apricot halves in fruit juice
150g/5oz/1¼ cups self-raising (self-rising) flour
75g/3oz/1½ cups fresh breadcrumbs
90g/3½oz/½ cup light muscovado (brown) sugar
5ml/1 tsp ground cinnamon
30ml/2 tbsp sunflower oil
175ml/6fl oz/¾ cup skimmed milk

1 Preheat the oven to 180°C/350°F/Gas 4. Lightly oil a 900ml/1½ pint/3¾ cup ovenproof bowl. Carefully spoon in the golden syrup.

2 Drain the apricots and reserve the juice. Arrange about 8 halves, rounded side up, in the bowl. Purée the rest of the apricots with the juice and set aside.

3 Mix together the flour, breadcrumbs, sugar and cinnamon in a mixing bowl, then beat in the oil and milk. Spoon into the ovenproof bowl on top of the apricots.

4 Bake the mixture for 50–55 minutes, or until firm to the touch and golden on top. Run a knife around the pudding to loosen it from the bowl, then turn it out on to a plate. Serve with the puréed fruit as an accompaniment.

> **Cook's tips**
> To make fresh breadcrumbs, use bread that is a couple of days old and process in a blender or food processor, or use a grater.

Plum Batter Pudding Energy 139Kcal/594kJ; Protein 5.5g; Carbohydrate 30.2g, of which sugars 16.3g; Fat 0.5g, of which saturates 0.1g; Cholesterol 2mg; Calcium 144mg; Fibre 2.4g; Sodium 123mg.
Apricot Sponge Energy 348Kcal/1485kJ; Protein 7.6g; Carbohydrate 79.1g, of which sugars 37.2g; Fat 2.4g, of which saturates 0.6g; Cholesterol 3mg; Calcium 242mg; Fibre 2.5g; Sodium 310mg.

Mango & Amaretti Strudel

Fresh mango and crushed amaretti wrapped in wafer-thin filo pastry make a special treat. The dessert looks impressive, but takes very little time to make.

Serves 4
1 large mango
grated rind of 1 lemon
2 amaretti
25g/1oz/2 tbsp demerara
   (raw) sugar
60ml/4 tbsp wholemeal
   (whole-wheat) breadcrumbs
2 sheets of filo pastry, each
   measuring 48 x 28cm/
   19 x 11in
25g/1oz/2 tbsp butter or
   20g/¾oz/4 tsp soft margarine,
   melted
15ml/1 tbsp chopped almonds
icing (confectioners') sugar,
   for dusting

1 Preheat the oven to 190°C/375°F/Gas 5. Lightly grease a baking sheet. Cut the flesh from the mango and chop into small cubes. Place in a bowl and sprinkle with the grated lemon rind.

2 Crush the amaretti and mix them with the sugar and breadcrumbs in a bowl.

3 Lay one sheet of filo pastry on a flat surface and brush with a quarter of the melted butter or margarine. Top with the second sheet, brush with one-third of the remaining fat, then fold both sheets over, if necessary, to make a rectangle measuring 28 x 24cm/11 x 9½in. Brush with half the remaining fat.

4 Sprinkle the filo with the amaretti mixture, leaving a border on each long side. Arrange the mango over the top.

5 Carefully roll up the filo from one long side, Swiss-roll (jelly-roll) fashion, to enclose the amaretti mixture. Lift the strudel on to the baking sheet, seam side down. Brush with the remaining melted fat and sprinkle with the chopped almonds.

6 Bake the strudel for 20–25 minutes until light golden brown, then transfer to a board. Dust with the icing sugar, slice diagonally and serve.

Blueberry Frangipane Flan

A lemon pastry case is filled with a sweet almond filling, dotted with blueberries.

Serves 6
30ml/2 tbsp ground coffee
45ml/3 tbsp milk
50g/2oz/¼ cup unsalted
   (sweet) butter
50g/2oz/¼ cup caster
   (superfine) sugar
1 egg
115g/4oz/1 cup ground almonds
15ml/1 tbsp plain
(all-purpose) flour, sifted
225g/8oz/2 cups blueberries
30ml/2 tbsp jam
15ml/1 tbsp brandy

For the pastry
175g/6oz/1½ cups plain
   (all-purpose) flour
115g/4oz/½ cup unsalted (sweet)
   butter or margarine
25g/1oz/2 tbsp caster
   (superfine) sugar
finely grated rind of ½ lemon
15ml/1 tbsp chilled water

1 Preheat the oven to 190°C/375°F/Gas 5. To make the pastry, sift the flour into a bowl and rub in the butter. Stir in the sugar and lemon rind, then add the water and mix to a firm dough. Wrap in clear film (plastic wrap) and chill for 20 minutes.

2 Roll out the pastry on a lightly floured work surface and use to line a 23cm/9in loose-based flan tin (tart pan). Line the pastry with baking parchment and baking beans and bake for 10 minutes. Remove the paper and beans and bake for a further 10 minutes. Remove from the oven.

3 Meanwhile, make the filling. Put the ground coffee in a bowl. Bring the milk almost to the boil, then pour over the coffee and leave to infuse for 4 minutes. Cream the butter and sugar until pale. Beat in the egg, then add the almonds and flour. Finely strain in the coffee-flavoured milk and fold in.

4 Spread the coffee mixture into the pastry case. Scatter the blueberries over and push down slightly into the mixture. Bake for 30 minutes, until firm, covering with foil after 20 minutes.

5 Heat the jam and brandy in a small pan until melted. Brush over the flan and remove from the tin.

Chocolate, Date & Almond Filo Coil

Experience the allure of the Middle East with this delectable dessert. Crisp filo pastry conceals a chocolate and rose water filling studded with dates and almonds.

Serves 6

275g/10oz filo pastry, thawed if frozen
50g/2oz/¼ cup butter, melted
icing (confectioners') sugar, cocoa powder (unsweetened) and ground cinnamon, for dusting

For the filling

75g/3oz/6 tbsp butter
115g/4oz dark (bittersweet) chocolate, broken up into pieces
115g/4oz/1⅓ cup ground almonds
115g/4oz/⅔ cup chopped dates
75g/3oz/⅔ cup icing (confectioners') sugar
10ml/2 tsp rose water
2.5ml/½ tsp ground cinnamon

1 Preheat the oven to 180°C/350°F/Gas 4. Grease a 22cm/8½in round cake tin (pan). To make the filling, melt the butter with the chocolate in a heatproof bowl set over a pan of barely simmering water, then remove from the heat and stir in the remaining ingredients to make a thick paste. Leave to cool.

2 Lay one sheet of filo on a clean, flat surface. Brush with melted butter, then lay a second sheet on top and brush with more butter.

3 Roll a handful of the chocolate and almond mixture into a long sausage shape and place along one long edge of the layered filo. Roll up the pastry tightly around the filling to make a roll.

4 Fit the filo roll in the cake tin, in such a way that it sits snugly against the outer edge. Make more filo rolls in the same way, adding them to the tin from the outside towards the centre, until the coil fills the tin.

5 Brush the coil with the remaining melted butter. Bake for 30–35 minutes until the pastry is golden brown and crisp. Transfer the coil to a serving plate. Serve warm, dusted with icing sugar, cocoa and cinnamon.

Peach Leaf Pie

Juicy, lightly spiced peach slices are covered with a crust made entirely from individual pastry leaves to make this spectacular pie.

Serves 8

1.2kg/2½lb ripe peaches
juice of 1 lemon
115g/4oz/½ cup granulated sugar
45ml/3 tbsp cornflour (cornstarch)
1.5ml/¼ tsp grated nutmeg
2.5ml/½ tsp ground cinnamon
25g/1oz/2 tbsp butter, diced
1 egg, beaten with 15ml/1 tbsp water, to glaze

For the pastry

225g/8oz/2 cups plain (all-purpose) flour
4ml/¾ tsp salt
115g/4oz/½ cup cold butter, diced
40g/1½oz/3 tbsp white vegetable fat, diced
75–90ml/5–6 tbsp chilled water

1 Make the pastry. Sift the flour and salt into a large mixing bowl. Add the butter and vegetable fat, and rub in with your fingertips or cut in with a pastry blender until the mixture resembles coarse breadcrumbs.

2 Sprinkle over the dry ingredients just enough of the water to bind the mixture and use a fork to bring it together to form a soft dough. Gather the dough into two balls, one slightly larger than the other. Wrap separately in clear film (plastic wrap) and chill for 30 minutes.

3 Meanwhile, put a baking sheet in the oven and preheat to 220°C/425°F/Gas 7.

4 Drop a few peaches at a time into a large pan of boiling water, leave for 20 seconds, then transfer to a bowl of cold water. When the peaches are cool, peel off the skins. Slice the peaches and mix with the lemon juice, sugar, cornflour and spices in a bowl. Set aside.

5 On a lightly floured surface, roll out the larger piece of pastry to a thickness of 3mm/⅛in. Use to line a 23cm/9in pie plate. Chill until required.

6 Roll out the second piece of pastry and cut out leaf shapes about 7.5cm/3in long. Cut out enough to completely cover the top of the dish. Mark veins with a knife.

7 Brush the base of the pastry case with egg glaze. Add the peach mixture, piling it into a dome in the centre. Dot the surface with the diced butter.

8 To assemble the pie top, start from the outside edge. Make a ring of leaves around the edge, attaching each leaf to the pastry base with a dab of egg glaze. Place a second ring of leaves above, staggering the positions. Continue with rows of leaves until the pie is covered. Brush with egg glaze.

9 Bake the pie on the hot baking sheet for about 10 minutes. Lower the oven temperature to 180°C/350°F/Gas 4 and continue to bake for 35–40 minutes more, or until golden. Serve hot with cream, if you wish.

Filo Coil Energy 543Kcal/2267kJ; Protein 8.2g; Carbohydrate 55.4g, of which sugars 32.4g; Fat 33.6g, of which saturates 15g; Cholesterol 46mg; Calcium 108mg; Fibre 3.2g; Sodium 133mg.
Peach Leaf Pie Energy 390Kcal/1638kJ; Protein 4.4g; Carbohydrate 53.8g, of which sugars 27.2g; Fat 19g, of which saturates 10.7g; Cholesterol 52mg; Calcium 62mg; Fibre 3.2g; Sodium 152mg.

Chocolate Pecan Pie

A delicious version of an American favourite, this pie is great for any occasion.

Serves 6
200g/7oz/1¾ cups plain
  (all-purpose) flour
75ml/5 tbsp caster
  (superfine) sugar
90g/3½oz/scant ½ cup unsalted
  (sweet) butter, softened
1 egg, beaten
finely grated rind of 1 orange

For the filling
200g/7oz/¾ cup golden
  (light corn) syrup
45ml/3 tbsp light muscovado
  (brown) sugar
150g/5oz plain (semisweet)
  chocolate, chopped into
  small pieces
50g/2oz/¼ cup butter
3 eggs, beaten
5ml/1 tsp vanilla extract
175g/6oz/1½ cups shelled
  pecan nuts

1 Sift the flour into a bowl and stir in the sugar. Work in the butter evenly with your fingertips until combined.

2 Beat the egg and orange rind in a bowl, then stir into the mixture to make a firm dough. Add a little water if the mixture is too dry, and knead briefly.

3 Roll out the pastry on a lightly floured surface and use to line a deep, 20cm/8in loose-based flan tin (tart pan). Chill for about 30 minutes.

4 Preheat the oven to 180°C/350°F/Gas 4. Make the filling. Melt the syrup, sugar, chocolate and butter in a small pan.

5 Remove the pan from the heat and beat in the eggs and vanilla extract. Sprinkle the pecan nuts into the pastry case and carefully pour over the chocolate mixture.

6 Place the tin on a baking sheet and bake the pie for 50–60 minutes or until the filling is set.

7 Leave the pie in the tin for 10 minutes, then remove the tin's sides and transfer to a plate. Serve the pie on its own, or with a little single (light) cream.

Chocolate Almond Meringue Pie

This dreamy dessert offers a velvety chocolate filling on a light orange pastry case, topped with fluffy meringue.

Serves 6
175g/6oz/1½ cups plain
  (all-purpose) flour
50g/2oz/⅓ cup ground rice
150g/5oz/10 tbsp unsalted
  (sweet) butter
finely grated rind of 1 orange
1 egg yolk
flaked almonds and melted
  chocolate, to decorate

For the filling
150g/5oz plain (semisweet)
  chocolate, broken into squares
50g/2oz/¼ cup unsalted butter,
  softened
75g/3oz/6 tbsp caster
  (superfine) sugar
10ml/2 tsp cornflour (cornstarch)
4 egg yolks
75g/3oz/¾ cup ground almonds

For the meringue
3 egg whites
150g/5oz/¾ cup caster
  (superfine) sugar

1 Sift the flour and ground rice into a bowl. Rub in the butter to resemble breadcrumbs. Stir in the orange rind. Add the egg yolk; bring the dough together. Roll out and use to line a 23cm/9in round flan tin (tart pan). Chill for 30 minutes.

2 Preheat the oven to 190°C/375°F/Gas 5. Prick the pastry base all over with a fork, cover with baking parchment, weighed down with baking beans, and bake blind for 10 minutes. Remove the pastry case; take out the baking beans and paper.

3 Make the filling. Melt the chocolate in a heatproof bowl over hot water. Cream the butter with the sugar in a bowl, then beat in the cornflour and egg yolks. Fold in the almonds, then the chocolate. Spread in the pastry case. Bake for 10 minutes more.

4 Make the meringue. Whisk the egg whites until stiff, then gradually add half the sugar. Fold in the remaining sugar. Spoon the meringue over the chocolate filling, lifting it up with the back of the spoon to form peaks. Reduce the oven temperature to 180°C/350°F/Gas 4 and bake the pie for 15–20 minutes or until the topping is pale gold. Serve, sprinkled with almonds and drizzled with melted chocolate.

Choc. Pecan Pie Energy 843Kcal/3524kJ; Protein 11.6g; Carbohydrate 90.8g, of which sugars 64.8g; Fat 50.8g, of which saturates 19.1g; Cholesterol 178mg; Calcium 112mg; Fibre 3g; Sodium 282mg.
Meringue Pie Energy 792Kcal/3312kJ; Protein 11.4g; Carbohydrate 87g, of which sugars 56g; Fat 46.4g, of which saturates 23.5g; Cholesterol 241mg; Calcium 128mg; Fibre 2.6g; Sodium 248mg.

Rhubarb Meringue Pie

Tangy rhubarb contrasts
beautifully with meringue.

Serves 6
675g/1½lb rhubarb, chopped
250g/9oz/1¼ cup caster
  (superfine) sugar
grated rind and juice of 3 oranges
3 eggs, separated
75ml/5 tbsp cornflour (cornstarch)

For the pastry
200g/7oz/1¾ cups plain
  (all-purpose) flour
25g/1oz/¼ cup ground walnuts
115g/4oz/½ cup butter, diced
30ml/2 tbsp sugar
1 egg yolk, beaten with
  15ml/1 tbsp water

1 To make the pastry, sift the flour into a bowl and add the walnuts. Rub in the butter until the mixture resembles very fine breadcrumbs. Stir in the sugar and egg yolk mixture to make a firm dough. Knead lightly, wrap and chill for 30 minutes.

2 Preheat the oven to 190°C/375°F/Gas 5. Roll out the pastry on a lightly floured surface and use to line a 23cm/9in fluted flan tin (tart pan). Prick the base all over with a fork. Line the pastry with foil and baking beans, then bake for 15 minutes.

3 Meanwhile, to make the filling, put the chopped rhubarb in a large pan with 75g/3oz/6 tbsp of the sugar. Add the orange rind. Cover and cook over a low heat until tender.

4 Remove the foil and beans from the pastry case, then brush all over with a little egg yolk. Bake the pastry case for about 15 minutes, or until the pastry is crisp and golden.

5 Mix together the cornflour and the orange juice in a mixing bowl. Remove the rhubarb from the heat, stir in the cornflour mixture, then return the pan to the heat and bring to the boil, stirring constantly. Cook for 1–2 minutes more. Cool slightly, then beat in the remaining egg yolks. Pour into the pastry case.

6 Whisk the egg whites until they form soft peaks, then whisk in the remaining sugar, 15ml/1 tbsp at a time. Swirl over the filling and bake for 25 minutes until the meringue is golden.

Apple, Raisin & Maple Pies

Calvados accentuates the
apple flavour of these
elegant puff pastry pies.

Serves 4
350g/12oz puff pastry
beaten egg or milk, to glaze
whipped cream, flavoured with
  orange liqueur and sprinkled
  with grated orange rind, to serve

For the filling
75g/3oz/6 tbsp soft light
  brown sugar
30ml/2 tbsp lemon juice
45ml/3 tbsp maple syrup
150ml/¼ pint/⅔ cup water
45ml/3 tbsp Calvados
6 small eating apples, halved,
  peeled and cored
75g/3oz/½ cup raisins

1 Make the filling. Mix the sugar, lemon juice, maple syrup and water in a pan. Heat over medium heat until the sugar has dissolved, then bring to the boil and cook until reduced by half. Stir in the Calvados.

2 Cut four of the apples into eight even segments. Add the apple pieces to the syrup and simmer for 5–8 minutes until just tender. Lift the apple pieces out of the syrup using a slotted spoon and set them aside.

3 Chop the remaining apples and add to the syrup with the raisins. Simmer until the mixture is thick, then cool.

4 Preheat the oven to 200°C/400°F/Gas 6. Roll out the pastry on a floured surface and stamp out eight 15cm/6in rounds with a fluted cutter. Use half the pastry to line four 10cm/4in individual flan tins (mini tart pans). Spoon in the raisin mixture and level the surface.

5 Arrange the apple segments on top of the raisin mixture. Brush the edge of each pastry case with egg or milk and cover with a pastry lid. Trim, seal and flute the edges.

6 Cut attractive shapes from the pastry trimmings and use to decorate the pies. Brush over the tops with beaten egg or milk, then bake for 30–35 minutes until golden. Serve hot, with the liqueur-flavoured cream.

Rhubarb Pie Energy 567Kcal/2388kJ; Protein 8.4g; Carbohydrate 89.5g, of which sugars 52.6g; Fat 22.1g, of which saturates 11.1g; Cholesterol 136mg; Calcium 202mg; Fibre 2.8g; Sodium 168mg.
Apple, Raisin & Maple Energy 545Kcal/2294kJ; Protein 5.8g; Carbohydrate 82.8g, of which sugars 51.6g; Fat 21.6g, of which saturates 0g; Cholesterol 0mg; Calcium 75mg; Fibre 2g; Sodium 316mg.

Bakewell Tart

Although the pastry base makes this a tart, in the English village of Bakewell, where it originated, it is traditionally called Bakewell Pudding.

Serves 4
225g/8oz puff pastry
30ml/2 tbsp raspberry or
  apricot jam

2 eggs, plus 2 egg yolks
115g/4oz/generous ½ cup caster
  (superfine) sugar
115g/4oz/½ cup butter, melted
50g/2oz/⅔ cup ground almonds
  a few drops of almond extract
icing (confectioners') sugar,
  for dusting

1 Preheat the oven to 200°C/400°F/Gas 6. Roll out the pastry on a lightly floured surface and use to line an 18cm/7in pie plate. Trim the edge.

2 Re-roll the pastry trimmings and cut out wide strips of pastry. Use these to decorate the edge of the pastry case by gently twisting them around the rim, joining the strips together as necessary. Prick the pastry case all over, then spread the jam over the base.

3 Whisk the eggs, egg yolks and sugar together in a bowl until the mixture is thick and pale.

4 Gently stir the melted butter, ground almonds and almond extract into the whisked egg mixture.

5 Pour the mixture into the pastry case and bake for 30 minutes, or until the filling is just set and is lightly browned. Dust with icing sugar before serving hot, warm or cold.

> **Cook's Tip**
> Since this pastry case is not baked blind before being filled, place a baking sheet in the oven while it preheats, then place the tart on the hot sheet. This will ensure that the base of the pastry case cooks right through.

Treacle Tart

An old-fashioned favourite, with its sticky filling and twisted lattice topping, this tart is perfect with custard.

Serves 4–6
260g/9½oz/generous ¾ cup
  golden (light corn) syrup
75g/3oz/1½ cups fresh
  white breadcrumbs

grated rind of 1 lemon
30ml/2 tbsp lemon juice

For the pastry
150g/5oz/1¼ cups plain
  (all-purpose) flour
2.5ml/½ tsp salt
130g/4½oz/9 tbsp chilled butter,
  diced
45–60ml/3–4 tbsp chilled water

1 Make the pastry. Combine the flour and salt in a bowl. Rub or cut in the butter until the mixture resembles coarse breadcrumbs. With a fork, stir in just enough water to bind the dough. Gather into a smooth ball, knead lightly until smooth then wrap in clear film (plastic wrap) and chill for at least 20 minutes.

2 On a lightly floured surface, roll out the pastry to a thickness of 3mm/⅛in. Transfer to a 20cm/8in fluted flan tin (tart pan) and trim off the overhang. Chill the pastry case for 20 minutes. Reserve the pastry trimmings.

3 Put a baking sheet in the oven and preheat to 200°C/400°F/Gas 6. To make the filling, warm the syrup in a pan until it melts.

4 Remove the syrup from the heat and stir in the breadcrumbs and lemon rind. Leave to stand for 10 minutes, then add more breadcrumbs if the mixture is too thin and moist. Stir in the lemon juice, then spread the mixture evenly in the pastry case.

5 Roll out the pastry trimmings and cut into 10–12 thin strips. Twist the strips into spirals, then lay half of them on the filling. Arrange the remaining strips at right angles to form a lattice. Press the ends on to the rim.

6 Place the tart on the hot baking sheet and bake for 10 minutes. Lower the oven temperature to 190°C/375°F/Gas 5. Bake for 15 minutes more, until golden. Serve warm.

Treacle Tart Energy 420Kcal/1764kJ; Protein 4.1g; Carbohydrate 63.5g, of which sugars 35.1g; Fat 18.4g, of which saturates 11.3g; Cholesterol 46mg; Calcium 62mg; Fibre 1.1g; Sodium 344mg.
Bakewell Tart Energy 700Kcal/2919kJ; Protein 10.8g; Carbohydrate 57.1g, of which sugars 36.7g; Fat 49.9g, of which saturates 17.1g; Cholesterol 257mg; Calcium 110mg; Fibre 0.9g; Sodium 394mg.

Prune Tart with Custard Filling

Armagnac makes a great
partner for prunes but fresh
orange juice works well, too.

icing (confectioners') sugar, for
  dusting
thick cream, to serve

Serves 6–8
225g/8oz/1 cup pitted prunes
50ml/2fl oz/¼ cup Armagnac or
  other brandy
4 egg yolks
300ml/½ pint/1¼ cups milk
a few drops of vanilla extract
15g/½oz/2 tbsp cornflour
  (cornstarch)
25g/1oz/¼ cup flaked (sliced)
  almonds

For the pastry
175g/6oz/1½ cups plain
  (all-purpose) flour, sifted, plus
  extra for dusting
pinch of salt
90g/3½oz/½ cup caster
  (superfine) sugar
115g/4oz/½ cup unsalted
  (sweet) butter, at room
  temperature
1 egg

1 Place the prunes in a bowl with the Armagnac and leave in a
warm place to soak.

2 Place the flour, salt, 50g/2oz/¼ cup of the sugar, the butter
and egg, reserving 5ml/1 tsp egg white, in a food processor and
process until blended.

3 Turn out on a clean, lightly floured surface and bring the
mixture together into a ball. Leave for 10 minutes to rest.

4 Flour a 28 x 18cm/11 x 7in loose-based flan tin (tart pan).
Roll out the pastry and line the tin; don't worry if you have to
push it into shape, as this pastry is soft and easy to mould. Chill
for 10–20 minutes. Meanwhile, preheat the oven to
200°C/400°F/Gas 6.

5 Line the pastry case with baking parchment and fill with baking
beans, then bake for 15 minutes. Remove the paper and beans,
and bake for 10–15 minutes. Brush the base of the pastry with
the reserved egg white while it is still hot. Set aside to cool slightly.

6 Bring the milk and vanilla extract to the boil. In a bowl, whisk
the egg yolks and remaining sugar until thick, pale and fluffy, then
whisk in the cornflour. Strain in the milk and whisk until there
are no lumps.

7 Return to the pan and bring to the boil, whisking all the time
to remove any lumps. Cook for about 2 minutes until thick and
smooth, then set aside to cool. Press clear film (plastic wrap) on
to the surface of the custard to prevent a skin forming.

8 Stir any prune liquid into the custard, then spread over the
pastry case. Arrange the prunes on top, sprinkle with the flaked
almonds and dust with icing sugar, and return to the oven for
10 minutes until golden and glazed. Remove from the oven and
leave to cool. Serve hot or at room temperature with cream.

> **Cook's Tip**
> Let the prunes soak for at least an hour to absorb the brandy.

Moroccan Serpent Cake

This famous Moroccan
pastry is filled with lightly
fragrant almond paste.

Serves 8
8 sheets of filo pastry
50g/2oz/¼ cup butter, melted
1 egg, beaten
5ml/1 tsp ground cinnamon
icing (confectioners') sugar,
  for dusting

For the almond paste
about 50g/2oz/¼ cup butter,
  melted
225g/8oz/2⅔ cups ground
  almonds
2.5ml/½ tsp almond extract
50g/2oz/½ cup icing
  (confectioners') sugar
1 egg yolk, beaten
15ml/1 tbsp rose water or orange
  flower water

1 Make the almond paste. Mix the melted butter with the
ground almonds and almond extract in a bowl. Add the sugar,
egg yolk and rose or orange flower water, mix well and knead
until soft and pliable. Chill for 10 minutes.

2 Break the paste into 10 even-size balls and, with your hands,
roll them into 10cm/4in sausages. Chill again.

3 Preheat the oven to 180°C/350°F/Gas 4. Place two sheets of
filo pastry on the work surface so that they overlap slightly to
form an 18 x 56cm/7 x 22in rectangle. Brush the overlapping
edges with butter to secure and then lightly brush all over.
Cover with another two sheets of filo in the same way.

4 Place five almond paste sausages along the lower edge of the
filo sheet and roll up tightly, tucking in the ends. Repeat with the
remaining filo and almond paste, so that you have two rolls.
Shape the first roll into a loose coil, then transfer to a baking
sheet brushed with butter. Attach the second roll and continue
coiling the filo to make a snake. Tuck the end under.

5 Beat the egg with half the cinnamon; brush over the pastry.
Bake in the oven for 25 minutes until golden. Carefully invert
the snake on to another baking sheet and return to the oven
for 5–10 minutes more. Transfer to a serving plate, dust with
icing sugar, then sprinkle with the remaining cinnamon.

Prune Tart Energy 362Kcal/1518kJ; Protein 7.1g; Carbohydrate 42.1g, of which sugars 23.6g; Fat 18.1g, of which saturates 9.1g; Cholesterol 157mg; Calcium 117mg; Fibre 2.5g; Sodium 122mg.
Serpent Cake Energy 341Kcal/1417kJ; Protein 7.7g; Carbohydrate 18.3g, of which sugars 8g; Fat 26.9g, of which saturates 8g; Cholesterol 54mg; Calcium 94mg; Fibre 2.5g; Sodium 83mg.

Lime Sorbet

Light and tangy, this iced dessert is a good choice to serve after a substantial main course. Use an ice cream scoop to give the dish a professional-looking finish.

Serves 4
250g/9oz/1¼ cups granulated
  sugar
600ml/1 pint/2½ cups water
grated rind of 1 lime
175ml/6fl oz/¾ cup freshly
  squeezed lime juice
15–30ml/1–2 tbsp freshly
  squeezed lemon juice
icing (confectioners') sugar,
  to taste
slivers of lime rind, to decorate

1 In a small heavy pan, dissolve the granulated sugar in the water, without stirring, over medium heat. When the sugar has dissolved, boil for 5–6 minutes. Remove from the heat and leave to cool.

2 Combine the cooled sugar syrup with the lime rind and juice in a measuring jug (cup) or bowl. Stir well. Taste and adjust the flavour by adding lemon juice and some icing sugar, if necessary. Do not over-sweeten.

3 Pour the mixture into a freezer container and freeze for about 3 hours, until softly set.

4 Remove from the container and chop roughly into 7.5cm/3in pieces. Place in a food processor and process until smooth. Return the mixture to the freezer container and freeze again until set. Repeat this freezing and chopping process two or three times, until a smooth consistency is obtained.

5 Alternatively, use an ice cream maker to freeze the mixture, following the manufacturer's instructions.

6 Transfer the sorbet to the refrigerator about 20–30 minutes before serving to soften slightly. Serve in scoops, decorated with slivers of lime rind.

Creole Ambrosia

With layers of sliced orange and fresh coconut, this refreshing fruit dessert makes a change from the more traditional fruit salad.

Serves 6
6 oranges
1 coconut
25g/1oz/2 tbsp caster
  (superfine) sugar

1 Peel the oranges, removing all the white pith, then slice the flesh thinly, picking out any seeds with the point of a knife. Do this on a plate to catch the juice.

2 Pierce the "eyes" of the coconut and pour away the milk, then crack open the coconut with a hammer. (This is best done outside on a stone surface.)

3 Remove the coconut flesh from the shell with a sharp knife, then grate half the flesh coarsely, either with a hand grater or in a food processor fitted with a grating blade.

4 Layer the grated coconut and orange slices in a glass bowl, starting and finishing with the coconut. After each orange layer, sprinkle on a little sugar and pour over some of the reserved orange juice.

5 Leave to stand for 2 hours, either at room temperature or in the refrigerator in hot weather, before serving.

> **Cook's Tip**
> To cleanly remove the rind and pith from an orange, first cut a slice off either end of the fruit with a sharp knife. Stand it on a board and, working downwards, cut off the peel in wide strips.

> **Variation**
> Use mangoes instead of oranges for a more exotic flavour. Peel the mangoes, then slice the flesh away from the stone (pit).

Creole Ambrosia Energy 160Kcal/668kJ; Protein 2.7g; Carbohydrate 14.7g, of which sugars 14.7g; Fat 10.5g, of which saturates 8.9g; Cholesterol 0mg; Calcium 79mg; Fibre 5g; Sodium 13mg.
Lime Sorbet Energy 259Kcal/1106kJ; Protein 0.5g; Carbohydrate 68.6g, of which sugars 68.6g; Fat 0g, of which saturates 0g; Cholesterol 0mg; Calcium 38mg; Fibre 0.1g; Sodium 4mg.

Watermelon Sorbet

This pretty pink sorbet makes a fresh-tasting dessert, but it could also be served before the main course at a smart dinner party, to cleanse the palate.

Serves 6

1kg/2¼lb piece watermelon
200g/7oz/1 cup caster (superfine) sugar
120ml/4fl oz/½ cup water
juice of 1 lemon
2 egg whites
mint leaves, to decorate

1 Using a sharp knife, cut the watermelon into wedges, then cut the flesh away from the rind. Cube the flesh, picking out all the seeds at the same time.

2 Purée three-quarters of the flesh in a food processor or blender, but mash the last quarter on a plate – this will give the sorbet more texture.

3 Stir the sugar with the lemon juice and water in a pan over very low heat until the sugar dissolves and the syrup is clear.

4 Mix all the watermelon and the syrup in a large bowl and transfer to a freezer container.

5 Freeze for 1–1½ hours, until the edges begin to set. Beat the mixture, return to the freezer and freeze for a further 1 hour.

6 Whisk the egg whites to soft peaks. Beat the iced mixture again and fold in the egg whites. Return to the freezer for a further hour, then beat once more and freeze until firm.

7 Transfer the sorbet to the refrigerator about 20–30 minutes before serving. Serve in scoops decorated with mint leaves.

> **Cook's Tip**
> Work quickly when beating the frozen mixture – you do not want it to completely melt before you return it to the freezer.

Blackcurrant Sorbet

Blackcurrants produce a vibrant and intensely flavoured sorbet that is ideal for rounding off an *al-fresco* summer meal.

Serves 4–6

90g/3½oz/½ cup caster (superfine) sugar
120ml/4fl oz/½ cup water
500g/1¼lb blackcurrants
juice of ½ lemon
15ml/1 tbsp egg white
mint leaves, to decorate

1 Place the sugar and water in a pan over medium-high heat and bring to the boil, stirring until the sugar has dissolved. Continue to boil the syrup for 2 minutes, then remove the pan from the heat and set aside to cool.

2 Remove the blackcurrants from their stalks, by pulling them through the tines of a fork.

3 Put the blackcurrants and lemon juice in a blender or food processor fitted with a metal blade, and process until smooth. Alternatively, chop the blackcurrants coarsely, then add the lemon juice. Mix in the sugar syrup.

4 Press through a sieve (strainer) to remove the seeds.

5 Pour the blackcurrant purée into a non-metallic freezer container. Cover with clear film (plastic wrap) or a lid and freeze until the sorbet is nearly firm, but still a bit slushy.

6 Cut the sorbet into pieces and put in the blender or food processor. Process until smooth, then, with the machine running, add the egg white and process until well mixed. Transfer the sorbet back to the freezer container and freeze until almost firm. Chop the sorbet again and process until smooth. Return to the freezer again until firm.

7 Serve immediately or freeze, tightly covered, for up to one week. Allow to soften for 5–10 minutes at room temperature before serving, decorated with mint leaves.

Watermelon Sorbet Energy 187Kcal/798kJ; Protein 2g; Carbohydrate 46.7g, of which sugars 46.7g; Fat 0.5g, of which saturates 0.2g; Cholesterol 0mg; Calcium 30mg; Fibre 0.2g; Sodium 26mg.
Blackcurrant Sorbet Energy 84Kcal/361kJ; Protein 1.3g; Carbohydrate 21.2g, of which sugars 21.2g; Fat 0g, of which saturates 0g; Cholesterol 0mg; Calcium 58mg; Fibre 3g; Sodium 14mg.

Chocolate Sorbet with Red Fruits

Mouthwatering chocolate-flavoured sorbet tastes and looks stunning when served with a selection of luscious red berries.

Serves 6

475ml/16fl oz/2 cups water
45ml/3 tbsp clear honey
90g/3½oz/½ cup caster (superfine) sugar

75g/3oz/⅔ cup cocoa powder (unsweetened)
50g/2oz plain (semisweet) or dark (bittersweet) chocolate, chopped into small pieces
400g/14oz soft red fruits, such as raspberries, redcurrants or strawberries

1 Put the water in a pan with the honey, sugar and cocoa. Heat gently, stirring occasionally, until the sugar has completely dissolved.

2 Remove the pan from the heat, add the chocolate pieces and stir until melted. Leave until cool.

3 Pour the chocolate mixture into a freezer container and freeze until slushy. Whisk quickly until smooth, then return the mixture to the freezer again and freeze until almost firm. Whisk the iced mixture for a second time, cover the container and freeze until firm.

4 Alternatively, use an ice cream maker to freeze the mixture, following the manufacturer's instructions.

5 Remove the sorbet from the freezer 10–15 minutes before serving to soften slightly. Serve in scoops, in chilled dessert bowls, with the soft fruits.

> **Cook's Tip**
> Chocolate curls make an attractive decoration and are very easy to create. Simply chill a bar of chocolate, then use a vegetable peeler to shave off curls along the length of the bar.

Ginger & Kiwi Sorbet

Freshly grated root ginger gives a lively, aromatic flavour to this exotic sorbet, while the black seeds of the kiwi fruit add interesting texture and colour.

Serves 6

50g/2oz fresh root ginger
115g/4oz/generous ½ cup caster (superfine) sugar
300ml/½ pint/1¼ cups water
5 kiwi fruit
fresh mint sprigs or chopped kiwi fruit, to decorate

1 Peel the ginger and grate it finely. Put the sugar and water in a pan and heat gently until the sugar has dissolved. Add the ginger and cook for 1 minute, then leave to cool. Strain into a bowl and chill until very cold.

2 Peel the kiwi fruit, place in a blender and process to form a smooth purée. Add the purée to the chilled syrup and mix well.

3 Pour the kiwi mixture into a freezer container and freeze until slushy. Beat the mixture, then freeze again. Repeat this beating process one more time, then cover the container and freeze until firm.

4 Alternatively, use an ice cream maker. Freeze the mixture following the manufacturer's instructions, then transfer to a freezer container and freeze until required.

5 Remove the sorbet from the freezer 10–15 minutes before serving, to allow it to soften slightly. Spoon into glass bowls, then decorate with mint sprigs or pieces of chopped kiwi fruit and serve immediately.

> **Cook's Tip**
> Fresh ginger root is widely available and is easy to spot with its knobbly shape and pale brown skin. Look for smooth skin and firm solid flesh. Any left over can be wrapped and stored in the refrigerator for up to three weeks. Use a sharp knife for peeling.

Chocolate Sorbet Energy 179Kcal/758kJ; Protein 3.8g; Carbohydrate 31.2g, of which sugars 29.7g; Fat 5.3g, of which saturates 3.1g; Cholesterol 1mg; Calcium 44mg; Fibre 3.4g; Sodium 123mg.
Ginger & Kiwi Sorbet Energy 100Kcal/426kJ; Protein 0.7g; Carbohydrate 25.3g, of which sugars 25.2g; Fat 0.3g, of which saturates 0g; Cholesterol 0mg; Calcium 23mg; Fibre 1g; Sodium 3mg.

Chilli Sorbet

Served at a dinner party, as a palate tingling appetizer or a zingy dessert, this unusual sorbet is sure to become a talking point.

Serves 6
1 fresh medium-hot red chilli
finely grated rind and juice of
  2 lemons
finely grated rind and juice of
  2 limes
200g/7oz/1 cup caster (superfine)
  sugar
750ml/1¼ pints/3 cups water
lemon or lime rind, to decorate

1 Cut the chilli in half, removing all the seeds and any pith with a small sharp knife. Chop the flesh very finely.

2 Put the chilli, lemon and lime rind, sugar and water in a heavy pan. Heat gently and stir while the sugar dissolves. Bring to the boil, then simmer for 2 minutes without stirring. Leave to cool.

3 Add the lemon and lime juice to the chilli syrup and chill until very cold.

4 Pour the mixture into a freezer container and freeze for 3–4 hours, beating twice as it thickens. Return to the freezer until ready to serve.

5 Alternatively, use an ice cream maker. Freeze the mixture until it holds its shape. Scrape into a freezer container and freeze.

6 Soften slightly at room temperature before spooning into glasses and decorating with thinly pared lemon or lime rind.

> **Cook's Tips**
> • *Wash your hands immediately after handling the chilli to avoid getting chilli juice in your eyes, should you rub them.*
> • *For an added kick to this sorbet, drizzle each portion with a little tequila or vodka before serving.*

Lemon Sorbet

This is probably the most classic sorbet of all. Cooling and deliciously smooth, it literally melts in the mouth.

Serves 6
200g/7oz/1 cup caster
  (superfine) sugar
300ml/½ pint/1¼ cups water
4 lemons, well scrubbed
1 egg white

1 Put the sugar and water in a pan and bring to the boil, stirring occasionally until the sugar has just dissolved.

2 Using a swivel vegetable peeler, pare the rind thinly from two of the lemons so that it falls straight into the pan. Simmer for 2 minutes without stirring, then take the pan off the heat. Leave to cool, then chill.

3 Squeeze the juice from all the lemons and add to the syrup.

4 Strain the syrup into a shallow freezer container, reserving the rind. Freeze the mixture for 4 hours until it is mushy.

5 Scoop the sorbet into a food processor and process until smooth. Lightly whisk the egg white with a fork until it is just frothy. Spoon the sorbet back into the container, beat in the egg white and return the mixture to the freezer for 4 hours.

6 Alternatively, use an ice cream maker. Strain the lemon syrup, reserving the rind, and churn until thick. Add the egg white to the mixture and churn for a further 10–15 minutes until firm enough to scoop.

7 Scoop into bowls. Decorate with strips of the reserved rind.

> **Cook's Tip**
> *Cut one-third off the top of a lemon and reserve as a lid. Squeeze the juice out of the rest. Remove any membrane and use the shell as a ready-made container for the sorbet.*

Chilli Sorbet Energy 150Kcal/640kJ; Protein 0.5g; Carbohydrate 39.4g, of which sugars 39.4g; Fat 0.1g, of which saturates 0g; Cholesterol 0mg; Calcium 23mg; Fibre 0g; Sodium 3mg.
Lemon Sorbet Energy 135Kcal/574kJ; Protein 0.7g; Carbohydrate 35.1g, of which sugars 35.1g; Fat 0g, of which saturates 0g; Cholesterol 0mg; Calcium 19mg; Fibre 0g; Sodium 13mg.

Spiced Sorbet Pears

Pears poached in wine make an elegant dessert at any time of the year. In this recipe the cooked pears are hollowed out and filled with a delicious sorbet.

Serves 6
550ml/18fl oz/2½ cups red wine
2 cinnamon sticks, halved
115g/4oz/generous ½ cup caster (superfine) sugar
6 plump pears

1 Put the wine, cinnamon sticks and sugar in a heavy pan that is big enough for the pears. Heat gently to dissolve the sugar.

2 Peel the pears, leaving the stalks attached, and stand upright in the syrup, taking care not to pack them too tightly. Cover and simmer very gently for 10–20 minutes until just tender, turning so they colour evenly.

3 Lift out the pears with a slotted spoon and set aside to cool. Boil the cooking juice briefly until reduced to 350ml/12fl oz/ 1½ cups. Set aside and leave to cool.

4 Cut a deep 2.5cm/1in slice off the top of each pear and reserve. Use an apple corer to remove the cores. Using a teaspoon, scoop out the centre of each pear, leaving a thick shell. Put the scooped-out flesh in a food processor or blender. Put the hollowed pears and their lids in the freezer.

5 Strain the reduced cooking juice, then set 75ml/5 tbsp aside for serving and add the rest to the food processor. Blend until smooth. Pour the mixture into a freezer container and freeze for 3–4 hours, beating twice as it thickens. Alternatively, use an ice cream maker and churn until the mixture holds its shape.

6 Using a teaspoon, pack the sorbet into the frozen pears, piling it up high. Top with the lids and return to the freezer overnight.

7 Remove the pears from the freezer and leave them to stand for about 30 minutes before serving. The pears should have softened but the sorbet should remain icy. Spoon the reserved syrup around each pear to serve.

Chocolate Sorbet

A cooling treat for chocolate lovers. Serve with crisp little biscuits (cookies) as a light way to end a meal.

Serves 6
150g/5oz dark (bittersweet) chocolate, chopped
115g/4oz plain (semisweet) chocolate, grated
225g/8oz/1 cup caster (superfine) sugar
475ml/16fl oz/2 cups water
chocolate curls, to decorate

1 Put all of the chocolate in a food processor, fitted with a metal blade, and process for approximately 20–30 seconds, or until finely chopped.

2 Place the sugar and water in a pan over medium heat. Bring to the boil, stirring until all of the sugar has completely dissolved. Boil for about 2 minutes, then remove the pan from the heat.

3 While the machine is running, carefully add the hot sugar-and-water syrup to the chocolate in the food processor. Keep the food processor running for 1–2 minutes until the chocolate is completely melted and the mixture is smooth, scraping down the bowl once.

4 Strain the chocolate mixture into a large measuring jug (cup) or bowl. Leave to cool completely, then chill, making sure that you stir the mixture occasionally.

5 Pour the chilled mixture into a freezer container and freeze until it is slushy.

6 Whisk until smooth, then freeze again until almost firm. Whisk for a second time and return to the freezer.

7 Allow to soften slightly before serving decorated with the chocolate curls.

Spiced Sorbet Pears Energy 198Kcal/835kJ; Protein 0.6g; Carbohydrate 35.2g, of which sugars 35.2g; Fat 0.2g, of which saturates 0g; Cholesterol 0mg; Calcium 33mg; Fibre 3.3g; Sodium 12mg.
Chocolate Sorbet Energy 301Kcal/1266kJ; Protein 2.3g; Carbohydrate 48.1g, of which sugars 47.7g; Fat 12.4g, of which saturates 7.4g; Cholesterol 3mg; Calcium 25mg; Fibre 1.1g; Sodium 4mg.

Frozen Clementines

These pretty, sorbet-filled fruits store well in the freezer, so they make an ideal dessert to prepare in advance for a dinner party. Try to use organic citrus fruit, which will not be coated with anti-fungal wax.

Makes 12
16 large clementines or
  small oranges
175g/6oz/¾ cup caster
  (superfine) sugar
105ml/7 tbsp water
juice of 2 lemons
a little fresh orange juice, if
  necessary
fresh mint leaves, to decorate

1 Carefully slice the tops off 12 of the clementines to make lids. Place the lids on a baking sheet. Loosen the fruit flesh with a sharp knife then carefully scoop it out into a bowl, keeping the shells intact. Scrape out the membrane from the shells, then add the shells to the baking sheet and place in the freezer.

2 Put the sugar and water in a heavy pan and heat gently, stirring until the sugar dissolves. Boil for 3 minutes without stirring, then cool. Stir in the lemon juice.

3 Grate the rind from the remaining four clementines. Squeeze the fruits and add the juice and rind to the lemon syrup.

4 Process the clementine flesh in a food processor, then press it through a sieve (strainer) to extract the juice. Add this to the syrup. You need about 900ml/1½ pints/3¾ cups of liquid. Make up to the required amount with orange juice if necessary.

5 Pour the mixture into a freezer container and freeze for 3–4 hours, beating twice as the sorbet thickens. Alternatively, use an ice cream maker and churn the mixture until it holds its shape.

6 Spoon the citrus sorbet into the fruit shells, position the lids on top and return to the freezer for several hours, until solid.

7 Transfer to the refrigerator about 30 minutes before serving, to soften slightly. Decorate with fresh mint leaves to serve.

Orange & Yogurt Ice

With this low-fat ice, you can indulge in a dessert without feeling too guilty.

Serves 6
90ml/6 tbsp water
10ml/2 tsp powdered gelatine
115g/4oz/generous ½ cup caster
  (superfine) sugar

250ml/8fl oz/1 cup freshly
  squeezed orange juice from
  a carton or bottle
500ml/17fl oz/generous 2 cups
  bio yogurt
cones or meringue nests,
  blueberries and fresh mint
  sprigs, to serve

1 Put 30ml/2 tbsp of the water in a small bowl and sprinkle the powdered gelatine over the top. Set aside until spongy. Meanwhile, put the sugar in a small pan, add the remaining water and heat through gently until the sugar has dissolved.

2 Remove the pan from the heat, add the gelatine and stir until completely dissolved. Cool, stir in the orange juice and chill for 15–30 minutes.

3 Spoon the yogurt into a bowl, gradually add the chilled orange juice mixture and mix well. Pour the mixture into a freezer container. Freeze for 6 hours or until firm, beating twice with a fork or in a food processor to break up the ice crystals.

4 Alternatively, use an ice cream maker. Freeze the mixture until starting to thicken. Switch off the machine, remove the paddle, if necessary, add the yogurt and mix well. Replace the paddle and continue to churn the ice cream for 15–20 minutes until thick. Scrape it into a freezer container and freeze until firm.

5 Scoop the yogurt ice into cones or meringue nests and decorate with blueberries and mint.

> **Cook's Tip**
> Meringue nests are not difficult to make, but if you do not have the time, bought ones are a perfectly acceptable alternative.

Frozen Clementines Energy 117Kcal/499kJ; Protein 1.8g; Carbohydrate 28.9g, of which sugars 28.9g; Fat 0.2g, of which saturates 0g; Cholesterol 0mg; Calcium 83mg; Fibre 2.7g; Sodium 9mg.
Orange & Yogurt Ice Energy 137Kcal/583kJ; Protein 4.6g; Carbohydrate 30g, of which sugars 30g; Fat 0.9g, of which saturates 0.4g; Cholesterol 1mg; Calcium 173mg; Fibre 0.1g; Sodium 75mg.

Summer Berry Frozen Yogurt

Any frozen summer fruits will work well for this dish.

Serves 6

350g/12oz/3 cups frozen
  summer fruits

200ml/7fl oz/scant 1 cup Greek
  (US strained plain) yogurt
25g/1oz icing (confectioners')
  sugar

1 Put all the ingredients into a food processor and process until combined but still quite chunky. Spoon the mixture into six 150ml/¼ pint/⅔ cup ramekin dishes. Cover each dish with clear film (plastic wrap) and place in the freezer for about 2 hours, or until firm.

2 To turn out the frozen yogurts, dip the dishes briefly in hot water and invert them on to small serving plates. Tap the base of the dishes and the yogurts will come out easily. Serve immediately.

Watermelon Ice

This refreshing dessert is perfect after a spicy meal.

Serves 4–6

105ml/7 tbsp water

90ml/6 tbsp caster (superfine)
  sugar
4 kaffir lime leaves, torn into small
  pieces
500g/1¼lb watermelon

1 Put the water, sugar and lime leaves in a pan. Heat gently until the sugar dissolves, then pour into a bowl and set aside to cool.

2 Cut the watermelon into wedges. Cut the flesh from the rind, remove the seeds and chop the flesh. Process the flesh to a slush in a food processor. Mix in the sugar syrup. Chill for 3–4 hours.

3 Strain into a freezer container and freeze for 2 hours, then beat with a fork to break up the ice crystals. Return to the freezer for 3 hours more, beating every 30 minutes, then freeze until firm. Place in the refrigerator 30 minutes before serving.

Elderflower & Lime Yogurt Ice

Fragrant elderflowers have a wonderful flavour, but they are in season for only a very short time. Fortunately, good-quality ready-made elderflower cordial is readily available and combines beautifully with limes to make a lovely iced dessert.

Serves 6

4 egg yolks
50g/2oz/¼ cup caster
  (superfine) sugar

10ml/2 tsp cornflour (cornstarch)
300ml/½ pint/1¼ cups milk
finely grated rind and juice of
  2 limes
150ml/¼ pint/⅔ cup elderflower
  cordial
200ml/7fl oz/scant 1 cup Greek
  (US strained plain) yogurt
150ml/¼ pint/⅔ cup double
  (heavy) cream
grated lime rind, to decorate

1 Whisk the egg yolks in a bowl with the sugar, cornflour and a little of the milk. Pour the remaining milk into a heavy pan, bring it to the boil, then pour it over the yolk mixture, whisking constantly. Return the mixture to the pan and cook over a very gentle heat, stirring constantly until the custard thickens. Do not let it boil or it may curdle.

2 Pour the custard into a bowl and add the lime rind and juice. Pour in the elderflower cordial and mix lightly. Cover the surface of the mixture closely with baking parchment. Leave to cool, then chill until very cold.

3 Whip together the yogurt and cream and fold into the custard. Pour the mixture into a freezer container and freeze for 3–4 hours, beating twice as it thickens. Scoop into individual dishes and return to the freezer until ready to serve.

4 Alternatively, use an ice cream maker. Stir the yogurt and cream into the custard and churn until it thickens. Transfer the yogurt ice into individual dishes and freeze until required.

5 Transfer the yogurt ice to the refrigerator 30 minutes before serving. Decorate with the grated lime rind and serve.

Summer Berry Yogurt Energy 71Kcal/295kJ; Protein 2.6g; Carbohydrate 8.5g, of which sugars 8.5g; Fat 3.5g, of which saturates 1.7g; Cholesterol 0mg; Calcium 62mg; Fibre 0.7g; Sodium 28mg.
Watermelon Ice Energy 85Kcal/363kJ; Protein 0.5g; Carbohydrate 21.6g, of which sugars 21.6g; Fat 0.3g, of which saturates 0.1g; Cholesterol 0mg; Calcium 14mg; Fibre 0.1g; Sodium 3mg.
Elderflower & Lime Ice Energy 219Kcal/912kJ; Protein 4.3g; Carbohydrate 12.4g, of which sugars 10.9g; Fat 17.7g, of which saturates 10.6g; Cholesterol 37mg; Calcium 125mg; Fibre 0g; Sodium 54mg.

Ice Cream with Sweet Pine Nut Sauce

The delicious combination of lightly toasted pine nuts, tangy lemon and butter makes an easy sauce, perfect for enlivening vanilla ice cream and lemon sorbet.

Serves 4
75g/3oz/5 tbsp pine nuts
25g/1oz/2tbsp unsalted (sweet) butter
30ml/2 tbsp clear honey
30ml/2 tbsp light muscovado (brown) sugar
finely grated rind and juice of 1 lemon
250ml/8fl oz/1 cup lemon sorbet
250ml/8fl oz/1 cup vanilla ice cream

1 Toast the nuts lightly, shaking them until evenly coloured, then chop roughly. Melt the butter in a small, heavy pan with the honey and sugar. Remove from the heat. Stir in the lemon rind and juice.

2 Stir in the chopped pine nuts. Pour the sauce into a small jug (pitcher). Leave to cool until ready to serve.

3 To serve, alternate small scoops of the lemon sorbet and the vanilla ice cream in four tall serving glasses. Generously spoon the pine nut sauce over the ices and serve immediately.

Cook's Tips
• The sauce will be very thin while it is still warm, but it becomes thicker as it cools. It is best to serve the sauce before it has turned cold.
• Pine nuts, which are the seeds of a Mediterranean pine tree, have a softish, oily texture and an attractive, delicate flavour. You can toast the pine nuts in a variety of ways. Spread them on a baking sheet and toast in the oven or under the grill (broiler) for about 5 minutes, shaking them frequently. Alternatively, put the pine nuts in a dry non-stick frying pan and lightly toast over a medium heat, shaking often. Keep a close eye on them as they can over-brown very quickly.

Mascarpone & Raspberry Ripple

Mascarpone makes a wonderfully smooth base for ice cream, which is made even more delicious when mixed with a tangy lemon syrup and streaked with raspberry purée.

Serves 8
250g/9oz/1¼ cups caster (superfine) sugar
450ml/¾ pint/scant 2 cups water
finely grated rind and juice of 1 lemon
350g/12oz/2 cups raspberries, plus extra to decorate
500g/1¼lb/2½ cups mascarpone

1 Put 225g/8oz/1 cup of the sugar in a heavy pan. Pour in the water and heat gently until the sugar dissolves. Bring to the boil, add the lemon rind and juice and boil for 3 minutes, without stirring, to make a syrup. Leave to cool.

2 Crush the raspberries lightly with a fork until broken up but not completely puréed, then stir in the remaining sugar.

3 Beat the mascarpone in a large bowl until smooth, gradually adding the lemon syrup.

4 Pour the mascarpone mixture into a freezer container and freeze until it begins to thicken. Beat to break down the ice crystals, then return to the freezer. When beginning to thicken again, repeat the beating process for a second time, then return to the freezer until the ice cream is frozen but still soft.

5 Alternatively, use an ice cream maker. Churn the mixture until thick, then transfer to a freezer container.

6 Spoon the crushed raspberries over the ice cream. Using a metal spoon, fold into the ice cream until rippled, making sure you reach the corners. Freeze for several hours or overnight until firm.

7 To serve, scoop the ice cream into glasses and decorate with the extra raspberries.

Ice Cream Energy 419Kcal/1756kJ; Protein 5.6g; Carbohydrate 48.1g, of which sugars 47.4g; Fat 23.4g, of which saturates 7.9g; Cholesterol 29mg; Calcium 71mg; Fibre 0.4g; Sodium 88mg. **Mascarpone & Rasp. Ripple** Energy 217Kcal/916kJ; Protein 10.1g; Carbohydrate 36.9g, of which sugars 36.9g; Fat 5.1g, of which saturates 3.3g; Cholesterol 15mg; Calcium 100mg; Fibre 1.1g; Sodium 277mg.

Chocolate Flake Ice Cream

This enticing ice cream, speckled with chocolate, is difficult to resist. Serve with slices of tropical fruit, such as pineapple and mango, for a perfect balance.

Serves 6
300ml/½ pint/1¼ cups whipping cream, chilled
90ml/6 tbsp Greek (US strained plain) yogurt
75–90ml/5–6 tbsp caster (superfine) sugar
few drops of vanilla extract
150g/5oz/10 tbsp flaked or roughly grated chocolate
flaked chocolate pieces, to decorate

1 Have ready a 600–900ml/1–1½ pint/2½–3¾ cup freezer container, preferably with a lid.

2 Softly whip the cream in a large bowl then fold in the yogurt, sugar, vanilla extract and chocolate. Stir gently to mix thoroughly, and then transfer to the freezer container.

3 Smooth the surface of the ice cream, then cover and freeze. Gently stir with a fork every 30 minutes for up to 4 hours until the ice cream is too hard to stir.

4 Alternatively, use an ice cream maker. Freeze the cream and chocolate mixture following the manufacturer's instructions.

5 Transfer to the refrigerator 15 minutes before serving to soften slightly. Serve in scoops, decorated with chocolate flakes.

Cook's Tips
• *Transferring the ice cream to the refrigerator for a short time before serving allows the full flavour of the dessert to develop and makes it easier to scoop it into neat balls.*
• *Use a metal scoop to serve the ice cream, dipping the scoop briefly in warm water between servings.*

Chocolate Ice Cream

To make this popular classic, use good quality chocolate to give the best flavour.

Serves 6
750ml/1¼ pints/3 cups milk
10cm/4in piece of vanilla pod (bean)
4 egg yolks
150g/5oz/¾ cup granulated sugar
225g/8oz dark (bittersweet) chocolate, melted

1 To make the custard, heat the milk with the vanilla pod in a small pan. Remove from the heat as soon as small bubbles start to form. Do not boil.

2 Beat the egg yolks with a wire whisk or electric beater. Gradually incorporate the sugar, and continue beating for about 5 minutes until the mixture is pale yellow. Strain the milk and slowly add it to the egg mixture, drop by drop.

3 Pour the mixture into a double boiler with the melted chocolate. Stir over moderate heat until the water in the pan is boiling, and the custard thickens enough to lightly coat the back of a spoon. Remove from the heat and allow to cool.

4 Pour the mixture into a freezer container and freeze until set, about 3 hours. Remove from the container and chop roughly into 7.5cm/3in pieces. Place in the bowl of a food processor and process until smooth. Return to the freezer container, and freeze again until firm. Repeat the freezing-chopping process 2 or 3 times, until a smooth consistency is reached, then freeze until required. Alternatively, use an ice cream maker and freeze the mixture following the manufacturer's instructions.

Cook's Tip
If you do not have a double boiler, cook the custard in a heatproof bowl set over a pan of water. Make sure that the custard does not boil, otherwise it will curdle.

Choc. Ice Cream Energy 388Kcal/1634kJ; Protein 8.2g; Carbohydrate 55.8g, of which sugars 55.5g; Fat 16.3g, of which saturates 8.7g; Cholesterol 144mg; Calcium 191mg; Fibre 0.9g; Sodium 64mg.
Choc. Flake Ice Energy 385Kcal/1600kJ; Protein 3.3g; Carbohydrate 30.6g, of which sugars 30.4g; Fat 28.7g, of which saturates 17.6g; Cholesterol 54mg; Calcium 66mg; Fibre 0.6g; Sodium 25mg.

White Chocolate Raspberry Ripple

A truly luscious treat that always impresses. Note that an ice cream maker is required for this recipe.

Serves 6
250ml/8fl oz/1 cup milk
475ml/16fl oz/2 cups whipping cream
7 egg yolks
30ml/2 tbsp granulated sugar
225g/8oz good white chocolate, chopped into small pieces

5ml/1 tsp vanilla extract
mint sprigs, to decorate

For the sauce
275g/10oz raspberry preserve or 275g/10oz frozen raspberries in light syrup
10ml/2 tsp golden (light corn) syrup
15ml/1 tbsp lemon juice
15ml/1 tbsp cornflour (cornstarch), if using frozen fruit in syrup, mixed with 15ml/1 tbsp water

1 For the sauce, put the preserve in a pan with the golden syrup, the lemon juice and the water but not the cornflour. If using frozen fruit, press the fruit and its syrup through a sieve (strainer) into a pan and add all the other sauce ingredients. Bring to the boil, stirring. Simmer for 1–2 minutes. Pour into a bowl, cool, then chill.

2 In a pan, combine the milk and 250ml/8fl oz/1 cup of the cream and bring to the boil. In a bowl, beat the yolks and sugar with a hand-held mixer for 2–3 minutes until thick and creamy. Gradually pour the hot milk mixture over the yolks and return to the pan. Cook over a medium heat, stirring constantly, until the custard coats the back of a wooden spoon.

3 Remove the pan from the heat and stir in the white chocolate until melted and smooth. Pour the remaining cream into a large bowl. Strain in the hot custard, mix well, then stir in the vanilla extract. Cool, then freeze in an ice cream maker.

4 When frozen but soft, transfer one-third of the ice cream to a freezerproof bowl. Set aside half the raspberry sauce, spooning a third of the rest over the ice cream. Cover with another third of the ice cream and more sauce. Repeat. With a knife, lightly marble the mixture. Cover and freeze. Let the ice cream soften for 15 minutes. Serve with the rest of the raspberry sauce, and the mint.

Chocolate Ripple Ice Cream

This creamy, dark chocolate ice cream, unevenly rippled with swirls of rich chocolate sauce, will stay deliciously soft even after freezing.

Serves 4–6
4 egg yolks
75g/3oz/6 tbsp caster (superfine) sugar
5ml/1 tsp cornflour (cornstarch)

300ml/½ pint/1¼ cups semi-skimmed (low-fat) milk
250g/9oz dark (bittersweet) chocolate, broken into squares
25g/1oz/2 tbsp butter, diced
30ml/2 tbsp golden (light corn) syrup
90ml/6 tbsp single (light) cream or cream and milk mixed
300ml/½ pint/1¼ cups whipping cream

1 Put the egg yolks, sugar and cornflour in a bowl and whisk until thick and foamy. Pour the milk into a heavy pan, bring just to the boil, then gradually pour the milk on to the yolk mixture, whisking constantly.

2 Return the mixture to the pan and cook over a gentle heat, stirring constantly until the custard thickens and is smooth. Pour back into the bowl and stir in 150g/5oz of the chocolate until melted. Cover the custard closely, leave to cool, then chill.

3 Put the remaining chocolate in a pan with the butter and golden syrup. Heat gently, stirring, until melted. Stir in the single cream or cream and milk mixture. Heat gently, stirring, until smooth then leave to cool.

4 Whip the cream until it has thickened, but is still soft enough to fall from a spoon. Fold it into the custard, pour into a freezer container and freeze for 5 hours until thick, beating twice with a fork or in a food processor during this time.

5 Alternatively, use an ice cream maker. Stir the whipped cream into the cooled custard and churn the mixture for 20–25 minutes until thick.

6 Add alternate spoonfuls of ice cream and sauce to a large freezer container. Freeze for 5–6 hours until firm.

White Choc. Ripple Energy 735Kcal/3066kJ; Protein 10.3g; Carbohydrate 63.3g, of which sugars 61g; Fat 50.8g, of which saturates 29.2g; Cholesterol 321mg; Calcium 242mg; Fibre 1.2g; Sodium 110mg.
Choc. Ripple Energy 594Kcal/2474kJ; Protein 7.3g; Carbohydrate 48.3g, of which sugars 47.2g; Fat 42.6g, of which saturates 25.2g; Cholesterol 209mg; Calcium 140mg; Fibre 1.1g; Sodium 87mg.

Chocolate Ice Cream with Lime Sabayon

Sabayon sauce has a light, foamy texture that perfectly complements the rich, smooth flavour of ice cream. This tangy lime version is particularly delicious when spooned generously over chocolate ice cream.

Serves 4
2 egg yolks
65g/2½oz/5 tbsp caster
   (superfine) sugar
finely grated rind and juice of
   2 limes
60ml/4 tbsp white wine or
   apple juice
45ml/3 tbsp single (light) cream
500ml/17fl oz/2¼ cups chocolate
   chip or dark (bittersweet)
   chocolate ice cream
pared strips of lime rind,
   to decorate

1 Put the egg yolks and sugar in a heatproof bowl and beat until combined. Beat in the lime rind and juice, then the white wine or apple juice.

2 Whisk the mixture over a pan of gently simmering water until the sabayon is smooth and thick, and the mixture leaves a trail when the whisk is lifted from the bowl. Lightly whisk in the cream. Remove the bowl from the pan and cover with a lid or plate.

3 Working quickly, scoop the ice cream into four glasses. Spoon the sabayon sauce over the ice cream, decorate with the strips of lime rind and serve immediately.

Variation
The tangy lime sauce marries just as well with vanilla ice cream. It is also very good served with individual servings of sliced tropical fruit – pineapple, papaya and kiwi would look pretty. Try the sabayon sauce as a topping for a selection of soft summer fruits, too.

Rocky Road Ice Cream

A gloriously rich ice cream with lots of texture.

Serves 6
115g/4oz plain (semisweet)
   chocolate, chopped into small
   pieces
150ml/¼ pint/⅔ cup milk
300ml/½ pint/1¼ cups double
   (heavy) cream
115g/4oz/2 cups marshmallows,
   chopped
115g/4oz/½ cup glacé (candied)
   cherries, chopped
50g/2oz/½ cup crumbled
   shortbread
30ml/2 tbsp chopped walnuts
chocolate sauce and wafers, to
   serve (optional)

1 Melt the chocolate in the milk in a pan over a gentle heat, stirring from time to time. Pour into a bowl and leave to cool.

2 Whip the cream in a separate bowl until it just holds its shape. Beat in the chocolate mixture, a little at a time, until the mixture is smooth and creamy.

3 Pour the chocolate mixture into a freezer container and transfer to the freezer. Freeze until ice crystals form around the edges, then whisk with a strong hand whisk or hand-held electric mixer until smooth. Alternatively, use an ice cream maker and churn the mixture until almost frozen, following the manufacturer's instructions.

4 Stir the marshmallows, glacé cherries, crumbled shortbread and nuts into the iced mixture, then return to the freezer container and freeze until firm.

5 Allow the ice cream to soften at room temperature for 15–20 minutes before serving in scoops. Add a wafer and chocolate sauce to each portion, if you wish.

Cook's Tip
Do not allow the mixture to freeze too hard before step 4, otherwise it will be difficult to stir in the remaining ingredients.

Choc. Ice Cream Energy 395Kcal/1648kJ; Protein 6.8g; Carbohydrate 38.3g, of which sugars 38.2g; Fat 23.8g, of which saturates 13.5g; Cholesterol 107mg; Calcium 157mg; Fibre 0g; Sodium 84mg.
Rocky Road Ice Cream Energy 545Kcal/2271kJ; Protein 4.7g; Carbohydrate 48.3g, of which sugars 40.6g; Fat 38.4g, of which saturates 22g; Cholesterol 77mg; Calcium 85mg; Fibre 1g; Sodium 57mg.

Crème Fraîche & Honey Ice

This delicately flavoured ice cream is lovely served on its own, but is also good with a fruit pie or crumble.

Serves 4
4 egg yolks
60ml/4 tbsp clear flower honey
5ml/1 tsp cornflour (cornstarch)

300ml/½ pint/1¼ cups semi-skimmed (low-fat) milk
7.5ml/1½ tsp vanilla extract
250g/9oz/generous 1 cup crème fraîche
nasturtium, pansy or herb flowers, to decorate

1 Whisk the egg yolks, honey and cornflour in a bowl until thick and foamy. Pour the milk into a heavy pan, bring to the boil, then gradually pour on to the yolk mixture in the bowl, whisking constantly.

2 Return the mixture to the pan and cook over a gentle heat, stirring all the time until the custard thickens and is smooth. Pour it back into the bowl, then chill.

3 Stir in the vanilla extract and crème fraîche. Pour into a freezer container. Freeze for 6 hours or until firm enough to scoop, beating once or twice with a fork or in a food processor to break up the ice crystals.

4 Alternatively, use an ice cream maker. Stir the vanilla extract and crème fraîche into the chilled honey custard mixture and churn until thick and firm enough to scoop, following the manufacturer's instructions.

5 Serve in glass dishes and decorate with nasturtiums, pansies or herb flowers.

Cook's Tip
Measure the honey carefully and use level spoonfuls; if you are over-generous, the honey flavour will dominate and the ice cream will be too sweet.

Classic Vanilla Ice Cream

Nothing beats the creamy simplicity of true vanilla ice cream. Vanilla pods are expensive, but well worth buying for the superb flavour they impart.

Serves 4
1 vanilla pod (bean)
300ml/½ pint/1¼ cups semi-skimmed (low-fat) milk
4 egg yolks
75g/3oz/6 tbsp caster (superfine) sugar
5ml/1 tsp cornflour (cornstarch)
300ml/½ pint/1¼ cups double (heavy) cream

1 Using a small knife, slit the vanilla pod lengthways. Pour the milk into a heavy pan, add the vanilla pod and bring to the boil. Remove from the heat and leave for 15 minutes to allow the flavours to infuse.

2 Lift the vanilla pod up. Holding it over the pan, scrape the black seeds out of the pod with a small knife so that they fall back into the milk. Set the vanilla pod aside and bring the milk back to the boil.

3 Whisk the egg yolks, sugar and cornflour in a bowl until the mixture is thick and foamy. Gradually pour on the hot milk, whisking constantly. Return the mixture to the pan and cook over a gentle heat, stirring constantly.

4 When the custard is thick and smooth, pour it back into the bowl. Leave to cool, then chill.

5 Whip the cream until it has thickened but still falls from a spoon. Fold it into the custard and pour into a freezer container. Freeze for 6 hours or until firm enough to scoop, beating twice with a fork or in a food processor.

6 Alternatively, use an ice cream maker. Stir the cream into the custard and churn the mixture until thick.

7 Serve scooped into dishes, bowls or bought cones.

Crème Fraîche Ice Energy 386Kcal/1602kJ; Protein 6.9g; Carbohydrate 16.5g, of which sugars 16.3g; Fat 33g, of which saturates 19.5g; Cholesterol 277mg; Calcium 151mg; Fibre 0g; Sodium 57mg.
Classic Vanilla Energy 546Kcal/2264kJ; Protein 6.8g; Carbohydrate 25.6g, of which sugars 24.4g; Fat 47.1g, of which saturates 27.4g; Cholesterol 309mg; Calcium 160mg; Fibre 0g; Sodium 60mg.

Orange Flower Water Ice Cream

Delicately perfumed with orange flower water, this nutty ice cream is filled with flavours popular in the Middle East.

Serves 4–6
4 egg yolks
75g/3oz/6 tbsp caster
  (superfine) sugar
5ml/1 tsp cornflour (cornstarch)

300ml/½ pint/1¼ cups
  semi-skimmed (low-fat) milk
300ml/½ pint/1¼ cups whipping
  cream
150g/5oz/1¼ cups cashew nuts,
  finely chopped
15ml/1 tbsp orange flower water
grated rind of ½ orange, plus
  spirals of orange rind, to
  decorate

1 Whisk the egg yolks, sugar and cornflour in a bowl until thick. Pour the milk into a pan and bring it to the boil. Whisk it into the egg yolk mixture.

2 Return to the pan and cook over a low heat, stirring constantly, until very smooth. Pour back into the bowl. Leave to cool, then chill.

3 Heat the cream in a pan. When it has come to the boil, stir in the chopped cashew nuts. Leave to cool.

4 Stir the orange flower water and grated orange rind into the chilled custard. Process the cashew nut cream in a food processor or blender until it forms a fine paste, then stir it into the custard mixture.

5 Pour the mixture into a freezer container and freeze for 6 hours, beating twice with a fork or whisking briefly with an electric mixer, to break up the ice crystals and obtain a smooth consistency.

6 Alternatively, use an ice cream maker and churn the mixture until it is firm enough to scoop.

7 To serve, scoop the ice cream into dishes and decorate with orange rind curls.

Coconut & Lemon Grass Ice Cream

The combination of cream and coconut milk makes for a wonderfully rich ice cream. The lemon grass flavouring adds a subtle tang to the dish.

Serves 4
2 lemon grass stalks
475ml/16fl oz/2 cups double
  (heavy) cream
120ml/4fl oz/½ cup coconut milk
4 large (US extra large) eggs
105ml/7 tbsp caster
  (superfine) sugar
5ml/1 tsp vanilla extract

1 Cut the lemon grass stalks in half lengthways. Use a mallet or rolling pin to mash the pieces, breaking up the fibres so that all the flavour is released.

2 Pour the cream and coconut milk into a pan. Add the lemon grass stalks and heat gently, stirring frequently, until the mixture starts to simmer.

3 Put the eggs, sugar and vanilla extract in a large bowl. Using an electric whisk, whisk until the mixture is very light and fluffy.

4 Strain the cream mixture into a heatproof bowl that will fit over a pan of simmering water. Whisk in the egg mixture, then place the bowl over the pan and continue to whisk until the mixture thickens. Remove from the heat and leave to cool. Chill the coconut custard in the refrigerator for 3–4 hours.

5 Pour the mixture into a freezer container. Freeze for 4 hours, beating two or three times at hourly intervals with a fork to break up the ice crystals.

6 Alternatively, use an ice cream maker. Pour the chilled mixture into the machine and churn until it is firm enough to scoop. Serve immediately, or scrape into a freezer container and transfer to the freezer.

7 About 30 minutes before serving, transfer the container to the refrigerator so that the ice cream softens slightly. Serve in scoops.

Coc. & Lemon Grass Energy 773Kcal/3200kJ; Protein 8.4g; Carbohydrate 30.9g, of which sugars 30.9g; Fat 69.4g, of which saturates 41.3g; Cholesterol 353mg; Calcium 109mg; Fibre 0g; Sodium 131mg.
Or. Fl. Water Energy 410Kcal/1696kJ; Protein 9.8g; Carbohydrate 9.2g, of which sugars 5.1g; Fat 37.4g, of which saturates 16.7g; Cholesterol 190mg; Calcium 114mg; Fibre 0.8g; Sodium 113mg.

Brandied Fruit & Rice Ice Cream

This combines spicy rice pudding with a creamy egg custard.

Serves 4–6

50g/2oz/¼ cup ready-to-eat pitted prunes, chopped
50g/2oz/¼ cup ready-to-eat dried apricots, chopped
50g/2oz/¼ cup glacé (candied) cherries, chopped
30ml/2 tbsp brandy
150ml/¼ pint/⅔ cup single (light) cream

For the rice mixture

40g/1½oz/generous ¼ cup pudding (short grain) rice
450ml/¾ pint/scant 2 cups milk
1 cinnamon stick, halved, plus extra to decorate
4 cloves

For the custard

4 egg yolks
75g/3oz/6 tbsp caster (superfine) sugar
5ml/1 tsp cornflour (cornstarch)
300ml/½ pint/1¼ cups milk

1 Put the chopped dried fruit in a bowl. Pour over the brandy. Cover and leave to soak for 3 hours or overnight, if possible.

2 Put the rice, milk and spices in a pan. Bring to the boil, then simmer gently for 30 minutes, stirring occasionally until most of the milk has been absorbed. Lift out the spices. Let the rice cool.

3 Whisk the egg yolks, sugar and cornflour in a bowl until thick and foamy. Heat the milk in a heavy pan, then gradually pour it on to the yolks, whisking constantly. Pour back into the pan and cook, stirring until the custard thickens. Leave to cool, then chill.

4 Mix the chilled custard, rice and cream together. Pour into a freezer container and freeze for 4–5 hours until mushy, then beat lightly with a fork to break up the ice crystals.

5 Fold in the fruits then freeze for 2–3 hours until firm enough to scoop. Alternatively, use an ice cream maker. Mix the chilled custard, rice and cream together and churn until thick. Spoon the ice cream into a freezer container and fold in the fruits. Freeze for 2–3 hours until firm.

6 Serve scoops of ice cream decorated with cinnamon sticks.

Coffee Ice Cream

This classic ice cream is always a favourite and, despite its simplicity, has an air of sophistication and elegance about it.

Serves 8

600ml/1 pint/2½ cups fresh ready-made custard
150ml/¼ pint/⅔ cup strong black coffee
300ml/½ pint/1¼ cups double (heavy) cream

1 Put the custard in a large bowl and stir in the coffee. In a separate bowl, whip the cream until it has a soft texture but is not stiff, and then fold the whipped cream evenly into the coffee and custard mixture.

2 Pour the mixture into a freezer container and cover with a tight-fitting lid or clear film (plastic wrap) and place in the freezer for about 2 hours until beginning to freeze.

3 Remove the ice cream from the freezer and beat with a fork to break up the ice crystals.

4 Return the ice cream to the freezer, freeze for a further 2 hours, then beat again with a fork. Return to the freezer until completely frozen.

5 Alternatively, use an ice cream maker. Pour the coffee and custard mixture into the machine and churn until firm.

6 Serve scooped into individual dishes.

> **Cook's Tips**
> • For a good flavour, it is best to make the coffee from ground coffee beans brewed in a cafetière, for instance, or made by the filter method. Coffee made from instant granules is perfectly adequate as long you make it quite strong.
> • Coffee beans make a complementary decoration for individual portions of ice cream.

Brandied Fruit & Rice Energy 293Kcal/1228kJ; Protein 8g; Carbohydrate 36.7g, of which sugars 30.7g; Fat 13.4g, of which saturates 7.2g; Cholesterol 166mg; Calcium 207mg; Fibre 1.1g; Sodium 73mg.
Coffee Ice Cream Energy 260Kcal/1076kJ; Protein 2.6g; Carbohydrate 12.9g, of which sugars 10.2g; Fat 21.5g, of which saturates 12.5g; Cholesterol 53mg; Calcium 87mg; Fibre 0.1g; Sodium 39mg.

Chocolate Mint Ice Cream Pie

This chocolate-flavoured cereal pie case is incredibly easy to make and offers a simple way to turn ready-made ice cream into a smart-looking dessert.

Serves 8
75g/3oz plain (semisweet) chocolate chips
40g/1½oz/3 tbsp butter or margarine
50g/2oz crisped rice cereal
1 litre/1¾ pints/4 cups mint-chocolate-chip ice cream
chocolate curls, to decorate

1 Line a 23cm/9in pie tin (pan) with foil. Place a round of baking parchment over the foil in the bottom of the tin.

2 Put the chocolate chips and butter or margarine in a heatproof bowl that will fit over a pan of simmering water. Place the bowl over the pan and melt the chocolate and butter.

3 Remove the bowl from the heat and gently stir in the cereal, a little at a time.

4 Press the chocolate-cereal mixture evenly over the base and up the sides of the prepared tin, forming a 1cm/½in rim. Chill until completely hard.

5 Carefully remove the cereal case from the tin and peel off the foil and paper. Return the case to the pie tin.

6 Remove the ice cream from the freezer. Let it soften for 10 minutes and spread it evenly in the cereal case. Freeze until firm.

7 Sprinkle the ice cream with chocolate curls just before serving.

> **Variation**
> Use any flavour of ice cream that marries well with chocolate – coffee, orange or raspberry ripple would be a good choice. Try plain, milk or white chocolate for the base.

Pecan-Topped Coffee Ice Cream

Heavenly ice cream, topped with sweetened nuts.

Serves 4–6
300ml/½ pint/1¼ cups milk
1 tbsp demerara (raw) sugar
25g/1oz/3 tbsp finely ground coffee or 15ml/1 tbsp instant coffee granules
1 egg plus 2 yolks
300ml/½ pint/1¼ cups double (heavy) cream
15ml/1 tbsp caster (superfine) sugar

For the pecans
115g/4oz/1 cup pecan halves
50g/2oz/¼ cup soft dark brown sugar

1 Heat the milk and demerara sugar to boiling point. Remove from the heat and sprinkle on the coffee. Leave to stand for 2 minutes, then stir, cover and cool.

2 In a heatproof bowl, beat the egg and extra yolks until the mixture is thick and pale.

3 Strain the coffee mixture into a clean pan, heat to boiling point, then pour on to the eggs in a steady stream, beating constantly. Set the bowl over a pan of gently simmering water and stir until it thickens. Cool, then chill in the refrigerator.

4 Whip the cream with the caster sugar. Fold it into the coffee custard and freeze in a covered container. Beat twice at hourly intervals, then leave to freeze firm.

5 To caramelize the nuts, preheat the oven to 180°C/350°F/Gas 4. Spread the nuts on a baking sheet in a layer. Toast them in the oven for 10–15 minutes until they release their fragrance.

6 Dissolve the brown sugar in 30ml/2 tbsp water in a heavy pan, shaking over a low heat until it dissolves. When the syrup begins to bubble, add the pecans and cook for 1–2 minutes over medium heat until the syrup coats the nuts.

7 Spread the nuts on a lightly oiled baking sheet, separating them with the tip of a knife. Leave to cool. Soften the ice cream in the refrigerator for 30 minutes, then serve with the nuts.

Coffee Ice Cream Energy 478Kcal/1980kJ; Protein 6.3g; Carbohydrate 15.6g, of which sugars 15.4g; Fat 43.9g, of which saturates 19.1g; Cholesterol 170mg; Calcium 115mg; Fibre 0.9g; Sodium 48mg.
Chocolate Mint Energy 378Kcal/1573kJ; Protein 6.1g; Carbohydrate 32g, of which sugars 27.2g; Fat 25.9g, of which saturates 15.5g; Cholesterol 11mg; Calcium 183mg; Fibre 0.2g; Sodium 108mg.

White Chocolate Parfait

The ultimate cold dessert – white and dark chocolate in one mouthwatering slice.

Serves 10

225g/8oz white chocolate, chopped
600ml/1 pint/2½ cups whipping cream
120ml/4fl oz/½ cup milk
10 egg yolks
15ml/1 tbsp caster (superfine) sugar
25g/1oz/scant ½ cup desiccated (dry unsweetened shredded) coconut
120ml/4fl oz/½ cup canned sweetened coconut milk
150g/5oz/1¼ cups unsalted macadamia nuts

For the chocolate icing

225g/8oz plain (semisweet) chocolate
75g/3oz/6 tbsp butter
20ml/generous 1 tbsp golden (light corn) syrup
175ml/6fl oz/¾ cup whipping cream
curls of fresh coconut, to decorate

1 Line the base and sides of a 1.4 litre/2⅓ pint/6 cup terrine mould (25 × 10cm/10 × 4in) with clear film (plastic wrap).

2 Place the white chocolate and 120ml/4fl oz/½ cup of the cream in the top of a double boiler or in a heatproof bowl set over hot water. Stir until melted and smooth. Set aside.

3 Put 250ml/8fl oz/1 cup of the cream and the milk in a pan and bring to boiling point.

4 Meanwhile, whisk the egg yolks and caster sugar together in a large bowl, until thick and pale.

5 Add the hot cream mixture to the yolks, beating constantly. Pour back into the pan and cook over a low heat for 2–3 minutes, until thickened. Stir constantly and do not boil. Remove the pan from the heat. Add the melted chocolate, desiccated coconut and coconut milk, then stir well and leave to cool.

6 Whip the remaining cream until thick, then fold into the chocolate and coconut mixture.

7 Put 475ml/16fl oz/2 cups of the parfait mixture in the prepared mould and spread evenly. Cover and freeze for about 2 hours, until just firm. Cover the remaining mixture and chill.

8 Scatter the macadamia nuts evenly over the frozen parfait. Pour in the remaining parfait mixture. Cover the terrine and freeze for 6–8 hours or overnight, until the parfait is firm.

9 To make the icing, melt the chocolate with the butter and syrup in the top of a double boiler set over hot water. Stir occasionally. Heat the cream in a pan, until just simmering, then stir into the chocolate mixture. Remove from the heat; cool.

10 To turn out the parfait, wrap the terrine in a hot towel and invert on to a plate. Lift off the mould and clear film and place the parfait on a rack over a baking sheet. Pour the chocolate icing over the top and quickly smooth it down the sides with a palette knife. Leave to set slightly, then freeze for 3–4 hours. To serve, slice with a knife dipped in hot water and decorate with coconut curls.

Iced Praline Torte

This lovely torte will serve you well on any occasion.

Serves 8

115g/4oz/1 cup almonds
115g/4oz/generous ½ cup caster (superfine) sugar
115g/4oz/⅔ cup raisins
90ml/6 tbsp rum or brandy
115g/4oz dark (bittersweet) chocolate, broken into squares
30ml/2 tbsp milk
450ml/¾ pint/scant 2 cups double (heavy) cream
30ml/2 tbsp strong black coffee
16 sponge fingers

To finish

150ml/¼ pint/⅔ cup double (heavy) cream
50g/2oz/½ cup flaked (sliced) almonds, toasted
15g/½oz dark (bittersweet) chocolate, melted

1 To make the praline, oil a baking sheet. Put the nuts into a heavy pan with the sugar and heat gently until the sugar melts and coats the nuts. Cook slowly until the nuts brown and the sugar caramelizes. Transfer the nuts quickly to the sheet; leave until cold. Break up and grind to a fine powder in a blender.

2 Soak the raisins in 45ml/3 tbsp of the rum or brandy for at least an hour to soften and absorb the rum. Melt the chocolate with the milk in a bowl over a pan of hot, but not boiling water. Remove and leave until cold. Lightly grease a 1.2 litre/2 pint/5 cup loaf tin (pan) and line it with baking parchment.

3 Whisk the cream in a bowl until it holds soft peaks. Whisk in the chocolate. Fold in the praline and the raisins, with any liquid.

4 Mix the coffee and remaining rum or brandy in a shallow dish. Dip in the sponge fingers and arrange half in a layer over the base of the prepared loaf tin. Cover with the chocolate mixture and add another layer of soaked sponge fingers. Leave in the freezer overnight.

5 To finish, whip the double cream. Dip the tin briefly in warm water and turn the torte out on to a serving plate. Cover with the whipped cream, sprinkle the top with toasted almonds and drizzle with melted chocolate. Freeze until needed.

White Choc. Parfait Energy 792Kcal/3280kJ; Protein 9.2g; Carbohydrate 34.8g, of which sugars 34.5g; Fat 69.4g, of which saturates 36g; Cholesterol 301mg; Calcium 165mg; Fibre 1.7g; Sodium 169mg.
Praline Torte Energy 636Kcal/2650kJ; Protein 7.7g; Carbohydrate 49.5g, of which sugars 43.5g; Fat 43.9g, of which saturates 22.3g; Cholesterol 134mg; Calcium 104mg; Fibre 1.9g; Sodium 47mg.

Mocha, Prune & Armagnac Terrines

A sophisticated iced dessert for entertaining in style.

Serves 6
115g/4oz/½ cup ready-to-eat pitted prunes, chopped
90ml/6 tbsp Armagnac
90g/3½oz/½ cup caster (superfine) sugar
150ml/¼ pint/⅔ cup water
45ml/3 tbsp coffee beans
150g/5oz plain (semisweet) chocolate, broken into pieces
300ml/½ pint/1¼ cups double (heavy) cream
cocoa powder (unsweetened), for dusting

1 Put the prunes in a small bowl. Pour over 75ml/5 tbsp of the Armagnac and leave to soak for at least 3 hours at room temperature, or overnight in the refrigerator. Line the bases of six 100ml/3½fl oz/scant ½ cup ramekins with baking parchment.

2 Put the sugar and water in a heavy pan and heat gently until the sugar dissolves, stirring occasionally. Add the soaked prunes and any of the Armagnac that remains in the bowl; simmer the prunes gently in the syrup for 5 minutes.

3 Using a slotted spoon, lift the prunes out of the pan and set them aside. Add the coffee beans to the syrup and simmer gently for 5 minutes.

4 Lift out the coffee beans and put about a third of them in a bowl. Spoon over 120ml/4fl oz/½ cup of the syrup and stir in the remaining Armagnac.

5 Add the chocolate to the pan containing the remaining syrup and leave until melted. Whip the cream until it just holds its shape. Using a large metal spoon, fold the chocolate mixture and prunes into the cream until just combined. Spoon the mixture into the lined ramekins, cover and freeze for at least 3 hours.

6 To serve, loosen the edges of the ramekins with a knife then dip in very hot water for 2 seconds and invert on to serving plates. Decorate the plates with the coffee bean syrup and a dusting of cocoa powder.

Double Chocolate Snowball

An ideal party dessert as it can be prepared ahead and decorated on the day.

8 eggs
50ml/2fl oz/¼ cup orange-flavoured liqueur (optional)

Serves 12–14
350g/12oz plain (semisweet) chocolate, chopped
285g/10½oz/1½ cups caster (superfine) sugar
275g/10oz/1¼ cups unsalted (sweet) butter, diced

For the chocolate cream
200g/7oz good-quality white chocolate, broken into pieces
475ml/16fl oz/2 cups double (heavy) or whipping cream
30ml/2 tbsp orange-flavoured liqueur (optional)

1 Preheat the oven to 180°C/350°F/Gas 4. Line a 1.75 litre/3 pint/7½ cup round ovenproof bowl with foil, smoothing the sides. In a bowl over a pan of simmering water, melt the plain chocolate. Add the sugar and stir until it dissolves. Strain into a medium bowl. Using an electric mixer at low speed, beat in the butter, then the eggs, one at a time. Stir in the liqueur, if using, and pour into the lined bowl. Tap to release large air bubbles.

2 Bake for 1¼–1½ hours until the surface is firm and slightly risen, but cracked. The centre will set on cooling. Transfer to a rack to cool. Cover with a plate, then cover completely with clear film (plastic wrap) and chill overnight. To unmould, remove the plate and film and invert the mould on to a plate; shake firmly to release. Peel off foil. Cover until ready to decorate.

3 Work the white chocolate in a food processor to form fine crumbs. In a small pan, heat 120ml/4fl oz/½ cup of the cream until just beginning to simmer. With the processor running, pour in the cream until the chocolate has melted. Strain into a bowl and cool to room temperature, stirring occasionally.

4 Beat the remaining cream until soft peaks form, add the liqueur, if using, and beat for 30 seconds or until the cream just holds its shape. Fold a spoonful of cream into the chocolate then fold in the remaining cream. Spoon into an icing (pastry) bag fitted with a star tip and pipe rosettes over the surface.

Mocha Terrines Energy 495Kcal/2060kJ; Protein 2.6g; Carbohydrate 38.9g, of which sugars 38.7g; Fat 33.9g, of which saturates 20.9g; Cholesterol 70mg; Calcium 47mg; Fibre 1.7g; Sodium 16mg.
D. Choc. Snowball Energy 640Kcal/2661kJ; Protein 6.7g; Carbohydrate 46.2g, of which sugars 46g; Fat 49g, of which saturates 29.3g; Cholesterol 199mg; Calcium 94mg; Fibre 0.6g; Sodium 185mg.

White Chocolate Mousse with Dark Sauce

In this delicious dessert, creamy, white chocolate mousse is set off by a dark rum and chocolate sauce.

Serves 6–8

200g/7oz white chocolate, broken into squares
2 eggs, separated
60ml/4 tbsp caster (superfine) sugar
300ml/½ pint/1¼ cups double (heavy) cream
15ml/1 tbsp/1 sachet powdered gelatine
150ml/¼ pint/⅔ cup Greek (US strained plain) yogurt
10ml/2 tsp vanilla extract

For the sauce

50g/2oz plain (semisweet) chocolate, broken into squares
30ml/2 tbsp dark rum
60ml/4 tbsp single (light) cream

1 Line a 1 litre/1¾ pint/4 cup loaf tin (pan) with baking parchment or clear film (plastic wrap). Melt the chocolate in a heatproof bowl over hot water, then remove from the heat.

2 Whisk the egg yolks and sugar in a bowl until pale and thick, then beat in the melted chocolate.

3 Heat the cream in a small pan until almost boiling, then remove from the heat. Sprinkle the powdered gelatine over, stirring gently until it is completely dissolved. Then pour on to the chocolate mixture, whisking vigorously to mix until smooth.

4 Whisk the yogurt and vanilla extract into the mixture. In a clean, grease-free bowl, whisk the egg whites until stiff, then fold them into the mixture. Turn into the prepared loaf tin, level the surface and chill until set.

5 Make the sauce. Melt the chocolate with the rum and cream in a heatproof bowl over barely simmering water. Cool.

6 Remove the mousse from the tin with the aid of the lining. Serve sliced with the chocolate sauce poured around.

Rich Chocolate Mousse with Glazed Kumquats

Perfumed kumquats, glazed in orange liqueur, turn this mousse into a special treat.

Serves 6

225g/8oz plain (semisweet) chocolate, broken into squares
4 eggs, separated
30ml/2 tbsp orange-flavoured liqueur
90ml/6 tbsp double (heavy) cream

For the glazed kumquats

275g/10oz/2¾ cups kumquats
115g/4oz/generous ½ cup granulated sugar
150ml/¼ pint/⅔ cup water
15ml/1 tbsp orange-flavoured liqueur

1 To make the glazed kumquats, halve the fruit lengthways and place cut side up in a shallow serving dish.

2 Place the sugar in a small pan with the water. Heat gently, stirring constantly, until the sugar has dissolved, then bring to the boil and boil rapidly, without stirring, until a golden-brown caramel forms.

3 Remove the pan from the heat and very carefully stir in 60ml/4 tbsp boiling water. Stir in the orange-flavoured liqueur, then pour the caramel sauce over the kumquat slices and leave to cool. Once completely cold, cover and chill.

4 Line a shallow 20cm/8in round cake tin (pan) with clear film (plastic wrap). Melt the chocolate in a bowl over a pan of barely simmering water, then remove the bowl from the heat.

5 Beat the egg yolks and liqueur into the chocolate, then gently fold in the cream. In a separate mixing bowl, whisk the egg whites until stiff, then gently fold them into the chocolate mixture. Pour the mixture into the prepared tin and level the surface. Chill for several hours until set.

6 Turn the mousse out on to a plate and cut into slices. Serve with the glazed kumquats alongside.

White Choc. Mousse Energy 433Kcal/1796kJ; Protein 6g; Carbohydrate 25g, of which sugars 24.9g; Fat 34.4g, of which saturates 20.5g; Cholesterol 103mg; Calcium 133mg; Fibre 0.2g; Sodium 69mg.
Rich Choc. Mousse Energy 431Kcal/1805kJ; Protein 6.9g; Carbohydrate 49.8g, of which sugars 49.5g; Fat 22.3g, of which saturates 12.4g; Cholesterol 150mg; Calcium 71mg; Fibre 1.7g; Sodium 56mg.

Frozen Strawberry Mousse Cake

Children will love this pretty dessert – it tastes just like an ice cream.

Serves 4–6

425g/15oz can strawberries in syrup
15ml/1 tbsp/1 sachet powdered gelatine

6 trifle sponge cakes
45ml/3 tbsp strawberry jam
200ml/7fl oz/scant 1 cup crème fraîche
200ml/7fl oz/⁷⁄₈ cup whipped cream, to decorate

1 Strain the syrup from the strawberries into a large heatproof bowl. Sprinkle over the gelatine and stir well. Stand the bowl in a pan of hot water and stir until the gelatine has dissolved.

2 Leave to cool, then chill for just under 1 hour, until beginning to set. Meanwhile, cut the sponge cakes in half lengthways and spread the cut surfaces with the strawberry jam.

3 Carefully whisk the crème fraîche into the strawberry jelly, then whisk in the canned strawberries. Line a deep, 20cm/8in loose-based cake tin (pan) with baking parchment.

4 Pour half the strawberry mousse mixture into the tin, arrange the sponge cakes over the surface, and then spoon over the remaining mousse mixture, pushing down any sponge cakes that rise up.

5 Freeze for 1–2 hours until the mousse is firm. Remove the cake from the tin and carefully peel away the lining paper. Transfer to a serving plate. Decorate the mousse with whirls of whipped cream and a few strawberry leaves and a fresh strawberry, if they are available.

> **Variation**
> *Replace the crème fraîche with a mix of lightly whipped double (heavy) cream and low-fat yogurt for a less rich cake.*

Bitter Chocolate Mousse

A classic and ever-popular dessert, little chocolate mousses make a stylish and memorable finish to any dinner party.

Serves 8

225g/8oz plain (semisweet) chocolate, chopped into small pieces
60ml/4 tbsp water

30ml/2 tbsp orange-flavoured liqueur or brandy
25g/1oz/2 tbsp unsalted (sweet) butter, cut into small pieces
4 eggs, separated
90ml/6 tbsp whipping cream
1.5ml/¼ tsp cream of tartar
45ml/3 tbsp caster (superfine) sugar
crème fraîche and chocolate curls, to decorate

1 Melt the chocolate with the water in a heatproof bowl set over a pan of barely simmering water, stirring until completely smooth. Remove from the heat and whisk in the liqueur or brandy and butter.

2 With a hand-held electric mixer, beat the egg yolks for 2–3 minutes until thick and creamy, then slowly beat into the melted chocolate until well blended. Set aside.

3 Whip the cream until soft peaks form and stir a spoonful into the chocolate mixture to lighten it. Fold in the remaining cream.

4 In a grease-free bowl, beat the egg whites slowly until frothy. Add the cream of tartar, increase the speed and continue beating until they form soft peaks. Gradually sprinkle over the sugar and continue beating until the whites are stiff and glossy.

5 Using a rubber spatula or large metal spoon, stir a quarter of the egg whites into the chocolate mixture, then gently fold in the remaining whites, cutting down to the bottom, along the sides and up to the top in a semicircular motion until they are just combined. Gently spoon into eight individual dishes. Chill for at least 2 hours or until set.

6 Spoon a little crème fraîche over each mousse and decorate with the chocolate curls.

Cherry Syllabub

This recipe follows the style of the earliest syllabubs from the sixteenth and seventeenth centuries, producing a frothy, creamy layer over a liquid one. Ripe cherries sprinkled with fiery Kirsch form the delicious bottom layer.

Serves 4

225g/8oz ripe dark cherries, pitted and chopped
30ml/2 tbsp Kirsch
2 egg whites
75g/3oz/6 tbsp caster (superfine) sugar
30ml/2 tbsp fresh lemon juice
150ml/¼ pint/⅔ cup sweet white wine
300ml/½ pint/1¼ cups double (heavy) cream

1 Divide the chopped cherries among six tall dessert glasses and sprinkle over the Kirsch.

2 In a clean, grease-free bowl, whisk the egg whites until stiff. Gently fold in the sugar, lemon juice and wine.

3 In a separate bowl (but using the same whisk), lightly beat the cream then fold into the egg white mixture.

4 Spoon the cream mixture over the cherries, then chill overnight. Serve straight from the refrigerator.

> **Cook's Tip**
> *Be careful not to over-beat the egg whites otherwise they will separate, which will spoil the consistency of the dessert. Whip the cream until it is just forming soft peaks.*

> **Variation**
> *You can use crushed fresh raspberries or chopped ripe peaches or strawberries instead of the cherries. Ratafia biscuits (almond macaroons) make the perfect accompaniment.*

Apricot & Orange Jelly

A light and refreshing dessert for a summer's day.

Serves 4

350g/12oz well-flavoured fresh ripe apricots, stoned (pitted)
50–75g/2–3oz/about ⅓ cup granulated sugar
about 300ml/½ pint/1¼ cups freshly squeezed orange juice
15ml/1 tbsp/1 sachet powdered gelatine
single (light) cream, to serve
finely chopped candied orange peel, to decorate

1 Put the apricots in a pan with the sugar and 120ml/4fl oz/½ cup of the orange juice. Place over medium heat and stir until the sugar has dissolved. Simmer very gently until the apricots are tender.

2 Press the apricot mixture through a nylon sieve (strainer) into a small measuring jug (cup) using a spoon.

3 Pour 45ml/3 tbsp of the orange juice into a small heatproof bowl, sprinkle over the gelatine and leave for about 5 minutes, until softened.

4 Place the bowl over a pan of hot water and heat until the gelatine has dissolved. Slowly pour into the apricot mixture, stirring constantly. Make up to 600ml/1 pint/2½ cups with the remaining orange juice.

5 Pour the apricot mixture into four individual dishes and chill until set.

6 To serve, pour a thin layer of cream over the surface, and decorate with candied orange peel.

> **Cook's Tip**
> *Make sure that the gelatine is completely dissolved in the orange juice – there should be no sign of any granules and the liquid should be completely clear. The mixture must not boil.*

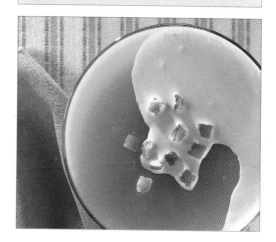

Cherry Syllabub Energy 514Kcal/2132kJ; Protein 3.3g; Carbohydrate 29.6g, of which sugars 29.6g; Fat 40.3g, of which saturates 25.1g; Cholesterol 103mg; Calcium 60mg; Fibre 0.5g; Sodium 54mg.
Apricot & Orange Jelly Energy 104Kcal/442kJ; Protein 1.2g; Carbohydrate 26g, of which sugars 26g; Fat 0.2g, of which saturates 0g; Cholesterol 0mg; Calcium 27mg; Fibre 1.6g; Sodium 10mg.

Rhubarb & Orange Fool

This traditional English dessert is extremely easy to make, yet is utterly mouthwatering with its distinctive taste and texture.

Serves 4
30ml/2 tbsp freshly squeezed
    orange juice
5ml/1 tsp finely shredded
    orange rind
1kg/2¼lb (about 10–12 stems)
    rhubarb, chopped
15ml/1 tbsp redcurrant jelly
45ml/3 tbsp caster (superfine)
    sugar
150g/5oz/⅔ cup ready-to-serve
    thick and creamy custard
150ml/¼ pint/⅔ cup double
    (heavy) cream, whipped
crisp biscuits (cookies), to serve

1 Place the orange juice and rind, the rhubarb, redcurrant jelly and sugar in a pan. Cover and simmer gently for about 8 minutes, stirring occasionally, until the rhubarb is just tender but not mushy.

2 Remove the pan from the heat, transfer the rhubarb to a bowl and leave to cool completely.

3 Drain the cooled rhubarb to remove some of the liquid. Reserve a few pieces of the rhubarb and a little orange rind for decoration. Purée the remaining rhubarb in a food processor or blender, or push through a sieve (strainer).

4 Stir the custard into the purée, then fold in the whipped cream. Spoon the fool into individual bowls, cover and chill. Just before serving, top with the reserved fruit and rind. Serve with crisp, sweet biscuits.

Variation
This dessert also works well with gooseberries – another classic English fruit – instead of the rhubarb. Cook the gooseberries with about 60ml/4 tbsp water instead of the orange juice and increase the sugar to taste. Leave out the grated orange rind as well, and decorate with chopped nuts.

Apricots with Orange Cream

Creamy mascarpone cheese, delicately flavoured with orange juice, makes a delicious topping for chilled apricots. Here, the apricots themselves are infused with the subtle flavours of orange and cinnamon, with dessert wine added for a taste of sweet luxury.

Serves 4
450g/1lb/2 cups ready-to-eat
    dried apricots
strip of orange peel
1 cinnamon stick
45ml/3 tbsp caster (superfine)
    sugar
450ml/¾ pint/scant 2 cups
    water
150ml/¼ pint/⅔ cup sweet
    dessert wine
115g/4oz/½ cup mascarpone
    cheese
45ml/3 tbsp orange juice
pinch of ground cinnamon
    and fresh mint sprig,
    to decorate

1 Place the apricots, orange peel, cinnamon stick and 15ml/1 tbsp of the sugar in a pan and cover with the water. Bring to the boil, cover and simmer gently for 25 minutes, or until the fruit is tender.

2 Remove from the heat and stir in the dessert wine. Leave until cold, then chill for at least 3–4 hours or overnight.

3 Mix together the mascarpone cheese, orange juice and the remaining sugar in a bowl and beat thoroughly until the mixture is smooth, then chill.

4 Just before serving the dessert, remove the cinnamon stick and orange peel.

5 Serve with a spoonful of the orange cream sprinkled with cinnamon and decorated with a sprig of fresh mint.

Cook's Tip
The sweet wine Muscat de Beaumes de Venise is a good choice for this recipe, but any sweet muscat wine would do.

Gooseberry & Orange Flower Cream

Fresh-tasting gooseberries and fragrant orange flower water give this dessert an attractive flavour. For the most effective presentation, serve the cream in individual dishes, prettily decorated with mint sprigs.

Serves 4

500g/1¼lb gooseberries, trimmed
300ml/½ pint/1¼ cups double (heavy) cream
about 115g/4oz/1 cup icing (confectioners') sugar, to taste
30ml/2 tbsp orange flower water
fresh mint sprigs, to decorate
almond biscuits (cookies), to serve

1 Place the gooseberries in a heavy pan, cover and cook over a low heat, shaking the pan occasionally, until the gooseberries are tender. Tip the gooseberries into a bowl, crush them, then leave to cool completely.

2 Beat the cream until soft peaks form, then fold in half the gooseberries. Sweeten the mixture with icing sugar to taste, and add the orange flower water. Sweeten the remaining gooseberries to taste.

3 Layer the cream mixture and the crushed gooseberries in four dessert dishes or tall glasses, and then cover and chill. Decorate with mint sprigs and serve accompanied by almond biscuits.

Cook's Tip
If you prefer, the cooked gooseberries can be thoroughly puréed and then strained. This will give the cream a much smoother texture.

Variation
The orange flower water can be replaced by elderflower cordial and homemade custard used instead of the cream.

Rose Petal Cream

This old-fashioned dessert, which is set with rennet, is traditionally called a junket. The finished dish has a lovely, smooth texture and a light, fragrant taste. Do not be tempted to move the dish while it is setting, otherwise it will separate.

Serves 4

600ml/1 pint/2½ cups milk
45ml/3 tbsp caster (superfine) sugar
several drops triple-strength rose water
10ml/2 tsp rennet
60ml/4 tbsp double (heavy) cream
sugared rose petals, to decorate (optional)

1 Gently heat all of the milk and 30ml/2 tbsp of the sugar, making sure that you stir continuously, until the sugar has melted and the temperature reaches 36.9°C/98.4°F, or the milk feels lukewarm.

2 Stir rose water to taste into the milk, then remove the pan from the heat before stirring in the rennet.

3 Pour the milk into a serving dish and leave undisturbed for 2–3 hours, until the junket has set.

4 Stir the remaining sugar into the cream, then carefully spoon in an even layer over the junket. Decorate with sugared rose petals, if you wish.

Cook's Tips
• Use only rose petals taken from bushes that have not been sprayed with chemicals of any kind.
• To make sugared rose petals for the decoration, lightly whisk an egg white, then, using a clean paintbrush, paint both sides of clean rose petals with the egg white. Either dip the petals in a bowl of caster (superfine) sugar to coat well or sprinkle sugar on both sides and shake off the excess. Leave to dry out completely, then store in an airtight container or jar.

Gooseberry Cream Energy 518Kcal/2151kJ; Protein 2.7g; Carbohydrate 37.3g, of which sugars 37.3g; Fat 40.8g, of which saturates 25.1g; Cholesterol 103mg; Calcium 88mg; Fibre 3g; Sodium 21mg.
Rose Petal Cream Energy 188Kcal/788kJ; Protein 5.4g; Carbohydrate 19.1g, of which sugars 19.1g; Fat 10.6g, of which saturates 6.6g; Cholesterol 29mg; Calcium 193mg; Fibre 0g; Sodium 69mg.

Chocolate Blancmange

An old-fashioned dessert that deserves a revival. Serve with pouring cream for a touch of luxury.

Serves 4
60ml/4 tbsp cornflour (cornstarch)
600ml/1 pint/2½ cups milk
45ml/3 tbsp sugar
50–115g/2–4oz plain (semisweet) chocolate, chopped
few drops of vanilla extract
white and plain (semisweet) chocolate curls, to decorate

1 Rinse a 750ml/1¼ pint/3 cup fluted mould with cold water and leave it upside down to drain. Blend the cornflour to a smooth paste with a little of the milk in a medium bowl.

2 Bring the remaining milk to the boil, preferably in a non-stick pan, then pour on to the blended paste, stirring constantly, until smooth in consistency.

3 Pour all the milk back into the pan and bring slowly to the boil over a low heat, stirring constantly until the mixture boils and thickens. Remove the pan from the heat, then add the sugar, chopped chocolate and vanilla extract and stir until the sauce is smooth, all the sugar has dissolved and the chocolate pieces have melted completely.

4 Carefully pour the chocolate mixture into the mould, cover the top closely with dampened baking parchment (to prevent the formation of a skin) and leave in a cool place for several hours to set.

5 To unmould the blancmange, place a large serving plate upside down on top of the mould. Holding the plate and mould firmly together, turn them both over. Give both plate and mould a gentle but firm shake to loosen the blancmange, then carefully lift off the mould.

6 To serve, sprinkle the chocolate curls over the top.

Tiramisu in Chocolate Cups

The Italian favourite served in an elegant new way.

Serves 6
1 egg yolk
30ml/2 tbsp caster (superfine) sugar
2.5ml/½ tsp vanilla extract
250g/9oz/generous 1 cup mascarpone cheese
120ml/4fl oz/½ cup strong black coffee

15ml/1 tbsp cocoa powder (unsweetened), plus extra for dusting
30ml/2 tbsp coffee liqueur
16 amaretti

For the chocolate cups
175g/6oz plain (semisweet) chocolate, chopped
25g/1oz/2 tbsp unsalted (sweet) butter

1 Make the chocolate cups. Cut out six 15cm/6in rounds of baking parchment. Melt the chocolate with the butter in a heatproof bowl over a pan of simmering water. Stir until smooth, then spread a spoonful of the chocolate mixture over each circle, to within 2cm/¾in of the edge.

2 Carefully lift each paper round and drape it over an upturned teacup or ramekin so that the edges curve into frills. Leave until completely set, then carefully peel away the paper.

3 Make the filling. Using a hand-held electric mixer, beat the egg yolk and sugar in a bowl until smooth, then stir in the vanilla extract. Soften the mascarpone if necessary, then stir it into the egg yolk mixture. Beat until smooth.

4 In a separate bowl, mix the coffee, cocoa and liqueur. Break up the amaretti roughly, then stir them into the mixture.

5 Place the chocolate cups on individual plates. Divide half the amaretti mixture among them, then spoon over half the mascarpone mixture.

6 Spoon over the remaining amaretti mixture (including any free liquid), top with the rest of the mascarpone mixture and dust lightly with cocoa. Chill for 30 minutes before serving.

Choc. Blancmange Energy 230Kcal/975kJ; Protein 5.9g; Carbohydrate 40.6g, of which sugars 26.6g; Fat 6.2g, of which saturates 3.7g; Cholesterol 10mg; Calcium 192mg; Fibre 0.3g; Sodium 74mg.
Tiramisu Energy 351Kcal/1469kJ; Protein 6.9g; Carbohydrate 34.5g, of which sugars 29.6g; Fat 20.4g, of which saturates 12.1g; Cholesterol 62mg; Calcium 33mg; Fibre 1.2g; Sodium 86mg.

Chocolate Cones with Apricot Sauce

Glamorous chocolate cones with a luxurious filling.

Serves 6
250g/9oz plain (semisweet) chocolate, chopped into small pieces
350g/12oz/1½ cups ricotta cheese
45ml/3 tbsp double (heavy) cream
30ml/2 tbsp brandy
30ml/2 tbsp icing (confectioners') sugar
finely grated rind of 1 lemon
pared strips of lemon rind, to decorate

For the sauce
175g/6oz/⅔ cup apricot jam
45ml/3 tbsp lemon juice

1 Cut twelve 10cm/4in double thickness rounds from baking parchment and shape each into a cone. Secure in place with masking tape.

2 Melt the chocolate in a bowl over a pan of simmering water. Cool slightly, then spoon a little into each cone, swirling and brushing it to coat the paper evenly.

3 Support each cone point downwards in a cup or glass held on its side, to keep it level. Leave in a cool place until the cones are completely set. Unless it is a very hot day, do not put the cones in the refrigerator, as this may spoil their appearance.

4 Make the sauce. Combine the apricot jam and lemon juice in a small pan. Place over a gentle heat until melted, stirring occasionally, then press through a sieve (strainer) into a small bowl. Set aside to cool.

5 Beat the ricotta cheese in a bowl until softened, then beat in the cream, brandy and icing sugar. Stir in the grated lemon rind. Spoon the mixture into a piping (pastry) bag. Fill the cones, then carefully peel off the baking parchment.

6 Spoon a pool of apricot sauce on to six dessert plates. Arrange the cones in pairs on the plates. Decorate with a scattering of pared lemon rind strips and serve immediately.

Chocolate Vanilla Timbales

These elegantly turned-out timbales look particularly impressive if they are set in fluted moulds. It's worth investing in some.

Serves 6
350ml/12fl oz/1½ cups semi-skimmed (low-fat) milk
30ml/2 tbsp cocoa powder (unsweetened), plus extra for dusting
2 eggs
10ml/2 tsp vanilla extract
45ml/3 tbsp caster (superfine) sugar
15ml/1 tbsp/1 sachet powdered gelatine
45ml/3 tbsp hot water
fresh mint sprigs, to decorate

For the sauce
115g/4oz/½ cup light Greek (US strained plain) yogurt
25ml/1½ tbsp vanilla extract

1 Place the milk and cocoa in a pan and stir until the milk is boiling. Separate the eggs and beat the egg yolks with the vanilla extract and sugar in a bowl, until the mixture is pale and smooth. Gradually pour in the chocolate milk, beating well.

2 Return the mixture to the pan and stir constantly over a gentle heat, without boiling, until it is slightly thickened and smooth in consistency.

3 Remove the pan from the heat. Pour the gelatine into the hot water and stir until it is completely dissolved, then quickly stir it into the milk mixture. Put this mixture aside and allow it to cool until almost setting.

4 Whisk the egg whites until they hold soft peaks. Fold the egg whites quickly into the milk mixture. Spoon the timbale mixture into six individual moulds and chill them until set.

5 To serve, run a knife around the edge, dip the moulds quickly into hot water and turn out on to serving plates. For the sauce, stir together the yogurt and vanilla extract and spoon on to the plates next to the timbales. Lightly dust with cocoa and decorate with mint sprigs.

Choc. Cones Energy 461Kcal/1932kJ; Protein 7.8g; Carbohydrate 53.8g, of which sugars 53.4g; Fat 24.2g, of which saturates 14.8g; Cholesterol 37mg; Calcium 24mg; Fibre 1.1g; Sodium 13mg.
Choc. Vanilla Timbales Energy 89Kcal/372kJ; Protein 6.2g; Carbohydrate 3.7g, of which sugars 3.1g; Fat 5.9g, of which saturates 2.8g; Cholesterol 67mg; Calcium 115mg; Fibre 0.6g; Sodium 110mg.

Mocha Velvet Cream Pots

These dainty pots of chocolate heaven are a great way to round off a meal.

Serves 8
15ml/1 tbsp instant coffee
 powder
475ml/16fl oz/2 cups milk
75g/3oz/6 tbsp caster
 (superfine) sugar

225g/8oz plain (semisweet)
 chocolate, chopped into
 small pieces
10ml/2 tsp vanilla extract
30ml/2 tbsp coffee-flavoured
 liqueur (optional)
7 egg yolks
whipped cream and crystallized
 mimosa balls, to decorate

1 Preheat the oven to 160°C/325°F/Gas 3. Place eight 120ml/4fl oz/½ cup custard cups or ramekins in a roasting pan. Set the pan aside.

2 Put the instant coffee in a pan. Stir in the milk, then add the sugar and place the pan over medium heat. Bring to the boil, stirring constantly, until both the coffee and the sugar have dissolved completely.

3 Remove the pan from the heat and add the chocolate. Stir until it has melted and the sauce is smooth. Stir in the vanilla extract and coffee liqueur, if using.

4 In a bowl, whisk the egg yolks to blend them lightly. Slowly whisk in the chocolate mixture until well mixed, then strain the mixture into a large jug (pitcher) and divide equally among the cups or ramekins. Pour enough boiling water into the roasting pan to come halfway up the sides of the cups or ramekins. Carefully place the roasting pan in the oven.

5 Bake for 30–35 minutes, until the custard is just set and a knife inserted into the custard comes out clean. Remove the cups or ramekins from the roasting pan and allow to cool. Place on a baking sheet, cover and chill completely.

6 Decorate the pots with whipped cream and crystallized mimosa balls, if you wish.

Chocolate & Chestnut Pots

The chestnut purée adds substance and texture to these mousses. Crisp, delicate biscuits (cookies), such as langues-de-chat, provide a good foil to the richness.

Serves 6
250g/9oz plain (semisweet)
 chocolate
60ml/4 tbsp Madeira
25g/1oz/2 tbsp butter, diced
2 eggs, separated
225g/8oz/scant 1 cup
 unsweetened chestnut purée
crème fraîche or whipped double
 (heavy) cream, to decorate

1 Make a few chocolate curls for decoration by rubbing a grater along the length of the bar of chocolate. Break the rest of the chocolate into squares and melt it in a pan with the Madeira over a gentle heat. Remove from the heat and add the butter, a few pieces at a time, stirring until melted and smooth.

2 Beat the egg yolks quickly into the mixture, then beat in the chestnut purée, mixing until smooth.

3 Whisk the egg whites in a clean, grease-free bowl until stiff. Stir about 15ml/1 tbsp of the whites into the chestnut mixture to lighten it, then fold in the rest smoothly and evenly.

4 Spoon the mixture into six small ramekin dishes and chill until set.

5 Remove the pots from the refrigerator about 30 minutes before serving to allow the flavours to "ripen". Serve the pots topped with a generous spoonful of crème fraîche or whipped cream and decorated with chocolate curls.

Cook's Tips
• If Madeira is not available, use brandy or rum instead.
• These chocolate pots can be frozen successfully for up to 2 months, making them ideal for a prepare-ahead dessert.

Mocha Velvet Energy 261Kcal/1095kJ; Protein 6g; Carbohydrate 30.5g, of which sugars 30.2g; Fat 13.7g, of which saturates 6.7g; Cholesterol 182mg; Calcium 106mg; Fibre 0.7g; Sodium 36mg.
Choc. & Chestnut Energy 348Kcal/1455kJ; Protein 5g; Carbohydrate 41.4g, of which sugars 29.9g; Fat 18g, of which saturates 9.9g; Cholesterol 75mg; Calcium 42mg; Fibre 2.6g; Sodium 56mg.

Coffee, Vanilla & Chocolate Stripe

This looks really special layered in wine glasses and decorated with cream.

Serves 6
285g/10½oz/1½ cups caster (superfine) sugar
90ml/6 tbsp cornflour (cornstarch)

900ml/1½ pints/3¾ cups milk
3 egg yolks
75g/3oz/6 tbsp unsalted (sweet) butter, at room temperature
20ml/generous 1 tbsp instant coffee powder
10ml/2 tsp vanilla extract
30ml/2 tbsp cocoa powder (unsweetened)

1 To make the coffee layer, place 90g/3½oz/½ cup of the sugar and 30ml/2 tbsp of the cornflour in a heavy pan. Gradually add one-third of the milk, whisking until well blended. Over a medium heat, whisk in one of the egg yolks and bring to the boil, whisking. Boil for 1 minute.

2 Remove the pan from the heat. Stir in 25g/1oz/2 tbsp of the butter and the instant coffee. Set aside the pan to cool slightly.

3 Divide the coffee mixture among six wine glasses. Smooth the tops before the mixture sets. Wipe any dribbles on the insides and outsides of the glasses with damp kitchen paper.

4 To make the vanilla layer, place half of the remaining sugar and cornflour in a heavy pan. Whisk in half the milk. Over a medium heat, whisk in another egg yolk and bring to the boil, whisking. Boil for 1 minute.

5 Remove the pan from the heat and stir in 25g/1oz/2 tbsp of the butter and the vanilla. Leave to cool slightly, then spoon into the glasses on top of the coffee layer. Smooth the tops.

6 To make the chocolate layer, place the remaining sugar and cornflour in a heavy pan. Gradually whisk in the remaining milk until blended. Over a medium heat, whisk in the last egg yolk and bring to the boil, whisking. Boil for 1 minute. Remove from the heat, stir in the remaining butter and the cocoa. Leave to cool slightly, then spoon on top of the vanilla layer. Chill to set.

Steamed Custard in Nectarines

Steaming nectarines or peaches brings out their natural colour and sweetness, so this is a good way of making the most of underripe or less flavourful fruit.

Serves 4–6
6 nectarines
1 large (US extra large) egg
45ml/3 tbsp palm sugar or light muscovado (brown) sugar
30ml/2 tbsp coconut milk

1 Cut the nectarines in half. Using a teaspoon, scoop out the stones (pits) and a little of the surrounding flesh.

2 Lightly beat the egg, then add the sugar and the coconut milk. Beat until the sugar has dissolved.

3 Transfer the nectarines to a steamer and carefully fill the cavities three-quarters full with the custard mixture. Steam over a pan of simmering water for 5–10 minutes. Remove from the heat and leave to cool completely before transferring to plates and serving.

Cook's Tip
Palm sugar, also known as jaggery, is made from the sap of certain Asian palm trees, such as coconut and palmyrah. It is available from Asian food stores. If you buy it as a cake or large lump, grate it before use.

Variations
• *To add extra colour to this dessert, drizzle the cold fruit with a raspberry sauce. To make the sauce, simply purée fresh raspberries, then press through a sieve (strainer) to remove the seeds. Sweeten with icing (confectioners') sugar to taste.*
• *Serve the nectarines with chocolate hazelnut rounds – melt some plain (semisweet) chocolate and spread on to circles drawn on baking parchment. Sprinkle with flaked (sliced) hazelnuts and leave to set. Remove from the paper and serve alongside.*

Coffee, Vanilla & Choc. Energy 448Kcal/1891kJ; Protein 7.9g; Carbohydrate 71.1g, of which sugars 56.8g; Fat 16.8g, of which saturates 9.6g; Cholesterol 136mg; Calcium 228mg; Fibre 0.6g; Sodium 203mg. **Steamed Custard** Energy 103Kcal/438kJ; Protein 3.2g; Carbohydrate 21.6g, of which sugars 21.6g; Fat 1.1g, of which saturates 0.3g; Cholesterol 32mg; Calcium 21mg; Fibre 1.8g; Sodium 19mg.

Mango & Chocolate Crème Brûlée

Fresh mangoes, topped with a wickedly rich chocolate cream and a layer of crunchy caramel, make a fantastic dessert.

Serves 6
2 ripe mangoes, peeled, stoned (pitted) and chopped
300ml/½ pint/1¼ cups double (heavy) cream
300ml/½ pint/1¼ cups crème fraîche
1 vanilla pod (bean)
115g/4oz plain (semisweet) chocolate, chopped into small pieces
4 egg yolks
15ml/1 tbsp clear honey
90ml/6 tbsp demerara (raw) sugar, for the topping

1 Divide the mangoes among six flameproof dishes set on a baking sheet.

2 Mix the cream, crème fraîche and vanilla pod in a large heatproof bowl. Place the bowl over a pan of barely simmering water.

3 Heat the cream mixture for 10 minutes. Do not let the bowl touch the water or the cream may overheat. Remove the vanilla pod and stir in the chocolate, a few pieces at a time, until melted. When smooth, remove the bowl, but leave the pan of water over the heat.

4 Whisk the egg yolks and clear honey in a second heatproof bowl, then gradually pour in the chocolate cream, whisking constantly. Place over the pan of simmering water and stir constantly until the chocolate custard thickens enough to coat the back of a wooden spoon.

5 Remove from the heat and spoon the custard over the mangoes. Cool, then chill in the refrigerator until set.

6 Preheat the grill (broiler) to high. Sprinkle 15ml/1 tbsp demerara sugar evenly over each dessert and spray lightly with a little water. Grill (broil) briefly, as close to the heat as possible, until the sugar melts and caramelizes. Chill again before serving.

Almond Caramel Custard

Known as crème caramel in France and as flan in Spain, this classic baked custard has been given an unusual twist by adding a hint of almond, rather than vanilla. It tastes wonderful served with strawberries and cream.

Serves 6–8
250g/9oz/1¼ cups granulated sugar
425ml/15fl oz/1¾ cups double (heavy) cream
5ml/1 tsp almond extract
5 large (US extra large) eggs, plus 2 extra yolks

1 Put 175g/6oz/¾ cup of the sugar in a small heavy pan with just enough water to moisten the sugar. Bring to the boil over a high heat, swirling the pan until the sugar has dissolved. Boil for about 5 minutes, without stirring, until the syrup is a dark caramel colour.

2 Working quickly, pour the caramel into a 1 litre/1¾ pint/4 cup soufflé dish. Holding the dish with oven gloves, carefully swirl to coat the base and sides with the caramel. Set aside to cool.

3 Preheat the oven to 160°C/325°F/Gas 3. Put the cream and almond extract in a pan and bring just to the boil over a medium-high heat, stirring. Remove from the heat, cover and cool for 20 minutes.

4 In a bowl, whisk the eggs and egg yolks with the remaining sugar for 2–3 minutes until the mixture is creamy. Whisk in the warm cream and pour into the caramel-lined dish. Cover tightly with foil.

5 Place the dish in a roasting tin (pan) and pour in boiling water to come halfway up the side of the dish. Bake for 40–45 minutes until just set. To test whether it is set, insert a knife near the edge; if it comes out clean, the custard should be ready. Remove the soufflé dish from the tin and leave to cool for at least 30 minutes, then chill overnight.

6 To turn out, run a sharp knife around the edge of the dish. Invert on to a serving plate, then gently lift one edge of the dish, allowing the caramel to escape. Lift off the dish and serve.

Almond Caramel Energy 448Kcal/1864kJ; Protein 5.6g; Carbohydrate 33.6g, of which sugars 33.6g; Fat 33.4g, of which saturates 19.1g; Cholesterol 242mg; Calcium 66mg; Fibre 0g; Sodium 60mg.
Mango & Choc. Energy 670Kcal/2782kJ; Protein 5.2g; Carbohydrate 38.9g, of which sugars 38.4g; Fat 56g, of which saturates 34.6g; Cholesterol 261mg; Calcium 90mg; Fibre 1.8g; Sodium 31mg.

Chocolate Fudge Sundaes

A banana and ice cream treat, highlighted with coffee.

Serves 4
4 scoops each vanilla and coffee
  ice cream
2 small ripe bananas
whipped cream
toasted flaked (sliced) almonds

For the sauce
50g/2oz/¼ cup soft light
  brown sugar
120ml/4fl oz/½ cup golden (light
  corn) syrup
45ml/3 tbsp strong black coffee
5ml/1 tsp ground cinnamon
150g/5oz plain (semisweet)
  chocolate, chopped into pieces
75ml/2½fl oz/⅓ cup whipping
  cream
45ml/3 tbsp coffee-flavoured
  liqueur (optional)

1 Make the sauce. Place the sugar, syrup, coffee and cinnamon in a heavy pan. Bring to the boil, then boil for about 5 minutes, stirring the mixture constantly.

2 Turn off the heat and stir in the chocolate pieces. When the chocolate has melted and the mixture is smooth, stir in the cream and the coffee-flavoured liqueur, if using. Set the sauce aside to cool slightly.

3 Fill four glasses with a scoop each of vanilla and coffee ice cream.

4 Peel the bananas and slice them thinly. Sprinkle the sliced bananas over the ice cream. Pour the warm fudge sauce over the bananas, then top each sundae with a generous swirl of whipped cream. Sprinkle the sundaes with toasted almonds and serve at once.

> **Cook's Tip**
> You can make the chocolate sauce ahead of time and reheat it gently, until just warm, when you are ready to make the sundaes. Assemble the sundaes just before serving.

Pear & Gingerbread Sundaes

The best sundaes do not consist solely of ice cream, but are a feast of flavours that melt into each other, rather like a trifle. Poach the pears and chill them well in advance, so that the dessert can be assembled in minutes. As a finishing touch, serve with wafers.

Serves 4
65g/2½oz/5 tbsp light
  muscovado (brown) sugar
90ml/6 tbsp water
30ml/2 tbsp lemon juice
40g/1½oz/⅓ cup sultanas
  (golden raisins) or raisins
1.5ml/¼ tsp mixed (apple pie)
  spice
4 small pears
150g/5oz moist gingerbread or
  ginger cake
250ml/8fl oz/1 cup vanilla
  ice cream

1 Heat the sugar and water in a heavy pan until the sugar has dissolved. Add the lemon juice, sultanas or raisins and spice. Peel, quarter and core the pears, then add them to the pan.

2 Cover the pan and simmer very gently for 5–10 minutes until the pears are just tender. Cool the pears in the syrup. Using a slotted spoon, lift them out of the syrup and put them in a bowl. Pour the syrup into a jug (pitcher). Chill both the pears and syrup in the refrigerator.

3 Cut the gingerbread or ginger cake into four pieces and arrange in four glass dishes. Divide the pears among the glasses, then pile vanilla ice cream in the centre of each portion. Pour a little of the syrup over each sundae and serve.

> **Variation**
> This extremely quick and easy dessert can be made just as successfully with tart dessert apples. Peel, quarter and core the apples, then cook as for the pears, until just tender. Replace some of the water with clear apple juice to make the apple flavour more intense.

Pear & Gingerb'd Energy 404Kcal/1706kJ; Protein 5.2g; Carbohydrate 75.6g, of which sugars 63.7g; Fat 10.3g, of which saturates 3.8g; Cholesterol 15mg; Calcium 125mg; Fibre 4g; Sodium 120mg.
Choc. Fudge Energy 642Kcal/2690kJ; Protein 5.5g; Carbohydrate 85.9g, of which sugars 84g; Fat 33.1g, of which saturates 20.5g; Cholesterol 64mg; Calcium 115mg; Fibre 1.4g; Sodium 132mg.

Fig, Port & Clementine Sundaes

The distinctive flavours of
figs, cinnamon, clementines
and port are combined to
make a refreshing sundae
bursting with taste.

Serves six
6 clementines
30ml/2 tbsp clear honey
1 cinnamon stick, halved
15ml/1 tbsp light muscovado
   (brown) sugar
60ml/4 tbsp port
6 fresh figs
about 500ml/17fl oz/2¼ cups
   orange sorbet

1 Finely grate the rind from two clementines and put it in a
small, heavy pan. Using a small, sharp knife, cut the peel away
from all the clementines, then slice the flesh thinly.

2 Add the honey, cinnamon, sugar and port to the clementine
rind. Heat gently until the sugar has completely dissolved, in
order to make a syrup.

3 Put the clementine slices in a heatproof bowl and pour over
the syrup. Cool completely, then chill.

4 Slice the figs thinly and add to the clementines and syrup,
tossing the ingredients together gently. Leave for 10 minutes,
then discard the cinnamon stick.

5 Arrange half the fig and clementine slices around the sides of
six serving glasses. Half fill the glasses with scoops of sorbet.
Arrange the remaining fruit slices around the sides of the
glasses, then pile more sorbet into the centre. Pour over the
port syrup and serve.

> **Cook's Tip**
> This rich and yet refreshing combination of ingredients creates
> the ideal dessert for finishing off a hearty winter meal on a
> light and fruity note.

Banana & Apricot Caramel Trifle

Bananas are transformed
into a marvellous trifle.

Serves 6–8
300ml/½ pint/1¼ cups milk
1 vanilla pod (bean), or 4–5 drops
   vanilla extract
40g/1½oz/3 tbsp caster
   (superfine) sugar
20ml/4 tsp cornflour (cornstarch)
3 egg yolks

60ml/4 tbsp apricot jam
120ml/8 tbsp water
175–225g/6–8oz ginger cake,
   cubed
3 bananas, sliced, with one
   reserved for topping
115g/4oz/generous ½ cup
   granulated sugar
300ml/½ pint/1¼ cups double
   (heavy) cream
a few drops of lemon juice

1 Pour the milk into a small pan. Carefully split the vanilla pod
(if using) down the middle and scrape the seeds into the pan.

2 Add the vanilla pod or extract to the milk and bring just to
the boil, then remove the pan from the heat and set aside.
When the milk has cooled slightly, remove the vanilla pod.

3 Whisk together the sugar, cornflour and egg yolks until pale
and creamy. Whisk in the milk and return the mixture to the
pan. Heat to simmering point, stirring constantly, and cook over
a low heat until the custard coats the back of a wooden spoon
thickly. Leave to cool, covering the surface with clear film (plastic
wrap) to prevent a skin forming.

4 Put the apricot jam and 60ml/4 tbsp of the water in a pan
and heat gently for 2–3 minutes, stirring. Put the cake in a deep
serving bowl and pour on the apricot mixture. Cover with
sliced bananas, then the custard. Chill for 1–2 hours.

5 Melt the sugar in a small pan with the remaining water and
cook until just turning golden. Immediately pour on to a sheet
of foil. Leave to harden, then break the caramel into pieces.

6 Whip the cream, then spread over the custard. Chill the trifle
for 2–3 hours, then top with the remaining sliced banana,
dipped into lemon juice, and the cracked caramel pieces.

Chocolate Mandarin Trifle

Rich chocolate custard is combined with mandarin oranges to make a trifle that is too tempting to resist.

Serves 6–8
4 trifle sponges
14 amaretti
60ml/4 tbsp Amaretto di Saronno
 or sweet sherry
8 mandarin oranges

For the custard
200g/7oz plain (semisweet)
 chocolate, broken into squares

25g/1oz/2 tbsp cornflour
 (cornstarch) or custard powder
25g/1oz/2 tbsp caster
 (superfine) sugar
2 egg yolks
200ml/7fl oz/scant 1 cup milk
250g/9oz/generous 1 cup
 mascarpone

For the topping
250g/9oz/generous 1 cup
 mascarpone or fromage frais
chocolate shapes
mandarin slices

1 Break up the trifle sponges and place them in a large glass serving dish. Crumble the amaretti over and then sprinkle with Amaretto or sweet sherry.

2 Squeeze the juice from two of the mandarins and sprinkle into the dish. Segment the rest and put in the dish.

3 Make the custard. Melt the chocolate in a heatproof bowl over hot water. In a separate bowl, mix the cornflour or custard powder, sugar and egg yolks to a smooth paste.

4 Heat the milk in a small pan until almost boiling, then pour in a steady stream on to the egg yolk mixture, stirring constantly. Return to the pan and stir over a low heat until the custard has thickened slightly and is smooth.

5 Stir in the mascarpone until melted, then add the melted chocolate; mix well. Spread over the trifle, cool, then chill to set.

6 To finish, spread the mascarpone or fromage frais over the custard, then decorate with chocolate shapes and the remaining mandarin slices just before serving.

Blackcurrant & Meringue Trifles

Trifle with a twist, this quick and easy dessert is made using crushed meringues, cream and sorbet. Served in individual dishes, it is suitable for any occasion.

Serves 6
350ml/12fl oz/1½ cups
 blackcurrant sorbet
3 bought meringues

several sprigs of fresh mint, plus
 extra mint sprigs, to decorate
30ml/2 tbsp icing (confectioners')
 sugar
20ml/4 tsp freshly squeezed
 lemon juice
300ml/½ pint/1¼ cups double
 (heavy) or whipping cream
90ml/6 tbsp Greek (US strained
 plain) yogurt

1 Remove the blackcurrant sorbet from the freezer for about 20 minutes to soften slightly. Roughly break the meringues into small pieces.

2 Chop the mint finely and put it into a bowl. Add the icing sugar, lemon juice and cream. Whip until the mixture just holds its shape. Stir in the Greek yogurt, then carefully fold in the crushed meringues.

3 Spoon a little of the cream mixture into six small, deep dishes or glasses. Add layers of sorbet and cream mixture, ending with cream mixture. Decorate with mint sprigs.

Cook's Tip
The number this will serve will depend on the size of the dishes used. If you opt for large, bowl-shaped glasses, the mixture will probably serve four.

Variation
Leave out the chopped mint, if you prefer. The blackcurrant sorbet gives a good colour and flavour contrast to the cream mixture, but you could use any other flavourful sorbet instead.

Choc. Mandarin Energy 569Kcal/2394kJ; Protein 12.5g; Carbohydrate 80.3g, of which sugars 61.3g; Fat 23.1g, of which saturates 12.8g; Cholesterol 135mg; Calcium 162mg; Fibre 2.9g; Sodium 115mg.
Blackcurrant & Meringue Energy 405Kcal/1687kJ; Protein 2.8g; Carbohydrate 36.9g, of which sugars 36g; Fat 28.6g, of which saturates 17.5g; Cholesterol 69mg; Calcium 56mg; Fibre 0g; Sodium 47mg.

Lemon Soufflé with Blackberries

The simple fresh taste of cold lemon soufflé combines well with rich blackberry sauce, and the colour contrast looks wonderful, too. Blueberries or raspberries make equally delicious alternatives to blackberries.

Serves 6

grated rind of 1 lemon and juice of 2 lemons
15ml/1 tbsp/1 sachet powdered gelatine

5 eggs, separated
150g/5oz/³⁄₄ cup caster (superfine) sugar
few drops vanilla extract
400ml/14fl oz/1²⁄₃ cups whipping cream

For the sauce

175g/6oz/³⁄₄ cup blackberries (fresh or frozen)
30–45ml/2–3 tbsp caster (superfine) sugar
few fresh blackberries and blackberry leaves, to decorate

1 Place the lemon juice in a small pan and heat through. Sprinkle on the gelatine and leave to dissolve or heat further until clear. Allow to cool.

2 Put the lemon rind, egg yolks, sugar and vanilla into a large bowl and whisk until the mixture is very thick, pale and creamy.

3 Whisk the egg whites until stiff and almost peaky. Whip the cream until stiff.

4 Stir the gelatine mixture into the yolks, then fold in the whipped cream and lastly the egg whites. Turn into a 1.5 litre/2½ pint/6¼ cup soufflé dish and freeze for about 2 hours.

5 To make the sauce, place the blackberries in a pan with the sugar and cook for 4–6 minutes, until the juices begin to run and all the sugar has dissolved. Pass through a sieve (strainer) to remove the seeds, then chill.

6 When the soufflé is almost frozen, but still spoonable, scoop or spoon out on to individual plates and serve with the blackberry sauce, decorated with fresh blackberries and blackberry leaves.

Tangerine Trifle

An unusual variation on a traditional trifle – of course, you can add a little alcohol if you wish.

Serves 4

5 trifle sponges, halved lengthways
30ml/2 tbsp apricot jam
15–20 ratafia biscuits (almond macaroons)

142g/4³⁄₄oz packet tangerine jelly (flavoured gelatine)
300g/11oz can mandarin oranges, drained, reserving juice
600ml/1 pint/2½ cups fresh ready-made custard
whipped cream and shreds of orange rind, to decorate
caster (superfine) sugar, for sprinkling

1 Spread the halved sponge cakes with apricot jam and arrange in the base of a deep serving bowl or glass dish. Sprinkle over the ratafia biscuits.

2 Break up the jelly into a heatproof measuring jug (cup). Add the juice from the canned mandarins and place in a pan of hot water or in the microwave to dissolve. Stir until clear.

3 Make up to 600ml/1 pint/2½ cups with ice cold water, stir well and leave to cool for up to 30 minutes. Scatter the mandarin oranges over the cakes and ratafias.

4 Pour the jelly over the mandarin oranges, cake and ratafias and chill for 1 hour.

5 When the jelly has set, pour the custard smoothly over the top and chill again.

6 When ready to serve, pipe the whipped cream over the custard. Wash the orange rind shreds, sprinkle them with caster sugar and use to decorate the trifle.

Cook's Tip
For an even better flavour, use your own homemade custard.

Tangerine Trifle Energy 579Kcal/2451kJ; Protein 14.1g; Carbohydrate 111g, of which sugars 81.1g; Fat 10.3g, of which saturates 2.7g; Cholesterol 145mg; Calcium 241mg; Fibre 1.3g; Sodium 211mg.
Lemon Soufflé Energy 381Kcal/1592kJ; Protein 7.4g; Carbohydrate 35g, of which sugars 35g; Fat 24.6g, of which saturates 18.9g; Cholesterol 164mg; Calcium 104mg; Fibre 1g; Sodium 98mg.

Pear & Hazelnut Meringue Torte

This stunning dessert will raise gasps of admiration.

Serves 8–10
175g/6oz/³⁄₄ cup granulated sugar
1 vanilla pod (bean), split
475ml/16fl oz/2 cups water
4 ripe pears, peeled, halved and cored
30ml/2 tbsp hazelnut- or pear-flavoured liqueur
150g/5oz/1¹⁄₄ cups hazelnuts, toasted
6 egg whites

pinch of salt
350g/12oz/3 cups icing (confectioners') sugar
5ml/1 tsp vanilla extract
50g/2oz plain (semisweet) chocolate, melted

For the chocolate cream
275g/10oz plain (semisweet) chocolate, chopped into small pieces
475ml/16fl oz/2 cups whipping cream
60ml/4 tbsp hazelnut- or pear-flavoured liqueur

1 In a pan large enough to hold the pears in a single layer, combine the sugar, vanilla pod and water. Over a high heat, bring to the boil, stirring until the sugar dissolves. Lower the heat, add the pears to the syrup, cover and simmer gently for 12–15 minutes until tender. Remove the pan from the heat and allow the pears to cool in their poaching liquid. Carefully lift the pears out of the liquid and drain on kitchen paper. Transfer them to a plate, sprinkle with liqueur, cover and chill overnight.

2 Preheat the oven to 180°C/350°F/Gas 4. With a pencil, draw a 23cm/9in circle on each of two sheets of baking parchment. Turn the paper over on to two baking sheets (so that the pencil marks are underneath). Grind the toasted hazelnuts.

3 In a large bowl, beat the whites with a hand-held electric mixer until frothy. Add the salt and beat on high speed until soft peaks form. Reduce the mixer speed and gradually add the icing sugar, beating well after each addition until all the sugar has been added and the whites are stiff and glossy. Gently fold in the nuts and vanilla extract and spoon the meringue on to the circles on the baking sheets, smoothing the top and sides.

4 Bake for 1 hour until the tops are dry and firm. Turn off the oven and cool in the oven for 2–3 hours or overnight, until dry.

5 Make the chocolate cream. Melt the chocolate in a heatproof bowl set over a pan of simmering water and stir until melted and smooth. Cool to room temperature. Whip the cream in a bowl to soft peaks. Quickly fold the cream into the chocolate; fold in the liqueur. Spoon about one-third of the chocolate cream into an icing (pastry) bag fitted with a star tip. Set aside.

6 Thinly slice each pear half lengthways. Place one meringue layer on a serving plate. Spread with half the chocolate cream and arrange half the pears on top. Pipe rosettes around edge.

7 Top with the second meringue layer, spread with the remaining chocolate cream and arrange the remaining pear slices on top. Pipe a border of rosettes around the edge. Spoon the melted chocolate into a small paper cone and drizzle the chocolate over the pears. Chill for at least 1 hour before serving.

Raspberry Meringue Gâteau

A rich hazelnut meringue sandwiched with whipped cream and raspberries is the ultimate in elegance.

Serves 6
4 egg whites
225g/8oz/1 cup caster (superfine) sugar
a few drops of vanilla extract
5ml/1 tsp distilled malt vinegar
115g/4oz/1 cup roasted and chopped hazelnuts, ground

300ml/¹⁄₂ pint/1¹⁄₄ cups double (heavy) cream
350g/12oz/2 cups raspberries
icing (confectioners') sugar, for dusting
raspberries and mint sprigs, to decorate

For the sauce
225g/8oz/1¹⁄₃ cups raspberries
45–60ml/3–4 tbsp icing (confectioners') sugar, sifted
15ml/1 tbsp orange liqueur

1 Preheat the oven to 180°C/350°F/Gas 4. Grease two 20cm/8in sandwich tins (layer cake pans) and line the bases with baking parchment.

2 Whisk the egg whites in a large bowl until they hold stiff peaks, then gradually whisk in the caster sugar a tablespoon at a time, whisking well after each addition. Continue whisking the meringue mixture for a minute or two until very stiff, then fold in the vanilla extract, vinegar and ground hazelnuts.

3 Divide the meringue mixture between the prepared tins and spread level. Bake for 50–60 minutes, until crisp. Remove the meringues from the tins and leave them to cool on a wire rack.

4 Meanwhile, make the sauce. Process the raspberries with the icing sugar and liqueur in a blender or food processor, then press through a sieve (strainer) to remove seeds. Chill the sauce.

5 Whip the cream until it forms soft peaks, then gently fold in the raspberries. Sandwich the meringue rounds together with the raspberry cream.

6 Dust the top of the gâteau with icing sugar. Decorate with mint sprigs and serve with the raspberry sauce.

Pear & Hazelnut Energy 706Kcal/2960kJ; Protein 6.9g; Carbohydrate 86.1g, of which sugars 85.5g; Fat 37.4g, of which saturates 17.9g; Cholesterol 52mg; Calcium 97mg; Fibre 3.1g; Sodium 64mg.
Raspberry Gâteau Energy 354Kcal/1477kJ; Protein 4.2g; Carbohydrate 32.4g, of which sugars 32.2g; Fat 23.6g, of which saturates 10.6g; Cholesterol 41mg; Calcium 60mg; Fibre 2.2g; Sodium 35mg.

COLD DESSERTS

Chocolate Pavlova with Passion Fruit Cream

This meringue dish has a delicious chewy centre that is hard to resist.

Serves 6
4 egg whites
200g/7oz/1 cup caster
  (superfine) sugar
20ml/4 tsp cornflour (cornstarch)
45g/1¾oz/3 tbsp cocoa powder
  (unsweetened)
5ml/1 tsp vinegar
chocolate leaves, to decorate

For the filling
150g/5oz plain (semisweet)
  chocolate, chopped into
  small pieces
250ml/8fl oz/1 cup double
  (heavy) cream
150g/5oz/²⁄₃ cup Greek (US
  strained plain) yogurt
2.5ml/½ tsp vanilla extract
4 passion fruit

1 Preheat oven to 140°C/275°F/Gas 1. Cut a piece of baking parchment to fit a baking sheet. Draw on a 23cm/9in circle.

2 Whisk the egg whites in a clean, grease-free bowl until stiff. Gradually whisk in the sugar and continue to whisk until the mixture is stiff again. Whisk in the cornflour, cocoa and vinegar.

3 Place the baking parchment upside down on the baking sheet. Spread the mixture over the circle; make a slight dip in the centre. Bake for 1½–2 hours.

4 Make the filling. Melt the chocolate in a heatproof bowl over barely simmering water, then remove from the heat and cool slightly. In a separate bowl, whip the cream with the yogurt and vanilla extract until thick. Fold 60ml/4 tbsp into the chocolate, then set both mixtures aside.

5 Halve all the passion fruit and scoop out the pulp. Stir half into the plain cream mixture. Carefully transfer the meringue shell to a serving plate. Fill with the passion fruit cream, then spoon over the chocolate mixture and the remaining passion fruit pulp. Decorate with chocolate leaves. Serve immediately.

Meringue Squiggles

These delightful meringue shapes are easy to make, taste delicious and look fantastic. They're popular with children and adults alike and are great as a teatime treat or as a simple dessert with ice cream.

Makes 14–16
2 egg whites
90g/3½oz/scant ½ cup caster
  (superfine) sugar
multi-coloured sugar sprinkles,
  to decorate

1 Preheat the oven to 150°C/300°F/Gas 2. Line a large baking sheet with baking parchment.

2 Put the egg whites in a large bowl, reserving about 15ml/1 tbsp for decoration, and whisk until they form firm peaks. Add a spoonful of caster sugar and whisk briefly to combine. Add another spoonful and whisk again. Continue in this way until all the sugar has been incorporated.

3 Spoon the meringue mixture into a large piping (pastry) bag fitted with a large plain nozzle. Pipe wavy lines of meringue, about 13cm/5in long, on to the baking sheet and bake for about 1 hour, or until dry and crisp.

4 Carefully peel the meringues off the paper and transfer to a wire rack to cool.

5 Using a fine pastry brush, brush the tops of the meringues with the reserved egg white, then scatter over the multi-coloured sugar sprinkles to decorate.

> **Cook's Tip**
> If you prefer not to use raw egg white to decorate the meringue squiggles, use a sugar paste instead. Put 45g/1¾oz/3 tbsp icing (confectioners') sugar in a small bowl and add a few drops of water. Stir well to make a paste, then brush on to the meringues.

Choc. Pavlova Energy 541Kcal/2260kJ; Protein 7.3g; Carbohydrate 56.4g, of which sugars 52.3g; Fat 33.6g, of which saturates 20.4g; Cholesterol 59mg; Calcium 96mg; Fibre 1.9g; Sodium 146mg.
Meringue Squiggles Energy 24Kcal/101kJ; Protein 0.4g; Carbohydrate 5.9g, of which sugars 5.9g; Fat 0g, of which saturates 0g; Cholesterol 0mg; Calcium 3mg; Fibre 0g; Sodium 8mg.

Coffee Crêpes with Peaches & Cream

Summery peaches and brandy cream make a tasty filling for light crêpes.

Serves 6
75g/3oz/²⁄₃ cup plain
   (all-purpose) flour
25g/1oz/¼ cup buckwheat flour
1 egg, beaten
200ml/7fl oz/scant 1 cup milk
15g/½oz/1 tbsp butter, melted
100ml/3½fl oz/scant ½ cup
   brewed coffee, cooled
sunflower oil, for frying

For the filling
6 ripe peaches
300ml/½ pint/1¼ cups double
   (heavy) cream
15ml/1 tbsp brandy
225g/8oz/1 cup crème fraîche
65g/2½oz/5 tbsp unrefined
   caster (superfine) sugar
30ml/2 tbsp sifted icing
   (confectioners') sugar, for
   dusting (optional)

1 Sift the flours into a mixing bowl. Make a well in the middle and add the beaten egg, half the milk and the melted butter. Gradually mix in the flour, beating until the mixture is smooth, then beat in the remaining milk and the coffee.

2 Heat a drizzle of sunflower oil in a 15–20cm/6–8in crêpe pan. Pour in just enough batter to cover the base of the pan thinly, swirling the pan to spread the mixture evenly. Cook for 2–3 minutes until the underneath is golden brown, then flip the crêpe over using a metal spatula and cook the other side.

3 Slide the crêpe on to a plate. Continue making crêpes in this way, stacking and interleaving them with baking parchment.

4 To make the filling, halve the peaches and carefully remove the stones (pits). Cut the peaches into thick slices. Whip the cream and brandy together until soft peaks form. Beat the crème fraîche with the sugar until smooth. Beat 30ml/2 tbsp of the cream into the crème fraîche, then fold in the remainder.

5 Place the crêpes on plates. Spoon a little of the brandy cream on to one half of each crêpe and top with peach slices. Fold the crêpe over and dust with a little icing sugar, if you wish.

Devilish Chocolate Roulade

Indulge yourself with this wickedly rich roulade.

Serves 6–8
175g/6oz plain (semisweet)
   chocolate, chopped into
   small pieces
4 eggs, separated
115g/4oz/generous ½ cup caster
   (superfine) sugar
cocoa powder (unsweetened),
   for dusting

chocolate-dipped strawberries, to
   decorate

For the filling
225g/8oz plain (semisweet)
   chocolate, chopped into
   small pieces
45ml/3 tbsp brandy
2 eggs, separated
250g/9oz/generous 1 cup
   mascarpone

1 Preheat oven to 180°C/350°F/Gas 4. Grease a 33 × 23cm/13 × 9in Swiss roll tin (jelly roll pan) and line with baking parchment. Melt the chocolate in a bowl over a pan of hot water.

2 Whisk the egg yolks and sugar in a bowl until pale and thick, then stir in the melted chocolate. Place the egg whites in a clean, grease-free bowl. Whisk them to soft peaks, then fold lightly and evenly into the egg and chocolate mixture.

3 Scrape into the tin and spread to the corners. Bake for 15–20 minutes, until well risen and firm to the touch. Dust a sheet of baking parchment with cocoa. Turn the sponge out on to the paper, cover with a clean dish towel and cool.

4 Make the filling. Melt the chocolate with the brandy in a heatproof bowl over a pan of simmering water. Remove from the heat. Beat the egg yolks together, then beat into the chocolate mixture. In a separate bowl, whisk the whites to soft peaks, then fold them lightly and evenly into the filling.

5 Uncover the roulade, remove the lining paper and spread with the mascarpone. Spread the chocolate mixture over the top, then roll up carefully from a long side to enclose the filling. Transfer to a serving plate with the join underneath, top with fresh chocolate-dipped strawberries and chill before serving.

Coffee Crêpes Energy 578Kcal/2403kJ; Protein 6.5g; Carbohydrate 36.3g, of which sugars 23.1g; Fat 45.7g, of which saturates 28.8g; Cholesterol 150mg; Calcium 123mg; Fibre 2.1g; Sodium 63mg.
Chocolate Roulade Energy 486Kcal/2022kJ; Protein 10.2g; Carbohydrate 32.8g, of which sugars 32.4g; Fat 34.5g, of which saturates 19.9g; Cholesterol 189mg; Calcium 41mg; Fibre 1.3g; Sodium 143mg.

Cherries Jubilee

Fresh black or red cherries taste wonderful cooked lightly and served hot over ice cream. A great idea for a mid-week meal when time is short.

Serves 4
450g/1lb sweet fresh cherries
115g/4oz/generous ½ cup caster (superfine) sugar
pared rind of 1 lemon
300ml/½ pint/1¼ cups water, plus 15ml/1 tbsp
15ml/1 tbsp arrowroot
60ml/4 tbsp Kirsch
vanilla ice cream, to serve

1 Pit the cherries over a pan to catch the juice. Drop the pits into the pan as you work.

2 Add the sugar, lemon rind and 300ml/½ pint/1¼ cups water to the pan. Stir over a low heat until the sugar has dissolved, then bring to the boil and simmer for 10 minutes. Strain the syrup, then return to the pan. Add the cherries and cook for 3–4 minutes. Remove from the heat.

3 Blend the arrowroot to a paste with 15ml/1 tbsp cold water and stir into the cherries.

4 Return the pan to the heat. Bring to the boil, stirring all the time. Cook the sauce for a minute or two, stirring until thick and smooth.

5 Heat the Kirsch in a ladle over a flame, ignite and pour over the cherries. Spoon the cherries and hot sauce over scoops of ice cream and serve immediately.

> **Cook's Tips**
> • *If you don't have a cherry pitter, simply push the pits through with a skewer, keeping the fruit whole. Remember to do this over a pan (or plate), so that you can catch the juice.*
> • *When buying fresh cherries, look for well-coloured fruits and avoid any that are split, as they will be over-ripe.*

Warm Autumn Compote

An unusual combination of pears, figs and raspberries.

Serves 4
75g/3oz/6 tbsp caster (superfine) sugar
1 bottle red wine
1 vanilla pod (bean), split
1 strip pared lemon rind
4 pears
2 purple figs, quartered
225g/8oz/1⅓ cups raspberries
freshly squeezed lemon juice, to taste

1 Put the sugar and wine in a large pan and heat gently until the sugar has dissolved. Add the vanilla pod and lemon rind and bring to the boil, then simmer for 5 minutes.

2 Peel and halve the pears, then scoop out the cores, using a melon baller or a teaspoon. Add the pears to the syrup and poach for 15 minutes, carefully turning the pears several times so that they colour evenly. Add the figs to the pan and poach for a further 5 minutes, until the fruits are tender.

3 Transfer the poached pears and figs to a serving bowl using a slotted spoon, then sprinkle over the raspberries.

4 Return the syrup to the heat and boil rapidly to reduce slightly and concentrate the flavour. Add a little lemon juice to taste. Strain the syrup over the fruits and serve warm.

> **Variation/Cherry Compote**
> *Combine 120ml/4fl oz/½ cup red wine, 50g/2oz/¼ cup light muscovado (brown) sugar, 50g/2oz/¼ cup granulated sugar, 15ml/1 tbsp honey, two 2.5cm/1in strips of pared orange rind and 1.5ml/¼ tsp almond extract in a pan with 120ml/4fl oz/½ cup water. Stir over medium heat until the sugar dissolves, then increase the heat and boil until the liquid reduces slightly. Add 675g/1½lb pitted sweet fresh cherries and bring back to the boil, skimming off any foam. Reduce the heat slightly and simmer for 8–10 minutes. Serve lukewarm on ice-cream.*

Cherries Jubilee Energy 206Kcal/873kJ; Protein 1.2g; Carbohydrate 47.9g, of which sugars 47.9g; Fat 0.1g, of which saturates 0g; Cholesterol 0mg; Calcium 30mg; Fibre 1g; Sodium 3mg.
Autumn Compote Energy 298Kcal/1257kJ; Protein 1.9g; Carbohydrate 42.9g, of which sugars 42.9g; Fat 0.5g, of which saturates 0.1g; Cholesterol 0mg; Calcium 79mg; Fibre 5.5g; Sodium 27mg.

Russian Fruit Compote

Traditionally called "Kissel" in Russia, this fruit dish is made from the thickened juice of stewed red- or blackcurrants. This version uses the whole fruit with an added dash of blackberry liqueur to give added zing.

Serves 4

225g/8oz/2 cups red- or blackcurrants or a mixture of both
225g/8oz/1⅓ cups raspberries
50g/2oz/¼ cup caster (superfine) sugar
150ml/¼ pint/⅔ cup water
25ml/1½ tbsp arrowroot
15–30ml/1–2 tbsp Crème de Mûre
Greek (US strained plain) yogurt, to serve

1 Place the red- or blackcurrants, raspberries and sugar in a pan with the water. Cover the pan and cook gently over a low heat for 12–15 minutes, until the fruit is soft.

2 Blend the arrowroot with a little water in a bowl and stir into the fruit off the heat. Bring the syrup back to the boil, stirring frequently until thickened.

3 Remove from the heat and cool slightly, then gently stir in the Crème de Mûre liqueur.

4 Pour into four serving bowls and leave until cold, then chill. Serve topped with spoonfuls of Greek yogurt.

Cook's Tips
• If you have difficulty finding Crème de Mûre, use the more well-known blackcurrant liqueur, Crème de Cassis, instead.
• Unlike cornflour (cornstarch), arrowroot thickens a liquid without making it cloudy, producing a clear glossy sauce.
• When preparing clusters of currants, remove the fruit from the stalks by running them through the prongs of a fork. There is no need to trim the fruit.

Spiced Red Fruit Compote

A colourful mix of succulent red fruit, delicately flavoured with aromatic spices, this dish is guaranteed to bring a touch of summer warmth to a cold day.

Serves 4

4 ripe red plums, halved
225g/8oz/2 cups strawberries, halved
225g/8oz/1⅓ cups raspberries

30ml/2 tbsp light muscovado (brown) sugar
30ml/2 tbsp water
1 cinnamon stick
3 pieces star anise
6 cloves
natural (plain) yogurt or Greek (US strained plain) yogurt, to serve

1 Place the plums, strawberries and raspberries in a heavy pan with the sugar and the water.

2 Add the cinnamon stick, star anise and cloves to the pan and heat gently, without boiling, until the sugar dissolves and the fruit juices run.

3 Cover the pan and leave the fruit to infuse over a very low heat for about 5 minutes. Remove the spices from the compote before serving warm in individual dishes, with spoonfuls of natural or Greek yogurt.

Cook's Tip
Star anise is the dried fruit of a tree native to China and is dark red-brown in colour. As its name implies, the spice is star-shaped and has an aniseed-like taste. It is quite pungent, so don't be heavy-handed with it.

Variation
Try using peaches and cherries instead of the plums and strawberries, and add a dash of liqueur for good measure.

Russian Fruit Compote Energy 91Kcal/389kJ; Protein 1.4g; Carbohydrate 20.3g, of which sugars 20.3g; Fat 0.2g, of which saturates 0.1g; Cholesterol 0mg; Calcium 55mg; Fibre 3.4g; Sodium 4mg.
Red Fruit Compote Energy 70Kcal/298kJ; Protein 1.5g; Carbohydrate 16.5g, of which sugars 16.5g; Fat 0.3g, of which saturates 0.1g; Cholesterol 0mg; Calcium 31mg; Fibre 2.5g; Sodium 6mg.

Apricots in Marsala

Rich Marsala creates a
beautifully flavoured syrup
for the apricots. Serve with
amaretti to add to the
Italian tone of the dish.

Serves 4
12 apricots
50g/2oz/¼ cup caster
    (superfine) sugar
300ml/½ pint/1¼ cups Marsala
2 strips pared orange rind

1 vanilla pod (bean), split
250ml/8fl oz/1 cup water
150ml/¼ pint/⅔ cup double
    (heavy) or whipping cream
15ml/1 tbsp icing
    (confectioners') sugar
1.5ml/¼ tsp ground cinnamon
150ml/¼ pint/⅔ cup Greek
    (US strained plain) yogurt
amaretti, to serve

1 Halve and stone (pit) the apricots, then place in a bowl of
boiling water for about 30 seconds. Drain well, then slip off
their skins.

2 Place the caster sugar, Marsala, orange rind, vanilla pod and
water in a pan. Heat gently until the sugar dissolves. Bring to the
boil, without stirring, then simmer for 2–3 minutes.

3 Add the apricot halves to the pan and poach for 5–6 minutes,
or until just tender. Using a slotted spoon, transfer the apricots
to a serving dish.

4 Boil the syrup rapidly until reduced by half, then pour over
the apricots and leave to cool. Cover and chill. Remove the
orange rind and vanilla pod.

5 Whip the cream with the icing sugar and cinnamon until it
forms soft peaks. Gently fold in the yogurt. Spoon the cream
into a serving bowl and chill. Serve with the apricots.

> **Cook's Tip**
> Make sure that the apricots are completely covered by the
> syrup so that they don't discolour.

Prunes Poached in Red Wine

Bathed in a lightly aromatic
wine sauce, prunes are
transformed into something
special. Easy to make
and quite delicious, this is
a particularly useful fruit
dessert for the winter time.

Serves 8–10
900g/2lb large pitted prunes
1 unwaxed orange
1 unwaxed lemon
750ml/1¼ pints/3 cups fruity
    red wine

50g/2oz/¼ cup caster (superfine)
    sugar, or to taste
1 cinnamon stick
pinch of freshly grated nutmeg
2 or 3 cloves
5ml/1 tsp black peppercorns
1 bay leaf
475ml/16fl oz/2 cups water
strips of orange rind, to decorate
    (optional)
pouring (half-and-half) cream,
    to serve

1 Place the prunes in a bowl, cover with water and leave to
soak for a few hours.

2 Using a vegetable peeler, pare two or three strips of rind
from both the orange and lemon. Squeeze the juice from both
and put in a large pan.

3 Add the wine, sugar, spices, peppercorns, bay leaf and strips of
rind to the pan with the water.

4 Bring to the boil over a medium heat, stirring occasionally to
dissolve the sugar. Drain the prunes and add to the pan. Reduce
the heat to low and simmer, covered, for 10–15 minutes until
the prunes are tender. Remove from the heat and set aside
until cool.

5 Using a slotted spoon, transfer the prunes to a serving dish.
Return the cooking liquid to a medium-high heat and bring to
the boil. Boil for 5–10 minutes until slightly reduced and syrupy.

6 Pour or strain the hot syrup over the prunes. Cool, then chill
in the refrigerator. Serve with cream, decorated with strips of
orange rind, if you like.

Apricots in Marsala Energy 448Kcal/1870kJ; Protein 4.2g; Carbohydrate 36g, of which sugars 36g; Fat 24.1g, of which saturates 14.5g; Cholesterol 51mg; Calcium 104mg; Fibre 2.1g; Sodium 41mg.
Prunes in Red Wine Energy 198Kcal/837kJ; Protein 2.4g; Carbohydrate 36g, of which sugars 36g; Fat 0.4g, of which saturates 0g; Cholesterol 0mg; Calcium 39mg; Fibre 5.1g; Sodium 16mg.

Poached Pears in Red Wine

This makes a very pretty
dessert, as the pears take on
a red blush from the wine.

Serves 4
1 bottle red wine
150g/5oz/³⁄₄ cup caster
  (superfine) sugar
45ml/3 tbsp clear honey
juice of ¹⁄₂ lemon

1 cinnamon stick
1 vanilla pod (bean), split
5cm/2in piece of orange rind
1 clove
1 black peppercorn
4 firm, ripe pears
whipped double (heavy) cream or
  sour cream, to serve

1 Place the wine, sugar, honey, lemon juice, cinnamon stick,
vanilla pod, orange rind, clove and peppercorn in a pan just
large enough to hold the pears standing upright. Heat gently,
stirring occasionally, until the sugar has completely dissolved.

2 Meanwhile, peel the pears, leaving the stem intact. Cut a thin
slice off the base of each pear so that it will stand straight and
upright in the pan.

3 Place the pears in the wine mixture, then simmer, uncovered,
for 20–35 minutes, depending on their size and ripeness, until
the pears are just tender.

4 Carefully transfer the pears to a bowl using a slotted spoon.
Continue to boil the poaching liquid until reduced by about
half. Leave to cool, then strain the cooled liquid over the pears
and chill for at least 3 hours.

5 Place the pears in four individual serving dishes and spoon
over a little of the red wine syrup. Serve with whipped or
sour cream.

> **Cook's Tip**
> *Take care not to over-cook the pears. They need to be firm but
> tender – test them with a sharp knife after 20 minutes.*

Ginger Baked Pears

Based on a traditional
French dessert, this dish is
simplicity itself to make. In
France, this dish would be
served after a Sunday lunch.

Serves 4
4 large pears
300ml/¹⁄₂ pint/1 ¹⁄₄ cups whipping
  cream

50g/2oz/¹⁄₄ cup caster
  (superfine) sugar
2.5ml/¹⁄₂ tsp vanilla extract
1.5ml/¹⁄₄ tsp ground cinnamon
pinch of freshly grated nutmeg
5ml/1 tsp grated fresh
  root ginger

1 Preheat the oven to 190°C/375°F/Gas 5. Lightly butter a
large shallow baking dish.

2 Peel the pears, cut in half lengthways and remove the cores.
Arrange, cut side down, in a single layer, in the baking dish.

3 Mix together the cream, sugar, vanilla extract, cinnamon,
nutmeg and ginger and pour over the pears.

4 Bake for 30–35 minutes, basting from time to time, until the
pears are tender and browned on top and the cream is thick
and bubbly. Cool slightly before serving.

> **Cook's Tips**
> • *Try to find Comice or Anjou pears for an authentic touch. The
> Comice, with its pale yellow skin and russet flecks, has a lovely
> smooth, buttery texture. The Anjou, also known as Beurre, has
> soft, aromatic flesh and is very juicy.*
> • *This recipe is especially useful for slightly under-ripe fruit.*

> **Variation**
> *Add a little Poire William, the pear-flavoured eau de vie, to give
> a touch of luxury to the dish.*

Pears in Red Wine Energy 378Kcal/1595kJ; Protein 1g; Carbohydrate 65.7g, of which sugars 65.7g; Fat 0.2g, of which saturates 0g; Cholesterol 0mg; Calcium 53mg; Fibre 3.9g; Sodium 22mg.
Ginger Baked Pears Energy 435Kcal/1809kJ; Protein 2.3g; Carbohydrate 40.1g, of which sugars 40.1g; Fat 30.5g, of which saturates 18.9g; Cholesterol 79mg; Calcium 78mg; Fibre 5.5g; Sodium 27mg.

Poached Pears in Port Syrup

The perfect choice for autumn entertaining, this simple dessert has a beautiful rich colour and fantastic flavour thanks to the tastes of port and lemon.

175ml/6fl oz/³⁄₄ cup ruby port
50g/2oz/¹⁄₄ cup caster
   (superfine) sugar
1 cinnamon stick
60ml/4 tbsp cold water
cream, to serve

Serves 4

2 ripe, firm pears, such as
   Williams or Comice
pared rind of 1 lemon

To decorate

30ml/2 tbsp flaked (sliced)
   hazelnuts, toasted
fresh mint, pear or rose leaves

1 Peel the pears, cut them in half and remove the cores. Place the lemon rind, port, sugar, cinnamon stick and water in a shallow pan. Bring to the boil over a low heat. Add the pears, lower the heat, cover and poach for 5 minutes. Let the pears cool in the syrup.

2 When the pears are cold, transfer them to a bowl with a slotted spoon. Return the syrup to the heat. Boil rapidly until it has reduced to form a syrup that will coat the back of a spoon lightly. Remove the cinnamon stick and lemon rind and leave the syrup to cool.

3 To serve, place a pear half on a board, cut side down. Keeping it intact at the stalk end, slice the pear lengthways, then, using a palette knife, carefully transfer to a dessert plate. Press gently so that the pear fans out. Repeat with the remaining pears.

4 When all the pears have been fanned, spoon over the port syrup. Top each portion with a few hazelnuts and decorate with fresh mint, pear or rose leaves. Serve with cream.

Cook's Tip
Choose pears of a similar size, with the stalks intact, for the most attractive effect when fanned on the plate.

Exotic Fruit Skewers with Lime Cheese

Lightly charred exotic fruit, served with luscious lime-flavoured cream, make the perfect finale for an *al fresco* meal. The lemon grass skewers impart a subtle lemon tang to the fruit – and look fun.

8 fresh bay leaves
a nutmeg
60ml/4 tbsp maple syrup
50g/2oz/¹⁄₄ cup demerara
   (raw) sugar

For the lime cheese
150g/5oz/²⁄₃ cup curd (farmer's)
   cheese or low-fat soft cheese
120ml/4fl oz/¹⁄₂ cup double
   (heavy) cream
grated rind and juice of ¹⁄₂ lime
30ml/2 tbsp icing
   (confectioners') sugar

Serves 4

4 long fresh lemon grass stalks
1 mango, peeled, stoned (pitted)
   and cut into chunks
1 papaya, peeled, seeded and cut
   into chunks
1 star fruit, cut into thick slices
   and halved

1 Prepare the barbecue or preheat the grill (broiler). Cut the top of each lemon grass stalk into a point with a sharp knife. Discard the outer leaves, then use the back of the knife to bruise the length of each stalk to release the aromatic oils. Thread each stalk, skewer-style, with a variety of the fruit pieces and bay leaves.

2 Support a piece of foil on a baking sheet and roll up the edges to make a rim. Grease the foil, lay the kebabs on top and grate a little nutmeg over each. Drizzle the maple syrup over and dust liberally with the demerara sugar. Grill (broil) for 5 minutes, until lightly charred.

3 Meanwhile, make the lime cheese. Mix together the cheese, cream, grated lime rind and juice and icing sugar in a bowl.

4 Serve the lightly charred exotic fruit kebabs along with the lime cheese.

Poached Pears Energy 158Kcal/666kJ; Protein 0.4g; Carbohydrate 28.3g, of which sugars 28.3g; Fat 0.1g, of which saturates 0g; Cholesterol 0mg; Calcium 20mg; Fibre 2.2g; Sodium 6mg.
Exotic Fruit Energy 306Kcal/1276kJ; Protein 7.1g; Carbohydrate 28.8g, of which sugars 28.7g; Fat 19.4g, of which saturates 12g; Cholesterol 50mg; Calcium 100mg; Fibre 4.3g; Sodium 180mg.

Star Anise Fruits with Coconut Jelly

This simple yet rather unusual Eastern-influenced dessert is sure to impress the most jaded of palates. It is best served after any oriental-style meal, with plenty of extra exotic fruit.

Serves 4
For the coconut jelly
250ml/8fl oz/1 cup water
75g/3oz/6 tbsp caster (superfine) sugar

15ml/1 tbsp powdered gelatine
400ml/14fl oz/1²⁄₃ cups coconut milk

For the syrup and fruit
250ml/8fl oz/1 cup water
3 star anise
50g/2oz/¼ cup caster (superfine) sugar
1 star fruit, sliced
12 lychees, peeled and stoned (pitted)
115g/4oz/1 cup blackberries

1 Pour the water into a pan and add the caster sugar. Heat gently until the sugar has dissolved.

2 Sprinkle over the gelatine and continue to heat the mixture gently until the gelatine has dissolved, stirring occasionally.

3 Stir the coconut milk into the sugar syrup, remove from the heat and set aside to cool.

4 Grease an 18cm/7in square cake tin (pan). Line with clear film (plastic wrap). Carefully pour the coconut milk mixture into the lined cake tin and chill to set.

5 Make the syrup. Combine the water, star anise and sugar in a pan. Bring to the boil, stirring, then lower the heat and simmer for about 10–12 minutes or until syrupy.

6 Place the fruit in a heatproof bowl and pour over the hot syrup. Cool, then chill.

7 To serve, cut the coconut jelly into diamond shapes and remove from the tin. Arrange the coconut jelly diamonds on individual plates, adding a few of the fruits and their syrup to each portion.

Papayas in Jasmine Flower Syrup

The fragrant syrup can be prepared in advance, using fresh jasmine flowers from a house plant or the garden. It tastes fabulous with papayas, but is also good with other tropical fruit, such as mangoes or lychees, or even ripe peaches.

Serves 2
105ml/7 tbsp water
45ml/3 tbsp palm sugar or light muscovado (brown) sugar
20–30 jasmine flowers, plus a few extra to decorate (optional)
2 ripe papayas
juice of 1 lime

1 Place the water and sugar in a small pan. Heat gently, stirring occasionally, until the sugar has dissolved, then simmer, without stirring, over a low heat for 4 minutes.

2 Pour into a bowl, leave to cool slightly, then add the jasmine flowers. Leave to steep for at least 20 minutes.

3 Peel the papayas and slice in half lengthways. Scoop out and discard the seeds. Place the papayas on serving plates and squeeze over the lime.

4 Strain the syrup into a clean bowl, discarding the flowers. Spoon the syrup over the papayas. Decorate with a few fresh jasmine flowers, if you like.

Cook's Tip
Although scented white jasmine flowers are perfectly safe to eat, it is important to make sure that they have not been sprayed with pesticides or other harmful chemicals. Washing them may not remove all the residue.

Variation
Use the delicately flavoured syrup to turn simple ice cream into an exotic dessert – simply spoon over individual servings.

Star Anise Fruits Energy 184Kcal/787kJ; Protein 1.2g; Carbohydrate 47g, of which sugars 47g; Fat 0.4g, of which saturates 0.2g; Cholesterol 0mg; Calcium 61mg; Fibre 1.5g; Sodium 113mg.
Papayas in Syrup Energy 269Kcal/1143kJ; Protein 2.6g; Carbohydrate 67.5g, of which sugars 67.5g; Fat 0.5g, of which saturates 0g; Cholesterol 0mg; Calcium 127mg; Fibre 11g; Sodium 27mg.

Papaya Baked with Ginger

For an instant dessert with a difference, why not serve this hot papaya dish? Ginger enhances the flavour of the fruit while the nuts provide a crunchy contrast to the creamy, orange flesh.

Serves 4

2 ripe papayas
2 pieces preserved stem ginger
    in syrup, drained, plus 15ml/
    1 tbsp syrup from the jar

8 amaretti or other dessert biscuits
    (cookies), coarsely crushed
45ml/3 tbsp raisins
shredded, finely pared rind and
    juice of 1 lime
25g/1oz/¼ cup pistachio nuts,
    chopped
15ml/1 tbsp light muscovado
    (brown) sugar
60ml/4 tbsp crème fraîche, plus
    extra to serve

1 Preheat the oven to 200°C/400°F/Gas 6. Cut the papayas in half and scoop out their seeds. Place the halves in a baking dish and set aside. Cut the stem ginger into fine matchsticks.

2 Make the filling. Combine the crushed amaretti, stem ginger matchsticks and raisins in a bowl.

3 Stir in the lime rind and juice, two thirds of the nuts, then add the sugar and the crème fraîche. Mix well.

4 Fill the papaya halves and drizzle with the ginger syrup. Sprinkle with the remaining nuts. Bake for about 25 minutes or until tender. Serve with extra crème fraîche.

Variation
Use Greek (US strained plain) yogurt and toasted almonds instead of crème fraîche and pistachios.

Cook's Tip
Don't overcook papaya or the flesh will turn watery.

Tropical Fruit Gratin

This out-of-the-ordinary gratin is strictly for grown-ups. A colourful combination of fruit is topped with a simple sabayon before being quickly browned.

Serves 4

2 tamarillos
½ sweet pineapple
1 ripe mango
175g/6oz/1½ cups blackberries
120ml/4fl oz/½ cup sparkling
    white wine
115g/4oz/generous ½ cup caster
    (superfine) sugar
6 egg yolks

1 Cut each tamarillo in half lengthways and then into thick slices. Cut the rind and core from the pineapple and take spiral slices off the outside to remove the eyes. Cut the flesh into chunks. Peel the mango, cut it in half and cut the flesh from the stone (pit) in slices.

2 Divide all the fruit, including the blackberries, among four 14cm/5½in gratin dishes placed on a baking sheet and set aside. Heat the wine and sugar in a pan until the sugar has dissolved. Bring to the boil and cook for 5 minutes.

3 Put the egg yolks in a large heatproof bowl. Place the bowl over a pan of simmering water and whisk until pale. Slowly pour on the hot sugar syrup, whisking all the time, until the mixture thickens. Preheat the grill (broiler).

4 Spoon the mixture over the fruit. Place the baking sheet holding the dishes on a low shelf under the hot grill until the topping is golden. Serve hot.

Variation
Although boiling drives off the alcohol in the wine, children do not always appreciate the flavour, so substitute orange juice if making the gratin for them. White grape juice or pineapple juice would also work well.

Papaya with Ginger Energy 285Kcal/1197kJ; Protein 3.5g; Carbohydrate 45.5g, of which sugars 40.9g; Fat 11.1g, of which saturates 5.1g; Cholesterol 17mg; Calcium 94mg; Fibre 6.3g; Sodium 99mg.
Tropical Fruit Gratin Energy 313Kcal/1322kJ; Protein 6.2g; Carbohydrate 51.5g, of which sugars 51.4g; Fat 8.8g, of which saturates 2.5g; Cholesterol 302mg; Calcium 99mg; Fibre 4.3g; Sodium 27mg.

Oranges with Caramel Wigs

Naranjas con pelucas is a pretty variation on the normal orange salad. The slightly bitter, caramelized orange rind and syrup sits in perfect harmony with the sweet, juicy oranges.

Serves 6
6 oranges
115g/4oz/generous ½ cup caster (superfine) sugar
120ml/4fl oz/½ cup boiling water, plus extra hot and cold water

1 Using a vegetable peeler, thinly pare the rind off some of the oranges to make at least 12 long strips.

2 Using a sharp knife, peel all the oranges, discarding the pith. and reserving the juice that has collected. Freeze the oranges separately for 30 minutes.

3 Slice the oranges, pile back into their original shape and secure each with a cocktail stick (toothpick). Chill.

4 To make the wigs, simmer the rind for about 5 minutes, drain, rinse, and then repeat. Trim into shape with scissors.

5 Put half the sugar in a small pan and add 15ml/1 tbsp water. Heat gently until the mixture caramelizes, shaking the pan a little if one side starts to brown too fast. As soon as the mixture colours, dip the bottom of the pan into cold water. Add 30ml/2 tbsp hot water and the orange rind to the caramel, then stir until the caramel dissolves. Turn the rind on to a plate to cool.

6 Make a caramel syrup for serving. Put the remaining sugar in a small pan with 15ml/1 tbsp water, and make caramel as before. When it has coloured nicely, stand well back, pour in the boiling water and stir with a wooden spoon to dissolve. Add the reserved orange juice and pour into a serving jug (pitcher).

7 To serve, arrange the orange strips in a criss-cross pattern on top of each orange. Remove the cocktail sticks and pour a little caramel syrup round the base of each orange.

Bananas with Lime & Cardamom Sauce

Serve these bananas solo, with ice cream, or spoon them over folded crêpes.

Serves 4
6 small bananas
50g/2oz/¼ cup butter
seeds from 4 cardamom pods, crushed
50g/2oz/½ cup flaked (sliced) almonds
thinly pared rind and juice of 2 limes
50g/2oz/¼ cup light muscovado (brown) sugar
30ml/2 tbsp dark rum
vanilla ice cream, to serve

1 Peel the bananas and cut them in half lengthways. Heat half the butter in a large frying pan. Add half the bananas, and cook until the undersides are golden. Turn carefully, using a fish slice. Cook until golden.

2 As they cook, transfer the bananas to a heatproof serving dish. Cook the remaining bananas in the same way.

3 Melt the remaining butter, then add the cardamom seeds and almonds. Cook, stirring until golden.

4 Stir in the lime rind and juice, then the sugar. Cook, stirring, until the mixture is smooth and also slightly reduced. Stir in the rum. Pour the sauce over the bananas and serve with the vanilla ice cream.

> **Cook's Tip**
> Use green cardamom pods, split open, and scrape out the black seeds, then crush to help release the aromatic flavour.

> **Variation**
> Use orange or pineapple juice in place of the rum, if you prefer.

Oranges Energy 129Kcal/552kJ; Protein 1.6g; Carbohydrate 32.5g, of which sugars 32.5g; Fat 0.1g, of which saturates 0g; Cholesterol 0mg; Calcium 75mg; Fibre 2.3g; Sodium 8mg.
Bananas Energy 350Kcal/1462kJ; Protein 4.2g; Carbohydrate 41.9g, of which sugars 38.8g; Fat 17.6g, of which saturates 7.2g; Cholesterol 27mg; Calcium 46mg; Fibre 2.3g; Sodium 80mg.

Clementines in Cinnamon Caramel

The combination of sweet yet sharp clementines and caramel sauce, flavoured with a hint of spice, is divine. Serve with thick yogurt or crème fraîche to make a delicious dessert for family and friends.

Serves 4–6
8–12 clementines
225g/8oz/1 cup granulated
  sugar
300ml/½ pint/1¼ cups warm
  water
2 cinnamon sticks
30ml/2 tbsp orange-flavoured
  liqueur
25g/1oz/¼ cup shelled
  pistachio nuts

1 Using a vegetable peeler, pare the rind from two clementines, and cut it into fine strips. Set aside.

2 Peel the clementines, removing all the pith but keeping them intact. Put the fruits in a serving bowl.

3 Gently heat the sugar in a pan until it melts and turns a rich golden brown. Immediately turn off the heat.

4 Cover your hand with a dish towel and pour in the warm water (the mixture will bubble violently). Bring slowly to the boil, stirring until the caramel has dissolved. Add the shredded rind and whole cinnamon sticks, then simmer for 5 minutes. Stir in the orange-flavoured liqueur.

5 Leave the syrup to cool for about 10 minutes, then pour over the clementines. Cover the bowl and chill for several hours or overnight.

6 Blanch the pistachios in boiling water. Drain, cool and remove the dark outer skins. Scatter over the clementines and serve.

> **Cook's Tip**
> *Watch out when you add the water as the mixture will splutter.*

Hot Bananas with Rum & Raisins

A classic way of serving bananas, the rum is set alight just before serving. This gives the fruit a wonderful, distinctive flavour, making an irresistible dish.

Serves 4
40g/1½oz/scant ¼ cup
  seedless raisins
75ml/5 tbsp dark rum
50g/2oz/¼ cup unsalted (sweet)
  butter
60ml/4 tbsp soft light brown
  sugar
4 ripe bananas, peeled and
  halved lengthways
1.5ml/¼ tsp grated nutmeg
1.5ml/¼ tsp ground cinnamon
30ml/2 tbsp slivered almonds,
  toasted
chilled cream or vanilla ice cream,
  to serve (optional)

1 Put the raisins in a bowl with the rum. Leave them to soak for about 30 minutes to plump up.

2 Melt the butter in a frying pan, add the sugar and stir until the sugar has dissolved. Add the bananas and cook for a few minutes until they are tender.

3 Sprinkle the nutmeg and cinnamon over the bananas, then pour in the rum and raisins. Carefully set alight using a long taper and stir gently to mix.

4 Scatter with the almonds and serve immediately with chilled cream or vanilla ice cream, if you like.

> **Cook's Tips**
> • *Choose almost-ripe bananas with evenly coloured skins, either all yellow or just green at the tips. Over-ripe bananas will not hold their shape so well when cooked.*
> • *Setting light to the rum, known as flambéeing, dispels most of the alcohol content but imparts to the bananas an intense flavour. You must, of course, take great care when lighting the rum and it is essential that you use a long taper.*

Hot Bananas Energy 362Kcal/1516kJ; Protein 3.2g; Carbohydrate 46.4g, of which sugars 43.9g; Fat 14.8g, of which saturates 7g; Cholesterol 27mg; Calcium 39mg; Fibre 1.9g; Sodium 85mg.
Clementines Energy 216Kcal/915kJ; Protein 1.7g; Carbohydrate 48.1g, of which sugars 48g; Fat 2.4g, of which saturates 0.3g; Cholesterol 0mg; Calcium 50mg; Fibre 1.2g; Sodium 28mg.

Apple Fritters

Make sure you buy plenty of apples for this recipe. The fritters taste so good you'll probably have to cook an extra batch. The fritters are delicious eaten on their own, but you could serve them with a sprinkling of lemon juice or natural (plain) yogurt for a tangy finish.

Serves 4–6
130g/4½oz/generous 1 cup plain (all-purpose) flour
10ml/2 tsp baking powder
1.5ml/¼ tsp salt
150ml/¼ pint/⅔ cup milk
1 egg, beaten
vegetable oil, for deep-frying
150g/5oz/¾ cup granulated sugar
5ml/1 tsp ground cinnamon
2 large tart eating apples, peeled, cored and cut in 5mm/¼in slices
icing sugar, for dusting

1 Sift the flour, baking powder and salt into a bowl. Beat in the milk and egg with a wire whisk.

2 Place at least 7.5cm/3in of oil in a heavy frying pan and heat to 185°C/360°F or until a cube of bread dropped into the oil turns brown in 1–2 minutes.

3 Mix the granulated sugar and cinnamon in a shallow bowl or plate. Toss the apple slices in the sugar mixture to coat all over.

4 Dip the apple slices in the batter, using a fork or slotted spoon. Drain off the excess batter. Fry, in batches, in the hot oil for 4–5 minutes, until golden brown on both sides. Drain the fritters on kitchen paper and keep warm.

5 Place the icing sugar in a sieve (strainer) and sprinkle over the fritters, tapping the side of the sieve with your hand. Serve hot.

> **Variation**
> Use 2 or 3 medium pears, sliced, in place of the apples.

Fruit Kebabs with Mango & Yogurt Sauce

These mixed fresh fruit kebabs make a versatile dessert that is as attractive as it is healthy.

Serves 4
½ pineapple, peeled, cored and cubed
2 kiwi fruit, peeled and cubed
175g/6oz/1½ cups strawberries, hulled and cut in half, if large
½ mango, peeled, stoned (pitted) and cubed

For the sauce
120ml/4fl oz/½ cup fresh mango purée, from 1–1½ peeled and stoned (pitted) mangoes
120ml/4fl oz/½ cup thick natural (plain) yogurt
5ml/1 tsp caster (superfine) sugar
few drops vanilla extract
15ml/1 tbsp finely chopped mint leaves

1 Make the sauce. Beat together the mango purée, yogurt, sugar and vanilla with an electric mixer.

2 Stir in the chopped mint. Cover the sauce and place in the refrigerator until required.

3 Thread the prepared fruit on to twelve 15cm/6in wooden skewers, alternating the pineapple, kiwi fruit, strawberries and mango cubes.

4 Arrange the kebabs on a large serving tray with the mango and yogurt sauce in the centre.

> **Variations**
> • Vary the type of fruit as you wish – melon, grapes and papaya would be suitable. The fruit must have a firm enough texture to stand up to being skewered.
> • Try replacing the mango cubes with ripe peaches and serve with a pink sauce, by adding puréed and strained raspberries to the sauce instead of the mango purée. Leave out the mint.

Fruit Kebabs Energy 120Kcal/513kJ; Protein 3g; Carbohydrate 27.1g, of which sugars 26.9g; Fat 0.8g, of which saturates 0.2g; Cholesterol 0mg; Calcium 97mg; Fibre 3.7g; Sodium 32mg.
Apple Fritters Energy 303Kcal/1275kJ; Protein 4.1g; Carbohydrate 46.1g, of which sugars 29.6g; Fat 12.7g, of which saturates 1.9g; Cholesterol 33mg; Calcium 79mg; Fibre 1g; Sodium 25mg.

Golden Pineapple with Papaya Sauce

Pineapple cooked in this way takes on a superb flavour and is sensational when served with the papaya sauce.

Serves 6
I sweet pineapple
melted butter, for greasing
   and brushing
2 pieces drained, preserved stem
ginger in syrup, cut into fine
   matchsticks, plus 30ml/2 tbsp
   of the syrup from the jar
30ml/2 tbsp demerara
   (raw) sugar
pinch of ground cinnamon
fresh mint sprigs, to decorate

For the sauce
I ripe papaya, peeled and seeded
175ml/6fl oz/¾ cup apple juice

I Peel the pineapple and take spiral slices off the outside to remove the eyes. Cut the flesh crossways into six slices, each 2.5cm/1in thick. Line a baking sheet with a sheet of foil, rolling up the sides to make a rim. Grease the foil with melted butter. Preheat the grill (broiler).

2 Arrange the pineapple slices on the lined baking sheet. Brush with melted butter, then top with the ginger matchsticks, sugar and cinnamon. Drizzle over the stem ginger syrup. Grill (broil) for 5–7 minutes or until the slices are golden and lightly charred on top.

3 Meanwhile, make the sauce. Cut a few slices from the papaya and set aside, then purée the rest with the apple juice in a blender or food processor.

4 Press the purée through a sieve (strainer) placed over a bowl, then stir in any juices from cooking the pineapple. Serve the pineapple slices with a little sauce drizzled around each plate. Decorate with the reserved papaya slices and the mint sprigs.

> **Cook's Tip**
> Try the papaya sauce with savoury dishes, too. It tastes great with grilled chicken and game birds as well as pork and lamb.

Thai Fried Pineapple

A very simple and quick Thai dessert – the pineapple is fried in butter, brown sugar and lime juice, then sprinkled with toasted coconut. The slightly sharp taste of the fruit makes this a very refreshing treat at the end of a meal.

Serves 4
I pineapple
40g/1½oz/3 tbsp butter
15ml/1 tbsp desiccated (dry
   unsweetened shredded)
   coconut
60ml/4 tbsp soft light brown
   sugar
60ml/4 tbsp freshly squeezed
   lime juice
lime slices or quarters,
   to decorate
thick and creamy natural (plain)
   yogurt, to serve

I Using a sharp knife, cut the top off the pineapple and peel off the skin, taking care to remove the eyes as you work around the fruit. Cut the pineapple in half lengthways, and cut out and discard the woody core. Then slice the flesh lengthways into 1cm-1½in-wide wedges.

2 Heat the butter in a large, heavy frying pan or wok. When it has melted, add the pineapple wedges and cook over a medium heat for 1–2 minutes on each side, or until they have turned pale golden in colour.

3 Meanwhile, dry-fry the coconut in a small frying pan until lightly browned, shaking the pan frequently to cook evenly. Remove from the heat and set aside.

4 Sprinkle the sugar into the pan with the pineapple, add the lime juice and cook, stirring constantly, until the sugar has completely dissolved.

5 Divide the pineapple wedges and cooking juices among four individual bowls. Sprinkle each serving with some of the fried coconut, decorate with the lime slices and serve immediately with the natural yogurt.

Golden Pineapple Energy 130Kcal/558kJ; Protein 1g; Carbohydrate 32.9g, of which sugars 32.9g; Fat 0.4g, of which saturates 0g; Cholesterol 0mg; Calcium 49mg; Fibre 3.4g; Sodium 21mg.
Thai Pineapple Energy 238Kcal/1004kJ; Protein 1.2g; Carbohydrate 36.2g, of which sugars 36.2g; Fat 11g, of which saturates 7.2g; Cholesterol 21mg; Calcium 47mg; Fibre 2.9g; Sodium 67mg.

Fried Bananas

A favourite with children and adults alike, these delicious banana treats are particularly popular in South-east Asia.

Serves 4
115g/4oz/1 cup plain
  (all-purpose) flour
2.5ml/½ tsp bicarbonate of soda
  (baking soda)
pinch of salt

30ml/2 tbsp granulated sugar
1 egg, beaten
90ml/6 tbsp water
30ml/2 tbsp desiccated (dry
  unsweetened shredded)
  coconut or 15ml/1 tbsp
  sesame seeds
4 firm bananas
vegetable oil, for deep-frying
fresh mint sprigs, to decorate
30ml/2 tbsp clear honey, to serve
  (optional)

1 Sift the flour, bicarbonate of soda and salt into a large bowl. Stir in the granulated sugar and the egg, and whisk in just enough of the water to make quite a thin batter.

2 Whisk the coconut or sesame seeds into the batter so that they are evenly distributed.

3 Peel the bananas. Carefully cut each one in half lengthways, then in half crossways to make 16 pieces of about the same size. Don't do this until you are ready to cook because, once peeled, bananas quickly discolour.

4 Heat the oil in a wok or deep-fryer to a temperature of 190°C/375°F or until a cube of bread dropped into the oil browns in about 45 seconds. Dip the banana pieces in the batter, then gently drop a few into the oil. Deep-fry until golden brown, then lift out and drain well on kitchen paper.

5 Cook the remaining banana pieces in the same way. Serve immediately with honey, if using, and decorated with mint.

> **Variation**
> This recipe works well with pineapple rings or apple wedges.

Toffee Bananas

Work quickly when dipping the fruit in the caramel, as it will cool and set quickly.

Serves 4
4 firm bananas
75g/3oz/⅔ cup plain
  (all-purpose) flour
50g/2oz/½ cup cornflour
  (cornstarch)

10ml/2 tsp baking powder
175ml/6fl oz/¾ cup water
5ml/1 tsp sesame oil
groundnut (peanut), sunflower or
  corn oil, for deep-frying

For the caramel
200g/7oz/1 cup granulated sugar
30ml/2 tbsp sesame seeds
60ml/4 tbsp water

1 Peel the bananas, then cut them diagonally into thick slices. Sift the flours and baking powder into a large bowl. Quickly beat in the water and sesame oil, taking care not to overmix. Stir in the bananas until coated.

2 Heat the oil in a deep pan to a temperature of 180°C/350°F or until a cube of bread turns pale brown in 45 seconds.

3 Using a fork, remove a piece of banana from the batter, allowing the excess batter to drain off. Gently lower the coated piece into the hot oil. Add more pieces but do not overcrowd the pan. Fry for about 2 minutes or until the coating is golden.

4 Remove the cooked fritters from the oil with a slotted spoon and drain on kitchen paper. Cook the rest in the same way.

5 When all the banana pieces have been fried, make the caramel. Mix the sugar, sesame seeds and water in a pan. Heat gently, stirring occasionally, until the sugar has dissolved. Increase the heat slightly and continue cooking, without stirring, until the syrup becomes a light caramel. Remove from the heat.

6 Have ready a bowl of iced water. Working quickly, drop one fritter at a time into the hot caramel. Flip over with a fork, remove immediately and plunge into the iced water. Remove from the water quickly (using your fingers for speed, but taking care) and drain on a wire rack while coating the rest.

Fried Bananas Energy 385Kcal/1616kJ; Protein 5.9g; Carbohydrate 53.9g, of which sugars 29.7g; Fat 17.7g, of which saturates 5.8g; Cholesterol 48mg; Calcium 59mg; Fibre 3g; Sodium 22mg.
Toffee Bananas Energy 551Kcal/2324kJ; Protein 4.7g; Carbohydrate 101.6g, of which sugars 73.5g; Fat 16.7g, of which saturates 2.2g; Cholesterol 0mg; Calcium 111mg; Fibre 2.3g; Sodium 13mg.

Ruby Plum Mousse

Red plums and ruby port give this lovely mousse its delicate flavour. The dessert is topped with a scattering of chopped pistachios, adding a splash of colour and interest.

Serves 6

450g/1lb ripe red plums
40g/1½oz/3 tbsp granulated sugar
75ml/5 tbsp water
60ml/4 tbsp ruby port
15ml/1 tbsp/1 sachet powdered gelatine
3 eggs, separated
115g/4oz/generous ½ cup caster (superfine) sugar
150ml/¼ pint/⅔ cup double (heavy) cream
skinned and chopped pistachio nuts, to decorate

1 Place the plums and granulated sugar in a pan with 30ml/2 tbsp water. Cook the fruit and sugar over a low heat until the fruit has softened.

2 Press the fruit through a sieve (strainer) in order to remove the stones (pits) and skins. Leave the fruit to cool, and then stir in the port.

3 Put the remaining water in a small bowl, sprinkle over the gelatine and leave to soften.

4 Stand the bowl in a pan of hot water and leave until dissolved. Stir into the plum purée.

5 Place the egg yolks and caster sugar in a bowl and whisk until thick and mousse-like.

6 Fold in the plum purée, then whip the cream and fold in gently.

7 Whisk the egg whites until they hold stiff peaks, then carefully fold in using a metal spoon.

8 Divide among six glasses and chill until set.

9 To serve, decorate the plum mousses with a sprinkling of chopped pistachio nuts.

Mango & Lime Fool

Canned mangoes are used here for convenience, but the dish tastes even better if made with fresh ones. Choose a variety like the voluptuous Alphonso mango, which is wonderfully fragrant and tastes indescribably delicious.

Serves 4

400g/14oz can sliced mango
grated rind of 1 lime
juice of ½ lime
150ml/¼ pint/⅔ cup double (heavy) cream
90ml/6 tbsp Greek (US strained plain) yogurt
fresh mango slices, to decorate (optional)

1 Drain the canned mango slices and put them in the bowl of a food processor. Add the grated lime rind and the lime juice. Process until the mixture forms a smooth purée. Alternatively, mash the mango slices with a potato masher, then press through a sieve (strainer) into a bowl with the back of a wooden spoon. Stir in the lime rind and juice.

2 Pour the cream into a mixing bowl and add the yogurt. Whisk until the mixture is thick and then quickly whisk in the mango mixture.

3 Spoon into tall glasses and chill for 1–2 hours. Just before serving, decorate each glass with fresh mango slices, if you like.

Cook's Tip
When mixing the cream and yogurt mixture with the mango purée, whisk just enough to combine, so as not to lose the lightness of the whipped cream mixture. If you prefer, fold the mixtures together lightly, so that the fool is rippled.

Variation
This fool can also be made with canned apricots, using orange rind and juice in place of the lime.

Plum Mousse Energy 309Kcal/1293kJ; Protein 4.1g; Carbohydrate 36.1g, of which sugars 36.1g; Fat 16.3g, of which saturates 9.1g; Cholesterol 129mg; Calcium 51mg; Fibre 1.2g; Sodium 44mg.
Mango & Lime Fool Energy 289Kcal/1203kJ; Protein 2.4g; Carbohydrate 21.4g, of which sugars 21.3g; Fat 22.4g, of which saturates 13.7g; Cholesterol 51mg; Calcium 62mg; Fibre 0.7g; Sodium 27mg.

Gooseberry & Elderflower Fool

Gooseberries and elderflowers are a match made in heaven, each bringing out the flavour of the other. Serve with amaretti or other dessert biscuits for dipping.

Serves 6
450g/1lb/4 cups gooseberries, trimmed
30ml/2 tbsp water

50–75g/2–3oz/¼–⅓ cup caster (superfine) sugar
30ml/2 tbsp elderflower cordial
400g/14oz fresh ready-made custard
green food colouring (optional)
300ml/½ pint/1¼ cups double (heavy) cream
crushed amaretti, to decorate

1 Put the gooseberries and water in a pan. Cover and cook for 5–6 minutes or until the berries pop open.

2 Add the sugar and elderflower cordial to the gooseberries, then stir vigorously or mash until the fruit forms a pulp. Remove the pan from the heat, spoon the gooseberry pulp into a bowl and set aside to cool.

3 Stir the custard into the fruit. Add a few drops of food colouring, if using. Whip the cream to soft peaks, then fold it into the mixture and chill. Serve the fool in dessert glasses, decorated with crushed amaretti, and accompanied by amaretti.

Cook's Tip
In the summer, you can always make your own elderflower cordial by leaving freshly picked elderflower heads to infuse in water with sugar and lemon for 24 hours. Use immediately.

Variation
Use puréed raspberries, sweetened to taste, instead of the cooked gooseberries and omit the elderflower cordial.

Clementine Jelly

Jelly isn't only for children: this adult version has a clean fruity taste and can be made extra special by adding a dash of white rum or Cointreau.

Serves 4
12 clementines
clear grape juice (see method for amount)
15ml/1 tbsp powdered gelatine
25g/1oz/2 tbsp caster (superfine) sugar
whipped cream, to decorate

1 Squeeze the juice from eight of the clementines and pour into a jug (pitcher). Make up to 600ml/1 pint/2½ cups with the grape juice, then strain the mixture through a sieve (strainer).

2 Pour half the juice mixture into a pan. Sprinkle the gelatine on top, leave to stand for 5 minutes, then heat gently until the gelatine has completely dissolved. Stir in the sugar, then the remaining juice; set aside.

3 Pare the rind very thinly from the remaining fruit and set it aside. Using a small sharp knife, cut between the membrane and fruit to separate the citrus segments. Discard the membrane and white pith.

4 Place half the segments in four dessert glasses and cover with some of the liquid fruit jelly. Leave in the refrigerator to set.

5 When the jellies are set, arrange the remaining segments on top. Carefully pour over the remaining liquid jelly and chill until set. Cut the pared clementine rind into fine shreds. Serve the jellies topped with a generous spoonful of whipped cream scattered with clementine rind shreds.

Variation
Use four ruby grapefruit instead of clementines, if you prefer. Squeeze the juice from half of them and segment the rest, discarding any bitter white pith.

Gooseberry Fool Energy 333Kcal/1381kJ; Protein 3.4g; Carbohydrate 15.5g, of which sugars 13.1g; Fat 28.4g, of which saturates 16.7g; Cholesterol 70mg; Calcium 107mg; Fibre 1.9g; Sodium 40mg.
Clementine Jelly Energy 97Kcal/414kJ; Protein 1.3g; Carbohydrate 24.1g, of which sugars 24.1g; Fat 0.2g, of which saturates 0g; Cholesterol 0mg; Calcium 51mg; Fibre 1.5g; Sodium 9mg.

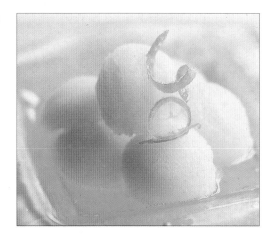

Mango Sorbet

A light and refreshing dessert that's surprisingly easy to make.

175ml/6fl oz/³⁄₄ cup water
1 large mango, peeled, stoned (pitted) and cubed
60ml/4 tbsp orange juice
fresh mint sprigs, to decorate

Serves 6
150g/5oz/³⁄₄ cup caster (superfine) sugar
a large pared strip of orange rind

1 Combine the sugar, orange rind and the water in a pan. Bring to the boil, stirring to dissolve the sugar. Leave to cool.

2 Purée the mango cubes with the orange juice in a blender or food processor. There should be about 475ml/16fl oz/2 cups of purée after processing. Add the mango purée to the cooled sugar syrup and stir to mix well. Strain, then chill.

3 When cold, tip the mixture into a freezer container and freeze until firm around the edges.

4 Spoon the semi-frozen mixture into the food processor and process until smooth. Return to the freezer until solid.

5 Allow the sorbet to soften slightly at room temperature for 15–20 minutes before serving, decorated with mint sprigs.

Apple & Cider Water Ice

With its very English ingredients, this dessert has a subtle apple flavour with just a hint of cider. As the apple purée is very pale, almost white, add just a few drops of green food colouring to echo the pale green of the apple skin.

Serves 6
500g/1¼lb green-skinned eating apples
150g/5oz/³⁄₄ cup caster (superfine) sugar
300ml/½ pint/1¼ cups water
250ml/8fl oz/1 cup strong dry (hard) cider
few drops of green food colouring (optional)
strips pared lime rind, to decorate

1 Quarter, core and roughly chop the apples. Put them in a pan. Add the caster sugar and half the water. Cover and simmer for 10 minutes or until the apples are soft.

2 Press the mixture through a sieve (strainer) placed over a bowl. Discard the apple skins. Stir the cider and the remaining water into the purée. Add a little colouring, if you like.

3 Pour into a shallow freezer container and freeze for 6 hours, beating with a fork once or twice to break up the ice crystals. Alternatively, churn in an ice cream maker until firm.

4 Scoop into dishes and decorate with strips of lime rind.

Variations/Banana Sorbet & Passion Fruit Sorbet
• *Banana Sorbet: peel and cube 4 or 5 large bananas. Purée with 30ml/2 tbsp lemon juice to make 475ml/16fl oz/2 cups. If you like, replace the orange rind with 2 or 3 whole cloves.*
• *Passion Fruit Sorbet: halve 16 or more passion fruit and scoop out the seeds and pulp (there should be about 475ml/16fl oz/2 cups). Work in a blender or food processor until the seeds are like coarse pepper. Omit the orange juice and rind. Add the passion fruit to the sugar syrup, then press through a wire sieve (strainer) before freezing.*

Variation/Strawberry & Champagne Water Ice
Put 500g/1¼lb/5 cups strawberries in a food processor or blender and process to a purée, then press through a sieve (strainer) into a bowl. Stir in 150g/5oz/³⁄₄ cup caster (superfine) sugar and 350ml/12fl oz/1½ cups champagne or sparkling white wine, mixing well until the sugar has dissolved. Pour into a shallow freezer container and freeze for 3 hours. Stiffly whisk an egg white in a grease-free bowl. Remove the ice from the freezer and beat well with a fork, then fold in the egg white. Return to the freezer for 3 hours more. Serve decorated with mint sprigs.

Banana Honey Yogurt Ice

Using Greek yogurt instead of cream in this dessert creates a cool dish with a more refreshing and less sugary taste.

Serves 4–6
4 ripe bananas, roughly chopped
15ml/1 tbsp lemon juice
30ml/2 tbsp clear honey
250g/9oz/generous 1 cup Greek
  (US strained plain) yogurt
2.5ml/½ tsp ground cinnamon
crisp biscuits (cookies), flaked
  (sliced) hazelnuts and banana
  slices, to serve

1 Place the bananas in a food processor or blender with the lemon juice, honey, yogurt and cinnamon. Process until the mixture is smooth and creamy.

2 Pour the mixture into a freezer container. Freeze until almost solid. Spoon back into the food processor. Process until smooth.

3 Pour back into the freezer container and freeze until firm. Allow to soften at room temperature for 15 minutes, then serve with crisp biscuits, flaked hazelnuts and banana slices.

Cook's Tip/Almond Biscuits
For a special touch, make your own almond biscuits (cookies) to serve with the ice. Rub 175g/6oz/¾ cup butter into 225g/8oz/2 cups self-raising (self-rising) flour. Stir in 115g/4oz/generous ½ cup caster (superfine) sugar and 2.5ml/½ tsp ground cinnamon, then add 1 egg yolk and 30ml/2 tbsp water and mix to a dough. Roll out to 1cm/½ in thick, sprinkle with 50g/2oz/½ cup flaked (sliced) almonds, and continue to roll until thin. Cut into rounds, then bake at 180°C/350°F/Gas 4 for 10–15 minutes until golden.

Variation
Use maple syrup in place of the clear honey for a change.

Fruity Ricotta Creams

Ricotta is an Italian soft cheese with a smooth texture and a mild, slightly sweet flavour. Served here with candied fruit peel and delicious chocolate, it is quite irresistible.

Serves 4
350g/12oz/1½ cups ricotta
  cheese
30–45ml/2–3 tbsp Cointreau or
  other orange liqueur
10ml/2 tsp grated lemon rind
30ml/2 tbsp icing
  (confectioners') sugar
150ml/¼ pint/⅔ cup double
  (heavy) cream
150g/5oz/scant 1 cup candied
  peel, such as orange, lemon and
  grapefruit, finely chopped
50g/2oz plain (semisweet)
  chocolate, finely chopped
chocolate curls, to decorate
amaretti, to serve (optional)

1 Using the back of a wooden spoon, push the ricotta through a fine sieve (strainer) into a large bowl.

2 Add the liqueur, lemon rind and icing sugar to the ricotta and beat well until the mixture is light and smooth.

3 Whip the cream in a large bowl until it forms soft peaks.

4 Gently fold the cream into the ricotta mixture with the candied peel and chopped chocolate.

5 Spoon the mixture into four individual glass dishes and chill for about 1 hour. Decorate the ricotta creams with chocolate curls and serve with amaretti, if you like.

Cook's Tips
• For this uncooked, Italian-style dessert, you need to buy candied fruits in large pieces from a good delicatessen – tubs of chopped candied peel are too tough to eat raw, and should only be used in baking.
• The desserts can also be topped with a sprinkling of raspberries to add an extra fruitiness.

Banana Ice Energy 119Kcal/502kJ; Protein 3.4g; Carbohydrate 18.6g, of which sugars 17.2g; Fat 4.4g, of which saturates 2.2g; Cholesterol 0mg; Calcium 66mg; Fibre 0.7g; Sodium 31mg.
Ricotta Creams Energy 546Kcal/2276kJ; Protein 9.4g; Carbohydrate 43.1g, of which sugars 43g; Fat 36.7g, of which saturates 22.6g; Cholesterol 89mg; Calcium 75mg; Fibre 2.1g; Sodium 115mg.

Banana & Mascarpone Creams

If you are a fan of cold banana custard, then you'll love this recipe. It is a grown-up version of an old favourite. No one will guess that the secret is simply ready-made custard.

Serves 4–6
250g/9oz/generous 1 cup mascarpone
300ml/½ pint/1¼ cups fresh ready-made custard
150ml/¼ pint/²/₃ cup Greek (US strained plain) yogurt
4 bananas
juice of 1 lime
50g/2oz/½ cup pecan nuts, coarsely chopped
120ml/4fl oz/½ cup maple syrup

1 Combine the mascarpone, custard and yogurt in a large bowl and beat together until smooth. Make this mixture up to several hours ahead, if you like. Cover and chill, then stir well before using.

2 Slice the bananas diagonally and place in a separate bowl. Pour over the lime juice and toss together until the bananas are coated in the juice.

3 Divide half the custard mixture among four or six dessert glasses and top each portion with a generous spoonful of the banana and lime mixture.

4 Spoon the remaining custard mixture into the glasses and top with the rest of the bananas. Sprinkle the nuts over the top. Drizzle maple syrup over each dessert and chill for 30 minutes before serving.

Variations
Use clear honey instead of maple syrup and walnuts instead of pecan nuts, if you like. Also, try layering in some crumbled biscuits, such as amaretti or ratafia biscuits (almond macaroons), shortbread crumbs or crushed meringues.

Lemon Coeur à la Crème with Cointreau Oranges

This zesty dessert is the ideal choice to follow all kinds of main courses, but in particular a rich dish such as a meat roast.

Serves 4
225g/8oz/1 cup cottage cheese
250g/9oz/generous 1 cup mascarpone
50g/2oz/¼ cup caster (superfine) sugar
grated rind and juice of 1 lemon
spirals of orange rind, to decorate

For the Cointreau oranges
4 oranges
10ml/2 tsp cornflour (cornstarch)
15ml/1 tbsp icing (confectioners') sugar
60ml/4 tbsp Cointreau

1 Put the cottage cheese in a food processor or blender and process until smooth. Add the mascarpone, caster sugar, lemon rind and juice and process briefly to mix the ingredients.

2 Line four coeur à la crème moulds with muslin (cheesecloth), and divide the mixture among them. Level the surface of each, then place the moulds on a plate to catch any liquid that drains from the cheese. Cover and chill overnight.

3 Make the Cointreau oranges. Squeeze the juice from two oranges and pour into a measuring cup. Make the juice up to 250ml/8fl oz/1 cup with water, then pour into a small pan. Blend a little of the juice mixture with the cornflour and add to the pan with the icing sugar. Heat the sauce, stirring until thick.

4 Using a sharp knife, peel the remaining oranges. Cut between the membrane and fruit to separate the orange segments. Discard the membrane and white pith. Add the segments to the pan, stir to coat, then set aside. When cool, stir in the Cointreau. Cover and chill overnight.

5 Turn the moulds out on to plates and surround with the oranges. Serve decorated with spirals of orange rind.

Banana Creams Energy 457Kcal/1902kJ; Protein 12.4g; Carbohydrate 32.1g, of which sugars 30g; Fat 32.1g, of which saturates 9.1g; Cholesterol 19mg; Calcium 177mg; Fibre 1.2g; Sodium 142mg.
Lemon Coeur Energy 333Kcal/1400kJ; Protein 14.3g; Carbohydrate 36.8g, of which sugars 34.5g; Fat 11.4g, of which saturates 7g; Cholesterol 35mg; Calcium 137mg; Fibre 2.1g; Sodium 178mg.

Peach Melba Syllabub

If you are making these sophisticated temptations for a dinner party, cook the peaches and raspberries the day before to allow the fruit to chill. Whip up the syllabub at the very last minute to make a delicious, light-as-a-cloud topping.

Serves 6

4 peaches, peeled, stoned (pitted) and sliced
300ml/½ pint/1¼ cups blush or red grape juice
115g/4oz/⅔ cup raspberries
raspberry or mint leaves, to decorate
ratafia biscuits (almond macaroons) or other small crisp biscuits (cookies), to serve

For the syllabub
60ml/4 tbsp peach schnapps
30ml/2 tbsp blush or red grape juice
300ml/½ pint/1¼ cups double (heavy) cream

1 Place the peach slices in a large pan. Add the grape juice. Bring to the boil, then cover, lower the heat and simmer for 5–7 minutes or until tender.

2 Add the raspberries and remove from the heat. Set aside in the refrigerator until cold. Divide the peach and raspberry mixture among six dessert glasses.

3 For the syllabub, place the peach schnapps and grape juice in a large bowl and whisk in the cream until it forms soft peaks.

4 Spoon the syllabub on top of the fruit and decorate each portion with a fresh raspberry or mint leaf. Serve with ratafias or other crisp biscuits.

Variations
Use pears and sliced kiwi fruit in place of peaches and raspberries. Instead of the syllabub, try topping the fruit with whipped cream flavoured with Advocaat and finely chopped preserved stem ginger.

Fragrant Fruit Salad

A medley of colourful and exotic fruit, this fresh-tasting salad is the perfect dessert for a dinner party.

Serves 6

130g/4½oz/scant ¾ cup sugar
thinly pared rind and juice of 1 lime
150ml/¼ pint/⅔ cup water
60ml/4 tbsp brandy
5ml/1 tsp instant coffee granules or powder dissolved in 30ml/2 tbsp boiling water
1 small pineapple
1 papaya
2 pomegranates
1 medium mango
2 passion fruit or kiwi fruit
strips of lime rind, to decorate

1 Put the sugar and lime rind in a small pan with the water. Heat gently until the sugar dissolves, then bring to the boil and simmer for 5 minutes. Leave to cool, then strain into a large serving bowl, discarding the lime rind. Stir in the lime juice, brandy and dissolved coffee.

2 Using a sharp knife, cut the plume and stalk ends from the pineapple. Cut off the peel, then remove the central core and discard. Slice the flesh into bitesize pieces and add to the bowl.

3 Halve the papaya and scoop out the seeds. Cut away the skin, then slice the papaya. Halve the pomegranates and scoop out the seeds. Add to the bowl.

4 Cut the mango lengthways into three pieces, along each side of the stone (pit). Peel the skin off the flesh. Cut into chunks and add to the bowl.

5 Halve the passion fruit and scoop out the flesh using a teaspoon, or peel and chop the kiwi fruit. Add to the bowl and serve, decorated with lime rind.

Cook's Tip
Allow the salad to stand at room temperature for an hour before serving so the flavours can blend.

Peach Melba Energy 329Kcal/1363kJ; Protein 2g; Carbohydrate 17g, of which sugars 17g; Fat 27g, of which saturates 16.7g; Cholesterol 69mg; Calcium 45mg; Fibre 1.6g; Sodium 17mg.
Fragrant Fruit Salad Energy 218Kcal/930kJ; Protein 1.4g; Carbohydrate 49.8g, of which sugars 49.8g; Fat 0.4g, of which saturates 0g; Cholesterol 0mg; Calcium 60mg; Fibre 4.4g; Sodium 10mg.

Exotic Fruit Salad with Passion Fruit Dressing

Passion fruit makes a superb dressing for any fruit, but really brings out the flavour of exotic varieties. You can easily double the recipe and serve the rest for breakfast.

Serves 6
1 mango
1 papaya
2 kiwi fruit

coconut or vanilla ice cream,
  to serve

For the dressing
3 passion fruit
thinly pared rind and juice of
  1 lime
5ml/1 tsp hazelnut or walnut oil
15ml/1 tbsp clear honey

1 Peel the mango, cut it into three slices, then cut the flesh into chunks and place it in a large bowl. Peel the papaya and cut it in half. Scoop out the seeds, then chop the flesh.

2 Cut both ends off each kiwi fruit, then stand them on a board. Using a small sharp knife, cut off the skin from top to bottom. Cut each kiwi fruit in half lengthways, then cut into thick slices. Combine all the fruit in a large bowl.

3 Make the dressing. Cut each passion fruit in half and scoop the seeds out into a sieve (strainer) set over a small bowl. Press the seeds well to extract all their juices.

4 Lightly whisk the remaining dressing ingredients into the passion fruit juice, then pour the dressing over the fruit in the bowl. Mix gently to combine. Leave to chill for approximately 1 hour before serving with generous scoops of coconut or vanilla ice cream.

> **Cook's Tip**
> A clear golden honey scented with orange blossom or acacia blossom would be perfect for the dressing.

Ruby Fruit Salad

After a rich main course, this port-flavoured fruit salad is light and refreshing.

Serves 8
115g/4oz/generous ½ cup caster
  (superfine) sugar
1 cinnamon stick
4 cloves
pared rind of 1 orange

300ml/½ pint/1¼ cups water
300ml/½ pint/1¼ cups port
2 oranges
1 small ripe Ogen, Charentais
  or honeydew melon
4 small bananas
2 eating apples
225g/8oz seedless grapes

1 Put the sugar, spices, pared orange rind and the water into a pan and stir over a gentle heat to dissolve the sugar. Then bring to the boil, cover with a lid and simmer for 10 minutes. Leave to cool, then add the port.

2 Strain the liquid (to remove the spices and orange rind) into a bowl. With a sharp knife, cut off all the skin and pith from the oranges. Then, holding each orange over the bowl to catch the juice, cut away the segments by slicing between the membrane that divides each segment and allowing the segments to drop into the syrup. Squeeze the remaining pith to release any juice.

3 Cut the melon in half, remove the seeds and scoop out the flesh with a melon baller, or cut into small cubes. Add the melon to the syrup.

4 Peel the bananas and cut them diagonally in 1cm/½in slices. Quarter and core the apples, then peel if the skin is tough. Cut into small cubes. Halve the grapes if large or leave them whole. Stir all the fruit into the syrup, cover with clear film (plastic wrap) and chill for 1 hour before serving.

> **Cook's Tip**
> The port-flavoured syrup is very versatile and will marry well with any combination of fruit that is available.

Exotic Fruit Salad Energy 64Kcal/270kJ; Protein 1g; Carbohydrate 14.2g, of which sugars 14g; Fat 0.8g, of which saturates 0.1g; Cholesterol 0mg; Calcium 25mg; Fibre 2.8g; Sodium 7mg.
Ruby Fruit Salad Energy 209Kcal/886kJ; Protein 1.7g; Carbohydrate 42.1g, of which sugars 41g; Fat 0.3g, of which saturates 0.1g; Cholesterol 0mg; Calcium 48mg; Fibre 2.4g; Sodium 12mg.

Raspberry Trifle

This ever-popular dessert looks wonderful served in a glass bowl so that you can see all the layers. Use fresh or frozen raspberries.

Serves 6–8
175g/6oz trifle sponges, or 2.5cm/1in cubes of plain Victoria sponge or coarsely crumbled sponge fingers
60ml/4 tbsp medium sherry
115g/4oz raspberry jam
275g/10oz/1⅔ cups raspberries
450ml/¾ pint/scant 2 cups custard, flavoured with 30ml/ 2 tbsp medium or sweet sherry
300ml/½ pint/1¼ cups whipping cream
15ml/1tbsp icing (confectioners') sugar
toasted flaked (sliced) almonds and mint leaves, to decorate

1 Spread half of the sponges, cake cubes or sponge fingers over the bottom of a large serving bowl. (A glass bowl is best for presentation.)

2 Sprinkle half of the sherry over the cake to moisten it. Spoon over half of the jam, dotting it evenly over the cake cubes.

3 Reserve a few raspberries for decoration. Make a layer of half of the remaining raspberries on top.

4 Pour over half of the custard, covering the fruit and cake. Repeat the layers. Cover and chill for at least 2 hours.

5 Before serving, whip the cream with the icing sugar until it forms soft peaks. Spoon the sweetened whipped cream evenly over the top of the custard. To decorate, sprinkle with toasted flaked almonds and arrange the reserved raspberries and the mint leaves on top. Serve as soon as possible.

Variation
Use other ripe summer fruit such as apricots, peaches, nectarines and strawberries in the trifle, with jam and liqueur to complement the fruit.

Mangoes with Sticky Rice

Glutinous rice is just as good in desserts as in savoury dishes. The delicate fragrance and velvety flesh of mangoes complement the rice especially well. You need to start preparing this dish the day before serving.

Serves 4
115g/4oz/⅔ cup white glutinous rice
175ml/6fl oz/¾ cup thick coconut milk
40g/1½oz/3 tbsp granulated sugar
pinch of salt
2 ripe mangoes
strips of pared lime rind, to decorate

1 Rinse the glutinous rice thoroughly in several changes of cold water, then leave to soak overnight in a bowl of fresh cold water.

2 Drain the rice well and spread it out evenly in a steamer lined with muslin. Cover and steam over a pan of simmering water for about 20 minutes, or until the rice is tender.

3 Reserve 45ml/3 tbsp of the cream from the top of the coconut milk. Pour the remainder into a pan and add the sugar and salt. Heat, stirring constantly, until the sugar has dissolved, then bring to the boil. Remove the pan from the heat, pour the coconut milk into a bowl and leave to cool.

4 Transfer the cooked rice to a bowl and pour over the cooled coconut milk. Stir well; leave to stand for 10–15 minutes. Meanwhile, peel the mangoes, cut the flesh away from the central stones (pits) and cut into slices.

5 Spoon the rice on to individual serving plates. Arrange the mango slices on one side, then drizzle with the reserved coconut cream. Decorate with strips of lime rind and serve.

Cook's Tip
The thickest part of coconut milk always rises to the top. When you open it, spoon off this top layer to use for serving.

Raspberry Trifle Energy 330Kcal/1382kJ; Protein 5.1g; Carbohydrate 35.9g, of which sugars 29.1g; Fat 17.7g, of which saturates 9.9g; Cholesterol 90mg; Calcium 102mg; Fibre 1.1g; Sodium 59mg.
Mangoes with Rice Energy 200Kcal/846kJ; Protein 3.1g; Carbohydrate 46g, of which sugars 24.3g; Fat 0.8g, of which saturates 0.2g; Cholesterol 0mg; Calcium 32mg; Fibre 2g; Sodium 51mg.

Tropical Fruit with Maple Butter

This dish turns exotic fruit
into comfort food.

Serves 4
1 large mango
1 large papaya
1 small pineapple
2 bananas
115g/4oz/½ cup unsalted
  (sweet) butter
60ml/4 tbsp pure maple syrup
ground cinnamon, for sprinkling

1 Peel the mango and cut the flesh into large pieces. Halve the
papaya and scoop out the seeds. Cut into thick slices, then peel.
Peel and core the pineapple and slice into thin wedges. Peel the
bananas, then halve them lengthways.

2 Cut the butter into small dice and place in a blender or food
processor with the maple syrup, then process until creamy.

3 Place the mango, papaya, pineapple and banana on a grill
(broiler) rack and brush with the maple syrup butter. Cook
under a medium heat for about 10 minutes, until just tender,
turning the fruit occasionally and brushing it with the butter.

4 Arrange the fruit on a serving platter and dot with the
remaining butter. Sprinkle over a little cinnamon and serve hot.

Variation/Tropical Fruits in Cinnamon Syrup

*Sprinkle a third of 450g/1lb/2¼ cups caster (superfine) sugar over
the base of a large pan. Add 1 cinnamon stick and half of the
following: about 675g/1½lb papayas, peeled, seeded and cut into
thin pieces; about 675g/1½lb mangoes, peeled, stoned (pitted) and
cut lengthways into thin pieces; about 225g/8oz star fruit, thinly
sliced. Sprinkle half the remaining sugar over the fruit pieces. Add
the remaining fruit, sprinkled with the remaining sugar. Cover and
cook over a medium-low heat for 35–45 minutes, until the sugar
melts. Shake the pan occasionally, but do not stir (the fruit will
collapse). Simmer, uncovered, for 10 minutes, until the fruit is
becoming translucent. Remove from the heat and cool. Transfer to a
bowl and chill, covered, overnight. Serve with yogurt or crème fraîche.*

Blueberry Pancakes

These are rather like the
thick American breakfast
pancakes – though they can,
of course, be eaten at any
time of the day.

Makes 6–8
115g/4oz/1 cup self-raising
  (self-rising) flour
pinch of salt
45–60ml/3–4 tbsp caster
  (superfine) sugar
2 eggs
120ml/4fl oz/½ cup milk
15–30ml/1–2 tbsp oil
115g/4oz/1 cup fresh or frozen
  blueberries, plus extra
  to decorate
maple syrup, to serve
lemon wedges, to decorate

1 Sift the flour into a bowl with the salt and sugar. Beat
together the eggs thoroughly. Make a well in the middle of the
flour and stir in the eggs.

2 Gradually blend in a little of the milk to make a smooth
batter. Then whisk in the rest of the milk and whisk for
1–2 minutes. Allow to rest for 20–30 minutes.

3 Heat a few drops of oil in a pancake pan or heavy frying pan
until just hazy. Pour about 30ml/2 tbsp of the batter and swirl
the batter around until it makes an even shape.

4 Cook for 2–3 minutes and when almost set on top, sprinkle
over 15–30ml/1–2 tbsp blueberries. As soon as the base is
loose and golden brown, turn the pancake over.

5 Cook on the second side for only about 1 minute, until
golden and crisp. Slide the pancake on to a plate and serve
drizzled with maple syrup. Continue with the rest of the
batter. Serve decorated with lemon wedges and a few
extra blueberries.

Cook's Tip
*Instead of blueberries you could use blackberries or raspberries.
If you use canned fruit, make sure it is very well drained.*

Tropical Fruit Energy 470Kcal/1974kJ; Protein 2.7g; Carbohydrate 64g, of which sugars 62.7g; Fat 24.4g, of which saturates 15.1g; Cholesterol 61mg; Calcium 90mg; Fibre 7.7g; Sodium 229mg.
Blueberry Pancakes Energy 111Kcal/468kJ; Protein 3.5g; Carbohydrate 18.2g, of which sugars 7.5g; Fat 3.2g, of which saturates 0.8g; Cholesterol 48mg; Calcium 84mg; Fibre 0.9g; Sodium 76mg.

Apple Soufflé Omelette

Apples sautéed until they are slightly caramelized make a delicious autumn filling for these light-as-air sweet pancakes. Great for an impromptu supper.

Serves 2

4 eggs, separated
30ml/2 tbsp single (light) cream
15ml/1 tbsp caster
  (superfine) sugar
15g/½oz/1 tbsp butter
icing (confectioners') sugar, for
  dredging

For the filling

1 eating apple, peeled, cored
  and sliced
25g/1oz/2 tbsp butter
30ml/2 tbsp soft light brown
  sugar
45ml/3 tbsp single (light) cream

1 Make the filling. Sauté the apple slices in the butter and sugar until just tender. Stir in the cream and keep warm while making the omelette.

2 Place the egg yolks in a bowl with the cream and sugar and beat well. Whisk the egg whites until they form stiff peaks, then fold into the yolk mixture.

3 Melt the butter in a large heavy frying pan, pour in the soufflé mixture and spread evenly. Cook for 1 minute until golden underneath, then cover the pan handle with foil and place under a hot grill (broiler) to brown the top.

4 Slide the omelette on to a plate, add the apple mixture, then fold over. Sift the icing sugar over thickly, then mark in a criss-cross pattern with a hot metal skewer. Serve immediately.

> **Cook's Tips**
> • When cooking the top, remove the omelette as soon as it is browned. Do not overcook at this stage otherwise the light texture of the omelette will be damaged.
> • Try replacing the apples with fresh raspberries or strawberries when they are in season.

Rhubarb-Strawberry Crisp

Strawberries, cinnamon and ground almonds make this a luxurious and delicious version of rhubarb crumble that's sure to go down well with all the family.

Serves 4

225g/8oz strawberries, hulled
450g/1lb rhubarb, diced
90g/3½oz/½ cup granulated
  sugar
15ml/1 tbsp cornflour
  (cornstarch)
85ml/3fl oz/⅓ cup fresh
  orange juice
115g/4oz/1 cup plain (all-
  purpose) flour
90g/3½oz/1 cup rolled oats
115g/4oz/½ cup light muscovado
  (brown) sugar
2.5ml/½ tsp ground cinnamon
50g/2oz/½ cup ground
  almonds
150g/5oz/10 tbsp cold butter
1 egg, lightly beaten
single (light) cream or natural
  (plain) yogurt, to serve

1 If the strawberries are large, cut them in half. Combine the strawberries, rhubarb and granulated sugar in a 2.4 litre/4 pint/10 cup baking dish. Preheat the oven to 180°C/350°F/Gas 4.

2 In a small bowl, blend the cornflour with the orange juice. Pour this mixture over the fruit and stir gently to coat. Set the baking dish aside while making the crumble topping.

3 In a bowl, toss together the flour, oats, muscovado sugar, cinnamon and ground almonds. With a pastry blender or two knives, cut in the butter until the mixture resembles coarse breadcrumbs. Stir in the beaten egg.

4 Spoon the oat mixture evenly over the fruit and press down gently. Cook in the oven for 50–60 minutes, until the top is golden brown. Serve warm with single cream or yogurt.

> **Cook's Tip**
> Rolled oats and ground almonds not only add interesting texture to the topping, but also turn this dish into a healthier version of traditional crumble.

Apple Omelette Energy 469Kcal/1952kJ; Protein 14.1g; Carbohydrate 27.5g, of which sugars 27.5g; Fat 34.8g, of which saturates 18.1g; Cholesterol 444mg; Calcium 107mg; Fibre 0.6g; Sodium 274mg.
Rh.-Strawb. Crisp Energy 808Kcal/3390kJ; Protein 11.8g; Carbohydrate 103g, of which sugars 60.9g; Fat 41.7g, of which saturates 20.5g; Cholesterol 128mg; Calcium 240mg; Fibre 5.6g; Sodium 269mg.

Stuffed Peaches with Mascarpone Cream

Peaches with an almond-flavoured filling and topped with a rich cream make a delicious Italian-style dessert for summer entertaining.

Serves 4

4 large peaches, halved and stoned (pitted)
40g/1½oz amaretti, crumbled
30ml/2 tbsp ground almonds
45ml/3 tbsp sugar
15ml/1 tbsp cocoa powder (unsweetened)
150ml/¼ pint/⅔ cup sweet white wine
25g/1oz/2 tbsp butter

For the mascarpone cream
25g/1oz/2 tbsp caster (superfine) sugar
3 egg yolks
15ml/1 tbsp sweet white wine
225g/8oz/1 cup mascarpone
150ml/¼ pint/⅔ cup double (heavy) cream

1 Preheat the oven to 200°C/400°F/Gas 6. Using a teaspoon, scoop some of the flesh from the cavities in the peaches, to make a reasonable space for the stuffing. Chop the scooped-out flesh.

2 Mix together the amaretti, ground almonds, sugar, cocoa and peach flesh. Now add enough wine to make the mixture into a thick paste.

3 Place the peaches in a buttered ovenproof dish and fill them with the stuffing. Dot with the butter, then pour the remaining wine into the dish. Bake in the oven for 35 minutes.

4 Make the mascarpone cream. Beat the sugar and egg yolks until thick and pale. Stir in the wine, then fold in the mascarpone. Whip the double cream to form soft peaks and fold into the mixture.

5 Remove the stuffed peaches from the oven and leave to cool completely. Serve at room temperature, along with the mascarpone cream.

Summer Pudding

Unbelievably simple to make and totally delicious, this is a real warm-weather classic. It's also a productive way of using up leftover bread.

Serves 4

about 8 slices white bread, at least one day old
800g/1¾lb mixed summer fruits
about 25g/1oz/2 tbsp granulated sugar
30ml/2 tbsp water

1 Remove the crusts from the bread. Cut a round from one slice of bread to fit in the base of a 1.2 litre/2 pint/5 cup round ovenproof bowl and place in position. Cut strips of bread about 5cm/2in wide and use to line the sides of the bowl, overlapping the strips as you work.

2 Gently heat the fruit, sugar and the water in a large heavy pan, shaking the pan occasionally, until the juices begin to run.

3 Reserve about 45ml/3 tbsp fruit juice, then spoon the fruit and remaining juice into the prepared bowl, taking care not to dislodge the bread lining.

4 Cut the remaining bread to fit entirely over the fruit. Stand the bowl on a plate and cover with a saucer or small plate that will just fit inside the top of the bowl. Place a heavy weight on top. Chill the pudding and the reserved fruit juice overnight.

5 Run a knife carefully around the inside of the bowl rim, then invert the pudding on to a cold serving plate. Pour over the reserved juice, making sure that all the bread is completely covered, and serve.

Cook's Tips
• Use a good mix of summer fruits for this pudding – red- and blackcurrants, raspberries, strawberries and loganberries.
• Summer pudding freezes well so make an extra one to enjoy during the winter.

Stuffed Peaches Energy 641Kcal/2670kJ; Protein 12.7g; Carbohydrate 40.9g, of which sugars 36g; Fat 45.3g, of which saturates 23.9g; Cholesterol 290mg; Calcium 102mg; Fibre 2.7g; Sodium 132mg.
Summer Pudding Energy 211Kcal/893kJ; Protein 6.2g; Carbohydrate 46.5g, of which sugars 21.3g; Fat 1.2g, of which saturates 0g; Cholesterol 0mg; Calcium 96mg; Fibre 3g; Sodium 293mg.

Autumn Pudding

As its name suggests, this is a tasty seasonal variation of summer pudding, using apples, blackberries and plums – a great combination.

Serves 6
10 slices white or brown bread, at least one day old
1 cooking apple, peeled, cored and sliced
225g/8oz ripe red plums, halved and stoned (pitted)
225g/8oz blackberries
75g/3oz/6 tbsp caster (superfine) sugar
60ml/4 tbsp water
natural (plain) yogurt or Greek (US strained plain) yogurt, to serve

1 Remove the crusts from the bread. Cut a round from one slice of bread to fit in the base of a 1.2 litre/2 pint/5 cup round ovenproof bowl and place in position.

2 Cut the remaining slices of bread in half and use to line the bowl, overlapping the pieces as you work. Save some pieces of bread for the top.

3 Place the apple, plums, blackberries, caster sugar and the water in a pan. Heat gently until the sugar dissolves, then simmer for 10 minutes, until soft. Remove from the heat.

4 Spoon the fruit into the bread-lined bowl, reserving the juice. Cut the remaining bread to fit entirely over the fruit, then gently spoon over the reserved fruit juice.

5 Stand the bowl on a plate and cover with a saucer or small plate that will just fit inside the top of the bowl. Place a heavy weight on top. Chill the pudding overnight. Turn out on to a serving plate and serve with natural or Greek yogurt.

> **Cook's Tip**
> *Choose good-quality bread, with slices at least 5mm/¼in thick so that it supports the fruit when the pudding is turned out.*

Baked Lattice Peaches

Nectarines also work well in this lovely recipe.

Serves 6
3 peaches
juice of ½ lemon
75g/3oz/scant ½ cup white marzipan
375g/13oz ready-rolled puff pastry
a large pinch of ground cinnamon
beaten egg, to glaze
caster (superfine) sugar, for sprinkling

For the caramel sauce
50g/2oz/¼ cup caster (superfine) sugar
30ml/2 tbsp water
150ml/¼ pint/⅔ cup double (heavy) cream

1 Preheat the oven to 190°C/375°F/Gas 5. Pour boiling water over the peaches to cover. Leave for 60 seconds, then drain and peel. Toss the fruit in the lemon juice to prevent browning.

2 Divide the marzipan into six pieces and shape each to form a small round. Cut the peaches in half and remove their stones (pits). Fill the cavity in each peach with a marzipan round.

3 Unroll the puff pastry and cut in half. Set one half aside, then cut out six rounds from the rest, making each one slightly larger than a peach half. Sprinkle a little cinnamon on each pastry round, then place a peach half, marzipan-side down, on top.

4 Cut the remaining pastry into lattice pastry, using a special cutter if you have one. If not, simply cut small slits in rows all over the pastry. Cut the lattice pastry into six equal squares.

5 Dampen the edges of the pastry rounds with water, then drape a lattice pastry square over each peach half. Press the pastry edges to seal, then trim and decorate with pastry leaves made from the trimmings. Transfer to a baking sheet. Brush with beaten egg, sprinkle with sugar and bake for 20 minutes.

6 Meanwhile, make the sauce. Heat the sugar with the water in a small pan until it dissolves. Boil until the syrup turns dark golden. Stand back and add the cream. Heat gently, stirring until smooth. Serve the peach pastries with the sauce.

Autumn Pudding Energy 182Kcal/775kJ; Protein 4.4g; Carbohydrate 41.5g, of which sugars 20.4g; Fat 1g, of which saturates 0g; Cholesterol 0mg; Calcium 77mg; Fibre 2.6g; Sodium 237mg.
Lattice Peaches Energy 452Kcal/1886kJ; Protein 5.1g; Carbohydrate 43.8g, of which sugars 21.4g; Fat 30.4g, of which saturates 8.5g; Cholesterol 34mg; Calcium 64mg; Fibre 0.8g; Sodium 203mg.

Apple Charlottes

These tempting little fruit
Charlottes are a wonderful
way to use windfalls.

Serves 4
175g/6oz/¾ cup butter
450g/1lb cooking apples
225g/8oz eating apples
60ml/4 tbsp water

130g/4½oz/scant ⅔ cup caster
 (superfine) sugar
2 egg yolks
pinch of grated nutmeg
9 thin slices white bread,
 crusts removed
extra-thick double (heavy) cream
 or custard, to serve

1 Preheat the oven to 190°C/375°F/Gas 5. Put a knob (pat) of
the butter in a pan. Peel and core the apples, dice them finely
and put them in the pan with the water. Cover and cook for
10 minutes or until the cooking apples have pulped down. Stir
in 115g/4oz/½ cup of the caster sugar. Boil, uncovered, until any
liquid has evaporated and what remains is a thick pulp. Remove
from the heat, beat in the egg yolks and nutmeg and set aside.

2 Melt the remaining butter in a separate pan over a low heat
until the white curds start to separate from the clear yellow
liquid. Remove from the heat. Leave to stand for a few minutes,
then strain the clear clarified butter through a sieve (strainer)
lined with muslin (cheesecloth), discarding the curds.

3 Brush four 150ml/¼ pint/⅔ cup individual Charlotte moulds
or round tins (pans) with a little of the clarified butter; sprinkle
with the remaining caster sugar. Cut the bread slices into
2.5cm/1in strips. Dip the strips into the remaining clarified
butter; use to line the moulds or tins. Overlap the strips on
the base to give the effect of a swirl and let the excess bread
overhang the tops of the moulds or tins.

4 Fill each bread case with apple pulp. Fold the excess bread
over the top of each mould or tin to make a lid and press
down lightly. Bake for 45–50 minutes or until golden. Run a
knife between each Charlotte and its mould or tin, then turn
out on to dessert plates. Serve immediately with extra-thick
double cream or custard.

Rhubarb Spiral Cobbler

Orange in the fruit filling
and in the topping gives this
pudding added zest.

Serves 4
675g/1½lb rhubarb, sliced
50g/2oz/¼ cup caster (superfine)
 sugar
45ml/3 tbsp orange juice

For the topping
200g/7oz/1¾ cups self-raising
 (self-rising) flour

30ml/2 tbsp caster
 (superfine) sugar
about 200g/7oz/scant 1 cup
 natural (plain) yogurt
grated rind of 1 medium orange
30ml/2 tbsp demerara
 (raw) sugar
5ml/1 tsp ground ginger
yogurt or fresh ready-made
 custard, to serve

1 Preheat the oven to 200°C/400°F/Gas 6. Cook the rhubarb,
sugar and orange juice in a covered pan until tender. Transfer to
an ovenproof dish.

2 Make the topping. Put the flour in a mixing bowl, add the
caster sugar and mix together. Stir in enough of the yogurt to
bind to a soft dough.

3 Roll out on a floured surface to a 25cm/10in square. Mix
together the orange rind, demerara sugar and ginger in a bowl,
then sprinkle the mixture evenly over the surface of the dough.

4 Roll up quite tightly, then cut into about ten slices, using a
sharp knife. Arrange the slices over the rhubarb.

5 Bake in the oven for 15–20 minutes, or until the spirals
are well risen and golden brown. Serve warm, with yogurt
or fresh custard.

> **Variation**
> For a cinnamon cobbler topping, leave out the orange rind and
> replace the ginger with ground cinnamon.

Apple Charlottes Energy 686Kcal/2874kJ; Protein 7.5g; Carbohydrate 79.2g, of which sugars 50.8g; Fat 40g, of which saturates 23.6g; Cholesterol 194mg; Calcium 111mg; Fibre 3.6g; Sodium 591mg.
Rhubarb Cobbler Energy 317Kcal/1355kJ; Protein 8.7g; Carbohydrate 72.6g, of which sugars 35.5g; Fat 1.3g, of which saturates 0.4g; Cholesterol 1mg; Calcium 443mg; Fibre 3.9g; Sodium 229mg.

Blackberry Cobbler

Make the most of the fresh autumn blackberries with this delicious dessert. Break through the scrumptious topping to reveal the dark, juicy fruit. Serve with whipped cream for a truly satisfying dish to herald in a new season.

Serves 8
800g/1¾lb/6 cups blackberries
200g/7oz/1 cup granulated sugar
20g/¾oz/scant ¼ cup plain
  (all-purpose) flour
grated rind of 1 lemon
30ml/2 tbsp granulated sugar
  mixed with 1.5ml/¼ tsp grated
  nutmeg

For the topping
225g/8oz/2 cups plain (all-purpose) flour
200g/7oz/1 cup granulated sugar
15ml/1 tbsp baking powder
pinch of salt
250ml/8fl oz/1 cup milk
115g/4oz/½ cup butter, melted

1 Preheat the oven to 180°C/350°F/Gas 4. In a bowl, combine the blackberries, sugar, flour and lemon rind. Stir gently to blend. Transfer to a 2.4 litre/4 pint/10 cup baking dish.

2 Make the topping. Sift the flour, sugar, baking powder and salt into a large bowl. Combine the milk and butter in a jug (pitcher).

3 Gradually stir the milk mixture into the dry ingredients and stir until the batter is just smooth.

4 Spoon the batter over the berries, levelling the top and spreading to the edges.

5 Sprinkle the surface with the sugar and nutmeg mixture. Bake for about 50 minutes, until the topping is set and lightly browned. Serve immediately.

> **Cook's Tip**
> Use half blackberries and half raspberries or tayberries for the filling, to ring the changes.

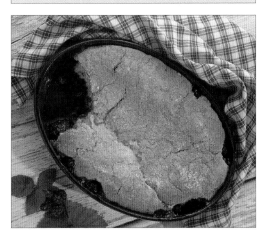

Black Cherry Clafoutis

This favourite French recipe has been reproduced with all manner of fruit, but you simply can't beat the classic version using slightly tart black cherries.

Serves 6
25g/1oz/2 tbsp butter,
  for greasing
450g/1lb/generous 2 cups black
  cherries, pitted
25g/1oz/¼ cup plain
  (all-purpose) flour
50g/2oz/½ cup icing
  (confectioners') sugar, plus
  extra for dusting
4 eggs, beaten
250ml/8fl oz/1 cup full cream
  (whole) milk
30ml/2 tbsp Kirsch

1 Preheat the oven to 180°C/350°F/Gas 4. Use the butter to thickly grease a 1.2 litre/2 pint/5 cup ovenproof dish. Sprinkle the cherries over the base.

2 Sift the flour and icing sugar together into a large mixing bowl and gradually whisk in the eggs until the mixture is smooth. Whisk in the milk until blended, then stir in the Kirsch.

3 Pour the batter carefully over the cherries, then bake for 35–45 minutes or until just set and lightly golden.

4 Allow the pudding to cool for about 15 minutes. Dust liberally with icing sugar just before serving.

> **Cook's Tip**
> Traditionally, the cherries are left whole, but you may prefer to pit the fruit first, to make the dish easier to eat.

> **Variations**
> Try other liqueurs in this dessert. Almond-flavoured liqueur is delicious teamed with cherries, as is raspberry or orange liqueur.

Blackberry Cobbler Energy 463Kcal/1952kJ; Protein 5.2g; Carbohydrate 86.6g, of which sugars 63.3g; Fat 13g, of which saturates 7.9g; Cholesterol 32mg; Calcium 153mg; Fibre 4.1g; Sodium 107mg.
Cherry Clafoutis Energy 201Kcal/843kJ; Protein 6.7g; Carbohydrate 23.8g, of which sugars 20.7g; Fat 8.9g, of which saturates 4.3g; Cholesterol 142mg; Calcium 89mg; Fibre 0.8g; Sodium 91mg.

Lemon & Lime Cheesecake

This tangy cheesecake is a citrus sensation.

Makes 8 slices
150g/5oz/1½ cups digestive biscuits (graham crackers)
40g/1½oz/3 tbsp butter

For the topping
grated rind and juice of 2 lemons
10ml/2 tsp powdered gelatine
250g/9oz/generous 1 cup ricotta cheese
75g/3oz/6 tbsp caster (superfine) sugar
150ml/¼ pint/⅔ cup double (heavy) cream
2 eggs, separated

For the lime syrup
pared rind and juice of 3 limes
75g/3oz/6 tbsp caster (superfine) sugar
5ml/1 tsp arrowroot mixed with 30ml/2 tbsp water
green food colouring (optional)

1 Lightly grease a 20cm/8in round springform cake tin (pan). Place the biscuits in a food processor or blender and process until they form fine crumbs. Melt the butter in a large pan, then stir in the crumbs until well coated. Spoon into the prepared cake tin, press the crumbs down well in an even layer, then chill.

2 Make the topping. Place the lemon rind and juice in a small pan and sprinkle over the gelatine. Leave for 5 minutes. Heat gently until the gelatine has dissolved, then set aside to cool slightly. Beat the ricotta cheese and sugar in a bowl. Stir in the cream and egg yolks, then whisk in the cooled gelatine mixture.

3 Whisk the egg whites in a grease-free bowl until they form soft peaks. Fold them into the cheese mixture. Spoon on to the biscuit base, level the surface and chill for 2–3 hours.

4 Meanwhile, make the lime syrup. Place the lime rind and juice and sugar in a small pan. Bring to the boil, stirring, then boil the syrup for 5 minutes. Stir in the arrowroot mixture and continue to stir until the syrup boils again and thickens slightly. Tint pale green with a little food colouring, if you like. Cool, then chill.

5 Spoon the lime syrup over the set cheesecake. Remove from the tin and cut into slices to serve.

Pomegranate Jewelled Cheesecake

This light cheesecake has a stunning pomegranate glaze.

Serves 8
225g/8oz oat biscuits (crackers)
75g/3oz/6 tbsp unsalted (sweet) butter, melted

For the filling
45ml/3 tbsp orange juice
15ml/1 tbsp powdered gelatine
250g/9oz/generous 1 cup mascarpone cheese
200g/7oz/scant 1 cup full-fat soft cheese
75g/3oz/⅔ cup icing (confectioners') sugar, sifted
200ml/7fl oz/scant 1 cup coconut cream
2 egg whites

For the topping
2 pomegranates, peeled and seeds separated
grated rind and juice of 1 orange
30ml/2 tbsp caster (superfine) sugar
15ml/1 tbsp arrowroot, mixed to a paste with 30ml/2 tbsp Kirsch
red food colouring (optional)

1 Grease a 23cm/9in springform cake tin (pan). Crumb the biscuits in a food processor or blender. Add the butter and process briefly. Spoon into the tin, press in well, then chill.

2 Make the filling. Pour the orange juice into a heatproof bowl, sprinkle the gelatine on top and set aside for 5 minutes. Place the bowl in a pan of hot water; stir until the gelatine dissolves.

3 In a bowl, beat together both cheeses and the icing sugar, then gradually beat in the coconut cream. Whisk the egg whites in a grease-free bowl to soft peaks. Quickly stir the melted gelatine into the coconut mixture and fold in the egg whites. Pour over the biscuit base, level and chill until set.

4 Make the topping. Place the pomegranate seeds in a pan and add the orange rind and juice and sugar. Bring to the boil, then lower the heat, cover and simmer for 5 minutes. Add the arrowroot paste and heat, stirring, until thickened. Stir in a few drops of food colouring, if using. Cool, stirring occasionally.

5 Pour the glaze over the top of the set cheesecake, then chill. Remove from the tin and cut into slices to serve.

Lemon & Lime Energy 366Kcal/1526kJ; Protein 6g; Carbohydrate 33.8g, of which sugars 23.5g; Fat 23.9g, of which saturates 13.8g; Cholesterol 105mg; Calcium 44mg; Fibre 0.4g; Sodium 166mg.
Pomegranate Energy 407Kcal/1702kJ; Protein 8.2g; Carbohydrate 37.3g, of which sugars 26.1g; Fat 26.1g, of which saturates 15.2g; Cholesterol 56mg; Calcium 57mg; Fibre 1.1g; Sodium 336mg.

Pear Tarte Tatin with Cardamom

Cardamom is a spice that is equally at home in sweet and savoury dishes. It is delicious with pears, and brings out their flavour beautifully in this easy-to-make tart.

Serves 4–6
50g/2oz/¼ cup butter, softened
50g/2oz/¼ cup caster
*   (superfine) sugar*
seeds from 10 green
*   cardamom pods*
225g/8oz fresh ready-made
*   puff pastry*
3 ripe, large round pears
single (light) cream, to serve

1 Preheat the oven to 220°C/425°F/Gas 7. Spread the butter over the base of an 18cm/7in heavy ovenproof omelette pan. Sprinkle the butter with the sugar, then sprinkle the cardamom seeds evenly over the top.

2 On a lightly floured work surface, roll out the pastry to a circle slightly larger than the pan. Prick the pastry all over with a fork, place on a baking sheet and chill.

3 Peel the pears, cut in half lengthways and remove the cores. Arrange the pears, rounded side down, in the pan. Place over medium heat and cook until the sugar melts and begins to bubble with the juice from the pears.

4 Once the sugar has caramelized, remove the pan from the heat. Carefully place the pastry on top, tucking in the edges with a knife. Bake for 25 minutes.

5 Leave the tart in the pan for about 2 minutes until the juices have stopped bubbling.

6 Invert a serving plate over the pan then, wearing oven gloves to protect your hands, firmly hold the pan and plate together and quickly shaking them to release the tart. It may be necessary to slide a spatula underneath the pears to loosen them. Allow the tart to cool slightly, then serve warm, with single cream.

Fresh Lemon Tart

Serve at room temperature to enjoy the zesty lemon flavour to the full.

Serves 6–8
350g/12oz ready-made rich
*   sweet shortcrust pastry*

For the filling
3 eggs
115g/4oz/½ cup caster
*   (superfine) sugar*
115g/4oz/1 cup ground almonds
105ml/7 tbsp double
*   (heavy) cream*
grated rind and juice of 2 lemons

For the topping
2 thin-skinned unwaxed lemons,
*   thinly sliced*
200g/7oz/1 cup caster
*   (superfine) sugar*
105ml/7 tbsp water

1 Roll out the pastry and line a deep 23cm/9in fluted flan tin (tart pan). Prick the base and chill for 30 minutes.

2 Preheat the oven to 200°C/400°F/Gas 6. Line the pastry with baking parchment and baking beans and bake blind for 10 minutes. Remove the paper and beans and return the pastry case to the oven for 5 minutes more.

3 Meanwhile, make the filling. Beat the eggs, caster sugar, almonds and cream in a bowl until smooth. Beat in the lemon rind and juice. Pour the filling into the pastry case. Lower the oven temperature to 190°C/375°F/Gas 5 and bake for 20 minutes or until the filling has set and the pastry is golden.

4 Make the topping. Place the lemon slices in a pan and pour over water to cover. Simmer for 15–20 minutes or until the skins are tender, then drain. Place the sugar in a pan and stir in the measured water. Heat gently until the sugar has dissolved, stirring constantly, then boil for 2 minutes. Add the lemon slices and cook for 10–15 minutes until the skins become candied.

5 Lift out the candied lemon slices and arrange them over the top of the tart. Return the syrup to the heat and boil until reduced to a thick glaze. Brush this over the tart and allow to cool completely before serving.

Lemon Tart Energy 528Kcal/2212kJ; Protein 7.8g; Carbohydrate 61.7g, of which sugars 42.3g; Fat 29.6g, of which saturates 5.6g; Cholesterol 89mg; Calcium 91mg; Fibre 1.9g; Sodium 104mg.
Tarte Tatin Energy 265Kcal/1106kJ; Protein 2.5g; Carbohydrate 30.1g, of which sugars 16.8g; Fat 16.1g, of which saturates 4.3g; Cholesterol 18mg; Calcium 36mg; Fibre 1.7g; Sodium 170mg.

FRUIT DESSERTS

Fresh Fig Filo Tart

Figs cook wonderfully well and taste superb in this tart – the riper the figs, the better.

Serves 6–8

five 35 x 25cm/14 x 10in sheets filo pastry, thawed if frozen
25g/1oz/2 tbsp butter, melted, plus extra for greasing
6 fresh figs, cut into wedges
75g/3oz/²⁄₃ cup plain (all-purpose) flour
75g/3oz/6 tbsp caster (superfine) sugar
4 eggs
450ml/³⁄₄ pint/scant 2 cups milk
2.5ml/½ tsp almond extract
15ml/1 tbsp icing (confectioners') sugar, for dusting
whipped cream or Greek (US strained plain) yogurt, to serve

1 Preheat the oven to 190°C/375°F/Gas 5. Grease a 25 x 16cm/10 x 6¼in baking tin (pan) with butter. Brush each filo sheet in turn with melted butter and use to line the prepared tin.

2 Using scissors, cut off any excess pastry, leaving a little overhanging the edge. Arrange the figs in the filo case.

3 Sift the flour into a bowl and stir in the caster sugar. Add the eggs and a little of the milk and whisk until smooth. Gradually whisk in the remaining milk and the almond extract. Pour the mixture over the figs; bake for 1 hour or until the batter has set and is golden.

4 Remove the tart from the oven and allow it to cool in the tin on a wire rack for 10 minutes. Dust with the icing sugar and serve with whipped cream or Greek yogurt.

> **Cook's Tip**
> Filo pastry dries out quickly, so keep the sheets not currently being used covered under a clean damp dish towel. Also, work as quickly as possible. If the filo should turn dry and brittle, simply brush it with melted butter to moisten.

Filo-Topped Apple Pie

With its crisp, melt-in-the-mouth filo topping and minimal butter, this is a really light dessert, making it the perfect choice for those trying to combine a sweet tooth with a healthy eating plan. There's certainly no loss of flavour in this tasty variation on a traditional theme, so feel free to serve it to family and friends who will soon discover it tastes as good as it looks.

Serves 6

900g/2lb cooking apples
75g/3oz/6 tbsp caster (superfine) sugar
grated rind of 1 lemon
15ml/1 tbsp lemon juice
75g/3oz/½ cup sultanas (golden raisins)
2.5ml/½ tsp ground cinnamon
4 large sheets filo pastry, thawed if frozen
25g/1oz/2 tbsp butter, melted
icing (confectioners') sugar, for dusting

1 Peel, core and dice the apples. Place the apples in a pan with the caster sugar and lemon rind. Drizzle the lemon juice over.

2 Bring to the boil, stir well, then cook for 5 minutes, until the apples have softened.

3 Stir in the sultanas and cinnamon. Spoon the mixture into a 1.2 litre/2 pint/5 cup pie dish; level the top. Allow to cool.

4 Preheat the oven to 180°C/350°F/Gas 4. Place a pie funnel in the centre of the fruit. Brush each sheet of filo with melted butter.

5 Scrunch the filo up loosely and place on the fruit to cover it completely. Bake for 20–30 minutes until the filo is golden.

6 To serve, dust the pie with the icing sugar.

> **Cook's Tip**
> For a delightful change of flavour and texture, substitute flaked (sliced) almonds – plain or toasted – for some or all of the sultanas (golden raisins) in the pie.

Fig Tart Energy 213Kcal/900kJ; Protein 5.8g; Carbohydrate 36.7g, of which sugars 20g; Fat 5.9g, of which saturates 2.5g; Cholesterol 102mg; Calcium 89mg; Fibre 1.8g; Sodium 65mg.
Apple Pie Energy 210Kcal/892kJ; Protein 2.1g; Carbohydrate 44.8g, of which sugars 35.3g; Fat 3.8g, of which saturates 2.2g; Cholesterol 9mg; Calcium 39mg; Fibre 3g; Sodium 32mg.

One-Crust Rhubarb Pie

This method can be used for all sorts of fruit and is really foolproof. It doesn't matter how rough the pie looks when it goes into the oven; it always comes out looking fantastic!

Serves 6

350g/12oz shortcrust pastry, thawed if frozen
1 egg yolk, beaten
25g/1oz/3 tbsp semolina
25g/1oz/¼ cup hazelnuts, coarsely chopped
30ml/2 tbsp golden granulated sugar

For the filling

450g/1lb rhubarb, cut into 2.5cm/1in pieces
75g/3oz/6 tbsp caster (superfine) sugar
1–2 pieces preserved stem ginger in syrup, drained and finely chopped

1 Preheat the oven to 200°C/400°F/Gas 6. Roll out the pastry to a circle 35cm/14in across. Lay it over the rolling pin and transfer it to a large baking sheet. Brush a little egg yolk over the pastry. Scatter the semolina over the centre, leaving a wide rim all round the edge.

2 Make the filling. Place the rhubarb pieces, caster sugar and chopped ginger in a large bowl and mix well.

3 Pile the rhubarb mixture into the middle of the pastry. Fold the rim roughly over the filling so that it almost covers it. Some of the fruit will remain visible in the centre.

4 Brush the pastry rim with any remaining egg yolk to glaze, then scatter the hazelnuts and golden sugar over the top. Bake the pie for 30–35 minutes or until the pastry is golden brown. Serve hot or warm.

> **Cook's Tip**
> *Egg yolk glaze brushed on to pastry gives it a nice golden sheen. However, be careful not to drip the glaze on the baking sheet, or it will burn and be difficult to remove.*

Apricot Parcels

These little filo parcels contain a special apricot and mincemeat filling. A good way to use up any mincemeat and marzipan that have been in your cupboard since Christmas!

Makes 8

350g/12oz filo pastry, thawed if frozen
50g/2oz/¼ cup butter, melted
8 apricots, halved and stoned (pitted)
60ml/4 tbsp luxury mincemeat
12 ratafia biscuits (almond macaroons), crushed
30ml/2 tbsp grated marzipan
icing (confectioners') sugar, for dusting

1 Preheat the oven to 200°C/400°F/Gas 6. Cut the filo pastry into 32 x 18cm/7in squares. Brush four of the squares with a little melted butter and stack them, giving each layer a quarter turn so that the stack acquires a star shape. Repeat this stacking process to make eight stars.

2 Place an apricot half, hollow up, in the centre of each pastry star. Mix together the mincemeat, crushed ratafias and marzipan and spoon a little of the mixture into the hollow of each apricot.

3 Top with another apricot half, then bring the corners of each pastry star together and squeeze to make a gathered purse.

4 Place the purses on a baking sheet and brush each with a little melted butter. Bake for 15–20 minutes or until the pastry is golden and crisp. Lightly dust with icing sugar to serve.

> **Cook's Tips**
> • *Whipped cream, flavoured with a little brandy, makes an ideal accompaniment to the delicious parcels.*
> • *If ratafias are not available, use amaretti instead or simply leave them out, as the mincemeat adds lots of flavour.*

Rhubarb Pie Energy 389Kcal/1633kJ; Protein 5.6g; Carbohydrate 49.7g, of which sugars 19.6g; Fat 20.1g, of which saturates 5.6g; Cholesterol 42mg; Calcium 139mg; Fibre 2.5g; Sodium 239mg.
Apricot Parcels Energy 214Kcal/902kJ; Protein 3.2g; Carbohydrate 34.9g, of which sugars 15.2g; Fat 7.9g, of which saturates 4.1g; Cholesterol 14mg; Calcium 56mg; Fibre 1.7g; Sodium 83mg.

Pear & Polenta Cake

Polenta gives the light sponge topping and sliced pears a nutty corn flavour that complements the fruit perfectly. Serve as a dessert with custard or cream.

Makes 10 slices
butter or margarine, for greasing
175g/6oz/¾ cup golden caster (superfine) sugar

4 ripe pears
juice of ½ lemon
30ml/2 tbsp clear honey
3 eggs
seeds from 1 vanilla pod (bean)
120ml/4fl oz/½ cup sunflower oil
115g/4oz/1 cup self-raising (self-rising) flour
50g/2oz/⅓ cup instant polenta

1 Preheat the oven to 180°C/350°F/Gas 4. Generously grease and line a 21cm/8½in round cake tin (pan). Sprinkle 30ml/2 tbsp of the golden caster sugar over the base of the prepared tin.

2 Peel and core the pears. Cut them into chunky slices and toss in the lemon juice. Arrange them on the base of the prepared cake tin. Drizzle the honey over the pears and set aside.

3 Mix together the eggs, seeds from the vanilla pod and the remaining golden caster sugar in a bowl.

4 Beat the egg mixture until thick and creamy, then gradually beat in the oil. Sift together the flour and polenta and fold into the egg mixture.

5 Pour the mixture carefully into the tin over the pears. Bake for about 50 minutes or until a skewer inserted into the centre comes out clean. Cool in the tin for 10 minutes, then turn the cake out on to a plate, peel off the lining paper, invert and slice.

Cook's Tip
Use the tip of a small, sharp knife to scrape out the vanilla seeds. If you do not have a vanilla pod, use 5ml/1 tsp pure vanilla extract instead.

Apricot & Pear Filo Roulade

A truly delicious mix of dried and fresh fruit and almonds, all wrapped up in light-as-a-feather filo pastry, makes a really great dessert. This dish is also amazingly quick to prepare and cook. Use your imagination and vary the fruits you use, depending on what is in season or what you have readily to hand.

Serves 4–6
115g/4oz/½ cup ready-to-eat dried apricots, chopped
30ml/2 tbsp apricot jam
5ml/1 tsp freshly squeezed lemon juice
50g/2oz/¼ cup soft brown sugar
2 medium pears, peeled, cored and chopped
50g/2oz/½ cup ground almonds
30ml/2 tbsp slivered almonds
25g/1oz/2 tbsp butter
8 sheets filo pastry
icing (confectioners') sugar, to dust

1 Put the dried apricots, apricot jam, lemon juice, brown sugar and prepared pears into a pan and heat gently, stirring all the time, for 5–7 minutes.

2 Remove the pan with the fruit mixture from the heat and cool. Mix in the ground and slivered almonds. Preheat the oven to 200°C/400°F/Gas 6. Melt the butter in a pan.

3 Lightly grease a baking sheet. Layer the filo pastry on the baking sheet, brushing each separate layer carefully with the melted butter.

4 Spoon the fruit-and-nut filling down the pastry, placing the filling just to one side of the centre and within 2.5cm/1in of each end.

5 Lift the other side of the pastry up by sliding a metal spatula underneath. Fold this pastry over the filling, tucking the edge under. Seal the ends neatly and brush all over with melted butter again.

6 Bake for 15–20 minutes, until golden. Dust with icing sugar and serve immediately.

Apricot & Pear Energy 212Kcal/890kJ; Protein 3.7g; Carbohydrate 31.3g, of which sugars 24.7g; Fat 8.8g, of which saturates 2.6g; Cholesterol 9mg; Calcium 59mg; Fibre 3.3g; Sodium 34mg.
Pear & Polenta Energy 256Kcal/1077kJ; Protein 3.7g; Carbohydrate 38.9g, of which sugars 26.7g; Fat 10.5g, of which saturates 1.5g; Cholesterol 57mg; Calcium 65mg; Fibre 1.8g; Sodium 66mg.

Dutch Apple Cake

The apple topping makes this cake really moist. It is just as good hot as it is cold.

50g/2oz/¼ cup butter, melted
2 eggs, beaten
150ml/¼ pint/⅔ cup milk

Makes 8–10 slices
250g/9oz/2¼ cups self-raising (self-rising) flour
10ml/2 tsp baking powder
5ml/1 tsp ground cinnamon
130g/4½oz/generous ½ cup caster (superfine) sugar

For the topping
2 eating apples
15g/½oz/1 tbsp butter, melted
60ml/4 tbsp demerara (raw) sugar
1.5ml/¼ tsp ground cinnamon

1 Preheat the oven to 200°C/400°F/Gas 6. Grease and line a 20cm/8in round cake tin (pan). Sift the flour, baking powder and cinnamon into a large mixing bowl. Stir in the caster sugar. In a separate bowl, whisk the melted butter, eggs and milk together, then stir the mixture into the dry ingredients.

2 Pour the cake mixture into the prepared tin, smooth the surface, then make a shallow hollow in a ring around the edge of the mixture.

3 Make the topping. Peel and core the apples, slice them into wedges and slice the wedges thinly. Arrange the slices around the edge of the cake mixture, in the hollowed ring. Brush with the melted butter, then scatter the demerara sugar and ground cinnamon over the top.

4 Bake for 45–50 minutes or until the cake has risen well, is golden and a skewer inserted into the centre comes out clean.

5 Serve immediately, or remove from the tin, peel off the lining paper and cool on a wire rack before serving cold with cream.

Variation
Add a few seedless raisins to the sliced apples if you like.

Exotic Fruit Tranche

This is a good way to make the most of a small selection of exotic fruit.

Serves 8
175g/6oz/1½ cups plain (all-purpose) flour
50g/2oz/¼ cup unsalted (sweet) butter
25g/1oz/2 tbsp white vegetable fat
50g/2oz/¼ cup caster (superfine) sugar
2 egg yolks
about 15ml/1 tbsp water
115g/4oz/scant ½ cup apricot jam, strained and warmed

For the filling
150ml/¼ pint/⅔ cup double (heavy) cream, plus extra to serve
250g/9oz/generous 1 cup mascarpone
25g/1oz/2 tbsp icing (confectioners') sugar, sifted
grated rind of 1 orange
450g/1lb/3 cups mixed prepared fruits, such as mango, papaya, star fruit, kiwi fruit and blackberries
90ml/6 tbsp apricot jam, strained
15ml/1 tbsp white or coconut rum

1 Sift the flour into a bowl and rub in the butter and white vegetable fat until the mixture resembles fine breadcrumbs. Stir in the caster sugar. Add the egg yolks and enough cold water to make a soft dough. Thinly roll out the pastry between two sheets of clear film (plastic wrap) and use the pastry to line a 35 x 12cm/14 x 4½in fluted tranche tin or a 23cm/9in flan tin (tart pan). Allow the excess pastry to hang over the edge of the tin, and chill for 30 minutes.

2 Preheat the oven to 200°C/400°F/Gas 6. Prick the base of the pastry case and line with baking parchment and baking beans. Bake for 10–12 minutes. Lift out the paper and beans and return the pastry case to the oven for 5 minutes. Trim off the excess pastry and brush the inside of the case with the warmed apricot jam to form a seal. Cool on a wire rack.

3 Make the filling. Whip the cream to soft peaks, then stir it into the mascarpone with the icing sugar and orange rind. Spread in the cooled pastry case and top with the prepared fruits. Warm the apricot jam with the rum and drizzle or brush over the fruits to make a glaze. Serve with extra cream.

Dutch Apple Cake Energy 225Kcal/951kJ; Protein 3.7g; Carbohydrate 40g, of which sugars 21.4g; Fat 6.8g, of which saturates 3.8g; Cholesterol 52mg; Calcium 105mg; Fibre 1g; Sodium 145mg.
Fruit Tranche Energy 429Kcal/1801kJ; Protein 6.4g; Carbohydrate 53.3g, of which sugars 36.9g; Fat 22.2g, of which saturates 12.7g; Cholesterol 99mg; Calcium 105mg; Fibre 2.1g; Sodium 136mg.

Indian Kulfi Ice Cream

This famous Indian ice cream is traditionally made by slowly boiling milk until it has reduced to about one-third of the original quantity. Although you can save time by using condensed milk, nothing beats this delicious ice cream when made in the authentic manner.

Serves 4
1.5 litres/2½ pints/6¼ cups milk
3 cardamom pods
25g/1oz/2 tbsp caster (superfine) sugar
50g/2oz/½ cup pistachio nuts, skinned, plus a few to decorate
a few pink rose petals, to decorate

1 Pour the milk into a large, heavy pan. Bring to the boil, lower the heat and simmer gently for 1 hour, stirring occasionally.

2 Put the cardamom pods in a mortar and crush them with a pestle. Add the pods and the seeds to the milk and continue to simmer for 1–1½ hours or until the milk has reduced to about 475ml/16fl oz/2 cups.

3 Strain the flavoured milk into a jug (pitcher), stir in the sugar and leave to cool.

4 Grind half the pistachio nuts to a smooth powder in a blender, nut grinder or cleaned coffee grinder. Cut the remaining pistachios into thin slivers and reserve for decoration. Stir the ground nuts into the milk mixture.

5 Pour the milk and pistachio mixture into four kulfi moulds. (If you do not have suitable moulds, use plastic cups instead.) Freeze overnight until firm.

6 To unmould the kulfi, half fill a plastic container or bowl with very hot water, stand the moulds in the water and count to ten. Immediately lift out the moulds and invert them on to a baking sheet to turn out the ice creams.

7 Transfer the ices to a platter or individual plates. Scatter sliced pistachios and rose petals over the top and serve immediately.

Italian Coffee Granita

Very popular in Italy, a granita is a cross between a frozen drink and a flavoured ice. The consistency should be slushy, not solid. Granitas are simple to make at home with the help of a food processor.

Serves 4–5
475ml/16fl oz/2cups water
115g/4oz/½ cup granulated sugar
250ml/8fl oz/1 cup very strong espresso coffee, cooled
whipped cream, to garnish (optional)

1 Heat the water with the sugar over low heat until the sugar dissolves. Bring to the boil, then remove from the heat and allow to cool.

2 Combine the coffee with the sugar syrup. Place in a shallow freezer container and freeze until solid.

3 Plunge the bottom of the frozen container into very hot water for a few seconds. Turn the frozen mixture out and chop it into large chunks.

4 Place the mixture in a food processor fitted with a metal blade, and process until it forms small crystals. Spoon the granita into individual bowls or glasses and top with whipped cream, if you like.

Variation/Lemon Granita

Heat 475ml/16fl oz/2 cups water with 115g/4oz/½ cup granulated sugar over low heat until the sugar dissolves. Bring to the boil. Remove from the heat, and cool. Combine the juice and grated rind of 1 lemon (scrubbed before grating) with the sugar syrup. Place in a shallow container or freezer tray and freeze until solid. Plunge the bottom of the frozen container into very hot water for a few seconds. Turn the frozen mixture out, then chop it into chunks. Process the mixture in a metal-bladed food processor until it forms small crystals. Serve immediately, spooned into individual serving dishes.

Coffee Granita Energy 93Kcal/396kJ; Protein 0.6g; Carbohydrate 24.2g, of which sugars 24g; Fat 0g, of which saturates 0g; Cholesterol 0mg; Calcium 16mg; Fibre 0g; Sodium 4mg.
Kulfi Ice Cream Energy 347Kcal/1443kJ; Protein 14.7g; Carbohydrate 24.4g, of which sugars 24.1g; Fat 21.6g, of which saturates 10.4g; Cholesterol 53mg; Calcium 460mg; Fibre 0.8g; Sodium 228mg.

Dondurma Kaymalki

This sweet, pure white ice cream comes from the Middle East, where it is traditionally thickened with sahlab and flavoured with orange flower water and mastic, a resin used in chewing gum. As sahlab and mastic are both difficult to obtain in the West, cornflour and condensed milk have been used in this delicious version.

Serves 4–6
45ml/3 tbsp cornflour
  (cornstarch)
600ml/1 pint/2½ cups milk
213g/7½oz can sweetened
  condensed milk
15ml/1 tbsp clear honey
10ml/2 tsp orange flower water
a few sugared almonds, to serve

1 Put the cornflour in a pan and mix to a smooth paste with a little of the milk. Stir in the remaining milk and the condensed milk and bring the mixture to the boil, stirring until it has thickened and is smooth. Pour the mixture into a bowl.

2 Stir in the honey and orange flower water. Cover with a plate to prevent a skin forming, leave to cool, then chill.

3 Pour the mixture into a freezer container and freeze for 6–8 hours, beating twice with a fork, electric whisk or in a food processor to break up the ice crystals.

4 Alternatively, use an ice cream maker and churn the mixture until firm enough to scoop.

5 To serve, scoop the ice cream into dishes and serve with a few sugared almonds.

> **Cook's Tip**
> *If you have made the ice cream by hand, transfer it to the refrigerator 30 minutes before you are ready to scoop. Rose water can be used instead of orange flower water.*

Classic Italian Tiramisu

Tiramisu has become one of the principal desserts that people associate with Italy, its birthplace. The word "tiramisu" actually means "pick me up" in Italian and this rich coffee dessert is guaranteed to do just that. Tiramisu has many variations, with the only constant ingredient being the mascarpone, but this particular recipe is certainly a tasty version.

Serves 6–8
500g/1¼lb mascarpone
5 eggs, separated, at room
  temperature
90g/3½oz/½ cup caster
  (superfine) sugar
pinch of salt
savoyard or sponge fingers, for
  lining
120ml/4fl oz/½ cup strong
  espresso coffee
60ml/4 tbsp brandy or rum
  (optional)
cocoa powder (unsweetened),
  to sprinkle

1 Beat the mascarpone in a small bowl until soft. In a separate bowl, beat the egg yolks with the sugar (reserving 15ml/1 tbsp) until the mixture is pale yellow and fluffy. Gradually beat in the softened mascarpone.

2 Using an electric whisk or wire whisk, beat the egg whites with the salt until they form stiff peaks. Fold the egg whites into the mascarpone mixture.

3 Line one large or 6–8 individual serving dishes with a layer of sponge fingers.

4 Add the reserved sugar to the coffee, and stir in the brandy or rum, if using.

5 Sprinkle the coffee over the sponge lining: it should be moist but not saturated. Cover with half of the egg mixture. Add a layer of sponge fingers moistened with coffee, and cover with the remaining egg mixture.

6 Sprinkle with cocoa powder. Chill for at least 1 hour, preferably more, before serving.

Dondurma Kaymalki Energy 218Kcal/917kJ; Protein 6.4g; Carbohydrate 33g, of which sugars 26.1g; Fat 7.5g, of which saturates 4.8g; Cholesterol 27mg; Calcium 222mg; Fibre 0g; Sodium 97mg.
Tiramisu Energy 294Kcal/1231kJ; Protein 12.2g; Carbohydrate 27g, of which sugars 21.4g; Fat 14.3g, of which saturates 7.1g; Cholesterol 202mg; Calcium 43mg; Fibre 0.2g; Sodium 65mg.

Iced Tiramisu

This favourite Italian combination is not usually served as a frozen dessert, but in fact it does make a marvellous ice cream.

Serves 4
150g/5oz/³⁄₄ cup caster
    (superfine) sugar
150ml/¼ pint/²⁄₃ cup water
250g/9oz/generous 1 cup
    mascarpone
200g/7oz/scant 1 cup virtually
    fat-free fromage frais or cream
    cheese
5ml/1 tsp vanilla extract
10ml/2 tsp instant coffee,
    dissolved in 30ml/2 tbsp
    boiling water
30ml/2 tbsp coffee liqueur or
    brandy
75g/3oz sponge fingers
cocoa powder (unsweetened) and
    chocolate curls, to decorate

1 Put 115g/4oz/generous ½ cup of the sugar into a small pan. Add the water and bring to the boil, stirring until the sugar has dissolved. Leave the syrup to cool, then chill.

2 Put the mascarpone into a bowl. Beat with a spoon until it is soft, then stir in the fromage frais. Add the chilled sugar syrup, a little at a time, then stir in the vanilla extract.

3 Spoon the mixture into a freezer container and freeze for 4 hours, beating twice with a fork, electric whisk or in a food processor to break up the ice crystals. Alternatively, use an ice cream maker and churn the mascarpone mixture until it is thick but too soft to scoop.

4 Meanwhile, put the coffee in a bowl, sweeten with the remaining sugar, then add the liqueur. Stir well, then cool. Crumble the sponge fingers and toss in the coffee mixture.

5 Spoon a third of the ice cream into a 900ml/1½ pint/3¾ cup freezer container, spoon over half the crumbled sponge, then top with half the remaining ice cream. Sprinkle over the rest of the crumbled sponge, then cover with the remaining ice cream.

6 Freeze for 2–3 hours until firm enough to scoop. Serve dusted with cocoa powder and decorated with chocolate curls.

Zabaglione

This airy Italian egg dish, fortified with sweet wine, is a traditional old Italian favourite. Said to have originated in the Venice region, it is usually eaten warm with biscuits (cookies) or fruit. If you serve it with fruit, then strawberries or raspberries are especially good choices.

Serves 3–4
3 egg yolks
40g/1½oz/3 tbsp caster
    (superfine) sugar
75ml/5 tbsp Marsala or white
    dessert wine
pinch of grated orange rind

1 In the top half of a double boiler, or in a heatproof bowl, away from the heat, whisk the egg yolks with the sugar until pale yellow.

2 Beat the Marsala or white dessert wine into the egg and sugar mixture.

3 Place the pan or bowl over a pan of simmering water and continue whisking for 6–8 minutes, or until the custard is a frothy, light mass and evenly coats the back of a spoon. Take care that you do not let the upper container touch the hot water, or the zabaglione may curdle.

4 Stir in the orange rind.

5 Spoon into individual dishes and serve immediately.

> **Variations**
> • Add a little ground cinnamon with the Marsala, if you like.
> • Grated lemon rind or a drop of vanilla extract may be added for flavouring instead of orange rind.
> • Substitute a mixture of 15ml/1 tbsp Kirsch, Chartreuse, brandy, rum or Kümmel and 60ml/4 tbsp white wine for the Marsala or dessert wine.

Iced Tiramisu Energy 362Kcal/1526kJ; Protein 11.7g; Carbohydrate 54.5g, of which sugars 50.3g; Fat 10.5g, of which saturates 6.1g; Cholesterol 69mg; Calcium 78mg; Fibre 0.2g; Sodium 35mg.
Zabaglione Energy 108Kcal/452kJ; Protein 2.3g; Carbohydrate 12.9g, of which sugars 12.9g; Fat 4.1g, of which saturates 1.2g; Cholesterol 151mg; Calcium 26mg; Fibre 0g; Sodium 10mg.

Caribbean Chocolate Ring with Rum Syrup

This delectable dish brings you a taste of the Caribbean.

Serves 8–10
115g/4oz/½ cup unsalted (sweet) butter, plus extra for greasing
115g/4oz/scant ½ cup light muscovado (brown) sugar
2 eggs, beaten
2 ripe bananas, mashed
30ml/2 tbsp desiccated (dry unsweetened shredded) coconut
30ml/2 tbsp sour cream
115g/4oz/1 cup self-raising (self-rising) flour
45ml/3 tbsp cocoa powder (unsweetened)
2.5ml/½ tsp bicarbonate of soda (baking soda)

For the syrup
115g/4oz/generous ½ cup caster (superfine) sugar
60ml/4 tbsp water
30ml/2 tbsp dark rum
50g/2oz plain (semisweet) chocolate, chopped
mixture of tropical fruits and chocolate shapes or curls, to decorate

1 Preheat the oven to 180°C/350°F/Gas 4. Grease a 1.5 litre/ 2½ pint/6¼ cup ring tin (pan) with butter.

2 Cream the butter and sugar in a bowl until light and fluffy. Add the eggs gradually, beating well, then mix in the bananas, coconut and sour cream. Sift the flour, cocoa and bicarbonate of soda over the mixture and fold in thoroughly.

3 Transfer to the prepared tin and spread evenly. Bake for 45–50 minutes, until firm to the touch. Cool for 10 minutes in the tin, then turn out to finish cooling on a wire rack.

4 Make the syrup. Place the sugar in a small pan. Add the water and heat gently, stirring occasionally until dissolved. Bring to the boil and boil rapidly, without stirring, for 2 minutes. Remove from the heat.

5 Add the rum and chocolate to the syrup and stir until smooth, then spoon evenly over the top and sides of the cake. Decorate the ring with tropical fruits and chocolate shapes.

Old English Trifle

A wonderful combination of fruit, custard and cake laced with alcohol, this traditional English dessert is always popular.

Serves 6
75g/3oz day-old sponge cake, broken into bite-size pieces
8 ratafia biscuits (almond macaroons), broken into halves
100ml/3½fl oz/scant ½ cup medium sherry
30ml/2 tbsp brandy
350g/12oz prepared fruit such as raspberries, strawberries or peaches
300ml/½ pint/1¼ cups double (heavy) cream
40g/1½oz/⅓ cup toasted flaked (sliced) almonds
strawberries, to decorate

For the custard
4 egg yolks
25g/1oz/2 tbsp caster (superfine) sugar
450ml/¾ pint/scant 2 cups single (light) or whipping cream
few drops of vanilla extract

1 Put the sponge cake and ratafia biscuits in a glass serving dish, then sprinkle over the sherry and brandy and leave until the liquid has been absorbed.

2 Make the custard. Whisk the egg yolks and sugar together. Bring the cream to the boil in a heavy pan, then pour on to the egg yolk mixture, stirring constantly.

3 Return the mixture to the pan and heat very gently, stirring all the time with a wooden spoon, until the custard thickens enough to coat the back of the spoon; do not allow to boil. Leave to cool, stirring occasionally.

4 Arrange the fruit in an even layer over the soaked sponge cake in the serving dish, then strain the custard over the fruit and leave to set.

5 Lightly whip the cream, spread it over the custard, then chill the trifle well. Decorate with flaked almonds and strawberries just before serving.

Caribbean Choc. Ring Energy 315Kcal/1319kJ; Protein 4g; Carbohydrate 40.5g, of which sugars 31g; Fat 15.6g, of which saturates 9.7g; Cholesterol 65mg; Calcium 72mg; Fibre 1.6g; Sodium 172mg.
Trifle Energy 632Kcal/2616kJ; Protein 8.4g; Carbohydrate 24.9g, of which sugars 18.4g; Fat 53.1g, of which saturates 28.4g; Cholesterol 258mg; Calcium 155mg; Fibre 1.4g; Sodium 116mg.

Frozen French Raspberry Mousse

Fill the centre of this lovely French dessert with extra raspberries, if you like.

Serves 6

350g/12oz/2 cups raspberries
40g/1½oz/3 tbsp icing (confectioners') sugar
2 egg whites
1.5ml/¼ tsp cream of tartar
90g/3½oz/scant ½ cup granulated sugar
25ml/1½ tbsp lemon juice
250ml/8fl oz/1 cup whipping cream
15ml/1 tbsp framboise or Kirsch
fresh mint leaves, to decorate

1 Put the raspberries in a food processor fitted with a metal blade and process until smooth. Press through a sieve (strainer).

2 Pour about a third of the purée into a small bowl, stir in the icing sugar, then cover and chill. Reserve the remaining purée for the mousse.

3 Half-fill a medium pan with hot water and place over a low heat (do not allow the water to boil). Combine the egg whites, cream of tartar, sugar and lemon juice in a heatproof bowl that just fits into the pan without touching the water. Using an electric whisk, beat at medium-high speed until the beaters leave tracks on the base of the bowl, then beat at high speed for about 7 minutes until the mixture is very thick and forms stiff peaks.

4 Remove the bowl from the pan and continue beating the egg white mixture for a further 2–3 minutes until it is cool. Fold in the reserved raspberry purée.

5 Whip the cream until it forms soft peaks and fold gently into the raspberry mixture with the framboise or Kirsch. Spoon into a 1.4 litre/2½ pint/6 cup ring mould, then cover and freeze for at least 4 hours or overnight.

6 To unmould, dip the mould in warm water for about 5 seconds and turn the mousse out on to a plate. Decorate with mint sprigs and serve with the sweetened raspberry purée.

Peach & Ginger Pashka

A low-fat version of the Russian Easter favourite – a glorious cheese dessert flavoured with peaches and preserved stem ginger.

Serves 4

350g/12oz/1½ cups low-fat cottage cheese
2 ripe peaches or nectarines
90g/3½oz/scant ½ cup low-fat natural (plain) yogurt
2 pieces preserved stem ginger in syrup, drained and chopped, plus 30ml/2 tbsp syrup from the jar
2.5ml/½ tsp vanilla extract

To decorate

1 peach or nectarine, peeled and sliced
10ml/2 tsp slivered almonds, toasted

1 Drain the cottage cheese and rub it through a fine sieve (strainer) into a bowl. Remove the stones (pits) from the peaches or nectarines and roughly chop.

2 Mix together the chopped peaches or nectarines in a large bowl with the low-fat cottage cheese, yogurt, preserved stem ginger, syrup and vanilla extract.

3 Line a new, clean flower pot or a sieve (strainer) with a piece of clean, fine cloth, such as muslin (cheesecloth).

4 Add the cheese mixture and wrap over the cloth to cover. Place a saucer on top and weigh down. Stand over a bowl in a cool place and leave to drain overnight.

5 To serve, unwrap the cloth and turn the pashka out on to a serving plate. Decorate the pashka with peach or nectarine slices and toasted almonds.

> **Cook's Tip**
> Rather than making one large pashka, line four to six cups or ramekins with the clean cloth or muslin (cheesecloth) and divide the mixture evenly among them.

Raspberry Mousse Energy 271Kcal/1135kJ; Protein 2.7g; Carbohydrate 27.3g, of which sugars 27.3g; Fat 17g, of which saturates 10.6g; Cholesterol 44mg; Calcium 51mg; Fibre 1.5g; Sodium 34mg.
Pashka Energy 157Kcal/660kJ; Protein 13.3g; Carbohydrate 14.7g, of which sugars 14.6g; Fat 5.1g, of which saturates 2.3g; Cholesterol 14mg; Calcium 165mg; Fibre 1g; Sodium 302mg.

Chilled Fruity Zucotto Sponge

An Italian-style dessert with a rich ricotta, fruit, chocolate and nut filling, zucotto is encased in a moist, chocolate and liqueur-flavoured sponge.

Serves 8
3 eggs
75g/3oz/6 tbsp caster
  (superfine) sugar
75g/3oz/⅔ cup plain
  (all-purpose) flour
25g/1oz/¼ cup cocoa powder
  (unsweetened)
90ml/6 tbsp Kirsch
250g/9oz/generous 1 cup
  ricotta cheese

50g/2oz/½ cup icing
  (confectioners') sugar
50g/2oz plain (semisweet)
  chocolate, finely chopped
50g/2oz/½ cup blanched
  almonds, chopped and toasted
75g/3oz/scant ½ cup natural
  glacé (candied) cherries,
  quartered
2 pieces preserved stem ginger,
  finely chopped
150ml/¼ pint/⅔ cup double
  (heavy) cream
cocoa powder (unsweetened), for
  dusting

1 Preheat the oven to 180°C/350°F/Gas 4. Grease and line a 23cm/9in cake tin (pan). Whisk the eggs and sugar in a heatproof bowl over a pan of simmering water until the whisk leaves a trail. Remove the bowl from the heat and continue to whisk the mixture for 2 minutes.

2 Sift the flour and cocoa into the bowl and fold it in with a large metal spoon. Spoon the mixture into the prepared tin and bake for about 20 minutes until just firm. Leave to cool.

3 Cut the cake horizontally into three layers. Set aside 30ml/ 2 tbsp of the Kirsch. Drizzle the remaining Kirsch over the layers.

4 Beat the ricotta cheese in a bowl until softened, then beat in the icing sugar, chopped chocolate, toasted almonds, cherries, stem ginger and reserved Kirsch.

5 Pour the cream into a separate bowl and whip it lightly. Using a large metal spoon, fold the cream into the ricotta mixture. Chill. Cut a 20cm/8in circle from one sponge layer, using a plate as a guide, and set it aside.

6 Use the remaining sponge to make the case for the zucotto. Cut the cake to fit the bottom of a 2.8–3.4 litre/5–6 pint/ 12½–15 cup freezerproof mixing bowl. Cut more sponge for the sides of the bowl, fitting the pieces together and taking them about one-third of the way up.

7 Spoon the ricotta filling into the bowl up to the height of the sponge, and level the surface.

8 Fit the reserved circle of sponge on top of the filling. Trim off the excess sponge around the edges. Cover the bowl and freeze overnight.

9 Transfer the zucotto to the refrigerator 45 minutes before serving, so that the filling softens slightly. Invert it on to a serving plate and peel away the clear film (plastic wrap). Dust with cocoa powder and serve immediately in slices.

Coconut Rice with Fruit Coulis

Desserts similar to this coconut treat are served in countries all over the Far East, often accompanied by fresh tropical fruit, such as mangoes, pineapple and guavas.

Serves 4–6
75g/3oz/scant ½ cup jasmine
  rice, soaked overnight in
  175ml/6fl oz/¾ cup water
350ml/12fl oz/1½ cups
  coconut milk

150ml/¼ pint/⅔ cup single
  (light) cream
50g/2oz/¼ cup caster
  (superfine) sugar
raspberries and fresh mint leaves,
  to decorate

For the coulis
75g/3oz/¾ cup blackcurrants,
  stalks removed
25g/1oz/2 tbsp caster
  (superfine) sugar
75g/3oz/½ cup fresh or
  frozen raspberries

1 Put the rice and its soaking water into a food processor and process for a few minutes until the mixture is soupy.

2 Heat the coconut milk and cream in a non-stick pan. When the mixture is on the point of boiling, stir in the rice mixture. Cook over a very gentle heat for 10 minutes, stirring constantly.

3 Stir the sugar into the coconut rice mixture and continue cooking for a further 10–15 minutes, or until thick and creamy.

4 Line a rectangular tin (pan) with non-stick baking parchment. Pour the coconut rice mixture into the pan, cool, then chill in the refrigerator until the dessert is set and firm.

5 Meanwhile, make the coulis. Put the blackcurrants in a bowl and sprinkle with the sugar. Set aside for 30 minutes. Turn the blackcurrants and raspberries into a sieve (strainer) set over a bowl. Using a spoon, press the fruit so that the juices collect in the bowl. Taste the coulis and add more sugar if necessary.

6 Cut the coconut cream into diamonds. Spoon a little coulis on to individual plates, arrange the diamonds on top and decorate with raspberries and mint leaves. Serve immediately.

Zucotto Sponge Energy 391Kcal/1631kJ; Protein 8.7g; Carbohydrate 33.8g, of which sugars 26.1g; Fat 22.7g, of which saturates 11.4g; Cholesterol 111mg; Calcium 66mg; Fibre 1.4g; Sodium 64mg.
Coconut Rice Energy 165Kcal/696kJ; Protein 2.3g; Carbohydrate 28.7g, of which sugars 18.8g; Fat 5.1g, of which saturates 3.2g; Cholesterol 14mg; Calcium 59mg; Fibre 0.8g; Sodium 73mg.

Coconut Custard

This traditional dessert
from South-east Asia can
be baked or steamed and
is often served with sweet
sticky rice and a selection
of fresh fruit. Mangoes and
tamarillos go particularly
well with the flavours.

Serves 4
4 eggs
75g/3oz/6 tbsp soft light brown
  sugar
250ml/8fl oz/1 cup coconut milk
5ml/1 tsp vanilla, rose or
  jasmine extract
fresh mint leaves and icing
  (confectioners') sugar,
  to decorate
sliced fruit, to serve

1 Preheat the oven to 150°C/300°F/Gas 2. Whisk the eggs and
sugar in a bowl until smooth. Add the coconut milk and extract
and whisk well.

2 Strain the mixture into a jug (pitcher), then pour it into four
individual heatproof glasses or ramekins or an ovenproof dish.

3 Stand the glasses, ramekins or dish in a roasting pan. Fill the
pan with hot water to reach halfway up the sides of the glasses,
ramekins or dish.

4 Bake for about 35–40 minutes, or until the custards are set.
Test with a fine skewer or cocktail stick (toothpick).

5 Remove the roasting pan from the oven, lift out the glasses,
ramekins or dish and leave to cool.

6 If you like, turn out the custard(s) on to serving plate(s).
Decorate with the mint leaves and a dusting of icing sugar, and
serve with sliced fruit.

Cook's Tip
*Before turning out the custard(s), first ease the edge of the
custard away from the side of the dish with a sharp knife.*

Zabaglione Ice Cream Torte

For anyone who likes
zabaglione, the famous,
whisked Italian dessert, this
simple iced version is an
absolute must! Its taste and
texture are just as good, and
there's no last-minute
whisking to worry about.

Serves 10
175g/6oz amaretti
115g/4oz/1½ cup ready-to-eat
  dried apricots, finely chopped

65g/2½oz/5 tbsp unsalted
  (sweet) butter, melted

For the ice cream
65g/2½oz/5 tbsp light
  muscovado (brown) sugar
75ml/5 tbsp water
5 egg yolks
250ml/8fl oz/1 cup
  double (heavy) cream
75ml/5 tbsp Madeira or cream
  sherry
poached fruit, to serve

1 Put the amaretti in a strong plastic bag and crush finely with a
rolling pin. Turn into a bowl and stir in the apricots and melted
butter until evenly combined.

2 Using a dampened spoon, pack the mixture on to the
bottom and up the sides of a 24cm/9½in loose-based flan tin
(tart pan) about 4cm/1½in deep. Chill.

3 Make the ice cream. Put the sugar and water in a small, heavy
pan and heat, stirring, until the sugar has dissolved. Bring to the
boil and boil for 2 minutes without stirring.

4 Whisk the egg yolks in a heatproof bowl until pale, then
gradually whisk in the sugar syrup. Put the bowl over a pan of
simmering water and continue to whisk for about 10 minutes
or until the mixture leaves a trail when the whisk is lifted.

5 Remove from the heat and carry on whisking for a further
5 minutes or until the mixture is cold. In a separate bowl, whip
the cream with the Madeira or sherry until it stands in peaks.

6 Using a large metal spoon, fold the cream into the whisked
mixture. Spoon it into the lined tin, level the surface, cover and
freeze overnight. Serve sliced, with a little poached fruit.

Coconut Custard Energy 161Kcal/681kJ; Protein 6.5g; Carbohydrate 22.7g, of which sugars 22.7g; Fat 5.7g, of which saturates 1.7g; Cholesterol 190mg; Calcium 57mg; Fibre 0g; Sodium 140mg.
Zabaglione Torte Energy 333Kcal/1387kJ; Protein 3.4g; Carbohydrate 25.8g, of which sugars 18.2g; Fat 23.9g, of which saturates 13.6g; Cholesterol 149mg; Calcium 60mg; Fibre 1g; Sodium 110mg.

French Chocolate Soufflés

These stylish French soufflés are actually extremely easy to make.

Serves 6
175g/6oz plain (semisweet) chocolate, chopped
150g/5oz/10 tbsp unsalted (sweet) butter, cut into small pieces
4 large (US extra large) eggs, separated
30ml/2 tbsp orange liqueur (optional)
1.5ml/¼ tsp cream of tartar
40g/1½oz/3 tbsp caster (superfine) sugar
icing (confectioners') sugar, for dusting
sprigs of redcurrants and white chocolate roses, to decorate

For the sauce
75g/3oz white chocolate, chopped
90ml/6 tbsp whipping cream
15–30ml/1–2 tbsp orange liqueur
grated rind of ½ orange

1 Generously butter six 150ml/¼ pint/⅔ cup ramekins, custard cups or small ovenproof dishes. Sprinkle each with a little sugar and tap out any excess. Place the dishes on a baking sheet.

2 Melt the chocolate and butter in a heavy pan over a very low heat, stirring until smooth. Remove from the heat and cool slightly, then beat in the egg yolks and orange liqueur, if using. Set aside, stirring occasionally.

3 Preheat the oven to 220°C/425°F/Gas 7. In a grease-free bowl, whisk the egg whites slowly until frothy. Add the cream of tartar, increase the speed and whisk to form soft peaks. Gradually whisk in the sugar until the whites are stiff and glossy. Stir a third of the whites into the cooled chocolate mixture, then fold this into the remaining whites. Spoon into the dishes.

4 Make the sauce. Put the white chocolate and cream in a small pan. Place over a low heat and cook, stirring constantly until smooth. Remove from the heat and stir in the liqueur and orange rind, then pour into a serving jug (pitcher); keep warm.

5 Bake the soufflés for 10–12 minutes until risen and set, but still slightly wobbly in the centre. Dust with icing sugar and decorate with redcurrants and chocolate roses. Serve with the sauce.

Crema Catalana

This fabulous Spanish dessert consists of a creamy custard topped with a net of brittle sugar – a Spanish variation on the theme of the crème brûlée. *Cremat* is the Catalan word for "burnt", and this was probably part of this dish's original name.

Serves 4
475ml/16fl oz/2 cups milk
pared rind of ½ lemon
1 cinnamon stick
4 large (US extra large) egg yolks
105ml/7 tbsp caster (superfine) sugar
25ml/1½ tbsp cornflour (cornstarch)
ground nutmeg, for sprinkling

1 Put the milk in a pan with the lemon rind and cinnamon stick. Bring to the boil, then simmer for 10 minutes. Remove the lemon rind and cinnamon. Put the egg yolks and 45ml/3 tbsp sugar in a bowl, and whisk until pale yellow. Add the cornflour and mix well.

2 Stir a few tablespoons of the hot milk into the egg yolk mixture, then pour back into the remaining milk. Return to the heat and cook gently, stirring, for about 5 minutes, until thickened and smooth. Do not boil.

3 Pour the custard into four shallow ovenproof dishes, measuring about 13cm/5in in diameter. Cool, then chill for a few hours, until firm.

4 No more than 30 minutes before you intend to serve the desserts, sprinkle the top of each one with 15ml/1 tbsp of the sugar and a little nutmeg.

5 Preheat the grill (broiler) to high. Place the dishes under the grill, on the highest shelf, and cook until the sugar caramelizes. This will take only a few seconds and they will caramelize unevenly, but this is normal. Do not leave them under the grill for too long in an attempt to make the effect even.

6 Leave the custards to cool for a few minutes before serving.

Chocolate Soufflés Energy 543Kcal/2256kJ; Protein 7.1g; Carbohydrate 35g, of which sugars 34.7g; Fat 42.3g, of which saturates 25g; Cholesterol 198mg; Calcium 80mg; Fibre 0.7g; Sodium 218mg.
Crema Catalana Energy 241Kcal/1020kJ; Protein 7.1g; Carbohydrate 38.8g, of which sugars 33g; Fat 7.6g, of which saturates 2.9g; Cholesterol 209mg; Calcium 181mg; Fibre 0g; Sodium 65mg.

Classic Crème Brûlée

This dessert actually originated in Cambridge, England, but has become associated with France and is widely eaten there. Add a little liqueur, if you like, but it is equally delicious without it.

Serves 6
1 vanilla pod (bean)
1 litre/1¾ pints/4 cups double (heavy) cream
6 egg yolks
90g/3½oz/½ cup caster (superfine) sugar
30ml/2 tbsp almond or orange liqueur (optional)
75g/3oz/6 tbsp soft light brown sugar

1 Preheat the oven to 150°C/300°F/Gas 2. Place six 120ml/4fl oz/½ cup ramekins, custard cups or small ovenproof dishes in a roasting pan and set aside.

2 With a small sharp knife, split the vanilla pod lengthways and scrape the black seeds into a medium pan. Add the cream and bring just to the boil over a medium heat, stirring. Remove from the heat and cover. Set aside for 15–20 minutes.

3 In a bowl, whisk the egg yolks, caster sugar and liqueur, if using, until well blended. Whisk in the hot cream and strain into a large jug (pitcher). Divide the custard among the dishes.

4 Pour enough boiling water into the roasting pan to come halfway up the sides of the dishes. Cover the pan with foil and bake for about 30 minutes until the custards are just set. Remove from the pan and leave to cool. Return to the dry roasting pan and chill.

5 Preheat the grill (broiler). Sprinkle the sugar evenly over the surface of each custard and grill (broil) for 30–60 seconds until the sugar melts and caramelizes. Do not let the sugar burn or allow the custard to curdle.

6 Place in the refrigerator to set the crust and chill completely before serving.

Crème Caramel

One of the most popular French desserts, this is a slightly lighter version of the traditional recipe.

Serves 6–8
250g/9oz/1¼ cups granulated sugar
60ml/4 tbsp water
1 vanilla pod (bean) or 10ml/2 tsp vanilla extract
400ml/14fl oz/1⅔ cups milk
250ml/8fl oz/1 cup whipping cream
5 large (US extra large) eggs
2 egg yolks

1 Put 175g/6oz/¾ cup of the sugar in a small heavy pan with the water to moisten. Bring to the boil over a high heat, swirling the pan to dissolve the sugar. Boil, without stirring, for 4–5 minutes until the syrup turns a dark caramel colour.

2 Immediately pour the caramel into a 1 litre/1¾ pint/4 cup soufflé dish. Holding the dish with oven gloves, quickly swirl the dish to coat the base and sides with the caramel and set aside. (The caramel will harden quickly.) Place in a roasting pan.

3 Preheat the oven to 160°C/325°F/Gas 3. With a knife, split the vanilla pod lengthways and scrape the black seeds into a medium pan. Add the milk and cream and bring just to the boil over a medium-high heat, stirring frequently. Remove the pan from the heat, cover and set aside for 15–20 minutes.

4 In a bowl, whisk the eggs and egg yolks with the remaining sugar for 2–3 minutes until creamy. Whisk in the hot milk and carefully strain the mixture into the lined dish. Cover with foil.

5 Pour enough boiling water into the roasting pan to come halfway up the sides of the filled dish. Bake the custard for 40–45 minutes until just set. Remove from the roasting pan and cool for at least 30 minutes, then chill overnight.

6 Run a sharp knife around the edge of the dish, cover with a serving plate, hold together tightly and invert. Lift one edge of the dish, allowing the caramel to run out, then remove the dish.

Crème Brûlée Energy 996Kcal/4116kJ; Protein 5.7g; Carbohydrate 31.6g, of which sugars 31.6g; Fat 95g, of which saturates 57.2g; Cholesterol 430mg; Calcium 120mg; Fibre 0g; Sodium 47mg.
Crème Caramel Energy 326Kcal/1367kJ; Protein 7.1g; Carbohydrate 35.9g, of which sugars 35.9g; Fat 18.3g, of which saturates 9.8g; Cholesterol 205mg; Calcium 118mg; Fibre 0g; Sodium 77mg.

Baked Apples with Marsala

In this recipe, the famous fortified wine from Italy – Marsala – is cooked down with the juice from the apples and the butter to make a rich, sticky sauce. For a truly indulgent dessert treat, serve up these delicious Italian-style apples with a spoonful of extra-thick cream.

Serves 6
4 medium cooking apples
50g/2oz/⅓ cup ready-to-eat
    dried figs
150ml/¼ pint/⅔ cup Marsala
50g/2oz/¼ cup butter, softened

1 Preheat the oven to 180°C/350°F/Gas 4. Using an apple corer, carefully remove the cores from the centre of the apples and discard.

2 Place the apples in a small, shallow baking dish and stuff the figs into the hollows of each apple.

3 Top each apple with a quarter of the butter and pour over the Marsala.

4 Cover the dish tightly with foil and bake in the preheated oven for 30 minutes.

5 Remove the foil from the apples and bake for a further 10 minutes, or until the apples are tender and the juices have reduced slightly.

6 Serve immediately with any remaining pan juices drizzled over the top.

Variation
Substitute vin santo for the Marsala for a different, but equally rich, flavour. Literally holy wine, vin santo is an intensely aromatic dessert wine from Veneto and Tuscany in Italy.

Roast Peaches with Amaretto

This lovely dish from Italy is an excellent dessert to serve in summer, when peaches are at their juiciest and most fragrant. The apricot and almond flavour of the amaretto liqueur subtly enhances the sweet, fruity taste of ripe peaches.

Serves 4
4 ripe peaches
45ml/3 tbsp Amaretto di
    Saronno liqueur
45ml/3 tbsp clear honey
crème fraîche or whipped cream,
    to serve

1 Preheat the oven to 190°C/375°F/Gas 5. Cut the peaches in half and remove the stones (pits).

2 Place the peaches, cut side up, in a roasting pan. In a small bowl, mix the amaretto liqueur with the honey, and drizzle over the halved peaches, covering them evenly.

3 Bake the peaches in the preheated oven for 20–25 minutes, or until tender. Place two peach halves on each individual plate and drizzle with the pan juices. Serve immediately with crème fraîche or whipped cream.

Cook's Tips
• If you are having difficulty removing the stones (pits), use a small sharp knife to help prise them out, but take care not to damage the peach flesh.
• You can cook these peaches over a barbecue. Place them on sheets of foil, drizzle over liqueur, then scrunch the foil around them to seal. Cook for 15–20 minutes.

Variation
Nectarines are also delicious served in this way. To ring the changes, use a different flavoured liqueur – orange liqueur, such as Grand Marnier, would work well.

Baked Apples Energy 134Kcal/560kJ; Protein 0.5g; Carbohydrate 11.1g, of which sugars 11.1g; Fat 7g, of which saturates 4.3g; Cholesterol 18mg; Calcium 24mg; Fibre 1.3g; Sodium 57mg.
Roast Peaches Energy 98Kcal/418kJ; Protein 1.2g; Carbohydrate 20.7g, of which sugars 20.7g; Fat 0.1g, of which saturates 0g; Cholesterol 0mg; Calcium 9mg; Fibre 1.7g; Sodium 4mg.

Australian Hazelnut Pavlova

This dessert dish is created from meringue – enhanced with the added interest of hazelnuts – topped with a mixture of fresh fruits and cream. A delicious Australian speciality.

Serves 4–6

3 egg whites
175g/6oz/3/4 cup caster (superfine) sugar
5ml/1 tsp cornflour (cornstarch)
5ml/1 tsp white wine vinegar
40g/1 1/2oz/5 tbsp chopped roasted hazelnuts
250ml/8fl oz/1 cup double (heavy) cream
15ml/1 tbsp orange juice
30ml/2 tbsp natural (plain) thick and creamy yogurt
2 ripe nectarines, stoned (pitted) and sliced
225g/8oz/1 1/3 cups raspberries
15–30ml/1–2 tbsp redcurrant jelly, warmed

1 Preheat the oven to 140°C/275°F/Gas 1. Lightly grease a baking sheet. Draw a 20cm/8in circle on a sheet of baking parchment. Place pencil-side down on the baking sheet.

2 Place the egg whites in a clean, grease-free bowl and whisk with an electric whisk until stiff.

3 Whisk in the sugar 15ml/1 tbsp at a time, whisking well after each addition.

4 Add the cornflour, vinegar and hazelnuts and fold in carefully with a large metal spoon.

5 Spoon the meringue on to the marked circle and spread out, making a dip in the centre.

6 Bake for about 1 1/4–1 1/2 hours, until crisp. Leave to cool, then transfer to a serving platter.

7 Whip the cream and orange juice until just thick, stir in the yogurt and spoon on to the meringue.

8 Place the fruit on top of the cream and drizzle over the redcurrant jelly. Serve immediately.

Chocolate Fruit Fondue

Fondues originated in Switzerland and are best known as a way of enjoying various cheeses. However, the fondue is a very simple and tasty way of preparing all kinds of food and one that is ideally suited to sweet dishes. This particular version makes a fun dessert that also looks extremely attractive and appealing.

Serves 6–8

16 fresh strawberries
4 rings fresh pineapple, cut into wedges
2 small nectarines, stoned (pitted)
and cut into wedges
1 kiwi fruit, halved and thickly sliced
small bunch of black seedless grapes
2 bananas, chopped
1 small eating apple, cored and cut into wedges
lemon juice, for brushing
225g/8oz plain (semisweet) chocolate
15g/1/2oz/1 tbsp butter
150ml/1/4 pint/2/3 cup single (light) cream
45ml/3 tbsp Irish cream liqueur
15ml/1 tbsp chopped pistachio nuts

1 Arrange the fruit on a serving platter and brush the banana and apple pieces with a little lemon juice. Cover and chill.

2 Place the chocolate, butter, cream and liqueur in a bowl over a pan of simmering water. Stir until smooth.

3 Pour into a warmed serving bowl and sprinkle with the pistachio nuts.

4 To eat, guests skewer the fruits on to forks, then dip them into the hot sauce.

> **Variations**
> *Other delicious dippers for this fondue include cubes of sponge cake, sweet biscuits (cookies) such as amaretti, miniature marshmallows, ready-to-eat dried fruit, such as apricots, crêpes torn into pieces and popcorn.*

Hazelnut Pavlova Energy 411Kcal/1715kJ; Protein 4.6g; Carbohydrate 40.3g, of which sugars 39.4g; Fat 26.8g, of which saturates 14.3g; Cholesterol 57mg; Calcium 69mg; Fibre 1.9g; Sodium 49mg.
Chocolate Fondue Energy 305Kcal/1282kJ; Protein 3.6g; Carbohydrate 39.7g, of which sugars 38.9g; Fat 15.2g, of which saturates 8.1g; Cholesterol 16mg; Calcium 51mg; Fibre 2.7g; Sodium 37mg.

French Floating Islands

Bring a touch of French elegance to the table with delicate meringues floating on a vanilla custard.

Serves 4–6
1 vanilla pod (bean)
600ml/1 pint/2½ cups milk
8 egg yolks
50g/2oz/¼ cup granulated sugar

For the meringues
4 large (US extra large) egg whites
1.5ml/¼ tsp cream of tartar
225g/8oz/1 cup caster (superfine) sugar

For the caramel
150g/5oz/¾ cup granulated sugar
45ml/3 tbsp water

1 Split the vanilla pod lengthways and scrape the seeds into a pan. Add the milk and bring just to the boil over a medium heat, stirring frequently. Cover and set aside for 15–20 minutes.

2 In a medium bowl, whisk the egg yolks and sugar for 2–3 minutes until thick and creamy. Whisk in the hot milk and return the mixture to the pan. With a wooden spoon, stir over a medium-low heat until the sauce begins to thicken and coat the back of the spoon (do not allow to boil). Immediately strain into a chilled bowl, allow to cool, stirring occasionally and then chill.

3 Half-fill a large wide pan with water and bring just to simmering point. In a grease-free bowl, whisk the egg whites until frothy. Add the cream of tartar and continue whisking to form soft peaks. Gradually whisk in the sugar, until stiff and glossy.

4 Using two tablespoons, form egg-shaped meringues and poach for 2–3 minutes, turning once until just firm. Using a slotted spoon, transfer the meringues to a baking sheet lined with kitchen paper to drain.

5 Pour the cold custard into individual serving dishes and arrange the meringues on top. Put the sugar into a small pan with the water. Boil, without stirring, until the syrup turns a dark caramel colour. Immediately drizzle the caramel over the meringues and custard. Serve cold.

Peach Melba

The story goes that the great French chef, Auguste Escoffier, created this dessert in honour of the opera singer Nellie Melba.

Serves 6
50g/2oz/¼ cup caster (superfine) sugar
1 litre/1¾ pints/4 cups water
1 vanilla pod (bean), split
3 large peaches

For the sauce
450g/1lb/2⅔ cups fresh or frozen raspberries
15ml/1 tbsp lemon juice
25–40g/1–1½oz/2–3 tbsp caster (superfine) sugar
30–45ml/2–3 tbsp raspberry liqueur (optional)
vanilla ice cream, to serve
mint leaves and fresh raspberries, to decorate

1 Put the sugar, water and vanilla pod in a pan large enough to hold the peach halves in a single layer. Bring to the boil, over a medium heat, stirring occasionally to dissolve the sugar.

2 Cut the peaches in half and remove the peach stones (pits). Add the peach halves to the syrup, cut-sides down, adding more water, if needed, to cover the fruit. Press a piece of baking parchment against the surface, reduce the heat to medium-low, then cover and simmer for 12–15 minutes until tender – the time will depend on the ripeness of the fruit. Remove the pan from the heat and leave the peaches to cool in the syrup.

3 Remove the peaches from the syrup and peel off the skins. Place on several thicknesses of kitchen paper to drain (reserve the syrup for another use), then cover and chill.

4 Put the raspberries, lemon juice and sugar in a blender or food processor fitted with the metal blade. Process for 1 minute, scraping down the sides once. Press through a fine sieve (strainer) into a small bowl, then stir in the raspberry liqueur, if using, and put in the refrigerator to chill.

5 To serve, place a peach half, cut-side up, on a plate, fill with a scoop of ice cream and spoon the raspberry sauce over the top. Decorate with mint and a few fresh raspberries.

Floating Islands Energy 414Kcal/1755kJ; Protein 9.5g; Carbohydrate 78.7g, of which sugars 78.7g; Fat 9g, of which saturates 3.2g; Cholesterol 275mg; Calcium 190mg; Fibre 0g; Sodium 100mg.
Peach Melba Energy 93Kcal/398kJ; Protein 1.9g; Carbohydrate 22.2g, of which sugars 22.2g; Fat 0.3g, of which saturates 0.1g; Cholesterol 0mg; Calcium 31mg; Fibre 3g; Sodium 4mg.

Apple-Stuffed Crêpes

Spain's dairy country lies along the cooler northern coast and crêpes are extremely popular there. The Asturias, which run east to west along the coast, are apple and cider country, too, and crêpes, which are known as *frisuelos*, are made with a variety of sweet fillings, such as this succulent apple one.

Serves 4
115g/4oz/1 cup plain
  (all-purpose) flour
pinch of salt
2 large (US extra large) eggs
175ml/6fl oz/³/4 cup milk
120ml/4fl oz/¹/2 cup sweet
  (hard) cider
butter, for frying
4 eating apples
50g/2oz/¹/4 cup caster (superfine)
  sugar
120ml/8 tbsp clear honey
150ml/¹/4 pint/²/3 cup double
  (heavy) cream, to serve

Crêpes Suzette

These classic French crêpes are an absolute winner.

Serves 4
115g/4oz/1 cup plain
  (all-purpose) flour
1 egg
1 egg yolk
300ml/¹/2 pint/1¹/4 cups
  skimmed milk
15g/¹/2oz/1 tbsp unsalted (sweet)

butter, melted, plus extra butter
  for frying

For the sauce
25g/1oz/2 tbsp unsalted (sweet)
  butter
50g/2oz/¹/4 cup caster (superfine)
  sugar
juice of 2 oranges
juice of ¹/2 lemon
60ml/4 tbsp orange liqueur

1 Sift the flour into a bowl and make a well in the centre. Add the egg and the extra yolk to the well. Stir with a wooden spoon to incorporate the flour from around the edges. Gradually beat in the milk to form a smooth batter. Stir in the melted butter, transfer to a measuring jug (cup) and chill.

2 Heat a 20cm/8in shallow frying pan, add a little butter and heat until sizzling. Pour in a little of the batter, tilting the pan to cover the base thinly.

3 Cook the crêpes over a medium heat for 1–2 minutes until lightly browned underneath, then flip over and cook for 1 minute. Repeat this process until you have eight crêpes.

4 Make the sauce. Melt the butter in a heavy frying pan. Stir in the caster sugar and cook over a medium heat, tilting the pan occasionally, until the mixture is golden brown. Add the orange and lemon juices and stir until the caramel has dissolved.

5 Add a crêpe to the pan. Using kitchen tongs, fold it in half, then in half again. Slide to the side of the pan. Repeat with the remaining crêpes.

6 When all the crêpes have been folded in the sauce, pour over the liqueur and set it alight. Shake the pan until the flames die down. Divide the crêpes and sauce among individual plates.

1 Make the batter. Sift the flour and salt into a large bowl. Add the eggs and milk and beat until smooth. Stir in the cider. Leave to stand for 30 minutes.

2 Heat a small heavy non-stick frying pan. Add a little butter and ladle in enough batter to coat the pan thinly.

3 Cook the crêpe for about 1 minute until it is golden underneath, then flip it over and cook the other side until golden. Slide the crêpe on to a plate, then repeat with the remaining batter to make seven more. Set the crêpes aside and keep warm.

4 Make the apple filling. Cut the apples into quarters and remove the cores, then cut them into thick slices. Heat 15g/¹/2oz butter in a large frying pan. Add the apples to the pan and cook until golden on both sides. Transfer the slices to a bowl with a slotted spoon and sprinkle with sugar.

5 Fold each pancake in half, then fold in half again to form a cone. Fill each with some of the fried apples. Place two filled pancakes on each dessert plate. Drizzle each with 15ml/1 tbsp honey and serve at once, accompanied by cream.

Crêpes Suzette Energy 336Kcal/1410kJ; Protein 7.8g; Carbohydrate 44.6g, of which sugars 22.7g; Fat 11.6g, of which saturates 6.2g; Cholesterol 122mg; Calcium 156mg; Fibre 0.9g; Sodium 118mg.
Apple-Stuffed Crêpes Energy 411Kcal/1736kJ; Protein 7.8g; Carbohydrate 70.3g, of which sugars 48.4g; Fat 12.2g, of which saturates 6.5g; Cholesterol 119mg; Calcium 123mg; Fibre 2g; Sodium 123mg.

Chocolate Profiteroles

This mouth-watering dessert is served in cafés throughout France. Sometimes the profiteroles are filled with whipped cream instead of ice cream.

Serves 4–6
275g/10oz plain (semisweet) chocolate
120ml/4fl oz/½ cup warm water
750ml/1¼ pints/3 cups vanilla ice cream

For the profiteroles
110g/3¾oz/scant 1 cup plain (all-purpose) flour
1.5ml/¼ tsp salt
pinch of freshly grated nutmeg
75g/3oz/6 tbsp unsalted (sweet) butter, cut into 6 pieces, plus extra for greasing
175ml/6fl oz/¾ cup water
3 eggs

1 Preheat the oven to 200°C/400°F/Gas 6 and butter a baking sheet.

2 Make the profiteroles. Sift together the flour, salt and nutmeg. In a medium pan, bring the butter and the water to the boil. Remove from the heat and add the dry ingredients all at once. Beat with a wooden spoon for about 1 minute until blended and the mixture starts to pull away from the sides of the pan, then set the pan over a low heat and cook the mixture for about 2 minutes, beating constantly. Remove from the heat.

3 Beat one egg in a small bowl and set aside. Add the remaining eggs, one at a time, to the flour mixture, beating well. Add the beaten egg gradually until the dough is smooth and shiny; it should fall slowly when dropped from a spoon.

4 Using a tablespoon, drop the dough on to the baking sheet in 12 mounds. Bake for 25–30 minutes until the pastry is well risen and browned. Turn off the oven and leave the puffs to cool with the oven door open.

5 Melt the chocolate and warm water in a bowl over a pan of hot water. Split the profiteroles in half and put a small scoop of ice cream in each. Pour the sauce over the top and serve.

Middle Eastern Pestiños

The Arabs invented sweet bites like these to eat after the main course.

Makes about 30
225g/8oz/2 cups plain (all-purpose) flour, plus extra for dusting
60ml/4 tbsp sunflower oil
15ml/1 tbsp aniseed, lightly crushed
40g/1½oz/3 tbsp caster (superfine) sugar
250ml/8fl oz/1 cup water
60ml/4 tbsp anisette or other anis spirit, such as Ricard
3 small (US medium) eggs

For the anis syrup
60ml/4 tbsp clear honey
60ml/4 tbsp anisette or other anis spirit, such as Ricard

1 Preheat the oven to 190°C/375°F/Gas 5. Sift the flour on to a sheet of baking parchment. Heat the oil in a small pan with the crushed aniseed, until the aniseed releases its aroma. Strain the oil into a larger pan and add the sugar, water and anisette. Heat to a rolling boil.

2 Remove the pan from the heat and add the sifted flour, all in one go. Beat vigorously with a wooden spoon until the mixture leaves the sides of the pan clean. Leave to cool.

3 Meanwhile lightly beat the eggs. Gradually incorporate the egg into the dough mixture, beating hard. You may not need to use all the egg – the paste should be soft but not sloppy. Reserve any remaining beaten egg.

4 Grease and flour two baking sheets. Fit a plain nozzle to a piping (pastry) bag and pipe small rounds of dough about 2.5cm/1in across on the sheets, spacing them about 2.5cm/1in apart. Brush with the remaining beaten egg.

5 Bake for about 30 minutes, or until lightly brown and an even texture all the way through. (Lift one off the sheet to test.)

6 Make the syrup. Melt the honey in a small pan and stir in the anisette. Just before serving, use a slotted spoon to dunk the pestiños into the syrup.

Pestiños Energy 70Kcal/296kJ; Protein 1.3g; Carbohydrate 9.9g, of which sugars 4.2g; Fat 2.1g, of which saturates 0.3g; Cholesterol 19mg; Calcium 14mg; Fibre 0.2g; Sodium 8mg.
Profiteroles Energy 647Kcal/2707kJ; Protein 11.7g; Carbohydrate 68.2g, of which sugars 52.4g; Fat 36.9g, of which saturates 22.7g; Cholesterol 155mg; Calcium 182mg; Fibre 1.7g; Sodium 189mg.

Lemon Ricotta Cake

This delicious lemon dessert originated in Sardinia.

Serves 6–8

75g/3oz/6 tbsp butter, plus extra
   for greasing
175g/6oz/³⁄₄ cup granulated
   sugar
75g/3oz/generous ¹⁄₃ cup
   ricotta cheese
3 eggs, separated
175g/6oz/1½ cups plain
   (all-purpose) flour, plus extra
   for dusting
grated rind of 1 lemon
45ml/3 tbsp fresh lemon
   juice
7.5ml/1½ tsp baking powder
icing (confectioners') sugar, for
   dusting

1 Grease a 23cm/9in round cake or springform tin (pan). Line the bottom with baking parchment. Grease the paper with butter, then lightly dust with flour. Set aside. Preheat the oven to 180°C/350°F/Gas 4.

2 Cream the butter and sugar together until smooth. Beat in the ricotta cheese.

3 Beat in the egg yolks, one at a time. Add 30ml/2 tbsp of the flour, together with the lemon rind and juice. Sift the baking powder into the remaining flour and beat into the batter just until it is well blended.

4 In a grease-free bowl, beat the egg whites until they form stiff peaks. Fold them carefully into the batter.

5 Turn the mixture into the prepared tin. Bake for 45 minutes, or until a cake tester inserted in the centre of the cake comes out clean. Allow the cake to cool for 10 minutes before turning it out on to a rack to cool. Dust the cake generously with icing sugar before serving.

> **Cook's Tip**
> Serve this cake with single (light) cream and a bowl of summer fruit to make a delectable dessert.

Classic American Cheesecake

Popular throughout America, this type of cheesecake with a crumb base is simple to make and tastes wonderful. You can decorate the dish with fruit and serve it with cream, if you like, but it tastes delicious just as it is.

Serves 8

25g/1oz/½ cup digestive biscuit
   (graham cracker) crumbs
900g/2lb/4 cups cream cheese
250g/9oz/1¼ cups caster
   (superfine) sugar
grated rind of 1 lemon
45ml/3 tbsp fresh lemon juice
5ml/1 tsp vanilla extract
4 eggs, at room temperature

1 Preheat the oven to 160°C/325°F/Gas 3. Grease a 23cm/8in springform cake tin (pan). Place on a round of foil that is 13cm/5in larger than the diameter of the pan. Press the foil up the sides of the tin to seal tightly.

2 Sprinkle the crumbs in the base of the tin. Press to form an even layer.

3 With an electric whisk, beat the cream cheese until smooth. Add the sugar, lemon rind and juice and vanilla extract, and beat until blended. Beat in the eggs, one at a time. Beat just enough to blend thoroughly.

4 Pour the mixture into the prepared tin. Place the tin in a roasting pan and pour in enough hot water to come 2.5cm/1in up the side of the filled tin.

5 Bake for about 1½ hours until the top of the cake is golden brown. Remove from the roasting pan. Leave to cool in the tin.

6 Run a knife around the edge to loosen, then remove the rim of the tin. Chill for at least 4 hours before serving.

> **Cook's Tip**
> Make sure the foil is wrapped high enough up the tin's side.

Ricotta Cake Energy 275Kcal/1156kJ; Protein 5.4g; Carbohydrate 40.2g, of which sugars 23.5g; Fat 11.4g, of which saturates 6.4g; Cholesterol 95mg; Calcium 55mg; Fibre 0.7g; Sodium 85mg.
Cheesecake Energy 668Kcal/2772kJ; Protein 7g; Carbohydrate 34.8g, of which sugars 33.1g; Fat 56.9g, of which saturates 34.5g; Cholesterol 203mg; Calcium 144mg; Fibre 0.1g; Sodium 393mg.

Greek Honey & Lemon Cake

Capture the flavour of Greece with this luscious cake, drenched in honey and lemon juice. The semolina in the recipe gives the cake an excellent texture.

Makes 16 slices
40g/1½oz/3 tbsp sunflower
  margarine
60ml/4 tbsp clear honey
finely grated rind and juice
  of 1 lemon
150ml/½ pint/⅔ cup skimmed
  milk
150g/5oz/1¼ cups plain
  (all-purpose) flour
7.5ml/1½ tsp baking powder
2.5ml/½ tsp grated nutmeg
50g/2oz/⅓ cup semolina
2 egg whites
10ml/2 tsp sesame seeds

1 Preheat the oven to 200°C/400°F/Gas 6. Lightly oil a 19cm/7½in square deep cake tin (pan) and line the base with baking parchment.

2 Place the margarine and 45ml/3 tbsp of the honey in a pan and heat gently until melted. Reserve 15ml/1 tbsp lemon juice, then stir in the rest with the lemon rind and milk.

3 Stir together the flour, baking powder and nutmeg in a large mixing bowl, then add the milk mixture with the semolina. Beat well together.

4 Whisk the egg whites until they form soft peaks, then fold evenly into the semolina mixture.

5 Spoon into the tin and sprinkle with sesame seeds. Bake for 25–30 minutes, until golden brown.

6 Mix the reserved honey and lemon juice and drizzle over the cake while warm. Cool in the tin, then cut into fingers to serve.

> **Cook's Tip**
> Use Greek honey for an authentic touch, or use a good-quality, fragrant, flower-flavoured honey.

American Chocolate Cheesecake

This popular variation of the American classic is made with a crunchy cinnamon and chocolate base.

Serves 10–12
175g/6oz plain (semisweet)
  chocolate, chopped
115g/4oz dark (bittersweet)
  chocolate, chopped
1.2kg/2½lb/5 cups cream cheese,
  at room temperature
200g/7oz/1 cup caster
  (superfine) sugar
10ml/2 tsp vanilla extract
4 eggs, at room temperature
175ml/6fl oz/¾ cup sour
  cream

For the base
75g/3oz/1½ cups chocolate
  biscuit (cookie) crumbs
75g/3oz/6 tbsp butter, melted
2.5ml/½ tsp ground cinnamon

1 Preheat the oven to 180°C/350°F/Gas 4. Grease a 23cm/9in springform cake tin (pan).

2 Make the base. Mix the chocolate wafer crumbs with the butter and cinnamon. Press evenly over the bottom of the tin.

3 Melt the plain and dark chocolate in the top of a double boiler, or in a heatproof bowl set over hot water. Set aside.

4 With an electric whisk, beat the cream cheese until smooth, then beat in the sugar and vanilla extract. Add the eggs, one at a time, scraping the bowl with a spatula when necessary.

5 Add the sour cream to the cheese mixture, then stir in the melted chocolate, mixing well.

6 Pour into the tin. Bake for 1 hour. Allow to cool in the tin, then remove from the tin. Chill before serving.

> **Variation**
> For a chocolate-orange cheesecake, replace the vanilla extract with finely grated orange rind. Serve with sliced oranges coated in a light sugar syrup, flavoured with shredded orange rind.

Choc. Cheesecake Energy 717Kcal/2972kJ; Protein 5.2g; Carbohydrate 37.5g, of which sugars 34.9g; Fat 61.8g, of which saturates 38.4g; Cholesterol 118mg; Calcium 131mg; Fibre 0.7g; Sodium 362mg.
Honey & Lemon Cake Energy 80Kcal/339kJ; Protein 2g; Carbohydrate 13g, of which sugars 3.4g; Fat 2.6g, of which saturates 0.5g; Cholesterol 1mg; Calcium 30mg; Fibre 0.4g; Sodium 33mg.

Christmas Pudding

Christmas day wouldn't seem the same without this traditional British dessert. It is absolutely delicious served with brandy or rum butter, whisky sauce, custard or whipped cream. Top with a decorative sprig of holly for a festive touch.

Serves 8

115g/4oz/½ cup butter, plus extra for greasing
225g/8oz/generous 1 cup soft dark brown sugar
50g/2oz/½ cup self-raising (self-rising) flour
5ml/1 tsp mixed spice (pumpkin pie spice)
1.5ml/¼ tsp grated nutmeg
2.5ml/½ tsp ground cinnamon
2 eggs
115g/4oz/2 cups fresh white breadcrumbs
175g/6oz/1 cup sultanas (golden raisins)
175g/6oz/generous 1 cup raisins
115g/4oz/½ cup currants
25g/1oz/3 tbsp mixed (candied) peel, chopped finely
25g/1oz/¼ cup chopped almonds
1 small cooking apple, peeled, cored and coarsely grated
finely grated rind of 1 orange or lemon
juice of 1 orange or lemon, made up to 150ml/¼ pint/⅔ cup with brandy, rum or sherry

1 Cut a disc of baking parchment to fit the base of one 1.2 litre/2 pint/5 cup heatproof bowl or two 600ml/1 pint/2½ cup heatproof bowls and butter each disc and bowl.

2 Whisk the butter and sugar together until soft. Beat in the flour, spices and eggs. Stir in the remaining ingredients thoroughly. The mixture should have a soft dropping consistency.

3 Turn the mixture into the greased bowl(s) and level the top with a spoon. Cover neatly with another disc of buttered baking parchment.

4 Make a pleat across the centre of a large piece of baking parchment and cover the bowl(s) with it, tying it in place with string under the rim. Cut off the excess paper. Pleat a piece of foil in the same way and cover the bowl(s) with it, tucking it around the bowl neatly, under the paper frill. Tie another piece of string around and across the top, as a handle.

5 Place the bowl(s) in a steamer over a pan of simmering water and steam for 6 hours. Alternatively, put into a large pan and pour round enough boiling water to come halfway up the bowl(s) and cover the pan with a tight-fitting lid. Check the water is simmering and remember to top it up with boiling water as it evaporates.

6 When the pudding(s) have cooked, leave to cool completely. Then remove the foil and paper. Wipe the bowls(s) clean and replace the paper and foil with clean pieces, ready for reheating.

Cook's Tip
To reheat, steam for 2 hours. Turn on to a plate and leave to stand for 5 minutes, before removing the bowl (the steam will rise to the top and help to loosen the pudding). The dish can be made up to a month in advance; store in a cool, dry place.

Queen of Puddings

This hot pudding was developed from a seventeenth-century recipe by Queen Victoria's chefs and named in her honour.

Serves 4

75g/3oz/1½ cups fresh breadcrumbs
50g/2oz/¼ cup caster (superfine) sugar, plus 5ml/1 tsp grated rind of 1 lemon
600ml/1 pint/2½ cups milk
4 eggs
45ml/3 tbsp raspberry jam, warmed

1 Preheat the oven to 160°C/325°F/Gas 3. Stir the breadcrumbs, half of the sugar and the lemon rind together in a bowl. Bring the milk to the boil in a pan, then stir into the breadcrumb mixture.

2 Separate three of the eggs and beat the yolks with the whole egg. Stir into the breadcrumb mixture, pour into a buttered baking dish and leave to stand for 30 minutes, then bake the pudding for 50–60 minutes, until set.

3 Whisk the three egg whites in a large, clean grease-free bowl until stiff but not dry, then gradually whisk in the remaining sugar until the mixture is thick and glossy, taking care that you do not overwhisk.

4 Spread the jam over the pudding, then spoon over the meringue to cover the top completely.

5 Sprinkle the remaining sugar over the meringue, then bake for a further 15 minutes, until the meringue is beginning to turn a light golden colour.

Cook's Tip
Ring the changes by using another flavoured jam, lemon curd, marmalade or fruit purée.

Christmas Pudding Energy 530Kcal/2236kJ; Protein 6.3g; Carbohydrate 89.9g, of which sugars 74.4g; Fat 15.6g, of which saturates 8g; Cholesterol 78mg; Calcium 116mg; Fibre 2.2g; Sodium 259mg.
Queen of Puddings Energy 297Kcal/1259kJ; Protein 13.7g; Carbohydrate 45g, of which sugars 31g; Fat 8.5g, of which saturates 3.2g; Cholesterol 199mg; Calcium 242mg; Fibre 0.4g; Sodium 281mg.

Chestnut Pudding

This is an Italian speciality, made during the months of October and November, when fresh sweet chestnuts are gathered.

Serves 4–5

450g/1lb fresh sweet chestnuts
300ml/½ pint/1¼ cups milk
115g/4oz/generous ½ cup caster (superfine) sugar
2 eggs, separated, at room temperature
25g/1oz/¼ cup cocoa powder (unsweetened)
2.5ml/½ tsp vanilla extract
50g/2oz/½ cup icing (confectioners') sugar, sifted
whipped cream and marrons glacés (candied chestnuts), to decorate

1 Cut a cross in the side of the chestnuts, then drop them into a pan of boiling water. Cook for 5–6 minutes. Remove with a slotted spoon and peel while still warm.

2 Place the peeled chestnuts in a heavy or non-stick pan with the milk and half of the caster sugar. Cook over low heat, stirring occasionally, until soft. Remove from the heat and allow to cool, then press the pan contents through a sieve (strainer).

3 Preheat the oven to 180°C/350°F/Gas 4. Beat the egg yolks with the remaining caster sugar until the mixture is pale yellow and fluffy. Beat in the cocoa powder and the vanilla.

4 In a separate clean bowl, whisk the egg whites with a wire whisk or electric whisk until they form soft peaks. Gradually beat in the sifted icing sugar and continue beating until the mixture forms stiff peaks.

5 Fold the chestnut and egg yolk mixtures together. Fold in the egg whites. Turn the mixture into one large or several individual buttered ovenproof moulds or bowls. Place on a baking sheet and bake in the oven for 12–20 minutes, depending on the size.

6 Remove the moulds or bowls from the oven. Allow to cool for 10 minutes then carefully turn out. Serve decorated with whipped cream and marrons glacés.

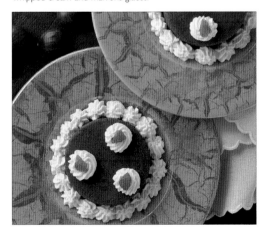

Bread Pudding with Pecan Nuts

A version of the British classic bread pudding, deliciously flavoured with pecan nuts and orange rind.

Serves 6

400ml/14fl oz/1⅔ cups milk
400ml/14fl oz/1⅔ cups single (light) or whipping cream
150g/5oz/¾ cup caster (superfine) sugar
3 eggs, beaten to mix
10ml/2 tsp grated orange rind
5ml/1 tsp vanilla extract
24 slices day-old French bread, 1cm/½in thick
75g/3oz/½ cup toasted pecan nuts, chopped
icing (confectioners') sugar, for sprinkling
whipped cream or sour cream and maple syrup, to serve

1 Put 350ml/12fl oz/1½ cups each of the milk and cream in a pan. Add the sugar. Warm over low heat, stirring to dissolve the sugar. Remove from the heat and cool. Add the eggs, orange rind and vanilla and mix well.

2 Arrange half of the bread slices in a buttered 23–25cm/ 9–10in baking dish. Sprinkle two-thirds of the pecans over the bread. Arrange the remaining bread slices on top and sprinkle over the rest of the pecans.

3 Pour the egg mixture evenly over the bread slices. Soak for 30 minutes. Press the top layer of bread down into the liquid once or twice.

4 Preheat the oven to 180°C/350°F/Gas 4. If the top layer of bread slices looks dry and all the liquid has been absorbed, moisten with the remaining milk and cream.

5 Place the baking dish in a roasting pan. Add enough boiling water to the pan to come halfway up the sides of the dish. Transfer to the oven and bake for 40 minutes or until the pudding is set and golden brown on top.

6 Sprinkle the top with sifted icing sugar and serve warm, with whipped cream or sour cream and maple syrup.

Chestnut Pudding Energy 356Kcal/1506kJ; Protein 7.4g; Carbohydrate 70.8g, of which sugars 43.6g; Fat 6.8g, of which saturates 2.4g; Cholesterol 80mg; Calcium 149mg; Fibre 4.3g; Sodium 113mg.
Bread Pudding Energy 731Kcal/3085kJ; Protein 20.9g; Carbohydrate 106.3g, of which sugars 35g; Fat 27.9g, of which saturates 10.8g; Cholesterol 136mg; Calcium 336mg; Fibre 3.8g; Sodium 906mg.

Sachertorte

This glorious gâteau was created in Vienna in 1832 by Franz Sacher, a royal chef.

Serves 10–12

225g/8oz dark (bittersweet) chocolate, broken into squares
150g/5oz/10 tbsp unsalted (sweet) butter, softened
115g/4oz/generous ½ cup caster (superfine) sugar
8 eggs, separated
115g/4oz/1 cup plain (all-purpose) flour

For the glaze
225g/8oz/generous ¾ cup apricot jam
15ml/1 tbsp lemon juice

For the icing
225g/8oz plain dark chocolate, broken into squares
200g/7oz/1 cup caster (superfine) sugar
15ml/1 tbsp golden (light corn) syrup
250ml/8fl oz/1 cup double (heavy) cream
5ml/1 tsp vanilla extract

1 Preheat the oven to 180°C/350°F/Gas 4. Grease a 23cm/9in round springform cake tin (pan) and line with baking parchment. Melt the chocolate in a heatproof bowl.

2 Cream the butter and sugar in a bowl until pale and fluffy. Add the egg yolks, one at a time, beating after each addition. Beat in the melted chocolate. Sift the flour over the mixture. Fold in evenly.

3 Whisk the egg whites until stiff, then stir a quarter into the chocolate mixture to lighten it. Fold in the remaining whites. Turn the mixture into the cake tin and smooth level. Bake for 50–55 minutes, or until firm. Turn out on to a wire rack to cool.

4 Heat the apricot jam with the lemon juice in a small pan until melted, then sieve. Slice the cake horizontally into two equal layers. Brush the cut surfaces and sides of each layer with the apricot glaze, then sandwich together, with the jam-covered surfaces against each other. Place on a wire rack.

5 Mix the icing ingredients in a heavy pan. Heat gently, stirring until thick. Simmer for 3–4 minutes, without stirring, until the mixture registers 95°C/200°F on a sugar thermometer. Pour quickly over the cake and spread evenly. Leave to set.

Peaches with Amaretti Stuffing

Peaches are both plentiful and luscious all over Italy. They are sometimes prepared hot, as in this traditional dish, which also adds the distinctive Italian signature of amaretti. Use properly ripened, good quality peaches – forced, over-hard supermarket fruit can produce a disappointing result.

Serves 4
4 ripe fresh peaches
juice of ½ lemon
65g/2½oz/⅔ cup amaretti, crushed
30ml/2 tbsp Marsala, brandy or peach brandy
25g/1oz/2 tbsp butter, at room temperature
2.5ml/½ tsp vanilla extract
30ml/2 tbsp granulated sugar
1 egg yolk

1 Preheat the oven to 180°C/350°F/Gas 4. Wash the peaches. Cut them in half and remove the stones (pits). Enlarge the hollow left by the stones with a small spoon.

2 Sprinkle the peach halves with the lemon juice.

3 Soften the amaretti crumbs in the Marsala or brandy for a few minutes.

4 Beat the butter until soft. Stir in the amaretti mixture and all the remaining ingredients.

5 Arrange the peach halves in a baking dish in one layer, hollow side upwards.

6 Divide the amaretti mixture into 8 parts, and fill the hollows, mounding the stuffing up in the centre.

7 Bake for 35–40 minutes. Serve hot or cold.

> **Cook's Tip**
> Serve these peaches with Zabaglione – made with the same wine or spirit – for a sensational dinner party dessert.

Spiced Peach Crumble

Fruit crumbles of various kinds have long been a traditional British family dessert. This peach crumble recipe offers a twist to the tradition, with rolled oats added for extra taste and crunchiness.

Serves 6

1.3kg/3lb ripe but firm peaches, peeled, stoned (pitted) and sliced
50g/2oz/¼ cup caster (superfine) sugar
2.5ml/½ tsp ground cinnamon
5ml/1 tsp lemon juice
whipped cream or vanilla ice cream, for serving (optional)

For the topping

115g/4oz/1 cup plain (all-purpose) flour
1.5ml/¼ tsp ground cinnamon
1.5ml/¼ tsp ground allspice
75g/3oz/scant 1 cup rolled oats
175g/6oz/¾ cup soft light brown sugar
115g/4oz/½ cup butter

1 Preheat the oven to 190°C/375°F/Gas 5. Make the topping for the fruit crumble. Sift the flour and the spices into a large mixing bowl.

2 Add the oats and sugar and stir to combine thoroughly. Cut or rub in the butter until the mixture resembles coarse breadcrumbs.

3 Toss the peaches with the sugar, cinnamon and lemon juice and place in a 20–23cm/8–9in diameter ovenproof dish.

4 Sprinkle the topping over the fruit in an even layer. Bake for 30–35 minutes.

5 Serve with cream or ice cream, if you like.

> **Variation**
> Try using fresh apricots instead of peaches, but leave the skins on the apricots. This dish also works well if you substitute nutmeg for cinnamon.

Mexican Sopaipillas

These golden pillows of fried pastry from Mexico can be served as a dessert with honey or plain with soups.

Makes about 30

225g/8oz/2 cups plain (all-purpose) flour
15ml/1 tsp baking powder
5ml/1 tsp salt
25g/1oz/2 tbsp white cooking fat or margarine
175ml/6fl oz/¾ cup warm water
oil, for deep frying
clear honey, for drizzling
ground cinnamon, for sprinkling
crème fraîche or thick double (heavy) cream, to serve

1 Sift the flour, baking powder and salt into a mixing bowl. Rub in the cooking fat or margarine until the mixture resembles fine breadcrumbs. Gradually add enough of the water to form a dough. Wrap the dough in clear film (plastic wrap) and leave for 1 hour.

2 Working with half the dough at a time, roll it out to a square, keeping it as even and as thin as possible. Cut into 7.5cm/3in squares. When both pieces of the dough have been rolled and cut, set the squares aside.

3 Heat the oil for deep frying to 190°C/375°F, or until a cube of dried bread added to the oil floats and turns golden after 1 minute. Add a few pastry squares, using tongs to push them down into the oil. Cook in batches until golden on both sides, turning them once, and drain on kitchen paper.

4 When all the sopaipillas have been cooked, arrange them on a large serving plate, drizzle with honey and sprinkle lightly with ground cinnamon. Serve warm, with dollops of crème fraîche or thick double cream.

> **Variation**
> Instead of drizzling honey over the sopaipillas, try using a mixture of 50g/2oz/¼ cup caster (superfine) sugar and 10ml/2 tsp ground cinnamon.

Peach Crumble Energy 495Kcal/2090kJ; Protein 6.2g; Carbohydrate 84g, of which sugars 60.3g; Fat 17.4g, of which saturates 10g; Cholesterol 41mg; Calcium 76mg; Fibre 5.2g; Sodium 126mg.
Sopaipillas Energy 107Kcal/442kJ; Protein 0.7g; Carbohydrate 5.8g, of which sugars 0.1g; Fat 9.1g, of which saturates 1.1g; Cholesterol 0mg; Calcium 11mg; Fibre 0.2g; Sodium 72mg.

Coconut Dumplings with Apricot Sauce

Based on a simple Asian recipe, these delicate little dumplings are very quick to cook. The sharp flavour of the sauce offsets the creamy dumplings beautifully.

Serves 4
75g/3oz/6 tbsp low-fat cottage cheese
1 egg white
15ml/1 tbsp low-fat spread
15ml/1 tbsp light muscovado (brown) sugar

30ml/2 tbsp self-raising (self-rising) wholemeal (whole-wheat) flour
finely grated rind of ½ lemon
15ml/1 tbsp desiccated (dry unsweetened shredded) coconut, toasted

For the sauce
225g/8oz can apricot halves in natural juice
15ml/1 tbsp lemon juice

1 Half-fill a steamer with boiling water and put it on to boil. If you do not own a steamer, place a heatproof plate over a pan of boiling water.

2 Beat together the cottage cheese, egg white and low-fat spread until they are evenly mixed.

3 Stir in the sugar, flour, lemon rind and coconut, mixing everything evenly to a fairly firm dough.

4 Place 8–12 spoonfuls of the mixture in the steamer or on the plate, leaving a space between them.

5 Cover the steamer or pan tightly with a lid or a plate and steam for about 10 minutes, until the dumplings have risen and are firm to the touch.

6 Make the sauce. Purée the can of apricots and stir in the lemon juice. Pour into a small pan and heat until boiling, then serve with the dumplings. Sprinkle with extra coconut to serve.

Apple & Walnut Crumble

An American favourite, combining delicious apples with crunchy walnuts for a simple, but tasty, dessert.

Serves 6
butter or margarine, for greasing
900g/2lb eating apples, peeled and sliced
grated rind of ½ lemon
15ml/1 tbsp fresh lemon juice

115g/4oz/scant ½ cup soft light brown sugar
75g/3oz/⅔ cup plain (all-purpose) flour
1.5ml/¼ tsp salt
1.5ml/¼ tsp grated nutmeg
2.5ml/½ tsp ground cardamom
2.5ml/½ tsp ground cinnamon
30ml/2 tbsp butter or margarine
20g/¾oz/3 tbsp walnut pieces, chopped

1 Preheat the oven to 180°C/350°F/Gas 4. Grease a 23cm/9in oval gratin dish or shallow baking dish. Toss the apples with the lemon rind and juice. Arrange the apples evenly in the bottom of the prepared dish.

2 Combine the brown sugar, flour, salt, nutmeg, cardamom and cinnamon in a mixing bowl. Rub in the butter or margarine with your fingertips until the mixture resembles coarse breadcrumbs. Stir in the chopped walnuts.

3 Using a large spoon, sprinkle the walnut and spice mixture evenly over the apples. Cover the dish with a piece of foil and bake for 30 minutes.

4 Remove the foil and continue baking for about 30 minutes more, until the apples are tender and the crumble topping is crisp. Serve warm.

Variations
To vary the crumble topping, replace the walnuts with rolled oats or use wholemeal (whole-wheat) flour instead of plain flour. For a citrus-flavoured crumble, replace the spices with finely grated lemon or orange rind. Try replacing some of the apples with blackberries, or add a handful of raisins to the filling.

Coconut Dumplings Energy 134Kcal/565kJ; Protein 4.4g; Carbohydrate 19.5g, of which sugars 13.9g; Fat 4.7g, of which saturates 2.9g; Cholesterol 3mg; Calcium 66mg; Fibre 1.3g; Sodium 130mg.
Apple & Walnut Crumble Energy 231Kcal/977kJ; Protein 2.2g; Carbohydrate 43.3g, of which sugars 33.7g; Fat 6.7g, of which saturates 0.2g; Cholesterol 0mg; Calcium 37mg; Fibre 2.9g; Sodium 45mg.

Spiced Apple Crumble

Any fruit can be used in this popular British dessert, but you can't beat the favourites of blackberry and apple. Hazelnuts and cardamom seeds give extra flavour.

Serves 4–6
450g/1lb cooking apples
115g/4oz/1 cup blackberries
grated rind and juice of 1 orange
50g/2oz/¼ cup light muscovado
 (brown) sugar

For the topping
175g/6oz/1½ cups plain
 (all-purpose) flour
75g/3oz/6 tbsp butter, plus extra
 for greasing
75g/3oz/6 tbsp caster
 (superfine) sugar
25g/1oz/¼ cup chopped
 hazelnuts
2.5ml/½ tsp crushed cardamom
 seeds
fresh custard, to serve

1 Preheat the oven to 200°C/400°F/Gas 6. Generously butter a 1.2 litre/2 pint/5 cup baking dish.

2 Peel and core the apples, then slice them into the prepared baking dish. Level the surface, then scatter the blackberries over. Sprinkle the orange rind and light muscovado sugar evenly over the top, then pour over the orange juice. Set aside.

3 Make the topping. Sift the flour into a bowl and rub in the butter until the mixture resembles coarse breadcrumbs. Stir in the caster sugar, hazelnuts and cardamom seeds. Scatter the topping over the top of the fruit.

4 Press the topping around the edges of the dish to seal in the juices. Bake for 30–35 minutes or until the crumble is golden. Serve hot, with custard.

> **Variations**
> *This wonderfully good-natured pudding can be made with all sorts of fruit. Try plums, apricots, peaches or pears, alone or in combination with apples. Rhubarb makes a delectable crumble, especially when partnered with bananas.*

Apple Strudel

Packed with spiced apples and nuts, this Austrian dessert is traditionally made with paper-thin layers of buttered strudel pastry, but featherlight filo pastry makes an easy substitute.

Serves 4–6
75g/3oz/¾ cup hazelnuts,
 chopped and roasted
30ml/2 tbsp nibbed almonds,
 roasted

50g/2oz/4 tbsp demerara (raw)
 sugar
2.5ml/½ tsp ground cinnamon
grated rind and juice of ½ lemon
2 large cooking apples, peeled,
 cored and chopped
50g/2oz/⅓ cup sultanas (golden
 raisins)
4 large sheets filo pastry
50g/2oz/4 tbsp unsalted (sweet)
 butter, melted
icing (confectioners') sugar, for
 dusting

1 Preheat the oven to 190°C/375°F/Gas 5. In a bowl mix together the hazelnuts, almonds, sugar, cinnamon, lemon rind and juice, apples and sultanas. Set aside.

2 Lay one sheet of filo pastry on a clean dish towel and brush with melted butter. Lay a second sheet on top and brush again with melted butter. Repeat with the remaining two sheets.

3 Spread the fruit and nut mixture over the pastry, leaving a 7.5cm/3in border at the shorter ends. Fold the ends in over the filling. Roll up from one long edge, using the dish towel.

4 Transfer the strudel to a greased baking sheet, placing it seam side down. Brush with butter and bake for 30–35 minutes, until golden and crisp. Dust with icing sugar and serve hot with cream, custard or yogurt.

> **Cook's Tip**
> *Filo or strudel pastry is fiddly and time consuming to make, so it makes sense to use the ready-made version, which is very good and is now widely available. The filo dries out quickly, so keep the sheets covered with a damp dish towel as you work.*

Apple Crumble Energy 333Kcal/1401kJ; Protein 3.9g; Carbohydrate 52.4g, of which sugars 30.1g; Fat 13.4g, of which saturates 6.8g; Cholesterol 27mg; Calcium 71mg; Fibre 3g; Sodium 80mg.
Apple Strudel Energy 287Kcal/1199kJ; Protein 4.4g; Carbohydrate 29.1g, of which sugars 19.2g; Fat 17.8g, of which saturates 5.2g; Cholesterol 18mg; Calcium 60mg; Fibre 2.4g; Sodium 55mg.

Blueberry Pie

American blueberries or European bilberries can be used for this scrumptious pie. You may need to add a little more sugar if you are lucky enough to find native bilberries.

Serves 6

2 x 225g/8oz ready-rolled shortcrust pastry sheets, thawed if frozen

800g/1³⁄₄lb/7 cups blueberries
75g/3oz/6 tbsp caster (superfine) sugar, plus extra for sprinkling
45ml/3 tbsp cornflour (cornstarch)
grated rind and juice of ½ orange
grated rind of ½ lemon
2.5ml/½ tsp ground cinnamon
15g/½oz/1 tbsp unsalted (sweet) butter, diced
beaten egg, to glaze
whipped cream, to serve

1 Preheat the oven to 200°C/400°F/Gas 6. Use one sheet of pastry to line a 23cm/9in pie dish, leaving the excess pastry hanging over the edges.

2 Mix the blueberries, caster sugar, cornflour, orange rind and juice, lemon rind and cinnamon in a large bowl. Spoon into the pastry case and dot with the butter. Dampen the rim of the pastry case (pie shell) with a little water and top with the remaining pastry sheet.

3 Cut the pastry edge at 2.5cm/1in intervals, then fold each section over on itself to form a triangle and create a sunflower edge. Trim off the excess pastry and cut out decorations from the trimmings. Stick them to the pastry lid with a little of the beaten egg.

4 Glaze the pastry with the egg and sprinkle with caster sugar. Bake for 30–35 minutes or until golden. Serve warm or cold with whipped cream.

> **Variation**
> Substitute a crumble topping for the pastry lid. The contrast with the juicy blueberry filling is sensational.

Lemon Meringue Pie

A lovely lemon-filled tart, heaped with soft meringue, this classic British dessert never fails to please.

Serves 6

115g/4oz/1 cup plain (all-purpose) flour
pinch of salt
50g/2oz/¼ cup butter
50g/2oz/¼ cup lard
15ml/1 tbsp caster (superfine) sugar
about 15ml/1 tbsp iced water

For the filling

3 large (US extra large) egg yolks
25g/1oz/2 tbsp caster (superfine) sugar
grated rind and juice of 1 lemon
25g/1oz/1½ cup fresh white breadcrumbs
250ml/8fl oz/1 cup milk

For the topping

3 large (US extra large) egg whites
115g/4oz/generous ½ cup caster (superfine) sugar

1 Sift the flour and salt into a bowl. Rub in the butter and lard until the mixture resembles fine breadcrumbs. Stir in the sugar and add enough iced water to make a soft dough. Roll out the pastry on a lightly floured surface and line a 21cm/8½in pie plate or tin (pan). Chill until required.

2 Meanwhile make the filling. Place all the ingredients in a bowl, mix lightly and leave to soak for 1 hour.

3 Preheat the oven to 200°C/400°F/Gas 6. Beat the filling until smooth and pour into the chilled pastry case (pie shell). Bake for 20 minutes or until the filling has just set and the pastry is golden. Remove from the oven and cool, in the tin, on a wire rack for 30 minutes or until a skin has formed on the surface. Lower the oven temperature to 180°C/350°F/Gas 4.

4 Make the topping. Whisk the egg whites in a grease-free bowl until they form stiff peaks. Whisk in the caster sugar to form a glossy meringue. Spoon on top of the set lemon filling and spread to completely cover. Swirl the meringue slightly.

5 Bake the pie for 20–25 minutes or until the meringue is crisp and golden brown. Cool slightly on a wire rack before serving.

Blueberry Pie Energy 458Kcal/1915kJ; Protein 4.7g; Carbohydrate 60g, of which sugars 20.4g; Fat 23.8g, of which saturates 1.3g; Cholesterol 5mg; Calcium 95mg; Fibre 5.6g; Sodium 143mg.
Lemon Meringue Pie Energy 357Kcal/1497kJ; Protein 6.8g; Carbohydrate 42.8g, of which sugars 25.1g; Fat 18.9g, of which saturates 9g; Cholesterol 129mg; Calcium 108mg; Fibre 0.7g; Sodium 137mg.

Boston Banoffee Pie

A great American creation, you simply press the biscuity pastry into the tin, rather than rolling it out. Just add the fudge-toffee filling and sliced banana topping and it'll prove irresistible.

Serves 6

115g/4oz/½ cup butter, diced
200g/7oz can skimmed, sweetened condensed milk
115g/4oz/scant ½ cup soft brown sugar
30ml/2 tbsp golden (light corn) syrup
2 small bananas, sliced
a little lemon juice
whipped cream, to decorate
5ml/1 tsp grated plain (semisweet) chocolate

For the pastry

150g/5oz/1¼ cups plain (all-purpose) flour
115g/4oz/½ cup butter, diced
50g/2oz/¼ cup caster (superfine) sugar

1 Make the pastry. Preheat the oven to 160°C/325°F/Gas 3. In a food processor, process the flour and diced butter until it forms crumbs. Stir in the caster sugar and mix to form a soft, pliable dough.

2 Press into a 20cm/8in loose-based flan tin (tart pan). Bake for 30 minutes.

3 Make the filling. Place the butter in a pan with the condensed milk, brown sugar and syrup. Heat gently, stirring, until the butter has melted and the sugar has completely dissolved.

4 Bring the mixture to a gentle boil, then cook for 7–10 minutes, stirring constantly, until the mixture thickens and turns a light caramel colour.

5 Pour the hot caramel filling into the pastry case (pie shell) and leave until completely cold.

6 Sprinkle the banana slices with lemon juice and arrange in overlapping circles on top of the filling, leaving a gap in the centre. Pipe a generous swirl of whipped cream in the centre and sprinkle with the grated chocolate.

American Pumpkin Pie

This spicy sweet pie is served at Thanksgiving, or at Hallowe'en to use the pulp from the hollowed-out pumpkin lanterns.

Serves 8

900g/2lb piece of pumpkin flesh
2 large (US extra large) eggs
75g/3oz/6 tbsp soft light brown sugar
60ml/4 tbsp golden (light corn) syrup
250ml/8fl oz/1 cup double (heavy) cream
15ml/1 tbsp mixed (pumpkin pie) spice
2.5ml/½ tsp salt
icing (confectioners') sugar, for dusting

For the pastry

200g/7oz/1¾ cups plain (all-purpose) flour
2.5ml/½ tsp salt
90g/3½oz/scant ½ cup butter, diced
1 egg yolk
15ml/1 tbsp chilled water

1 Make the pastry. Sift the flour and salt into a mixing bowl. Rub or cut in the butter until the mixture resembles fine breadcrumbs, then mix in the egg yolk and enough chilled water to make a soft dough. Roll into a ball, then wrap it in clear film (plastic wrap) and chill for at least 30 minutes.

2 Cut the pumpkin flesh into cubes and place in a heavy pan. Cover with water, bring to the boil and simmer for 15–20 minutes until tender. Mash the pumpkin until smooth, then spoon into a sieve (strainer) and set over a bowl to drain.

3 Preheat the oven to 200°C/400°F/Gas 6. Roll out the pastry and use to line a 23cm/9in loose-based flan tin (tart pan). Prick the base all over with a fork. Line with foil and baking beans. Chill the pastry case (pie shell) for 15 minutes. Bake for 10 minutes. Remove the foil and beans and bake for a further 5 minutes.

4 Lower the oven temperature to 190°C/375°F/Gas 5. Turn the pumpkin pulp into a mixing bowl and beat in the eggs, sugar, syrup, cream, spice and salt until smooth. Pour into the pastry case. Bake for 40 minutes, or until the filling has set. Dust the surface with icing sugar and serve at room temperature.

Banoffee Pie Energy 608Kcal/2547kJ; Protein 6.4g; Carbohydrate 78.5g, of which sugars 58.9g; Fat 32g, of which saturates 20.1g; Cholesterol 82mg; Calcium 169mg; Fibre 1.1g; Sodium 299mg.
Pumpkin Pie Energy 416Kcal/1736kJ; Protein 5.3g; Carbohydrate 38.2g, of which sugars 18.6g; Fat 28g, of which saturates 16.9g; Cholesterol 114mg; Calcium 98mg; Fibre 1.9g; Sodium 360mg.

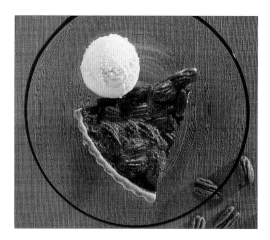

Mississippi Pecan Pie

This fabulous dessert started life in the United States but has become an international favourite.

Serves 6–8
115g/4oz/1 cup plain
(all-purpose) flour
50g/2oz/4 tbsp butter, cubed
25g/1oz/2 tbsp caster
(superfine) sugar
1 egg yolk
30ml/2 tbsp water

For the filling
175g/6oz/¹⁄₂ cup golden (light
corn) syrup
50g/2oz/¹⁄₄ cup dark muscovado
(molasses) sugar
50g/2oz/4 tbsp butter
3 eggs, lightly beaten
2.5ml/¹⁄₂ tsp vanilla extract
150g/5oz/1¹⁄₄ cups pecan nuts
fresh cream or ice cream, to serve

1 Place the flour in a bowl and add the butter. Rub in the butter with your fingertips until the mixture resembles breadcrumbs, then stir in the sugar, egg yolk and the water. Mix to a dough and knead lightly on a floured surface until smooth.

2 Roll out the pastry and use to line a 20cm/8in loose-based fluted flan tin (tart pan). Prick the base, then line with baking parchment and fill with baking beans. Chill for 30 minutes. Preheat the oven to 200°C/400°F/Gas 6.

3 Bake the pastry case (pie shell) for 10 minutes. Remove the paper and beans and bake for a further 5 minutes. Reduce the oven temperature to 180°C/350°F/Gas 4.

4 Meanwhile, heat the syrup, sugar and butter in a pan until the sugar dissolves. Remove from the heat and cool slightly. Whisk in the eggs and vanilla extract and stir in the pecans. Pour into the pastry case and bake for 35–40 minutes, until the filling is set. Serve with cream or ice cream.

> **Cook's Tip**
> *Cooking the pastry before filling stops it from turning soggy.*

Key Lime Pie

This American dish hails from the Florida Keys.

Makes 10 slices
225g/8oz/2 cups plain
(all-purpose) flour
115g/4oz/¹⁄₂ cup chilled
butter, diced
25g/1oz/2 tbsp caster
(superfine) sugar
2 egg yolks
pinch of salt
30ml/2 tbsp cold water
shredded, thinly pared lime rind
and mint leaves, to decorate

For the filling
4 eggs, separated
400g/14oz can condensed milk
grated rind and juice of 3 limes
a few drops of green food
colouring (optional)
25g/1oz/2 tbsp caster
(superfine) sugar

For the topping
300ml/¹⁄₂ pint/1¹⁄₄ cups double
(heavy) cream
2 or 3 limes, thinly sliced

1 Sift the flour into a bowl and rub in the butter until the mixture resembles breadcrumbs. Add the sugar, egg yolks, salt and water. Mix to a soft dough. Roll out the pastry on a lightly floured surface and use to line a deep 21cm/8¹⁄₂in fluted flan tin (tart pan), letting excess pastry hang over the edge. Prick the pastry base. Chill for 30 minutes. Preheat the oven to 200°C/400°F/Gas 6. Trim off the excess pastry and line the pastry case (pie shell) with parchment and baking beans. Bake blind for 10 minutes. Remove the paper and beans and return the pastry case to the oven for 10 minutes.

2 Meanwhile, make the filling. Beat the egg yolks in a bowl until light and creamy, then beat in the condensed milk, lime rind and juice. Add the food colouring, if using, and beat until the mixture is thick. In a grease-free bowl, whisk the egg whites to stiff peaks. Whisk in the caster sugar, then fold into the lime mixture.

3 Lower the oven to 160°C/325°F/Gas 3. Pour the filling into the pastry case. Bake for 20–25 minutes, until it has set and starts to brown. Cool, then chill. Before serving, whip the cream and spoon it around the edge of the pie. Cut the lime slices once from the centre to the edge, twist each one and arrange on the cream. Decorate with lime rind and mint.

Pecan Pie Energy 409Kcal/1705kJ; Protein 6g; Carbohydrate 39.4g, of which sugars 28.2g; Fat 26.4g, of which saturates 8.4g; Cholesterol 123mg; Calcium 56mg; Fibre 1.3g; Sodium 163mg.
Key Lime Pie Energy 510Kcal/2126kJ; Protein 9.2g; Carbohydrate 46.6g, of which sugars 29.4g; Fat 33.2g, of which saturates 19.5g; Cholesterol 196mg; Calcium 182mg; Fibre 0.7g; Sodium 163mg.

Apple Pie

An English and American classic, delicious on its own or with a dollop of cream.

Serves 8

900g/2lb tart cooking apples
25g/1oz/¼ cup plain
   (all-purpose) flour
90g/3½oz/½ cup sugar
25ml/1½ tbsp fresh lemon juice
2.5ml/½ tsp ground cinnamon
2.5ml/½ tsp ground allspice
1.5ml/¼ tsp ground ginger
1.5ml/¼ tsp grated nutmeg
1.5ml/¼ tsp salt
50g/2oz/4 tbsp butter, diced

For the pastry

225g/8oz/2 cups plain
   (all-purpose) flour
5ml/1 tsp salt
75g/3oz/6 tbsp cold butter, cut
   into pieces
50g/2oz/4 tbsp cold lard, cut
   into pieces
60–120ml/4–8 tbsp iced water

1 Make the pastry. Sift the flour and salt into a bowl. Add the butter and lard and cut in with a pastry blender or rub with your fingertips until the mixture resembles coarse breadcrumbs. Stir in just enough iced water to bind the dough. Form into two balls, wrap in clear film (plastic wrap) and chill for 20 minutes.

2 On a lightly floured surface, roll out one dough ball to 3mm/⅛in thick. Transfer to a 23cm/9in pie tin (pan) and trim the edge. Place a baking sheet in the centre of the oven and preheat to 220°C/425°F/Gas 7.

3 Peel, core and slice the apples into a bowl. Toss with the flour, sugar, lemon juice, spices and salt. Spoon into the pastry case (pie shell) and dot with butter.

4 Roll out the remaining dough. Place on top of the pie and trim to leave a 2cm/¾in overhang. Fold the overhang under the bottom dough and press to seal. Crimp the edge. Roll out the leftover pastry and cut out leaf shapes and roll balls. Arrange on top of the pie. Cut steam vents.

5 Bake for 10 minutes. Reduce the heat to 180°C/350°F/Gas 4 and bake for 40–45 minutes more until golden. If the pie browns too quickly, protect the top with foil.

Apple & Orange Pie

Oranges add an evocative Mediterranean twist to an Anglo-American favourite.

Serves 4–6

3 navel oranges
1kg/2¼lb cooking apples, peeled, cored and thickly sliced
30ml/2 tbsp demerara
   (raw) sugar
beaten egg, to glaze
caster (superfine) sugar,
   for sprinkling

For the pastry

275g/10oz/2½ cups plain
   (all-purpose) flour
2.5ml/½ tsp salt
150g/5oz/10 tbsp chilled
   butter, diced
about 45ml/4 tbsp chilled
   water

1 Make the pastry. Sift the flour and salt into a large bowl. Rub in the butter with your fingertips, until the mixture resembles fine breadcrumbs. Mix in the water and knead lightly to form a firm dough. Wrap the dough in clear film (plastic wrap) and chill for at least 30 minutes.

2 Roll out the pastry on a lightly floured work surface to a shape 2cm/¾in larger than the top of a 1.2 litre/2 pint/5 cup pie dish. Cut off a narrow strip around the edge of the pastry, brush it with a little cold water and firmly attach it to the rim of the pie dish.

3 Preheat the oven to 190°C/375°F/Gas 5. Using a sharp knife, cut a thin slice of peel and pith from both ends of each orange. Place cut side down on a plate and cut off the peel and pith in strips. Remove any bits of remaining pith. Cut out each segment leaving the membrane behind. Squeeze the remaining juice from the membrane.

4 Mix together the orange segments and juice, the apples and sugar in the pie dish. Place a pie funnel in the centre of the dish. Dampen the pastry strip on the rim of the dish and cover with the pastry. Press the edges to the pastry strip.

5 Brush the top with beaten egg to glaze. Bake for 35 minutes, or until golden. Sprinkle with caster sugar before serving.

Apple Pie Energy 364Kcal/1528kJ; Protein 3.5g; Carbohydrate 46.6g, of which sugars 22.3g; Fat 19.6g, of which saturates 10.7g; Cholesterol 39mg; Calcium 58mg; Fibre 2.8g; Sodium 344mg.
Apple & Orange Pie Energy 444Kcal/1865kJ; Protein 5.7g; Carbohydrate 61.2g, of which sugars 26.3g; Fat 21.4g, of which saturates 13.1g; Cholesterol 53mg; Calcium 108mg; Fibre 5.2g; Sodium 324mg.

Shoofly Pie

A wonderful sweet pie from the American Deep South.

Serves 8
115g/4oz/1 cup plain
 (all-purpose) flour
115g/4oz/scant ½ cup soft dark
 brown sugar
1.5ml/¼ tsp each salt, ground
 ginger, cinnamon, mace, and
 nutmeg
75g/3oz/6 tbsp cold butter, diced

2 eggs
185g/6½oz/½ cup black treacle
 (molasses)
120ml/4fl oz/½ cup boiling water
1.5ml/½ tsp bicarbonate of soda
 (baking soda)

For the pastry
115g/4oz/½ cup cream cheese
115g/4oz/½ cup butter, diced
115g/4oz/1 cup plain
 (all-purpose) flour

1 Preheat the oven to 190°C/375°F/Gas 5. Meanwhile make the pastry. Put the cream cheese and butter in a mixing bowl. Sift over the flour. Rub in with your fingertips or cut in with a pastry blender to bind the dough together. Wrap in clear film (plastic wrap) and chill for at least 30 minutes.

2 Make the filling. Mix the flour, brown sugar, salt, spices and butter in a bowl. Rub in with your fingertips until the mixture resembles coarse breadcrumbs, then set aside.

3 Roll out the dough thinly on a lightly floured surface to a thickness of about 3mm/⅛in and use to line a 23cm/9in pie plate. Trim and flute the pastry edges. Spoon one-third of the filling mixture into the pastry case (pie shell).

4 Whisk the eggs with the treacle in a large bowl. Put a baking sheet in the oven to preheat.

5 Pour the boiling water into a small bowl and stir in the bicarbonate of soda; it will foam. Pour immediately into the egg mixture and whisk to blend. Pour into the pastry case and sprinkle the remaining filling mixture over the top in an even layer.

6 Place the pie on the hot baking sheet and bake for about 35 minutes, or until browned. Leave to cool and serve warm.

Italian Chocolate Ricotta Pie

Savour the full richness of Italy with this de luxe tart.

Serves 6
225g/8oz/2 cups plain
 (all-purpose) flour
30ml/2 tbsp cocoa powder
 (unsweetened)
50g/2oz/¼ cup caster
 (superfine) sugar
115g/4oz/½ cup unsalted
 (sweet) butter
60ml/4 tbsp dry sherry

For the filling
2 egg yolks
115g/4oz/generous ½ cup caster
 (superfine) sugar
500g/1¼lb/2½ cups ricotta
 cheese
finely grated rind of 1 lemon
90ml/6 tbsp dark chocolate
 chips
75ml/5 tbsp mixed (candied)
 chopped peel
45ml/3 tbsp chopped
 angelica

1 Sift the flour and cocoa into a bowl. Stir in the sugar. Rub in the butter with your fingers. Work in the sherry to form a firm dough.

2 Preheat the oven to 200°C/400°F/Gas 6. Roll out three-quarters of the pastry on a lightly floured surface and line a 24cm/9½in loose-based flan tin (tart pan).

3 Make the filling. Beat the egg yolks and sugar in a bowl, then beat in the ricotta to mix thoroughly. Stir in the lemon rind, chocolate chips, mixed peel and angelica.

4 Scrape the ricotta mixture into the pastry case (pie shell) and level the surface. Roll out the remaining pastry and cut into strips. Arrange these in a lattice over the pie.

5 Bake for 15 minutes. Lower the oven temperature to 180°C/350°F/Gas 4 and cook for a further 30–35 minutes, until golden brown and firm. Cool the pie in the tin, then serve.

> **Cook's Tip**
> This dish is best served at room temperature, so if made in advance, chill it, then bring to room temperature before serving.

Ricotta Pie Energy 701Kcal/2938kJ; Protein 14.2g; Carbohydrate 83.4g, of which sugars 54.1g; Fat 35.6g, of which saturates 21.3g; Cholesterol 144mg; Calcium 115mg; Fibre 3g; Sodium 223mg.
Shoofly Pie Energy 472Kcal/1975kJ; Protein 5.2g; Carbohydrate 53g, of which sugars 31g; Fat 28.1g, of which saturates 17.1g; Cholesterol 112mg; Calcium 201mg; Fibre 0.9g; Sodium 248mg.

Butternut Squash & Maple Pie

This American-style pie has a crisp shortcrust pastry case and a creamy filling, sweetened with maple syrup and flavoured with fresh ginger and a dash of brandy.

Serves 10
1 small butternut squash
60ml/4 tbsp water
2.5cm/1in piece fresh root ginger, peeled and grated

275g/10oz shortcrust pastry
120ml/4fl oz/½ cup double (heavy) cream
90ml/6 tbsp maple syrup
40g/1½oz/3 tbsp light muscovado (brown) sugar
3 eggs, lightly beaten
30ml/2 tbsp brandy
1.5ml/¼ tsp grated nutmeg
beaten egg, to glaze

1 Halve the squash, peel and scoop out the seeds. Cut the flesh into cubes and put in a pan with the water. Cover and cook gently for 15 minutes. Uncover, stir in the ginger and cook for a further 5 minutes until the liquid has evaporated and the squash is tender. Cool slightly, then purée in a food processor.

2 Roll out the pastry and use to line a 23cm/9in flan tin (tart pan). Re-roll the trimmings, then cut into maple leaf shapes. Brush the edge of the pastry case with beaten egg and attach the leaf shapes at regular intervals to make a decorative rim. Cover with clear film (plastic wrap) and chill for 30 minutes.

3 Put a heavy baking sheet in the oven and preheat to 200°C/400°F/Gas 6. Prick the pastry base, line with foil and fill with baking beans. Bake blind on the baking sheet for 12 minutes.

4 Remove the foil and beans and bake for a further 5 minutes. Brush the base of the pastry case with beaten egg and return to the oven for about 3 minutes. Lower the oven temperature to 180°C/350°F/Gas 4.

5 Mix 200g/7oz/scant 1 cup of the butternut purée with the cream, syrup, sugar, eggs, brandy and nutmeg. (Discard any remaining purée.) Pour into the pastry case. Bake for about 30 minutes, until the filling is lightly set. Cool slightly and serve.

Lemon Tartlets

These classic French tartlets make a most delicious dessert. A luscious lemon curd is encased in rich pastry and decorated with caramelized lemon slices.

Makes 12
6 eggs, beaten
350g/12oz/1½ cups caster (superfine) sugar
115g/4oz/½ cup butter
grated rind and juice of 4 lemons
icing (confectioners') sugar, for dusting (optional)
175ml/6fl oz/¾ cup double (heavy) cream, to serve

For the pastry
225g/8oz/2 cups plain (all-purpose) flour
115g/4oz/½ cup chilled butter, diced
30ml/2 tbsp icing (confectioners') sugar
1 egg, beaten
5ml/1 tsp vanilla extract
15ml/1 tbsp chilled water

For the topping
2 lemons, well scrubbed
75ml/5 tbsp apricot jam

1 Preheat the oven to 200°C/400°F/Gas 6. Make the pastry. Sift the flour into a large mixing bowl. Using your fingertips, lightly rub the butter into the flour until the mixture resembles fine breadcrumbs. Add the icing sugar and stir well to mix.

2 Add the egg, vanilla extract and most of the chilled water, then work to a soft dough. Add a few more drops of water if necessary. Knead quickly and lightly, while still in the bowl, until a smooth dough forms.

3 Lightly butter twelve 10cm/4in tartlet tins (muffin pans). Roll out the pastry on a lightly floured work surface to a thickness of 3mm/⅛in.

4 Using a 10cm/4in fluted pastry (cookie) cutter, cut out 12 rounds and press them into the tartlet tins. Prick the bases all over with a fork and then transfer the tins to a baking sheet.

5 Line the pastry cases (pie shells) with baking parchment and fill with baking beans. Bake the pastry cases for 10 minutes. Remove the paper and beans. Set the tins aside while you make the filling.

6 Put the eggs, sugar and butter in a pan, and stir over a low heat until all the sugar has dissolved. Add the lemon rind and juice, and continue cooking, stirring constantly, until the lemon curd has thickened slightly.

7 Pour the lemon curd mixture into the pastry cases. Bake for 15 minutes, or until the curd filling is almost set.

8 Prepare the topping while the lemon tartlets are cooking. Cut the lemons into 12 slices, then cut the slices in half.

9 Push the jam through a fine sieve (strainer), then transfer to a small pan and heat. Place two lemon slices in the centre of each tartlet, overlapping them if you wish. Lightly brush the top of the tartlet with the strained jam, then put under the grill (broiler) and heat for 5 minutes, or until the top is caramelized and golden. Serve with cream.

Squash & Maple Pie Energy 266Kcal/1109kJ; Protein 4g; Carbohydrate 26.2g, of which sugars 13.7g; Fat 16.1g, of which saturates 4.6g; Cholesterol 74mg; Calcium 56mg; Fibre 1.4g; Sodium 92mg.
Lemon Tartlets Energy 391Kcal/1639kJ; Protein 5.7g; Carbohydrate 52.1g, of which sugars 37.8g; Fat 19.2g, of which saturates 10.9g; Cholesterol 152mg; Calcium 64mg; Fibre 0.6g; Sodium 162mg.

Jam Tart

Jam tarts are popular in Italy and Britain, traditionally decorated with pastry strips.

Serves 6–8
200g/7oz/1¾ cups plain
  (all-purpose) flour
pinch of salt
50g/2oz/¼ cup granulated sugar

115g/4oz/½ cup butter or
  margarine, chilled
1 egg
1.5ml/¼ tsp grated lemon rind
350g/12oz/1¼ cups fruit jam,
  such as raspberry, apricot or
  strawberry
1 egg, lightly beaten with 30ml/
  2 tbsp whipping cream

1 Make the pastry. Put the flour, salt and sugar in a mixing bowl. Using a pastry blender or two knives, cut the butter into the dry ingredients until the mixture resembles coarse crumbs.

2 Beat the egg with the lemon rind in a cup, and pour it over the flour mixture. Combine with a fork until the dough holds together. If it is too crumbly, mix in 15–30ml/1–2 tbsp water.

3 Gather the dough into two balls, one slightly larger than the other, and flatten into discs. Wrap in waxed paper, and put in the refrigerator for at least 40 minutes.

4 Lightly grease a shallow 23cm/9in flan tin (tart pan), preferably with a removable base. Roll out the larger ball of pastry on a lightly floured surface to about 3mm/⅛in thick.

5 Roll the pastry around the rolling pin and transfer to the prepared tin. Trim the edges evenly with a small knife. Prick the bottom with a fork. Chill for at least 30 minutes.

6 Preheat the oven to 190°C/375°F/Gas 5. Spread jam thickly over the base of the pastry. Roll out the remaining pastry. Cut the pastry into strips about 1cm/½in wide. Arrange over the jam in a lattice pattern. Trim the edges of the strips, pressing them lightly on to the pastry case (pie shell).

7 Brush the pastry with the egg and cream mix. Bake for about 35 minutes, or until the pastry is golden. Cool before serving.

Pear & Almond Cream Tart

This tart is equally successful made with other kinds of fruit – variations can be seen in almost every good French pâtisserie.

Serves 6
350g/12oz shortcrust or sweet
  shortcrust pastry
3 firm pears
lemon juice
15ml/1 tbsp peach brandy or
  water

60ml/4 tbsp peach preserve,
  strained

For the almond cream filling
115g/4oz/¾ cup blanched whole
  almonds
50g/2oz/¼ cup caster
  (superfine) sugar
65g/2½oz/5 tbsp butter
1 egg, plus 1 egg white
few drops almond extract

1 Roll out the pastry thinly and use to line a 23cm/9in flan tin (tart pan). Chill the pastry case (pie shell). Meanwhile, make the filling. Put the almonds and sugar in a food processor and pulse until finely ground (not a paste). Add the butter and process until creamy. Add the egg, egg white and almond extract and mix well.

2 Place a baking sheet in the oven and preheat to 190°C/ 375°F/Gas 5. Peel the pears, halve them, remove the cores and rub with lemon juice. Put the pear halves, cut-side down, on a board and slice thinly crossways, keeping the slices together.

3 Pour the almond cream filling into the pastry case. Slide a metal spatula under one pear half and press the top with your fingers to fan out the slices. Transfer to the tart, placing the fruit on the filling like spokes of a wheel. If you like, remove a few slices from each half before arranging and use to fill in any gaps in the centre.

4 Place on the baking sheet and bake for 50–55 minutes until the filling is set and well browned. Cool on a rack.

5 Meanwhile, heat the brandy or water and the preserve in a small pan, then brush over the top of the hot tart to glaze. Serve the tart warm, or at room temperature.

Jam Tart Energy 340Kcal/1434kJ; Protein 3.4g; Carbohydrate 56.4g, of which sugars 37.3g; Fat 12.8g, of which saturates 7.7g; Cholesterol 54mg; Calcium 49mg; Fibre 0.8g; Sodium 117mg.
Pear Tart Energy 558Kcal/2326kJ; Protein 8.6g; Carbohydrate 50.3g, of which sugars 24.4g; Fat 37.2g, of which saturates 6.8g; Cholesterol 55mg; Calcium 92mg; Fibre 4.2g; Sodium 189mg.

Tarte Tatin

This upside-down apple tart was first made by two sisters at their restaurant in the Loire Valley in France.

Serves 8–10
225g/8oz puff or shortcrust pastry
10–12 large eating apples
lemon juice
115g/4oz/½ cup butter, cut into pieces
90g/3½oz/½ cup caster (superfine) sugar
1.5ml/½ tsp ground cinnamon
crème fraîche or whipped cream, to serve

1 On a lightly floured surface, roll out the pastry into a 28cm/11in round, less than 5mm/¼in thick. Transfer to a lightly floured baking sheet and chill.

2 Peel the apples, cut them in half lengthways and core. Sprinkle them generously with lemon juice.

3 Preheat the oven to 230°C/450°F/Gas 8. In a 25cm/10in tarte tatin tin (pan), cook the butter, sugar and cinnamon over medium heat until the sugar has dissolved, stirring occasionally. Continue cooking for 6–8 minutes, until the mixture turns a caramel colour. Remove from the heat and arrange the apple halves in the tin, fitting them in tightly since they will shrink.

4 Return the apple-filled tin to the heat and bring to a simmer over a medium heat for 20–25 minutes until the apples are tender and coloured. Remove the tin from the heat and cool slightly.

5 Place the pastry on top of the apple-filled pan and tuck the edges of the pastry inside the edge of the tin around the apples.

6 Pierce the pastry in two or three places, then bake for 25–30 minutes until the pastry is golden. Cool for 10–15 minutes.

7 To serve, run a sharp knife around edge of the tin to loosen the pastry. Cover with a serving plate and, holding them tightly, carefully invert the tin and plate together (do this over the sink in case any caramel drips). Lift off the tin and loosen any apples that stick with a spatula. Serve the tart warm with cream.

Tarte au Citron

This classic lemon tart is served in restaurants all over France. The rich, citrus flavour of the filling gives the tart a truly gourmet feel, making it the perfect dessert for a dinner party.

Serves 8–10
350g/12oz shortcrust or sweet shortcrust pastry
grated rind of 2 or 3 lemons
150ml/¼ pint/⅔ cup freshly squeezed lemon juice
90g/3½oz/½ cup caster (superfine) sugar
60ml/4 tbsp crème fraîche or double (heavy) cream
4 eggs, plus 3 egg yolks
icing (confectioners') sugar, for dusting

1 Preheat the oven to 190°C/375°F/Gas 5. Roll out the pastry thinly and use to line a 23cm/9in flan tin (tart pan). Prick the base of the pastry with a fork.

2 Line the pastry case (pie shell) with foil and fill with baking beans. Bake for about 15 minutes until the edges are set and dry. Remove the foil and beans and continue baking for a further 5–7 minutes until golden.

3 Place the lemon rind, juice and sugar in a bowl. Beat until combined and then gradually add the crème fraîche or double cream and beat until well blended.

4 Beat in the eggs, one at a time, then beat in the egg yolks and pour the filling into the pastry case. Bake for 15–20 minutes, until the filling is set. If the pastry begins to brown too much, cover the edges with foil.

5 Leave to cool and dust with a little icing sugar before serving.

> **Variation**
> *Replace half the lemon juice and rind with orange juice and rind.*

Tarte Tatin Energy 228Kcal/954kJ; Protein 1.6g; Carbohydrate 23.7g, of which sugars 15.7g; Fat 15g, of which saturates 6g; Cholesterol 25mg; Calcium 23mg; Fibre 1.1g; Sodium 141mg.
Tarte au Citron Energy 259Kcal/1082kJ; Protein 5.3g; Carbohydrate 26.2g, of which sugars 10.1g; Fat 15.6g, of which saturates 5.6g; Cholesterol 128mg; Calcium 55mg; Fibre 0.7g; Sodium 172mg.

Honey & Pine Nut Tart

Wonderful tarts of all descriptions are to be found throughout France, and this recipe recalls the flavours of the south.

Serves 6

115g/4oz/½ cup butter, diced
115g/4oz/generous ½ cup caster
  (superfine) sugar
3 eggs, beaten
175g/6oz/⅔ cup sunflower honey
grated rind and juice of 1 lemon
225g/8oz/2⅔ cups pine nuts

pinch of salt
icing (confectioners') sugar,
  for dusting

For the pastry

225g/8oz/2 cups plain
  (all-purpose) flour
115g/4oz/½ cup butter, diced
30ml/2 tbsp icing
  (confectioners') sugar
1 egg
15ml/1 tbsp chilled water
crème fraîche or vanilla ice
  cream, to serve (optional)

1 Preheat the oven to 180°C/350°F/Gas 4. Make the pastry. Sift the flour into a large mixing bowl and rub or cut in the butter until the mixture resembles fine breadcrumbs.

2 Stir in the icing sugar. Add the egg and water and mix to form a soft dough. Knead lightly until smooth.

3 Roll out the pastry on a lightly floured surface and use to line a 23cm/9in flan tin (tart pan). Prick the base with a fork, then chill for 10 minutes. Line with baking parchment and fill with baking beans. Bake for 10 minutes. Remove the paper and beans and set the pastry case aside.

4 Cream the butter and caster sugar together until light and fluffy. Beat in the eggs one at a time. In a small pan, gently heat the honey until it melts, then add it to the butter mixture with the lemon rind and juice. Mix well. Stir in the pine nuts and salt, blending well, then pour the filling evenly into the pastry case.

5 Bake for about 45 minutes, or until the filling is lightly browned and set. Leave the tart to cool slightly in the tin, then remove and dust generously with icing sugar. Serve warm, or at room temperature, with crème fraîche or vanilla ice cream, if you like.

Almond & Pine Nut Tart

Strange though it may seem, this traditional tart is an Italian version of the homely Bakewell tart from Derbyshire in England.

Serves 8

115g/4oz/½ cup butter, softened
115g/4oz/generous ½ cup caster
  (superfine) sugar
1 egg, plus 2 egg yolks
150g/5oz/1¼ cups ground
  almonds
115g/4oz/1⅓ cups pine nuts
60ml/4 tbsp seedless raspberry
  jam

icing (confectioners') sugar,
  for dusting

For the pastry

175g/6oz/1½ cups plain
  (all-purpose) flour
65g/2½oz/5 tbsp caster
  (superfine) sugar
1.5ml/¼ tsp baking powder
pinch of salt
115g/4oz/½ cup chilled
  butter, diced
1 egg yolk

1 Make the pastry. Sift the flour, sugar, baking powder and salt on to a clean, dry cold surface or marble pastry board. Make a well in the centre and put in the diced butter and egg yolk. Gradually work the flour mixture into the butter and egg yolk, using just your fingertips, until you have a soft, pliable dough.

2 Press the dough into a 23cm/9in loose-based fluted flan tin (tart pan). Chill for 30 minutes.

3 Cream the butter and sugar with an electric whisk until light, then use a wooden spoon to beat in the egg and egg yolks a little at a time, alternating with the almonds. Beat in the pine nuts.

4 Preheat the oven to 160°C/325°F/Gas 3. Spread the jam evenly over the pastry case (pie shell), then spoon in the filling. Bake for 30–35 minutes until golden, or until a skewer inserted in the centre of the tart comes out clean.

5 Transfer to a wire rack and leave to cool, then carefully remove the side of the tin, leaving the tart on the tin base. Dust with icing sugar and serve with whipped cream.

Honey & Pine Nut Energy 899Kcal/3750kJ; Protein 13.4g; Carbohydrate 78.4g, of which sugars 49.8g; Fat 61.4g, of which saturates 22.8g; Cholesterol 209mg; Calcium 97mg; Fibre 1.9g; Sodium 285mg.
Almond & Pine Nut Energy 643Kcal/2675kJ; Protein 10.2g; Carbohydrate 47.7g, of which sugars 30.5g; Fat 47g, of which saturates 17.3g; Cholesterol 161mg; Calcium 108mg; Fibre 2.3g; Sodium 193mg.

Greek Chocolate Mousse Tartlets

Irresistible Greek-style tartlets with a lightweight chocolate and yogurt filling.

Serves 6

175g/6oz/1½ cups plain
  (all-purpose) flour
30ml/2 tbsp cocoa powder
  (unsweetened)
30ml/2 tbsp icing
  (confectioners') sugar
115g/4oz/½ cup butter
60ml/4 tbsp water

melted dark (bittersweet)
  chocolate, to decorate

For the filling

200g/7oz white chocolate
120ml/4fl oz/½ cup milk
10ml/2 tsp powdered gelatine
25g/1oz/2 tbsp caster
  (superfine) sugar
5ml/1 tsp vanilla extract
2 eggs, separated
250g/9oz/generous 1 cup Greek
  (US strained plain) yogurt

1 Preheat the oven to 190°C/375°F/Gas 5. Sift the flour, cocoa and icing sugar into a large bowl.

2 Place the butter in a pan with the water and heat gently until just melted. Cool, then stir into the flour to make a smooth dough. Chill until firm.

3 Roll out the pastry and line six deep 10cm/4in loose-based flan tins (tart pans). Prick the base of the pastry cases (pie shells), cover with baking parchment, weigh down with baking beans and bake blind for 10 minutes. Remove the beans and paper, return to the oven and bake for 15 minutes until firm. Leave to cool.

4 Make the filling. Melt the broken-up chocolate in a heatproof bowl over hot water. Pour the milk into a pan, sprinkle over the gelatine and heat gently, stirring, until the gelatine has dissolved. Remove from the heat and stir in the chocolate.

5 Whisk the sugar, vanilla and egg yolks in a large bowl, then beat in the chocolate mixture. Beat in the yogurt until mixed.

6 Whisk the egg whites in a clean, grease-free bowl until stiff, then fold into the chocolate mixture. Spoon into the pastry cases and leave to set. Drizzle with melted chocolate to serve.

Alsace Plum Tart

Fruit tarts are typical of the Alsace region of France.

Serves 6–8

450g/1lb ripe plums, halved
  and stoned (pitted)
30ml/2 tbsp Kirsch or plum brandy
30ml/2 tbsp seedless raspberry
  jam
2 eggs
50g/2oz/¼ cup caster
  (superfine) sugar
175ml/6fl oz/¾ cup double
  (heavy) cream

grated rind of ½ lemon
1.5ml/¼ tsp vanilla extract

For the pastry

200g/7oz/1¾ cups plain
  (all-purpose) flour
pinch of salt
25g/1oz/¼ cup icing
  (confectioners') sugar
90g/3½oz/scant ½ cup butter,
  diced
2 egg yolks
15ml/1 tbsp chilled water

1 Make the pastry. Sift the flour, salt and sugar into a bowl. Rub or cut in the butter until the mixture resembles fine breadcrumbs. Mix the egg yolks and water together, sprinkle over the dry ingredients and mix to a soft dough.

2 Lightly knead for a few seconds until smooth. Wrap in clear film (plastic wrap) and chill for 30 minutes. Preheat the oven to 200°C/400°F/Gas 6. Mix the plums with the Kirsch or plum brandy in a bowl. Set aside for 30 minutes.

3 Roll out the pastry thinly and use to line a 23cm/9in flan tin (tart pan). Cover and chill for 30 minutes. Prick the base and line with foil. Add baking beans and bake for 15 minutes until slightly dry and set. Remove the foil and beans. Lightly brush the base of the pastry case (pie shell) with a thin layer of jam, bake for 5 minutes more, then transfer to a wire rack to cool.

4 Lower the oven temperature to 180°C/350°F/Gas 4. Beat the eggs and sugar until well combined, then beat in the cream, lemon rind, vanilla and any juice from the plums. Arrange the plums, cut side down, in the pastry case, then pour over the custard. Bake for 30 minutes, or until a knife inserted in the centre comes out clean. Serve the tart warm.

Mousse Tartlets Energy 555Kcal/2320kJ; Protein 11.9g; Carbohydrate 55g, of which sugars 32.2g; Fat 34g, of which saturates 19.7g; Cholesterol 105mg; Calcium 242mg; Fibre 1.5g; Sodium 263mg.
Alsace Plum Tart Energy 396Kcal/1652kJ; Protein 5.5g; Carbohydrate 37.2g, of which sugars 18.2g; Fat 25.2g, of which saturates 14.7g; Cholesterol 155mg; Calcium 74mg; Fibre 1.7g; Sodium 104mg.

Almond & Raspberry Swiss Roll

An airy whisked sponge cake is rolled up with a mouthwatering fresh cream and raspberry filling to make a stunning dessert.

Serves 8

oil, for greasing
4 eggs, separated
115g/4oz/generous ½ cup caster (superfine) sugar
25g/1oz/¼ cup ground almonds
40g/1½oz/⅓ cup plain (all-purpose) flour, sifted
caster (superfine) sugar, for sprinkling
250ml/8fl oz/1 cup double (heavy) cream
275g/10oz/1½ cups fresh raspberries
16 flaked (sliced) almonds, toasted, to decorate

1 Preheat the oven to 190°C/375°F/Gas 5. Grease a 33 × 23cm/13 × 9in Swiss roll tin (jelly roll pan) and line with baking parchment, cut to fit.

2 In a large bowl, beat the egg yolks with half the caster sugar until light and foamy. Lightly fold in the almonds and flour. Whisk the egg whites until they form stiff peaks. Gradually whisk in the remaining sugar to form a stiff meringue. Stir half the meringue mixture into the egg yolk mixture, then fold in the rest.

3 Pour the mixture into the prepared tin, level the surface and bake for 10 minutes or until risen and spongy to the touch.

4 Sprinkle a sheet of baking parchment with caster sugar. Turn out the cake on to this. Leave to cool with the tin still in place.

5 Lift the tin off the cooled cake and peel off the lining. Whip the cream until it holds its shape. Fold in 250g/9oz/1¼ cups of the raspberries, and spread the cream and raspberry mixture over the cooled cake, leaving a narrow border around the edge.

6 Carefully roll up the cake from a short end, using the paper as a guide. Sprinkle the roll liberally with caster sugar.

7 To serve, slice the roll and top each portion with the remaining raspberries and the toasted almonds.

Lemon Curd Roulade

This featherlight roulade, filled with tangy lemon curd, is a delicious dessert.

Serves 8

4 eggs, separated
115g/4oz/generous ½ cup caster (superfine) sugar
finely grated rind of 2 lemons
5ml/1 tsp vanilla extract
25g/1oz/¼ cup ground almonds
40g/1½oz/⅓ cup plain (all-purpose) flour, sifted
45g/1¾oz/3 tbsp icing (confectioners') sugar, for dusting

For the lemon curd cream
300ml/½ pint/1¼ cups double (heavy) cream
60ml/4 tbsp lemon curd

1 Preheat the oven to 190°C/375°F/Gas 5. Grease a 33 × 23cm/13 × 9in Swiss roll tin (jelly roll pan) and line with baking parchment, cut to fit.

2 In a large bowl, beat the egg yolks with half the caster sugar until light and foamy. Beat in the lemon rind and vanilla extract, then lightly fold in the ground almonds and flour.

3 Whisk the egg whites in a grease-free bowl until they form stiff peaks. Gradually whisk in the remaining caster sugar to form a stiff meringue. Stir half the meringue mixture into the egg yolk mixture, then fold in the rest.

4 Pour into the prepared tin, level the surface with a metal spatula and bake for 10 minutes or until risen and spongy to the touch. Cover loosely with a sheet of baking parchment and a damp dish towel. Leave to cool in the tin. Make the lemon curd cream. Whip the cream, then lightly fold in the lemon curd.

5 Sift the icing sugar liberally over a piece of baking parchment, then turn the sponge out on to it. Peel off the lining paper and spread the lemon curd cream over the surface of the sponge, leaving a border around the edge.

6 Using the baking parchment underneath as a guide, roll up the sponge from one of the long sides. Place on a serving platter, with the seam underneath, and cut into slices to serve.

Swiss Roll Energy 293Kcal/1222kJ; Protein 5.3g; Carbohydrate 21.2g, of which sugars 17.3g; Fat 21.5g, of which saturates 11.4g; Cholesterol 138mg; Calcium 60mg; Fibre 1.3g; Sodium 44mg.
Roulade Energy 337Kcal/1401kJ; Protein 5g; Carbohydrate 24.5g, of which sugars 18.9g; Fat 25.1g, of which saturates 13.6g; Cholesterol 148mg; Calcium 55mg; Fibre 0.4g; Sodium 50mg.

Bizcocho Borracho

The name of this moist Spanish dessert translates as "drunken cake" – very appropriate as it is steeped in a delicious, brandy-soaked syrup. The cake can be layered with cream, but this version is made in a mould, then turned out. Pipe with whipped cream if you like.

Serves 6–8
butter, for greasing
90g/3½oz/¾ cup plain
   (all-purpose) flour
6 large (US extra large) eggs
90g/3½oz/½ cup caster
   (superfine) sugar
finely grated rind of 1 lemon
90ml/6 tbsp toasted flaked
   (sliced) almonds
250ml/8fl oz/1 cup whipping
   cream, to serve

For the syrup
115g/4oz/generous ½ cup caster
   (superfine) sugar
15ml/1 tbsp water
120ml/4fl oz/½ cup boiling water
105ml/7 tbsp Spanish brandy

1 Starting 1–2 days ahead, preheat the oven to 200°C/400°F/ Gas 6. Butter a shallow tin (pan), about 28 × 18cm/11 × 7in. Line the tin with baking parchment and butter well.

2 Sift the flour a couple of times into a bowl. Separate the eggs, putting the whites in a large, grease-free bowl. Put the yolks in a food processor with the sugar and lemon rind and beat until light. Whisk the whites to soft peaks, then work a little white into the yolk mixture.

3 Drizzle two spoonfuls of the yolk mixture across the whites, sift some flour over the top and cut in gently with a large spoon. Continue folding together in this way until all the egg yolk mixture and flour have been incorporated.

4 Turn the mixture into the prepared tin and and level the surface. Bake for 12 minutes. Leave the cake to set for 5 minutes, then turn out on to a wire rack. Peel off the paper and leave to cool completely.

5 Make the syrup. Place 50g/2oz/¼ cup of the sugar in a small pan with the water. Heat until it caramelizes, shaking the pan a little if one side starts to brown too fast. As soon as the syrup colours, dip the base of the pan into a bowl of cold water. Add the remaining sugar and pour in the boiling water. Bring back to a simmer, stirring until the sugar has dissolved. Pour into a measuring jug (cup) and add the brandy.

6 Put the cake back in the tin and drizzle half the syrup over. Cut the cake into scallops with a spoon and layer half in the bottom of a 700ml/1½ pint/3 cup mould or cake tin (pan). Sprinkle 30ml/2 tbsp almonds over the top, and push them into the cracks. Top with the remaining cake and 30ml/2 tbsp nuts.

7 Pour the remaining syrup over the cake, cover with foil and weight down the top. Chill until ready to serve.

8 To serve, whip the cream. Run a knife round the mould and turn the cake out on to a long dish. Sprinkle with the remaining almonds and serve with the cream.

Marbled Swiss Roll

A sensational combination of chocolate sponge and rich walnut buttercream.

Serves 6–8
90g/3½oz/¾ cup plain
   (all-purpose) flour
15ml/1 tbsp cocoa powder
   (unsweetened)
25g/1oz plain (semisweet)
   chocolate, grated
25g/1oz white chocolate, grated
3 eggs
115g/4oz/generous ½ cup caster
   (superfine) sugar
30ml/2 tbsp boiling water

For the filling
75g/3oz/6 tbsp unsalted (sweet)
   butter or margarine, softened
175g/6oz/1½ cups icing
   (confectioners') sugar
15ml/1 tbsp cocoa powder
   (unsweetened)
2.5ml/½ tsp vanilla extract
45ml/3 tbsp chopped walnuts

1 Preheat the oven to 200°C/400°F/Gas 6. Grease a 30 × 20cm/ 12 × 8in Swiss roll tin (jelly roll pan) and line with baking parchment. Sift half the flour with the cocoa into bowl. Stir in the grated plain chocolate. Sift the remaining flour into another bowl; stir in the grated white chocolate.

2 Whisk the eggs and sugar in a heatproof bowl, set over a pan of hot water, until it holds its shape when the whisk is lifted.

3 Remove from the heat and turn half the mixture into a separate bowl. Fold the white chocolate mixture into one half, then fold the plain chocolate mixture into the other. Stir 15ml/ 1 tbsp boiling water into each half to soften the mixtures.

4 Place alternate spoonfuls of mixture in the tin and swirl lightly together for a marbled effect. Bake for 12–15 minutes, or until firm. Turn out on to a sheet of baking parchment and cover with a damp, clean dish towel. Cool.

5 Make the filling. Beat the butter, icing sugar, cocoa and vanilla together in a bowl until smooth, then mix in the walnuts. Uncover the sponge, peel off the lining and spread the surface with the filling. Roll up carefully from a long side, using the paper underneath as a guide, then place on a serving plate.

Bizcocho Borracho Energy 294Kcal/1235kJ; Protein 8.3g; Carbohydrate 36.3g, of which sugars 27.4g; Fat 10.6g, of which saturates 1.7g; Cholesterol 143mg; Calcium 78mg; Fibre 1.2g; Sodium 56mg.
Marbled Swiss Roll Energy 361Kcal/1518kJ; Protein 5.6g; Carbohydrate 51.1g, of which sugars 42g; Fat 16.4g, of which saturates 7.4g; Cholesterol 92mg; Calcium 67mg; Fibre 1.1g; Sodium 125mg.

Chocolate Mousse Strawberry Layer Cake

To ring the changes, try replacing the strawberries with raspberries or blackberries, and use a complementary liqueur.

Serves 10
oil, for greasing
115g/4oz good-quality white chocolate, chopped
120ml/4fl oz/½ cup whipping or double (heavy) cream
120ml/4fl oz/½ cup milk
15ml/1 tbsp rum essence or vanilla extract
115g/4oz/½ cup unsalted (sweet) butter, softened
175g/6oz/¾ cup granulated sugar
3 eggs

275g/10oz/2½ cups plain (all-purpose) flour, plus extra for dusting
5ml/1 tsp baking powder
pinch of salt
675g/1½lb fresh strawberries, sliced, plus extra for decoration
750ml/1¼ pints/3 cups whipping cream
30ml/2 tbsp rum or strawberry-flavour liqueur

For the mousse
250g/9oz good-quality white chocolate, chopped
350ml/12fl oz/1½ cups whipping or double (heavy) cream
30ml/2 tbsp rum or strawberry-flavoured liqueur

1 Preheat the oven to 180°C/350°F/Gas 4. Grease and flour two 23cm/9in cake tins (pans). Line the base of the tins with baking parchment. Melt the chocolate and cream in a double boiler over a low heat, stirring until smooth. Stir in the milk and rum essence or vanilla extract; set aside to cool.

2 In a large bowl, beat the butter and sugar together with an electric whisk until light and creamy. Add the eggs one at a time, beating well after each addition.

3 In a small bowl, stir together the flour, baking powder and salt. Alternately add the flour and melted chocolate to the egg mixture, just until blended. Pour evenly into the tins.

4 Bake for 20–25 minutes until a metal skewer inserted into the centre comes out clean. Cool in the tins on a wire rack for 10 minutes. Turn the cakes out on to the rack, peel off the lining and leave to cool completely.

5 Make the mousse. Melt the chocolate and cream in a medium pan over low heat, stirring frequently, until smooth. Stir in the rum or strawberry-flavoured liqueur and pour into a bowl. Chill until just set. Using a wire whisk, whip the mixture lightly until it has a "mousse" consistency.

6 Using a large knife, carefully slice both cake layers in half horizontally. Sandwich the four layers together with the mousse and strawberries.

7 To decorate the cake, whip the cream with the rum or liqueur to form firm peaks. Spread half the flavoured cream over the top and sides of the cake. Spoon the remaining cream into a piping (pastry) bag with a star nozzle and pipe scrolls on top. Decorate with strawberries and serve.

Strawberry Roulade

A roulade packed with summer fruit is the perfect choice for a family supper.

Serves 6
oil, for greasing
4 egg whites
115g/4oz/generous ½ cup golden caster (superfine) sugar
75g/3oz/⅔ cup plain (all-purpose) flour, sifted

30ml/2 tbsp orange juice
caster (superfine) sugar, for sprinkling
115g/4oz/1 cup strawberries, chopped
150g/5oz/⅔ cup low-fat fromage frais or cream cheese
strawberries, to decorate

1 Preheat the oven to 200°C/400°F/Gas 6. Grease a 33 × 23cm/13 × 9in Swiss roll tin (jelly roll pan) and line with baking parchment, cut to fit.

2 Place the egg whites in a grease-free bowl and whisk to form soft peaks. Gradually whisk in the sugar. Fold in half of the sifted flour, then fold in the rest of the flour with the orange juice.

3 Spoon the mixture into the prepared tin, spreading evenly. Bake for 15–18 minutes, or until the sponge is golden brown and firm to the touch.

4 Meanwhile, spread out a sheet of baking parchment and sprinkle with caster sugar. Turn out the cake on to this and peel off the lining paper. Roll up the sponge loosely from one short side, with the paper inside. Leave to cool.

5 Unroll and remove the paper. Stir the strawberries into the fromage frais and spread over the sponge. Roll up and serve decorated with strawberries.

> **Cook's Tip**
> Cooling the cake rolled up in paper makes it easier to roll up again once spread with the filling.

Strawberry Roulade Energy 164Kcal/695kJ; Protein 4.7g; Carbohydrate 34.8g, of which sugars 25.1g; Fat 1.6g, of which saturates 0.9g; Cholesterol 5mg; Calcium 54mg; Fibre 0.6g; Sodium 53mg.
Layer Cake Energy 964Kcal/4008kJ; Protein 10.9g; Carbohydrate 69g, of which sugars 48g; Fat 72.1g, of which saturates 44.1g; Cholesterol 210mg; Calcium 253mg; Fibre 1.6g; Sodium 174mg.

Chocolate Pecan Torte

A luscious chocolate cake, topped with chocolate-glazed pecan nuts, makes a memorable dessert.

Serves 16
200g/7oz dark (bittersweet) or plain (semisweet) chocolate, chopped into small pieces
150g/5oz/10 tbsp unsalted (sweet) butter, cut into pieces, plus extra for greasing
4 eggs
90g/3¹/₂oz/¹/₂ cup caster (superfine) sugar
10ml/2 tsp vanilla extract
115g/4oz/1 cup ground pecan nuts
10ml/2 tsp ground cinnamon
24 toasted pecan nut halves, to decorate

For the glaze
115g/4oz dark (bittersweet) or plain (semisweet) chocolate, chopped into small pieces
50g/2oz/¹/₄ cup unsalted (sweet) butter, cut into pieces
30ml/2 tbsp clear honey
pinch of ground cinnamon

1 Preheat the oven to 180°C/350°F/Gas 4. Grease a 20cm/8in springform tin (pan); line with baking parchment. Wrap the tin in foil to prevent water from seeping in. Melt the chocolate and butter, stirring until smooth. Beat the eggs, sugar and vanilla in a mixing bowl until the mixture is frothy. Stir in the melted chocolate, nuts and cinnamon. Pour into the tin.

2 Place the tin in a roasting pan. Pour in boiling water to come 2cm/³/₄in up the side of the springform tin. Bake for 25–30 minutes, until the edge of the cake is set but the centre is still soft. Remove the tin from the water bath and lift off the foil. Cool the cake in the tin on a wire rack.

3 Make the glaze. Heat all the ingredients in a small pan until melted, stirring until smooth. Remove from the heat. Half-dip the toasted pecan halves in the glaze and place on a baking sheet lined with baking parchment until set.

4 Remove the cake from the tin, place on the rack and pour the remaining glaze over. Decorate the outside of the torte with the chocolate-dipped pecans and leave to set. Transfer to a plate when ready to serve, and slice into thin wedges.

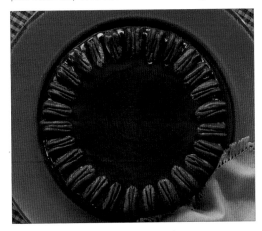

Chocolate Layer Cake

Round off a meal in style with this heavenly cake.

Serves 10–12
cocoa powder (unsweetened), for dusting
225g/8oz can cooked whole beetroot (beets), drained and juice reserved
115g/4oz/¹/₂ cup unsalted (sweet) butter, softened
500g/1¹/₄lb/2¹/₂ cups light brown sugar, firmly packed
3 eggs
15ml/1 tbsp vanilla extract
75g/3oz plain (semisweet) chocolate, melted
250g/9oz/2¹/₄ cups plain (all-purpose) flour
10ml/2 tsp baking powder
2.5ml/¹/₂ tsp salt
120ml/4fl oz/¹/₂ cup buttermilk
chocolate curls (optional)

For the chocolate ganache
475ml/16fl oz/2 cups whipping or double (heavy) cream
500g/1¹/₄lb good-quality chocolate, chopped
15ml/1 tbsp vanilla extract

1 Preheat the oven to 180°C/350°F/Gas 4. Grease two 23cm/9in cake tins (pans); dust the base and sides with cocoa. Grate the beetroot and add to the beet juice. Using an electric whisk, beat the butter, sugar, eggs and vanilla for 3–5 minutes until pale and fluffy. Reduce the speed and beat in the chocolate.

2 In a bowl, sift the flour, baking powder and salt. With the mixer on low speed, alternately beat in the flour mixture in fourths and buttermilk in thirds. Add the beetroot and juice and beat for 1 minute. Divide between the tins and bake for 30–35 minutes. Cool for 10 minutes, then unmould. Cool completely.

3 Make the ganache. Heat the cream in a heavy pan over medium heat, stirring occasionally, until it just begins to boil. Remove from the heat and add the chocolate, stirring constantly until smooth. Stir in the vanilla. Strain into a bowl and chill for about 1 hour, stirring every 10 minutes, until spreadable.

4 Place one cake on a plate and spread with one-third of the ganache. Add the other cake, upside down, and spread the remaining ganache over the top and sides. Top with chocolate curls. Allow the ganache to set for 30 minutes, then chill.

Layer Cake Energy 733Kcal/3073kJ; Protein 7.7g; Carbohydrate 93.5g, of which sugars 77.1g; Fat 39.1g, of which saturates 23.6g; Cholesterol 113mg; Calcium 116mg; Fibre 2.2g; Sodium 116mg.
Chocolate Pecan Torte Energy 308Kcal/1282kJ; Protein 3.6g; Carbohydrate 20.5g, of which sugars 20.1g; Fat 24.2g, of which saturates 10.8g; Cholesterol 75mg; Calcium 25mg; Fibre 1g; Sodium 95mg.

Easy Blueberry Cake

Ready-made cake mixes make life extremely easy and are available in most supermarkets. Simply top with blueberries or an equivalent favourite fruit, as detailed here, to serve up as a simple, yet totally scrumptious, dessert.

Serves 6–8
oil, for greasing
225g/8oz packet sponge
 cake mix
1 egg, if needed
115g/4oz/1 cup blueberries

1 Preheat the oven to 190°C/375°F/Gas 5. Grease a 20cm/8in cake tin (pan). Make up the sponge cake mix according to the instructions on the packet, using the egg if required. Spoon the mixture into the prepared cake tin (pan).

2 Bake the cake according to the instructions provided on the packet. Ten minutes before the end of the cooking time, sprinkle the blueberries over the top of the cake and then return the cake to the oven to finish cooking. (You must work quickly when adding the blueberries – the cake should be out of the oven for as short a time as possible, otherwise it may sink in the middle.)

3 Leave the cake to cool in the tin for 2–3 minutes, then carefully remove from the tin and transfer to a wire rack. Leave to cool completely before serving.

Cook's Tip
This cake is especially delicious served with either vanilla or blueberry ice cream.

Variation
The blueberry topping can be replaced with other fresh fruit, such as raspberries or blackberries.

Simple Chocolate Cake

An easy-to-make chocolate cake that is transformed into a terrific dessert when served with cream or mixed summer fruit.

Serves 6–8
115g/4oz plain (semisweet)
 chocolate, broken into squares
45ml/3 tbsp milk
150g/5oz/⅔ cup unsalted (sweet)
 butter or margarine, softened,
 plus extra for greasing
150g/5oz/¾ cup light muscovado
 (brown) sugar
3 eggs

200g/7oz/1¾ cups self-raising
 (self-rising) flour
15ml/1 tbsp cocoa powder
 (unsweetened)
icing (confectioners') sugar and
 cocoa powder, for dusting

For the buttercream
75g/3oz/6 tbsp unsalted (sweet)
 butter or margarine, softened
175g/6oz/1½ cups icing
 (confectioners') sugar
15ml/1 tbsp cocoa powder
 (unsweetened)
2.5ml/½ tsp vanilla extract

1 Preheat the oven to 180°C/350°F/Gas 4. Grease two 18cm/7in round sandwich cake tins (layer pans) and line the base of each with baking parchment. Melt the chocolate with the milk in a heatproof bowl set over a pan of simmering water.

2 Cream the butter or margarine with the sugar in a mixing bowl until pale and fluffy. Add the eggs one at a time, beating well after each addition. Stir in the chocolate mixture.

3 Sift the flour and cocoa over the mixture and fold in with a metal spoon until evenly mixed. Turn into the prepared tins, level the surfaces and bake for 35–40 minutes or until well risen and firm. Turn out on to wire racks and leave to cool.

4 Make the buttercream. Beat the butter or margarine, icing sugar, cocoa powder and vanilla extract together in a bowl until the mixture is smooth.

5 Spread buttercream over one of the cakes, then top with the second layer. Dust with a mixture of icing sugar and cocoa just before serving.

Chocolate Orange Marquise

Here is a cake for people who are passionate about chocolate. The rich, dense flavour is accentuated by fresh orange to make it a truly delectable treat.

Serves 6–8

200g/7oz/1 cup caster (superfine) sugar
60ml/4 tbsp freshly squeezed orange juice

350g/12oz dark (bittersweet) chocolate, broken into squares
225g/8oz/1 cup unsalted (sweet) butter, diced, plus extra for greasing
5 eggs
finely grated rind of 1 orange
45g/1³⁄₄oz/3 tbsp plain (all-purpose) flour
icing (confectioners') sugar and finely pared strips of orange rind, to decorate

1 Preheat the oven to 180°C/350°F/Gas 4. Grease a 23cm/9in shallow cake tin (pan) with a depth of 6cm/2½in. Line the base of the tin with baking parchment.

2 Place 90g/3½oz/½ cup of the sugar in a pan. Add the orange juice and stir over a low heat until dissolved.

3 Remove from the heat and stir in the chocolate until melted, then add the butter, piece by piece, until melted.

4 Whisk the eggs with the remaining sugar in a large bowl, until the mixture is pale and very thick. Add the orange rind, then lightly fold the chocolate mixture into the egg mixture. Sift the flour over the top and fold in.

5 Pour the mixture into the prepared tin. Place in a roasting pan, then pour hot water into the roasting pan to reach about halfway up the sides of the cake tin.

6 Bake for 1 hour, or until the cake is firm to the touch. Remove the tin from the roasting pan and cool for 20 minutes. Turn out the cake on to a baking sheet, place a serving plate upside down on top, then carefully turn the plate and baking sheet over together. Dust with a little icing sugar, decorate with strips of orange rind and serve slightly warm or chilled.

Chocolate & Cherry Polenta Cake

Polenta and almonds add an unusual nutty texture to this tasty dessert. It is delicious served on its own, but also tastes good served with thin cream or yogurt.

Serves 8

50g/2oz/⅓ cup quick-cook polenta
about 120ml/4fl oz/½ cup boiling water
oil, for greasing
200g/7oz plain (semisweet) chocolate, broken into squares

5 eggs, separated
175g/6oz/³⁄₄ cup caster (superfine) sugar
115g/4oz/1 cup ground almonds
50g/2oz/½ cup plain (all-purpose) flour
finely grated rind of 1 orange
115g/4oz/½ cup glacé (candied) cherries, halved
icing (confectioners') sugar, for dusting

1 Place the polenta in a heatproof bowl and pour over just enough of the boiling water to cover. Stir well, then cover the bowl and leave to stand for about 30 minutes, until the polenta has absorbed all the excess moisture.

2 Preheat the oven to 190°C/375°F/Gas 5. Grease a deep 22cm/8½in round cake tin (pan) and line the base with baking parchment. Melt the chocolate in a heatproof bowl set over a pan of hot water.

3 Whisk the egg yolks with the sugar in a bowl until thick and pale. Beat in the chocolate, then fold in the polenta, ground almonds, flour and orange rind.

4 Whisk the egg whites in a clean bowl until stiff. Stir 15ml/1 tbsp of the whites into the chocolate mixture, then fold in the rest. Finally, fold in the cherries.

5 Scrape the mixture into the prepared tin and bake for 45–55 minutes or until well risen and firm to the touch. Turn the cake out on to a wire rack and leave to cool. Dust with icing sugar just before serving.

Marquise Energy 553Kcal/2309kJ; Protein 3.1g; Carbohydrate 59.1g, of which sugars 54.4g; Fat 35.5g, of which saturates 22g; Cholesterol 63mg; Calcium 41mg; Fibre 1.3g; Sodium 176mg.
Polenta Cake Energy 420Kcal/1764kJ; Protein 9.6g; Carbohydrate 56.4g, of which sugars 45.5g; Fat 18.8g, of which saturates 5.8g; Cholesterol 120mg; Calcium 89mg; Fibre 2.2g; Sodium 53mg.

Chocolate Fudge Gâteau

A glorious dessert that is
sure to delight everyone.

Serves 8–10
275g/10oz/2½ cups self-raising
  wholemeal (self-rising whole-
  wheat) flour
50g/2oz/½ cup cocoa powder
  (unsweetened)
45ml/3 tbsp baking powder
225g/8oz/1 cup caster
  (superfine) sugar
few drops of vanilla extract
135ml/9 tbsp sunflower oil

350ml/12fl oz/1½ cups water
sifted cocoa powder
  (unsweetened), for sprinkling
25g/1oz/¼ cup chopped nuts

For the chocolate fudge
50g/2oz/¼ cup soya
  margarine
45ml/3 tbsp water
250g/9oz/2 cups icing
  (confectioners') sugar
30ml/2 tbsp cocoa powder
  (unsweetened)
15–30ml/1–2 tbsp hot water

1 Preheat the oven to 160°C/325°F/Gas 3. Grease a deep
20cm/8in round cake tin (pan), line with baking parchment and
grease the paper lightly with a little sunflower oil.

2 Sift the flour, cocoa and baking powder into a mixing bowl.
Add the sugar and vanilla extract, then gradually beat in the oil.
Gradually add the water, beating constantly to produce a thick
batter. Pour into the prepared tin and level the surface.

3 Bake the cake for about 45 minutes or until a fine metal
skewer inserted in the centre comes out clean. Leave in the tin
for about 5 minutes, before turning out on to a wire rack. Peel
off the lining and cool. Cut in half to make two equal layers.

4 Make the chocolate fudge. Place the margarine and water in
a pan and heat gently until the margarine has melted. Remove
from the heat and sift in the icing sugar and cocoa powder,
beating until shiny, adding more hot water if needed. Pour into a
bowl and cool until firm enough to spread and pipe.

5 Sandwich the cake layers together with two-thirds of the
chocolate fudge. Pipe the remaining chocolate fudge over the
cake. Sprinkle with cocoa powder and decorate with the nuts.

Iced Chocolate Nut Gâteau

A divine dessert of rich
chocolate ice cream encased
in brandy-soaked sponge.

Serves 6–8
75g/3oz/¾ cup shelled hazelnuts
about 32 sponge fingers
150ml/¼ pint/⅔ cup cold strong
  black coffee
30ml/2 tbsp brandy

475ml/16fl oz/2 cups double
  (heavy) cream
75g/3oz/⅔ cup icing
  (confectioners') sugar, sifted
150g/5oz plain (semisweet)
  chocolate, chopped into small
  pieces
icing (confectioners') sugar and
  cocoa powder (unsweetened),
  for dusting

1 Preheat the oven to 200°C/400°F/Gas 6. Spread out the
hazelnuts on a baking sheet and toast them in the oven for
5 minutes until golden. Turn the nuts on to a clean dish towel
and rub off the skins while still warm. Cool, then chop finely.

2 Line a 1.2 litre/2 pint/5 cup loaf tin (pan) with clear film
(plastic wrap) and cut the sponge fingers to fit the base and
sides. Reserve the remaining fingers. Mix the coffee with the
brandy in a shallow dish. Dip the sponge fingers briefly into the
coffee mixture and return to the tin, sugar side down, to fit.

3 Whip the cream with the icing sugar until it holds soft peaks.
Fold half the chopped chocolate into the cream with the
hazelnuts. Use a gentle figure-of-eight action to distribute the
chocolate and nuts evenly.

4 Melt the remaining chocolate in a bowl set over a pan of
barely simmering water. Cool, then fold into the cream mixture.
Spoon into the tin.

5 Moisten the remaining fingers in the coffee mixture – take care
not to soak the fingers, otherwise they will collapse. Lay the
moistened fingers over the filling. Wrap and freeze until firm.

6 To serve, remove from the freezer 30 minutes before serving
to allow the ice cream to soften slightly. Turn out on to a
serving plate and dust with icing sugar and cocoa powder.

Devil's Food Cake with Orange Frosting

The classic combination of chocolate and orange makes this dessert irresistible.

Serves 8–10

50g/2oz/½ cup cocoa powder (unsweetened)
175ml/6fl oz/¾ cup boiling water
175g/6oz/¾ cup butter, at room temperature
350g/12oz/1½ cups soft dark brown sugar
3 eggs, at room temperature
225g/8oz/2 cups plain (all-purpose) flour
25ml/1½ tsp bicarbonate of soda (baking soda)
1.5ml/¼ tsp baking powder
175ml/6fl oz/¾ cup sour cream
pared orange rind, shredded and blanched, to decorate

For the frosting
285g/10½oz/1½ cups granulated sugar
2 egg whites
60ml/4 tbsp frozen orange juice concentrate
15ml/1 tbsp fresh lemon juice
grated rind of 1 orange

1 Preheat the oven to 180°C/350°F/Gas 4. Line two 23cm/9in cake tins (pans) with baking parchment and grease. In a bowl, mix the cocoa and the boiling water until smooth. Set aside.

2 With an electric whisk, cream the butter and sugar until light and fluffy. Add the eggs, one at a time, beating well.

3 When the cocoa mixture is lukewarm, stir into the butter mixture. Sift together the flour, bicarbonate of soda and baking powder twice. Fold into the cocoa mixture in three batches, alternately with the sour cream.

4 Pour into the tins. Bake for 30–35 minutes, until the cakes pull away from the sides. Stand for 15 minutes before turning out.

5 Make the frosting. Place all the ingredients in a bowl set over hot water. With an electric whisk, beat until the mixture holds soft peaks. Remove from the heat and continue beating until thick enough to spread. Sandwich the cake with frosting, then spread over the top and sides. Decorate with orange rind.

Pineapple Upside-Down Cake

Made with handy canned pineapple, this is a favourite year-round dessert. For an added splash of colour, place a halved candied cherry in the middle of each pineapple ring before cooking.

Serves 8

115g/4oz/½ cup butter
225g/8oz/1 cup muscovado (molasses) sugar
450g/16oz can pineapple rings, drained
4 eggs, separated
grated rind of 1 lemon
pinch of salt
90g/3½oz/½ cup granulated sugar
85g/3¼oz/¾ cup plain (all-purpose) flour
5ml/1 tsp baking powder
whipped cream, to serve

1 Preheat the oven to 180°C/350°F/Gas 4. Melt the butter in an ovenproof cast-iron frying pan, about 25cm/10in in diameter. Remove 15ml/1 tbsp of the melted butter and set aside.

2 Add the sugar to the frying pan and stir until blended. Place the drained pineapple slices on top in one layer. Set aside.

3 In a bowl, whisk together the egg yolks, reserved butter and lemon rind until smooth and well blended. Set aside.

4 With an electric whisk, beat the egg whites with the salt until stiff. Fold in the granulated sugar, 30ml/2 tbsp at a time. Fold in the egg yolk mixture.

5 Sift the flour and baking powder together. Fold into the egg mixture in three batches. Pour the batter over the pineapple and level the surface.

6 Bake for about 30 minutes or until a metal skewer inserted into the centre of the cake comes out clean.

7 While still hot, place an upside-down serving plate on top of the frying pan. Using oven gloves, firmly hold the pan and plate together, then flip over to turn out the cake. Serve hot or cold with whipped cream.

Devil's Food Cake Energy 537Kcal/2262kJ; Protein 6.5g; Carbohydrate 86.2g, of which sugars 68.5g; Fat 20.9g, of which saturates 12.5g; Cholesterol 105mg; Calcium 101mg; Fibre 1.3g; Sodium 200mg.
Upside-Down Cake Energy 358Kcal/1508kJ; Protein 4.6g; Carbohydrate 55.2g, of which sugars 47.1g; Fat 14.8g, of which saturates 8.3g; Cholesterol 126mg; Calcium 63mg; Fibre 1g; Sodium 126mg.

Carrot Cake with Maple Butter Frosting

A good, quick dessert cake for a family supper.

Serves 12
450g/1lb carrots, peeled
175g/6oz/1½ cups plain
   (all-purpose) flour
10ml/2 tsp baking powder
2.5ml/½ tsp bicarbonate of soda
   (baking soda)
5ml/1 tsp salt
10ml/2 tsp ground cinnamon
4 eggs
10ml/2 tsp vanilla extract
225g/8oz/1 cup muscovado
   (molasses) sugar

90g/3½oz/½ cup granulated
   sugar
300ml/½ pint/1¼ cups sunflower
   oil, plus extra for greasing
115g/4oz/1 cup walnuts, finely
   chopped
65g/2½oz/½ cup raisins
walnut halves, for decorating
   (optional)

For the frosting
75g/3oz/6 tbsp unsalted (sweet)
   butter, at room temperature
350g/12oz/3 cups icing
   (confectioners') sugar
50ml/2fl oz/¼ cup maple syrup

1 Preheat the oven to 180°C/350°F/Gas 4. Line a 28 x 20cm/ 11 x 8in rectangular cake tin (pan) with baking parchment and grease. Grate the carrots and set aside.

2 Sift the flour, baking powder, bicarbonate of soda, salt and cinnamon into a bowl. Set aside.

3 With an electric whisk, beat the eggs until blended. Add the vanilla, sugars and oil; beat to incorporate. Fold in the flour mixture in three batches. Fold in the carrots, walnuts and raisins.

4 Pour into the prepared tin and bake for 40–45 minutes until springy to the touch. Stand for 10 minutes, then turn out.

5 Make the frosting. Cream the butter with half the sugar until soft. Add the syrup, then beat in the remaining sugar. Spread the frosting over the top of the cake. Using a metal spatula, make decorative ridges in the frosting. Cut into squares. Decorate with walnut halves, if you like.

Black & White Pound Cake

A great dish for feeding a crowd, served with fresh custard or pouring cream.

Serves 16
115g/4oz plain (semisweet)
   chocolate, broken into squares
350g/12oz/3 cups plain
   (all-purpose) flour, plus extra
   for dusting

5ml/1 tsp baking powder
450g/1lb/2 cups butter, at room
   temperature, plus extra
   for greasing
650g/1lb 7oz/3⅓ cups sugar
15ml/1 tbsp vanilla extract
10 eggs, at room temperature
icing (confectioners') sugar,
   for dusting

1 Preheat the oven to 180°C/350°F/Gas 4. Line the base of a 25cm/10in straight-sided ring mould with baking parchment and grease. Dust with flour spread evenly with a brush.

2 Melt the chocolate in a heatproof bowl set over a pan of hot water. Stir occasionally. Set aside.

3 In a bowl, sift together the flour and baking powder. In another bowl, cream the butter, sugar and vanilla extract with an electric whisk until light and fluffy. Add the eggs, two at a time, then gradually incorporate the flour mixture on low speed.

4 Spoon half of the batter into the prepared pan. Stir the chocolate into the remaining batter, then spoon into the pan. Using a metal spatula, swirl the two batters together to create a marbled effect.

5 Bake for about 1¾ hours until a metal skewer inserted into the centre comes out clean. Cover with foil halfway through baking. Allow to stand for 15 minutes, then turn out and transfer to a cooling rack. To serve, dust with icing sugar.

> **Cook's Tip**
> This delicious cake is also known as Marbled Cake because of its distinctive appearance.

Carrot Cake Energy 595Kcal/2495kJ; Protein 5.5g; Carbohydrate 79.6g, of which sugars 68.2g; Fat 30.5g, of which saturates 6.4g; Cholesterol 77mg; Calcium 82mg; Fibre 1.8g; Sodium 90mg.
Pound Cake Energy 527Kcal/2205kJ; Protein 6.7g; Carbohydrate 64.2g, of which sugars 47.5g; Fat 28.9g, of which saturates 16.9g; Cholesterol 179mg; Calcium 77mg; Fibre 0.9g; Sodium 218mg.

Lemon Coconut Layer Cake

The flavours of lemon and coconut complement each other beautifully in this light dessert cake.

Serves 8–10

115g/4oz/1 cup plain
  (all-purpose) flour
pinch of salt
8 eggs
350g/12oz/1¾ cups granulated
  sugar
15ml/1 tbsp grated orange rind
grated rind of 2 lemons
juice of 1 lemon

40g/1½oz/½ cup desiccated (dry
  unsweetened) coconut
30ml/2 tbsp cornflour (cornstarch)
75g/3oz/6 tbsp butter

For the frosting

115g/4oz/½ cup unsalted (sweet)
  butter, at room temperature
115g/4oz/1 cup icing
  (confectioners') sugar
grated rind of 1 lemon
90–120ml/6–8 tbsp freshly
  squeezed lemon juice
400g/14oz desiccated (dry
  unsweetened) coconut

1 Preheat the oven to 180°C/350°F/Gas 4. Line three 20cm/8in cake tins (pans) with baking parchment and grease. In a bowl, sift together the flour and salt and set aside.

2 Place six of the eggs in a large heatproof bowl set over hot water. With an electric whisk, beat until frothy. Gradually beat in 150g/5oz/¾ cup of the granulated sugar until the mixture doubles in volume and is thick enough to leave a ribbon trail when the beaters are lifted; this takes about 10 minutes.

3 Remove the bowl from the hot water. Fold in the orange rind, half the grated lemon rind and 15ml/1 tbsp of the lemon juice until blended. Fold in the coconut.

4 Sift over the flour mixture in three batches, folding in thoroughly after each addition. Divide the mixture between the prepared tins.

5 Bake for 25–30 minutes until the cakes pull away from the sides of the tin. Allow to stand for 3–5 minutes, then turn out on to a wire rack to cool.

6 In a bowl, blend the cornflour with a little cold water. Whisk in the remaining eggs until just blended. Set aside.

7 In a pan, combine the remaining lemon rind and juice, the remaining sugar, the butter and 250ml/8fl oz/1 cup of water.

8 Bring the mixture to the boil over a medium heat. Whisk in the eggs and cornflour, and return to the boil. Whisk constantly for about 5 minutes, until thick. Remove from the heat. Cover with baking parchment to stop a skin forming and set aside.

9 Make the frosting. Cream the butter and icing sugar until smooth. Stir in the lemon rind and enough lemon juice to give a thick, spreading consistency.

10 Sandwich the three cake layers together with the cooled lemon custard mixture. Spread the frosting over the top and sides of the cake. Cover the cake with the coconut, pressing it gently into the frosting to keep in place.

Marmalade Cake

Orange marmalade and cinnamon give this moist cake a deliciously warm flavour. Served as a dessert, with thick yogurt or even fresh custard, it is sure to go down well with the whole family.

Serves 8

200g/7oz/1¾ cups plain
  (all-purpose) flour
5ml/1 tsp baking powder
6.25ml/1¼ tsp ground cinnamon

90g/3½oz/scant ½ cup butter or
  margarine, plus extra
  for greasing
50g/2oz/¼ cup soft light
  brown sugar
60ml/4 tbsp chunky orange
  marmalade
1 egg, beaten
about 45ml/3 tbsp milk
50g/2oz/½ cup icing
  (confectioners') sugar
about 15ml/1 tbsp warm water
thinly pared and shredded orange
  and lemon rind, to decorate

1 Preheat the oven to 160°C/325°F/Gas 3. Butter a 900ml/1½ pint/3¾ cup loaf tin (pan), then line the base with baking parchment and grease.

2 Sift the flour, baking powder and cinnamon into a mixing bowl, then rub in the butter with your fingertips until the mixture resembles fine breadcrumbs. Stir in the sugar.

3 Mix together the marmalade, egg and most of the milk, then stir into the bowl to make a soft dropping (pourable) consistency, adding a little more milk if necessary.

4 Transfer the mixture to the prepared tin and bake for about 1¼ hours until firm to the touch. Leave the cake to cool for 5 minutes, then turn on to a wire rack.

5 Carefully peel off the lining paper and leave the cake on the rack to cool completely.

6 When the cake is cold, make the icing. Sift the icing sugar into a bowl and mix in the water a little at a time to make a thick glaze. Drizzle the icing over the top of the cake and decorate with the orange and lemon rind.

Layer Cake Energy 698Kcal/2912kJ; Protein 8.9g; Carbohydrate 63g, of which sugars 51.8g; Fat 47.5g, of which saturates 34.7g; Cholesterol 193mg; Calcium 78mg; Fibre 6.4g; Sodium 188mg.
Marmalade Cake Energy 250Kcal/1050kJ; Protein 3.5g; Carbohydrate 38g, of which sugars 19g; Fat 10.4g, of which saturates 6.2g; Cholesterol 48mg; Calcium 56mg; Fibre 0.8g; Sodium 86mg.

Tuscan Citrus Sponge

This tangy cake comes from the little Tuscan town of Pitigliano. It is a light whisked sponge made with matzo and potato flours rather than traditional wheat flour.

Serves 6–8

12 eggs, separated
300g/11oz/1½ cups caster (superfine) sugar
120ml/4fl oz/½ cup fresh orange juice
grated rind of 1 orange
grated rind of 1 lemon
50g/2oz/½ cup potato flour, sifted
90g/3½oz/¾ cup fine matzo meal or matzo meal flour, sifted
icing (confectioners') sugar, for dusting
orange juice and segments of orange, to serve

1 Preheat the oven to 160°C/325°F/Gas 3. Whisk the egg yolks until pale and frothy, then whisk in the sugar, orange juice, orange rind and lemon rind.

2 Fold the sifted flours or flour and meal into the egg and sugar mixture. In a clean bowl, whisk the egg whites until stiff, then fold into the egg yolk mixture.

3 Pour the cake mixture into a deep, ungreased 25cm/10in cake tin (pan) and bake for about 1 hour, or until a cocktail stick (toothpick), inserted in the centre, comes out clean. Leave to cool in the tin.

4 When cold, turn out the cake and invert on to a serving plate. Dust with a little icing sugar and serve in wedges with orange segments, moistened with a little fresh orange juice.

> **Cook's Tips**
> • When testing to see if the cake is cooked, if you don't have a cocktail stick (toothpick) to hand, use a strand of raw dried spaghetti instead – it will work just as well.
> • If you cannot find matzo meal, try fine polenta instead.

Greek Yogurt & Fig Cake

Baked fresh figs, thickly sliced, make a delectable base for a featherlight sponge. Figs that are a bit on the firm side work best for this particular recipe. Serve with yogurt as a finale to a Greek-style meal.

Serves 6–8

6 firm fresh figs, thickly sliced
45ml/3 tbsp clear honey, plus extra for glazing cooked figs
200g/7oz/scant 1 cup butter, softened, plus extra for greasing
175g/6oz/¾ cup caster (superfine) sugar
grated rind of 1 lemon
grated rind of 1 orange
4 eggs, separated
225g/8oz/2 cups plain (all-purpose) flour
5ml/1 tsp baking powder
5ml/1 tsp bicarbonate of soda (baking soda)
250ml/8fl oz/1 cup Greek (US strained plain) yogurt

1 Preheat the oven to 180°C/350°F/Gas 4. Grease a 23cm/9in cake tin (pan) and line the base with baking parchment. Arrange the figs over the base of the tin and drizzle over the honey.

2 In a large mixing bowl, cream the butter and caster sugar with the lemon and orange rinds until the mixture is pale and fluffy, then gradually beat in the egg yolks.

3 Sift the dry ingredients together. Add a little to the creamed mixture, beat well, then beat in a spoonful of Greek yogurt. Repeat this process until all the dry ingredients and Greek yogurt have been incorporated.

4 Whisk the egg whites in a grease-free bowl until they form stiff peaks. Stir half the whites into the cake mixture to soften it slightly, then fold in the rest. Pour the mixture over the figs in the tin, then bake for 1¼ hours or until golden and a skewer inserted in the centre of the cake comes out clean.

5 Turn the cake out on to a wire rack, peel off the lining paper and leave to cool. Drizzle the figs with extra honey before serving warm or cold.

Angel Food Cake

This beautifully light cake is wonderful served with fresh fruit.

Serves 12–14

115g/4oz/1 cup self-raising (self-rising) flour, sifted
285g/10½oz/1½ cups caster (superfine) sugar
300ml/½ pint/1¼ cups egg whites (about 10–11 eggs)
6.5ml/1¼ tsp cream of tartar
1.5ml/¼ tsp salt
5ml/1 tsp vanilla extract
1.5ml/¼ tsp almond extract
icing (confectioners') sugar, for dusting

1 Preheat the oven to 160°C/325°F/Gas 3. Sift the flour before measuring, then sift it four times with 90g/3½oz/½ cup of the sugar. Transfer to a bowl.

2 Beat the egg whites with an electric whisk until foamy. Sift the cream of tartar and salt over and continue to beat until the whites hold soft peaks when the beaters are lifted.

3 Add the remaining sugar in three batches, beating well after each addition. Stir in the vanilla and almond extracts. Add the flour mixture, ½ cup at a time, folding in gently with a large metal spoon after each addition.

4 Transfer to an ungreased 25cm/10in straight-sided ring mould and bake for about 1 hour until delicately browned on top.

5 Turn the ring mould upside down on to a cake rack and leave to cool for 1 hour. If the cake does not turn out, run a spatula around the edge to loosen it. Invert on to a serving plate.

6 When cool, lay a star-shaped template on top of the cake, sift with icing sugar, then lift off.

Cook's Tip

Sifting the flour over and over again lets plenty of air into the mixture and is the key to the cake's lightness.

Sponge Cake with Fruit & Cream

Called Génoise, this French cake is used as the base for both simple and elaborate creations. You could simply dust it with icing sugar, or layer it with fresh fruits to serve as a seasonal dessert.

Serves 6

butter, for greasing
115g/4oz/1 cup plain (all-purpose) flour
pinch of salt
4 eggs, at room temperature
115g/4oz/generous ½ cup caster (superfine) sugar
2.5ml/½ tsp vanilla extract
50g/2oz/4 tbsp butter, melted or clarified and cooled

For the filling
450g/1lb fresh strawberries or raspberries
30–60ml/2–4 tbsp caster (superfine) sugar
475ml/16fl oz/2 cups whipping cream
5ml/1 tsp vanilla extract

1 Preheat the oven to 180°C/350°F/Gas 4. Lightly butter a 23cm/9in springform or deep cake tin (pan). Line the base with baking parchment), and dust lightly with flour. Sift the flour and salt together twice.

2 Half-fill a medium pan with hot water and set over a low heat (do not allow the water to boil). Put the eggs in a heatproof bowl that just fits into the pan without touching the water. Using an electric whisk, beat the eggs at medium-high speed, gradually adding the sugar, for 8–10 minutes until the mixture is very thick and pale and leaves a ribbon trail when the beaters are lifted. Remove the bowl from the pan, add the vanilla extract and continue beating until the mixture is cool.

3 Fold in the flour mixture in three batches, using a balloon whisk or metal spoon. Before the third addition of flour, stir a large spoonful of the mixture into the melted or clarified butter to lighten it, then fold the butter into the remaining mixture with the last addition of flour. Work quickly, but gently, so the mixture does not deflate. Pour into the prepared tin, smoothing the top so the sides are slightly higher than the centre.

4 Bake in the oven for about 25–30 minutes until the top of the cake springs back when touched and the edge begins to shrink away from the sides of the tin. Cool the cake in its tin on a wire rack for 5–10 minutes, then turn the cake out on to the rack to cool completely. Peel off the lining paper.

5 Make the filling. Slice the strawberries, place in a bowl, sprinkle with 15–30ml/1–2 tbsp of the sugar and set aside. Beat the cream with 15–30ml/1–2 tbsp of the sugar and the vanilla extract until it holds soft peaks.

6 To assemble the cake (up to 4 hours before serving), split the cake horizontally, using a serrated knife. Place the top, cut side up, on a serving plate. Spread with a third of the cream and cover with an even layer of sliced strawberries.

7 Place the bottom half of the cake, cut side down, on top of the filling and press lightly. Spread the remaining cream over the top and sides of the cake. Chill until ready to serve. Serve the remaining strawberries with the cake.

Angel Food Cake Energy 117Kcal/500kJ; Protein 3.1g; Carbohydrate 27.7g, of which sugars 21.4g; Fat 0.1g, of which saturates 0g; Cholesterol 0mg; Calcium 24mg; Fibre 0.3g; Sodium 49mg.
Sponge Cake Energy 592Kcal/2466kJ; Protein 8.8g; Carbohydrate 45.8g, of which sugars 31.2g; Fat 42.9g, of which saturates 25.5g; Cholesterol 228mg; Calcium 125mg; Fibre 2.5g; Sodium 121mg.

Baked Chocolate & Raisin Cheesecake

This classic cheesecake will disappear in a flash.

Serves 8–10
75g/3oz/⅔ cup plain (all-purpose) flour
45ml/3 tbsp cocoa powder (unsweetened)
75g/3oz/½ cup semolina
50g/2oz/¼ cup caster (superfine) sugar
115g/4oz/½ cup unsalted (sweet) butter, softened

For the filling
225g/8oz/1 cup cream cheese
120ml/4fl oz/½ cup natural (plain) yogurt
2 eggs, beaten
75g/3oz/6 tbsp caster (superfine) sugar
finely grated rind of 1 lemon
75g/3oz/½ cup raisins
45ml/3 tbsp plain (semisweet) chocolate chips

For the topping
75g/3oz plain (semisweet) chocolate, chopped into small pieces
30ml/2 tbsp golden (light corn) syrup
40g/1½oz/3 tbsp butter

1 Preheat the oven to 150°C/300°F/Gas 2. Sift the flour and cocoa into a mixing bowl and stir in the semolina and sugar. Using your fingertips, work the butter into the flour mixture until it makes a firm dough.

2 Press the dough into the base of a 22cm/8½in springform tin (pan). Prick all over with a fork and bake in the oven for 15 minutes. Remove the tin but leave the oven on.

3 Make the filling. In a large bowl, beat the cream cheese with the yogurt, eggs and sugar until evenly mixed. Stir in the lemon rind, raisins and chocolate chips.

4 Smooth the cream cheese mixture over the chocolate base and bake for a further 35–45 minutes or until the filling is pale gold and just set. Cool in the tin on a wire rack.

5 Make the topping. Melt the chocolate, syrup and butter in a bowl over simmering water, then pour over the cheesecake. Leave until set. Remove the cheesecake from the tin and serve.

Blueberry-Hazelnut Cheesecake

Ground hazelnuts give this cheesecake an unusual base.

Serves 6–8
350g/12oz blueberries
15ml/1 tbsp clear honey
75g/3oz/6 tbsp granulated sugar
juice of 1 lemon
175g/6oz/¾ cup cream cheese, at room temperature
1 egg
5ml/1 tsp hazelnut liqueur (optional)
120ml/4fl oz/½ cup whipping cream

For the base
175g/6oz/1⅔ cups ground hazelnuts
75g/3oz/⅔ cup plain (all-purpose) flour
pinch of salt
50g/2oz/4 tbsp butter, plus extra for greasing
65g/2½oz/5 tbsp light muscovado (brown) sugar
1 egg yolk

1 Make the base. Put the hazelnuts in a large bowl. Sift in the flour and salt, then stir to mix. Set aside. Beat the butter with the sugar until light and fluffy. Beat in the egg yolk. Gradually fold in the nut mixture, in three batches, until well combined.

2 Press the dough into a greased 23cm/9in pie or tart dish, spread evenly against the sides. Form a rim around the top edge that is slightly thicker than the sides. Cover and chill for 30 minutes.

3 Preheat the oven to 180°C/350°F/Gas 4. Meanwhile, make the topping. Combine the blueberries, honey, 15ml/1 tbsp of the granulated sugar and 5ml/1 tsp of the lemon juice in a heavy pan. Cook for 5–7 minutes over low heat, stirring, until the berries have given off some liquid but retain their shape. Remove from the heat and set aside. Place the pastry base in the oven and bake for 15 minutes. Remove and allow to cool while making the filling.

4 In a bowl, beat the cream cheese with the remaining granulated sugar until light and fluffy. Add the egg, 15ml/1 tbsp of the lemon juice, the liqueur, if using, and the cream and beat until blended.

5 Pour the mixture into the pastry base. Bake for 25 minutes until just set. Cool on a wire rack, then cover and chill for at least 1 hour. Spread the blueberry mixture over the top.

Chocolate & Raisin Energy 441Kcal/1841kJ; Protein 5.8g; Carbohydrate 41.4g, of which sugars 29.3g; Fat 29.3g, of which saturates 17.7g; Cholesterol 93mg; Calcium 86mg; Fibre 1.4g; Sodium 243mg.
Blueberry-Hazelnut Energy 476Kcal/1978kJ; Protein 6.6g; Carbohydrate 31g, of which sugars 23.4g; Fat 37.1g, of which saturates 15g; Cholesterol 99mg; Calcium 109mg; Fibre 3.1g; Sodium 121mg.

Raspberry & White Chocolate Cheesecake

An unbeatable combination: raspberries teamed with mascarpone and white chocolate on a crunchy ginger and pecan nut base.

Serves 8

50g/2oz/4 tbsp unsalted (sweet) butter
225g/8oz/2⅓ cups ginger nut biscuits (gingersnaps), crushed
50g/2oz/½ cup chopped pecan nuts or walnuts

For the filling
275g/10oz/1¼ cups mascarpone
175g/6oz/¾ cup fromage frais or soft white (farmer's) cheese
2 eggs, beaten
40g/1½oz/3 tbsp caster (superfine) sugar
250g/9oz white chocolate, broken into squares
225g/8oz/1⅓ cups fresh or frozen raspberries

For the topping
115g/4oz/½ cup mascarpone cheese
75g/3oz/⅓ cup fromage frais or soft white (farmer's) cheese
white chocolate curls and raspberries, to decorate

1 Preheat the oven to 150°C/300°F/Gas 2. Melt the butter in a pan, then stir in the crushed biscuits and nuts. Press into the base of a 23cm/9in springform cake tin (pan).

2 Make the filling. Beat the mascarpone and fromage frais in a bowl, then beat in the eggs and caster sugar until evenly mixed.

3 Melt the white chocolate gently in a heatproof bowl over hot water. Stir the chocolate into the cheese mixture with the raspberries.

4 Turn into the prepared tin and spread evenly, then bake for about 1 hour or until just set. Switch off the oven, but do not remove the cheesecake. Leave it until cold and completely set.

5 Remove the cheesecake from the tin. Make the topping. Mix the mascarpone with the fromage frais and spread over the cheesecake. Decorate with chocolate curls and raspberries.

Luxury White Chocolate Cheesecake

A luscious dessert for a special occasion.

Serves 16–20

150g/5oz (about 16–18) digestive biscuits (graham crackers)
50g/2oz/½ cup blanched hazelnuts, toasted
50g/2oz/¼ cup unsalted (sweet) butter, melted, plus extra for greasing
2.5ml/½ tsp ground cinnamon
white chocolate curls, to decorate
cocoa powder (unsweetened), for dusting (optional)

For the filling
350g/12oz fine white chocolate, chopped into small pieces
120ml/4fl oz/½ cup whipping cream or double (heavy) cream
675g/1½lb/3 cups cream cheese, softened
50g/2oz/¼ cup granulated sugar
4 eggs
30ml/2 tbsp hazelnut-flavoured liqueur or 15ml/1 tbsp vanilla extract

For the topping
450ml/¾ pint/scant 2 cups sour cream
50g/2oz/¼ cup granulated sugar
15ml/1 tbsp hazelnut-flavoured liqueur or 5ml/1 tsp vanilla extract

1 Preheat the oven to 180°C/350°F/Gas 4. Grease a deep 23cm/9in springform tin (pan).

2 Put the biscuits and hazelnuts in a food processor and process to form fine crumbs. Pour in the butter and cinnamon. Process just until blended. Using the back of a spoon, press on to the base and to within 1cm/½in of the top of the sides of the cake tin.

3 Bake the crumb crust for 5–7 minutes, until just set. Cool in the tin on a wire rack. Lower the oven temperature to 150°C/300°F/Gas 2 and place a baking sheet inside to heat up.

4 Make the filling. Melt the white chocolate and cream in a small pan over a low heat, until smooth, stirring frequently. Set aside to cool slightly.

5 Using an electric whisk, beat the cream cheese and sugar in a large bowl until smooth. Add the eggs one at a time, beating well. Slowly beat in the white chocolate mixture and liqueur or vanilla extract.

6 Pour the filling into the baked crust. Place the tin on the hot baking sheet. Bake for 45–55 minutes; do not allow the top to brown. Transfer to a wire rack while preparing the topping. Increase the oven temperature to 200°C/400°F/Gas 6.

7 Make the topping. In a small bowl whisk the sour cream, sugar and liqueur or vanilla extract until mixed. Pour over the cheesecake, spreading it evenly, and return to the oven. Bake for a further 5–7 minutes. Turn off the oven, but do not open the door for 1 hour.

8 Serve the cheesecake at room temperature, decorated with the white chocolate curls. Dust with cocoa powder, if you like.

Rasp. & White Choc. Energy 551Kcal/2305kJ; Protein 12.8g; Carbohydrate 53.9g, of which sugars 41.4g; Fat 33.1g, of which saturates 17g; Cholesterol 88mg; Calcium 170mg; Fibre 1.4g; Sodium 195mg.
Luxury White Choc. Energy 421Kcal/1746kJ; Protein 5.3g; Carbohydrate 22.3g, of which sugars 18.1g; Fat 34.6g, of which saturates 20g; Cholesterol 98mg; Calcium 124mg; Fibre 0.3g; Sodium 206mg.

Iced Lime Cheesecake

This deliciously tangy, iced cheesecake has the advantage of not needing gelatine to set the filling.

Serves 10
175g/6oz almond biscuits (cookies), broken up
65g/2½oz/5 tbsp unsalted (sweet) butter, plus extra for greasing

8 limes
115g/4oz/generous ½ cup caster (superfine) sugar
90ml/6 tbsp water
200g/7oz/scant 1 cup cottage cheese
250g/9oz/generous 1 cup mascarpone
300ml/½ pint/1¼ cups double (heavy) cream

1 Lightly grease the base and sides of a 20cm/8in springform cake tin (pan) and line with baking parchment. Put the biscuits in a strong plastic bag and crush finely with a rolling pin.

2 Melt the butter in a small pan and stir in the biscuit crumbs until evenly combined. Spoon the mixture into the tin and pack down with the back of a spoon. Freeze while making the filling.

3 Finely grate the rind and squeeze the juice from five of the limes. Heat the sugar and water in a small, heavy pan, stirring until the sugar has dissolved. Boil for 2 minutes, without stirring, then remove from the heat. Stir in the lime juice and rind; cool.

4 Press the cottage cheese through a sieve (strainer) into a large bowl. Beat in the mascarpone, then the lime syrup. Lightly whip the cream and fold into the cheese mixture. Pour into a shallow freezer container, cover and freeze until thick.

5 Meanwhile, using a sharp knife, remove all the peel and pith from the remaining limes, then cut the flesh into thin slices. Arrange the slices around the sides of the tin, against the lining.

6 Pour the mixture into the tin and level the surface. Cover with clear film (plastic wrap) and freeze the cheesecake overnight. About 1 hour before serving, transfer the cheesecake to a serving plate and put in the refrigerator to soften slightly.

Ricotta Cheesecake

This refreshing, Sicilian-style cheesecake makes good use of ricotta's firm texture. Here, the cheese is enriched with eggs and cream and enlivened with grated orange and lemon rind.

Serves 8
450g/1lb/2 cups ricotta cheese
120ml/4fl oz/½ cup double (heavy) cream
2 eggs
1 egg yolk

75g/3oz/6 tbsp caster (superfine) sugar
finely grated rind of 1 orange and 1 lemon, plus extra to decorate

For the pastry
175g/6oz/1½ cups plain (all-purpose) flour
45ml/3 tbsp caster (superfine) sugar
115g/4oz/½ cup chilled butter, diced
1 egg yolk

1 Make the pastry. Sift the flour and sugar on to a cold work surface. Make a well in the centre and add the butter and egg yolk. Work the flour into the butter and egg yolk.

2 Gather the dough together, reserve a quarter and press the rest into a 23cm/9in loose-based, fluted flan tin (tart pan) and chill. Preheat the oven to 190°C/375°F/Gas 5.

3 Beat the cheese with the cream, eggs and egg yolk, sugar and citrus rinds in a large bowl.

4 Prick the base of the pastry case, then line with foil and fill with baking beans. Bake for 15 minutes, transfer to a wire rack, remove the foil and beans and allow the pastry to cool in the tin.

5 Spoon the cheese and cream filling into the pastry case (pie shell) and level the surface. Roll out the reserved dough and cut into long, even strips. Arrange the strips on the top of the filling in a lattice pattern, sticking them in place with water.

6 Bake the cheesecake for 30–35 minutes until golden and set. Transfer to a wire rack and leave to cool, then remove the side of the tin. Transfer to a plate and decorate with citrus rind.

Iced Lime Energy 385Kcal/1602kJ; Protein 6.4g; Carbohydrate 28g, of which sugars 20.5g; Fat 28.1g, of which saturates 17.2g; Cholesterol 69mg; Calcium 71mg; Fibre 0.3g; Sodium 165mg.
Ricotta Energy 449Kcal/1873kJ; Protein 9.9g; Carbohydrate 34.8g, of which sugars 18.1g; Fat 31.1g, of which saturates 18.4g; Cholesterol 173mg; Calcium 62mg; Fibre 0.7g; Sodium 112mg.

Marbled Chocolate Cheesecake

This attractive-looking dessert will be a big hit.

Serves 6

butter or margarine, for greasing
50g/2oz/½ cup cocoa powder
(unsweetened)
75ml/5 tbsp hot water

900g/2lb/4 cups cream cheese, at room temperature
200g/7oz/1 cup caster (superfine) sugar
4 eggs
5ml/1 tsp vanilla extract
75g/3oz digestive biscuits (graham crackers), crushed

1 Preheat the oven to 180°C/350°F/Gas 4. Line a deep 20cm/8in cake tin (pan) with baking parchment. Grease the paper.

2 Sift the cocoa powder into a bowl. Pour over the hot water and stir to dissolve.

3 In another bowl, beat the cheese until smooth, then beat in the sugar, followed by the eggs, one at a time. Do not overmix.

4 Divide the mixture evenly between two bowls. Stir the chocolate mixture into one bowl, then add the vanilla extract to the remaining mixture.

5 Pour a cup or ladleful of the plain mixture into the centre of the tin; it will spread out into an even layer. Slowly pour over a cupful of chocolate mixture in the centre. Continue to alternate the cake mixtures in this way until both are used up. Draw a thin metal skewer through the cake mixture for a marbled effect.

6 Place the tin in a roasting pan and pour in hot water to come 4cm/1½in up the sides of the cake tin. Bake the cheesecake for about 1½ hours, until the top is golden. (The cake will rise during baking but will sink later.) Cool in the tin on a wire rack.

7 Run a knife around the inside edge of the cheesecake. Invert a flat plate over the tin and turn out the cake. Sprinkle the crushed biscuits evenly over the cake, gently invert another plate on top, and turn over again. Cover and chill for 3 hours, preferably overnight, before serving.

Brandied Apple Charlotte

Loosely based on a traditional Apple Charlotte, this iced version combines brandy-steeped dried apple with a spicy ricotta cream to make an unusual and very tasty dessert.

Serves 8–10

130g/4½oz/¾ cup dried apples
75ml/5 tbsp brandy
50g/2oz/¼ cup unsalted (sweet) butter
115g/4oz/scant ½ cup light muscovado (brown) sugar
2.5ml/½ tsp mixed spice (apple pie spice)
60ml/4 tbsp water
75g/3oz/½ cup sultanas (golden raisins)
300g/11oz Madeira cake, cut into 1cm/½in slices
250g/9oz/generous 1 cup ricotta cheese
30ml/2 tbsp lemon juice
150ml/¼ pint/⅔ cup double (heavy) or whipping cream
icing (confectioners') sugar and fresh mint sprigs, to decorate

1 Roughly chop the dried apples, then transfer them to a clean bowl. Pour over the brandy and set aside for about 1 hour until most of the brandy has been absorbed.

2 Melt the butter in a frying pan. Add the sugar and stir over a low heat for 1 minute. Add the mixed spice, water and soaked apples, with any remaining brandy. Cook gently for 5 minutes, stirring occasionally, until the apples are tender. Stir in the sultanas and leave to cool.

3 Use the Madeira slices to line the sides of a 20cm/8in square or 20cm/8in round springform or loose-based cake tin (pan). Place in the freezer while you make the filling.

4 Beat the ricotta in a bowl until it has softened, then stir in the apple mixture and lemon juice. Whip the cream in a separate bowl and fold it in. Spoon the mixture into the lined tin and level the surface. Cover and freeze overnight.

5 Transfer the charlotte to the refrigerator 1 hour before serving. Turn it out on to a serving plate, dust with sugar, and decorate with mint sprigs.

Marbled Chocolate Energy 923Kcal/3828kJ; Protein 11.3g; Carbohydrate 44.4g, of which sugars 36.5g; Fat 79.3g, of which saturates 47.8g; Cholesterol 274mg; Calcium 206mg; Fibre 1.3g; Sodium 653mg.
Apple Charlotte Energy 373Kcal/1558kJ; Protein 5g; Carbohydrate 40.6g, of which sugars 34g; Fat 20.4g, of which saturates 12.4g; Cholesterol 42mg; Calcium 41mg; Fibre 1.2g; Sodium 152mg.

Maple & Walnut Meringue Gâteau

This simple dessert is a real treat for all meringue lovers. Before serving the gâteau, allow it to thaw slightly in the refrigerator in order to enjoy the full flavour.

Serves 10–12
4 egg whites
200g/7oz/1 cup light muscovado (brown) sugar
150g/5oz/1¼ cups walnut pieces
600ml/1 pint/2½ cups double (heavy) cream
150ml/¼ pint/⅔ cup maple syrup, plus extra to serve

1 Preheat the oven to 140°C/275°F/Gas 1. Draw three 23cm/9in circles on separate sheets of baking parchment. Invert the sheets on to three baking sheets.

2 Whisk the egg whites in a grease-free bowl until stiff. Whisk in the sugar, about 15ml/1 tbsp at a time, whisking well after each addition until the meringue is stiff and glossy.

3 Spread the meringue on to the baking parchment to within 1cm/½in of the edge of each marked circle. Bake for about 1 hour or until crisp, swapping the baking sheets around halfway through cooking. Leave to cool.

4 Set aside 45ml/3 tbsp of the walnuts. Finely chop the remainder. Whip the cream with the maple syrup until it forms soft peaks. Fold in the chopped walnuts. Use about a third of the mixture to sandwich the meringues together on a flat, freezerproof serving plate.

5 Using a palette knife, spread the remaining cream mixture over the top and sides of the gâteau. Sprinkle with the reserved walnuts and freeze overnight.

6 Transfer the gâteau to the refrigerator about 1 hour before serving so that the cream filling softens slightly.

7 Just before serving, drizzle a little of the extra maple syrup over the gâteau. Serve in slices.

Crunchy Apple & Almond Flan

A tasty apple tart with a delicious crunchy topping.

Serves 8
115g/4oz/1 cup plain (all-purpose) flour
1.5ml/¼ tsp mixed spice (apple pie spice)
50g/2oz/¼ cup butter, diced
50g/2oz/¼ cup demerara (raw) sugar
50g/2oz/½ cup flaked (sliced) almonds
675g/1½lb cooking apples

25g/1oz/3 tbsp raisins
sifted icing (confectioners') sugar, for dusting

For the pastry
175g/6oz/1½ cups plain (all-purpose) flour
75g/3oz/6 tbsp butter, diced
25g/1oz/¼ cup ground almonds
25g/1oz/2 tbsp caster (superfine) sugar
1 egg yolk
15ml/1 tbsp cold water
1.5ml/¼ tsp almond extract

1 Make the pastry. Put the flour in a mixing bowl and rub in the butter until it resembles fine breadcrumbs. Stir in the almonds and sugar. Whisk the egg yolk, water and almond extract together, then mix into the flour mixture to form a soft dough. Knead until smooth, wrap in clear film (plastic wrap) and leave in a cool place for 20 minutes.

2 Meanwhile, make the topping. Sift the flour and spice into a mixing bowl and rub in the butter. Stir in the sugar and almonds.

3 Roll out the pastry on a lightly floured surface and use to line a 23cm/9in loose-based flan tin (tart pan), making a lip around the top edge. Trim off the excess pastry. Chill for 15 minutes.

4 Place a baking sheet in the oven and preheat to 190°C/375°F/Gas 5. Peel, core and thinly slice the apples. Arrange over the pastry in overlapping circles, then sprinkle over the raisins.

5 Cover the apples with the crunchy topping mixture, pressing it on lightly. Place the flan on the hot baking sheet and bake for 25–30 minutes, or until the top is golden brown and the apples are tender. Leave the flan to cool in the tin for 10 minutes. Serve warm or cold, dusted with sifted icing sugar.

Chilled Chocolate & Date Slice

This richly flavoured dessert is wonderful served in wedges, accompanied by fresh orange segments.

Serves 6–8

115g/4oz/½ cup unsalted (sweet) butter, melted
225g/8oz ginger nut biscuits (gingersnaps) finely crushed
50g/2oz/⅔ cup stale sponge cake crumbs
75ml/5 tbsp orange juice
115g/4oz/⅔ cup stoned (pitted) dates
25g/1oz/¼ cup finely chopped nuts
175g/6oz dark (bittersweet) chocolate
300ml/½ pint/1¼ cups whipping cream
grated chocolate and icing (confectioners') sugar, to decorate
single (light) cream, to serve (optional)

1 Mix the butter and ginger biscuit crumbs in a bowl, then press the mixture on to the sides and base of an 18cm/7in loose-based flan tin (tart pan). Chill while making the filling.

2 Put the cake crumbs in a bowl. Pour over 60ml/4 tbsp of the orange juice, stir well with a wooden spoon and leave to soak. Put the dates in a pan and add the remaining orange juice. Warm the mixture over a low heat. Mash the warm dates thoroughly and stir in the cake crumbs, with the chopped nuts.

3 Mix the chocolate with 60ml/4 tbsp of the cream in a heatproof bowl. Place the bowl over a pan of barely simmering water and stir occasionally until melted. In a separate bowl, whip the rest of the cream to soft peaks, then fold in the melted chocolate.

4 Add the cooled date, crumb and nut mixture to the cream and chocolate and mix lightly but thoroughly. Pour into the tin. Using a spatula, level the mixture. Chill until just set, then mark the tart into portions, using a sharp knife dipped in hot water. Return the tart to the refrigerator and chill until firm.

5 To decorate, scatter the grated chocolate over the surface and dust with icing sugar. Serve with cream, if you wish.

Kiwi Ricotta Cheese Tart

It is well worth taking your time arranging the kiwi fruit topping in neat rows for this exotic tart – the results will be truly impressive.

Serves 8

50g/2oz/½ cup blanched almonds
90g/3½oz/½ cup plus 15ml/1 tbsp caster (superfine) sugar
900g/2lb/4 cups ricotta cheese
250ml/8fl oz/1 cup whipping cream
1 egg
3 egg yolks
15ml/1 tbsp plain (all-purpose) flour
pinch of salt
30ml/2 tbsp rum
grated rind of 1 lemon
40ml/2½ tbsp lemon juice
50ml/2fl oz/¼ cup clear honey
5 kiwi fruit

For the pastry

150g/5oz/1¼ cups plain (all-purpose) flour
15ml/1 tbsp caster (superfine) sugar
2.5ml/½ tsp salt
2.5ml/½ tsp baking powder
75g/3oz/6 tbsp cold butter, cut into small pieces
1 egg yolk
45–60ml/3–4 tbsp whipping cream

1 Make the pastry. Sift the flour, sugar, salt and baking powder into a bowl. Cut in the butter until the mixture resembles coarse crumbs. Mix the egg yolk and cream together. Stir in just enough to bind the dough.

2 Transfer to a lightly floured surface, flatten slightly, wrap in baking parchment and chill for 30 minutes. Preheat the oven to 220°C/425°F/Gas 7.

3 On a lightly floured surface, roll out the dough 3mm/⅛in thick and use to line a 23cm/9in springform tin (pan). Crimp the edge of the pastry.

4 Prick the base of the dough all over with a fork. Line with baking parchment and fill with baking beans. Bake for 10 minutes. Remove the paper and beans and bake for a further 6–8 minutes until golden. Allow to cool. Reduce the heat to 180°C/350°F/Gas 4.

5 Grind the almonds finely with 15ml/1 tbsp of the sugar in a food processor or blender.

6 With an electric whisk, beat the ricotta until creamy. Add the cream, egg, yolks, remaining sugar, flour, salt, rum, lemon rind and 30ml/2 tbsp of the lemon juice. Beat to combine. Stir in the ground almonds until well blended.

7 Pour the mixture into the pastry case (pie shell) and bake for about 1 hour until golden. Allow to cool, then chill, loosely covered, for 2–3 hours. Remove from the tin.

8 Combine the honey and remaining lemon juice for the glaze. Set aside.

9 Peel the kiwis. Halve them lengthways, then cut crossways into 5mm/¼in slices. Arrange the slices in rows across the top of the tart. Just before serving, brush with the glaze.

Chocolate & Date Energy 575Kcal/2394kJ; Protein 5.1g; Carbohydrate 51.3g, of which sugars 37.5g; Fat 40.2g, of which saturates 22.8g; Cholesterol 78mg; Calcium 87mg; Fibre 1.8g; Sodium 214mg.
Kiwi Ricotta Tart Energy 645Kcal/2686kJ; Protein 16.9g; Carbohydrate 41.1g, of which sugars 25.2g; Fat 46.2g, of which saturates 25.7g; Cholesterol 231mg; Calcium 93mg; Fibre 1.4g; Sodium 83mg.

Raspberry Tart

A lovely, summery dessert, this glazed fruit tart really does taste as good as it looks.

Serves 8
4 egg yolks
65g/2¾oz/5 tbsp granulated sugar
45g/1¾oz/3 tbsp plain
  (all-purpose) flour
300ml/½ pint/1¼ cups milk
pinch of salt
2.5ml/½ tsp vanilla extract
450g/1lb/2½ cups fresh raspberries

75ml/5 tbsp redcurrant jelly
15ml/1 tbsp fresh orange juice

For the pastry
150g/5oz/1¼ cups plain
  (all-purpose) flour
2.5ml/½ tsp baking powder
1.5ml/¼ tsp salt
15ml/1 tbsp sugar
grated rind of ½ orange
90ml/6 tbsp cold butter, diced
1 egg yolk
45ml/3 tbsp whipping cream

1 Make the pastry. Sift the flour, baking powder and salt into a bowl. Stir in the sugar and orange rind. Add the butter and rub in until the mixture resembles coarse breadcrumbs. With a fork, stir in the egg yolk and just enough cream to bind the dough. Gather into a ball, wrap in clear film (plastic wrap) and chill.

2 Make the custard filling. Beat the egg yolks and sugar until thick and lemon-coloured. Gradually stir in the flour.

3 In a pan, bring the milk and salt just to the boil, and remove from the heat. Whisk into the egg yolk mixture, return to the pan, and continue whisking over medium-high heat until just bubbling for 3 minutes to thicken. Transfer at once to a bowl and stir in the vanilla. Cover closely with baking parchment.

4 Preheat the oven to 200°C/400°F/Gas 6. Roll out the dough on a lightly floured surface to 3mm/⅛in thick. Use to line a 25cm/10in flan tin (tart pan) and trim the edge. Prick the pastry case (pie shell) all over with a fork and line with baking parchment. Fill with baking beans and bake for 15 minutes. Remove the paper and beans. Bake for 6–8 minutes more until golden. Cool.

5 Spread the filling in the pastry case. Top with the raspberries. Melt the jelly and orange juice together and brush on to glaze.

Lemon & Orange Tart

A tasty combination of refreshing citrus fruit and crisp, nutty pastry, this useful tart can be served at any time of the year.

Serves 8–10
115g/4oz/1 cup plain
  (all-purpose) flour, sifted
115g/4oz/1 cup wholemeal
  (whole-wheat) flour

25g/1oz/3 tbsp ground hazelnuts
25g/1oz/¼ cup icing
  (confectioners') sugar, sifted
pinch of salt
115g/4oz/½ cup unsalted
  (sweet) butter
30–45ml/2–3 tbsp water
60ml/4 tbsp lemon curd
300ml/½ pint/1¼ cups whipped
  cream or fromage frais
4 oranges, peeled and thinly sliced

1 Place the flours, hazelnuts, sugar, salt and butter in a food processor and process in short bursts until the mixture resembles breadcrumbs. Add the cold water and process until the mixture comes together as a dough.

2 Turn out on to a lightly floured surface and knead gently until smooth. Roll out and line a 25cm/10in loose-based flan tin (tart pan). Ease the pastry gently into the corners without stretching it. Chill for 20 minutes. Preheat the oven to 190°C/375°F/Gas 5.

3 Line the pastry with baking parchment and fill with baking beans. Bake blind for 15 minutes, remove the paper and beans and continue cooking for a further 5–10 minutes, until the pastry is crisp. Allow to cool.

4 Whisk the lemon curd into the cream or fromage frais and spread over the base of the pastry. Arrange the orange slices on top of the filling in overlapping, concentric circles. Remove the tart from the tin, transfer to a serving plate and serve at room temperature.

> **Variation**
> Fresh raspberries or halved strawberries would also team up well with the lemon-flavoured filling.

Raspberry Energy 322Kcal/1353kJ; Protein 6.5g; Carbohydrate 40.6g, of which sugars 22g; Fat 16.1g, of which saturates 8.8g; Cholesterol 158mg; Calcium 120mg; Fibre 2.2g; Sodium 97mg.
Lemon & Orange Energy 336Kcal/1400kJ; Protein 4.2g; Carbohydrate 27.9g, of which sugars 10.7g; Fat 23.9g, of which saturates 13.8g; Cholesterol 57mg; Calcium 69mg; Fibre 2.4g; Sodium 85mg.

Sticky Tart

This is quite a filling tart, so it is best served after a light main course.

Serves 4–6

250g/9oz/¾ cup golden (light corn) syrup
75g/3oz/1½ cups fresh white breadcrumbs
grated rind of 1 lemon
30ml/2 tbsp fresh lemon juice

For the pastry
150g/5oz/1¼ cups plain (all-purpose) flour
2.5ml/½ tsp salt
75g/3oz/6 tbsp cold butter or margarine, cut into pieces
45–60ml/3–4 tbsp iced water

1 Make the pastry. Combine the flour and salt in a bowl. Add the butter or margarine and rub in or cut in with a pastry blender until the mixture resembles coarse breadcrumbs.

2 With a fork, stir in just enough iced water to bind the mixture into a dough. Gather into a ball, wrap in baking parchment and chill for at least 20 minutes.

3 Roll out the dough on a lightly floured surface to 3mm/⅛in thick. Use to line a 20cm/8in loose-based flan tin (tart pan) and trim off the excess pastry. Chill for at least 20 minutes.

4 Place a baking sheet above the centre of the oven and heat to 200°C/400°F/Gas 6.

5 In a pan, warm the syrup until thin and runny. Remove from the heat and stir in the breadcrumbs and lemon rind. Set aside for 10 minutes to allow the bread to absorb the syrup.

6 Add more breadcrumbs if the mixture is thin. Stir in the lemon juice and spread evenly in the pastry case (pie shell).

7 Place the tart on the hot baking sheet and bake in the oven for 10 minutes. Lower the heat to 190°C/375°F/Gas 5. Continue to bake for about 15 minutes until the top is golden. Remove from the tin and serve warm or cold.

Chocolate Pear Tart

Serve slices of this tart drizzled with cream for a special treat.

Serves 8

115g/4oz plain (semisweet) chocolate, grated
3 large firm, ripe pears
1 egg
1 egg yolk
120ml/4fl oz/½ cup single (light) cream
2.5ml/½ tsp vanilla extract
40g/1½oz/3 tbsp caster (superfine) sugar

For the pastry
115g/4oz/1 cup plain (all-purpose) flour
pinch of salt
25g/1oz/2 tbsp caster (superfine) sugar
115g/4oz/½ cup cold unsalted (sweet) butter, cut into pieces
1 egg yolk
15ml/1 tbsp fresh lemon juice

1 Make the pastry. Sift the flour and salt into a bowl. Add the sugar and butter. Cut in with a pastry blender until the mixture resembles coarse crumbs. With a fork, stir in the egg yolk and lemon juice until the mixture forms a dough. Gather into a ball, wrap in baking parchment, and chill for at least 20 minutes.

2 Place a baking sheet in the oven and preheat to 200°C/400°F/Gas 6. On a lightly floured surface, roll out the dough to 3mm/⅛in thick and trim the edge. Use to line a 25cm/10in loose-based flan tin (tart pan).

3 Sprinkle the base of the pastry with the grated chocolate.

4 Peel, halve and core the pears. Cut in thin slices crossways, then fan them out slightly. Transfer the pear halves to the tart with the help of a metal spatula and arrange on top of the chocolate in a pattern resembling the spokes of a wheel.

5 Whisk together the egg and egg yolk, cream and vanilla extract. Spoon over the pears, then sprinkle with sugar.

6 Bake for 10 minutes. Reduce the heat to 180°C/350°F/Gas 4 and continue to cook for about 20 minutes until the custard is set and the pears begin to caramelize. Serve warm.

Sticky Tart Energy 347Kcal/1462kJ; Protein 4g; Carbohydrate 62.1g, of which sugars 33.7g; Fat 10.8g, of which saturates 6.6g; Cholesterol 27mg; Calcium 60mg; Fibre 1.1g; Sodium 284mg.
Choc. Pear Tart Energy 357Kcal/1492kJ; Protein 4.5g; Carbohydrate 39.9g, of which sugars 28.8g; Fat 21.1g, of which saturates 12.3g; Cholesterol 114mg; Calcium 66mg; Fibre 2.9g; Sodium 107mg.

Rich Chocolate-Berry Tart

A gorgeous way to serve
fresh summer berries.

Serves 10

115g/4oz/1/2 cup unsalted (sweet)
   butter, softened
90g/3 1/2oz/1/2 cup caster
   (superfine) sugar
2.5ml/1/2 tsp salt
15ml/1 tbsp vanilla extract
50g/2oz/1/2 cup cocoa powder
   (unsweetened)
215g/7 1/2oz/scant 2 cups plain
   (all-purpose) flour
450g/1lb fresh berries for topping

For the chocolate filling
475ml/16fl oz/2 cups double
   (heavy) cream
150g/5oz/1/2 cup seedless
   blackberry preserve
225g/8oz plain (semisweet)
   chocolate, chopped
25g/1oz/2 tbsp unsalted (sweet)
   butter

For the blackberry sauce
225g/8oz fresh or frozen
   blackberries or raspberries
15ml/1 tbsp lemon juice
25g/1oz/2 tbsp caster (superfine)
   sugar
30ml/2 tbsp blackberry liqueur

I Make the pastry. Place the butter, sugar, salt and vanilla in a food processor and process until creamy. Add the cocoa and process for 1 minute. Add the flour all at once and process for 10–15 seconds, until just blended. Place a piece of clear film (plastic wrap) on a work surface. Turn out the dough on to the clear film. Use the clear film to help shape the dough into a flat disc and wrap tightly. Chill for 1 hour.

2 Lightly grease a 23cm/9in loose-based flan tin (tart pan). Roll out the dough between two sheets of clear film to a 28cm/11in round, about 5mm/1/4in thick. Peel off the top sheet of clear film and invert the dough into the prepared tin. Ease the dough into the tin. Remove the clear film.

3 With floured fingers, press the dough on to the base and side of the tin, then roll a rolling pin over the edge of the tin to cut off any excess dough. Prick the base of the dough with a fork. Chill for 1 hour. Preheat the oven to 180°C/350°F/Gas 4. Line the pastry case (pie shell) with foil or baking paper and fill with baking beans. Bake for 10 minutes, then lift out the foil and beans and bake for 5 minutes more, until just set (the pastry may look underdone on the base, but will dry out). Place on a wire rack to cool completely.

4 Make the filling. Place the cream and blackberry preserve in a medium pan over medium heat and bring to the boil. Remove from the heat and add the chocolate, stirring until smooth. Stir in the butter and strain into the cooled tart, then level the surface. Leave the tart to cool completely.

5 Make the sauce. In a food processor, combine the blackberries, lemon juice and sugar and process until smooth. Strain into a small bowl and add the blackberry-flavour liqueur. If the sauce is too thick, thin with a little water.

6 To serve, remove the tart from the tin. Place on a serving plate and arrange the berries on the top of the tart. With a pastry brush, brush the berries with a little of the blackberry sauce to glaze lightly. Serve the remaining sauce separately.

Chocolate Lemon Tart

In this easy-to-make recipe, the chocolate-flavoured pastry is pressed into the tin rather than rolled out, helping to speed up the preparation. With a simple lemon filling, this is a great dessert for the busy cook.

Serves 8–10

175g/6oz/1 1/2 cups plain
   (all-purpose) flour
10ml/2 tsp cocoa powder
   (unsweetened)
25g/1oz/1/4 cup icing
   (confectioners') sugar

2.5ml/1/2 tsp salt
115g/4oz/1/2 cup unsalted
   (sweet) butter or margarine,
   plus extra for greasing
15ml/1 tbsp water

For the filling
225g/8oz/1 cup caster
   (superfine) sugar
6 eggs
grated rind of 2 lemons
175ml/6fl oz/3/4 cup freshly
   squeezed lemon juice
175ml/6fl oz/3/4 cup double
   (heavy) or whipping cream
chocolate curls, to decorate

I Grease a 25cm/10in loose-based flan tin (tart pan). Sift the flour, cocoa, icing sugar and salt into a bowl. Set aside.

2 Melt the butter or margarine and water in a pan over a low heat. Add the flour mixture and stir until the flour has absorbed all the liquid and the dough is smooth.

3 Press the dough evenly over the base and side of the prepared tin. Chill the pastry case (pie shell).

4 Preheat the oven to 190°C/375°F/Gas 5, and place a baking sheet inside to heat up. Make the filling. Whisk the caster sugar and eggs in a bowl until the sugar has dissolved. Add the lemon rind and juice and mix well. Stir in the cream. Taste and add more lemon juice or sugar if needed, for a sweet taste with a touch of tartness.

5 Pour the filling into the pastry shell and place the tin on the hot baking sheet. Bake for 20–25 minutes or until the filling is set. Cool the tart on a rack, then remove from the tin. Decorate with the chocolate curls and serve.

Choc. Lemon Tart Energy 379Kcal/1585kJ; Protein 6.1g; Carbohydrate 40.5g, of which sugars 27g; Fat 22.6g, of which saturates 12.9g; Cholesterol 163mg; Calcium 68mg; Fibre 0.7g; Sodium 127mg.
Choc.-Berry Tart Energy 653Kcal/2722kJ; Protein 6g; Carbohydrate 58.9g, of which sugars 41.8g; Fat 44.9g, of which saturates 27.7g; Cholesterol 96mg; Calcium 95mg; Fibre 3.5g; Sodium 152mg.

Peach Tart with Almond Cream

Peaches and almonds form a natural flavour partnership.

Serves 8–10

115g/4oz/²⁄₃ cup blanched almonds
30ml/2 tbsp plain (all-purpose) flour
90g/3½oz/scant ½ cup unsalted (sweet) butter, slightly soft
130g/4½oz/scant ¾ cup granulated sugar
1 egg
1 egg yolk
2.5ml/½ tsp vanilla extract or 10ml/2 tsp rum
4 large ripe peaches, skinned

For the pastry

150g/5oz/1¼ cups plain (all-purpose) flour
4ml/¾ tsp salt
90g/3½oz/scant ½ cup cold unsalted (sweet) butter, cut into pieces
1 egg yolk
30–45ml/2–3 tbsp iced water

1 Make the pastry. Sift the flour and salt into a bowl. Add the butter and cut in with a pastry blender until the mixture resembles breadcrumbs. With a fork, stir in the egg yolk and just enough iced water to bind the dough. Gather into a ball, wrap in baking parchment and chill for at least 20 minutes. Place a baking sheet in the oven and preheat to 200°C/400°F/Gas 6.

2 On a lightly floured surface, roll out the pastry to 3mm/⅛in thick. Transfer to a 25cm/10in flan tin (tart pan). Trim the edge, prick the pastry base and chill.

3 Grind the almonds finely with the flour. With an electric whisk, cream the butter and 90g/3½oz/½ cup of the sugar until light and fluffy. Gradually beat in the egg and yolk. Stir in the almonds and vanilla or rum. Spread in the pastry case (pie shell).

4 Halve the peaches and remove the stones (pits). Cut crossways into thin slices and arrange on top of the almond cream like the spokes of a wheel. Press down gently to fan out. Bake for 10–15 minutes until the pastry begins to brown. Lower the heat to 180°C/350°F/Gas 4 and continue baking for about 15 minutes until the filling sets. Ten minutes before the end of the cooking time, sprinkle with the remaining sugar.

Chocolate Apricot Linzer Tart

This makes an excellent dinner party dessert.

Serves 10–12

50g/2oz/⅓ cup blanched almonds
115g/4oz/generous ½ cup caster (superfine) sugar
175g/6oz/1½ cups plain (all-purpose) flour
30ml/2 tbsp cocoa powder (unsweetened)
5ml/1 tsp ground cinnamon
2.5ml/½ tsp salt
5ml/1 tsp grated orange rind
225g/8oz/1 cup unsalted (sweet) butter, cut into small pieces
75g/3oz/½ cup chocolate chips
icing (confectioners') sugar, for dusting

For the apricot filling

350g/12oz/1½ cups dried apricots
120ml/4fl oz/½ cup orange juice
40g/1½oz/3 tbsp granulated sugar
50g/2oz/2 tbsp apricot jam
2.5ml/½ tsp almond extract

1 For the filling, simmer the apricots, orange juice and 175ml/6fl oz/¾ cup water, stirring, until the liquid is absorbed. Stir in the remaining ingredients. Strain into a bowl, cool, cover and chill.

2 Grease a 28cm/11in loose-based flan tin (tart pan). Grind the almonds and half the sugar in a food processor. Sift in the flour, cocoa, cinnamon and salt, add the remaining sugar and process. Add the rind and butter. Process for 15–20 seconds until the mixture resembles breadcrumbs. Add 30ml/2 tbsp iced water and pulse, adding a little more water until the dough holds together.

3 Turn out and knead the dough on a lightly floured surface. Halve and press one piece on to the base and sides of the tin. Prick the base with a fork. Chill for 20 minutes. Roll out the rest of the dough between sheets of clear film (plastic wrap) to a 28cm/11in round, then slide on to a baking sheet and chill for 30 minutes.

4 Preheat the oven to 180°C/350°F/Gas 4. Spread the filling in the pastry case (pie shell) and sprinkle with chocolate chips. Cut the dough round into 1cm/½in strips. Leave to soften, then place the strips over the filling, 1cm/½in apart, to form a lattice. Press the ends on to the side of the tart and trim. Bake for 35–40 minutes, until golden. Cool on a rack and dust with icing sugar.

Linzer Tart Energy 368Kcal/1539kJ; Protein 4.4g; Carbohydrate 44.3g, of which sugars 32.8g; Fat 20.4g, of which saturates 11.4g; Cholesterol 40mg; Calcium 69mg; Fibre 3.1g; Sodium 147mg.
Peach Tart Energy 350Kcal/1459kJ; Protein 5.9g; Carbohydrate 31.5g, of which sugars 17.5g; Fat 23.1g, of which saturates 10.4g; Cholesterol 98mg; Calcium 73mg; Fibre 2g; Sodium 121mg.

Apricot & Almond Tart

This dish shows how well almonds and apricots combine.

Serves 6

115g/4oz/½ cup butter or margarine
115g/4oz/generous ½ cup caster (superfine) sugar
1 egg, beaten
50g/2oz/⅓ cup ground rice
50g/2oz/½ cup ground almonds
few drops of almond extract
450g/1lb fresh apricots, halved and stoned (pitted)
sifted icing (confectioners') sugar, for dusting (optional)
apricot slices and fresh mint sprigs, to decorate (optional)

For the pastry
115g/4oz/1 cup brown rice flour
115g/4oz/1 cup cornmeal
115g/4oz/½ cup butter or margarine
25g/1oz/2 tbsp caster (superfine) sugar
1 egg yolk

1 Make the pastry. Place the rice flour and cornmeal in a large mixing bowl and stir to mix. Lightly rub in the butter or margarine until the mixture resembles fine breadcrumbs. Add the sugar, the egg yolk and enough chilled water to make a smooth, soft but not sticky dough. Wrap the dough in clear film (plastic wrap) and chill for 30 minutes.

2 Preheat the oven to 180°C/350°F/Gas 4. Line a 24cm/9½in loose-based flan tin (tart pan) with the pastry by pressing it gently over the base and up the sides, making sure that there are no holes in the pastry. Trim the edge of the pastry with a sharp knife.

3 Make the almond filling. Place the butter or margarine and sugar in a bowl and cream together with a wooden spoon until the mixture is light and fluffy. Gradually add the beaten egg to the mix, beating well after each addition. Fold in the ground rice and almonds and the almond extract and mix well to incorporate.

4 Spoon the mixture into the pastry case, spreading it evenly, then arrange the apricot halves cut side down on top. Place the tart on a baking sheet and bake for 40–45 minutes until the filling and pastry are cooked and lightly browned. Serve warm or cold, dusted with icing sugar and decorated with apricots and mint.

Strawberry Tart

This summery tart is best assembled just before serving, but you can bake the pastry case earlier in the day. You can also make the filling ahead of time so that the tart can be put together in just a few minutes – perfect for easy entertaining.

Serves 6
350g/12oz rough puff or puff pastry
225g/8oz/1 cup cream cheese
grated rind of ½ orange
30ml/2 tbsp orange liqueur or orange juice
45–60ml/3–4 tbsp icing (confectioners') sugar, plus extra for dusting (optional)
450g/1lb/4 cups strawberries, hulled

1 Roll out the pastry on a lightly floured surface to a thickness of about 3mm/⅛in and use to line a 28 x 10cm/11 x 4in tranche tin or shallow rectangular tin (pan). Trim the edges of the pastry neatly with a knife, then chill for 30 minutes. Preheat the oven to 200°C/400°F/Gas 6.

2 Prick the base of the pastry all over. Line with foil, fill with baking beans and bake for 15 minutes. Remove the foil and beans and bake for a further 10 minutes until the pastry is browned. Gently press down on the pastry base to deflate it, then leave to cool on a wire rack.

3 Using a hand-held electric whisk or food processor, beat well together the cream cheese, orange rind, liqueur or orange juice and icing sugar.

4 Spread the cheese filling in the pastry case (pie shell). Halve the strawberries and arrange them on top of the cheese filling. Dust with icing sugar, if you like, just before serving.

Cook's Tip
Ready-made puff pastry is available in most supermarkets. If you use the frozen version, thaw it thoroughly before using.

Apricot & Almond Energy 640Kcal/2670kJ; Protein 8.4g; Carbohydrate 66.2g, of which sugars 30.7g; Fat 39g, of which saturates 20.9g; Cholesterol 147mg; Calcium 89mg; Fibre 3.1g; Sodium 251mg.
Strawberry Energy 434Kcal/1805kJ; Protein 5.2g; Carbohydrate 34.4g, of which sugars 13.5g; Fat 32.2g, of which saturates 11.1g; Cholesterol 36mg; Calcium 87mg; Fibre 0.8g; Sodium 299mg.

Coffee Custard Tart

For sheer decadence, this creamy tart is hard to beat.

Serves 6–8

1 vanilla pod (bean)
30ml/2 tbsp ground coffee
300ml/½ pint/1¼ cups single (light) cream
150ml/¼ pint/⅔ cup milk
2 eggs, plus 2 egg yolks
50g/2oz/¼ cup caster (superfine) sugar
whipped cream, to serve

For the pastry

175g/6oz/1½ cups plain (all-purpose) flour
30ml/2 tbsp icing (confectioners') sugar
115g/4oz/½ cup butter, diced
75g/3oz/¾ cup walnuts, chopped
1 egg yolk
5ml/1 tsp vanilla extract
10ml/2 tsp chilled water

1 Make the pastry. Sift the flour and sugar into a mixing bowl. Rub or cut in the butter until the mixture resembles fine breadcrumbs. Stir in the walnuts.

2 In a small bowl, mix together the egg yolk, vanilla and water. Add to the flour mixture and mix to a smooth dough. Wrap in clear film (plastic wrap); chill for 20 minutes. Put a heavy baking sheet in the oven and preheat the oven to 200°C/400°F/Gas 6.

3 Roll out the pastry and use to line a 20cm/8in loose-based flan tin (tart pan). Trim the edges. Chill for 20 minutes.

4 Prick the pastry base all over with a fork. Line with foil and fill with baking beans. Place on the baking sheet and bake for 10 minutes. Remove the foil and beans, bake for 10 minutes more, then reduce the oven temperature to 150°C/300°F/Gas 2.

5 Meanwhile, split the vanilla pod and scrape out the seeds. Put both in a pan with the coffee, cream and milk. Heat until almost boiling, remove from the heat, cover and infuse for 10 minutes. Whisk the eggs, egg yolks and caster sugar together in a bowl.

6 Bring the coffee mixture back to the boil, then pour on to the egg mixture, stirring. Strain into the tin. Bake for 40–45 minutes until lightly set, then cool. Top with whirls of cream to serve.

Yorkshire Curd Tart

The distinguishing characteristic of Yorkshire curd tarts is allspice, or "clove pepper" as it was known locally. This tart tastes superb and does not taste too sweet.

Serves 8

90g/3½oz/scant ½ cup soft light brown sugar
large pinch of ground allspice
3 eggs, beaten
grated rind and juice of 1 lemon
40g/1½oz/3 tbsp butter, melted
450g/1lb/2 cups curd (farmer's) cheese
75g/3oz/½ cup raisins
whipped cream, to serve (optional)

For the pastry

225g/8oz/2 cups plain (all-purpose) flour
115g/4oz/½ cup butter, diced
1 egg yolk
15–30ml/1–2 tbsp chilled water

1 Make the pastry. Place the flour in a large mixing bowl and rub or cut in the butter until the mixture resembles fine breadcrumbs. Stir the egg yolk into the flour and add just enough of the water to bind the mixture together to form a dough.

2 Put the dough on a floured surface, knead lightly and briefly, then form into a ball. Roll out the pastry thinly and use to line a 20cm/8in fluted loose-based flan tin (tart pan). Cover with clear film (plastic wrap) and chill for about 15 minutes.

3 Preheat the oven to 190°C/375°F/Gas 5. Mix the sugar with the ground allspice in a bowl, then stir in the eggs, lemon rind and juice, butter, curd cheese and raisins. Mix well.

4 Pour the filling into the pastry case (pie shell), then bake for 40 minutes, or until the pastry is cooked and the filling is lightly set and golden brown. Cut the tart into wedges while it is still slightly warm, and serve with cream, if you like.

Cook's Tip
Although it is not traditional, mixed spice (apple pie spice) would make a good substitute for the ground allspice.

Coffee Custard Energy 408Kcal/1698kJ; Protein 8.1g; Carbohydrate 29.6g, of which sugars 12.8g; Fat 29.5g, of which saturates 13.8g; Cholesterol 176mg; Calcium 119mg; Fibre 1g; Sodium 129mg.
Yorkshire Curd Energy 419Kcal/1753kJ; Protein 14.1g; Carbohydrate 42.2g, of which sugars 20.8g; Fat 23.6g, of which saturates 13.9g; Cholesterol 151mg; Calcium 132mg; Fibre 1.1g; Sodium 398mg.

Orange Sweetheart Tart

A real treat to eat, this tart has a crisp shortcrust pastry case, spread with apricot jam and filled with frangipane, then topped with tangy orange slices.

Serves 8

200g/7oz/1 cup sugar
250ml/8fl oz/1 cup fresh orange juice, strained
2 large navel oranges
75g/3oz/½ cup blanched almonds
50g/2oz/¼ cup butter

1 egg
15ml/1 tbsp plain (all-purpose) flour
45ml/3 tbsp apricot jam

For the pastry

175g/6oz/1½ cups plain (all-purpose) flour
2.5ml/½ tsp salt
75g/3oz/6 tbsp chilled butter, diced
45ml/3 tbsp chilled water

1 Make the pastry. Sift the flour and salt into a mixing bowl. Add the butter and rub in with your fingertips until the mixture resembles fine breadcrumbs. Sprinkle over the water and mix to a dough. Knead the dough on a lightly floured surface for a few seconds until smooth. Wrap the dough in clear film (plastic wrap) and chill for at least 30 minutes.

2 After the pastry has rested, roll it out on a floured surface to a thickness of about 5mm/¼in. Use to line a 20cm/8in heart-shaped tart tin (pan). Trim the pastry edges and chill again for a further 30 minutes.

3 Preheat the oven to 200°C/400°F/Gas 6, with a baking sheet placed in the centre. Line the pastry case (pie shell) with baking parchment or foil and fill with baking beans. Bake blind for 10 minutes. Remove the parchment or foil and beans and cook for 10 minutes more, or until it is light and golden.

4 Put 150g/5oz/¾ cup of the sugar into a heavy pan and pour in the orange juice. Bring to the boil, stirring until the sugar has dissolved, then boil steadily for about 10 minutes, or until the liquid is thick and syrupy.

5 Cut the unpeeled oranges into 5mm/¼in slices. Add to the syrup. Simmer for 10 minutes, or until glazed. Transfer the slices to a wire rack placed over a plate to dry, reserving the syrup. When the orange slices are cool, cut in half.

6 Grind the almonds finely in a food processor. With an electric whisk, cream the butter and remaining sugar until light. Beat in the egg and 30ml/2 tbsp of the orange syrup. Stir in the almonds, then add the flour.

7 Melt the jam over a low heat, then brush it evenly over the the pastry case. Pour in the ground almond mixture. Bake for 20 minutes, or until set. Leave to cool in the tin.

8 Starting at the top of the heart shape and working down to the point, arrange the orange slices on the surface of the tart in an overlapping pattern, cutting them to fit. Boil the remaining syrup until thick and brush on top to glaze. Leave to cool.

Red Grape & Cheese Tartlets

The natural partnership of fruit and cheese is the hallmark of this simple recipe. Look out for small, pale, mauve-coloured or red grapes. These are often seedless, and sweeter than large black varieties.

Makes 6

225g/8oz/1 cup curd (farmer's) cheese
150ml/¼ pint/⅔ cup double (heavy) cream
2.5ml/½ tsp vanilla extract

30ml/2 tbsp icing (confectioners') sugar
200g/7oz/2 cups red grapes, halved, seeded if necessary
60ml/4 tbsp apricot jam
15ml/1 tbsp water

For the pastry

200g/7oz/1¾ cups plain (all-purpose) flour
15ml/1 tbsp caster (superfine) sugar
150g/5oz/10 tbsp butter
2 egg yolks
15ml/1 tbsp chilled water

1 Make the pastry. Sift the flour and sugar into a mixing bowl. Rub or cut in the butter until the mixture resembles fine breadcrumbs. Add the egg yolks and water and mix to a dough. Knead lightly until smooth. Wrap in clear film (plastic wrap) and chill for 30 minutes.

2 Preheat the oven to 200°C/400°F/Gas 6. Roll out the pastry and use to line six deep 10cm/4in fluted tartlet tins (muffin pans). Prick the bases, line with foil and fill with baking beans. Bake for 10 minutes, remove the foil and beans, then bake for a further 5 minutes until golden. Remove the pastry cases (pie shells) from the tins and cool.

3 Meanwhile, beat the curd cheese with the double cream, vanilla extract and icing sugar in a small bowl. Divide the mixture among the pastry cases. Smooth the surface and arrange the halved grapes attractively on top.

4 Press the apricot jam through a sieve (strainer) into a small pan. Add the water and heat, stirring constantly, until smooth and glossy. Generously spoon the apricot glaze over the grapes. Leave to cool, then chill before serving.

Orange Sweetheart Energy 405Kcal/1699kJ; Protein 6.4g; Carbohydrate 53.7g, of which sugars 36.8g; Fat 19.8g, of which saturates 9g; Cholesterol 81mg; Calcium 98mg; Fibre 2g; Sodium 123mg.
Grape & Cheese Energy 559Kcal/2330kJ; Protein 10.4g; Carbohydrate 45.1g, of which sugars 19.7g; Fat 39.3g, of which saturates 23.9g; Cholesterol 164mg; Calcium 123mg; Fibre 1.3g; Sodium 331mg.

Plum & Almond Tart

Plums and marzipan are terrific together and here they are used as a delicious topping for light puff pastry. Simplicity itself to make, this tart is the perfect dessert for an informal gathering.

Serves 4
375g/13oz ready-rolled puff pastry, thawed if frozen
115g/4oz marzipan
6–8 plums, stoned (pitted) and sliced
icing (confectioners') sugar, for dusting
crème fraîche, to serve

1 Preheat the oven to 190°C/375°F/Gas 5. Unroll the pastry on to a large baking sheet. Using a small, sharp knife, score a border 5cm/2in from the edge of the pastry, without cutting all the way through.

2 Roll out the marzipan into a rectangle, to fit just within the pastry border, then lay it on top of the pastry, pressing down lightly with the tips of your fingers.

3 Sprinkle the sliced plums on top of the marzipan in an even layer and bake for 20–25 minutes, or until the pastry is risen and golden brown.

4 Carefully transfer the tart to a wire rack to cool slightly, then dust lightly with icing sugar. To serve, cut into squares or wedges and serve with crème fraîche.

Cook's Tip
Puff pastry is particularly light because the dough is folded and rolled a number of times, trapping air between the layers.

Variation
Apricots and peaches also have a natural affinity with almonds, so they can be successfully substituted for the plums.

Yellow Plum Tart

In this pretty tart, glazed yellow plums sit on top of a delectable almond filling.

Serves 8
175g/6oz/1½ cups plain (all-purpose) flour
pinch of salt
75g/3oz/6 tbsp butter, chilled
30ml/2 tbsp caster (superfine) sugar
a few drops of vanilla extract
45ml/3 tbsp chilled water
cream or custard, to serve

For the filling
75g/3oz/6 tbsp caster (superfine) sugar
75g/3oz/6 tbsp butter, softened
75g/3oz/¾ cup ground almonds
1 egg, beaten
30ml/2 tbsp plain (all-purpose) flour
450g/1lb yellow plums or greengages, halved and pitted

For the glaze
45ml/3 tbsp apricot jam
15ml/1 tbsp water

1 Sift the flour and salt into a bowl, then rub in the chilled butter until the mixture resembles fine breadcrumbs. Stir in the sugar, vanilla and enough water to make a soft dough. Knead the dough gently on a lightly floured surface until smooth, then wrap in clear film (plastic wrap) and chill for 10 minutes.

2 Preheat the oven to 200°C/400°F/Gas 6. Roll out the pastry and use to line a 23cm/9in fluted flan tin (tart pan), allowing the excess pastry to overhang the top. Prick the base with a fork and line with baking parchment and baking beans. Bake blind for 10 minutes, remove the paper and beans, then cook for a further 10 minutes. Allow to cool. Trim off any excess pastry.

3 Make the filling. Whisk or beat together all the ingredients except the plums. Spread over the pastry base. Arrange the plums on top, placing them cut side down. Make a glaze. Press the jam through a sieve (strainer) and heat with the water. Stir well, then brush a little of the glaze over the top of the fruit.

4 Bake for 50–60 minutes, until the almond filling is cooked and the plums are tender. Warm any remaining jam glaze and brush over the top. Cut into slices and serve with cream or custard.

Plum & Almond Energy 478Kcal/2003kJ; Protein 7.1g; Carbohydrate 58.1g, of which sugars 24.6g; Fat 26.7g, of which saturates 0.3g; Cholesterol 0mg; Calcium 79mg; Fibre 1.3g; Sodium 297mg.
Yellow Plum Energy 365Kcal/1529kJ; Protein 5.7g; Carbohydrate 39.3g, of which sugars 19.6g; Fat 21.7g, of which saturates 10.4g; Cholesterol 64mg; Calcium 80mg; Fibre 2.4g; Sodium 126mg.

Chocolate & Pine Nut Tart

Orange-flavoured pastry
makes this a real winner.

Serves 8
200g/7oz/1¾ cups plain
  (all-purpose) flour
50g/2oz/¼ cup caster
  (superfine) sugar
pinch of salt
grated rind of ½ orange
115g/4oz/½ cup unsalted (sweet)
  butter, cut into small pieces
3 egg yolks, lightly beaten
15–30ml/1–2 tbsp chilled water

For the filling
2 eggs
45ml/3 tbsp caster
  (superfine) sugar
grated rind of 1 orange
15ml/1 tbsp orange liqueur
250ml/8fl oz/1 cup whipping cream
115g/4oz plain (semisweet)
  chocolate, cut into small pieces
75g/3oz/¾ cup pine nuts, toasted

For the decoration
thinly pared rind of 1 orange
50g/2oz/¼ cup granulated sugar

1 Process the flour, sugar, salt and orange rind in a food processor, add the butter and process again for 30 seconds. Add the yolks and pulse until the dough begins to stick together. If it seems dry, gradually add the water. Knead, then wrap and chill for 2–3 hours.

2 Grease a 23cm/9in loose-based flan tin (tart pan). Roll out the dough on a floured surface into a 28cm/11in round. Ease it into the tin and roll a rolling pin over the edge to trim. Prick the base. Chill for 1 hour. Preheat the oven to 200°C/400°F/Gas 6.

3 Line the pastry with foil, fill with baking beans and bake blind for 5 minutes. Remove the foil and beans and bake for 5 minutes more, then cool. Lower the temperature to 180°C/350°F/Gas 4.

4 Beat the eggs, sugar, orange rind and liqueur in a bowl. Stir in the cream. Sprinkle the chocolate and pine nuts over the base of the tart. Pour in the filling. Bake for 20–30 minutes, until golden.

5 Make the decoration. Cut the orange rind into strips. Dissolve the sugar in 120ml/4fl oz/½ cup water over a medium heat, add the rind and boil for 5 minutes. Remove from the heat and stir in 15ml/1 tbsp cold water. Brush the orange syrup over the tart and decorate with the caramelized strips. Serve warm.

Fruit Tartlets

The cream and fresh fruit
topping contrast beautifully
with the chocolate pastry.

Makes 8
215g/7½oz/¾ cup redcurrant or
  grape jelly
15ml/1 tbsp fresh lemon juice
175ml/6fl oz/¾ cup whipping
  cream
675g/1½lb fresh fruit, such as
  strawberries, raspberries, kiwi
  fruit, peaches, grapes or
  blueberries, peeled and sliced
  as necessary

For the pastry
150g/5oz/10 tbsp cold butter, cut
  into pieces
65g/2½oz/5 tbsp dark brown
  sugar
45ml/3 tbsp cocoa powder
  (unsweetened)
175g/6oz/1½ cups plain
  (all-purpose) flour
1 egg white

1 Make the pastry. Place the butter, brown sugar and cocoa in a medium pan over low heat. When the butter has melted, remove from the heat and sift over the flour. Stir with a wooden spoon to combine, then add just enough egg white to bind the mixture. Gather into a ball, wrap in baking parchment and chill for at least 30 minutes.

2 Preheat the oven to 180°C/350°F/Gas 4. Grease eight 7.5cm/3in tartlet tins (muffin pans). Roll out the dough between two sheets of baking parchment and stamp out eight 10cm/4in rounds with a fluted cutter.

3 Line the tartlet tins with dough rounds. Prick the pastry bases with a fork. Chill for 15 minutes.

4 Bake for 20–25 minutes until firm. Leave to cool, then remove from the tins.

5 Melt the jelly with the lemon juice. Brush a thin layer over the base of the tartlets. Whip the cream and spread a thin layer in the tartlet cases (shells). Arrange the fruit on top. Brush evenly with the glaze and serve.

Choc. & Pine Nut Energy 543Kcal/2261kJ; Protein 7.8g; Carbohydrate 42.7g, of which sugars 23.5g; Fat 38.6g, of which saturates 19.2g; Cholesterol 187mg; Calcium 84mg; Fibre 1.3g; Sodium 118mg.
Fruit Tartlets Energy 440Kcal/1841kJ; Protein 5.4g; Carbohydrate 49.3g, of which sugars 32g; Fat 26g, of which saturates 16.1g; Cholesterol 63mg; Calcium 83mg; Fibre 3.5g; Sodium 192mg.

Black Bottom Pie

A totally wicked rum and chocolate creation.

Serves 6–8
250g/9oz/2¼ cups plain (all-purpose) flour
150g/5oz/10 tbsp unsalted (sweet) butter
2 egg yolks
15–30ml/1–2 tbsp chilled water

For the filling
3 eggs, separated
20ml/4 tsp cornflour (cornstarch)
75g/3oz/6 tbsp golden caster (superfine) sugar
400ml/14fl oz/1⅔ cups milk
150g/5oz plain (semisweet) chocolate, chopped into small pieces
5ml/1 tsp vanilla extract
1 sachet powdered gelatine
45ml/3 tbsp water
30ml/2 tbsp dark rum
175ml/6fl oz/¾ cup whipping cream
chocolate curls, to decorate

1 Sift the flour into a bowl and rub in the butter until the mixture resembles coarse breadcrumbs. Stir in the egg yolks with just enough chilled water to bind the mixture to a soft dough. Roll out on a lightly floured surface and line a deep 23cm/9in flan tin (tart pan). Chill for about 30 minutes.

2 Preheat the oven to 190°C/375°F/Gas 5. Prick the pastry all over with a fork, cover with baking parchment weighed down with baking beans and bake blind for 10 minutes. Remove the baking beans and paper, return the pastry case (pie shell) to the oven and bake for 10 minutes, until golden. Cool in the tin.

3 Make the filling. Mix the egg yolks, cornflour and 25g/1oz/2 tbsp of the sugar in a bowl. Heat the milk in a pan until almost boiling, then beat into the egg mixture. Return to the clean pan and stir over a low heat until the custard has thickened and is smooth. Pour half the custard into a bowl.

4 Put the chocolate in a heatproof bowl. Place over a pan of barely simmering water until the chocolate has melted, stirring occasionally until smooth. Stir the melted chocolate into the custard in the bowl, with the vanilla extract.

5 Spread the chocolate filling in the pastry case and cover closely with dampened clear film (plastic wrap) to prevent a skin forming. Allow to cool, then chill until set.

6 Sprinkle the gelatine over the water in a bowl, leave until spongy, then place the bowl over a pan of simmering water until all the gelatine has dissolved. Stir into the remaining custard, then add the rum.

7 Whisk the egg whites in a clean, grease-free bowl until peaks form. Whisk in the remaining sugar, a little at a time, until stiff, then fold the egg whites quickly but evenly into the rum-flavoured custard.

8 Spoon the custard over the chocolate layer in the pastry shell. Level the mixture, making sure that none of the chocolate custard is visible. Chill the pie until the top layer has set, then remove the pie from the tin. Whip the cream, spread it over the top and sprinkle with chocolate curls, to decorate.

Coconut Cream Pie

A delicately flavoured tart, suitable for any occasion.

Serves 8
200g/7oz/2½ cups desiccated (dry unsweetened) coconut
115g/4oz/generous ½ cup caster (superfine) sugar
60ml/4 tbsp cornflour (cornstarch)
pinch of salt
600ml/1 pint/2½ cups milk
50ml/2fl oz/¼ cup whipping cream
2 egg yolks
25g/1oz/2 tbsp unsalted (sweet) butter
10ml/2 tsp vanilla extract

For the pastry
115g/4oz/1 cup plain (all-purpose) flour
1.5ml/¼ tsp salt
40g/1½oz/3 tbsp cold butter, cut into pieces
25g/1oz/2 tbsp cold lard
30–45ml/2–3 tbsp chilled water

1 Make the pastry. Sift the flour and salt into a bowl. Add the butter and lard and cut in with a pastry blender or two knives until the mixture resembles coarse breadcrumbs. With a fork, stir in just enough water to bind the dough. Gather into a ball, wrap in baking parchment and chill for at least 20 minutes.

2 Preheat the oven to 220°C/425°F/Gas 7. Roll out the dough to 3mm/⅛in thick. Transfer to a 23cm/9in flan tin (tart pan). Trim and flute the edges. Prick the base. Line with baking parchment and fill with baking beans. Bake for 10–12 minutes. Remove the paper and beans, reduce the heat to 180°C/350°F/Gas 4 and bake for a further 10–15 minutes until brown.

3 Spread 75g/3oz/1 cup of the coconut on a baking sheet. Toast in the oven for 6–8 minutes, stirring often, until golden. Set aside.

4 Put the sugar, cornflour and salt in a pan. In a bowl, whisk together the milk, cream and egg yolks. Add the egg mixture to the pan. Cook over low heat, stirring constantly, until the mixture comes to the boil. Boil for 1 minute, then remove from the heat. Add the butter, vanilla and remaining coconut.

5 Pour into the pastry case (pie shell). When the filling is cool, sprinkle the toasted coconut in a ring in the centre.

Coconut Cream Energy 445Kcal/1857kJ; Protein 6.3g; Carbohydrate 38.4g, of which sugars 20.6g; Fat 30.7g, of which saturates 21.7g; Cholesterol 82mg; Calcium 136mg; Fibre 3.9g; Sodium 98mg.
Black Bottom Energy 545Kcal/2276kJ; Protein 9.3g; Carbohydrate 51.3g, of which sugars 25.1g; Fat 34.2g, of which saturates 20g; Cholesterol 189mg; Calcium 148mg; Fibre 1.4g; Sodium 173mg.

Chocolate, Banana & Toffee Pie

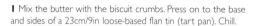

As an alternative to the coffee topping, just decorate the pie with whipped cream and extra banana slices.

Serves 6
65g/2½oz/5 tbsp unsalted (sweet) butter, melted
250g/9oz milk chocolate digestive biscuits (graham crackers), crushed
chocolate curls, to decorate

For the filling
397g/13½oz can condensed milk
150g/5oz plain (semisweet) chocolate, chopped
120ml/4fl oz/½ cup crème fraîche
15ml/1 tbsp golden (light corn) syrup

For the topping
2 bananas
250ml/8fl oz/1 cup crème fraîche
10ml/2 tsp strong black coffee

1 Mix the butter with the biscuit crumbs. Press on to the base and sides of a 23cm/9in loose-based flan tin (tart pan). Chill.

2 Make the filling. Place the unopened can of condensed milk in a deep pan of boiling water, making sure that it is completely covered. Lower the heat and simmer, covered for 2 hours, topping up the water as necessary. The can must remain covered at all times.

3 Remove the pan from the heat and set aside, covered, until the can has cooled down completely in the water. Do not attempt to open the can until it is completely cold.

4 Gently melt the chocolate with the crème fraîche and golden syrup in a heatproof bowl over a pan of simmering water. Stir in the caramelized condensed milk and beat together until thoroughly combined. Pour the chocolate filling into the biscuit crust and spread it evenly.

5 Slice the bananas evenly and arrange them over the chocolate filling in an attractive pattern.

6 Stir the crème fraîche and coffee together in a bowl, then spoon the mixture over the bananas. Sprinkle the chocolate curls on top.

Rhubarb Pie

This pie is as attractive as it is delicious.

Serves 6
175g/6oz/1½ cups plain (all-purpose) flour
2.5ml/½ tsp salt
10ml/2 tsp caster (superfine) sugar
75g/3oz/6 tbsp cold butter or margarine
30ml/2 tbsp single (light) cream

For the filling
1kg/2¼lb fresh rhubarb, cut into 2.5cm/1in slices
30ml/2 tbsp cornflour (cornstarch)
1 egg
275g/10oz/1½ cups caster (superfine) sugar
15ml/1 tbsp grated orange rind

1 Make the pastry. Sift the flour, salt and sugar into a bowl. Add the butter or margarine and rub in until the mix resembles breadcrumbs. Sprinkle the flour mixture with enough chilled water, about 45ml/3 tbsp, to bind the ingredients into a dough that just holds together. If the dough is too crumbly, mix in a little more chilled water. Gather the dough into a ball, flatten into a round, place in a plastic bag and chill for 20 minutes.

2 Roll out the pastry between two sheets of baking parchment to 3mm/⅛in thick. Use to line a 23cm/9in pie dish or tin (pan). Trim around the edge, leaving a 1cm/½in overhang. Fold the overhang under the edge and flute. Chill the pastry case (pie shell) and trimmings for 30 minutes.

3 Make the filling. Put the rhubarb in a bowl, sprinkle with the cornflour and toss to coat. Preheat the oven to 220°C/425°F/ Gas 7. Beat the egg with the sugar in a bowl until blended, then mix in the orange rind. Stir the sugar mixture into the rhubarb and mix well, then spoon the fruit into the prepared pastry case.

4 Roll out the pastry trimmings and make decorative shapes with a cutter. Arrange on top of the pie. Brush the shapes and the edge of the case with cream. Bake for 30 minutes. Reduce the temperature to 160°C/325°F/Gas 3 and bake for 15–20 minutes more, until the pastry is golden brown and the rhubarb is tender.

Choc., Ban. & Toffee Energy 900Kcal/3758kJ; Protein 11.5g; Carbohydrate 90g, of which sugars 73.2g; Fat 57.4g, of which saturates 35.8g; Cholesterol 139mg; Calcium 275mg; Fibre 1.8g; Sodium 368mg.
Rhubarb Pie Energy 431Kcal/1823kJ; Protein 5.8g; Carbohydrate 78.4g, of which sugars 51.6g; Fat 12.7g, of which saturates 7.4g; Cholesterol 61mg; Calcium 233mg; Fibre 3.3g; Sodium 100mg.

Cherry Pie

The woven lattice is the perfect finishing touch, although you can cheat and use a lattice pastry roller if you prefer.

Serves 8
900g/2lb fresh Morello cherries, pitted, or 2 x 450g/1lb cans or jars, drained and pitted
65g/2½oz/generous ¾ cup caster (superfine) sugar
25g/1oz/¼ cup plain (all-purpose) flour
25ml/1½ tbsp fresh lemon juice
1.5ml/¼ tsp almond extract
25g/1oz/2 tbsp butter or margarine

For the pastry
225g/8oz/2 cups plain (all-purpose) flour
5ml/1 tsp salt
175g/6oz/1 cup lard or vegetable fat
60–75ml/4–5 tbsp chilled water

1 Make the pastry. Sift the flour and salt into a mixing bowl. Using a pastry blender, cut in the fat until the mixture resembles coarse breadcrumbs.

2 Sprinkle in the chilled water, a tablespoon at a time, tossing lightly with your fingertips or a fork, until the pastry comes together to form a ball.

3 Preheat the oven to 220°C/425°F/Gas 7. Divide the pastry in half and shape each half into a ball. On a lightly floured surface, roll out one of the balls to a circle about 30cm/12in in diameter.

4 Use the rolled-out dough to line a 23cm/9in pie tin (pan), easing the pastry in and being careful not to stretch it. Using scissors or a knife, trim off the excess pastry, leaving a 1cm/½in overhang around the pie tin.

5 Roll out the remaining pastry to 3mm/⅛in thick. Cut out eleven strips 1cm/½in wide.

6 Combine the cherries, sugar, flour, lemon juice and almond extract in a mixing bowl. Spoon the mixture into the pastry case (pie shell) and dot the top with the butter or margarine.

7 Make the lattice. Place five of the pastry strips evenly across the filling. Fold every other strip back. Lay the first strip across in the opposite direction. Continue in this pattern, folding back every other strip each time you add a cross strip.

8 Trim the ends of the lattice strips even with the case overhang. Press together so that the edge rests on the pie-tin rim. With your thumbs, flute the edge. Chill for 15 minutes.

9 Bake the pie for 30 minutes, covering the edge of the pastry case with foil, if necessary, to prevent over-browning. Allow to cool, in the tin, on a wire rack.

> **Cook's Tip**
> *Morello cherries are the sour tasting type. Dark red and juicy, they are particularly good for cooked dishes.*

Apple & Cranberry Lattice Pie

Use fresh or frozen cranberries for this classic American pie.

Serves 8
grated rind of 1 orange
45ml/3 tbsp fresh orange juice
2 large, tart cooking apples
115g/4oz/1 cup cranberries
65g/2½oz/½ cup raisins
25g/1oz/¼ cup walnuts, chopped
225g/8oz/1 cup granulated sugar
115g/4oz/½ cup dark brown sugar
15ml/1 tbsp quick-cooking tapioca

For the pastry
225g/8oz/2 cups plain (all-purpose) flour
2.5ml/½ tsp salt
75g/3oz/6 tbsp cold butter, diced
60ml/4 tbsp cold lard, cut into pieces
15ml/1 tbsp granulated sugar, for sprinkling

1 Make the pastry. Sift the flour and salt into a bowl. Add the butter and lard and rub in until the mixture resembles coarse crumbs. With a fork, stir in just enough iced water to bind the dough. Gather into two equal balls, wrap in baking parchment, and chill for at least 20 minutes.

2 Put the orange rind and juice into a mixing bowl. Peel and core the apples; grate into the bowl. Stir in the cranberries, raisins, walnuts, granulated sugar, brown sugar and tapioca.

3 Place a baking sheet in the oven and preheat to 200°C/400°F/Gas 6.

4 On a lightly floured surface, roll out one ball of dough to about 3mm/⅛in thick. Transfer to a 23cm/9in pie tin (pan) and trim the edge. Spoon the cranberry and apple mixture into the shell.

5 Roll out the remaining dough to a circle about 28cm/11in in diameter. With a serrated pastry wheel, cut the dough into ten strips, 2cm/¾in wide. Place five strips horizontally across the top of the tart at 2.5cm/1in intervals. Weave in six vertical strips. Trim the edges. Sprinkle the top with the sugar.

6 Bake for 20 minutes. Reduce the heat to 180°C/350°F/Gas 4 and bake for 15 minutes until the crust is golden.

Cherry Pie Energy 437Kcal/1830kJ; Protein 3.6g; Carbohydrate 53.6g, of which sugars 29.8g; Fat 24.6g, of which saturates 10.5g; Cholesterol 27mg; Calcium 66mg; Fibre 1.7g; Sodium 30mg.
Lattice Pie Energy 485Kcal/2044kJ; Protein 3.8g; Carbohydrate 79.2g, of which sugars 57.8g; Fat 19.3g, of which saturates 9.1g; Cholesterol 31mg; Calcium 74mg; Fibre 2g; Sodium 79mg.

Chocolate, Pear & Pecan Pie

A classic pie gets a tempting new twist.

Serves 8–10

3 small pears, peeled
150ml/¼ pint/⅔ cup water
165g/5½oz/¾ cup caster
  (superfine) sugar
pared rind of 1 lemon
50g/2oz plain (semisweet)
  chocolate, broken into pieces
50g/2oz/¼ cup butter, diced
225g/8oz/scant ¾ cup golden
  (light corn) syrup

3 eggs, beaten
5ml/1 tsp vanilla extract
150g/5oz/1¼ cups pecan nuts,
  chopped

For the pastry

175g/6oz/1½ cups plain
  (all-purpose) flour
115g/4oz/½ cup butter, diced
25g/1oz/2 tbsp caster
  (superfine) sugar
1 egg yolk, lightly beaten with
  10ml/2 tsp chilled water

1 Sift the flour into a bowl, rub in the butter and stir in the sugar. Add the egg yolk and mix to a dough, adding more water if necessary. Knead lightly, wrap and chill for 30 minutes.

2 Roll out the pastry and use to line a 23cm/9in flan tin (tart pan). Chill for 20 minutes. Preheat the oven to 200°F/400°C/Gas 6. Line the pie case (shell) with foil, fill with baking beans and bake for 10 minutes. Lift out the foil and beans and bake for 5 minutes more. Set aside to cool.

3 Halve and core the pears. Bring the water, 50g/2oz/¼ cup of the sugar and the lemon rind to the boil. Add the pears, cover and simmer for 10 minutes. Remove the pears from the pan.

4 Melt the chocolate over simmering water, beat in the butter and set aside. Heat the remaining sugar and syrup until the sugar has dissolved. Bring to the boil and simmer for 2 minutes. Whisk the eggs into the chocolate mixture until combined, then whisk in the syrup mixture. Stir in the vanilla and nuts.

5 Slice the pear halves lengthways without cutting all the way through. Arrange them in the pastry case and pour in the nut mixture. Bake for 25–30 minutes. Cool and serve sliced.

Chocolate Chiffon Pie

Decorate with chocolate curls for a pretty finish.

Serves 8

175g/6oz plain (semisweet)
  chocolate squares, chopped
25g/1oz dark (bittersweet)
  chocolate, chopped
250ml/8fl oz/1 cup milk
15ml/1 tbsp powdered gelatine
130g/4½oz/⅔ cup sugar

2 eggs, separated
5ml/1 tsp vanilla extract
350ml/12fl oz/1½ cups whipping
  cream
pinch of salt
whipped cream, to decorate

For the crust

75g/3oz/1½ cups digestive biscuit
  (graham cracker) crumbs
75g/3oz/6 tbsp butter, melted

1 Place a baking sheet in the oven and preheat to 180°C/350°F/Gas 4. Make the crust. Mix the biscuit crumbs and butter in a bowl. Press the crumbs evenly over the base and sides of a 23cm/9in pie tin (pan). Bake for 8 minutes. Allow to cool.

2 Grind the chocolate in a food processor or blender. Set aside. Place the milk in the top of a double boiler or in a heatproof bowl. Sprinkle over the gelatine. Let stand for 5 minutes to soften.

3 Set the top of the double boiler or heatproof bowl over hot water. Add 50g/2oz/¼ cup of the sugar, the chocolate and egg yolks. Stir until dissolved. Add the vanilla extract.

4 Place the top of the double boiler or the heatproof bowl in a bowl of ice and stir until the mixture reaches room temperature. Remove from the ice and set aside.

5 Whip the cream lightly. Set aside. With an electric whisk, beat the egg whites and salt until they hold soft peaks. Add the remaining sugar and beat only enough to blend. Fold a dollop of egg whites into the chocolate mixture, then pour back into the whites and gently fold in.

6 Fold in the cream and pour into the tin. Freeze for about 5 minutes until just set. If the centre sinks, fill with any remaining mixture. Chill for 3–4 hours. Decorate with whipped cream.

Choc. Chiffon Energy 509Kcal/2120kJ; Protein 5.5g; Carbohydrate 43.2g, of which sugars 37.8g; Fat 36.2g, of which saturates 21.7g; Cholesterol 121mg; Calcium 98mg; Fibre 0.8g; Sodium 158mg.
Choc., Pear & Pecan Energy 499Kcal/2090kJ; Protein 5.8g; Carbohydrate 59.9g, of which sugars 46.3g; Fat 28g, of which saturates 11g; Cholesterol 113mg; Calcium 68mg; Fibre 2.4g; Sodium 186mg.

Crunchy-Topped Coffee Meringue Pie

For a special treat, try this sweet pastry case filled with coffee custard and topped with meringue – crisp on the outside and soft and chewy underneath.

Serves 6

30ml/2 tbsp ground coffee
350ml/12fl oz/1½ cups milk
25g/1oz/¼ cup cornflour (cornstarch)
130g/4½oz/⅔ cup caster (superfine) sugar
4 egg yolks
15g/½oz/1 tbsp butter

For the pastry
175g/6oz/1½ cups plain (all-purpose) flour
15ml/1 tbsp icing (confectioners') sugar
75g/3oz/6 tbsp butter, diced
1 egg yolk
finely grated rind of ½ orange
15ml/1 tbsp orange juice

For the meringue
3 egg whites
1.5ml/¼ tsp cream of tartar
150g/5oz/¾ cup caster (superfine) sugar
15ml/1 tbsp demerara (raw) sugar
25g/1oz/¼ cup skinned hazelnuts

1 Preheat the oven to 200°C/400°F/Gas 6. Make the pastry. Sift the flour and icing sugar into a bowl. Rub or cut in the butter until the mixture resembles fine breadcrumbs. Add the egg yolk, orange rind and juice and mix to form a firm dough. Wrap in clear film (plastic wrap) and chill for 20 minutes.

2 Roll out the pastry and use to line a 23cm/9in loose-based flan tin (tart pan). Cover again with clear film and chill for 30 minutes more.

3 Prick the pastry all over with a fork, line with foil, fill with baking beans and bake for about 10 minutes. Remove the foil and beans and bake for a further 5 minutes. Lower the oven temperature to 160°C/325°F/Gas 3.

4 Put the coffee in a small bowl. Heat 250ml/8fl oz/1 cup of the milk until near-boiling and pour over the coffee. Leave to infuse (steep) for 4–5 minutes, then strain. Blend the cornflour and sugar with the remaining milk in a pan and whisk in the coffee-flavoured milk.

5 Bring the mixture to the boil, stirring until thickened. Remove from the heat.

6 In a bowl, beat the egg yolks. Stir a little of the coffee mixture into the egg yolks, then add to the remaining coffee mixture in the pan with the butter. Cook the filling over a low heat for 4 minutes, or until very thick. Pour the coffee filling into the pastry case.

7 Make the meringue. Whisk the egg whites and cream of tartar in a small bowl until stiff peaks form. Whisk in the caster sugar, a spoonful at a time.

8 Spoon the meringue over the filling and spread right up to the edge of the pastry, swirling into peaks. Sprinkle with demerara sugar and hazelnuts, leaving some whole and chopping others into pieces. Bake for 30–35 minutes, or until the topping is golden brown and crisp. Serve warm or cold.

Plum Crumble Pie

Polenta adds a wonderful golden hue and crunchiness to the crumble topping for this pie, making a perfect contrast to the ripe, juicy plum filling.

Serves 6–8

10ml/2 tsp caster (superfine) sugar
15ml/1 tbsp polenta
450g/1lb dark plums
25g/1oz/¼ cup rolled oats
15ml/1 tbsp demerara (raw) sugar
custard or cream, to serve

For the pastry
115g/4oz/1 cup plain (all-purpose) flour, sifted
115g/4oz/1 cup wholemeal (whole-wheat) flour
150g/5oz/¾ cup caster (superfine) sugar
115g/4oz/1 cup polenta
5ml/1 tsp baking powder
pinch of salt
150g/5oz/10 tbsp butter, diced
1 egg, beaten
15ml/1 tbsp olive oil
about 60ml/4 tbsp chilled water

1 Make the pastry. Mix the dry ingredients in a large bowl. Rub or cut in the butter until the mixture resembles fine breadcrumbs. Stir in the egg, olive oil and chilled water to form a dough.

2 Grease a 23cm/9in springform cake tin (pan). Press two-thirds of the dough evenly over the base and sides of the tin. Wrap the remaining dough in clear film (plastic wrap) and chill.

3 Preheat the oven to 180°C/350°F/Gas 4. Sprinkle the sugar and polenta into the pastry case. Cut the plums in half and remove the stones (pits), then place the plums, cut side down, on top of the polenta base.

4 Unwrap the chilled dough, crumble with your fingers into a mixing bowl, then add the oats and mix lightly. Sprinkle the mixture over the plums. Sprinkle the demerara sugar on top.

5 Bake the pie for 50 minutes, or until golden. Leave for 15 minutes before removing the pie from the tin. Leave to cool for a few minutes before serving in slices with custard or cream.

Coffee Meringue Energy 540Kcal/2274kJ; Protein 9.5g; Carbohydrate 83.6g, of which sugars 57.4g; Fat 21g, of which saturates 10g; Cholesterol 203mg; Calcium 168mg; Fibre 1.2g; Sodium 160mg.
Plum Crumble Energy 426Kcal/1787kJ; Protein 6.4g; Carbohydrate 60.5g, of which sugars 26.5g; Fat 18.9g, of which saturates 10.2g; Cholesterol 64mg; Calcium 53mg; Fibre 3.2g; Sodium 127mg.

Cider Pie

Few can resist this delectable pie, with its rich cider filling. Suggest the season with pretty pastry decorations of apples, dotted around the edge of the pie.

Serves 6
600ml/1 pint/2½ cups cider (hard cider)
15g/½oz/1 tbsp butter
250ml/8fl oz/1 cup maple syrup
60ml/4 tbsp water
2 eggs, at room temperature, separated and yolks beaten
5ml/1 tsp grated nutmeg
icing (confectioners') sugar, for dusting

For the pastry
175g/6oz/1½ cups plain (all-purpose) flour
1.5ml/¼ tsp salt
10ml/2 tsp granulated sugar
115g/4oz/½ cup cold butter, diced
about 60ml/4 tbsp chilled water

1 Make the pastry. Sift the flour, salt and sugar into a mixing bowl. Rub or cut in the butter until the mixture resembles fine breadcrumbs.

2 Sprinkle the chilled water over the flour mixture. Combine with a fork until the dough holds together. If the dough is too crumbly, add a little more water. Gather the dough into a ball and flatten into a round. Wrap in clear film (plastic wrap) and chill for 30 minutes.

3 Meanwhile, pour the cider into a pan and boil until only 175ml/6fl oz/¾ cup, or approximately one-third, remains, then set aside to cool.

4 Roll out the pastry between two large sheets of baking parchment or clear film to 3mm/⅛in thick. Use to line a 23cm/9in pie dish.

5 Trim the edge, leaving a 1cm/½in overhang. Fold the overhang under to form a rim. Using a fork, press the rim down and scallop the edge. Chill for at least 20 minutes. Preheat the oven to 180°C/350°F/Gas 4.

6 Place the butter, maple syrup, water and reduced cider in a pan and simmer gently for 5–6 minutes. Cool slightly, then whisk in the beaten egg yolks.

7 Place the egg whites in a large bowl, and whisk vigorously until they form stiff peaks. Using a wooden spoon, gently fold in the cider mixture.

8 Pour the filling into the pastry case (pie shell) so that it fills the case evenly. Lightly dust with the grated nutmeg. Bake for 30–35 minutes, or until the filling is firmly set and golden. Dust with icing sugar and serve immediately.

Basque Apple Pie

The pastry for this Spanish pie has a cake-like texture.

Serves 6
215g/7½oz/scant 2 cups plain (all-purpose) flour, plus extra for rolling
5ml/1 tsp baking powder
pinch of salt
115g/4oz/½ cup cold unsalted (sweet) butter, cubed, plus extra for greasing
finely grated rind of ½ lemon
75g/3oz/6 tbsp caster (superfine) sugar, plus extra for sprinkling
2 small (US medium) eggs
3 eating apples, peeled, cored and cubed
ground cinnamon, for sprinkling

1 Sift the flour, baking powder and salt into a food processor. Add the butter and grated lemon rind and process briefly to combine, then add the sugar, 1 whole egg and the yolk of the second egg to the flour mixture and process to make a soft dough.

2 Divide the dough into two pieces, one portion nearly double the size of the other. Pat into two flat cakes. Wrap tightly in clear film (plastic wrap) and chill for at least 2 hours until firm.

3 Preheat the oven to 180°C/350°F/Gas 4. Place a baking sheet in the oven and grease a 20cm/8in loose-based flan tin (tart pan). Place the larger piece of dough on a lightly floured piece of clear film and cover with another piece of film. Roll out to a 25cm/10in round. Remove the film, transfer to the tin and press into the tin so that it stands just clear of the top.

4 Pack the tin with the apples and sprinkle with cinnamon. Roll out the second piece of dough in the same way, to exactly the same size as the tin. Lay the dough on top of the apples and fold the overlapping edges of the bottom piece of dough inward. Gently press the edges together with a fork, to seal.

5 Prick the dough a few times, brush with egg white and sprinkle with sugar. Place on the hot baking sheet and bake for 20 minutes. Reduce the temperature to 160°C/325°F/Gas 3 for a further 25–30 minutes until golden. Cool in the tin for 30 minutes, then remove from the tin. Cool on a wire rack.

Cook's Tip
Cut apple shapes from the pastry trimmings, bake them for 10 minutes alongside the pie, then arrange on top of the baked pie before dusting with icing sugar.

Basque Apple Pie Energy 232Kcal/984kJ; Protein 5.7g; Carbohydrate 45.4g, of which sugars 18.1g; Fat 4.4g, of which saturates 1.9g; Cholesterol 69mg; Calcium 69mg; Fibre 1.9g; Sodium 41mg.
Cider Pie Energy 452Kcal/1897kJ; Protein 5.1g; Carbohydrate 60.1g, of which sugars 37.8g; Fat 20g, of which saturates 11.9g; Cholesterol 110mg; Calcium 70mg; Fibre 0.9g; Sodium 275mg.

Peach & Brandy Pie

This fragrant fruit pie is simple but delicious.

450g/1lb puff pastry
vanilla ice cream, to serve

Serves 8
6 large, firm ripe peaches
40g/1½oz/3 tbsp butter
45ml/3 tbsp brandy
75g/3oz/6 tbsp caster (superfine)
  sugar

For the glaze
1 egg
5ml/1 tsp water
15ml/1 tbsp granulated sugar

1 Immerse the peaches in boiling water for about 30 seconds. Lift out with a slotted spoon, dip in cold water, then peel off the skins. Carefully halve and stone (pit) the peaches, then cut into slices.

2 Melt the butter in a frying pan, add the peaches and sprinkle with the brandy and sugar. Cook for 4 minutes, shaking the pan frequently, or until the the peaches are tender. Set the pan aside.

3 Cut the pastry into two pieces, one very slightly larger than the other. Roll out on a floured surface and cut the larger piece into a 30cm/12in round and the smaller one into a 28cm/11in round. Place on separate baking sheets lined with baking parchment. Cover with clear film (plastic wrap). Chill for 30 minutes.

4 Preheat the oven to 200°C/400°F/Gas 6. Remove the clear film from the pastry rounds. Spoon the peaches into the middle of the larger round and spread them out to within about 5cm/2in of the edge. Place the smaller round on top, shaping it in a mound over the peaches. Brush the edge of the larger pastry round with water, then fold this over the top pastry round. Press the edges to seal. Twist the edges together to make a pattern all the way round.

5 Make the glaze by mixing the egg and water together. Lightly brush it over the pastry and sprinkle evenly with the granulated sugar. Make five or six small crescent-shape slashes on the top of the pastry, radiating from the centre towards the edge. Bake the pie for about 45 minutes, or until the pastry is golden brown. Serve warm in slices with vanilla ice cream.

Fresh Cherry & Hazelnut Strudel

Serve this wonderful old-world treat as a warm dessert with crème fraîche.

250g/9oz/generous 1 cup
  ricotta cheese
8 large sheets of filo pastry,
  thawed if frozen
75g/3oz ratafia biscuits (almond
  macaroons), crushed
450g/1lb/2½ cups cherries, pitted
30ml/2 tbsp chopped hazelnuts
icing (confectioners') sugar,
  for dusting

Serves 6–8
75g/3oz/6 tbsp butter
75g/3oz/6 tbsp light muscovado
  (brown) sugar
3 egg yolks
grated rind of 1 lemon
1.5ml/¼ tsp grated nutmeg

1 Preheat the oven to 190°C/375°F/Gas 5. Beat 15g/½oz/ 1 tbsp of the butter with the sugar and egg yolks in a mixing bowl until light and fluffy. Beat in the lemon rind, grated nutmeg and ricotta cheese.

2 Melt the remaining butter in a small pan. Place a sheet of filo on a clean dish towel and brush it generously with melted butter. Place a second sheet on top and repeat the process. Continue until all the sheets of filo have been used, reserving some of the butter.

3 Sprinkle the crushed ratafias over the top of the filo, leaving a 5cm/2in border all round. Spoon the ricotta mixture over the ratafia biscuits, spreading it lightly, then sprinkle over the cherries.

4 Fold in the filo pastry border on all four sides, then, using the dish towel to help you, roll up the strudel, Swiss-roll (jelly-roll) style, beginning from one of the long sides of the pastry. Grease a large baking sheet with a little of the remaining melted butter.

5 Place the strudel, seam side down, on the baking sheet, brush with the remaining melted butter, and sprinkle the chopped hazelnuts over the surface.

6 Bake for 35–40 minutes, or until the strudel is golden and crisp. Dust with icing sugar and serve.

Cherry & Hazelnut Energy 317Kcal/1326kJ; Protein 6.5g; Carbohydrate 34.2g, of which sugars 22.9g; Fat 18.1g, of which saturates 9.1g; Cholesterol 109mg; Calcium 54mg; Fibre 1.2g; Sodium 93mg.
Peach & Brandy Energy 343Kcal/1437kJ; Protein 5.2g; Carbohydrate 39.2g, of which sugars 19.1g; Fat 18.7g, of which saturates 2.8g; Cholesterol 34mg; Calcium 50mg; Fibre 1.7g; Sodium 215mg.

Nectarine Puff Pastry Tarts

These simple, fresh fruit pastries are easy to put together, but the puff pastry gives them an elegant look. You could use peaches, apples or pears instead of the nectarines.

Serves 6

15g/½oz/1 tbsp butter, plus extra
 for greasing
225g/8oz rough puff or puff
 pastry
450g/1lb nectarines
25g/1oz/2 tbsp caster (superfine)
 sugar
freshly grated nutmeg
crème fraîche or lightly whipped
 cream, to serve (optional)

1 Lightly grease a large baking sheet and sprinkle very lightly with water.

2 On a lightly floured surface, roll out the rough puff pastry to a large rectangle, measuring about 40 x 25cm/16 x 10in, and cut into six smaller rectangles.

3 Transfer the pastry to the baking sheet. Using the back of a small knife, scallop the edges of each piece of pastry. Then, using the tip of the knife, score a line 1cm/½in from the edge of each rectangle to form a border.

4 Chill the shapes for 30 minutes. Meanwhile, preheat the oven to 200°C/400°F/Gas 6.

5 Halve the nectarines and remove the stones (pits), then cut the fruit into thin slices. Arrange the nectarine slices neatly in the centre of the pastry rectangles, leaving the border uncovered. Sprinkle the fruit with the caster sugar and a little freshly grated nutmeg.

6 Bake for 12–15 minutes until the edges of each pastry case (pie shell) are puffed up and the fruit is tender.

7 Transfer the tarts to a wire rack to cool slightly, then serve warm with crème fraîche or whipped cream, if you like.

Peach & Blueberry Pie

This pie features an unusual combination of fruits.

Serves 8

225g/8oz/2 cups plain
 (all-purpose) flour
pinch of salt
10ml/2 tsp sugar
150g/5oz/⅔ cup cold butter
1 egg yolk
30ml/2 tbsp milk, to glaze

For the filling

450g/1lb fresh peaches, peeled,
 stoned (pitted) and sliced
275g/10oz/2 cups blueberries
150g/5oz/¾ cup caster
 (superfine) sugar
30ml/2 tbsp lemon juice
40g/1½oz/⅓ cup plain
 (all-purpose) flour
large pinch of grated nutmeg
25g/1oz/2 tbsp butter, diced

1 Sift the flour, salt and sugar into a bowl and rub in the butter. Mix the egg yolk with 50ml/2fl oz/¼ cup water, sprinkle over the mixture and mix with a fork until the dough holds together. Add a little more water if necessary. Gather the dough into a ball and flatten into a round. Place in a plastic bag and chill for 20 minutes.

2 Roll out two-thirds of the pastry between sheets of baking parchment to 3mm/⅛in thick. Use to line a 23cm/9in pie dish. Trim the edge, leaving a 1cm/½in overhang. Fold the overhang under and press the edge to the rim of the pie dish.

3 Roll out the trimmings and remaining pastry to 5mm/¼in thick. Cut into 1cm/½in wide strips. Chill them and the pastry case (pie shell) for 20 minutes. Preheat the oven to 200°C/400°F/Gas 6.

4 Line the pastry case with baking parchment and fill with baking beans. Bake for 7–10 minutes, until just set. Remove the paper and beans. Prick the base with a fork, return to the oven and bake for 5 minutes more. Leave to cool slightly. Leave the oven on.

5 Make the filling. Combine the peaches, blueberries, sugar, lemon juice, flour and nutmeg. Spoon into the dish. Dot with the butter.

6 Weave a lattice top with the strips, pressing the ends in place. Brush with the milk. Bake for 15 minutes. Lower the temperature to 180°C/350°F/Gas 4 and bake for 30 minutes more.

Nectarine Tarts Energy 208Kcal/873kJ; Protein 3.2g; Carbohydrate 25.9g, of which sugars 12.5g; Fat 11.3g, of which saturates 1.3g; Cholesterol 5mg; Calcium 30mg; Fibre 0.9g; Sodium 133mg.
Peach & Blueberry Pie Energy 391Kcal/1640kJ; Protein 4.7g; Carbohydrate 53g, of which sugars 27.7g; Fat 19.3g, of which saturates 11.7g; Cholesterol 72mg; Calcium 86mg; Fibre 2.9g; Sodium 139mg.

Berry Brûlée Tarts

This quantity of pastry is enough for eight tartlets, so freeze half for another day. The brûlée topping is best added no more than two hours before serving.

Makes 4

250g/9oz/2¼ cups plain (all-purpose) flour
pinch of salt
25g/1oz/¼ cup ground almonds
15ml/1 tbsp icing (confectioners') sugar
150g/5oz/10 tbsp unsalted (sweet) butter, chilled and diced

I egg yolk
about 45ml/3 tbsp cold water

For the filling
4 egg yolks
15ml/1 tbsp cornflour (cornstarch)
50g/2oz/¼ cup caster (superfine) sugar
a few drops of vanilla extract
300ml/½ pint/1¼ cups creamy milk
225g/8oz/2 cups mixed berry fruits, such as strawberries, raspberries and redcurrants
50g/2oz/½ cup icing (confectioners') sugar

1 Mix the flour, salt, ground almonds and icing sugar in a bowl. Rub in the butter by hand or in a food processor until the mixture resembles fine breadcrumbs. Add the egg yolk and enough cold water to form a dough. Knead the dough gently, then cut it in half and freeze half for use later.

2 Cut the remaining pastry into four equal pieces and roll out thinly on a lightly floured surface. Use the pastry rounds to line four individual tartlet tins (muffin pans), allowing the excess pastry to hang over the edges. Chill for 30 minutes.

3 Preheat the oven to 200°C/400°F/Gas 6. Line the pastry with baking parchment and fill with baking beans. Bake blind for 10 minutes. Remove the paper and beans and return the tartlet cases to the oven for 5 minutes until golden. Allow the pastry to cool, then carefully trim off the excess pastry.

4 Beat the egg yolks, cornflour, caster sugar and vanilla in a bowl. Warm the milk in a heavy pan, pour it on to the egg yolks, whisking constantly, then return the mixture to the cleaned out pan.

5 Heat, stirring, until the custard thickens, but do not let it boil. Remove from the heat, press a piece of clear film (plastic wrap) directly on the surface of the custard and allow to cool.

6 Scatter the berries in the tartlet cases and spoon over the custard. Chill the tarts for 2 hours.

7 To serve, sift icing sugar generously over the tops of the tartlets. Preheat the grill (broiler) to the highest setting. Place the tartlets under the hot grill until the sugar melts and caramelizes. Allow the topping to cool and harden for about 10 minutes before serving.

Cook's Tip
If you have a culinary blow torch – and are confident about operating it safely – use it to melt the brûlée topping easily.

Mince Pies with Orange Cinnamon Pastry

Home-made mince pies are so much nicer than shop bought ones, especially with this tasty pastry. Serve with whipped cream, flavoured with liqueur, for a special festive treat.

Makes 18
225g/8oz/2 cups plain (all-purpose) flour
40g/1½oz/⅓ cup icing (confectioners') sugar

10ml/2 tsp ground cinnamon
150g/5oz/10 tbsp butter
grated rind of 1 orange
60ml/4 tbsp chilled water
225g/8oz/⅔ cup mincemeat
1 beaten egg, to glaze
icing (confectioners') sugar, for dusting

1 Make the pastry. Sift together the flour, icing sugar and cinnamon in a mixing bowl, then rub in the butter until it resembles breadcrumbs. (This can be done in a food processor.) Stir in the grated orange rind.

2 Mix to a firm dough with the chilled water. Knead lightly, then roll out to 5mm/¼in thick.

3 Using a 6cm/2½in round cutter, cut out 18 circles, re-rolling as necessary. Then cut out 18 smaller 5cm/2in circles.

4 Line two bun tins (muffin pans) with the 18 larger circles – they will fill one and a half tins. Spoon a small spoonful of mincemeat into each and top with the smaller pastry circles, pressing the edges lightly together to seal.

5 Glaze the tops of the pies with egg and chill for 30 minutes. Preheat the oven to 200°C/400°F/Gas 6.

6 Bake the pies for 15–20 minutes until they are golden brown. Transfer them to wire racks to cool. Serve just warm and dusted with icing sugar.

Berry Tarts Energy 743Kcal/3099kJ; Protein 13.6g; Carbohydrate 75.2g, of which sugars 20.6g; Fat 45g, of which saturates 23.8g; Cholesterol 342mg; Calcium 250mg; Fibre 4g; Sodium 282mg.
Mince Pies Energy 148Kcal/619kJ; Protein 1.3g; Carbohydrate 19.9g, of which sugars 10.3g; Fat 7.6g, of which saturates 4.4g; Cholesterol 18mg; Calcium 25mg; Fibre 0.6g; Sodium 53mg.

Mango & Tamarillo Pastries

These fruit-topped little pastries go down a treat at the end of a spicy meal. Exotic mango and tamarillos provide a refreshing taste, while the marzipan adds a delectable sweetness to the pastry and fruit.

Makes 8
225g/8oz ready-rolled puff pastry
(30 x 25cm/12 x 10in
rectangle)
1 egg yolk, lightly beaten
115g/4oz/½ cup white marzipan
40ml/8 tsp ginger or apricot
conserve
1 mango, peeled and thinly sliced
off the stone (pit)
2 tamarillos, halved and sliced
caster (superfine) sugar, for
sprinkling

1 Preheat the oven to 200°C/400°F/Gas 6. Unroll the pastry and cut it into 8 rectangles. Carefully transfer to a couple of baking sheets.

2 Using a sharp knife, score the surface of each piece of pastry into a diamond pattern, then brush with the egg yolk to glaze.

3 Cut eight thin slices of marzipan and lay one slice on each pastry rectangle. Top each with a teaspoon of the ginger or apricot conserve and spread over evenly.

4 Top each pastry rectangle with alternate slices of mango and tamarillo. Sprinkle the fruit with some of the caster sugar, then bake in the preheated oven for 15–20 minutes until the pastry is well puffed up and golden.

5 Transfer the pastries to a wire rack to cool. Sprinkle with more caster sugar before serving.

Variation
If you have difficulty finding tamarillos, use apricot slices instead or try a mix of plums and peaches.

Luxury Mince Pies

A luxury version of the festive favourite.

Makes 12–15
225g/8oz/⅔ cup mincemeat
50g/2oz/⅓ mixed chopped
(candied) peel
50g/2oz/¼ cup glacé (candied)
cherries, chopped
30ml/2 tbsp whisky
1 egg, beaten or a little milk

icing (confectioners') sugar,
for dusting
double (heavy) cream, to serve

For the pastry
1 egg yolk
5ml/1 tsp grated orange rind
15ml/1 tbsp caster (superfine)
sugar
10ml/2 tsp chilled water
225g/8oz/2 cups plain
(all-purpose) flour
150g/5oz/10 tbsp butter, diced

1 Make the pastry. Lightly beat the egg yolk in a bowl, then add the grated orange rind, caster sugar and water and mix together. Cover and set aside. Sift the flour into a separate mixing bowl.

2 Rub the butter into the flour until the mixture resembles fine breadcrumbs. Stir in the egg mixture and mix to a dough. Wrap in clear film (plastic wrap) and chill for 30 minutes.

3 Mix together the mincemeat, mixed peel and glacé cherries, then add the whisky.

4 Roll out three-quarters of the pastry. With a fluted pastry (cookie) cutter, stamp out rounds and line 12–15 patty tin (muffin pan) holes. Re-roll the trimmings and stamp out star shapes.

5 Preheat the oven to 200°C/400°F/Gas 6. Spoon a little filling into each pastry case (pie shell) and top with a star shape. Brush with a little beaten egg or milk and bake for 20–25 minutes, or until golden. Leave to cool.

6 If you like, lift the pastry star off each mince pie and place a dollop of thick cream on top of the filling before replacing the star. Lightly dust the mince pies with a little icing sugar.

Mince Pies Energy 195Kcal/818kJ; Protein 1.8g; Carbohydrate 26.3g, of which sugars 14.8g; Fat 9.5g, of which saturates 5.3g; Cholesterol 35mg; Calcium 36mg; Fibre 0.9g; Sodium 75mg.
Mango Pastries Energy 202Kcal/847kJ; Protein 3.2g; Carbohydrate 28.4g, of which sugars 18.3g; Fat 9.5g, of which saturates 0.4g; Cholesterol 25mg; Calcium 43mg; Fibre 1.2g; Sodium 95mg.

Fruit-Filled Empanadas

Imagine biting through crisp buttery pastry to discover a rich fruity filling flavoured with oranges and cinnamon. These are the stuff that dreams are made of.

Makes 12

275g/10oz/2½ cups plain
(all-purpose) flour
30ml/2 tbsp sugar
75g/3oz/6 tbsp chilled butter,
cubed
1 egg yolk

iced water
milk, to glaze
sugar, for sprinkling
whole almonds and orange
wedges, to serve

For the filling

30ml/2 tbsp butter
3 ripe plantains, peeled and
mashed
2.5ml/½ tsp ground cloves
5ml/1 tsp ground cinnamon
200g/7oz/1⅓ cups raisins
grated rind and juice of 2 oranges

1 Make the pastry. Combine the flour and sugar in a mixing bowl. Rub in the chilled cubes of butter until the mixture resembles fine breadcrumbs.

2 Beat the egg yolk and add to the flour mixture. Add enough iced water to make a smooth dough, then shape into a ball.

3 Make the filling. Melt the butter in a pan. Add the plantains, cloves and cinnamon and cook over medium heat for 2–3 minutes. Stir in the raisins with the orange rind and juice. Lower the heat so that the mixture barely simmers. Cook for about 15 minutes, until the raisins are plump and the juice has evaporated. Set the mixture aside to cool.

4 Preheat the oven to 200°C/400°F/Gas 6. Roll out the pastry on a lightly floured surface. Cut it into 10cm/4in rounds. Place the rounds on a baking sheet and spoon on a little of the filling. Dampen the rim of the pastry rounds with water, fold the pastry over the filling and crimp the edges to seal.

5 Brush the empanadas with milk. Bake in batches for about 15 minutes or until golden. Allow to cool a little, sprinkle with sugar and serve warm, with almonds and orange wedges.

Baked Sweet Ravioli

These sweet ravioli have a wonderful ricotta filling.

Serves 4

175g/6oz/¾ cup ricotta cheese
50g/2oz/¼ cup caster (superfine)
sugar
4ml/¾ tsp vanilla extract
small egg, beaten, plus 1 egg
yolk
15ml/1 tbsp mixed glacé
(candied) fruits

25g/1oz dark (bittersweet)
chocolate, finely chopped

For the pastry

225g/8oz/2 cups plain
(all-purpose) flour
65g/2½oz/5 tbsp caster
(superfine) sugar
90g/3½oz/scant ½ cup butter,
diced
1 egg
5ml/1 tsp finely grated lemon rind

1 Make the pastry. Place the flour and sugar in a food processor and gradually process in the butter. Keep the motor running while you add the egg and lemon rind to make a dough.

2 Transfer the dough to a sheet of clear film (plastic wrap), cover with another sheet of film and flatten into a round. Chill.

3 Press the ricotta through a sieve (strainer) into a bowl. Stir in the sugar, vanilla, egg yolk, glacé fruits and dark chocolate.

4 Bring the pastry back to room temperature. Divide in half and roll each between clear film to make rectangles measuring 15 x 56cm/6 x 22in. Preheat the oven to 180°C/350°F/Gas 4.

5 Arrange heaped tablespoonfuls of the filling in two rows along one of the pastry strips, leaving a 2.5cm/1in margin around each. Brush the pastry between the mounds of filling with beaten egg. Place the second strip of pastry on top and press down between each mound of filling to seal.

6 Use a 6cm/2½in plain pastry (cookie) cutter to cut around each mound of filling to make small circular ravioli. Gently pinch each ravioli with your fingertips to seal the edges. Place on a greased baking sheet and bake for 15 minutes until golden brown. Serve warm, sprinkled with lemon rind, if you wish.

Empanadas Energy 235Kcal/990kJ; Protein 3.2g; Carbohydrate 39.7g, of which sugars 21.6g; Fat 8.1g, of which saturates 4.8g; Cholesterol 35mg; Calcium 47mg; Fibre 1.4g; Sodium 66mg.
Ravioli Energy 628Kcal/2636kJ; Protein 13.1g; Carbohydrate 81.4g, of which sugars 38.5g; Fat 30.1g, of which saturates 17.7g; Cholesterol 162mg; Calcium 119mg; Fibre 2.1g; Sodium 186mg.

An Ice Bowl for a Sorbet

Nothing sets off a freshly scooped sorbet quite so effectively as an ice bowl inlaid with fresh flowers and leaves. Ice bowls are easy to make, inexpensive and stunning enough to grace any special celebration, from lunch party to country wedding.

Serves 8–10
ice cubes
cold water
selection of fresh edible flowers
*   and leaves*
18–20 scoops of sorbet, to serve

1 Place some ice cubes in the base of a 3.5 litre/6 pint/15 cup clear plastic or glass freezerproof bowl. Tuck some flowers and leaves around the ice. Position a smaller bowl so that it rests on the ice cubes, leaving an even space between the two bowls.

2 Pour cold water into the space between the bowls until the water level starts to come up the sides. Freeze for 2–3 hours until frozen.

3 Tuck more flowers and leaves between the two bowls, mixing the flowers and leaves so that they look attractive through the sides of the larger bowl.

4 Place some kitchen weights or food cans in the central bowl to stop it from rising, then fill the space between the bowls to the rim with more water. Freeze overnight until firm.

5 Release the inner bowl by pouring boiling water into it almost to the top. Quickly tip out the water and lift away the inner bowl. Repeat the process if the bowl won't come free instantly.

6 To remove the outer bowl, dip it quickly in a large bowl of very hot water until the ice bowl loosens. Return the ice bowl to the freezer.

7 Shortly before serving, scoop the sorbet into the bowl. Return to the freezer until ready to serve.

Lavender & Honey Ice Cream

Lavender and honey make a memorable partnership in this old-fashioned and elegant ice cream. Serve scooped into glasses or set in little moulds and top with lightly whipped cream. Pretty lavender flowers add the finishing touch.

Serves 6–8
90ml/6 tbsp clear honey
4 egg yolks
10ml/2 tsp cornflour (cornstarch)
8 lavender sprigs, plus extra
*   to decorate*
450ml/³⁄₄ pint/scant 2 cups milk
450ml/³⁄₄ pint/scant 2 cups
*   whipping cream*
thin biscuits (cookies), to serve

1 Put the honey, egg yolks, and cornflour in a bowl. Separate the lavender flowers from the stalks and add them with a little milk. Whisk lightly. Bring the remaining milk to the boil in a heavy pan. Add to the egg yolk mixture, stirring well.

2 Return the mixture to the pan and cook very gently, stirring until the mixture thickens. Pour the custard into a bowl, cover the surface closely with a circle of waxed paper and leave to cool, then chill until very cold.

3 Whip the cream and fold into the custard. Pour into a freezer container and freeze for 3–4 hours, beating twice as it thickens. Return to the freezer until ready to serve.

4 Alternatively, use an ice cream maker. Stir the cream into the custard, then churn the mixture until it holds its shape. Transfer to a freezer container and freeze until ready to serve.

5 Transfer the ice cream to the refrigerator 30 minutes before serving, so that it softens slightly. Scoop into small dishes, decorate with lavender flowers and serve with biscuits.

Cook's Tip
To make lavender sugar for flavouring desserts, leave some lavender in caster (superfine) sugar, then sieve before using.

Sorbet Energy 73Kcal/308kJ; Protein 0.2g; Carbohydrate 18.6g, of which sugars 17.5g; Fat 0.2g, of which saturates 0g; Cholesterol 0mg; Calcium 6mg; Fibre 0g; Sodium 8mg. **Lavender & Honey Ice Cream** Energy 308Kcal/1275kJ; Protein 4.5g; Carbohydrate 13.9g, of which sugars 12.8g; Fat 26.4g, of which saturates 15.6g; Cholesterol 163mg; Calcium 113mg; Fibre 0g; Sodium 45mg.

Classic Dark Chocolate Ice Cream

Rich, dark and wonderfully luxurious, this ice cream can be served solo or drizzled with warm chocolate sauce. If you are making it in advance, don't forget to soften the ice cream before serving so that the full flavour of the chocolate comes through.

Serves 4–6
4 egg yolks
75g/3oz/6 tbsp caster (superfine) sugar
5ml/1 tsp cornflour (cornstarch)
300ml/½ pint/1¼ cups semi-skimmed (low-fat) milk
200g/7oz dark (bittersweet) chocolate
300ml/½ pint/1¼ cups whipping cream
shaved chocolate, to decorate

1 Whisk the egg yolks, sugar and cornflour in a bowl until thick and foamy. Pour the milk into a pan, bring just to the boil, then gradually whisk it into the yolk mixture.

2 Return the mixture to the pan and cook over a gentle heat, stirring constantly until the custard thickens and is smooth. Remove the pan from the heat.

3 Break the chocolate into small pieces and stir into the hot custard until it has melted. Leave to cool, then chill.

4 Whip the cream until it has thickened but still falls from a spoon. Fold into the custard, then pour into a freezer container. Freeze for 6 hours or until firm enough to scoop, beating once or twice with a fork or in a food processor as it thickens.

5 Alternatively, use an ice cream maker. Mix the chocolate custard with the whipped cream. Churn until firm enough to scoop. Serve in scoops, decorated with chocolate shavings.

> **Cook's Tip**
> *For the best flavour use a good-quality chocolate with at least 75 per cent cocoa solids, such as fine Belgian chocolate.*

Spicy Pumpkin & Orange Bombe

In this fabulous bombe dessert, a mouthwatering pumpkin ice cream is encased in delicious sponge and served with an orange and whole-spice syrup.

Serves 8
115g/4oz/½ cup unsalted (sweet) butter or margarine, softened
115g/4oz/generous ½ cup caster (superfine) sugar
115g/4oz/1 cup self-raising (self-rising) flour
2.5ml/½ tsp baking powder
2 eggs

For the ice cream
450g/1lb fresh pumpkin, seeded and cubed
1 orange
300g/11oz/scant 1½ cups granulated sugar
300ml/½ pint/1¼ cups water
2 cinnamon sticks, halved
10ml/2 tsp whole cloves
30ml/2 tbsp orange flower water
300ml/½ pint/1¼ cups extra-thick double (heavy) cream
2 pieces preserved stem ginger, grated
icing (confectioners') sugar, for dusting

1 Preheat the oven to 180°C/350°F/Gas 4. Grease and base-line a 450g/1lb loaf tin (pan).

2 Make the sponge. Beat the butter or margarine, caster sugar, flour, baking powder and eggs in a bowl until creamy. Spoon the mixture into the prepared tin, then level the surface and bake for 30–35 minutes until firm in the centre. Leave in the tin for a few minutes then turn out and cool.

3 Make the ice cream. Steam the cubes of pumpkin for about 15 minutes, or until tender. Drain and blend in a food processor to form a smooth purée. Leave to cool.

4 Pare thin strips of rind from the orange, then cut into very fine shreds. Squeeze the orange and set the juice aside. Heat the sugar and water in a small, heavy pan until the sugar dissolves. Boil rapidly without stirring for 3 minutes.

5 Stir in the orange shreds and juice, cinnamon and cloves and heat gently for 5 minutes. Strain the syrup, reserving the orange shreds and spices. Measure 300ml/½ pint/1¼ cups of the syrup and reserve. Return the spices to the remaining syrup and stir in the orange flower water. Pour into a jug (pitcher) and cool.

6 Beat the pumpkin purée with 175ml/6fl oz/¾ cup of the measured strained syrup until evenly combined. Stir in the cream and ginger. Cut the cake into 1cm/½in slices. Dampen a 1.5 litre/2½ pint/6¼ cup deep bowl and line it with clear film (plastic wrap). Pour the remaining strained syrup into a shallow dish.

7 Dip the cake slices briefly in the syrup and use to line the prepared bowl, placing the coated sides against the bowl.

8 Pour the pumpkin mixture into a shallow container and freeze until firm. Scrape the ice cream into the sponge-lined bowl, level the surface and freeze until firm, preferably overnight.

9 To serve, invert the bombe on to a plate. Lift off the bowl and clear film. Dust with the icing sugar and serve with the spiced syrup spooned over.

Choc. Ice Cream Energy 349Kcal/1461kJ; Protein 4.8g; Carbohydrate 36.8g, of which sugars 35.8g; Fat 21.4g, of which saturates 11.9g; Cholesterol 162mg; Calcium 78mg; Fibre 0.7g; Sodium 29mg.
Pumpkin Bombe Energy 571Kcal/2387kJ; Protein 4.2g; Carbohydrate 67g, of which sugars 56.1g; Fat 33.6g, of which saturates 20.5g; Cholesterol 130mg; Calcium 122mg; Fibre 1g; Sodium 168mg.

White Chocolate Castles

These impressive and romantic-looking chocolate cases serve a wide variety of uses. They can be frozen with iced mousses or other desserts set in them, or, as in this recipe, filled with scoops of ice cream and succulent fresh blueberries.

Serves 6
225g/8oz white chocolate, broken into pieces
250ml/8fl oz/1 cup white chocolate ice cream
250ml/8fl oz/1 cup dark (bittersweet) chocolate ice cream
115g/4oz/1 cup blueberries
cocoa powder (unsweetened), for dusting

1 Put the white chocolate in a heatproof bowl, set it over a pan of gently simmering water and leave until melted. Line a baking sheet with baking parchment. Cut out six 30 x 13cm/12 x 5in strips of baking parchment, then fold each in half lengthways.

2 Stand a 7.5cm/3in pastry cutter on the baking sheet. Roll one strip of paper into a circle and fit inside the cutter with the folded edge on the base paper. Stick the edges together with tape.

3 Remove the cutter and make more paper collars in the same way, leaving the pastry cutter in place around the final collar.

4 Spoon a little of the melted chocolate into the base of the collar supported by the cutter. Using a teaspoon, spread the chocolate over the base and up the sides of the collar, making the top edge uneven. Carefully lift away the cutter.

5 Make five more chocolate cases in the same way, using the cutter for extra support each time. Leave the cases in a cool place or in the refrigerator to set.

6 Carefully peel away the paper from the sides of the chocolate cases then lift the cases off the base. Transfer to serving plates.

7 Using a teaspoon, scoop the ice creams into the cases and decorate with the fruit. Dust with cocoa powder and serve.

Strawberry Semi-Freddo

Serve this quick strawberry and ricotta dessert semi-frozen to enjoy the flavour at its best. The contrasting texture of crisp dessert biscuits (cookies) makes the perfect accompaniment.

Serves 4–6
250g/9oz/generous 2 cups strawberries
115g/4oz/scant ½ cup strawberry jam
250g/9oz/generous 1 cup ricotta cheese
200g/7oz/scant 1 cup Greek (US strained plain) yogurt
5ml/1 tsp natural vanilla extract
40g/1½oz/3 tbsp caster (superfine) sugar
extra strawberries and mint or lemon balm, to decorate

1 Put the strawberries in a bowl and mash them with a fork until broken into small pieces but not completely puréed. Stir in the strawberry jam. Drain off any whey from the ricotta.

2 Transfer the ricotta to a large bowl and stir in the Greek yogurt, vanilla extract and sugar. Using a dessertspoon, gently fold the mashed strawberries into the ricotta mixture to create a rippled effect.

3 Spoon into individual freezerproof dishes and freeze for at least 2 hours until almost solid. Alternatively, freeze until completely solid, then transfer the ice cream to the refrigerator for about 45 minutes to soften before serving.

4 Serve in small bowls with extra strawberries and decorated with mint or lemon balm.

Cook's Tip
Don't mash the strawberries too much or they'll become too liquid. Freeze in a large freezer container if you don't have suitable small dishes. Transfer to the refrigerator to thaw slightly, then scoop into glasses.

Choc. Castles Energy 351Kcal/1463kJ; Protein 6g; Carbohydrate 34.3g, of which sugars 34.2g; Fat 22g, of which saturates 13.1g; Cholesterol 0mg; Calcium 182mg; Fibre 1.2g; Sodium 84mg.
Strawberry Semi-Freddo Energy 181Kcal/764kJ; Protein 5.8g; Carbohydrate 29.6g, of which sugars 29.6g; Fat 5.3g, of which saturates 3.2g; Cholesterol 15mg; Calcium 91mg; Fibre 0.9g; Sodium 43mg.

Chocolate Meringues with Mixed Fruit Compote

A glamorous dinner party dessert that is hard to beat.

blackcurrants, redcurrants, raspberries and blackberries

Serves 6
105ml/7 tbsp unsweetened red grape juice
105ml/7 tbsp unsweetened apple juice
30ml/2 tbsp clear honey
450g/1lb/4 cups mixed fresh summer berries, such as

For the meringues
3 egg whites
150g/5oz/³/₄ cup caster (superfine) sugar
75g/3oz good-quality plain (semisweet) chocolate, finely grated
175g/6oz/³/₄ cup crème fraîche

1 Preheat the oven to 110°C/225°F/Gas ¼. Grease and line two large baking sheets with baking parchment, cutting the paper to fit.

2 Make the meringues. Whisk the egg whites in a large mixing bowl until stiff. Gradually whisk in half the sugar, then fold in the remaining sugar, using a metal spoon. Gently fold in the grated plain chocolate. Carefully spoon the meringue mixture into a large piping (pastry) bag fitted with a large star nozzle. Pipe small round whirls of the mixture on to the prepared baking sheets.

3 Bake the meringues for 2½–3 hours until they are firm and crisp. Remove from the oven. Carefully peel the meringues off the paper, then transfer them to a wire rack to cool.

4 Meanwhile, make the compote. Heat the fruit juices and honey in a pan until the mixture is almost boiling. Place the mixed berries in a large bowl and pour over the hot fruit juice and honey mixture. Stir gently to mix, then set aside and leave to cool. Once cool, cover the bowl with clear film (plastic wrap) and chill until required.

5 To serve, sandwich the cold meringues together with crème fraîche. Spoon the mixed fruit compote on to individual plates, top with the meringues and serve immediately.

Nectarine & Hazelnut Meringues

If it's indulgence you're seeking, look no further. Sweet nectarines and cream syllabub paired with crisp hazelnut meringues make a superb dessert that is quite irresistible.

Serves 5
3 egg whites
150g/5oz/³/₄ cup caster (superfine) sugar
50g/2oz/½ cup chopped hazelnuts, toasted
300ml/½ pint/1¼ cups double (heavy) cream
60ml/4 tbsp sweet dessert wine
2 nectarines, stoned (pitted) and sliced
fresh mint sprigs, to decorate

1 Preheat the oven to 140°C/275°F/Gas 1. Line two large baking sheets with baking parchment.

2 Whisk or beat the egg whites in a grease-free bowl until they form stiff peaks when the whisk or beaters are lifted. Gradually whisk in the caster sugar, a spoonful at a time, until the mixture forms a stiff, glossy meringue.

3 Fold in two-thirds of the chopped toasted hazelnuts, then spoon five large ovals on to each lined baking sheet. Sprinkle the remaining hazelnuts over five of the meringue ovals. Flatten the tops of the remaining five ovals.

4 Bake the meringues for 1–1¼ hours until crisp and dry, then carefully lift them off the baking parchment and leave them to cool completely on a wire rack.

5 Whip the cream with the dessert wine until the mixture forms soft peaks. Spoon some of the cream syllabub on to each of the plain meringues. Arrange a few nectarine slices on top of each syllabub-topped meringue.

6 Place each meringue on a dessert plate and add a hazelnut-topped meringue to each plate. Decorate the portions with mint sprigs and serve immediately.

Nect. & Hazel. Energy 540Kcal/2250kJ; Protein 5.1g; Carbohydrate 43.8g, of which sugars 43.6g; Fat 38.6g, of which saturates 20.5g; Cholesterol 82mg; Calcium 68mg; Fibre 1.3g; Sodium 54mg. **Choc. Meringues** Compote Energy 343Kcal/1442kJ; Protein 4g; Carbohydrate 50.2g, of which sugars 50g; Fat 15.4g, of which saturates 10.1g; Cholesterol 34mg; Calcium 61mg; Fibre 2.2g; Sodium 44mg.

Iced Christmas Torte

This makes an exciting alternative to traditional Christmas pudding – but don't feel that you have to limit it to the festive season.

Serves 8–10

75g/3oz/³/₄ cup dried cranberries
75g/3oz/scant ½ cup pitted prunes
50g/2oz/⅓ cup sultanas (golden raisins)
175ml/6fl oz/¾ cup port
2 pieces preserved stem ginger, finely chopped
25g/1oz/2 tbsp unsalted (sweet) butter
45ml/3 tbsp light muscovado (brown) sugar
90g/3½oz/scant 2 cups fresh white breadcrumbs
600ml/1 pint/2½ cups double (heavy) cream
30ml/2 tbsp icing (confectioners') sugar
5ml/1 tsp ground allspice
75g/3oz/¾ cup brazil nuts, finely chopped
sugared bay leaves and fresh cherries, to decorate

1 Put the cranberries, prunes and sultanas in a food processor and process briefly. Transfer them to a bowl and add the port and ginger. Leave to absorb the port for 2 hours.

2 Melt the butter in a frying pan. Add the sugar and heat gently until the sugar has dissolved. Add the breadcrumbs, stir lightly, then fry over a low heat for about 5 minutes, until lightly coloured and turning crisp. Leave to cool.

3 Turn the breadcrumbs into a food processor or blender and process to finer crumbs. Sprinkle a third into an 18cm/7in loose-based springform tin (pan) and freeze.

4 Whip the cream with the icing sugar and spice until the mixture is thick but not yet standing in peaks. Fold in the brazil nuts with the dried fruit mixture and any port remaining.

5 Spread a third of the mixture over the breadcrumb base in the tin, taking care not to dislodge the crumbs. Sprinkle with another layer of the breadcrumbs. Repeat the layering, finishing with a layer of the cream mixture. Freeze the torte overnight. Serve decorated with sugared bay leaves and fresh cherries.

Chocolate & Brandied Fig Torte

A seriously rich torte for chocolate lovers. If you dislike figs, use dried prunes, dates or apricots instead.

Serves 8

250g/9oz/1½ cups dried figs
60ml/4 tbsp brandy
200g/7oz gingersnap biscuits (cookies)
175g/6oz/¾ cup unsalted (sweet) butter, softened
150ml/¼ pint/⅔ cup milk
250g/9oz plain (semisweet) chocolate, broken into pieces
45ml/3 tbsp caster (superfine) sugar
cocoa powder (unsweetened), for dusting
whipped cream, to serve

1 Chop the figs and put them into a bowl, pour over the brandy and leave for 2–3 hours until most of the brandy has been absorbed. Break the biscuits into large chunks, put them in a strong plastic bag and crush them with a rolling pin.

2 Melt half the butter and stir in the crumbs until combined. Pack on to the bottom and up the sides of a 20cm/8in loose-based flan tin (tart pan) that is about 3cm/1¼in deep. Leave in the refrigerator to chill.

3 Pour the milk into a pan, add the chocolate pieces and heat gently until the chocolate has melted and the mixture is smooth, stirring frequently. Pour the chocolate mixture into a bowl and leave to cool.

4 In a separate bowl, beat the remaining butter with the caster sugar until the mixture is pale and creamy.

5 Add the chocolate mixture, whisking until it is well mixed. Fold in the figs, and any remaining brandy, and spoon the mixture into the chilled flan case. Level the surface, cover and freeze overnight.

6 Transfer the frozen torte to the refrigerator about 30 minutes before serving so that the filling softens slightly. Lightly dust the surface with cocoa powder and serve in slices, with dollops of lightly whipped cream.

Christmas Torte Energy 504Kcal/2098kJ; Protein 6.3g; Carbohydrate 38.4g, of which sugars 21g; Fat 36.4g, of which saturates 17.8g; Cholesterol 61mg; Calcium 92mg; Fibre 2.3g; Sodium 209mg.
Choc. & Fig Torte Energy 539Kcal/2257kJ; Protein 5g; Carbohydrate 63.9g, of which sugars 54.2g; Fat 29.7g, of which saturates 17.7g; Cholesterol 50mg; Calcium 172mg; Fibre 4.1g; Sodium 241mg.

Rhubarb & Ginger Wine Torte

The classic combination of rhubarb and ginger is used in this luxury frozen torte to make a dessert with a refreshingly tart flavour.

Serves 8

500g/1¼lb rhubarb, trimmed
115g/4oz/generous ½ cup caster (superfine) sugar
30ml/2 tbsp water
200g/7oz/scant 1 cup cream cheese
150ml/¼ pint/⅔ cups double (heavy) cream
40g/1½oz/¼ cup preserved stem ginger, finely chopped
a few drops of pink food colouring (optional)
250ml/8fl oz/1 cup ginger wine
175g/6oz sponge fingers
fresh mint or lemon balm sprigs, dusted with icing sugar, to decorate

1 Chop the rhubarb roughly and put it in a pan with the sugar and water. Cover and cook very gently for 5–8 minutes until the rhubarb is just tender. Process in a food processor or blender until smooth, then leave to cool.

2 Beat the cheese in a bowl until softened. Stir in the cream, rhubarb purée and ginger, then food colouring, if you like. Line a 900g/2lb/6–8 cup loaf tin (pan) with clear film (plastic wrap).

3 Pour the mixture into a shallow freezer container and freeze until firm. Alternatively, churn in an ice cream maker.

4 Pour the ginger wine into a shallow dish. Spoon a thin layer of ice cream over the bottom of the tin. Working quickly, dip the sponge fingers in the ginger wine, then lay them lengthways over the ice cream in a single layer, trimming to fit.

5 Spread another layer of ice cream over the top. Repeat the process, adding two to three more layers and finishing with ice cream. Cover and freeze overnight.

6 Transfer to the refrigerator 30 minutes before serving, to soften the torte slightly. To serve, briefly dip in very hot water then invert on to a flat dish. Peel off the lining and decorate.

Frozen Grand Marnier Soufflés

These sophisticated little desserts make a wonderful end to a meal.

Serves 8

200g/7oz/1 cup caster (superfine) sugar
6 large (US extra large) eggs, separated
250ml/8fl oz/1 cup milk
15g/½oz powdered gelatine, soaked in 45ml/3 tbsp cold water
45ml/3 tbsp water
450ml/¾ pint/scant 2 cups double (heavy) cream
60ml/4 tbsp Grand Marnier

1 Tie a double collar of waxed paper around eight ramekin dishes. Put 75g/3oz/6 tbsp of the sugar in a bowl with the egg yolks and whisk until pale.

2 Heat the milk until almost boiling and pour it on to the yolks, whisking all the time. Return the egg mixture to the pan and stir over a gentle heat until thick enough to coat the spoon.

3 Remove the pan from the heat and stir in the soaked gelatine. Pour into a bowl and leave to cool. Whisk occasionally, until it is on the point of setting.

4 Put the remaining sugar in a pan with the water and dissolve it over a low heat. Bring to the boil and boil rapidly until it reaches the soft ball stage or 119°C/238°F on a sugar thermometer. Remove from the heat.

5 In a clean bowl, whisk the egg whites until they are stiff. Pour the hot syrup on to the whites, whisking constantly. Set aside and leave to cool.

6 Whisk the cream until it holds soft peaks. Add the Grand Marnier to the cold custard and fold the custard into the cold meringue mixture, with the cream. Quickly pour into the prepared ramekin dishes. Freeze overnight.

7 Remove the paper collars. Leave the soufflés at room temperature for 30 minutes before serving.

Rhubarb & Ginger Energy 398Kcal/1658kJ; Protein 3.9g; Carbohydrate 29.4g, of which sugars 25.2g; Fat 26.8g, of which saturates 16.2g; Cholesterol 100mg; Calcium 132mg; Fibre 1.2g; Sodium 111mg.
Grand Marnier Energy 478Kcal/1991kJ; Protein 6.7g; Carbohydrate 33.7g, of which sugars 33.7g; Fat 34.9g, of which saturates 20.3g; Cholesterol 222mg; Calcium 99mg; Fibre 0g; Sodium 79mg.

Luxury Dark Chocolate Ravioli

Serve this special treat with cream and grated chocolate.

Serves 4
175g/6oz/1½ cups plain
  (all-purpose) flour
25g/1oz/¼ cup cocoa powder
  (unsweetened)
salt

30ml/2 tbsp icing (confectioners')
  sugar
2 large eggs, beaten
15ml/1 tbsp olive oil

For the filling
175g/6oz white chocolate, chopped
350g/12oz/1½ cups cream cheese
1 egg, plus 1 beaten egg to seal

1 Make the pasta. Sift the flour with the cocoa, salt and icing sugar on to a work surface. Make a well in the centre and pour in the eggs and oil. Mix together with your fingers. Knead until smooth. Cover and rest for at least 30 minutes.

2 For the filling, melt the white chocolate in a heatproof bowl placed over a pan of simmering water. Cool slightly. Beat the cream cheese in a bowl, then beat in the chocolate and egg. Spoon into a piping (pastry) bag fitted with a plain nozzle.

3 Cut the dough in half and wrap one portion in clear film (plastic wrap). Roll the pasta out thinly to a rectangle on a lightly floured surface, or use a pasta machine. Cover with a clean damp dish towel and repeat with the remaining pasta.

4 Pipe small mounds (about 5ml/1 tsp) of filling in rows, spacing them at 4cm/1½in intervals across one piece of the dough. Brush the dough between the mounds with beaten egg.

5 Using a rolling pin, lift the remaining sheet of pasta over the dough with the filling. Press down firmly between the pockets of filling, pushing out any trapped air. Cut the filled chocolate pasta into rounds with a ravioli cutter or sharp knife. Transfer to a floured dish towel. Leave for 1 hour to dry out.

6 Bring a frying pan of water to the boil and add the ravioli a few at a time, stirring to prevent sticking. Simmer gently for 3–5 minutes, remove with a perforated spoon and serve.

Chocolate Amaretto Marquise

This wickedly rich chocolate dessert is truly extravagant.

Serves 10–12
15ml/1 tbsp flavourless vegetable
  oil, such as groundnut (peanut)
  or sunflower
75g/3oz/7–8 amaretti, finely
  crushed
25g/1oz/¼ cup unblanched
  almonds, toasted and finely
  chopped
450g/1lb fine-quality plain or
  dark (bittersweet) chocolate,
  chopped into small pieces

75ml/5 tbsp Amaretto di Saronno
  liqueur
75ml/5 tbsp golden (light
  corn) syrup
475ml/16fl oz/2 cups double
  (heavy) cream
cocoa powder (unsweetened), for
  dusting

For the Amaretto cream
350ml/12fl oz/1½ cups whipping
  cream or double (heavy)
  cream
30–45ml/2–3 tbsp Amaretto di
  Saronno liqueur

1 Lightly oil a 23cm/9in heart-shaped or springform cake tin (pan). Line the bottom with baking parchment, then oil the paper. In a small bowl, combine the crushed amaretti and the chopped almonds. Sprinkle evenly on to the base of the tin.

2 Place the chocolate, Amaretto liqueur and golden syrup in a medium pan over a very low heat. Stir frequently until the chocolate has melted and the mixture is smooth. Remove from the heat and allow it to cool for about 6–8 minutes, until the mixture feels just warm to the touch.

3 Whip the cream until it just begins to hold its shape. Stir a large spoonful into the chocolate mixture, to lighten it, then quickly add the remaining cream and gently fold in. Pour into the prepared tin, on top of the amaretti mixture. Level the surface. Cover the tin with clear film (plastic wrap) and chill overnight.

4 To unmould, run a slightly warmed, thin-bladed sharp knife around the edge of the dessert, then unmould. Carefully peel off the paper, replacing any crust that sticks to it, and dust with cocoa. In a bowl, whip the cream and Amaretto liqueur to soft peaks. Serve separately.

Dark Choc. Ravioli Energy 894Kcal/3722kJ; Protein 16.2g; Carbohydrate 68.1g, of which sugars 34g; Fat 63.9g, of which saturates 36.5g; Cholesterol 226mg; Calcium 299mg; Fibre 2.1g; Sodium 424mg.
Choc. Marquise Energy 589Kcal/2444kJ; Protein 3.9g; Carbohydrate 38.2g, of which sugars 35.1g; Fat 46.4g, of which saturates 27.5g; Cholesterol 87mg; Calcium 63mg; Fibre 1.2g; Sodium 57mg.

Chocolate Puffs

Cream-filled choux pastry puffs are an exquisite treat.

Serves 4–6
65g/2½oz/9 tbsp plain (all-purpose) flour
150ml/¼ pint/⅔ cup water
50g/2oz/¼ cup butter
2 eggs, beaten

For the filling and icing
150ml/¼ pint/⅔ cup double (heavy) cream
225g/8oz/1½ cups icing (confectioners') sugar
15ml/1 tbsp cocoa powder (unsweetened)
30–60ml/2–4 tbsp water

1 Preheat the oven to 220°C/425°F/Gas 7. Sift the flour into a bowl. Put the water in a pan over a medium heat, add the butter and heat gently until it melts. Increase the heat and bring to the boil, then remove from the heat. Add all the flour at once and beat quickly until the mixture sticks together and becomes thick and glossy, leaving the side of the pan clean. Leave the mixture to cool slightly.

2 Add the eggs, a little at a time, to the mixture and beat by hand with a wooden spoon or with an electric whisk, until the mixture (choux pastry) is thick and glossy and drops reluctantly from a spoon. (You may not need to use all of the egg.) Spoon the choux pastry into a piping (pastry) bag fitted with a 2cm/¾in nozzle. Dampen two baking sheets with cold water.

3 Pipe walnut-size spoonfuls of the choux pastry on to the dampened baking sheets. Leave some space for them to rise. Cook for 25–30 minutes, until they are golden brown and well risen. Use a palette knife to lift the puffs on to a wire rack, and make a small hole in each one with the handle of a wooden spoon to allow the steam to escape. Leave to cool.

4 Make the filling and icing. Whip the cream until thick. Put it into a piping bag fitted with a plain or star nozzle. Push the nozzle into the hole in each puff and squirt a little cream inside. Put the icing sugar and cocoa in a small bowl and stir together. Add enough water to make a thick glossy icing. Spread a little icing on each puff and serve when set.

Strawberry & Kirsch Choux Ring

This spectacular ring is made from individual balls of choux pastry.

Serves 4–6
350g/12oz/generous 2 cups small whole strawberries
75g/3oz/6 tbsp granulated sugar
150ml/¼ pint/⅔ cup double (heavy) cream
30ml/2 tbsp Kirsch

10ml/2 tsp icing (confectioners') sugar, sifted, plus extra for dusting
whipped cream, to serve

For the pastry
150ml/¼ pint/⅔ cup water
50g/2oz/¼ cup butter
65g/2½oz/9 tbsp plain (all-purpose) flour, sifted
2 eggs, beaten

1 Preheat the oven to 220°C/425°F/Gas 7. Reserve half the strawberries and slice the rest. Draw a 15cm/6in circle on a sheet of parchment. Turn it over and press on to a greased baking sheet.

2 Make the pastry. Heat the water and butter in a pan until the butter melts, bring to the boil, add the flour and remove from the heat. Beat with a wooden spoon until the mixture forms a ball, leaving the pan-sides clean. Gradually beat in the eggs to form a smooth paste. Spoon/pipe the pastry in balls, making a circle on the baking sheet, using the drawn circle. The balls should just touch each other. Bake for 15 minutes, then lower the heat to 190°C/375°F/Gas 5 and cook for 20–25 minutes. Make one or two slits in the pastry to let the hot air escape. Leave to cool.

3 Heat the granulated sugar until it dissolves, then increase the heat and cook the syrup until it turns a gold colour and a spoonful hardens when dropped into a bowl of cold water. Using a fork, half-dip and turn each whole strawberry in the syrup. Leave the strawberries to cool on baking parchment.

4 Make the filling. Whip the cream in a bowl until it just starts to thicken. Stir in the Kirsch and icing sugar and continue whisking until stiff. With a wooden spoon, fold in the sliced strawberries. Slice the choux ring in half horizontally, spoon in the strawberry cream and replace the top. Dust with a little icing sugar. Serve with whipped cream and the dipped strawberries.

Choc. Puffs Energy 403Kcal/1687kJ; Protein 4.2g; Carbohydrate 48.4g, of which sugars 39.8g; Fat 22.8g, of which saturates 13.6g; Cholesterol 115mg; Calcium 62mg; Fibre 0.6g; Sodium 106mg.
Choux Ring Energy 324Kcal/1346kJ; Protein 4.1g; Carbohydrate 25.5g, of which sugars 17.2g; Fat 22.3g, of which saturates 13.2g; Cholesterol 115mg; Calcium 54mg; Fibre 1g; Sodium 84mg.

Sicilian Brioche with Hot Fudge Sauce

For sheer indulgence, this dessert is unbeatable. Warm brioche filled with ice cream and topped with a glorious hot fudge sauce will make anyone's day.

Serves 2
2 individual brioches
2 large scoops of best vanilla or
   coffee ice cream

For the hot fudge sauce
50g/2oz best dark (bittersweet)
   chocolate with 70% cocoa
   solids
15g/½oz/1 tbsp butter
75ml/5 tbsp boiling water
30ml/2 tbsp golden (light corn)
   syrup
150g/5oz/¾ cup soft light brown
   sugar, sifted
5ml/1 tsp vanilla extract

1 Preheat the oven to 200°C/400°F/Gas 6. Meanwhile, make the hot fudge sauce. Break up the chocolate and place in a heatproof bowl set over a pan of barely simmering water. Leave, without stirring, for about 10 minutes until the chocolate has completely melted, then stir in the butter.

2 Add the boiling water to the melted chocolate and butter, stir well to blend, then stir in the syrup, sugar and vanilla extract. Pour and scrape the chocolate mixture into a pan and bring to the boil, then turn down the heat and allow to barely bubble for 5 minutes.

3 Meanwhile, put the brioches on a baking sheet and warm them in the oven for approximately 5 minutes – or until they are slightly crisp on the outside but are still soft, fluffy and warm on the inside.

4 Remove the pan of chocolate sauce from the heat. Immediately split the brioches open and gently pull out a little of the insides. Generously fill each brioche base with ice cream and gently press on the tops.

5 Put the filled brioches into individual bowls or on to plates and pour over the hot fudge sauce. Serve immediately.

Chocolate Eclairs

A delicious version of a popular French dessert.

Makes 12
300ml/½ pint/1¼ cups double
   (heavy) cream
10ml/2 tsp icing (confectioners')
   sugar, sifted
1.5ml/¼ tsp vanilla extract
115g/4oz plain (semisweet)
   chocolate

30ml/2 tbsp water
25g/1oz/2 tbsp butter

For the pastry
65g/2½oz/9 tbsp plain
   (all-purpose) flour
pinch of salt
50g/2oz/¼ cup butter, diced
150ml/¼ pint/⅔ cup water
2 eggs, lightly beaten

1 Preheat the oven to 200°C/400°F/Gas 6. Grease a large baking sheet and line with baking parchment. Make the pastry. Sift the flour and salt on to a sheet of parchment. Heat the butter and water in a pan until the butter melts. Increase the heat to a rolling boil. Remove from the heat and beat in the flour with a wooden spoon. Return to a low heat, then beat the mixture until it forms a ball. Set the pan aside and allow to cool for 2–3 minutes.

2 Gradually beat in the beaten eggs until you have a smooth paste thick enough to hold its shape. Spoon the pastry into a piping (pastry) bag with a 2.5cm/1in plain nozzle. Pipe 10cm/4in lengths on to the prepared baking sheet. Bake for 25–30 minutes, until the pastries are well risen and golden brown. Remove from the oven and make a slit along the side of each to release steam. Lower the heat to 180°C/350°F/Gas 4 and bake for 5 minutes. Cool on a wire rack.

3 Make the filling. Whip the cream with the icing sugar and vanilla extract until it just holds its shape. Spoon into a piping bag fitted with a 1cm/½in plain nozzle and use to fill the éclairs.

4 Place the chocolate and water in a small bowl set over a pan of hot water. Melt, stirring until smooth. Remove from the heat and gradually stir in the butter. Dip the top of each éclair in the melted chocolate, place on a wire rack and leave in a cool place to set. Ideally, serve within 2 hours of making.

Brioche Energy 913Kcal/3853kJ; Protein 13.8g; Carbohydrate 163.3g, of which sugars 121.5g; Fat 27.2g, of which saturates 15.4g; Cholesterol 18mg; Calcium 257mg; Fibre 3g; Sodium 674mg.
Eclairs Energy 253Kcal/1050kJ; Protein 2.5g; Carbohydrate 11.6g, of which sugars 7.4g; Fat 22.2g, of which saturates 13.5g; Cholesterol 80mg; Calcium 29mg; Fibre 0.4g; Sodium 56mg.

Iced Strawberry & Lemon Gâteau

Perfect for summer entertaining, this glorious iced gâteau is layered with favourite fruit flavours.

Serves 8
115g/4oz/½ cup unsalted (sweet) butter, softened
115g/4oz/generous ½ cup caster (superfine) sugar
2 eggs
115g/4oz/1 cup self-raising (self-rising) flour
2.5ml/½ tsp baking powder

To finish
500ml/17fl oz/2¼ cups strawberry ice cream
300ml/½ pint/1¼ cups double (heavy) cream
200g/7oz/scant 1 cup good-quality lemon curd
30ml/2 tbsp lemon juice
500g/1¼lb/5 cups strawberries, hulled
25g/1oz/2 tbsp caster (superfine) sugar
45ml/3 tbsp Cointreau or other orange-flavoured liqueur

1 Preheat the oven to 180°C/350°F/Gas 4. Grease and line a 23cm/9in round springform cake tin (pan). In a bowl, beat the butter with the sugar, eggs, flour and baking powder until creamy.

2 Spoon the mixture into the prepared tin and bake for about 20 minutes or until just firm. Leave to cool for 5 minutes, then turn the cake out on a wire rack. Cool completely.

3 Line the sides of the cleaned cake tin with a strip of baking parchment. Using a sharp knife, carefully slice off the top of the cake where it has formed a crust. Save this for another use.

4 Fit the cake in the tin, cut-side down. Freeze the cake for 10 minutes, then cover with the ice cream and freeze until firm.

5 Whip the cream in a bowl until it forms soft peaks, then fold in the lemon curd and lemon juice. Spoon the mixture over the strawberry ice cream. Cover and freeze overnight.

6 About 45 minutes before serving, cut half the strawberries into thin slices. Purée the rest of the strawberries with the sugar and liqueur to make the sauce. Arrange the sliced strawberries over the frozen gâteau. Serve with the sauce.

Coffee Profiteroles

Irresistible coffee-flavoured choux puffs, with a liqueur-laced white chocolate sauce.

Serves 6
65g/2½oz/9 tbsp plain (all-purpose) flour
pinch of salt
50g/2oz/4 tbsp butter, diced
150ml/¼ pint/⅔ cup freshly brewed coffee
2 eggs, lightly beaten

250ml/8fl oz/1 cup double (heavy) cream, whipped

For the white chocolate sauce
50g/2oz/¼ cup granulated sugar
120ml/4fl oz/½ cup water
150g/5oz white chocolate, broken into pieces
25g/1oz/2 tbsp unsalted (sweet) butter
45ml/3 tbsp double (heavy) cream
30ml/2 tbsp coffee liqueur

1 Preheat the oven to 220°C/425°F/Gas 7. Sift the flour and salt on to a piece of baking parchment.

2 Place the butter in a pan with the coffee. Bring to a rolling boil, then remove from the heat and pour in the sifted flour in one go. Beat hard until the mixture leaves the side of the pan, forming a ball of thick paste. Leave to cool for 5 minutes.

3 Gradually add the eggs, beating well after each addition, until the mixture forms a stiff dropping consistency. Spoon into a piping (pastry) bag fitted with a 1cm/½in plain nozzle. Pipe 24 small buns on a dampened baking sheet, leaving plenty of room between them. Bake for 20 minutes, until risen.

4 Remove the buns from the oven and pierce the side of each one with a sharp knife to let out the steam.

5 Make the sauce. Put the sugar and water in a heavy pan, and heat gently until the sugar has completely dissolved. Bring to the boil and simmer for 3 minutes. Remove the pan from the heat, and add the white chocolate and butter, stirring constantly until smooth. Stir in the double cream and liqueur.

6 Spoon the whipped cream into a piping bag and fill the choux buns through the slits. Serve with the sauce poured over.

Profiteroles Energy 577Kcal/2393kJ; Protein 6g; Carbohydrate 34.3g, of which sugars 26g; Fat 46.4g, of which saturates 28.1g; Cholesterol 157mg; Calcium 123mg; Fibre 0.3g; Sodium 139mg. **Strawb. & Lemon Gâteau** Energy 653Kcal/2725kJ; Protein 6.5g; Carbohydrate 66.8g, of which sugars 49.9g; Fat 40.2g, of which saturates 24.6g; Cholesterol 150mg; Calcium 164mg; Fibre 1.2g; Sodium 224mg.

Death by Chocolate

One of the richest
chocolate cakes ever.

Serves 16–20
225g/8oz dark (bittersweet)
    chocolate, broken into squares
115g/4oz/½ cup unsalted (sweet)
    butter
150ml/¼ pint/⅔ cup milk
225g/8oz/1 cup light muscovado
    (brown) sugar
10ml/2 tsp vanilla extract
2 eggs, separated
150ml/¼ pint/⅔ cup sour
    cream
225g/8oz/2 cups self-raising
    (self-rising) flour
5ml/1 tsp baking powder

For the filling
60ml/4 tbsp seedless raspberry
    jam
60ml/4 tbsp brandy
400g/14oz dark (bittersweet)
    chocolate, broken into squares
200g/7oz/scant 1 cup unsalted
    (sweet) butter

For the topping
250ml/8fl oz/1 cup double
    (heavy) cream
225g/8oz dark (bittersweet)
    chocolate, broken into squares
plain (semisweet) and white
    chocolate curls, to decorate
chocolate-dipped physalis, to serve
    (optional)

1 Preheat the oven to 180°C/350°F/Gas 4. Grease and base-line a deep 23cm/9in springform cake tin (pan). Place the chocolate, butter and milk in a pan. Heat gently until smooth. Remove from the heat, beat in the sugar and vanilla, then cool.

2 Beat the egg yolks and cream in a bowl, then beat into the chocolate mixture. Sift the flour and baking powder over the surface and fold in. Whisk the egg whites in a grease-free bowl until stiff; fold into the mixture.

3 Scrape into the prepared tin and bake for 45–55 minutes, or until firm. Cool in the tin for 15 minutes, then turn out and cool.

4 Slice the cold cake across the middle to make three even layers. In a small pan, warm the jam with 15ml/1 tbsp of the brandy, then brush over two of the layers. Heat the remaining brandy in a pan with the chocolate and butter, stirring, until smooth. Cool until beginning to thicken.

5 Spread the bottom layer of the cake with half the chocolate filling, taking care not to disturb the jam. Top with a second layer, jam side up, and spread with the remaining filling. Top with the final layer and press lightly. Leave to set.

6 Make the topping. Heat the cream and chocolate together in a pan over a low heat, stirring frequently until the chocolate has melted. Pour into a bowl, leave to cool, then whisk until the mixture begins to hold its shape.

7 Spread the top and sides of the cake with the chocolate topping. Decorate with chocolate curls and chocolate-dipped physalis, if you like.

> **Cook's Tip**
> For chocolate-coated physalis, melt the chocolate in a bowl, then dip in the fruit, holding them by their tops. Leave to set.

White Chocolate Cappuccino Gâteau

A sensational, rich gâteau,
guaranteed to impress.

Serves 8
4 eggs
115g/4oz/generous ½ cup caster
    (superfine) sugar
15ml/1 tbsp strong black coffee
2.5ml/½ tsp vanilla extract
115g/4oz/1 cup plain
    (all-purpose) flour
75g/3oz white chocolate,
    coarsely grated

For the filling
120ml/4fl oz/½ cup double
    (heavy) cream or whipping
    cream
15ml/1 tbsp coffee liqueur

For the topping
15ml/1 tbsp coffee liqueur
1 quantity white chocolate frosting
white chocolate curls
cocoa powder (unsweetened) or
    ground cinnamon, for dusting

1 Preheat the oven to 180°C/350°F/Gas 4. Grease two 18cm/7in round sandwich cake tins (layer cake pans) and line the base of each with baking parchment.

2 Combine the eggs, caster sugar, coffee and vanilla extract in a large heatproof bowl. Place over a pan of hot water and whisk until pale and thick.

3 Sift half the flour over the mixture; fold in gently and evenly. Fold in the remaining flour with the grated white chocolate.

4 Divide the mixture between the prepared tins and smooth level. Bake for 20–25 minutes, until firm and golden brown, then turn out on to wire racks and leave to cool completely.

5 Make the filling. Whip the cream with the coffee liqueur in a bowl until it holds its shape. Spread over one of the cakes, then place the second layer on top.

6 Stir the coffee liqueur into the frosting. Spread over the top and sides of the cake, swirling with a palette knife. Top with curls of white chocolate and dust with cocoa or cinnamon. Transfer the cake to a serving plate and set aside until the frosting has set. Serve that day.

Death by Chocolate Energy 432Kcal/1809kJ; Protein 4.7g; Carbohydrate 49.9g, of which sugars 38.4g; Fat 24.7g, of which saturates 14.9g; Cholesterol 57mg; Calcium 99mg; Fibre 1.4g; Sodium 120mg.
Cappuccino Gâteau Energy 337Kcal/1418kJ; Protein 5.3g; Carbohydrate 50.5g, of which sugars 39.5g; Fat 13.6g, of which saturates 7.4g; Cholesterol 116mg; Calcium 61mg; Fibre 0.7g; Sodium 41mg.

Gâteau Saint-Honoré

This is named after the patron saint of bakers.

Serves 10
175g/6oz puff pastry

For the choux pastry
300ml/½ pint/1¼ cups water
115g/4oz/½ cup butter, diced
130g/4½oz/generous 1 cup plain
  (all-purpose) flour, sifted
2.5ml/½ tsp salt
4 eggs, lightly beaten
beaten egg, to glaze

For the filling
3 egg yolks
50g/2oz/¼ cup caster (superfine)
  sugar
30ml/2 tbsp plain (all-purpose) flour
30ml/2 tbsp cornflour (cornstarch)
300ml/½ pint/1¼ cups milk
150ml/¼ pint/⅔ cup double
  (heavy) cream
30ml/2 tbsp orange liqueur

For the caramel
225g/8oz/1 cup granulated sugar
120ml/4fl oz/½ cup water

1 Roll out the puff pastry, cut out a 20cm/8in circle, place on a lined baking sheet, prick all over and chill. Make the choux pastry. Heat the water and butter until the butter melts, bring to the boil, add the flour and salt, remove from the heat and beat until the mixture forms a ball. Beat in the eggs to form a paste.

2 Preheat the oven to 200°C/400°F/Gas 6. Using a piping (pastry) bag with a 1cm/½in nozzle, pipe a choux spiral on the puff pastry base. Pipe 16 choux buns on to a lined baking sheet. Brush with egg. Bake for 20 minutes and the base on the shelf below for 35 minutes. Pierce holes in the spiral, and one in the side of each bun. Return to the oven for 5 minutes to dry out. Cool on a rack.

3 Make the filling. Whisk the yolks and sugar until creamy. Whisk in the flours, then boil the milk and whisk that in. Return to the cleaned pan. Cook for 3 minutes, until thick, cover with damp parchment and cool. Whip the cream, fold in to the crème pâtissière with the liqueur and pipe into the buns. Make the caramel. Simmer the sugar and water until dissolved and golden. Transfer to a bowl of hot water to keep it liquid. Dip the bun bases in the caramel, put around the edge of the pastry case and pipe the remaining crème pâtissière into the centre. Drizzle the buns with the remaining caramel and leave to set for 2 hours.

Black Forest Gâteau

This classic gâteau makes a great dinner-party dessert.

Serves 8–10
6 eggs
200g/7oz/1 cup caster
  (superfine) sugar
5ml/1 tsp vanilla extract
50g/2oz/½ cup plain
  (all-purpose) flour
50g/2oz/½ cup cocoa powder
  (unsweetened)
115g/4oz/½ cup unsalted (sweet)
  butter, melted

grated chocolate, chocolate curls
  and morello cherries, to
  decorate

For the filling and topping
60ml/4 tbsp Kirsch
600ml/1 pint/2½ cups double
  (heavy) cream
30ml/2 tbsp icing (confectioners')
  sugar
2.5ml/½ tsp vanilla extract
675g/1½lb jar pitted morello
  cherries, well drained

1 Preheat the oven to 180°C/350°F/Gas 4. Grease three 19cm/7½in sandwich cake tins (layer cake pans). Line the bottom of each with baking parchment. Combine the eggs with the sugar and vanilla in a bowl and beat until pale and very thick.

2 Sift the flour and cocoa powder over the mixture and fold in lightly with a metal spoon. Gently stir in the melted butter.

3 Divide the mixture among the prepared cake tins, smoothing them level. Bake for 15–18 minutes, until the cakes have risen and are springy to the touch. Leave to cool in the tins for about 5 minutes, then turn out and cool completely. Remove the lining.

4 Prick each layer all over with a skewer, then sprinkle with Kirsch. Using a hand-held electric mixer, whip the cream until it starts to thicken, then gradually beat in the icing sugar and vanilla extract until the mixture begins to hold its shape.

5 Spread one cake layer with flavoured cream and top with about half the cherries. Repeat with the second cake layer, then place on top of the first layer. Top with the third cake layer. Spread the remaining cream all over the cake. Press grated chocolate over the sides and decorate with curls and cherries.

Gâteau Saint-Honoré Energy 466Kcal/1952kJ; Protein 7.3g; Carbohydrate 51.9g, of which sugars 30.9g; Fat 26.5g, of which saturates 12.5g; Cholesterol 186mg; Calcium 139mg; Fibre 0.5g; Sodium 221mg. **Black Forest** Energy 570Kcal/2371kJ; Protein 2.9g; Carbohydrate 44g, of which sugars 39.6g; Fat 42.8g, of which saturates 26.7g; Cholesterol 107mg; Calcium 67mg; Fibre 1.2g; Sodium 137mg.

Chocolate Truffle Tart

A dreamy chilled tart with a chocolate flavoured pastry case and a luscious filling, laced with brandy.

Serves 12

115g/4oz/1 cup plain (all-purpose) flour
40g/1¼oz/⅓ cup cocoa powder (unsweetened)
50g/2oz/¼ cup caster (superfine) sugar
2.5ml/½ tsp salt
115g/4oz/½ cup unsalted (sweet) butter, cut into pieces
1 egg yolk

15–30ml/1–2 tbsp iced water
25g/1oz good-quality white or milk chocolate, melted
whipped cream for serving (optional)

For the truffle filling
350ml/12fl oz/1½ cups double (heavy) cream
350g/12oz fine plain (bittersweet) chocolate, chopped
50g/2oz/4 tbsp unsalted (sweet) butter, cut into small pieces
30ml/2 tbsp brandy or liqueur

1 Make the pastry. Sift the flour and cocoa into a bowl. In a food processor fitted with a metal blade, process the flour mixture with the sugar and salt. Add the butter and process for a further 15–20 seconds, until the mixture resembles coarse breadcrumbs.

2 Lightly beat the yolk with the iced water in a bowl. Add to the flour mixture and pulse until the dough begins to stick together. Turn out the dough on to a sheet of clear film (plastic wrap). Use the film to help shape the dough into a flat disc. Wrap tightly. Chill for 1–2 hours, until firm.

3 Lightly grease a 23cm/9in flan tin (tart pan) with a removable base. Let the dough soften briefly, then roll it out between sheets of baking parchment or clear film (plastic wrap) to a 28cm/11in round, about 5mm/¼in thick. Peel off the top sheet and invert the dough into the tart tin. Remove the bottom sheet. Ease the dough into the tin. Prick with a fork. Chill for 1 hour.

4 Preheat the oven to 180°C/350°F/Gas 4. Line the tart with foil or baking parchment; fill with baking beans. Bake blind for 5–7 minutes. Lift out the foil with the beans, return the pastry case to the oven and bake for a further 5–7 minutes, until the pastry is just set. Cool completely in the tin on a rack.

5 Make the filling. In a medium pan, bring the cream to the boil over a medium heat. Remove the pan from the heat and stir in the chocolate until melted and smooth. Stir in the butter and brandy or liqueur. Strain into the prepared tart shell, tilting the tin slightly to level the surface. Do not touch the surface of the filling or it will spoil the glossy finish.

6 Spoon the melted chocolate into a paper piping (pastry) bag and cut off the tip. Drop rounds of chocolate over the surface of the tart and use a skewer or cocktail stick (toothpick) to draw a point gently through the chocolate to produce a marbled effect. Chill for 2–3 hours, until set.

7 Just before serving, allow the tart to soften slightly at room temperature, then serve with whipped cream, if you like.

Rich Chocolate & Coffee Pudding

This heavenly dessert boasts a rich sponge topping with a luscious sauce underneath.

Serves 6

90g/3½oz/¾ cup plain (all-purpose) flour
10ml/2 tsp baking powder
pinch of salt
50g/2oz/¼ cup butter or margarine
25g/1oz plain (semisweet) chocolate, chopped into small pieces
115g/4oz/generous ½ cup caster (superfine) sugar

75ml/2½fl oz/⅓ cup milk
1.5ml/¼ tsp vanilla extract
whipped cream, to serve

For the topping
30ml/2 tbsp instant coffee powder or granules
325ml/11fl oz/1⅓ cups hot water
90g/3½oz/½ cup soft dark brown sugar
65g/2½oz/5 tbsp caster (superfine) sugar
30ml/2 tbsp cocoa powder (unsweetened)

1 Preheat the oven to 180°C/350°F/Gas 4. Grease a 23cm/9in square non-stick baking tin (pan).

2 Sift the flour, baking powder and salt into a small bowl. Set aside.

3 Melt the butter or margarine, chocolate and caster sugar in a heatproof bowl set over a pan of simmering water, or in a double boiler, stirring occasionally. Remove the bowl from the heat.

4 Add the flour mixture and stir well. Stir in the milk and vanilla extract. Mix well, then pour into the prepared tin.

5 Make the topping. Dissolve the coffee in the water in a bowl. Allow to cool. Mix the brown sugar, caster sugar and cocoa powder in a bowl. Sprinkle the mixture over the pudding mixture in the tin.

6 Pour the coffee evenly over the surface. Bake for 40 minutes or until the pudding is risen and set on top. The coffee mixture will have formed a delicious creamy sauce underneath. Serve immediately with whipped cream.

Choc. & Coffee Pudding Energy 325Kcal/1371kJ; Protein 3g; Carbohydrate 60.6g, of which sugars 50.5g; Fat 9.5g, of which saturates 5.8g; Cholesterol 19mg; Calcium 66mg; Fibre 1.1g; Sodium 107mg.
Choc. Truffle Tart Energy 474Kcal/1969kJ; Protein 3.7g; Carbohydrate 32.5g, of which sugars 24.6g; Fat 36.8g, of which saturates 22.6g; Cholesterol 88mg; Calcium 48mg; Fibre 1.4g; Sodium 117mg.

Chocolate Tiramisu Tart

This tart has an utterly delicious creamy filling.

Serves 12–16

115g/4oz/½ cup butter
15ml/1 tbsp coffee-flavoured liqueur
175g/6oz/1½ cups plain (all-purpose) flour
25g/1oz/¼ cup cocoa powder (unsweetened), plus extra for dusting
25g/1oz/¼ cup icing (confectioners') sugar
pinch of salt
2.5ml/½ tsp vanilla extract

For the chocolate layer
350ml/12fl oz/1½ cups double (heavy) cream
15ml/1 tbsp golden (light corn) syrup
115g/4oz plain (semisweet) chocolate, chopped into pieces
25g/1oz/2 tbsp unsalted (sweet) butter, cut into small pieces
30ml/2 tbsp coffee-flavoured liqueur

For the filling
250ml/8fl oz/1 cup whipping cream
350g/12oz/1½ cups mascarpone, at room temperature
45ml/3 tbsp icing sugar
45ml/3 tbsp cold espresso or strong black coffee
45ml/3 tbsp coffee-flavoured liqueur
90g/3½oz plain (semisweet) chocolate, grated

1 Make the pastry. Grease a 23cm/9in springform tin (pan). Heat the butter and liqueur until the butter melts. Sift the flour, cocoa, icing sugar and salt into a bowl. Remove the butter mixture from the heat, stir in the vanilla and stir into the flour mixture until soft dough forms. Knead until smooth. Press on to the base and up the sides of the tin. Prick the dough. Chill for 40 minutes. Preheat the oven to 190°C/375°F/Gas 5. Bake the pastry case for 8–10 minutes. If the pastry puffs up, prick it with a fork and bake for 2–3 minutes more until set. Cool in the tin on a rack.

2 Mix the cream and syrup in a pan. Bring to a boil over medium heat. Off the heat, stir in the chocolate until melted. Beat in the butter and liqueur and pour into the pastry case. Cool and chill.

3 Make the filling. In one bowl, whip the cream until soft peaks form; in another, beat the cheese until soft, then beat in icing sugar until smooth. Add the coffee, liqueur, cream and chocolate. Spoon into the pastry case, on top of the chocolate layer. Level the surface. Chill until ready to serve, dusted with cocoa.

White Chocolate & Mango Cream Tart

A rich, exotic tart designed to tantalize the taste buds.

Serves 8

175g/6oz/1½ cups plain (all-purpose) flour
75g/3oz/1 cup sweetened, desiccated (dry unsweetened shredded) coconut
115g/4oz/½ cup butter, softened
30ml/2 tbsp caster (superfine) sugar
2 egg yolks
2.5ml/½ tsp almond extract
120ml/4fl oz/½ cup whipping cream, whipped to soft peaks

1 large mango, peeled and sliced
whipped cream and toasted almonds, to decorate

For the filling
150g/5oz good-quality white chocolate, chopped finely
120ml/4fl oz/½ cup whipping cream or double (heavy) cream
75ml/5 tbsp cornflour (cornstarch)
15ml/1 tbsp plain (all-purpose) flour
50g/2oz/¼ cup granulated sugar
350ml/12fl oz/1½ cups milk
5 egg yolks

1 Beat the flour, coconut, butter, sugar, egg yolks and almond extract in a bowl to form a soft dough. Grease a 23cm/9in flan tin (tart pan) with a removable base and press the pastry into the tin to line. Prick the base with a fork. Chill for 30 minutes.

2 Preheat the oven to 180°C/350°F/Gas 4. Line the pastry case with baking parchment; fill with baking beans and bake blind for 10 minutes. Remove the paper and beans and bake for a further 5–7 minutes, until golden. Cool in the tin on a wire rack.

3 Make the filling. In a small pan over a low heat, melt the white chocolate with the cream, stirring until smooth. Combine the cornflour, plain flour and sugar in another pan. Gradually stir in the milk and cook gently, stirring constantly, until thickened.

4 Beat the egg yolks in a small bowl. Slowly stir in some of the hot milk mixture. Return the yolk mixture to the rest of the sauce in the pan, stirring. Bring to a gentle boil, stirring, until thickened. Stir in the melted chocolate. Cool, then fold in the whipped cream. Spoon half the custard into the pastry case and arrange the mango on top. Cover with the rest of the custard. Remove from the tin and decorate with piped cream and nuts.

Tiramisu Energy 399Kcal/1657kJ; Protein 4.8g; Carbohydrate 24.4g, of which sugars 15.8g; Fat 30.9g, of which saturates 20.4g; Cholesterol 60mg; Calcium 49mg; Fibre 0.9g; Sodium 86mg.
Choc. & Mango Energy 802Kcal/3336kJ; Protein 12.3g; Carbohydrate 57.3g, of which sugars 30.3g; Fat 59.8g, of which saturates 41.9g; Cholesterol 217mg; Calcium 256mg; Fibre 3.1g; Sodium 195mg.

Mini Praline Pavlovas

Melt-in-the-mouth meringue topped with rich, velvety chocolate and nutty praline.

Makes 14
2 large (US extra large) egg
  whites
large pinch of ground cinnamon
90g/3¹/₂oz/¹/₂ cup caster
  (superfine) sugar
50g/2oz/¹/₂ cup pecan nuts,
  finely chopped

For the filling
50g/2oz/¹/₄ cup unsalted (sweet)
  butter, diced
100g/3¹/₂oz/scant 1 cup icing
  (confectioners') sugar, sifted
50g/2oz plain (semisweet)
  chocolate, broken into pieces

For the praline
50g/2oz/¹/₄ cup caster (superfine)
  sugar
15g/¹/₂oz/1 tbsp finely chopped
  toasted almonds

1 Preheat the oven to 140°C/275°F/Gas 1. Line two baking sheets with baking parchment. Whisk the egg whites until stiff. Stir the cinnamon into the sugar. Add a spoonful of sugar to the egg whites and whisk well. Continue whisking in the sugar, a spoonful at a time, until thick and glossy. Stir in the pecan nuts.

2 Place 14 spoonfuls of meringue on the prepared baking sheets, well spaced. Using the back of a wet teaspoon, make a small hollow in the top of each meringue. Bake in the oven for 45–60 minutes until dry and just beginning to colour. Cool.

3 Make the filling. Beat together the butter and icing sugar until light and creamy. Place the chocolate in a heatproof bowl. Set over a pan of barely simmering water and stir occasionally until melted. Cool the chocolate slightly, then add to the butter mixture and stir well. Divide the filling among the meringues.

4 Make the praline. Put the sugar in a small non-stick frying pan. Heat gently until the sugar melts to form a clear liquid. When the mixture begins to turn brown, stir in the nuts. When the mixture is a golden brown, remove from the heat and pour immediately on to a lightly oiled or non-stick baking sheet. Leave to cool completely and then break into small pieces. Sprinkle over the meringues and serve.

Dark Chocolate & Hazelnut Tart

The crisp, hazelnut-flavoured pastry tastes wonderful combined with a luxurious chocolate filling.

Serves 10
300ml/¹/₂ pint/1¹/₄ cups double
  (heavy) cream
150ml/¹/₄ pint/²/₃ cup creamy
  milk
150g/5oz dark (bittersweet)
  chocolate, chopped
4 eggs
50g/2oz/¹/₄ cup caster (superfine)
  sugar
5ml/1 tsp vanilla extract
15ml/1 tbsp plain
  (all-purpose) flour

115g/4oz/1 cup toasted
  hazelnuts
10ml/2 tsp icing (confectioners')
  sugar, for dusting

For the pastry
150g/5oz/1¹/₄ cups plain
  (all-purpose) flour
pinch of salt
40g/1¹/₂oz/3 tbsp caster
  (superfine) sugar
50g/2oz/¹/₂ cup ground hazelnuts,
  toasted
90g/3¹/₂oz/scant ¹/₂ cup butter,
  diced
1 egg, lightly beaten

1 Make the pastry. Sift the flour, salt and sugar into a mixing bowl, then mix in the toasted hazelnuts. Rub or cut in the butter until the mixture resembles fine breadcrumbs.

2 Make a well in the centre, add the beaten egg and mix to a firm dough. Knead the dough on a lightly floured surface for a few seconds until smooth. Wrap in clear film (plastic wrap) and chill for 30 minutes.

3 Roll out the pastry on a floured surface and use to line a 23cm/9in loose-based heart-shaped flan tin (tart pan). Trim the edges. Cover and chill for a further 30 minutes.

4 Re-roll the pastry trimmings into a long strip, about 30cm/12in long. Cut this into six strips, each 5mm/¹/₄in wide, and make two plaits (braids) with three pastry strips in each. Curve into a heart shape and press gently to join together at both ends. Carefully place the heart on a baking sheet lined with baking parchment, and chill.

5 Put a baking sheet in the oven and preheat to 200°C/400°F/Gas 6. Prick the base of the pastry case (pie shell) with a fork. Line with foil and baking beans and bake blind on the sheet for 10 minutes. Remove the foil and beans and bake for a further 5 minutes. Bake the pastry plait on the shelf below for 10 minutes, or until lightly browned.

6 Meanwhile, pour the cream and milk into a pan and bring to the boil. Add the chocolate and stir until melted. Whisk the eggs, caster sugar, vanilla and flour together in a bowl. Pour the hot chocolate cream over the egg mixture, whisking all the time. Stir in the chopped hazelnuts.

7 Pour the chocolate and hazelnut mixture into the pastry case and bake in the oven for 25 minutes, or until just set. Allow the tart to cool, then remove from the tin and transfer to a serving plate. Place the pastry rope on top of the tart, then lightly dust the surface with icing sugar.

Praline Cakes Energy 148Kcal/621kJ; Protein 1.3g; Carbohydrate 21.2g, of which sugars 21.1g; Fat 7g, of which saturates 2.7g; Cholesterol 8mg; Calcium 16mg; Fibre 0.3g; Sodium 32mg. **Choc. & Hazelnut Tart** Energy 544Kcal/2261kJ; Protein 8.8g; Carbohydrate 35.6g, of which sugars 22.5g; Fat 41.8g, of which saturates 19.2g; Cholesterol 158mg; Calcium 105mg; Fibre 2g; Sodium 106mg.

Marbled Caramel Chocolate Slice

This classic recipe is made even more special here with a decorative marbled chocolate topping.

Makes about 24
250g/9oz/2¼ cups plain
   (all-purpose) flour
75g/3oz/6 tbsp caster (superfine)
   sugar
175g/6oz/¾ cup unsalted (sweet)
   butter, softened

For the filling
90g/3½oz/scant ½ cup unsalted
   (sweet) butter, diced
90g/3½oz/½ cup light
   muscovado (brown) sugar
two 397g/14oz cans evaporated
   (unsweetened condensed) milk

For the topping
90g/3½oz plain (semisweet)
   chocolate
90g/3½oz milk chocolate
50g/2oz white chocolate

1 Preheat the oven to 180°C/350°F/Gas 4. Line and lightly grease a 33 × 23cm/13 × 9in Swiss roll tin (jelly roll pan). Put the flour and sugar in a bowl and rub in the butter until the mixture resembles fine breadcrumbs, then form into a dough.

2 Press the dough over the base of the tin. Prick all over with a fork and bake for about 20 minutes, or until firm to the touch and very light brown. Set aside and leave in the tin to cool.

3 Make the filling. Put the butter, muscovado sugar and milk in a pan and heat gently, stirring, until the sugar has dissolved, Simmer the mixture very gently, stirring constantly, for about 5–10 minutes, or until it has thickened and has turned a caramel colour. Remove from the heat.

4 Pour the filling mixture over the pastry base, spread evenly, then leave until cold.

5 Make the topping. Melt each type of chocolate separately in a microwave or in a heatproof bowl set over hot water. Spoon lines of plain and milk chocolate over the set caramel filling.

6 Add small spoonfuls of white chocolate. Use a skewer to form a marbled effect on the topping.

Mississippi Mud Pie

This is the ultimate in chocolate desserts.

Serves 6–8
3 eggs, separated
20ml/4 tsp cornflour (cornstarch)
75g/3oz/6 tbsp sugar
400ml/14fl oz/1²/₃ cups milk
150g/5oz plain (semisweet)
   chocolate, broken up
5ml/1 tsp vanilla extract
15ml/1 tbsp powdered gelatine

45ml/3 tbsp water
30ml/2 tbsp dark rum
175ml/6fl oz/¾ cup double
   (heavy) cream, whipped
a few chocolate curls, to decorate

For the pastry
250g/9oz/2¼ cups plain
   (all-purpose) flour
150g/5oz/10 tbsp butter, diced
2 egg yolks
15–30ml/1–2 tbsp chilled water

1 Make the pastry. Sift the flour into a bowl. Rub in the butter until "breadcrumbs" form. Stir in the yolks with enough chilled water to make a soft dough. Roll out and use to line a deep 23cm/9in flan tin (pie pan). Chill for 30 minutes. Preheat the oven to 190°C/375°F/Gas 5. Prick the pastry, line with foil and beans, and bake blind for 10 minutes. Remove the foil and beans, and return to the oven for 10 minutes until the pastry is crisp and golden. Cool.

2 Mix the yolks, cornflour and 30ml/2 tbsp of the sugar in a bowl. In a pan, bring the milk almost to a boil, then beat into the egg mixture. Return to the cleaned pan and stir over a low heat until the custard thickens. Pour half into a bowl. Melt the chocolate in a heatproof bowl set over a pan of hot water, then add to the custard in the bowl. Mix in the vanilla extract. Spread in the pastry case, cover with parchment to prevent a skin forming, cool, then chill until set. Sprinkle the gelatine over the water in a small bowl, leave until spongy, then place over a pan of simmering water until the gelatine dissolves. Stir into the remaining custard, with the rum.

3 Whisk the egg whites until stiff peaks form, whisk in the rest of the sugar, then fold into the gelatine and custard mix before it sets.

4 Spoon over the chocolate custard to cover. Chill until set, then remove from the tin. Spread whipped cream over the top, decorate with chocolate curls and serve immediately.

Mud Pie Energy 571Kcal/2385kJ; Protein 9.4g; Carbohydrate 53.5g, of which sugars 22.7g; Fat 36.2g, of which saturates 21.2g; Cholesterol 196mg; Calcium 160mg; Fibre 1.3g; Sodium 180mg.
Marbled Slice Energy 305Kcal/1279kJ; Protein 4.5g; Carbohydrate 39.8g, of which sugars 31.8g; Fat 15.3g, of which saturates 9.5g; Cholesterol 36mg; Calcium 125mg; Fibre 0.5g; Sodium 117mg.

Honeyed Goat's Milk Gelato

Goat's milk is much more widely available than it used to be and is more easily tolerated by some individuals than cow's milk. With this recipe, the milk is used to make a surprisingly rich iced dessert.

Serves 4
6 egg yolks
50g/2oz/¼ cup caster (superfine) sugar
10ml/2 tsp cornflour (cornstarch)
600ml/1 pint/2½ cups goat's milk
60ml/4 tbsp clear honey pomegranate seeds, to decorate

1 Whisk the egg yolks, sugar and cornflour in a bowl until the mixture is pale and thick. Pour the goat's milk into a heavy pan, bring it to the boil, and then gradually whisk it into the egg yolk mixture.

2 Return the custard mixture to the pan and cook over a gentle heat, stirring constantly, until the custard thickens and is smooth. Pour it back into a clean bowl and stir in the honey. Leave to cool, then chill.

3 Pour the mixture into a freezer container and freeze for 6 hours until just firm enough to scoop, beating twice with a fork or in a food processor to break up the ice crystals.

4 To serve, scoop the ice cream into dishes and decorate with a few pomegranate seeds.

> **Variation/Banana Gelato**
> *Make a syrup by heating 150ml/¼ pint/⅔ cup water and 115g/4oz/½ cup caster (superfine) sugar in a pan until the sugar dissolves completely. When the sugar syrup has cooled, add 3 mashed bananas and the juice of 1 lemon, plus 300ml/½ pint/1¼ cups vanilla-flavour soya dessert. Freeze for 6–7 hours until firm, beating twice within that time to break up any ice crystals.*

Raspberry Sorbet

This delicious sorbet is gloriously flavoured with both puréed and crushed fresh raspberries.

Serves 4
175g/6oz/¾ cup caster (superfine) sugar
150ml/¼ pint/⅔ cup water
500g/1¼lb/3½ cups raspberries, plus extra, to serve
500ml/17fl oz/generous 2 cups virtually fat-free fromage frais or low-fat cream cheese

1 Put the caster sugar and water in a small pan and bring to the boil, stirring until the sugar has dissolved. Pour into a jug (pitcher) and leave to cool.

2 Put 350g/12oz/2½ cups of the raspberries in a food processor or blender. Process to a purée, then press through a sieve (strainer) placed over a large bowl to remove the seeds. Stir the sugar syrup into the raspberry purée and chill the mixture until it is very cold.

3 Add the fromage frais to the purée and whisk until smooth.

4 Pour the mixture into a freezer container and freeze for 4 hours, beating twice as it freezes with a fork, electric whisk or in a food processor to break up the ice crystals.

5 Alternatively, use an ice cream maker, following the manufacturer's instructions. Churn the mixture until it is thick but too soft to scoop, then scrape into a freezer container. (If this quantity is too large for your machine, make it in two batches.)

6 Crush the remaining raspberries between your fingers and add them to the partially frozen ice cream. Mix lightly then freeze for 2–3 hours until firm.

7 Scoop the ice cream into individual dishes and serve with extra raspberries on top.

Raspberry Sherbet Energy 276Kcal/1181kJ; Protein 11.6g; Carbohydrate 60g, of which sugars 60g; Fat 0.6g, of which saturates 0.3g; Cholesterol 1mg; Calcium 163mg; Fibre 3.1g; Sodium 48mg.
Goat's Milk Gelato Energy 255Kcal/1075kJ; Protein 7.7g; Carbohydrate 33.4g, of which sugars 31.1g; Fat 11.1g, of which saturates 5.1g; Cholesterol 218mg; Calcium 181mg; Fibre 0g; Sodium 76mg.

Date & Tofu Ice

All you sceptics who claim to hate tofu, prepare to be converted by this creamy date and apple ice cream. Generously spiced with cinnamon, it not only tastes good but is packed with soya protein, contains no added sugar, is low in fat and free from all dairy products.

Serves 4

250g/9oz/1 ½ cups stoned (pitted) dates
600ml/1 pint/2 ½ cups apple juice
5ml/1 tsp ground cinnamon
285g/10½oz pack chilled tofu, drained and cubed
150ml/¼ pint/⅔ cup unsweetened soya milk

1 Put the dates in a pan. Pour in 300ml/½ pint/1 ¼ cups of the apple juice and leave to soak for 2 hours. Simmer for 10 minutes, then leave to cool. Using a slotted spoon, lift out one-quarter of the dates, chop roughly and set aside.

2 Purée the remaining dates in a food processor or blender. Add the cinnamon and process with enough of the remaining apple juice to make a smooth paste.

3 Add the cubes of tofu, a few at a time, processing after each addition. Finally, add the remaining apple juice and the soya milk.

4 Pour the mixture into a freezer container and freeze for 4 hours, beating twice to break up the ice crystals.

5 Alternatively, use an ice cream maker. Churn until thick, but not firm enough to scoop. Turn into a freezer container.

6 Stir in most of the chopped dates and freeze for 2–3 hours until firm. To serve, scoop the ice into dessert glasses and decorate with the remaining chopped dates.

> **Cook's Tip**
> As tofu is a non-dairy product, it will not blend completely, so don't be concerned if the mixture contains tiny flecks of tofu.

Coconut Ice

Despite its creamy taste, this ice cream contains neither cream nor egg and is very refreshing. Serve it with scoops of fresh summer fruits.

Serves 4–6

150ml/¼ pint/⅔ cup water
115g/4oz/generous ½ cup caster (superfine) sugar
2 limes
400ml/14fl oz can coconut milk
toasted coconut shavings, to decorate

1 Put the water in a small pan. Add the caster sugar and bring to the boil, stirring constantly until the sugar has completely dissolved. Remove the pan from the heat and leave the syrup to cool, then chill well.

2 Grate the limes finely, taking care to avoid the bitter pith. Squeeze the fruit and pour the juice and rind into the pan of syrup. Add the coconut milk.

3 Pour the mixture into a freezer container and freeze for 5–6 hours until firm, beating twice with a fork, electric whisk or in a food processor to break up the ice crystals.

4 Alternatively, use an ice cream maker and churn the mixture until firm enough to scoop, then transfer to a freezer container and freeze until required.

5 To serve, scoop the coconut ice into individual dishes and decorate with toasted coconut shavings.

> **Cook's Tip**
> To make toasted coconut shavings, you will need a peeled piece of fresh coconut. First, rinse the fresh coconut with cold water, then cut off thin slices using a vegetable peeler. Toast the slices under a moderate grill (broiler) until the coconut has curled and the edges have turned golden. Cool slightly, then use as a pretty decoration for the coconut ice.

Date & Tofu Ice Energy 290Kcal/1232kJ; Protein 9.1g; Carbohydrate 58.2g, of which sugars 57.9g; Fat 3.9g, of which saturates 0.5g; Cholesterol 0mg; Calcium 407mg; Fibre 2.5g; Sodium 24mg.
Coconut Ice Energy 90Kcal/386kJ; Protein 0.3g; Carbohydrate 23.3g, of which sugars 23.3g; Fat 0.2g, of which saturates 0.1g; Cholesterol 0mg; Calcium 30mg; Fibre 0g; Sodium 75mg.

Summer Fruit Salad Ice Cream

A combination of yogurt and luscious soft fruits, this mouthwatering ice cream makes a fresh, low-fat treat for summer days.

Serves 6

900g/2lb/6 cups mixed soft summer fruit, such as raspberries, strawberries, blackcurrants or redcurrants

2 eggs
250ml/8fl oz/1 cup low-fat Greek (US strained plain) yogurt
175ml/6fl oz/³⁄4 cup red grape juice
15ml/1 tbsp powdered gelatine

1 Reserve half the fruit for the decoration; purée the rest in a food processor, then strain it over a bowl to make a smooth purée.

2 Separate the eggs and whisk the yolks and the yogurt into the fruit purée.

3 Heat the grape juice until almost boiling, then remove it from the heat. Sprinkle the gelatine over the grape juice and stir to dissolve the gelatine completely.

4 Whisk the dissolved gelatine mixture into the fruit purée. Cool, then pour the mixture into a freezer container. Freeze until half-frozen and slushy in consistency.

5 Whisk the egg whites in a grease-free bowl until stiff. Quickly fold them into the half-frozen mixture.

6 Return to the freezer and freeze until almost firm. To serve, scoop into dishes and decorate with the reserved soft fruits.

Cook's Tip
Red grape juice has a good flavour and improves the colour of the ice, but if it is not available, use cranberry, apple or orange juice instead.

Christmas Cranberry Bombe

This healthy alternative to Christmas pudding is light and low in fat, but still very festive and luxurious.

Serves 6

250ml/8fl oz/1 cup buttermilk
60ml/4 tbsp half-fat crème fraîche
1 vanilla pod (bean)
2 eggs
30ml/2 tbsp clear honey
30ml/2 tbsp chopped angelica
30ml/2 tbsp mixed (candied) peel

· 10ml/2 tsp flaked (sliced) almonds, toasted

For the sorbet centre
175g/6oz/1½ cups fresh or frozen cranberries
150ml/¼ pint/²⁄3 cup fresh orange juice
finely grated rind of ½ orange
2.5ml/½ tsp mixed spice (apple pie spice)
50g/2oz/¼ cup golden caster (superfine) sugar

1 Heat the buttermilk, crème fraîche and vanilla pod in a pan until the mixture is almost boiling. Remove the vanilla pod.

2 Place the eggs in a heatproof bowl over a pan of hot water and whisk until they are pale and thick. Pour in the heated buttermilk in a thin stream, whisking hard. Continue whisking over the hot water until the mixture thickens slightly.

3 Whisk in the honey and leave to cool. Spoon the mixture into a freezer container and freeze until slushy, then turn into a bowl and stir in the chopped angelica, mixed peel and almonds. Spoon into a 1.2 litre/2 pint/5 cup freezerproof round bowl and hollow out the centre. Freeze until firm.

4 Meanwhile, make the sorbet centre. Put the cranberries, orange juice, rind and spice in a pan and cook gently until the cranberries are soft. Set some cranberries aside for decorating. Add the sugar to the rest, then purée in a food processor until almost smooth, but still with some texture. Leave to cool.

5 Fill the hollowed-out centre of the bombe with the cranberry mixture, smooth over and freeze until firm. To serve, allow to soften slightly at room temperature, then turn out and serve in slices, decorated with the reserved cranberries.

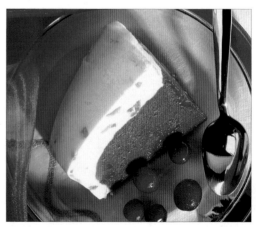

Frozen Apple & Blackberry Terrine

This pretty autumn fruit terrine is frozen so that you can enjoy a healthy dessert at any time of the year.

Serves 6

450g/1lb cooking or eating apples
300ml/½ pint/1¼ cups
  sweet (hard) cider
15ml/1 tbsp clear honey
5ml/1 tsp pure vanilla extract
200g/7oz/scant 2 cups fresh or
  frozen and thawed blackberries
15ml/1 tbsp powdered gelatine
2 egg whites
fresh apple slices and
  blackberries, to decorate

1 Peel, core and chop the apples and place them in a pan with half the cider. Bring the cider to the boil, then lower the heat, cover the pan and let the apples simmer gently until tender.

2 Transfer the apples to a food processor and process them to a smooth purée. Stir in the honey and vanilla extract. Add half the blackberries to half the apple purée, and process again until smooth. Press through a sieve (strainer) to remove the seeds.

3 Heat the remaining cider until almost boiling, then sprinkle the gelatine over and stir until the gelatine has dissolved completely. Add half the gelatine mixture to the apple purée and half to the blackberry and apple purée.

4 Leave both purées to cool until almost set. Whisk the egg whites until they are stiff. Quickly fold them into the apple purée. Remove half the purée to another bowl. Stir the remaining whole blackberries into half the apple purée, and then transfer this to a 1.75 litre/3 pint/7½ cup loaf tin (pan), packing it down firmly.

5 Top with the blackberry purée and spread it evenly. Finally, add a layer of the plain apple purée and smooth it evenly. If necessary, freeze each layer until firm before adding the next.

6 Freeze until firm. To serve, remove from the freezer and allow to stand at room temperature for about 20 minutes to soften. Serve in slices, decorated with apple slices and blackberries.

Plum & Port Sorbet

A melt-in-the-mouth sorbet with a wonderful taste and colour, this fat-free ice is a refreshing way to round off any meal.

Serves 4–6

900g/2lb ripe red plums, halved
  and stoned (pitted)
75g/3oz/6 tbsp caster
  (superfine) sugar
45ml/3 tbsp water
45ml/3 tbsp ruby port or red wine
crisp biscuits (cookies), to serve
  (optional)

1 Place the plums in a pan with the sugar and the water. Stir over a low heat until the sugar has melted, then cover and simmer gently for about 5 minutes, until the fruit is soft.

2 Turn the plum mixture into a blender or food processor and purée until smooth, then stir in the port. Allow to cool completely, then transfer to a freezer container and freeze until firm round the edges.

3 Remove from the freezer and process in the food processor or beat with an electric whisk to break up the ice crystals. Put back in the freezer and freeze until solid.

4 Before serving, allow the sorbet to stand for 15–20 minutes until softened slightly, then scoop on to individual dishes and serve with crisp biscuits, if you like.

Cook's Tip
If you prefer not to use alcohol, leave out the port and use fresh red grape juice instead for an equally delicious taste.

Variation
Use redcurrants and strawberries instead of the plums, pressing them through a sieve (strainer) after puréeing.

Apple & Blackberry Terrine Energy 67Kcal/283kJ; Protein 1.5g; Carbohydrate 12.4g, of which sugars 12.4g; Fat 0.2g, of which saturates 0g; Cholesterol 0mg; Calcium 21mg; Fibre 2.2g; Sodium 26mg.
Plum & Port Sorbet Energy 115Kcal/492kJ; Protein 1g; Carbohydrate 27.2g, of which sugars 27.2g; Fat 0.2g, of which saturates 0g; Cholesterol 0mg; Calcium 27mg; Fibre 2.4g; Sodium 4mg.

Rich Blackcurrant Coulis

A simple decorative trick makes these low-fat fruity desserts look stunning.

Serves 6-8
6 sheets leaf gelatine
475ml/16fl oz/2 cups water
450g/1lb/4 cups blackcurrants

225g/8oz/1 cup caster (superfine) sugar
150ml/¼ pint/⅔ cup ruby port
30ml/2 tbsp crème de cassis
120ml/4fl oz/½ cup single (light) cream, to decorate

1 In a small bowl, soak the gelatine in 75ml/5 tbsp of the water until soft. Place the blackcurrants, sugar and 300ml/½ pint/1¼ cups of the remaining water in a large pan. Bring to the boil, lower the heat and simmer for 20 minutes.

2 Strain, reserving the cooking liquid in a large jug (pitcher). Put half the blackcurrants in a bowl and pour over 60ml/4 tbsp of the reserved cooking liquid. (Freeze the remaining blackcurrants for another day.) Set the bowl and jug aside.

3 Squeeze the water out of the gelatine and place in a small pan with the port, cassis and remaining water. Heat gently to dissolve the gelatine but do not allow the mixture to boil. Pour the gelatine mixture into the jug of blackcurrant liquid, stirring until well mixed.

4 Run 6–8 jelly moulds under cold water, drain and place in a roasting pan. Fill with the port mixture. Chill for at least 6 hours until set. Turn the bowl of blackcurrants into a food processor, purée until smooth, then pass through a fine sieve (strainer) to make the coulis; adjust the sweetness.

5 Run a fine knife around each jelly. Dip each mould in hot water for 5–10 seconds, then turn the jelly out on to your hand. Place on a serving plate and spoon the coulis around the jelly.

6 To decorate, drop a little cream at intervals on to the coulis. Draw a cocktail stick (toothpick) through the cream dots, dragging each into a heart shape. Serve the desserts immediately.

Apple Foam with Blackberries

A light dessert, with a good contrast in flavour, texture and colour – weight watchers will love it.

Serves 4
225g/8oz blackberries
150ml/¼ pint/⅔ cup clear apple juice
5ml/1 tsp powdered gelatine
15ml/1 tbsp clear honey
2 egg whites

1 Place the blackberries in a pan with 60ml/4 tbsp of the apple juice and heat gently until the fruit is soft. Remove from the heat, cool and chill.

2 Sprinkle the gelatine over the remaining apple juice in another pan. Leave to soak for 5 minutes until spongy, then place over a low heat until the gelatine has completely dissolved. Stir in the honey.

3 Whisk the egg whites in a bowl until they hold stiff peaks. Continue whisking hard while gradually pouring in the hot gelatine mixture, until well mixed.

4 Quickly spoon the foam into rough mounds on individual plates. Chill in the refrigerator, then serve with the blackberries and juice spooned around the foam.

Cook's Tips
• Make sure that you dissolve the gelatine over a very low heat. It must not boil, or it will lose its setting ability.
• The egg white foam acts here as a flavourful, low-fat alternative to flavoured cream.

Variation
Any seasonal soft fruit can be used to accompany the apple foam if blackberries are not available.

Blackcurrant Coulis Energy 202Kcal/855kJ; Protein 1.3g; Carbohydrate 37g, of which sugars 37g; Fat 3.6g, of which saturates 2.3g; Cholesterol 10mg; Calcium 66mg; Fibre 2g; Sodium 10mg.
Apple Foam with Blackberries Energy 45Kcal/191kJ; Protein 2g; Carbohydrate 9.5g, of which sugars 9.5g; Fat 0.2g, of which saturates 0g; Cholesterol 0mg; Calcium 27mg; Fibre 1.8g; Sodium 33mg.

Fluffy Banana & Pineapple Mousse

This delicious mousse looks very impressive but is in fact easy to make, especially with a food processor. As an added bonus, it's surprisingly low in fat, so everyone can indulge in the dessert without feeling guilty.

Serves 6
2 ripe bananas
225g/8oz/1 cup cottage cheese
425g/15oz can pineapple chunks
*   or pieces in juice*
15ml/1 tbsp/1 sachet powdered
*   gelatine*
2 egg whites

1 Tie a double band of non-stick baking parchment around a 600ml/1 pint/2½ cup soufflé dish, so that it comes 5cm/2in above the rim.

2 Peel and chop one banana and place it in a blender or food processor with the cottage cheese. Process until smooth.

3 Drain the pineapple, reserving the juice. Reserve a few pieces or chunks of pineapple for decoration and add the rest to the mixture in the blender or food processor and process for a few seconds until finely chopped.

4 Dissolve the gelatine in 60ml/4 tbsp of the reserved pineapple juice. Stir the gelatine quickly into the fruit mixture.

5 Whisk the egg whites until they hold soft peaks and fold them into the mixture. Turn the mousse mixture into the prepared dish, smooth the surface and chill until set.

6 When the mousse is set, carefully remove the paper collar. Slice the remaining banana and use with the pineapple to decorate the mousse. Serve immediately.

> **Cook's Tip**
> *To make the preparation of this mousse even simpler, use a 1 litre/1¾ pint/4 cup serving dish, which will hold all the mixture without a paper collar.*

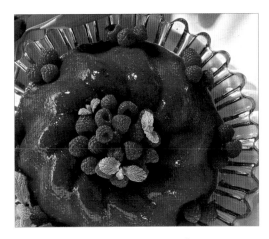

Minted Raspberry Bavarois

A sophisticated dessert that is low in fat, yet looks and tastes delectable.

Serves 6
450g/1lb/2⅔ cups fresh or frozen
*   and thawed raspberries*
25g/1oz/2 tbsp icing
*   (confectioners') sugar*
30ml/2 tbsp lemon juice
15ml/1 tbsp finely chopped
*   fresh mint*
30ml/2 tbsp/2 sachets powdered
*   gelatine*
75ml/5 tbsp boiling water
300ml/½ pint/1¼ cups custard,
*   made with skimmed milk*
250g/9oz/generous 1 cup Greek
*   (US strained plain) yogurt*
fresh mint sprigs, to decorate

1 Reserve a few raspberries for decoration. Place the raspberries, icing sugar and lemon juice in a blender or food processor and process until smooth.

2 Press the purée through a sieve (strainer) to remove the raspberry seeds. Add the mint. You should have about 600ml/ 1 pint/2½ cups of purée.

3 Sprinkle 5ml/1 tsp of the gelatine over 30ml/2 tbsp of boiling water and stir until the gelatine has dissolved. Stir into 150ml/ ¼ pint/⅔ cup of the fruit purée.

4 Pour this jelly into a 1 litre/1¾ pint/4 cup mould, and leave the mould to chill in the refrigerator until the jelly is just on the point of setting. Tip the tin to swirl the setting jelly around the sides, and then leave to chill until the jelly has set completely.

5 Stir the remaining fruit purée into the custard and yogurt. Dissolve the rest of the gelatine in 45ml/3 tbsp of boiling water and stir it in quickly.

6 Pour the raspberry custard into the mould and leave it to chill until it has set completely.

7 To serve, dip the mould quickly into hot water and then turn it out into a serving dish. Decorate the bavarois with the reserved raspberries and the mint sprigs.

Fluffy Mousse Energy 102Kcal/431kJ; Protein 6.2g; Carbohydrate 16.4g, of which sugars 15.7g; Fat 1.6g, of which saturates 0.9g; Cholesterol 6mg; Calcium 56mg; Fibre 0.7g; Sodium 134mg.
Raspb. Bavarois Energy 141Kcal/597kJ; Protein 5.1g; Carbohydrate 19.2g, of which sugars 17.5g; Fat 5.4g, of which saturates 2.2g; Cholesterol 1mg; Calcium 130mg; Fibre 1.9g; Sodium 53mg.

Cappuccino Coffee Cups

Coffee-lovers will adore this dessert – and the delicious pots of cappuccino-flavoured custard taste rich and creamy, even though they are low in calories. For a sophisticated finishing touch, decorate each pot with a coffee bean.

Serves 4
2 eggs
215g/7.7oz carton semi-skinned evaporated (unsweetened condensed) milk
25ml/1½ tbsp instant coffee granules or powder
30ml/2 tbsp caster (superfine) sugar
10ml/2 tsp powdered gelatine
60ml/4 tbsp light crème fraîche
cocoa powder (unsweetened) or ground cinnamon, to decorate

1 Separate one egg and reserve the white. Beat the yolk with the whole of the remaining egg. Put the evaporated milk, coffee granules, sugar and beaten eggs in a pan, then whisk until the ingredients are well combined.

2 Put the pan over a low heat and stir constantly until the mixture is hot, but not boiling. Cook, stirring constantly, without boiling, until the mixture is slightly thickened and smooth.

3 Remove the pan from the heat. Sprinkle the gelatine over the pan and whisk until the gelatine has completely dissolved. Carefully spoon the coffee custard into four individual dishes or glasses and chill until set.

4 Whisk the reserved egg white until stiff. Whisk in the crème fraîche, then spoon the mixture over the desserts. Sprinkle with cocoa or cinnamon and serve.

> **Variation**
> *Greek (US strained plain) yogurt can be used instead of the crème fraîche, if you prefer.*

Fresh Fruit Salad

A refreshing and colourful fruit salad, packed with Vitamin C, makes a healthy finale for any occasion.

Serves 6
2 eating apples
2 oranges
2 peaches
16–20 strawberries

30ml/2 tbsp freshly squeezed lemon juice
15–30ml/1–2 tbsp orange flower water
icing (confectioners') sugar, to taste (optional)
a few sprigs of fresh mint, to decorate

1 Peel and core the apples and cut into thin slices. Cut a thin slice of peel and pith from both ends of the oranges, then cut off the remaining peel and pit. Cut out each segment, leaving the membranes behind. Squeeze the juice from the membranes; reserve the juice and discard the membranes.

2 Blanch the peaches for 1 minute in boiling water, then peel off the skin and cut the flesh into thick slices.

3 Hull the strawberries, if you like, and halve or quarter if large. Place all the fruit in a large serving bowl.

4 Blend together the lemon juice, orange flower water and any orange juice. Taste and add a little icing sugar to sweeten, if you like. Pour the fruit juice mixture over the salad and serve decorated with mint leaves.

> **Cook's Tips**
> *• There are no rules with this fruit salad, and you could use almost any fruit that you like. Oranges, however, should form the base and apples give a delightful contrast in texture.*
> *• As far as healthy desserts go, a fruit salad is hard to beat. Low in calories, yet high in fibre and a good source of Vitamin C, fresh fruit is nutritionally important and serving it as a salad is an excellent way of including it in the diet.*

Coffee Cups Energy 205Kcal/866kJ; Protein 9g; Carbohydrate 32.9g, of which sugars 32.7g; Fat 5.1g, of which saturates 2.4g; Cholesterol 96mg; Calcium 206mg; Fibre 0g; Sodium 121mg.
Fresh Fruit Salad Energy 39Kcal/167kJ; Protein 1g; Carbohydrate 9.1g, of which sugars 9.1g; Fat 0.1g, of which saturates 0g; Cholesterol 0mg; Calcium 27mg; Fibre 1.8g; Sodium 5mg.

Fresh Citrus Jelly

Shimmering fresh fruit jellies really are worth the effort – they're packed with fresh flavour, natural colour and vitamins, plus they make a lovely fat-free dessert.

Serves 4
3 medium oranges
1 lemon
1 lime
75g/3oz/scant ½ cup golden caster (superfine) sugar
300ml/½ pint/1¼ cups water
15ml/1 tbsp/1 sachet powdered gelatine
extra slices of fruit, to decorate

1 With a sharp knife, cut all the peel and white pith from one orange and carefully remove the segments from between the membranes. Arrange the segments in the base of a 900ml/ 1½ pint/3¾ cup mould or dish.

2 Pare off some citrus rind, cut into shreds and reserve them for decoration. Grate the remaining rind from the lemon and lime and one orange. Place all the grated rind in a pan, with the sugar and the water.

3 Heat gently until the sugar has dissolved, without boiling. Remove from the heat. Squeeze the juice from all the rest of the fruit and stir it into the pan.

4 Strain the liquid into a measuring jug (cup) to remove the rind (you should have about 600ml/1 pint/2½ cups: if necessary, make up the amount with water). Sprinkle the gelatine over the liquid and stir until it has completely dissolved.

5 Pour a little of the jelly over the orange segments and chill until set. Leave the remaining jelly at room temperature to cool, but do not allow it to set.

6 Pour the remaining cooled jelly into the dish and chill until set. To serve, turn out the jelly on to a serving plate and decorate it with the reserved citrus rind shreds and extra slices of citrus fruit.

Strawberries in Spiced Grape Jelly

A subtle touch of cinnamon is combined with juicy strawberries and orange juice to make a fresh-tasting dessert that is fat free and vitamin rich.

Serves 4
475ml/16fl oz/2 cups red grape juice
1 cinnamon stick
1 small orange
15ml/1 tbsp powdered gelatine
225g/8oz/2 cups strawberries, chopped, plus extra to decorate

1 Pour the grape juice into a pan and add the cinnamon stick. Thinly pare the rind from the orange. Add most of it to the pan but shred some pieces and set them aside for the decoration.

2 Place the pan over a very low heat for 10 minutes, then remove the flavourings from the grape juice.

3 Squeeze the juice from the orange into a bowl and sprinkle over the powdered gelatine. When the mixture is spongy, stir into the grape juice until it has completely dissolved. Allow the jelly to cool until just beginning to set.

4 Stir in the strawberries and quickly turn into a 1 litre/1¾ pint/ 4 cup mould or serving dish. Chill until set.

5 To serve, dip the mould quickly into hot water and turn the jelly out on to a serving plate. Decorate with strawberries and shreds of orange rind.

> **Cook's Tip**
> *Do not wash strawberries until just before you hull them. Quickly dip them in water, then pat dry on kitchen paper.*

> **Variation**
> *Fresh raspberries can be used instead of strawberries.*

Citrus Jelly Energy 107Kcal/458kJ; Protein 1.1g; Carbohydrate 27.3g, of which sugars 27.3g; Fat 0.1g, of which saturates 0g; Cholesterol 0mg; Calcium 52mg; Fibre 1.5g; Sodium 6mg.
Strawberries in Grape Jelly Energy 81Kcal/344kJ; Protein 1.1g; Carbohydrate 19.8g, of which sugars 19.8g; Fat 0.2g, of which saturates 0g; Cholesterol 0mg; Calcium 46mg; Fibre 1.1g; Sodium 13mg.

Grapes in Grape-Yogurt Jelly

Grapes can do you a power of good and here they are combined with low-fat yogurt to make a stylish dessert for a dinner party.

Serves 4
250g/9oz/2¼ cups white seedless grapes
450ml/¾ pint/scant 2 cups unsweetened white grape juice
15ml/1 tbsp powdered gelatine
120ml/4fl oz/½ cup low-fat natural (plain) yogurt

1 Set aside four tiny bunches of grapes for decoration. Pull the rest off their stalks and cut them in half.

2 Divide the grapes among four stemmed glasses and tilt the glasses on one side, propping them firmly in a bowl of ice.

3 Place the grape juice in a pan and heat it until almost boiling. Remove it from the heat and sprinkle the gelatine over the surface, stirring to dissolve the gelatine.

4 Pour half the grape juice over the grapes and leave to set.

5 Cool the remaining grape juice until on the verge of setting, then stir in the low-fat natural yogurt.

6 Stand the set glasses upright and pour in the yogurt mixture. Chill to set, then decorate the rim of each glass with grapes, and serve.

Cook's Tip
For an easier version, stand the glasses upright rather than at an angle – then they can be put in the refrigerator to set rather than packed with ice.

Variation
You could always use small red grapes instead of green.

Orange-Blossom Jelly

A fresh orange jelly makes a delightful dessert; the natural fruit flavour combined with the smooth jelly has a wonderful cleansing quality.

Serves 4
65g/2½oz/5 tbsp caster (superfine) sugar
150ml/¼ pint/⅔ cup water
25g/1oz powdered gelatine
600ml/1 pint/2½ cups fresh orange juice
30ml/2 tbsp orange flower water
unsprayed edible flowers, to decorate (optional)

1 Place the caster sugar and water in a small pan and heat gently to dissolve the sugar. Pour into a heatproof bowl and leave to cool.

2 Sprinkle the gelatine over the surface of the syrup. Leave to stand until the gelatine has absorbed all the liquid.

3 Gently melt the gelatine over a pan of simmering water until it becomes clear and transparent. Leave to cool. When the gelatine mixture is cold, mix it with the orange juice and orange flower water.

4 Wet a jelly mould or bowl and pour in the jelly. Chill in the refrigerator for at least 2 hours, or until set.

5 To serve, dip the mould quickly into hot water and turn the jelly out on to a serving plate. Decorate the edge of the jelly with edible flowers, if you like.

Cook's Tips
• If you are entertaining, make this jelly extra-special by substituting Grand Marnier for the orange flower water.
• For a vegetarian version, use an alternative gelling agent such as agar-agar, which is produced from seaweed. Treat as for gelatine but bear in mind that agar-agar has to boil to dissolve.

Grapes in Jelly Energy 106Kcal/452kJ; Protein 2.1g; Carbohydrate 25.1g, of which sugars 25.1g; Fat 0.5g, of which saturates 0.2g; Cholesterol 0mg; Calcium 87mg; Fibre 0.5g; Sodium 34mg.
Orange-Blossom Jelly Energy 118Kcal/503kJ; Protein 0.8g; Carbohydrate 30.2g, of which sugars 30.2g; Fat 0.2g, of which saturates 0g; Cholesterol 0mg; Calcium 24mg; Fibre 0.2g; Sodium 16mg.

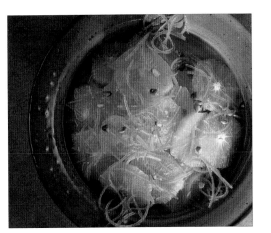

Mandarins in Orange Flower Syrup

Whole mandarins, bathed in a fragrant juice, create a healthy fruit dessert that's bursting with fresh flavours. A perfect, palate-tingling way to end any meal.

Serves 4
10 fresh mandarins
15ml/1 tbsp icing (confectioners') sugar
10ml/2 tsp orange flower water
15ml/1 tbsp unsalted pistachio nuts, shelled and chopped

1 Thinly pare a little of the rind from one mandarin with a vegetable peeler and cut it into fine shreds for decoration. Squeeze the juice from two of the mandarins and reserve.

2 Peel the remaining fruit, removing as much of the white pith as possible. Arrange the whole fruits in a wide dish.

3 Mix the reserved juice with the sugar and orange flower water, then pour over the fruit. Cover the dish and chill for at least 1 hour.

4 Blanch the shreds of rind in boiling water for 30 seconds. Drain and leave to cool.

5 Sprinkle the rind shreds and chopped pistachio nuts over the mandarins in the dish and serve.

Cook's Tips
• *The mandarins look very attractive if you leave them whole, especially if there is a large quantity for a special occasion, but you may prefer to separate the segments.*
• *This dish is suitable for any of the other small-size citrus fruits. Tangerines, clementines, mineolas and satsumas would all work very well instead of mandarins.*
• *If you want to serve the dish with an accompaniment, try yogurt-based ice cream or low-fat crème fraîche to keep on a healthy note.*

Chilled Oranges in Syrup

This popular classic is a refreshing way to serve up oranges, which are packed with Vitamin C and dietary fibre – vital for good health.

Serves 4
4 oranges
600ml/1 pint/2½ cups water
350g/12oz/1½ cups granulated sugar

30ml/2 tbsp freshly squeezed lemon juice
30ml/2 tbsp rose water
40g/1½oz/¼ cup unsalted pistachio nuts, shelled and chopped

1 Pare the rind from the oranges with a vegetable peeler, leaving the white pith on the fruit.

2 Cut the orange rind into fine strips and boil in water several times to remove the bitterness. Drain on kitchen paper.

3 Place the water, sugar and lemon juice in a pan. Bring to the boil, add the pared orange rind strips and simmer until the syrup thickens and turns to a syrup. Add the rose water, stir and leave to cool.

4 Peel away the pith from the oranges, then cut the fruit crossways into neat slices. Arrange in a serving dish and pour over the flavoured syrup.

5 Chill the oranges for 1–2 hours. Sprinkle with the pistachio nuts before serving.

Cook's Tips
• *Almonds could be substituted for the pistachio nuts, if you like, but don't be tempted to increase the quantity or you'll raise the level of fat.*
• *If they are available, use blood red oranges to add an interesting colour to the dish.*

Chilled Oranges Energy 449Kcal/1909kJ; Protein 3.6g; Carbohydrate 102.5g, of which sugars 102.2g; Fat 5.7g, of which saturates 0.8g; Cholesterol 0mg; Calcium 114mg; Fibre 2.7g; Sodium 64mg.
Mandarins in Syrup Energy 74Kcal/314kJ; Protein 1.6g; Carbohydrate 12.9g, of which sugars 12.8g; Fat 2.2g, of which saturates 0.3g; Cholesterol 0mg; Calcium 37mg; Fibre 1.4g; Sodium 24mg.

Crispy Mango Stacks with Raspberry Coulis

This makes an extremely healthy yet impressively attractive dessert – it is low in fat and also contains no added sugar. However, if the fresh raspberries prove to be a little sharp to the taste, then you may prefer to add a pinch of sugar to the fruit purée.

Serves 4

3 filo pastry sheets, thawed
  if frozen
2 small ripe mangoes
115g/4oz/²⁄₃ cup raspberries,
  thawed if frozen
45ml/3 tbsp water
50g/2oz/¹⁄₄ cup butter,
  melted

1 Preheat the oven to 200°C/400°F/Gas 6. Lay the filo sheets on a clean work surface and cut out four 10cm/4in rounds from each.

2 Brush each round with the melted butter and lay them out on two baking sheets.

3 Bake the filo rounds for 5 minutes, or until they are crisp and golden in colour. Place on wire racks to cool.

4 Peel the mangoes, then remove the stones (pits) and cut the flesh into thin slices. Put the fresh raspberries in a food processor along with the water and process until the mixture has formed a purée; press the raspberry purée through a sieve (strainer).

5 Place a filo pastry round on each of four individual plates. Top with a quarter of the mango and drizzle with a little of the raspberry purée.

6 Repeat layering in this way until all of the ingredients have been used, finishing off with a layer of mango and a drizzle of the raspberry purée.

7 Serve immediately; this dessert is best served straight away.

Strawberries with Cointreau

Strawberries and oranges make a brilliant partnership. This dish is a glamorous way to have a portion of your daily fruit intake.

Serves 4

1 unwaxed orange
40g/1¹⁄₂oz/3 tbsp granulated
  sugar
75ml/5 tbsp water
450g/1lb/3¹⁄₂ cups strawberries,
  hulled
45ml/3 tbsp Cointreau or other
  orange-flavoured liqueur
250ml/8fl oz/1 cup low-fat
  Greek (US strained plain)
  yogurt

1 With a vegetable peeler, remove wide strips of rind from the orange, taking care to avoid the pith. Stack two or three pieces at a time and cut into very thin strips.

2 Mix the sugar and water in a small pan. Heat gently, swirling the pan occasionally until the sugar has dissolved. Bring to the boil, add the orange rind strips, then simmer for 10 minutes. Remove the pan from the heat and set the syrup aside to cool completely.

3 Reserve four strawberries for decoration and cut the rest lengthways in halves or quarters. Put them in a bowl. Stir the Cointreau or chosen liqueur into the syrup and pour it over the fruit with the orange rind. Set aside for at least 30 minutes or for up to 2 hours.

4 Whip the yogurt briefly, then sweeten to taste with a little of the syrup from the strawberries.

5 Spoon the chopped strawberries into glass serving dishes and top with dollops of the sweetened Greek yogurt. Decorate with the reserved strawberries.

> **Variation**
> *Use a mixture of soft summer fruit to ring the changes.*

Mango Stacks Energy 194Kcal/815kJ; Protein 2.4g; Carbohydrate 23.6g, of which sugars 12g; Fat 10.7g, of which saturates 6.7g; Cholesterol 27mg; Calcium 40mg; Fibre 3.1g; Sodium 79mg.
Strawberries Energy 151Kcal/638kJ; Protein 4.5g; Carbohydrate 27.2g, of which sugars 27.2g; Fat 0.8g, of which saturates 0.3g; Cholesterol 1mg; Calcium 156mg; Fibre 1.8g; Sodium 62mg.

Cinnamon & Apricot Soufflés

Don't expect this to be difficult simply because it's a soufflé – it really couldn't be easier, and, best of all, it's relatively low in fat. The cinnamon gives the dish a subtle spicy flavour that makes you want to come back for more.

Serves 4

low-fat spread, for greasing
plain (all-purpose) flour,
*   for dusting*
3 eggs
115g/4oz/½ cup apricot fruit
*   spread*
finely grated rind of ½ lemon
5ml/1 tsp ground cinnamon, plus
*   extra to decorate*

1 Preheat the oven to 190°C/375°F/Gas 5. Lightly grease four individual soufflé dishes and dust them lightly with flour.

2 Separate the eggs and place the yolks in a bowl with the fruit spread, lemon rind and cinnamon.

3 Whisk hard until the mixture is thick and pale in colour.

4 Place the egg whites in a grease-free bowl and whisk them until they form soft peaks when the whisk is lifted.

5 Using a metal spoon or spatula, gradually fold the egg whites evenly into the yolk mixture.

6 Divide the soufflé mixture among the prepared dishes and bake for 10–15 minutes, until well risen and golden brown. Serve immediately, dusted with a little extra ground cinnamon.

> **Variations**
> • *Other fruit spreads would be delicious in this soufflé. Try peach or blueberry for a change.*
> • *Puréed, well-drained canned fruit can be used instead of the apricot spread, but make sure that the mixture is not too wet or the soufflés will not rise properly. Puréed fresh soft fruit can also be used but may need to be cooked before being puréed.*

Apricot Delight

A layered treat for those who are watching their fat intake.

Serves 4

two 400g/14oz cans apricots in
*   natural juice*
50ml/2fl oz/¼ cup fructose

15ml/1 tbsp lemon juice
25ml/1½ tbsp powdered gelatine
425g/15 oz/1¾ cups low-fat
*   custard*
150ml/¼ cup/⅔ cup low-fat
*   natural (plain) thick yogurt*
sliced apricot, fresh mint and yogurt
*   piping cream, to decorate*

1 Line the bottom of a 1.2 litre/2 pint/5 cup heart-shaped or round cake tin (pan) with baking parchment.

2 Drain the apricots, reserving the juice. Put the drained apricots in a food processor or blender. Add the fructose and 50ml/2fl oz/¼ cup of the apricot juice. Blend to a purée.

3 Measure 15ml/1 tbsp of the apricot juice into a small bowl. Add the lemon juice, then sprinkle 10ml/2 tsp of the gelatine over. Set aside for 5 minutes until softened.

4 Stir the gelatine into half the apricot purée and pour into the cake tin. Chill in the refrigerator for 1½ hours, or until firm.

5 Sprinkle the remaining gelatine over 50ml/2fl oz/¼ cup of the apricot juice. Soak and dissolve as before. Mix the remaining apricot purée with the custard, yogurt and gelatine. Pour on to the layer of set fruit purée and chill for 3 hours.

6 Dip the cake tin in hot water for a few seconds and unmould the heart on to a serving plate. Decorate with piped yogurt cream (see Cook's Tip box), apricot and mint.

> **Cook's Tip**
> *For yogurt piping cream, dissolve 10ml/2 tsp powdered gelatine in 45ml/3 tbsp water then mix with 300ml/½ pint/1¼ cups thick yogurt, 15ml/1 tbsp fructose and 2.5ml/½ tsp vanilla extract, chill for 30 minutes, then fold in a beaten egg white. Use to pipe.*

Cinn. & Apricot Soufflés Energy 143Kcal/604kJ; Protein 5.2g; Carbohydrate 22.8g, of which sugars 19.9g; Fat 4.2g, of which saturates 1.2g; Cholesterol 143mg; Calcium 30mg; Fibre 0.1g; Sodium 61mg.
Apricot Delight Energy 193Kcal/823kJ; Protein 5.8g; Carbohydrate 36.9g, of which sugars 33.2g; Fat 2.5g, of which saturates 0.2g; Cholesterol 3mg; Calcium 210mg; Fibre 1.9g; Sodium 85mg.

Souffléed Rice Pudding

The fluffy egg whites in this unusually light rice pudding make the portions seem much more substantial, without adding lots of extra unwanted fat.

Serves 4
65g/2½oz/⅓ cup pudding
   (short-grain) rice
45ml/3 tbsp clear honey
750ml/1¼ pints/3 cups semi-
   skimmed (low-fat) milk
1 vanilla pod (bean) or
   2.5ml/½ tsp vanilla extract
2 egg whites
5ml/1 tsp freshly grated nutmeg

1 Place the rice, honey and milk in a heavy or non-stick pan and bring the milk to the boil. Add the vanilla pod, if using.

2 Lower the heat, cover and simmer over the lowest possible heat for approximately 1–1¼ hours, stirring occasionally to prevent sticking, until most of the liquid has been absorbed.

3 Remove the vanilla pod, or, if using vanilla extract, add this to the rice mixture now. Set the pan aside, so that the mixture cools slightly. Preheat the oven to 220°C/425°F/Gas 7.

4 Place the egg whites in a grease-free bowl and whisk them until they hold soft peaks when the whisk is lifted.

5 Using a metal spoon or spatula, fold the egg whites evenly into the rice mixture, then turn into a 1 litre/1¾ pint/4 cup ovenproof dish.

6 Sprinkle with grated nutmeg and bake for 15–20 minutes, until the pudding has risen well and is golden brown. Serve hot.

Cook's Tip
If you like, use skimmed milk instead of semi-skimmed (low-fat), but take care when it is simmering as, with so little fat, it tends to boil over very easily.

Souffléed Orange Semolina

If your opinion of semolina is coloured by the memory of sloppy school puddings, treat yourself to a taste of this delicious version. Healthy grains have never tasted better.

Serves 4
50g/2oz/⅓ cup semolina
600ml/1 pint/2½ cups semi-
   skimmed (low-fat) milk
25g/1oz/2 tbsp light muscovado
   (brown) sugar
1 large orange
1 egg white

1 Preheat the oven to 200°C/400°F/Gas 6. Put the semolina in a non-stick pan and add the milk and sugar. Stir over a moderate heat until the semolina is thickened and smooth. Remove from the heat.

2 Pare a few thin pieces of rind from the orange, shred and reserve for decoration. Finely grate the remaining rind. Cut all the peel and white pith from the orange and separate the flesh into equal segments, cutting between the membranes. Discard the membranes and stir the segments of flesh into the semolina, with the grated orange rind.

3 Whisk the egg white in a grease-free bowl until stiff but not dry, then fold lightly and evenly into the mixture. Spoon into a 1 litre/1¾ pint/4 cup ovenproof dish and bake in the oven for 15–20 minutes, until risen and golden brown. Sprinkle over the orange shreds and serve immediately.

Cook's Tip
When using the rind of citrus fruit, scrub the fruit thoroughly before use, or buy unwaxed fruit.

Variation
For rosy-flecked semolina, use fresh raspberries in place of the orange segments and decorate with a few whole berries.

Orange Semolina Energy 159Kcal/676kJ; Protein 7.6g; Carbohydrate 27.8g, of which sugars 18.1g; Fat 2.8g, of which saturates 1.6g; Cholesterol 9mg; Calcium 204mg; Fibre 0.9g; Sodium 84mg.
Rice Pudding Energy 183Kcal/773kJ; Protein 9.1g; Carbohydrate 30.4g, of which sugars 17.4g; Fat 3.3g, of which saturates 2g; Cholesterol 11mg; Calcium 230mg; Fibre 0g; Sodium 112mg.

Hot Blueberry & Pear Soufflés

Blueberries are deliciously fragrant, with a flavour that is simultaneously sharp and sweet. Combining them with the slightly acidic, yet creamy, richness of pears is truly inspired. Make sure that you choose a good culinary pear.

Serves 6
low-fat spread, for greasing
150g/5oz/¾ cup caster (superfine) sugar, plus extra for dusting
350g/12oz/3 cups blueberries
2 medium pears, peeled, cored and finely diced
grated rind and juice of 1 pink grapefruit
3 egg whites
icing (confectioners') sugar, for dusting

1 Preheat the oven to 200°C/400°F/Gas 6. Grease six 150ml/¼ pint/⅔ cup soufflé dishes and dust with caster sugar. Put a baking sheet in the oven to heat.

2 Cook the blueberries and pears with the grapefruit rind and juice in a pan for 10 minutes. Press through a sieve (strainer) into a bowl. Stir in 50g/2oz/¼ cup of the caster sugar. Set aside to cool.

3 Put a spoonful of the blueberry and pear purée into each prepared dish and smooth the surface. Reserve the remaining purée and set the dishes aside.

4 Whisk the egg whites in a large grease-free bowl until they form stiff peaks. Very gradually whisk in the remaining caster sugar to make a stiff, glossy meringue mixture. Fold in the remaining blueberry and pear purée and spoon the flavoured meringue into the prepared dishes. Level the tops with a palette knife, and run a table knife around the edge of each dish.

5 Place the filled dishes on the hot baking sheet and bake in the oven for 10–15 minutes until the soufflés have risen well and are lightly browned.

6 Dust the tops of the soufflés with icing sugar. Serve immediately.

Mango & Ginger Clouds

The sweet, perfumed flavour of ripe mango combines beautifully with ginger, and this low-fat dessert makes the very most of them both.

Serves 6
3 ripe mangoes
3 pieces preserved stem ginger, plus 45ml/3 tbsp syrup from the jar
75g/3oz/½ cup silken tofu
3 egg whites
6 unsalted pistachio nuts, chopped

1 Cut the mango flesh from the stone (pit), remove the peel and chop the flesh.

2 Put the mango flesh in a food processor and add the ginger, syrup and tofu. Process until smooth. Spoon into a bowl.

3 Whisk the egg whites in a grease-free bowl until they form soft peaks. Fold them lightly into the mango mixture.

4 Spoon the mango mixture into either wide dishes or glasses and chill well before serving, sprinkled with the chopped pistachio nuts.

Cook's Tips
• *Tofu, which is made from soya beans, has a high protein content yet is low in fat. It looks rather like cheese and is useful for vegetarian cooking. Firm tofu can be cut into chunks, while silken tofu has a softer consistency and is good for sauces. Although tofu has little taste, it readily absorbs other flavours, so is quite versatile.*

Variation
Use toasted flaked (sliced) almonds or hazelnuts instead of the pistachios, or omit and decorate with extra mango slices.

Blueberry & Pear Energy 126Kcal/535kJ; Protein 2.2g; Carbohydrate 30.8g, of which sugars 30.8g; Fat 0.1g, of which saturates 0g; Cholesterol 0mg; Calcium 39mg; Fibre 2g; Sodium 34mg.
Mango & Ginger Clouds Energy 95Kcal/404kJ; Protein 3.5g; Carbohydrate 16.8g, of which sugars 16.5g; Fat 2.1g, of which saturates 0.3g; Cholesterol 0mg; Calcium 78mg; Fibre 2.1g; Sodium 66mg.

Bread & Sultana Custard

An old favourite gets the low-fat treatment and proves how successful this can be.

Serves 4

15ml/1 tbsp low-fat spread, plus extra for greasing
3 thin slices of bread, crusts removed
475ml/16fl oz/2 cups skimmed milk
2.5ml/½ tsp mixed spice (apple pie spice)
40g/1½oz/3 tbsp demerara (raw) sugar
2 eggs, whisked
75g/3oz/½ cup sultanas (golden raisins)
freshly grated nutmeg
a little icing (confectioners') sugar, for dusting

1 Preheat the oven to 180°C/350°F/Gas 4 and lightly grease an ovenproof dish. Spread the bread with low-fat spread and cut it into small pieces.

2 Place a layer of bread in the prepared dish, then continue layering until all the bread is used up.

3 Whisk together the skimmed milk, mixed spice, demerara sugar and eggs in a large mixing bowl. Pour the mixture over the complete surface of the bread. Sprinkle over the sultanas and leave to stand for 30 minutes.

4 Grate a little nutmeg over the top and bake for 30–40 minutes until the custard is just set and golden.

5 Serve the dessert immediately, dusted with icing sugar.

> **Variations**
> • White bread is the traditional choice for this dessert, but for a healthier dessert, use wholemeal (whole-wheat) or other mixed grain bread, as this would provide extra fibre.
> • Mix the sultanas with other dried fruits, such as chopped apricots or dates.

Poppyseed Custard with Red Fruit

Poppyseeds add a nutty flavour to this creamy custard without increasing the amount of fat too much.

Serves 6

low-fat spread, for greasing
600ml/1 pint/2½ cups skimmed milk
2 eggs
15ml/1 tbsp caster (superfine) sugar
15ml/1 tbsp poppyseeds
115g/4oz/1 cup each of strawberries, raspberries and blackberries
15ml/1 tbsp soft light brown sugar
60ml/4 tbsp red grape juice

1 Preheat the oven to 150°C/300°F/Gas 2. Grease a soufflé dish very lightly with low-fat spread. Heat the milk until just below boiling point, but do not boil. Beat the eggs in a bowl with the caster sugar and poppyseeds until creamy.

2 Whisk the milk into the egg mixture until very well mixed. Stand the prepared soufflé dish in a shallow roasting pan, then pour in hot water from a kettle to come halfway up the sides of the dish.

3 Pour the custard into the soufflé dish and bake in the preheated oven for 50–60 minutes, until the custard is just set and golden on top.

4 While the custard is cooking, mix the fruit with the brown sugar and fruit juice. Chill until ready to serve with the custard.

> **Variations**
> • If you don't like poppyseeds, sprinkle the surface of the custard with freshly grated nutmeg or ground cinnamon instead.
> • Vary the mixed fruit according to what is available. A combination of exotic fruits would also look and taste delicious with the custard – just mix with orange or tropical juice and leave out the sugar, if you like.
> • Cook the custard in individual ovenproof dishes, if you wish.

Bread & Sultana Energy 224Kcal/949kJ; Protein 9.6g; Carbohydrate 41.1g, of which sugars 30.6g; Fat 3.6g, of which saturates 0.9g; Cholesterol 100mg; Calcium 202mg; Fibre 0.7g; Sodium 209mg.
Poppyseed Energy 110Kcal/466kJ; Protein 6.8g; Carbohydrate 13.5g, of which sugars 13.5g; Fat 3.8g, of which saturates 0.9g; Cholesterol 67mg; Calcium 167mg; Fibre 1.6g; Sodium 71mg.

Orange Yogurt Brûlées

Luxurious treats, much lower in fat than classic brûlées, which are made with cream, eggs and lots of sugar. Proof that low-fat desserts can still be creamy and delicious.

Serves 4
2 oranges
150ml/¼ pint/⅔ cup low-fat Greek (US strained plain) yogurt
60ml/4 tbsp half-fat crème fraîche
40g/1½oz/3 tbsp golden caster (superfine) sugar
25g/1oz/2 tbsp light muscovado (brown) sugar

1 With a sharp knife, cut away all the peel and white pith from the oranges and chop the fruit. Alternatively, cut the oranges into segments, cutting the flesh away from the membranes.

2 Place the fruit in the bottom of four individual flameproof dishes. Mix together the yogurt and crème fraîche and spoon the mixture over the oranges.

3 Mix together the two sugars and sprinkle them evenly over the tops of the dishes.

4 Place the dishes under a preheated, very hot grill (broiler) for 3–4 minutes or until the sugar melts and turns to a rich golden brown. Serve warm or cold.

> **Cook's Tip**
> *You can now buy little gas blow torches for use in the kitchen. They make quick work of caramelizing the sugar on top of the brûlées – and are also fun to use!*

> **Variation**
> *Try replacing the oranges with peaches or raspberries.*

Tofu Berry Brûlée

Brûlée desserts are usually totally out of bounds on a low-fat diet, but this version is perfectly acceptable because it uses tofu, which is both low in fat and free from cholesterol.

Serves 4
300g/11oz packet silken tofu
45g/1¾oz/3 tbsp icing (confectioners') sugar
225g/8oz/2 cups red berry fruits, such as raspberries, strawberries and redcurrants
about 65g/2½oz/5 tbsp demerara (raw) sugar

1 Mix the tofu and the icing sugar in a food processor or a blender and process until smooth.

2 Stir in the fruits, then spoon the tofu and fruit mixture into a 900ml/1½ pint/3¾ cup flameproof dish. Flatten the top.

3 Sprinkle the top with enough demerara sugar to cover evenly. Place under a very hot grill (broiler) until the sugar melts and caramelizes. Chill before serving.

> **Cook's Tip**
> *You should choose silken tofu as firm tofu does not have a smooth enough texture for this kind of dish.*

> **Variation/Passion Fruit Brûlées**
> *Cut 4 passion fruit in half with a sharp knife. Use a teaspoon to scoop out the pulp and seeds; divide among 4 ovenproof ramekins. Spoon equal amounts of 300ml/½ pint/1¼ cups low-fat Greek (US strained plain) yogurt on top of the fruit and smooth the surface level. Chill for at least 2 hours. Put 75g/3oz /6 tbsp soft light brown sugar in a small pan with 15ml/1 tbsp water and heat gently, stirring, until the sugar has melted and caramelized. Pour over the yogurt; the caramel will harden within 1 minute. Keep the brûlées in a cool place until ready to serve.*

Orange Yogurt Energy 91Kcal/385kJ; Protein 2.9g; Carbohydrate 16.3g, of which sugars 16.1g; Fat 2.1g, of which saturates 1.3g; Cholesterol 1mg; Calcium 114mg; Fibre 1g; Sodium 39mg.
Tofu Berry Brûlée Energy 187Kcal/794kJ; Protein 7g; Carbohydrate 34.5g, of which sugars 34.2g; Fat 3.3g, of which saturates 0.4g; Cholesterol 0mg; Calcium 413mg; Fibre 1.4g; Sodium 7mg.

Raspberry Passion Fruit Swirls

Quick and nutritious, this attractive fruit and yogurt dessert is the ideal choice for mid-week entertaining when you haven't got much time on your hands.

Serves 4
350g/12oz/2 cups raspberries
2 passion fruit
400ml/14fl oz/1⅔ cups low-fat
  fromage frais or Greek (US
  strained plain) yogurt
25g/1oz/2 tbsp caster
  (superfine) sugar
raspberries and fresh mint sprigs,
  to decorate

1 Using a fork, mash the raspberries in a small bowl until the juice runs.

2 Place the fromage frais and sugar in a separate bowl. Halve the passion fruit and scoop out the seeds. Add to the fromage frais and mix well.

3 Place alternate spoonfuls of the raspberry pulp and the fromage frais mixture into stemmed glasses or serving dishes.

4 Stir lightly to create a swirled effect. Decorate each dessert with a whole raspberry and a sprig of fresh mint. Serve chilled.

Cook's Tip
Use frozen raspberries when fresh are not available, but thaw them first. If passion fruit isn't available, flavour the yogurt mixture with finely grated orange rind instead.

Variations
This is a good recipe for using over-ripe, slightly soft fruit. The raspberries can be replaced by any summer fruit very successfully. Add chopped nuts or crumbled amaretti for added texture, but watch the fat content.

Strawberry Rose Petal Pashka

This lighter version of a traditional Russian dessert is ideal for dinner parties. The rose decoration is worth trying to do as it makes the dish look extremely pretty.

Serves 4
350g/12oz/1½ cups low-fat
  cottage cheese
175ml/6fl oz/¾ cup low-fat
  natural (plain) yogurt
30ml/2 tbsp clear honey
2.5ml/½ tsp rose water
275g/10oz/2½ cups strawberries
handful of scented pink rose
  petals, to decorate

1 Drain any free liquid from the cottage cheese and turn the cheese into a sieve (strainer). Rub it through the sieve into a bowl. Stir the yogurt, honey and rose water into the cheese.

2 Roughly chop about half the strawberries and fold them into the cheese mixture.

3 Line a new, clean flowerpot or a sieve (strainer) with fine muslin (cheesecloth) and add the cheese mixture. Leave the mixture to drain over a bowl for several hours or overnight.

4 Invert the flowerpot or sieve on to a serving plate, turn out the pashka and lift off the muslin. Cut the remaining strawberries in half and arrange them around the pashka. Scatter the rose petals over the top. Serve chilled.

Cook's Tip
Allow yourself enough time to make this dessert – for the best results, it needs to be drained overnight, then chilled well.

Variation
Use small porcelain heart-shaped moulds with draining holes for a pretty alternative.

Fruit Swirls Energy 109Kcal/466kJ; Protein 9g; Carbohydrate 18.5g, of which sugars 18.5g; Fat 0.5g, of which saturates 0.2g; Cholesterol 1mg; Calcium 111mg; Fibre 2.1g; Sodium 37mg.
Pashka Energy 153Kcal/643kJ; Protein 13.8g; Carbohydrate 15.9g, of which sugars 15.9g; Fat 3.9g, of which saturates 2.3g; Cholesterol 15mg; Calcium 206mg; Fibre 0.8g; Sodium 304mg.

Lemon Hearts with Strawberry Sauce

These elegant little hearts are perfect for a romantic celebration, such as a Valentine's Day dinner.

Serves 6

low-fat spread, for greasing
175g/6oz/1¾ cup low-fat cottage
  cheese
150ml/¼ pint/⅔ cup half-fat
  crème fraîche
15ml/1 tbsp granulated sugar
finely grated rind of ½ lemon
30ml/2 tbsp lemon juice
10ml/2 tsp powdered gelatine
2 egg whites

For the sauce

225g/8oz/2 cups fresh or frozen
  and thawed strawberries, plus
  extra to decorate
15ml/1 tbsp lemon juice

1 Lightly grease six individual heart-shaped moulds. Press the cottage cheese through a sieve (strainer) into a bowl. Beat in the crème fraîche, sugar and lemon rind.

2 Pour the lemon juice into a small heatproof bowl and sprinkle the gelatine over the surface. When it has soaked in, place the bowl over a pan of hot water and stir to dissolve the gelatine completely.

3 Quickly stir the gelatine into the cheese mixture, making sure that it is mixed in evenly.

4 Beat the egg whites in a grease-free bowl until they form soft peaks. Quickly fold them into the cheese mixture.

5 Carefully spoon the mixture into the six prepared moulds, and chill until set.

6 Make the sauce. Mix the strawberries and lemon juice in a food processor or blender and process until smooth.

7 Pour the sauce on to serving plates and then carefully invert the lemon hearts to lie on top of the sauce. Decorate with slices of strawberry.

Rice Pudding with Mixed Berry Sauce

In this recipe, a compote of red berries contrasts brilliantly with creamy rice pudding to create a delicious yet nutritionally well-balanced dessert.

Serves 6

low-fat spread, for greasing
400g/14oz/2 cups pudding
  (short-grain) rice
325ml/11fl oz/scant 1½ cups
  skimmed milk
pinch salt
115g/4oz/scant ½ cup soft light
  brown sugar
5ml/1 tsp vanilla extract
2 eggs, beaten
grated rind of 1 lemon
5ml/1 tsp lemon juice
30ml/2 tbsp low-fat spread
strawberry leaves, to
  decorate

For the sauce

225g/8oz/2 cups strawberries,
  hulled and quartered
225g/8oz/1⅓ cups raspberries
115g/4oz/½ cup granulated
  sugar
grated rind of 1 lemon

1 Preheat the oven to 160°C/325°F/Gas 3. Grease a deep 2 litre/3½ pint/8 cup baking dish. Add the rice to a pan of boiling water and boil for 5 minutes. Drain. Transfer the rice to the prepared baking dish.

2 Combine the milk, salt, brown sugar, vanilla extract, eggs, and lemon rind and juice. Pour over the rice and stir.

3 Dot the surface of the rice mixture with the spread. Bake for about 50 minutes until the rice is cooked and creamy.

4 Meanwhile, make the sauce. Mix the berries and sugar in a small pan. Stir over low heat until the sugar dissolves completely and the fruit is becoming pulpy. Transfer to a bowl and stir in the lemon rind. Cool, then chill until required.

5 Remove the rice pudding from the oven and allow to cool. Serve with the berry sauce and decorate each serving with strawberry leaves.

Lemon Hearts Energy 90Kcal/376kJ; Protein 4.7g; Carbohydrate 6.9g, of which sugars 6.5g; Fat 4.9g, of which saturates 3.2g; Cholesterol 5mg; Calcium 68mg; Fibre 0.4g; Sodium 99mg.
Rice Pudding Energy 461Kcal/1942kJ; Protein 9.7g; Carbohydrate 100.2g, of which sugars 47g; Fat 3.4g, of which saturates 0.8g; Cholesterol 66mg; Calcium 121mg; Fibre 0.8g; Sodium 63mg.

Mexican Citrus Rice Pudding

Rice is a versatile, healthy ingredient and in this Mexican recipe it is transformed into a light and attractive dessert, perfect for a family meal.

Serves 4
75g/3oz/½ cup raisins
90g/3½oz/½ cup pudding (short-grain) rice
2.5cm/1in strip of pared lime or lemon rind
250ml/8fl oz/1 cup water

475ml/16fl oz/2 cups skimmed milk
225g/8oz/1 cup granulated sugar
1.5ml/¼ tsp salt
2.5cm/1in cinnamon stick
1 egg yolk, well beaten
15ml/1 tbsp low-fat spread
10ml/2 tsp toasted flaked (sliced) almonds, to decorate
orange segments, to serve

1 Put the raisins into a small bowl. Cover with warm water and set aside to soak.

2 Put the rice into a pan together with the pared lime or lemon rind and water. Bring slowly to the boil, then lower the heat. Cover the pan and simmer gently for about 20 minutes or until all the water has been absorbed.

3 Remove the rind from the rice and discard it. Add the milk, sugar, salt and cinnamon stick. Cook, stirring, over a very low heat until all the milk has been absorbed. Do not cover the pan during cooking.

4 Discard the cinnamon stick. Drain the raisins well. Add the raisins, egg yolk and low-fat spread to the rice, stirring constantly until the spread has been absorbed and the pudding is rich and creamy.

5 Cook the pudding for a few minutes longer. Transfer the rice to a serving dish and allow to cool.

6 Decorate with the toasted flaked almonds and serve with the orange segments.

Fruited Rice Ring

This unusual chilled rice dessert ring is topped with a tasty mix of dried fruits that have been simmered until meltingly soft. The delicious combination of the fruits and rice make this a dish rich in fibre.

Serves 4
65g/2½oz/5 tbsp pudding (short-grain) rice
900ml/1½ pint/3¾ cups semi-skimmed (low-fat) milk
1 cinnamon stick
175g/6oz/1 cup mixed dried fruit
175ml/6fl oz/¾ cup orange juice
45ml/3 tbsp caster (superfine) sugar
grated rind of 1 small orange

1 Place the rice, milk and cinnamon stick in a large pan and bring to the boil. Cover and simmer, stirring occasionally, for about 1½ hours, until all the liquid has disappeared and been absorbed by the rice.

2 Meanwhile, place the fruit and orange juice in a pan and bring to the boil. Cover and simmer very gently for about 1 hour, until tender and no free liquid remains.

3 Remove the cinnamon stick from the rice and stir in the sugar and orange rind.

4 Tip the fruit into the base of a lightly oiled 1.5 litre/2½ pint/6¼ cup ring mould. Spoon the rice over, smoothing down firmly. Chill until needed.

5 Run a knife around the edge of the mould and turn out the rice carefully on to a serving plate.

> **Cook's Tip**
> *If you do not have a ring mould, you can serve the dessert in individual dishes. Roughly cut up the cooked dried fruit at the end of step 2, then stir the fruit into the rice at step 4. Carefully spoon into the dishes and chill.*

Rice Pudding Energy 421Kcal/1786kJ; Protein 7.3g; Carbohydrate 95g, of which sugars 77g; Fat 3.4g, of which saturates 1g; Cholesterol 55mg; Calcium 195mg; Fibre 0.4g; Sodium 94mg.
Rice Ring Energy 369Kcal/1566kJ; Protein 10.2g; Carbohydrate 76.8g, of which sugars 63.8g; Fat 4.1g, of which saturates 2.4g; Cholesterol 13mg; Calcium 319mg; Fibre 1g; Sodium 123mg.

Spiced Pear & Blueberry Parcels

Baked in foil parcels, the pears and blueberries happily cook in their own juices, making this a low-fat method of turning fruit into a hot dessert.

Serves 4
4 firm, ripe pears
30ml/2 tbsp lemon juice
15ml/1 tbsp low-fat spread,
  melted
150g/5oz/1¼ cups blueberries
50g/2oz/¼ cup light muscovado
  (brown) sugar
ground black pepper

1 Prepare a barbecue or preheat the oven to 200°C/400°F/Gas 6. Peel the pears thinly. Cut in half lengthways. Scoop out the core from each half. Brush the pears with lemon juice, to stop them browning.

2 Cut four squares of double-thickness foil, each large enough to wrap a pear, and brush with melted spread. Place two pear halves on each square, cut side upwards. Gather the foil around the pears, to hold them level.

3 Mix the blueberries and sugar together and spoon them on top of the pears. Sprinkle with black pepper. Wrap the foil over and make sure it is properly sealed. Cook for 20–25 minutes on the rack of a fairly hot barbecue or in the preheated oven, until the fruit is tender.

Cook's Tip
To assemble the dessert in advance, place waxed paper inside the parcel, because the acid in the lemon juice may react with the foil and taint the flavour.

Variation
Add a dash of Kirsch just before sealing the parcel, to give a sophisticated flavour to the dessert.

Fruit & Spice Bread Pudding

Made with brown bread and skimmed milk, this is a very healthy and utterly delicious version of an old favourite.

Serves 4
6 medium slices wholemeal
  (whole-wheat) bread
low-fat spread, for greasing
50g/2oz apricot or strawberry
  jam

50g/2oz/⅓ cup sultanas
  (golden raisins)
50g/2oz/¼ cup ready-to-eat dried
  apricots, chopped
50g/2oz/¼ cup soft light brown
  sugar
5ml/1 tsp mixed (apple pie) spice
2 eggs
600ml/1 pint/2½ cups skimmed
  milk
finely grated rind of 1 lemon

1 Preheat the oven to 160°C/325°F/Gas 3. Lightly grease an ovenproof dish with the spread.

2 Remove and discard the crusts from the bread. Spread the bread slices with jam and cut into small triangles.

3 Place half the bread triangles in the greased ovenproof dish, arranging them in neat rows and overlapping the pointed ends.

4 Mix together the sultanas, apricots, sugar and spice and sprinkle half the fruit mixture over the bread in the dish. Top with the remaining bread triangles and then sprinkle over the remaining fruit.

5 Beat the eggs, milk and lemon rind together in a jug (pitcher) and pour over the bread. Set aside for about 30 minutes, to allow the bread to absorb some of the liquid.

6 Bake the pudding in the oven for 45–60 minutes, until lightly set and golden brown. Serve hot or cold.

Cook's Tip
If you like, serve with fat-free yogurt as an accompaniment.

Spiced Parcels Energy 143Kcal/605kJ; Protein 1.1g; Carbohydrate 32.6g, of which sugars 32.6g; Fat 1.8g, of which saturates 0.4g; Cholesterol 0mg; Calcium 41mg; Fibre 4.5g; Sodium 31mg.
Bread Pudding Energy 303Kcal/1287kJ; Protein 12.6g; Carbohydrate 58.1g, of which sugars 39.1g; Fat 4.1g, of which saturates 1g; Cholesterol 101mg; Calcium 267mg; Fibre 1.7g; Sodium 319mg.

Fruity Bread Pudding

A delicious family favourite from grandmother's kitchen, with a lighter, healthier touch for today.

Serves 4

75g/3oz/1/2 cup mixed dried fruit
150ml/1/4 pint/2/3 cup unsweetened apple juice
115g/4oz/3–4 slices day-old brown or white bread, cubed
5ml/1 tsp mixed spice (apple pie spice)
1 large banana, sliced
150ml/1/4 pint/2/3 cup skimmed milk
15ml/1 tbsp demerara (raw) sugar
fat-free natural (plain) yogurt, to serve (optional)

1 Preheat the oven to 200°C/400°F/Gas 6. Place the dried fruit in a small pan with the apple juice and bring to the boil.

2 Remove the pan from the heat and stir in the bread cubes, spice and banana. Spoon the mixture into a shallow 1.2 litre/2 pint/5 cup ovenproof dish and pour over the milk.

3 Sprinkle the top with demerara sugar and bake in the oven for 25–30 minutes, until firm and golden brown. Serve hot or cold, with yogurt, if you like.

Baked Apples in Honey & Lemon

A classic combination of flavours in a healthy, traditional dessert.

Serves 4

4 even-size cooking apples
15ml/1 tbsp clear honey
grated rind and juice of 1 lemon
15ml/1 tbsp low-fat spread
fresh custard, made with skimmed milk, to serve (optional)

1 Preheat the oven to 180°C/350°F/Gas 4. Using an apple corer, remove the cores from the apples, taking care not to go right through the bottoms of the apples.

2 Using a zester or a sharp knife with a narrow pointed blade, cut lines through the apple skin at intervals. Stand the apples in an ovenproof dish.

3 Place the honey in a bowl and mix in the lemon rind and juice and low-fat spread.

4 Spoon the mixture into the apples and cover the dish with foil or a lid. Bake in the oven for 40-45 minutes, or until the apples are tender. Serve with fresh custard made from skimmed milk, if you like.

> **Variation**
> *You can always add dried fruit, such as chopped apricots or raisins, to the hollowed out core instead of honey – dried fruit adds natural sweetness and ups the fibre and vitamin content.*

Baked Apples with Red Wine

These mouthwatering baked apples are packed with goodness. Flavoured with a delicious filling of dried fruit soaked in spiced red wine, they are certainly worthy of a dinner party.

Serves 6

65g/2½oz/scant ½ cup sultanas (golden raisins)
350ml/12fl oz/1½ cups red wine
pinch of grated nutmeg
pinch of ground cinnamon
50g/2oz/¼ cup granulated sugar
pinch of grated lemon rind
35ml/7 tsp low-fat spread
6 even-size cooking apples

1 Put the sultanas in a small bowl and pour over the wine. Stir in the grated nutmeg, ground cinnamon, sugar and lemon rind. Cover and leave to stand for about 1 hour.

2 Preheat the oven to 190°C/375°F/Gas 5. Use a little of the low-fat spread to grease a baking dish. Using an apple corer, remove the core of each apple, without cutting right through to the bottom.

3 Divide the sultana mixture among the apples, carefully packing it into the hollows. Spoon in a little extra spiced wine. Arrange the apples in the prepared baking dish.

4 Pour the remaining wine around the apples. Top the filling in each apple with 5ml/1 tsp of the remaining spread. Bake for 40–50 minutes, or until the apples are soft but not mushy. Serve hot or at room temperature.

> **Cook's Tips**
> • *If you want to reduce the fat content to almost nothing, do not top each apple with the spread. The fat does add a certain richness to the dish, but is not completely necessary as the wine provides enough moisture in which to cook the apples.*
> • *Make sure that the apples do not overcook, as this will ruin the look and texture of the dish. Test with a knife.*

Bread Pudding Energy 178Kcal/759kJ; Protein 4.4g; Carbohydrate 40.9g, of which sugars 27g; Fat 0.8g, of which saturates 0.1g; Cholesterol 1mg; Calcium 97mg; Fibre 1.1g; Sodium 176mg.
Apples/Honey & Lemon Energy 51Kcal/216kJ; Protein 0.5g; Carbohydrate 9.3g, of which sugars 9.3g; Fat 1.6g, of which saturates 0.4g; Cholesterol 0mg; Calcium 5mg; Fibre 1.2g; Sodium 26mg.
Apples/Red Wine Energy 149Kcal/627kJ; Protein 0.9g; Carbohydrate 22.3g, of which sugars 22.3g; Fat 2.5g, of which saturates 0.7g; Cholesterol 0mg; Calcium 20mg; Fibre 1.3g; Sodium 46mg.

Sultana & Couscous Puddings

Couscous makes an interesting alternative to rice. In this recipe, it is flavoured with fruit, then steamed in moulds and turned out to make unusual fat-free desserts.

Serves 4
50g/2oz/⅓ cup sultanas (golden raisins)
475ml/16fl oz/2 cups unsweetened apple juice
90g/3½oz/generous 1 cup couscous
2.5ml/½ tsp mixed spice (apple pie spice)
fresh skimmed milk custard, to serve (optional)

1 Lightly grease four 250ml/8fl oz/1 cup heatproof bowls. Place the sultanas and apple juice in a pan.

2 Bring the apple juice to the boil, then lower the heat and simmer the mixture gently for 2–3 minutes, to plump up the fruit. Lift out about half of the fruit and place it in the bottom of the bowls.

3 Add the couscous and mixed spice to the pan and bring the liquid back to the boil, stirring. Cover and leave over a low heat for 8–10 minutes, or until all the liquid has been absorbed.

4 Spoon the couscous into the bowls, level the surfaces, then cover the bowls tightly with foil. Place the bowls in a steamer over boiling water, cover and steam for about 30 minutes. Run a knife around the edges, turn the puddings out carefully and serve straight away, with skimmed milk custard, if you like.

> **Cook's Tips**
> • If you prefer, these delicious puddings can easily be cooked in a microwave oven instead of steaming over boiling water. To do this, simply use individual microwave-safe basins or teacups, cover them and then microwave on High for approximately 8–10 minutes.

Baked Peaches with Raspberry Sauce

It's always a good idea to round off a meal on a light and fruity note. Everyone will enjoy these stuffed peaches, which also look very pretty.

Serves 4
30ml/2 tbsp low-fat spread
50g/2oz/¼ cup granulated sugar
1 egg, beaten
25g/1oz/¼ cup ground almonds
6 ripe peaches
glossy leaves and plain or frosted raspberries, to decorate

For the sauce
350g/12oz/2 cups raspberries
15ml/1 tbsp icing (confectioners') sugar

1 Preheat the oven to 180°C/350°F/Gas 4. Beat the low-fat spread and sugar together in a bowl, then beat in the egg and ground almonds.

2 Cut the peaches in half and remove the stones (pits). With a spoon, scrape out some of the flesh from each peach half, slightly enlarging the hollow left by the stone. Save the excess peach flesh for the sauce.

3 Stand the peach halves on a baking sheet, supporting them with crumpled foil to keep them steady. Fill the hollow in each peach half with the almond mixture.

4 Bake in the preheated oven for 30 minutes, or until the almond filling is puffed and golden and the peaches are tender.

5 Meanwhile, make the sauce. Combine the raspberries and icing sugar in a food processor or blender. Add the reserved peach flesh and process until smooth. Press through a sieve (strainer) set over a bowl, to remove the fibres and seeds.

6 Allow the peaches to cool slightly. Spoon the sauce on to each plate and arrange two peach halves on top. Decorate with the leaves and raspberries and serve immediately.

Couscous Puddings Energy 131Kcal/555kJ; Protein 1.8g; Carbohydrate 32g, of which sugars 20.4g; Fat 0.4g, of which saturates 0g; Cholesterol 0mg; Calcium 21mg; Fibre 0.3g; Sodium 5mg.
Baked Peaches Energy 223Kcal/945kJ; Protein 6.1g; Carbohydrate 33.5g, of which sugars 33.3g; Fat 8.3g, of which saturates 1.6g; Cholesterol 48mg; Calcium 64mg; Fibre 4.8g; Sodium 72mg.

Strawberry & Apple Crumble

A high-fibre, low-fat version of the classic apple crumble that will appeal to both children and adults alike.

2.5ml/½ tsp ground cinnamon
30ml/2 tbsp orange juice
low-fat custard or yogurt, to serve
  (optional)

Serves 4
450g/1lb cooking apples
150g/5oz/1¼ cups strawberries,
  hulled
25g/1oz/2 tbsp caster
  (superfine) sugar

For the crumble
45g/1¾oz/3 tbsp plain
  (all-purpose) wholemeal
  (whole-wheat) flour
50g/2oz/⅔ cup rolled oats
30ml/2 tbsp low-fat spread

1 Preheat the oven to 180°C/350°F/Gas 4. Peel, core and cut the apples into approximately 5mm/¼in size slices. Halve the strawberries.

2 Toss together the apples, strawberries, sugar, cinnamon and orange juice. Transfer the mixture to a 1.2 litre/2 pint/5 cup ovenproof dish.

3 Make the crumble. Combine the flour and oats in a bowl and mix in the low-fat spread with a fork.

4 Sprinkle the crumble evenly over the fruit. Bake for 40–45 minutes, until golden brown and bubbling. Serve warm, with low-fat custard or yogurt, if you like.

Cook's Tip
Strawberries and apples are a good source of Vitamin C, which plays an important role in a healthy diet.

Variations
Blackberries, raspberries or redcurrants can be used instead of the strawberries very successfully.

Chunky Apple Bake

An apple a day keeps the doctor away, as they say. Apples are certainly a good source of Vitamin C and fibre, so this wholesome dish is full of goodness.

Serves 4
450g/1lb cooking apples
75g/3oz wholemeal (whole-
  wheat) bread, crusts removed
115g/4oz/½ cup low-fat cottage
  cheese
40g/1½oz/3 tbsp light
  muscovado (brown) sugar
200ml/7fl oz/scant 1 cup
  skimmed milk
5ml/1 tsp demerara (raw) sugar

1 Preheat the oven to 220°C/425°F/Gas 7. Peel the apples, cut them into quarters and remove the cores.

2 Using a sharp knife, roughly chop the apples into even-size pieces, about 1cm/½in in width and depth.

3 Cut the bread into 1cm/½in cubes. Do not use crusts as these will be too thick for the mixture.

4 Put the apples in a bowl and add the bread cubes, cottage cheese and muscovado sugar. Toss lightly to mix.

5 Stir in the skimmed milk and then turn the mixture into a wide ovenproof dish. Sprinkle demerara sugar over the top of the mixture.

6 Bake for 30–35 minutes, or until the apple bake is golden brown and bubbling. Serve hot.

Cook's Tip
You may need to adjust the amount of milk used, depending on the dryness of the bread; the staler it is, the more milk it will absorb. The texture should be very moist but not falling apart.

Strawb. & Apple Crumble Energy 200Kcal/846kJ; Protein 3.8g; Carbohydrate 38.7g, of which sugars 21g; Fat 4.4g, of which saturates 0.9g; Cholesterol 0mg; Calcium 41mg; Fibre 3.4g; Sodium 59mg.
Apple Bake Energy 170Kcal/721kJ; Protein 7.4g; Carbohydrate 32.7g, of which sugars 25.2g; Fat 1.9g, of which saturates 0.7g; Cholesterol 6mg; Calcium 120mg; Fibre 2.9g; Sodium 213mg.

Kumquat Compote

Warm, spicy and full of sun-
ripened ingredients, this is
the perfect winter dessert
to remind you of long
summer days – and to keep
you in good shape.

Serves 4
200g/7oz/2 cups kumquats
200g/7oz/scant 1 cup ready-to-
eat dried apricots
30ml/2 tbsp sultanas
(golden raisins)

400ml/14fl oz/1²⁄₃ cups water
1 orange
2.5cm/1in piece of fresh root
ginger
4 cardamom pods
4 cloves
30ml/2 tbsp clear honey
15ml/1 tbsp flaked (sliced)
almonds, toasted

1 Wash the kumquats, and, if they are large, cut them in half.
Place them in a pan with the dried apricots, sultanas and water.
Bring to the boil.

2 Pare the orange rind and add to the pan. Peel and grate the
ginger and add to the pan. Crush the cardamom pods and add
the seeds to the mixture, with the cloves.

3 Reduce the heat, cover the pan and leave to simmer gently
for about 30 minutes, or until the kumquats are tender, stirring
occasionally during cooking.

4 Squeeze the juice of the orange into the compote. Sweeten
with the honey, sprinkle with the almonds and serve warm.

Cook's Tips
• Kumquats, which look like tiny oranges, can be eaten whole
as their skins are thin and sweet tasting. They provide a
delicious, distinctive citrus flavour to sweet and savoury dishes.
Their season is short – if they are unavailable, use orange
segments or sliced, peeled clementines instead.
• Try a full-flavoured honey made from clover, acacia or thyme.

Baked Fruit Compote

This marvellous medley of
dried fruit is the ultimate
high-fibre dessert and is filled
with natural sweetness.

Serves 6
115g/4oz/²⁄₃ cup ready-to-eat
dried figs
115g/4oz/¹⁄₂ cup ready-to-eat
dried apricots
50g/2oz/¹⁄₂ cup ready-to-eat dried
apple rings
50g/2oz/¹⁄₄ cup ready-to-eat prunes

50g/2oz/¹⁄₂ cup ready-to-eat
dried pears
50g/2oz/¹⁄₂ cup ready-to-eat
dried peaches
300ml/¹⁄₂ pint/1¹⁄₄ cups
unsweetened apple juice
300ml/¹⁄₂ pint/1¹⁄₄ cups
unsweetened orange juice
6 cloves
1 cinnamon stick
a few toasted flaked (sliced)
almonds, to decorate

1 Preheat the oven to 180°C/350°F/Gas 4. Place the figs,
apricots, apple rings, prunes, pears and peaches in a shallow
ovenproof dish and stir to mix.

2 Mix together the unsweetened apple and orange juices and
pour evenly over the fruit. Add the cloves and cinnamon stick
and stir gently to mix. Make sure that all the fruit has been
thoroughly coated with the apple and orange juices.

3 Bake for about 30 minutes until the fruit mixture is hot,
stirring once or twice during cooking. Set aside and leave to
soak for 20 minutes. Discard the cloves and cinnamon stick.

4 Spoon the compote into serving bowls and serve warm or
cold, decorated with toasted flaked almonds.

Fresh Figs with Honey & Wine

Fresh figs are naturally
sweet, and they taste
wonderful in a honeyed
wine syrup.

Serves 6
450ml/³⁄₄ pint/scant 2 cups dry
white wine
75g/3oz/¹⁄₃ cup clear honey
50g/2oz/¹⁄₄ cup caster
(superfine) sugar

1 small orange
8 whole cloves
450g/1lb fresh figs
1 cinnamon stick
bay leaves, to decorate

For the sauce
300ml/¹⁄₂ pint/1¹⁄₄ cups low-fat
Greek (US strained plain) yogurt
5ml/1 tsp pure vanilla extract
5ml/1 tsp caster (superfine) sugar

1 Put the wine, honey and sugar in a heavy pan and heat gently
until the sugar dissolves.

2 Stud the orange with the cloves and add to the syrup with
the figs and cinnamon. Cover and simmer until the figs are soft.
Transfer to a serving dish and cool.

3 Flavour the yogurt with the vanilla and sugar and spoon into
a serving dish. With a sharp knife, cut one or two of the figs in
half, if you like, to show off their pretty centres. Decorate with
the bay leaves and serve with the yogurt.

Kumquat Energy 348Kcal/1482kJ; Protein 5.3g; Carbohydrate 80.7g, of which sugars 80.6g; Fat 2.8g, of which saturates 0.2g; Cholesterol 0mg; Calcium 110mg; Fibre 5.5g; Sodium 25mg.
Baked Fruit Energy 160Kcal/683kJ; Protein 3g; Carbohydrate 37.8g, of which sugars 37.8g; Fat 0.7g, of which saturates 0g; Cholesterol 0mg; Calcium 91mg; Fibre 4.7g; Sodium 24mg.
Fresh Figs Energy 225Kcal/954kJ; Protein 3.9g; Carbohydrate 41g, of which sugars 41g; Fat 1g, of which saturates 0.3g; Cholesterol 1mg; Calcium 191mg; Fibre 2.5g; Sodium 67mg.

Plum, Apple & Banana Scone Pie

A simple, satisfying dish, the scrumptious topping hides a delicious mix of fruits.

Serves 4
450g/1lb plums
1 cooking apple
1 large banana
150ml/¼ cup/⅔ cup water

115g/4oz/1 cup wholemeal (whole-wheat) flour
10ml/2 tsp baking powder
45ml/3 tbsp raisins
50ml/2fl oz/¼ cup soured milk or low-fat natural (plain) yogurt
low-fat natural yogurt, to serve (optional)

1 Preheat the oven to 180°C/350°F/Gas 4. Cut the plums in half and ease out the stones (pits). Peel, core and chop the apple, then slice the banana.

2 Mix together all of the cut-up fruit in a pan. Pour in the water. Bring the mixture to simmering point and cook gently for about 15 minutes, or until all of the fruit is completely soft.

3 Spoon the cooked fruit mixture into a pie dish. Level the top.

4 Mix the flour, baking powder and raisins in a bowl. Add the soured milk or yogurt and mix to make a very soft dough.

5 Transfer the scone dough to a lightly floured surface and divide it up into 6–8 portions. Pat the dough portions into flattish scones.

6 Cover the plum and apple mixture with the scones. Bake the pie for about 40 minutes, or until the scone topping is completely cooked through. Serve with yogurt, if you like.

Almond Tart

This lower-fat version of a favourite tart is easy to make and bursts with nutty flavour.

Serves 4
225g/8oz puff pastry
30ml/2 tbsp raspberry or apricot jam

2 eggs
2 egg yolks
generous 50g/2oz/¼ cup caster (superfine) sugar
115g/4oz/½ cup butter, melted
50g/2oz/½ cup ground almonds
few drops of almond extract
icing (confectioners') sugar, for sifting

1 Preheat the oven to 200°C/400°F/Gas 6. Roll out the pastry on a lightly floured surface and use it to line an 18cm/7in pie plate or loose-bottomed flan tin (tart pan). Spread the jam over the bottom of the pastry case.

2 Whisk the eggs, egg yolks and sugar together in a large bowl until thick and pale. Gently stir the butter, ground almonds and almond extract into the mixture.

3 Pour the mixture into the pastry case and bake for about 30 minutes, until the filling is just set and browned. Sift icing sugar over the top before serving the tart hot, warm or cold.

Apple Brown Betty

A traditional favourite, this tasty dish is made up of delicious layers of lightly spiced toasted breadcrumbs and apples. It is very warming and satisfying, yet at the same time low in fat. Delicious served with fat-free yogurt.

Serves 6
50g/2oz/¾ cup fresh breadcrumbs
low-fat spread, for greasing
175g/6oz/1 cup light muscovado (brown) sugar
2.5ml/½ tsp ground cinnamon
1.5ml/¼ tsp ground cloves
1.5ml/¼ tsp grated nutmeg
900g/2lb eating apples
juice of 1 lemon
30ml/2 tbsp low-fat spread
20g/¾oz/3 tbsp finely chopped walnuts

1 Preheat the grill (broiler). Spread the breadcrumbs on a baking sheet and toast under the grill until golden, stirring so that they colour evenly. Set aside.

2 Preheat the oven to 190°C/375°F/Gas 5. Grease a 2 litre/3½ pint/8 cup baking dish.

3 Place the sugar in a medium-size mixing bowl and add the ground cinnamon, cloves and grated nutmeg. Mix well together.

4 Peel, core and slice the apples. Toss the apple slices with the lemon juice to prevent them from turning brown.

5 Sprinkle about 45ml/3 tbsp of the breadcrumbs over the bottom of the prepared dish. Cover with one-third of the apples and sprinkle one-third of the sugar-spice mixture on top.

6 Add another layer of breadcrumbs and dot with one-quarter of the spread. Repeat the layers two more times, ending with a layer of breadcrumbs. Sprinkle with the nuts, and dot with the remaining spread.

7 Bake for 35–40 minutes, until the apples are tender and the top is golden brown. Serve warm.

Scone Pie Energy 211Kcal/895kJ; Protein 5.2g; Carbohydrate 42.7g, of which sugars 24.5g; Fat 3.4g, of which saturates 1.7g; Cholesterol 8mg; Calcium 44mg; Fibre 5.1g; Sodium 16mg.
Almond Tart Energy 577Kcal/2394kJ; Protein 10.6g; Carbohydrate 24.4g, of which sugars 4g; Fat 49.9g, of which saturates 17.1g; Cholesterol 257mg; Calcium 94mg; Fibre 0.9g; Sodium 391mg.
Apple Brown Betty Energy 232Kcal/987kJ; Protein 2.3g; Carbohydrate 48.5g, of which sugars 42.3g; Fat 4.6g, of which saturates 0.8g; Cholesterol 0mg; Calcium 36mg; Fibre 2.7g; Sodium 101mg.

Blueberry Buckle

This wholesome dessert is an American speciality. A great way to turn vitamin-rich, juicy blueberries into a hearty family dessert.

175ml/6fl oz/³/4 cup skimmed milk
450g/1lb/4 cups fresh blueberries
low-fat Greek (US strained plain) yogurt, to serve (optional)

Serves 8

low-fat spread, for greasing
225g/8oz/2 cups plain (all-purpose) flour
10ml/2 tsp baking powder
2.5ml/¹/2 tsp salt
30ml/2 tbsp low-fat spread
175g/6oz/³/4 cup caster (superfine) sugar
1 egg
2.5ml/¹/2 tsp vanilla extract

For the topping

115g/4oz/scant ¹/2 cup soft light brown sugar
50g/2oz/¹/2 cup plain (all-purpose) flour
2.5ml/¹/2 tsp salt
2.5ml/¹/2 tsp ground allspice
45ml/3 tbsp low-fat spread
10ml/2 tsp skimmed milk
5ml/1 tsp pure vanilla extract

1 Preheat the oven to 190°C/375°F/Gas 5. Grease a 23cm/9in round gratin dish or shallow baking dish. Sift the flour, baking powder and salt into a bowl. Set aside.

2 Cream the low-fat spread and the sugar. Beat in the egg and vanilla extract. Add the flour mixture alternately with the milk, beginning and ending with flour.

3 Pour the mixture into the prepared dish and sprinkle over the blueberries.

4 Make the topping. Mix the brown sugar, flour, salt and allspice in a bowl. Rub in the spread with your fingertips until the mixture resembles coarse breadcrumbs.

5 Mix the milk and vanilla extract together. Drizzle over the flour mixture and mix with a fork. Sprinkle the topping over the blueberries. Bake for 45 minutes, or until a skewer inserted in the centre comes out clean. Serve warm, with low-fat Greek yogurt, if you like.

Cornflake-Topped Peach Bake

With just a few basic storecupboard ingredients, this healthy, crisp-crusted dish can be rustled up in next to no time. Just the job for an instant family meal.

Serves 4

415g/14¹/2oz can peach slices in juice
30ml/2 tbsp sultanas (golden raisins)
1 cinnamon stick
strip of pared orange rind
30ml/2 tbsp low-fat spread
50g/2oz/1¹/2 cups cornflakes
10ml/2 tsp sesame seeds

1 Preheat the oven to 200°C/400°F/Gas 6. Drain the peaches, reserving the juice in a small pan. Arrange the peach slices in a shallow ovenproof dish.

2 Add the sultanas, cinnamon stick and orange rind to the juice and bring to the boil. Lower the heat and simmer, for 3–4 minutes, to reduce the liquid by half. Remove the cinnamon stick and rind and spoon the syrup over the peaches.

3 Melt the low-fat spread in a small pan, stir in the cornflakes and sesame seeds.

4 Spread the cornflake mixture over the fruit. Bake for 15–20 minutes, or until the topping is crisp and golden. Serve hot.

Variations

• Try experimenting with the breakfast cereal for the topping – the lowest-calorie breakfast cereals are usually those that are highest in fibre, so it is worth checking the labels for comparisons. Bran cereals are a good choice.
• You could use chopped nuts instead of the sesame seeds, but remember that this will increase the fat content.
• Any canned fruit can be used in place of the peaches. Apricots would be delicious, as would pineapple chunks. Make sure they are in their own natural juice.

Blueberry Buckle Energy 329Kcal/1396kJ; Protein 6.4g; Carbohydrate 73.8g, of which sugars 42.4g; Fat 2.9g, of which saturates 0.7g; Cholesterol 25mg; Calcium 133mg; Fibre 3g; Sodium 48mg.
Peach Bake Energy 152Kcal/641kJ; Protein 2.7g; Carbohydrate 26.5g, of which sugars 16.4g; Fat 4.6g, of which saturates 1.1g; Cholesterol 0mg; Calcium 29mg; Fibre 1.3g; Sodium 188mg.

Barbecued Bananas with Spicy Vanilla Spread

Baked bananas are a must for the barbecue. As they are baked in their own skins, they create a fat-free dessert, and need no preparation at all. The vanilla and brandy spread adds a touch of luxury to the dish.

Serves 4
4 bananas
6 green cardamom pods
1 vanilla pod (bean)
finely grated rind of 1 small orange
30ml/2 tbsp brandy
50g/2oz/¼ cup light muscovado (brown) sugar
40g/1½oz/3 tbsp cup low-fat spread

1 Place the bananas, in their skins, on the hot barbecue and leave for 6–8 minutes, turning occasionally, until the skins are a brownish-black.

2 Meanwhile, split the cardamom pods and remove the seeds. Place the seeds in a mortar and crush lightly with a pestle.

3 Split the vanilla pod lengthways and scrape out the tiny seeds. Mix with the cardamom seeds, orange rind, brandy, sugar and spread, to make a thick paste.

4 Using a sharp knife, slit the skin of each banana and gently open out slightly. Spoon a little of the paste along each banana and serve immediately.

> **Cook's Tips**
> • *If making this for children, use orange juice instead of the brandy or, if the fat content is no object, drizzle the cooked bananas with melted chocolate.*
> • *Bananas are a particularly nutritious fruit as they are rich in vitamins and minerals and have a good fibre content. Available throughout the year, they provide a healthy addition to the diet.*

Hot Spiced Bananas

Baking bananas in a rum and fruit syrup makes for a dessert with negligible fat and maximum flavour. Very easy to prepare, this dish is a delicious dish for impromptu entertaining.

Serves 6
low-fat spread, for greasing
6 ripe bananas
200g/7oz/1 cup light muscovado (brown) sugar
250ml/8fl oz/1 cup unsweetened pineapple juice
120ml/4fl oz/½ cup dark rum
2 cinnamon sticks
12 whole cloves

1 Preheat the oven to 180°C/350°F/Gas 4. Using low-fat spread, grease a 23cm/9in baking dish.

2 Peel the bananas and cut them diagonally into 2.5cm/1in pieces. Arrange the banana pieces evenly over the bottom of the prepared baking dish.

3 Mix the sugar and pineapple juice in a pan. Heat gently until the sugar has dissolved, stirring occasionally. Add the rum, cinnamon sticks and cloves. Bring to the boil, then remove the pan from the heat.

4 Pour the hot pineapple and spice mixture over the bananas in the baking dish. Bake in the preheated oven for about 25–30 minutes until the bananas are hot and very tender.

5 Divide the hot bananas between individual dishes, arranging them in a neat pattern. Serve immediately.

> **Cook's Tip**
> *For an accompaniment that won't add too much to the fat content of this dessert, make your own frozen yogurt by churning an extra low-fat yogurt in an ice-cream maker until it has thickened. Serve a scoop with each serving.*

Barbecued Bananas Energy 215Kcal/905kJ; Protein 1.9g; Carbohydrate 38.9g, of which sugars 36.6g; Fat 4.9g, of which saturates 1.4g; Cholesterol 1mg; Calcium 18mg; Fibre 1.1g; Sodium 75mg.
Spiced Bananas Energy 288Kcal/1221kJ; Protein 1.5g; Carbohydrate 62.4g, of which sugars 60.1g; Fat 0.3g, of which saturates 0.1g; Cholesterol 0mg; Calcium 27mg; Fibre 1.1g; Sodium 6mg.

Caribbean Bananas

Tender baked bananas for a a feel-good dessert.

Serves 4
30ml/2 tbsp low-fat spread
8 firm ripe bananas
juice of 1 lime
75g/3oz/6 tbsp soft dark brown
   sugar
5ml/1 tsp ground allspice
2.5ml/½ tsp ground ginger
seeds from 6 cardamoms, crushed
30ml/2 tbsp rum
pared lime rind, to decorate
half-fat crème fraîche, to serve
   (optional)

1 Preheat the oven to 200°C/400°F/Gas 6. Use a little of the spread to grease a shallow baking dish large enough to hold the bananas snugly in a single layer.

2 Peel the bananas and cut them in half lengthways. Arrange the bananas in the dish and pour over the lime juice.

3 Mix the sugar, allspice, ginger and crushed cardamom seeds in a bowl. Scatter the mixture over the bananas. Dot with the remaining low-fat spread. Bake, basting once, for 15 minutes, or until the bananas are soft.

4 Remove the dish from the oven. Warm the rum in a small pan or metal ladle, pour it over the bananas and set it alight.

5 As soon as the flames die down, decorate the dessert with the pared lime rind. Serve while still hot and add a dollop of low-fat crème fraîche to each portion, if you like.

Mulled Pears with Ginger & Brandy

Whole pears flavoured with spices and brandy – hard to beat as a simple yet elegant low-fat fruit dessert.

Serves 8
600ml/1 pint/2½ cups red wine
200g/7oz/1 cup sugar
1 cinnamon stick
6 cloves
finely grated rind of 1 orange
5ml/2 tsp grated fresh root ginger
8 even-size firm pears, with stems
15ml/1 tbsp brandy
25g/1oz/¼ cup almonds or
   hazelnuts, toasted, to decorate
low-fat whipped cream, to serve
   (optional)

1 Put all the ingredients except the pears, brandy and nuts into a pan large enough to hold the pears and heat slowly until the sugar has dissolved. Simmer for 5 minutes.

2 Peel the pears, leaving the stems on, and arrange upright in the pan. Cover and simmer for 45–50 minutes until tender.

3 Gently remove the pears from the syrup with a slotted spoon, being very careful not to dislodge the stems. Put the cooked pears in a serving bowl or individual bowls.

4 Boil the syrup until it thickens and reduces. Cool slightly, add the brandy and strain over the pears. Decorate with toasted nuts. Serve with whipped cream, if you like.

Floating Islands in Hot Plum Sauce

A low-fat version of the French classic that is simpler to make than it looks. The plum sauce can be made in advance, and reheated just before you cook the meringues.

Serves 4
450g/1lb red plums
300ml/½ pint/1¼ cups apple
   juice
2 egg whites
30ml/2 tbsp concentrated apple
   juice syrup
freshly grated nutmeg, to serve

1 Halve the plums and remove the stones (pits). Place them in a wide pan, with the apple juice.

2 Bring to the boil, then cover with a lid and leave to simmer gently for 20–30 minutes or until the plums are tender.

3 Place the egg whites in a grease-free, dry bowl and whisk until they form soft peaks.

4 Gradually whisk in the apple juice syrup, whisking until the meringue holds fairly firm peaks.

5 Using a tablespoon, scoop the meringue mixture into the gently simmering plum sauce. You may need to cook the "islands" in two batches.

6 Cover and allow to simmer gently for 2–3 minutes, until the meringues are just set. Serve immediately, sprinkled with a little freshly grated nutmeg.

Cook's Tips
• *To make a neatly shaped "island", scoop up a round of beaten egg white and lightly mould into an oval shape using two spoons before placing in the simmering sauce.*
• *A bottle of concentrated apple juice is a useful store-cupboard (pantry) sweetener, but if you don't have any, use a little honey instead.*

Caribbean Bananas Energy 310Kcal/1311kJ; Protein 2.9g; Carbohydrate 66g, of which sugars 61.4g; Fat 3.7g, of which saturates 1.1g; Cholesterol 0mg; Calcium 25mg; Fibre 2.2g; Sodium 52mg.
Mulled Pears Energy 233Kcal/982kJ; Protein 1.3g; Carbohydrate 41.5g, of which sugars 41.4g; Fat 1.9g, of which saturates 0.1g; Cholesterol 0mg; Calcium 43mg; Fibre 3.5g; Sodium 12mg.
Floating Islands Energy 97Kcal/417kJ; Protein 2.2g; Carbohydrate 23.3g, of which sugars 23.3g; Fat 0.2g, of which saturates 0g; Cholesterol 0mg; Calcium 22mg; Fibre 1.8g; Sodium 55mg.

Grilled Nectarines with Ricotta & Spice

An irresistibly delicious combination of fresh nectarines and smooth ricotta cheese flavoured with star anise, this fresh fruit dessert can be put together in minutes. Canned peach halves can be used if fresh ones are not available.

Serves 4

4 ripe nectarines or peaches
15ml/1 tbsp light muscovado (brown) sugar
115g/4oz/½ cup ricotta cheese or fromage frais
2.5ml/½ tsp ground star anise

1 Cut the nectarines in half and remove the stones (pits).

2 Arrange the nectarines, cut side upwards, in a wide flameproof dish or on a baking sheet.

3 Stir the sugar into the ricotta or fromage frais. Using a teaspoon, carefully spoon the mixture into the hollow of each nectarine half.

4 Sprinkle with the star anise. Place under a moderately hot grill (broiler) for 6–8 minutes, or until the nectarines are hot and bubbling. Serve warm.

Cook's Tips

• Star anise has a warm, rich flavour that instantly imparts a distinctive Oriental touch to all kinds of dessert dishes. Try making a fruit and star anise jam to make a tasty topping for grilled (broiled) fruit and pancakes or muffins. Simply simmer some fruits of your choice with sugar, fruit juices, a little fruit rind, spices to taste and a couple of star anise. Melon works particularly well with star anise. Store the jam cold in sterilized jars, or serve up immediately.
• If you can't obtain star anise, try ground cloves or mixed (apple pie) spice instead.

Cherry Pancakes

These pancakes are virtually fat free, and lower in calories and higher in fibre than traditional ones. They also freeze well, which is handy – layer the pancakes, separated by waxed paper, before freezing.

Serves 4

50g/2oz/½ cup plain (all-purpose) flour
50g/2oz/½ cup plain wholemeal (all-purpose whole-wheat) flour

pinch of salt
1 egg white
150ml/¼ pint/⅔ cup skimmed milk
150ml/¼ pint/⅔ cup water
a little oil, for frying

For the filling

425g/15oz can black cherries in juice
7.5ml/1½ tsp arrowroot

1 Sift the flours and salt into a bowl, adding any bran left in the sieve (strainer) to the bowl at the end.

2 Make a well in the centre of the flour and add the egg white. Gradually beat in the milk and the water, whisking hard until all the liquid is incorporated and the batter is smooth and bubbly.

3 Heat a non-stick pan with a small amount of oil until the pan is very hot. Pour in just enough batter to cover the base of the pan, swirling the pan to cover the base evenly.

4 Cook until the pancake is set and golden, and then turn to cook the other side. Remove to a sheet of kitchen paper and then cook the remaining batter to make about eight pancakes.

5 Drain the cherries, reserving the juice. Blend about 30ml/ 2 tbsp of the juice from the can of cherries with the arrowroot in a pan. Stir in the rest of the juice. Heat gently, stirring, until boiling. Stir over a moderate heat for about 2 minutes, until thickened and clear.

6 Add the cherries and stir until thoroughly heated. Spoon the cherries into the pancakes and fold them into quarters.

Grilled Nectarines Energy 118Kcal/499kJ; Protein 4.5g; Carbohydrate 16.5g, of which sugars 16.5g; Fat 4.3g, of which saturates 2.6g; Cholesterol 12mg; Calcium 11mg; Fibre 1.6g; Sodium 2mg.
Cherry Pancakes Energy 200Kcal/852kJ; Protein 4.9g; Carbohydrate 40.7g, of which sugars 21.7g; Fat 3.2g, of which saturates 0.4g; Cholesterol 1mg; Calcium 97mg; Fibre 1.4g; Sodium 41mg.

Crunchy Gooseberry Crumble

Combining gooseberries with an oat and nut crumble topping gives this popular family pudding a high-fibre slant. The result is a dessert that will both satisfy and delight everyone.

Serves 4

500g/1¼lb/5 cups gooseberries
50g/2oz/4 tbsp caster
*   (superfine) sugar*
75g/3oz/scant 1 cup rolled oats
75g/3oz/⅔ cup wholemeal
*   (whole-wheat) flour*
60ml/4 tbsp sunflower oil
50g/2oz/4 tbsp demerara
*   (raw) sugar*
30ml/2 tbsp chopped walnuts
low-fat natural (plain) yogurt or
*   custard, to serve*

1 Preheat the oven to 200°C/400°F/Gas 6. Place the gooseberries in a pan with the caster sugar. Cover the pan and cook over a low heat for 10 minutes, until the gooseberries are just tender. Transfer to an ovenproof dish.

2 Make the crumble. Place the oats, flour and oil in a bowl and stir with a fork until evenly mixed.

3 Stir in the demerara sugar and walnuts, then spread evenly over the gooseberries. Bake for 25–30 minutes, or until golden and bubbling. Serve hot with yogurt, or custard made with skimmed milk.

> **Cook's Tip**
> *The best gooseberries to use are the early cooking varieties, which are firm and green with a sour taste. The eating gooseberries vary more in colour and usually have softer flesh.*

> **Variation**
> *When gooseberries are out of season, try making this crumble with other fruits such as apples, plums or rhubarb.*

Tofu Berry "Cheesecake"

This summery "cheesecake" is a light and refreshing finish to any meal. Strictly speaking, it is not really a cheesecake at all, as it is based on tofu – but who would guess?

Serves 6

50g/2oz/4 tbsp low-fat spread
30ml/2 tbsp apple juice
115g/4oz/6 cups bran flakes or
*   other high-fibre cereal*

For the filling
275g/10oz/1¼ cups tofu or
*   skimmed-milk soft cheese*

200g/7oz/scant 1 cup low-fat
*   natural (plain) yogurt*
15ml/1 tbsp/1 sachet powdered
*   gelatine*
60ml/4 tbsp apple juice

For the topping
175g/6oz/1¾ cups mixed
*   summer soft fruit, such as*
*   strawberries, raspberries,*
*   redcurrants, blackberries, etc.*
*   (or frozen "fruits of the forest")*
30ml/2 tbsp redcurrant jelly
30ml/2 tbsp hot water

1 For the base, place the low-fat spread and apple juice in a pan and heat them gently until the spread has melted. Crush the cereal and stir it into the pan.

2 Turn into a 23cm/9in round flan tin (tart pan) and press down firmly. Leave to set.

3 Make the filling. Place the tofu or cheese and yogurt in a blender or food processor and process until smooth. Dissolve the gelatine in the apple juice and stir the juice immediately into the tofu mixture.

4 Spread the tofu mixture over the chilled cereal base, smoothing it evenly. Place in the refrigerator until the filling is firm and set.

5 Remove the flan tin and transfer the cheesecake to a serving plate. Arrange the mixed summer fruits over the top. Melt the redcurrant jelly with the hot water to make a glaze, allow it cool, then spoon over the fruit and serve.

Gooseberry Crumble Energy 406Kcal/1706kJ; Protein 7.3g; Carbohydrate 55.8g, of which sugars 30.5g; Fat 18.7g, of which saturates 1.8g; Cholesterol 0mg; Calcium 73mg; Fibre 6.2g; Sodium 11mg.
Tofu "Cheesecake" Energy 175Kcal/735kJ; Protein 8.1g; Carbohydrate 23.2g, of which sugars 13.7g; Fat 6.1g, of which saturates 1.4g; Cholesterol 1mg; Calcium 314mg; Fibre 2.8g; Sodium 241mg.

Apricot & Orange Roulade

Guests will be pleased to know that this elegant dessert has a very low fat content.

Serves 6
low-fat spread, for greasing
4 egg whites
115g/4oz/generous ½ cup golden caster (superfine) sugar
50g/2oz/½ cup plain (all-purpose) flour
finely grated rind of 1 small orange
45ml/3 tbsp orange juice

For the filling
115g/4oz/½ cup ready-to-eat dried apricots
150ml/¼ pint/⅔ cup orange juice
10ml/2 tsp icing (confectioners') sugar, for sprinkling
shreds of orange rind, to decorate

1 Preheat the oven to 200°C/400°F/Gas 6. Grease a 23 x 33cm/9 x 13in Swiss roll tin (jelly roll pan) and line it with baking parchment. Grease the paper.

2 Make the roulade. Pace the egg whites in a large clean bowl and whisk until they hold soft peaks. Gradually add the sugar, whisking vigorously between each addition.

3 Fold in the flour, orange rind and juice. Spoon the mixture into the prepared tin and spread it evenly.

4 Bake for 15–18 minutes, or until the sponge is firm and light golden in colour. Turn out on to a sheet of baking parchment and roll it up loosely from one short side. Leave to cool.

5 Roughly chop the dried apricots and put in a pan, with the orange juice. Cover the pan and leave to simmer until most of the liquid has been absorbed. Purée in a blender or food processor until smooth.

6 Unroll the roulade, spread the surface with the apricot mixture, then roll up. To decorate, arrange strips of paper diagonally across the roll, then sprinkle lightly with lines of icing sugar. Remove the paper, scatter the top of the roulade with orange rind and serve.

Filo Chiffon Pie

Filo pastry is low in fat and is very easy to use. Keep a pack in the freezer, ready to make impressive desserts like this one.

Serves 3
500g/1¼lb pink rhubarb
5ml/1 tsp mixed spice (apple pie spice)
finely grated rind and juice of 1 orange
15ml/1 tbsp caster (superfine) sugar
15g/½oz/1 tbsp butter
3 sheets filo pastry

1 Preheat the oven to 200°C/400°F/Gas 6. Trim the leaves and ends from the rhubarb sticks and chop them in to 2.5cm/1in pieces. Place in a bowl.

2 Add the mixed spice, orange rind and juice and sugar and toss well to coat evenly. Transfer the rhubarb to a 1 litre/1¾ pint/4 cup pie dish.

3 Melt the butter and brush it over the pastry sheets. Lift the pastry sheets on to the pie dish, butter-side up, and crumple to form a chiffon effect, covering the pie completely.

4 Place the dish on a baking sheet and bake in the oven for 20 minutes, until golden brown. Reduce the heat to 180°C/350°F/Gas 4 and bake for a further 10–15 minutes, until the rhubarb is tender. Serve warm.

> **Cook's Tip**
> When buying rhubarb, choose young, slender, pink stems, as these will be the most tender.

> **Variation**
> Other fruit, such as apples, pears or peaches, can be used in this pie – try it with whatever is in season.

Roulade Energy 164Kcal/697kJ; Protein 3.7g; Carbohydrate 39g, of which sugars 32.6g; Fat 0.3g, of which saturates 0g; Cholesterol 0mg; Calcium 42mg; Fibre 1.5g; Sodium 48mg.
Chiffon Pie Energy 109Kcal/461kJ; Protein 2.6g; Carbohydrate 15.8g, of which sugars 8.2g; Fat 4.4g, of which saturates 2.6g; Cholesterol 11mg; Calcium 174mg; Fibre 2.7g; Sodium 38mg.

Banana Ginger Parkin

This wholesome, moist parkin is totally scrumptious. The icing sets it off nicely, but you can leave this out to reduce the calorie content.

Makes 12 squares

200g/7oz/1¾ cups plain (all-purpose) flour
10ml/2 tsp bicarbonate of soda (baking soda)
10ml/2 tsp ground ginger
150g/5oz/1¼ cups medium oatmeal
60ml/4 tbsp dark muscovado (molasses) sugar
75g/3oz/6 tbsp sunflower margarine
150g/5oz/⅔ cup golden (light corn) syrup
1 egg, beaten
3 ripe bananas, mashed
75g/3oz/¾ cup icing (confectioners') sugar
preserved stem ginger, to decorate (optional)

1 Preheat the oven to 160°C/325°F/Gas 3. Grease and line an 18 × 28cm/7 × 11in cake tin (pan).

2 Sift together the flour, bicarbonate of soda and ginger into a mixing bowl, then stir in the oatmeal. Melt the sugar, margarine and syrup in a pan, then stir into the flour mixture. Beat in the egg and mashed bananas.

3 Spoon the mixture into the prepared tin and bake for about 1 hour, or until firm to the touch. Allow to cool in the tin, then turn out and cut into even-size squares.

4 Sift the icing sugar into a bowl and stir in just enough water to make a smooth, runny icing. Drizzle the icing over each square and top with pieces of stem ginger, if you like.

> **Cook's Tips**
> • This nutritious cake is ideal for packed lunches as it doesn't break up too easily.
> • The parkin improves with keeping – store in a tightly covered container for up to two months.

Banana Orange Loaf

For the best banana flavour and a really good, moist texture, make sure the bananas are very ripe.

Makes 1 loaf

90g/3½oz/generous ¾ cup wholemeal (whole-wheat) flour
90g/3½oz/generous ¾ cup plain (all-purpose) flour
5ml/1 tsp baking powder
5ml/1 tsp mixed (pumpkin pie) spice
45ml/3 tbsp chopped hazelnuts, toasted
2 large ripe bananas
1 egg
30ml/2 tbsp sunflower oil
30ml/2 tbsp clear honey
finely grated rind and juice of 1 small orange
4 orange slices, halved
10ml/2 tsp icing (confectioners') sugar

1 Preheat the oven to 180°C/350°F/Gas 4. Brush a 1 litre/¾ pint/4 cup loaf tin (pan) with sunflower oil and line the base with baking parchment.

2 Sift the flours with the baking powder and spice into a bowl.

3 Stir the hazelnuts into the dry ingredients. Peel and mash the bananas in a separate bowl and beat in the egg, oil, honey and the orange rind and juice. Stir the banana mixture evenly into the dry ingredients.

4 Spoon the mixture into the prepared tin and smooth the top. Bake for 40–45 minutes, or until firm and golden brown. Turn out and cool on a wire rack.

5 Sprinkle the orange slices with the icing sugar and grill (broil) until golden. Use to decorate the cake.

> **Cook's Tip**
> If you plan to keep the loaf for more than two or three days, omit the orange slices. Brush the cake with honey and sprinkle with chopped hazelnuts.

Parkin Energy 478Kcal/2025kJ; Protein 6.7g; Carbohydrate 101.7g, of which sugars 74.2g; Fat 7.6g, of which saturates 1.4g; Cholesterol 16mg; Calcium 56mg; Fibre 4.1g; Sodium 97mg.
Banana Loaf Energy 1465Kcal/6161kJ; Protein 35.1g; Carbohydrate 209.9g, of which sugars 80.2g; Fat 59.9g, of which saturates 7g; Cholesterol 190mg; Calcium 271mg; Fibre 16g; Sodium 84mg.

Three-Fruit Compote

A combination of dried and fresh fruit, flavoured with fragrant orange flower water, makes a super-fast, refreshing dessert. Using a melon-baller gives the compote a classy touch, but you could always cut the melon into cubes if you find it quicker.

Serves 6
175g/6oz/³⁄₄ cup ready-to-eat, dried apricots
300ml/¹⁄₂ pint/1¹⁄₄ cups water
1 small ripe pineapple
1 small ripe melon
15ml/1 tbsp orange flower water
fresh sprig of mint, to decorate

1 Put the apricots in a medium pan with the water. Bring to the boil, then simmer for 5 minutes. Transfer to a serving bowl and set aside to cool.

2 Peel and quarter the pineapple, then cut the core from each quarter and discard. Cut the flesh into chunks. Reserve any juices that collect.

3 Seed the melon and scoop balls from the flesh, again saving any juices that collect. Pour all the reserved fruit juices into the bowl of apricots with the orange flower water.

4 Add the pineapple and melon pieces to the bowl and mix well together. Chill the fruit salad lightly and decorate with mint just before serving.

> **Variation**
> A good fruit salad needn't be a boring mixture of multi-coloured fruits swimming in sweet syrup. Instead of the usual apple, orange and grape type of salad, give it a theme, such as red berry fruits or a variety of sliced green fruits – even a dish of just one fruit nicely prepared and sprinkled lightly with some sugar and fresh lemon juice can look beautiful and tastes delicious. Do not use more than three fruits in a salad, so that the flavours remain distinct.

Minted Pomegranate Yogurt

In this simple Moroccan recipe, the juicy, ruby seeds of pomegranates and tangy mint are added to plain yogurt to make a flavourful light dessert. The dish is fabulous served with a citrus fruit salad (as shown in the picture).

Serves 3–4
300ml/¹⁄₂ pint/1¹⁄₄ cups Greek (US strained plain) yogurt
2 or 3 ripe pomegranates
small bunch of fresh mint, finely chopped
honey or sugar, to taste (optional)
handful of pomegranate seeds and mint leaves, to decorate

1 Put the yogurt in a bowl and beat well. Cut open the pomegranates and scoop out the seeds, removing all the bitter pith. Fold the pomegranate seeds and chopped mint into the yogurt. Sweeten with a little honey or sugar, if using, then chill.

2 To serve, decorate the chilled yogurt with a sprinkling of pomegranate seeds and mint leaves.

Blackberries in Port

Pour this rich fruit compote over ice cream or serve it with a spoonful of clotted cream to create an attractive, rich dessert. Taking only minutes to make, it provides the perfect end to a dinner party.

Serves 4
300ml/¹⁄₂ pint/1¹⁄₄ cups ruby port
75g/3oz/6 tbsp caster (superfine) sugar
150ml/¹⁄₄ pint/²⁄₃ cup water
450g/1lb/4 cups fresh blackberries

1 Pour the port into a pan, then add the sugar and water. Stir over a gentle heat with a wooden spoon until the sugar has completely dissolved.

2 Remove the pan from the heat and stir in the blackberries. Set aside to cool, then pour into a bowl and cover with clear film (plastic wrap). Chill until ready to serve.

Three-Fruit Compote Energy 94Kcal/399kJ; Protein 1.9g; Carbohydrate 22.1g, of which sugars 22.1g; Fat 0.4g, of which saturates 0g; Cholesterol 0mg; Calcium 44mg; Fibre 3g; Sodium 31mg.
Pomegranate Yogurt Energy 103Kcal/430kJ; Protein 5.4g; Carbohydrate 5.1g, of which sugars 4.4g; Fat 7.8g, of which saturates 3.9g; Cholesterol 0mg; Calcium 140mg; Fibre 0.5g; Sodium 56mg.
Blackberries in Port Energy 220Kcal/924kJ; Protein 1.2g; Carbohydrate 34.3g, of which sugars 34.3g; Fat 0.2g, of which saturates 0g; Cholesterol 0mg; Calcium 59mg; Fibre 3.5g; Sodium 7mg.

Peach, Blackberry & Ice Cream Gratin

A wonderfully easy dessert in which the flavours of the peaches, blackberries, ice cream and brown sugar mingle together as they cook. Use large, ripe peaches to allow enough space for the filling.

Serves 4

4 large peaches
15ml/1 tbsp lemon juice
120ml/4fl oz/¹/₂ cup vanilla
   ice cream
115g/4oz/1 cup small
   blackberries
40g/1¹/₂oz/3 tbsp light
   muscovado (brown)
   sugar

1 Preheat the grill (broiler). Cut the peaches in half and remove the stones (pits). Cut a thin slice off the rounded side of each peach so that they sit flat on the surface.

2 Brush the cut surfaces with lemon juice and transfer to a shallow flameproof dish. Grill (broil) for 2 minutes. Remove from the heat; leave the grill on to maintain the temperature.

3 Using a small teaspoon, take small scoops of the ice cream and pack them into the peach halves, piling up in the centre. Add the blackberries, pushing them gently into the ice cream.

4 Sprinkle the filled peaches with the muscovado sugar and grill for a further 1–2 minutes until the sugar has dissolved and the ice cream is beginning to melt. Serve immediately.

Cook's Tips
• *Don't take the ice cream out of the freezer until just before you are ready to fill the peaches, and then work quickly. The ice cream must still be solid or it will melt too quickly when the dessert is under the hot grill (broiler).*
• *Other berries, such as fresh blueberries, can be used instead of blackberries, if you prefer.*

Pineapple Crush Ice Cream

Look out for pineapples that are labelled "extra sweet". This type has bright yellow flesh that is naturally sweet and juicy, and is ideal for this easy-to-make ice cream.

Serves 4–6

2 extra-sweet pineapples
50g/2oz/¹/₄ cup caster
   (superfine) sugar
300ml/¹/₂ pint/1¹/₄ cups
   whipping cream

1 Slice one pineapple in half lengthways through the leafy top, then scoop out the flesh from both halves, keeping the shells intact. Reserve the flesh. Stand the shells upside down to drain, wrap in clear film (plastic wrap) and chill until needed.

2 Trim the top off the remaining pineapple, cut the flesh into slices, then cut away the skin and any eyes. Remove the core from each slice, then finely chop the flesh from both pineapples. Purée 300g/11oz of the pineapple in a food processor or blender, reserving the remaining pineapple.

3 Using an ice-cream maker, churn the pineapple purée with the sugar for 15–20 minutes. Mix in the cream and churn until thick but too soft to scoop.

4 Add 175g/6oz/1¹/₂ cups of the chopped pineapple and continue to churn the ice cream until it is stiff enough to serve in scoops. Serve, offering any remaining pineapple separately.

Cook's Tip
To make the ice cream by hand, whip the cream until it is just thick. Fold in the purée and sugar, then freeze for 6 hours, beating twice. Fold in the pineapple and freeze for 2–3 hours.

Variation
This is also delicious mixed with meringues: crumble four meringue nests into the mixture when adding the pineapple.

Ice Cream Gratin Energy 138Kcal/583kJ; Protein 2.4g; Carbohydrate 26.8g, of which sugars 26.4g; Fat 2.8g, of which saturates 1.8g; Cholesterol 7mg; Calcium 55mg; Fibre 2.4g; Sodium 20mg.
Pineapple Ice Cream Energy 278Kcal/1159kJ; Protein 1.6g; Carbohydrate 23.5g, of which sugars 23.5g; Fat 20.4g, of which saturates 12.6g; Cholesterol 53mg; Calcium 58mg; Fibre 1.6g; Sodium 16mg.

Raspberry Yogurt Layer

If you are looking for a really speedy and healthy dessert, then this is the one for you. Low in fat and high in fibre, it is packed with goodness. Try it for your breakfast, too.

Serves 4
225g/8oz/1⅓ cups fresh or frozen and thawed raspberries
225g/8oz/1 cup low-fat natural (plain) yogurt
75g/3oz/¾ cup Swiss-style muesli (granola)

1 Reserve four raspberries for decoration, and then spoon a few raspberries into four stemmed glasses or glass dishes.

2 Top the raspberries with a spoonful of yogurt in each glass.

3 Sprinkle a generous layer of muesli over the yogurt. Now repeat with the raspberries and other ingredients. Top each with a whole raspberry.

> **Cook's Tips**
> • *This recipe can be made in advance and stored in the refrigerator for several hours without spoiling.*
> • *Muesli is made up of a mix of cereal, dried fruit and nuts and is therefore high in fibre. When buying muesli from the wide range available in stores, choose a type that is low in sugar to keep in tune with the healthy feel of the dish.*

> **Variations**
> • *This recipe can be made with whatever fruit is in season. Fresh strawberries, redcurrants or peaches would all taste delicious as would tropical fruit such as mango and banana. Layers of cooked, puréed apple or lightly poached plums also make a tasty substitute for the raspberries. For a last-minute dessert, canned fruit would be perfectly acceptable.*
> • *Instead of layers of muesli, try crushed digestive biscuits (graham crackers) or ginger nut biscuits (gingersnaps).*

Yogurt with Apricots & Pistachios

Add subtly honeyed apricots and chopped pistachio nuts to creamy yogurt and you have a dessert with a really distinctive and exotic flavour. This truly is an instant dish that can be whipped up in next to no time, and you can easily vary it, to taste, with whatever ingredients you happen to have to hand.

Serves 4
450g/1lb/2 cups Greek (US strained plain) yogurt
175g/6oz/¾ cup ready-to-eat dried apricots, chopped
15ml/1 tbsp clear honey
grated rind of ½ orange
30ml/2 tbsp unsalted pistachios, roughly chopped
ground cinnamon

1 Place the dried apricots in a pan, barely cover with water and simmer for just 3 minutes, to soften.

2 Drain the apricots and transfer to a bowl. Allow to cool, then mix with the honey.

3 Mix the yogurt with the apricots, orange rind and nuts.

4 Spoon into sundae dishes, sprinkle over a little cinnamon and chill until ready to serve.

> **Cook's Tip**
> *Straining the yogurt overnight will make the dessert thicker, if you prefer that consistency, although this obviously requires advance planning and so means that the dish is no longer a really quick, last-minute option. To strain the yogurt, simply leave it in a sieve (strainer) over a bowl in the refrigerator overnight. The next day, discard the liquid whey collected from the yogurt.*

> **Variation**
> *Sprinkle over a little demerara (raw) sugar or grated chocolate with the ground cinnamon for added flavour.*

Yogurt with Apricots Energy 255Kcal/1064kJ; Protein 10.3g; Carbohydrate 21.7g, of which sugars 21.5g; Fat 15.9g, of which saturates 6.4g; Cholesterol 0mg; Calcium 209mg; Fibre 3.2g; Sodium 126mg.
Raspberry Muesli Energy 114Kcal/483kJ; Protein 5.5g; Carbohydrate 20.4g, of which sugars 11.7g; Fat 2g, of which saturates 0.5g; Cholesterol 1mg; Calcium 142mg; Fibre 2.6g; Sodium 120mg.

Chocolate Banana Fools

This de luxe version of banana custard looks great served in glasses. Quick to put together, it can be made a few hours in advance and chilled until ready to serve.

Serves 4
115g/4oz plain (semisweet) chocolate, chopped
300ml/½ pint/1¼ cups fresh custard
2 bananas

1 Put the chocolate in a heatproof bowl and melt in the microwave on High for 1–2 minutes. Stir, then set aside to cool. Alternatively, put the chocolate in a heatproof bowl, set it over a pan of simmering water and leave until melted, stirring frequently.

2 Pour the custard into a bowl and gently fold in the melted chocolate to make a rippled effect.

3 Peel and slice the bananas and stir these into the chocolate and custard mixture. Spoon into four glasses and chill for 30 minutes–1 hour before serving.

Lemon Posset

This creamy dessert dates back to the Middle Ages.

Serves 4
600ml/1 pint/2½ cups double (heavy) cream

175g/6oz/¾ cup caster (superfine) sugar
grated rind and juice of 2 unwaxed lemons

1 Gently heat the cream and sugar together in a pan until the sugar has dissolved, then bring to the boil, stirring constantly.

2 Add the lemon juice and rind to the cream mixture and stir until it thickens.

3 Pour the posset into four heatproof serving glasses and chill until just set, then serve.

Coffee Mascarpone Creams

For the best results, use good quality coffee beans and make the coffee as strong as possible. These little desserts are very rich so you need a really robust shot of coffee to give the desired result. They are particularly good served with a glass of liqueur or a cup of espresso.

Serves 4
115g/4oz/½ cup mascarpone
45ml/3 tbsp strong espresso coffee
45g/1¾oz/3 tbsp icing (confectioners') sugar

1 Put the mascarpone in a bowl and add the coffee. Mix well until smooth and creamy. Sift in the icing sugar and stir until thoroughly combined.

2 Spoon the mixture into little china pots or ramekin dishes and chill for 30 minutes before serving.

Cook's Tip
Chocolate-dipped strawberries make a lovely accompaniment to these desserts. Melt some broken-up chocolate in a small deep heatproof bowl set over a pan of barely simmering water. While the chocolate is melting, line a baking sheet with baking parchment. Stir the melted chocolate until it is completely smooth. Holding a strawberry by its stalk, dip it partially or fully into the melted chocolate, allowing any excess chocolate to drip off, then place the fruit on the baking sheet. Repeat with the rest of the fruit. Leave to set and use on the same day.

Variation
You can flavour mascarpone with almost anything you like to make a quick but elegant dessert. Try replacing the coffee with the same quantity of orange juice, Marsala or honey.

Coffee Creams Energy 96Kcal/403kJ; Protein 2.7g; Carbohydrate 12.7g, of which sugars 12.7g; Fat 4.2g, of which saturates 2.6g; Cholesterol 12mg; Calcium 6mg; Fibre 0g; Sodium 1mg.
Banana Fools Energy 263Kcal/1106kJ; Protein 4g; Carbohydrate 40.9g, of which sugars 37g; Fat 9.5g, of which saturates 4.9g; Cholesterol 3mg; Calcium 81mg; Fibre 1.3g; Sodium 33mg.
Lemon Posset Energy 917Kcal/3797kJ; Protein 2.6g; Carbohydrate 48.3g, of which sugars 48.3g; Fat 80.6g, of which saturates 50.1g; Cholesterol 206mg; Calcium 97mg; Fibre 0g; Sodium 36mg.

Banana & Passion Fruit Whip

This very easy and quickly prepared dessert has a delicious tropical flavour. Serve with dainty, crisp biscuits (cookies) for a lovely contrast to the creamy texture.

Serves 4
2 ripe bananas
2 passion fruit
115g/4oz/¹/₂ cup fromage frais or mascarpone
150ml/¹/₄ pint/²/₃ cup double (heavy) cream
10ml/2 tsp clear honey

1 Peel the bananas, then mash them with a fork in a bowl to a smooth purée.

2 Halve the passion fruit and scoop out the pulp. Mix with the bananas and fromage frais. Whip the cream with the honey until it forms soft peaks.

3 Carefully fold the cream and honey mixture into the fruit mixture. Spoon into four glass dishes and serve immediately.

Frudités with Honey Dip

A colourful and tasty variation on the popular savoury crudités, this dessert is great fun for impromptu entertaining.

Serves 4
225g/8oz/1 cup Greek (US strained plain) yogurt
45ml/3 tbsp clear honey
selection of fresh fruit for dipping such as apples, pears, tangerines, grapes, figs, cherries, strawberries and kiwi fruit

1 Place the yogurt in a dish, beat until smooth, then partially stir in the honey, leaving a slight marbled effect.

2 Cut the various fruits into wedges or bite-size pieces or leave whole. Arrange the fruits on a platter with the bowl of dip in the centre. Serve chilled.

Quick Apricot Blender Whip

One of the speediest desserts you could make – as well as being one of the prettiest. Perfect for mid-week meals when you have run out of time.

Serves 4
400g/14oz can apricot halves in juice
15ml/1 tbsp Grand Marnier or brandy
175g/6oz/³/₄ cup Greek (US strained plain) yogurt
30ml/2 tbsp flaked (sliced) almonds

1 Drain the juice from the apricots and place the fruit and liqueur in a blender or food processor. Process the apricots to a smooth purée.

2 Spoon the fruit purée and yogurt in alternate spoonfuls into four tall glasses or glass dishes, swirling them together slightly to give a marbled effect.

3 Lightly toast the almonds in a dry, non-stick frying pan or under the grill (broiler) until they are golden. Allow them to cool slightly, then sprinkle them over the top of the desserts.

Cook's Tips
• Why not make quick petit four biscuits (cookies) to serve with this fruit whip? Roll out a carton of chocolate chip cookie dough on a floured surface to 1cm/¹/₂in thick. Using a small pastry (cookie) cutter, stamp out as many rounds as possible and transfer to a lightly greased baking sheet. Bake according to the packet instructions and leave to cool. Meanwhile, melt some plain (semisweet) chocolate in a bowl set over a pan of simmering water, then allow to cool. Use the chocolate to sandwich together the biscuits in pairs, then serve. These are delicious with any creamy dessert.
• For an even lighter dessert, use low-fat yogurt instead of Greek (US strained plain) yogurt, and replace the liqueur with a little fruit juice from the can of apricots.

Fruit Whip Energy 262Kcal/1086kJ; Protein 2.5g; Carbohydrate 15.4g, of which sugars 14.3g; Fat 21.6g, of which saturates 13.4g; Cholesterol 56mg; Calcium 41mg; Fibre 0.7g; Sodium 18mg.
Frudités Energy 141Kcal/595kJ; Protein 4g; Carbohydrate 20.9g, of which sugars 20.9g; Fat 5.9g, of which saturates 2.9g; Cholesterol 0mg; Calcium 90mg; Fibre 2g; Sodium 44mg.
Apricot Whip Energy 168Kcal/701kJ; Protein 4.8g; Carbohydrate 17.5g, of which sugars 17.3g; Fat 8.8g, of which saturates 2.6g; Cholesterol 0mg; Calcium 103mg; Fibre 1.5g; Sodium 42mg.

Brazilian Coffee Bananas

Rich and sinful-looking, this tasty dessert takes only about two minutes to make – just the job for a busy modern lifestyle.

Serves 4
4 small ripe bananas
15ml/1 tbsp instant coffee
  granules or powder
15ml/1 tbsp hot water
25g/1oz/2 tbsp dark muscovado
  (molasses) sugar
250g/9oz/1⅛ cups Greek (US
  strained plain) yogurt
15ml/1 tbsp toasted flaked
  (sliced) almonds

1 Peel and slice one banana and roughly mash the remaining three with a fork.

2 Dissolve the coffee in the hot water, then stir into the mashed bananas.

3 Spoon a little of the mashed banana mixture into four individual dishes and sprinkle with sugar. Top with a spoonful of yogurt, then repeat until all the ingredients are used up.

4 Swirl the last layer of yogurt for a marbled effect. Finish with a few banana slices and flaked almonds. Serve immediately – if possible, serve within about an hour of making.

Cook's Tip
Sprinkle the sliced banana, for the topping, with freshly squeezed lemon juice to prevent it from turning brown.

Variations
For a special occasion, add a dash of dark rum or brandy to the bananas for extra richness. Chocolate teams up with coffee and banana very well, so for a luxurious touch, drizzle some melted chocolate over the sliced banana and nut topping.

Figs with Ricotta Cream

Fresh, ripe figs are full of natural sweetness, and need little adornment. This simple recipe really makes the most of their beautiful, intense flavour.

Serves 4
4 ripe, fresh figs
115g/4oz/¼ cup ricotta or
  cottage cheese
45ml/3 tbsp crème fraîche
15ml/1 tbsp clear honey
2.5ml/½ tsp vanilla extract
freshly grated nutmeg, to decorate

1 Trim the stalks from the figs. Make four cuts through each fig from the stalk-end, cutting almost right through but leaving them intact at the base. Place on serving plates and open them out.

2 Mix together the ricotta or cottage cheese, crème fraîche, honey and vanilla.

3 Spoon a little ricotta cream on to each plate and sprinkle with grated nutmeg to serve.

Red Fruit Coulis with Meringue

A heavenly, vibrant sauce teamed with crisp meringue.

Serves 6
225g/8oz/2 cups redcurrants,
  removed from stalks
450g/1lb/2⅔ cups raspberries
50g/2oz/½ cup icing
  (confectioners') sugar
15ml/1 tbsp cornflour (cornstarch)
juice of 1 orange
6 ready-made meringues
double (heavy) cream, to serve

1 Place the fruit in a food processor or blender with the sugar and purée. Press through a fine sieve (strainer).

2 Blend the cornflour with the orange juice, then stir into the fruit purée. Transfer to a pan, simmer for 1–2 minutes, stirring, until smooth and thick. Cool, then spoon some coulis on to individual plates, swirl in a little cream and top with a meringue.

Coffee Bananas Energy 210Kcal/882kJ; Protein 5.9g; Carbohydrate 30.2g, of which sugars 28.1g; Fat 8.7g, of which saturates 3.5g; Cholesterol 0mg; Calcium 112mg; Fibre 1.3g; Sodium 46mg.
Figs with Ricotta Cream Energy 128Kcal/536kJ; Protein 4.6g; Carbohydrate 14.6g, of which sugars 14.6g; Fat 6g, of which saturates 3.7g; Cholesterol 17mg; Calcium 93mg; Fibre 1.5g; Sodium 102mg.
Red Fruit Coulis Energy 138Kcal/589kJ; Protein 2.4g; Carbohydrate 33.7g, of which sugars 31.4g; Fat 0.3g, of which saturates 0.1g; Cholesterol 0mg; Calcium 49mg; Fibre 3.2g; Sodium 25mg.

Fresh Pineapple Salad

A fragrant and fresh-tasting fruit salad, this dessert can be prepared very quickly, ahead of time. Orange flower water gives the salad its special quality – it is available from Middle Eastern food stores or good delicatessens.

Serves 4
1 small ripe pineapple
icing (confectioners') sugar,
    to taste
15ml/1 tbsp orange flower water,
    or more to taste
115g/4oz/generous ½ cup fresh
    dates, stoned (pitted) and
    quartered
225g/8oz/2 cups fresh
    strawberries, sliced
few fresh mint sprigs, to
    decorate

1 Peel the pineapple and, using the tip of a vegetable peeler, remove as many brown "eyes" as possible.

2 Cut the peeled pineapple into quarters, lengthways, remove the core, then slice.

3 Arrange the pineapple slices in a shallow glass bowl that is large enough to accommodate the dates and strawberries added in the next step. Sprinkle with the icing sugar and the orange flower water.

4 Add the dates and strawberries to the pineapple, cover and chill for at least 2 hours, stirring once or twice.

5 Serve the fruit salad slightly chilled, decorated with a few mint sprigs.

> **Cook's Tip**
> *Make sure that the dates you use are of a good enough quality or they could spoil the dish. Fresh dates should be plump with smooth, shiny brown skins. The flesh ought to have a rich, honey-like flavour and dense texture.*

Prune & Orange Pots

A handy storecupboard dessert, made in minutes. It can be served straight away, but for the best effect, chill for about half an hour before serving.

Serves 4
225g/8oz/1 cup ready-to-eat
    dried prunes
150ml/¼ pint/⅔ cup orange juice
225g/8oz/1 cup low-fat
    natural (plain) yogurt
shredded, pared orange rind, to
    decorate

1 Remove the pits from the prunes and roughly chop the flesh. Put the prunes in a pan with the orange juice.

2 Bring the juice to the boil, stirring. Reduce the heat, cover and leave to simmer for 5 minutes, until the prunes are tender and the liquid is reduced by half.

3 Remove from the heat, allow to cool slightly and then beat well with a wooden spoon, until the fruit breaks down to a rough purée.

4 Transfer the mixture to a bowl. Stir in the yogurt, swirling the yogurt and fruit purée together lightly, to give an attractive marbled effect.

5 Spoon the mixture into stemmed glasses or individual dishes, smoothing the tops.

6 Top each dish with a few shreds of orange rind, to decorate. Chill before serving.

> **Variations**
> *This dessert can also be made with other ready-to-eat dried fruit, such as apricots or peaches. For a special occasion, add a dash of brandy or Cointreau with the yogurt. Sprinkle the top of each serving with toasted flaked (sliced) almonds or crumbled amaretti to give added texture to the dessert.*

Prune & Orange Pots Energy 124Kcal/528kJ; Protein 4.5g; Carbohydrate 26.7g, of which sugars 26.7g; Fat 0.8g, of which saturates 0.3g; Cholesterol 1mg; Calcium 130mg; Fibre 3.3g; Sodium 57mg.
Pineapple Salad Energy 92Kcal/391kJ; Protein 1.3g; Carbohydrate 22.4g, of which sugars 22.4g; Fat 0.3g, of which saturates 0g; Cholesterol 0mg; Calcium 34mg; Fibre 2.3g; Sodium 7mg.

Grapefruit in Honey & Whisky

Create a simple yet elegant dessert by arranging a colourful fan of pink, red and white grapefruit segments in a sweet whisky sauce. This dessert is perfect after a rich meal.

Serves 4
1 pink grapefruit
1 red grapefruit
1 white grapefruit
50g/2oz/^{1}/4 cup sugar
150ml/^{1}/4 pint/^{2}/3 cup water
60ml/4 tbsp clear honey
45ml/3 tbsp whisky
fresh mint sprigs, to decorate

1 Cut a thin slice from each end of the grapefruits. Place cut side down on a plate and cut off the peel and pith in strips. Remove any remaining pith.

2 Cut out each segment, leaving the membrane behind. Put the segments into a shallow bowl.

3 Put the sugar and water into a heavy pan, bring to the boil, stirring constantly, until the sugar has dissolved, then simmer, without stirring, for 10 minutes, until thickened and syrupy.

4 Heat the honey in a pan and boil until it becomes a slightly deeper colour or begins to caramelize.

5 Remove the pan from the heat, add the whisky and, using a match or taper, carefully ignite, if you like, then pour the mixture into the sugar syrup.

6 Bring to the boil, and pour over the fruit. Cover and leave until cold. To serve, arrange the grapefruit segments on individual plates, alternating the colours, and pour over the syrup. Add the mint.

Variation
The whisky can be replaced with brandy, Cointreau or Grand Marnier, any of which will work just as well.

Watermelon, Ginger & Grapefruit Salad

This pretty pink salad ably proves that a dish doesn't need to be complicated to taste great. Here, sweet stem ginger brilliantly ties together the freshness of the watermelon and the tang of the grapefruit.

Serves 4
500g/1^{1}/4lb/2 cups diced
    watermelon flesh
2 red or pink grapefruit
2 pieces preserved stem ginger,
    plus 30ml/2 tbsp of the
    preserved stem ginger syrup
whipped cream, to serve

1 Remove any seeds from the watermelon with a knife and cut into bitesize chunks. Place in a serving bowl.

2 Cut a thin slice from each end of the grapefruit. Place cut side down on a plate and, using a sharp knife, cut off the peel and pith in strips. Remove any remaining pith. Cut out each segment, leaving the membrane behind; catch any juice in a bowl as you work.

3 Add the grapefruit segments and collected juice to the bowl of watermelon. Finely chop the stem ginger and add to the fruits in the bowl.

4 Spoon over the ginger syrup and toss the fruits lightly in the syrup to mix evenly. Chill before serving with a bowl of whipped cream.

Cook's Tip
Toss the fruits gently, otherwise the grapefruit segments will break up and the appearance of the dish will be spoiled.

Variation
Use blood oranges instead of the grapefruit and add orange rind shreds with the ginger.

Grapefruit Energy 154Kcal/649kJ; Protein 1.1g; Carbohydrate 32.7g, of which sugars 32.7g; Fat 0.1g, of which saturates 0g; Cholesterol 0mg; Calcium 35mg; Fibre 1.6g; Sodium 6mg. **Watermelon, Ginger & Grapefruit** Energy 85Kcal/362kJ; Protein 1.3g; Carbohydrate 20.3g, of which sugars 20.3g; Fat 0.5g, of which saturates 0.1g; Cholesterol 0mg; Calcium 28mg; Fibre 1.2g; Sodium 25mg.

Scented Red & Orange Fruit Salad

A lovely salad, bursting with colour and exotic tastes.

Serves 4–6
350–400g/12–14oz/3–3½ cups
  strawberries, hulled and halved
3 oranges, peeled and segmented

3 small blood oranges, peeled
  and segmented
1 or 2 passion fruit
120ml/4fl oz/½ cup
  dry white wine
sugar, to taste

1 Put the strawberries and oranges into a serving bowl. Halve the passion fruit and spoon the flesh into the fruit.

2 Pour the wine over the fruit and add sugar to taste. Toss gently, then chill until ready to serve.

Rhubarb & Ginger Trifles

Choose a good-quality jar of rhubarb compote for this speedy recipe; try to find one with large, chunky pieces of fruit.

Serves 4
12 ginger nut biscuits
  (gingersnaps)
50ml/2fl oz/¼ cup rhubarb
  compote
450ml/¾ pint/scant 2 cups extra
  thick double (heavy) cream

1 Put the ginger biscuits in a plastic bag and seal. Press the biscuits with a rolling pin until roughly crushed.

2 Set aside 30ml/2 tbsp of the crushed biscuits and divide the rest among four glasses.

3 Spoon the rhubarb compote on top of the crushed biscuits, then top with the cream. Place in the refrigerator and chill for about 30 minutes.

4 To serve, sprinkle the reserved crushed biscuits over the trifles and serve immediately.

Pistachio & Rose Water Oranges

This light and citrusy dessert is perfect to serve after a heavy main course, such as a hearty meat stew or a leg of roast lamb. Combining three favourite Middle Eastern ingredients, the dish is delicately fragrant and refreshing. If pistachio nuts are not available, use hazelnuts instead.

Serves 4
4 large oranges
30ml/2 tbsp rose water
30ml/2 tbsp shelled pistachio
  nuts, roughly chopped

1 Slice the top and bottom off one of the oranges to expose the flesh.

2 Using a small serrated knife, slice down between the pith and the flesh, working round the orange, neatly removing all the peel and pith.

3 Slice the orange horizontally into six rounds, reserving any juice. Repeat with the remaining oranges.

4 Arrange the orange rounds decoratively in a serving dish. Mix the reserved juice with the rose water and drizzle over the oranges.

5 Cover the dish with clear film (plastic wrap) and chill for about 30 minutes. Sprinkle the chopped pistachio nuts over the oranges to serve.

Cook's Tip
Rose-scented sugar is delicious sprinkled over fresh fruit salads. Wash and thoroughly dry a handful of fresh, unsprayed rose petals and place in a sealed container filled with caster (superfine) sugar for 2–3 days. Remove the rose petals, then use the sugar as a delicate flavouring.

Red & Orange Salad Energy 78Kcal/329kJ; Protein 2g; Carbohydrate 14.7g, of which sugars 14.7g; Fat 0.2g, of which saturates 0g; Cholesterol 0mg; Calcium 70mg; Fibre 3g; Sodium 12mg.
Trifles Energy 695Kcal/2874kJ; Protein 3.6g; Carbohydrate 27.1g, of which sugars 14.1g; Fat 64.3g, of which saturates 39.4g; Cholesterol 154mg; Calcium 98mg; Fibre 0.6g; Sodium 124mg.
Oranges Energy 101Kcal/424kJ; Protein 3g; Carbohydrate 13.4g, of which sugars 13.2g; Fat 4.3g, of which saturates 0.6g; Cholesterol 0mg; Calcium 79mg; Fibre 3g; Sodium 47mg.

Chargrilled Apples on Cinnamon Toasts

This delicious treat provides a truly fabulous finale to any kind of summertime barbecue. However, it can also, just as effectively, be cooked under the grill or broiler, which means that you can enjoy it at any time of year.

Serves 4

4 sweet dessert apples
juice of ½ lemon
4 individual English muffins
15ml/1 tbsp low-fat spread, melted
25g/1oz/2 tbsp golden caster (superfine) sugar
5ml/1 tsp ground cinnamon
low-fat Greek (US strained plain) yogurt, to serve (optional)

1 Core all of the dessert apples and then cut them horizontally into three or four thick, equal-sized slices. Sprinkle the slices with the lemon juice.

2 Cut the muffins into halves. Brush sparingly with melted low-fat spread on both sides.

3 Mix together the caster sugar and the ground cinnamon. Preheat the grill (broiler) at this stage if you are not using the barbecue.

4 Place the apple slices and the muffin halves on the hot barbecue – or under the grill – and cook them for about 3–4 minutes, turning once, until they are beginning to turn a golden brown colour.

5 Sprinkle half the cinnamon sugar over the apple slices and muffins and cook for 1 minute more, until they are a rich golden brown.

6 To serve, arrange the apple slices over the toasts and sprinkle them with the remaining cinnamon sugar. Serve hot, with low-fat Greek yogurt, if you like.

Greek Fig & Honey Pudding

This dessert is packed with sunny Greek flavours.

Serves 4

4 fresh or canned figs

2 x 225g/8oz tubs/2 cups Greek (US strained plain) yogurt
60ml/4 tbsp clear honey
30ml/2 tbsp chopped unsalted pistachio nuts

1 Chop the figs and place in the bottom of four stemmed wine glasses or deep, individual dessert bowls.

2 Spoon half a tub (120ml/4fl oz/½ cup) of the thick yogurt on top of the figs in the glasses or bowls. Chill in the refrigerator until ready to serve. Just before serving, drizzle 15ml/1 tbsp of honey over each portion and sprinkle with the pistachio nuts.

Passion Fruit Soufflés

Here, passion fruit adds an exotic twist to a classic.

Serves 4

softened butter, for greasing

200ml/7fl oz/scant 1 cup ready-made fresh custard
3 passion fruit, halved
2 egg whites

1 Preheat the oven to 200°C/400°F/Gas 6. Grease four 200ml/7fl oz/scant 1 cup ramekins or small ovenproof dishes with the butter.

2 Pour the custard into a mixing bowl. Scrape out the seeds and juice from the passion fruit and stir well into the custard.

3 Whisk the egg whites until stiff, and fold a quarter of them into the custard. Carefully fold in the remaining egg whites, then spoon the mixture into the dishes.

4 Place the dishes on a baking sheet and bake in the oven for 8–10 minutes, or until the soufflés are well risen. Serve immediately.

Chargrilled Apples on Cinnamon Toasts Energy 218Kcal/926kJ; Protein 5.6g; Carbohydrate 40.9g, of which sugars 17.4g; Fat 4.8g, of which saturates 0.4g; Cholesterol 0mg; Calcium 79mg; Fibre 2.5g; Sodium 92mg. **Greek Fig & Honey** Energy 292Kcal/1220kJ; Protein 10.9g; Carbohydrate 25.4g, of which sugars 25.2g; Fat 18.5g, of which saturates 7.7g; Cholesterol 0mg; Calcium 265mg; Fibre 2g; Sodium 152mg. **Fruit Soufflés** Energy 59Kcal/249kJ; Protein 3.1g; Carbohydrate 8.8g, of which sugars 7.1g; Fat 1g, of which saturates 0g; Cholesterol 1mg; Calcium 48mg; Fibre 0.4g; Sodium 53mg.

Fruit-Filled Soufflé Omelette

A melt-in-the-mouth dish, this dessert is surprisingly quick to make. The creamy omelette fluffs up in the pan, then is softly folded over to envelop its filling.

Serves 2

75g/3oz/³/₄ cup strawberries, hulled
45ml/3 tbsp Kirsch, brandy or Cointreau

3 eggs, separated
25g/1oz/2 tbsp caster (superfine) sugar
45ml/3 tbsp double (heavy) cream, whipped
a few drops of vanilla extract
25g/1oz/2 tbsp butter
icing (confectioners') sugar, sifted

1 Cut the strawberries in half and place in a bowl. Pour over 30ml/2 tbsp of the liqueur and set aside to marinate.

2 Beat the egg yolks and sugar together until pale and fluffy, then fold in the whipped cream and vanilla extract. Whisk the egg whites in a very large, grease-free bowl until stiff, then carefully fold into the yolks.

3 Melt the butter in an omelette pan. When sizzling, pour in the egg mixture and cook until set underneath, shaking occasionally. Spoon on the strawberries and liqueur and, tilting the pan, slide the omelette so that it folds over.

4 Slide the omelette on to a warm plate and spoon over the remaining liqueur. Dredge with icing sugar, cut in half and serve.

Apricot Pancakes

A simple, tasty dessert to keep all the family happy.

Serves 4

115g/4oz/1 cup plain (all-purpose) flour
pinch of salt
1 egg

300ml/½ pint/1¼ cups milk
a little oil, for frying

For the sauce
200g/7oz/scant 1 cup ready-to-eat dried apricots
150ml/¼ pint/²/₃ cup apple juice
300ml/½ pint/1¼ cups water

1 Make the sauce. Put the apricots in a pan with the apple juice and water and simmer, covered, for 10 minutes until tender. Cool slightly, then purée in a blender until smooth. Set aside.

2 Sift the flour and salt into a bowl and make a well in the centre. Add the egg and milk and, using a whisk, gradually incorporate the surrounding dry ingredients to form a batter.

3 Heat a lightly oiled, non-stick pan until very hot. Pour in just enough batter to cover the base of the pan, swirling the pan to cover the base evenly. Cook until the pancake is set and golden, and then turn to cook the other side. Keep warm while cooking more pancakes in the same way.

4 Serve the pancakes with the apricot sauce poured over.

Warm Pears in Cider

An easy way of making the most of autumn fruit.

Serves 4

1 lemon
50g/2oz/¼ cup caster (superfine) sugar

a little grated nutmeg
250ml/8fl oz/1 cup sweet (hard) cider
4 firm, ripe pears
freshly made custard, cream or ice cream, to serve

1 Carefully remove the rind from the lemon with a vegetable peeler, leaving any white pith behind.

2 Squeeze the juice from the lemon into a pan large enough to hold the pears. Add the rind, sugar, nutmeg and cider and heat through until the sugar has completely dissolved.

3 Carefully peel the pears, leaving the stalks on if possible, and place in the pan of cider. Poach the pears for 10–15 minutes until almost tender, turning frequently to cook evenly.

4 Transfer the pears to individual serving dishes using a slotted spoon. Simmer the liquid over a high heat until it reduces slightly and becomes syrupy.

5 Pour the warm syrup over the pears, and serve immediately with freshly made custard, cream or ice cream.

Cook's Tip
To get pears of just the right firmness, you may have to buy them slightly under-ripe and then wait a day or more. Soft pears are no good at all for this dish.

Variation
Try using sweet white wine instead of (hard) cider and replace the nutmeg with finely grated orange rind.

Soufflé Omelette Energy 434Kcal/1802kJ; Protein 10.2g; Carbohydrate 18.4g, of which sugars 18.4g; Fat 30.7g, of which saturates 16.4g; Cholesterol 343mg; Calcium 70mg; Fibre 0.4g; Sodium 189mg.
Apricot Pancakes Energy 276Kcal/1168kJ; Protein 7.6g; Carbohydrate 46.1g, of which sugars 24.2g; Fat 8.2g, of which saturates 1.5g; Cholesterol 50mg; Calcium 132mg; Fibre 4.1g; Sodium 42mg.
Pears in Cider Energy 136Kcal/574kJ; Protein 0.5g; Carbohydrate 30.8g, of which sugars 30.8g; Fat 0.2g, of which saturates 0g; Cholesterol 0mg; Calcium 28mg; Fibre 3.3g; Sodium 10mg.

Pineapple Flambé

Flambéing is a quick and tasty way to serve fruit. Setting light to the alcohol gives the dish a delicious, distinctive flavour.

Serves 4
1 large, ripe pineapple
40g/1½oz/3 tbsp unsalted (sweet) butter
40g/1½oz/3 tbsp light soft brown sugar
60ml/4 tbsp fresh orange juice
30ml/2 tbsp brandy or vodka
25g/1oz/4 tbsp slivered (sliced) almonds, toasted
crème fraîche, to serve

1 Slice off the top and base of the pineapple. Then cut down the sides, removing the skin and all the dark "eyes", but leaving the pineapple in a good shape.

2 Cut the pineapple into thin slices and, with an apple corer, remove the hard central core.

3 Heat the butter, sugar and orange juice in a large frying pan until the sugar has dissolved. Add the pineapple slices and cook for about 1–2 minutes, turning once to coat both sides.

4 Add the brandy or vodka and immediately set alight with a long match or taper. Allow the flames to die down and then sprinkle with the toasted almonds. Serve with crème fraîche.

> **Cook's Tip**
> *If you are serving this dish to children, you can leave out the alcohol – it will taste just as good.*

> **Variation**
> *For speed, use canned pineapple rings in natural juice and replace the orange with the same amount of canned juice.*

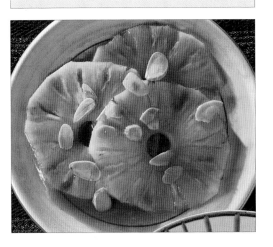

Grilled Pineapple with Rum Custard

This speedy dessert is perfect for any occasion.

Serves 4
1 ripe pineapple
25g/1oz/2 tbsp butter
fresh strawberries, sliced, to serve
a few pineapple leaves, to decorate

For the sauce
1 egg
2 egg yolks
25g/1oz/2 tbsp caster (superfine) sugar
30ml/2 tbsp dark rum
2.5ml/½ tsp freshly ground black pepper

1 Slice off the top and base of the pineapple. Then cut down the sides, removing the skin and all the dark "eyes", but leaving the pineapple in a good shape.

2 Preheat the grill (broiler) to medium heat. Cut the pineapple into thin slices and, with an apple corer, remove the hard central core. Dot the pineapple slices with butter and grill (broil) for about 5 minutes.

3 Make the sauce. Place all the ingredients in a heatproof bowl. Set over a pan of simmering water and whisk for about 3–4 minutes or until the mixture is foamy and cooked.

4 Scatter the sliced strawberries over the cooked pineapple, decorate with a few pineapple leaves and serve immediately, with the sauce poured over the top of each serving.

> **Cook's Tips**
> • *The sweetest pineapples are picked and exported when ripe. Contrary to popular belief, pineapples do not ripen well after picking. Choose fruit that smells sweet and yields to firm pressure from your thumbs.*
> • *Freshly ground black pepper may seem an unusual ingredient to team up with pineapple, until you realize that peppercorns are the fruit of a tropical vine. If the idea does not appeal, you can always leave out the pepper – but it's worth a try.*

Pineapple Flambé Energy 246Kcal/1032kJ; Protein 2.2g; Carbohydrate 29.9g, of which sugars 29.8g; Fat 12.1g, of which saturates 5.5g; Cholesterol 21mg; Calcium 55mg; Fibre 2.6g; Sodium 67mg.
Grilled Pineapple Energy 203Kcal/853kJ; Protein 3.7g; Carbohydrate 23g, of which sugars 23g; Fat 9.6g, of which saturates 4.4g; Cholesterol 162mg; Calcium 51mg; Fibre 1.8g; Sodium 63mg.

Ginger & Orange Crème Brûlée

With this cheat's version of crème brûlée, the creamy base is set the easy way, without lengthy cooking.

Serves 4–5
2 eggs, plus 2 egg yolks
300ml/½ pint/1¼ cups single (light) cream
25g/1oz/2 tbsp caster (superfine) sugar
5ml/1 tsp powdered gelatine

finely grated rind and juice of ½ orange
1 large piece preserved stem ginger, finely chopped
45–60ml/3–4 tbsp icing (confectioners') or caster (superfine) sugar
orange segments and sprig of mint, to decorate

1 Whisk the eggs and yolks together until pale. Bring the cream and sugar to the boil in a pan, remove from the heat and sprinkle on the gelatine. Stir until the gelatine has dissolved and then pour the cream mixture on to the eggs, whisking constantly.

2 Add the orange rind to the custard, with a little juice to taste, then stir in the chopped ginger.

3 Carefully pour into four or five ramekins or small flameproof dishes and leave in the refrigerator until set.

4 Some time before serving, sprinkle the sugar generously over the top of the custard and put under a very hot grill (broiler). Watch closely for the couple of moments it takes for the tops to caramelize. Allow to cool before serving.

5 Decorate with a few segments of orange and a sprig of mint.

Cook's Tips
• Not many people will guess that this recipe is a cheat – but take care not to over-chill the custard.
• For a milder ginger flavour, just add up to 5ml/1 tsp ground ginger instead of the stem ginger.

Oranges in Hot Coffee Syrup

This easy recipe features an unusual blend of flavours.

Serves 6
6 medium oranges
200g/7oz/1 cup sugar
50ml/2fl oz/¼ cup cold water
100ml/3½fl oz/scant ½ cup

boiling water
100ml/3½fl oz/scant ½ cup fresh strong brewed coffee
50g/2oz/½ cup pistachio nuts, chopped (optional)

1 Finely pare the rind from one orange, shred and reserve the rind. Peel the remaining oranges. Cut each orange crossways into slices, then re-form and hold in place with a cocktail stick (toothpick) through the centre.

2 Put the sugar and cold water in a pan. Heat gently, stirring constantly, until the sugar dissolves, then bring to the boil and cook until the syrup turns a pale golden colour.

3 Remove from the heat and carefully pour the boiling water into the pan. Return to the heat until the syrup has dissolved in the water. Stir in the coffee.

4 Add the oranges and the shredded rind to the coffee syrup. Simmer for 15–20 minutes, turning the oranges once during cooking. Sprinkle with pistachio nuts, if using, and serve hot.

Cook's Tip
Choose a pan in which the oranges will just fit in a single layer.

Spiced Poached Kumquats

Kumquats are at their best just before the Christmas season. Simply poached with spices, their marvellous spicy-sweet citrus flavour produces a refreshing dish that will give any meal a lift.

Serves 6
450g/1lb/4 cups kumquats
115g/4oz/generous ½ cup caster (superfine) sugar
150ml/¼ pint/⅔ cup water
1 small cinnamon stick
1 star anise

1 Cut the kumquats in half and discard the seeds. Place the kumquats in a pan with the sugar, water and spices. Cook over a gentle heat, stirring until the sugar has dissolved.

2 Increase the heat, cover the pan and boil the mixture for 8–10 minutes until the kumquats are tender.

3 Transfer to a serving bowl, cool, then chill before serving.

Cook's Tip
To bottle the kumquats, spoon them into warm, sterilized jars at the end of step 2, then seal and label.

Crème Brûlée Energy 231Kcal/962kJ; Protein 5.7g; Carbohydrate 17.4g, of which sugars 17.4g; Fat 15.9g, of which saturates 8.5g; Cholesterol 190mg; Calcium 83mg; Fibre 0g; Sodium 50mg.
Oranges in Syrup Energy 183Kcal/782kJ; Protein 2g; Carbohydrate 46.4g, of which sugars 46.3g; Fat 0.1g, of which saturates 0g; Cholesterol 0mg; Calcium 84mg; Fibre 2.3g; Sodium 10mg.
Poached Kumquats Energy 103Kcal/441kJ; Protein 0.8g; Carbohydrate 26.6g, of which sugars 26.6g; Fat 0.1g, of which saturates 0g; Cholesterol 0mg; Calcium 33mg; Fibre 0.9g; Sodium 4mg.

Chocolate Fudge Bananas

A fast dessert that's bound to go down well with kids.

Serves 4

4 bananas
15ml/1 tbsp lemon juice
grated chocolate, to decorate

For the sauce

150ml/¼ pint/⅔ cup double (heavy) cream
50g/2oz/¼ cup butter
50g/2oz/¼ cup granulated sugar
175g/6oz plain (semisweet) chocolate, broken into pieces

1 Make the sauce. Heat the cream with the butter and sugar in the top of a double boiler or in a heatproof bowl over a pan of hot water. Stir until smooth, then remove from the heat and stir in the chocolate until combined.

2 Peel the bananas and cut into large pieces. Toss in the lemon juice, then arrange on individual plates and pour over the sauce. Top with grated chocolate and serve immediately.

Almost Instant Banana Pudding

Ginger cake is the base for this scrummy quick dessert.

Serves 6–8

4 thick slices ginger cake
6 bananas
30ml/2 tbsp lemon juice

300ml/½ pint/1¼ cups whipping cream or fromage frais
60ml/4 tbsp fruit juice
40–50g/1½–2oz/3–4 tbsp soft brown sugar

1 Break up the cake into chunks and arrange in an ovenproof dish. Peel and slice the bananas and toss in the lemon juice.

2 Whip the cream and, when firm, gently whip in the juice. (If using fromage frais, just gently stir in the juice.) Fold in the bananas and spoon the mixture over the ginger cake.

3 Top with the soft brown sugar and place under a hot grill (broiler) for 2–3 minutes to caramelize. Serve immediately.

Baked Bananas with Ice Cream

Baked bananas make the perfect partners for delicious vanilla ice cream topped with a toasted hazelnut sauce. A quick and easy dessert that looks as good as it tastes.

Serves 4

4 large bananas
15ml/1 tbsp lemon juice
4 large scoops vanilla ice cream

For the sauce

25g/1oz/2 tbsp unsalted (sweet) butter
50g/2oz/½ cup hazelnuts, toasted and roughly chopped
45ml/3 tbsp golden (light corn) syrup
30ml/2 tbsp lemon juice

1 Preheat the oven to 180°C/350°F/Gas 4. Place the unpeeled bananas on a baking sheet and brush them with the lemon juice. Bake for about 20 minutes until the skins are starting to turn black and the flesh gives a little when the bananas are gently squeezed.

2 Meanwhile, make the sauce. Melt the butter in a small pan. Add the hazelnuts and cook gently for 1 minute. Add the syrup and lemon juice and heat, stirring, for 1 minute more.

3 To serve, slit each banana open with a knife and open out the skins. Transfer to individual plates and serve with scoops of ice cream and the sauce poured over.

> **Cook's Tip**
> Cook the bananas over the dying coals of a barbecue, if you like. Put them on the rack as soon as you have removed all the main course items.

> **Variation**
> Use almonds instead of hazelnuts, and add a little brandy.

Chocolate Fudge Energy 647Kcal/2696kJ; Protein 4.1g; Carbohydrate 64.8g, of which sugars 62.1g; Fat 43g, of which saturates 26.5g; Cholesterol 81mg; Calcium 48mg; Fibre 2.2g; Sodium 89mg.
Banana Pudding Energy 326Kcal/1361kJ; Protein 3.1g; Carbohydrate 37.6g, of which sugars 30.4g; Fat 19.1g, of which saturates 11.6g; Cholesterol 39mg; Calcium 40mg; Fibre 1.1g; Sodium 106mg.
Baked Bananas Energy 416Kcal/1740kJ; Protein 6.3g; Carbohydrate 50.7g, of which sugars 47.2g; Fat 21.1g, of which saturates 9.5g; Cholesterol 35mg; Calcium 117mg; Fibre 1.9g; Sodium 124mg.

Barbecued Pineapple Boats with Rum Glaze

Fresh pineapple has even more flavour when barbecued; this spiced rum glaze turns it into a very special dessert in a matter of minutes.

Serves 4
1 medium pineapple, about 600g/1lb 6oz
25g/1oz/2 tbsp dark muscovado (molasses) sugar
5ml/1 tsp ground ginger
45ml/3 tbsp low-fat spread, melted
30ml/2 tbsp dark rum

1 With a large, sharp knife, cut the pineapple lengthways into four equal wedges.

2 Cut out and discard the hard centre core from each wedge of pineapple. Take care when handling the pineapple's rough outer skin.

3 Cut between the flesh and skin, to release the flesh; keep the skin in place. Slice the flesh across, into chunks.

4 Push a bamboo skewer lengthways through each wedge and into the stalk, to hold the chunks in place.

5 Mix together the sugar, ginger, melted spread and rum and then brush over the pineapple.

6 Cook the wedges on a hot barbecue for about 3–4 minutes.

7 Pour the remaining glaze over the top and serve.

Variation
For an even simpler version of this recipe, cut the skin off the pineapple and then slice the whole pineapple into thick slices and cook as above.

Deep-Fried Cherries

Succulent fresh cherries coated with a simple batter and then quickly deep-fried make a delicious and unusual dessert. Serve with vanilla ice cream for a perfect ending to a summery meal.

Serves 4–6
450g/1lb ripe red cherries, with stalks
225g/8oz packet batter mix
1 egg
vegetable oil, for deep-frying

1 Gently wash the cherries and pat dry with kitchen paper. Tie the stalks together with fine string to form clusters of four or five cherries.

2 Make up the batter mix according to the instructions on the packet, beating in the egg. Pour the vegetable oil into a deep-fat fryer or large, heavy pan and heat to 190°C/375°F.

3 Working in batches, half-dip each cherry cluster into the batter and then carefully drop the cluster into the hot oil. Fry for 3–4 minutes, or until golden.

4 Remove the deep-fried cherries with a wire-mesh skimmer or slotted spoon and drain on a wire rack placed over crumpled kitchen paper, and serve immediately.

Cook's Tips
• *You can always make your own batter – it doesn't take much longer to put together. Sift 115g/4oz/1 cup plain (all-purpose) flour and a pinch of salt into a large bowl and make a well in the centre. Add 1 egg and 150ml/¼ pint/⅔ cup milk to the well and whisk them lightly together, then gradually whisk in the dry ingredients to make a smooth batter. You can flavour the batter with a little ground cinnamon, if you like.*
• *The cherry fritters taste even more delicious dusted with caster (superfine) sugar and served with whipped cream.*

Apples & Raspberries in Rose Syrup

Inspiration for this dessert stems from the fact that the apple and the raspberry belong to the rose family. The subtle flavours are shared here in an infusion of rose-scented tea.

Serves 4

5ml/1 tsp rose pouchong tea
900ml/1½ pints/3¾ cups
    boiling water
5ml/1 tsp rose water (optional)
50g/2oz/¼ cup granulated sugar
5ml/1 tsp lemon juice
5 eating apples
175g/6oz/1½ cups fresh
    raspberries

1 Warm a large tea pot. Add the rose pouchong tea, then pour on the boiling water, together with the rose water, if using. Allow to stand and infuse for 4 minutes.

2 Put the sugar and lemon juice into a stainless steel pan. Strain in the tea and stir to dissolve the sugar.

3 Peel and core the apples, then cut into quarters. Poach the apples in the syrup for about 5 minutes.

4 Transfer the apples and syrup to a large metal tray and leave to cool to room temperature.

5 Transfer the cooled apples and syrup to a bowl, add the raspberries and mix to combine. Spoon into individual dishes or bowls and serve warm.

> **Cook's Tip**
> Serve warm, not cold, to make the most of the delicate flavours.

> **Variation**
> Use orange blossom tea instead of the rose pouchong tea and replace the rose water with orange flower water.

Grilled Nectarines with Amaretto

Amaretto, the sweet almond-flavoured liqueur from Italy, adds a touch of luxury to this incredibly quick and easy dessert.

Serves 4-6

6 ripe nectarines
30ml/2 tbsp clear honey
60ml/4 tbsp Amaretto di Saronno
half-fat crème fraîche, to serve
    (optional)

1 Cut the nectarines in half, running a small sharp knife down the side of each fruit from top to bottom, through to the stone (pit). Gently ease the halves apart and remove the stones.

2 Place the nectarines cut side up in a flameproof dish and drizzle 2.5ml/½ tsp honey and 5ml/1 tsp Amaretto over each half.

3 Preheat the grill (broiler) until very hot, then grill (broil) the fruit until slightly charred. Serve with crème fraîche, if you like.

Nectarines with Marzipan & Yogurt

A luscious dessert that few can resist; marzipan and nectarines are a wonderful combination. The nectarines can be cooked on the barbecue, if you like.

Serves 4

4 firm, ripe nectarines or peaches
75g/3oz marzipan
75ml/5 tbsp low-fat Greek
    (US strained plain) yogurt
3 amaretti, crushed

1 Cut the nectarines in half, running a small sharp knife down the side of each fruit through to the stone (pit). Gently ease the nectarine halves apart and remove the stones.

2 Cut the marzipan into eight pieces and press one piece into the cavity of each nectarine half. Preheat the grill (broiler).

3 Spoon the yogurt on top and sprinkle with crushed amaretti. Place the fruits under the hot grill. Cook for 3–5 minutes, until the yogurt starts to melt. Serve immediately.

Grilled Nectarines Energy 93Kcal/394kJ; Protein 1.8g; Carbohydrate 18.8g, of which sugars 18.8g; Fat 0.1g, of which saturates 0g; Cholesterol 0mg; Calcium 10mg; Fibre 1.6g; Sodium 3mg. **Nectarines with Marzipan & Yogurt** Energy 161Kcal/682kJ; Protein 4.2g; Carbohydrate 28.5g, of which sugars 27.4g; Fat 4.4g, of which saturates 1.1g; Cholesterol 0mg; Calcium 49mg; Fibre 2.2g; Sodium 24mg. **Apples & Raspberries** Energy 104Kcal/447kJ; Protein 1.1g; Carbohydrate 26.2g, of which sugars 26.2g; Fat 0.3g, of which saturates 0.1g; Cholesterol 0mg; Calcium 23mg; Fibre 3.1g; Sodium 5mg.

Pistachio & Nougat Torte

In this easy-to-prepare torte, nougat is combined with nuts, honey and rose water to create a fragrantly flavoured iced dessert.

Serves 8
75g/3oz/½ cup unsalted pistachio nuts, shelled
150g/5oz nougat
300ml/½ pint/1¼ cups whipping cream
90ml/6 tbsp clear honey
30ml/2 tbsp rose water
250g/9oz/generous 1 cup fromage frais or mascarpone
8 trifle sponges
icing (confectioners') sugar, for dusting
fresh raspberries, poached apricots or cherries, to serve (optional)

1 Soak the pistachio nuts in boiling water for 2 minutes. Drain them thoroughly, then rub them between pieces of kitchen paper to remove the skins. Peel off any skins that remain, then chop the nuts roughly.

2 Using a small sharp knife or scissors, cut the nougat into small pieces. Pour the cream into a bowl, add the honey and rose water and whip until it is just beginning to hold its shape.

3 Stir in the fromage frais or mascarpone, chopped pistachio nuts and nougat, and mix well. Slice the trifle sponges horizontally into three very thin layers.

4 Line a 15–17cm/6–6½in square loose-based cake tin (pan) with baking parchment or clear film (plastic wrap). Arrange a layer of sponges on the bottom, trimming the pieces to fit.

5 Pack the prepared filling into the cake tin and level the surface. Cover with the remaining sponges, then cover and freeze overnight.

6 Transfer the torte to the refrigerator about one hour before serving, then invert the torte on to a serving plate and dust with icing sugar. Serve with raspberries, poached apricots or cherries, if you like.

White Chocolate & Brownie Torte

An exceedingly rich dessert, this quick dish is guaranteed to appeal to chocolate lovers. The great thing about this recipe is that it uses very few ingredients, making shopping a breeze.

Serves 10
300g/11oz white chocolate, broken into pieces
600ml/1 pint/2½ cups double (heavy) cream
250g/9oz rich chocolate brownies
cocoa powder (unsweetened), for dusting

1 Dampen the sides of a 20cm/8in springform tin (pan) and line with a strip of baking parchment. Put the chocolate in a small pan. Add 150ml/¼ pint/⅔ cup of the cream and heat very gently until the chocolate has melted. Stir until smooth, then pour into a bowl and leave to cool.

2 Break the chocolate brownies into chunky pieces and scatter these on the bottom of the prepared tin. Pack them down lightly to make a fairly dense base.

3 Whip the remaining cream until it forms peaks, then fold in the white chocolate mixture. Spoon into the tin to cover the layer of brownies, then tap the tin gently on the work surface to level the chocolate mixture. Cover and freeze overnight.

4 Transfer the torte to the refrigerator about 45 minutes before serving, then remove the tin to serve. Decorate with a light dusting of cocoa powder before serving.

Cook's Tips
• If you are unable to find good quality brownies, use a moist chocolate sponge instead.
• Serve with a fresh fruit salad as a foil to the richness. A simple mix of summer fruit topped with a purée made from lightly cooked raspberries is the perfect partner. Or try tropical fruit tossed in a syrup made by dissolving sugar in lemon juice and water, then adding chopped fresh ginger to taste.

Pistachio & Nougat Energy 462Kcal/1929kJ; Protein 8.8g; Carbohydrate 46.7g, of which sugars 38.1g; Fat 28g, of which saturates 14.2g; Cholesterol 134mg; Calcium 119mg; Fibre 0.9g; Sodium 129mg.
White Chocolate Energy 570Kcal/2365kJ; Protein 5.2g; Carbohydrate 31.1g, of which sugars 25.7g; Fat 48.1g, of which saturates 25.6g; Cholesterol 82mg; Calcium 129mg; Fibre 0g; Sodium 154mg.

Soft Fruit & Crushed Meringue Gâteau

This recipe takes five minutes to make but looks and tastes as though a lot of preparation went into the dish. Use a really good vanilla ice cream for the best result.

Serves 6
400g/14oz/3½ cups mixed small
   strawberries, raspberries
   or redcurrants
30ml/2 tbsp icing (confectioners')
   sugar
750ml/1¼ pints/3 cups vanilla
   ice cream
6 meringue nests, or 115g/4oz
   meringue

1 Dampen a 900g/2lb loaf tin (pan) and line it with clear film (plastic wrap). If using strawberries, chop them into small pieces. Put them in a bowl together with the raspberries or redcurrants and icing sugar. Toss until the fruit is beginning to break up, but do not let it become mushy.

2 Put the vanilla ice cream in a large bowl and break it up with a fork. Crumble the meringues into the bowl of ice cream and then add the fruit.

3 Fold all the ingredients together until evenly combined and lightly marbled. Pack into the prepared tin and press down gently to level. Cover and freeze overnight.

4 Transfer the tin to the refrigerator about 30 minutes before serving. To serve, turn out on to a plate and peel away the clear film. Serve in slices.

> **Cook's Tip**
> *To make your own meringues, whisk 2 egg whites until stiff. Gradually whisk in 90g/3½oz/½ cup caster (superfine) sugar, then put spoonfuls on to lined baking sheets and cook in the oven, preheated to 150°C/300°F/Gas 2, for 1 hour or until dry.*

Tangy Raspberry & Lemon Tartlets

Fresh raspberries and popular lemon curd are teamed up to create colourful, tangy tartlets. Buy the best lemon curd you can find.

Serves 4
175g/6oz ready-made shortcrust
   pastry, thawed if frozen
120ml/8 tbsp good quality
   lemon curd
115g/4oz/⅔ cup fresh
   raspberries
whipped cream, to serve

1 Preheat the oven to 190°C/375°F/Gas 5. Roll out the pastry and use to line four 9cm/3½in tartlet tins (muffin pans). Line each tin with a circle of baking parchment and fill with baking beans or uncooked rice.

2 Bake for 15–20 minutes, or until golden and cooked through. Remove the baking beans or rice and paper and take the pastry cases (pie shells) out of the tins. Leave to cool completely on a wire rack.

3 Set aside 12 raspberries for decoration and fold the remaining ones into the lemon curd. Spoon the mixture into the pastry cases and top with the reserved raspberries. Serve immediately with whipped cream.

> **Cook's Tips**
> *• To save on last-minute preparation, you can make the pastry cases (pie shells) for these little tartlets in advance and store them in an airtight container until ready to serve.*
> *• For an attractive finish, dust the raspberry topping with sifted icing (confectioners') sugar and decorate with mint sprigs or finely shredded lemon rind.*

> **Variation**
> *Stir a little whipped cream into the lemon for a luxurious touch.*

Soft Fruit & Meringue Energy 332Kcal/1397kJ; Protein 6.1g; Carbohydrate 52.4g, of which sugars 51g; Fat 10.8g, of which saturates 7.6g; Cholesterol 30mg; Calcium 141mg; Fibre 0.7g; Sodium 102mg.
Raspberry & Lemon Energy 289Kcal/1214kJ; Protein 3.1g; Carbohydrate 40.6g, of which sugars 13.8g; Fat 13.9g, of which saturates 4.3g; Cholesterol 13mg; Calcium 47mg; Fibre 1.6g; Sodium 195mg.

Ice Cream Croissants with Chocolate Sauce

A deliciously easy-to-make croissant "sandwich" with a tempting filling of vanilla custard, ice cream and chocolate sauce melting inside the warmed bread.

Makes 4
75g/3oz plain (semisweet) chocolate, broken into pieces
15g/½oz/1 tbsp unsalted (sweet) butter
30ml/2 tbsp golden (light corn) syrup
4 croissants
90ml/6 tbsp good quality ready-made vanilla custard
4 large scoops of vanilla ice cream
icing (confectioners') sugar, for dusting

1 Preheat the oven to 180°C/350°F/Gas 4. Put the chocolate in a small, heavy pan. Add the butter and syrup and heat very gently until smooth, stirring the mixture frequently.

2 Split each of the croissants in half horizontally and place the base halves on a baking sheet. Spoon over the ready-made custard so that it covers the croissant bases, cover with the lids and bake in the oven for approximately 5 minutes or until warmed through.

3 Remove the lids and place a scoop of ice cream in each croissant. Spoon half the chocolate sauce over the ice cream and press the lids down gently. Put the croissants in the oven for 1 minute more.

4 Dust the filled croissants with icing sugar, spoon over the remaining chocolate sauce and serve immediately.

> **Variation**
> Add a dash of brandy to the chocolate sauce and use coffee-flavoured ice cream instead of vanilla.

Syrupy Brioche Slices with Vanilla Ice Cream

Keep a few individual brioche rolls in the freezer so that you can whip them out to make this fabulous five-minute pudding.

Serves 4
butter, for greasing
finely grated rind and juice of 1 orange
50g/2oz/¼ cup caster (superfine) sugar
90ml/6 tbsp water
1.5ml/¼ tsp ground cinnamon
4 brioche rolls
15ml/1 tbsp icing (confectioners') sugar
400ml/14fl oz/1⅔ cups vanilla ice cream

1 Lightly grease a shallow flameproof dish and set aside. Put the orange rind and juice, sugar, water and cinnamon in a heavy pan. Heat gently, stirring, until the sugar has dissolved, then boil for 2 minutes without stirring.

2 Remove the syrup from the heat and pour it into a heatproof shallow dish. Preheat the grill (broiler).

3 Cut each brioche vertically into three thick slices. Dip one side of each brioche slice in the hot syrup and arrange in the greased flameproof dish, with the syrup-coated sides down. Reserve the remaining syrup. Grill (broil) the brioche until lightly toasted.

4 Turn over and dust with icing sugar. Grill for 2–3 minutes more until they begin to caramelize around the edges.

5 Transfer to individual plates and top with scoops of ice cream. Spoon over the remaining syrup and serve immediately.

> **Cook's Tip**
> For a slightly more tart taste, use grated lemon rind in the recipe instead of the orange rind.

Brioche Slices Energy 409Kcal/1725kJ; Protein 8.5g; Carbohydrate 68.4g, of which sugars 45.3g; Fat 12g, of which saturates 7.2g; Cholesterol 25mg; Calcium 175mg; Fibre 1.3g; Sodium 251mg.
Ice Cream Croissants Energy 498Kcal/2086kJ; Protein 8.7g; Carbohydrate 59.4g, of which sugars 35g; Fat 29.5g, of which saturates 14.6g; Cholesterol 55mg; Calcium 134mg; Fibre 1.5g; Sodium 341mg.

Chocolate Petits Fours

Serve these dainty biscuits (cookies) as a stylish way to finish a meal. If you do not have any amaretto liqueur, they will work well without it. Alternatively, you can substitute the same quantity of brandy or rum.

Serves 8
350g/12oz carton chocolate chip
   cookie dough
115g/4oz plain (semisweet)
   chocolate
30ml/2 tbsp Amaretto di Saronno
   liqueur
50g/2oz/¼ cup butter

1 Preheat the oven according to the instructions on the cookie dough packet. Roll out the cookie dough on a floured surface to 1cm/½in thick. Using a 2.5cm/1in cutter, stamp out as many rounds from the dough as possible and transfer them to a lightly greased baking sheet. Bake for about 8 minutes, or until cooked through. Transfer to a wire rack to cool completely.

2 Make the filling. Break the chocolate into small pieces and place in a heatproof bowl with the amaretto liqueur and butter. Sit the bowl over a pan of gently simmering water and stir occasionally, until the chocolate has melted. Remove from the heat and set aside to cool.

3 Spread a small amount of the filling on the flat bottom of one of the cookies and sandwich together with another. Repeat until all the cookies have been used.

Strawberry Cream Shortbreads

Simple to assemble, these pretty strawberry desserts are always popular. Serve them as soon as they are ready because the shortbread biscuits (cookies) will lose their lovely crisp texture if left to stand.

Serves 3
150g/5oz/generous 1 cup
   strawberries
450ml/¾ pint/scant 2 cups
   double (heavy) cream
6 round shortbread biscuits
fresh mint sprigs, to decorate
   (optional)

1 Reserve three strawberries for decoration. Hull the remaining strawberries and cut them in half.

2 Put the halved strawberries in a bowl and gently crush using the back of a fork. (Only crush the berries lightly; they should not be reduced to a purée.)

3 Put the cream in a large, clean bowl and whip to form soft peaks. Add the crushed strawberries and gently fold in to combine – do not overmix.

4 Halve the reserved strawberries, then spoon the strawberry and cream mixture on top of the shortbread biscuits. Decorate each one with half a strawberry and a mint sprig, if you like. Serve immediately.

> **Cook's Tip**
> Use whole strawberries for the decoration and give them a pretty frosted effect by painting with whisked egg white, then dipping in caster (superfine) sugar. Leave to dry before serving.

> **Variation**
> You can use any other berry you like for this dessert – try raspberries or blueberries. Two ripe, peeled peaches will also give great results.

Cherry Chocolate Brownies

This is a modern, quick version of the classic Black Forest gâteau. Choose really good-quality bottled fruits because this will make all the difference to the end result. Look out for bottled fruit at Christmas time in particular, when supermarket shelves are packed with different varieties.

Serves 4
4 chocolate brownies
300ml/½ pint/1¼ cups double
   (heavy) cream
20–24 bottled cherries in Kirsch
icing (confectioners') sugar, to
   decorate (optional)

1 Using a sharp knife, carefully cut the brownies in half horizontally to make two thin slices. Place one brownie square on each of four serving plates.

2 Pour the cream into a large bowl and whip until soft but not stiff, then divide half the whipped cream between the four brownie squares.

3 Divide half the cherries among the cream-topped brownies, then place the remaining brownie halves on top of the cherries. Press down lightly.

4 Spoon the remaining cream on top of the brownies, then top each one with more cherries. Dust with a little icing sugar, if you like, and serve immediately.

Shortbreads Energy 890Kcal/3673kJ; Protein 4.4g; Carbohydrate 22g, of which sugars 9.6g; Fat 87.8g, of which saturates 54.8g; Cholesterol 225mg; Calcium 105mg; Fibre 1g; Sodium 106mg.
Petit Fours Energy 337Kcal/1410kJ; Protein 3.3g; Carbohydrate 38.9g, of which sugars 24.1g; Fat 19.2g, of which saturates 10.3g; Cholesterol 15mg; Calcium 42mg; Fibre 1.2g; Sodium 192mg.
Brownies Energy 632Kcal/2619kJ; Protein 5g; Carbohydrate 31.1g, of which sugars 20.3g; Fat 53.5g, of which saturates 25.1g; Cholesterol 103mg; Calcium 78mg; Fibre 0.2g; Sodium 234mg.

Butterfly Pastries

Melt-in-the-mouth puff pastry interleaved with sugar, nuts and cinnamon produces an eye-catching accompaniment that teams well with ice creams, baked custards or fruit salads.

Makes about 12
500g/1¼lb packet ready-made puff pastry
1 egg, beaten
115g/4oz/generous ½ cup granulated sugar
25g/1oz/¼ cup chopped mixed nuts
5ml/1 tsp ground cinnamon

1 Preheat the oven to 200°C/400°F/Gas 6. Roll out the pastry on a lightly floured surface to a rectangle measuring 50 x 17cm/ 20 x 6½in. Cut widthways into four pieces. Brush each piece with beaten egg.

2 Mix 75g/3oz/6 tbsp of the sugar with the nuts and cinnamon in a bowl. Sprinkle this mixture evenly over three of the pieces of pastry. Place the pieces one on top of the other, ending with the uncoated piece, placing this one egg side down on the top. Press lightly together with the rolling pin.

3 Cut the stack of pastry sheets widthways into 5mm/¼in slices. Carefully place one strip on a non-stick baking sheet and place the next strip over it at an angle. Place a third strip on top at another angle so that it looks like a butterfly. Don't worry if the strips separate slightly when you move them.

4 Press the centre very flat. Sprinkle with a little of the reserved sugar. Continue in this way with the rest of the pastry.

5 Bake for 10–15 minutes, or until golden brown all over. Cool completely on the baking sheet before serving.

Cook's Tip
If using frozen puff pastry, thaw it first, but keep it chilled. Handle the dough lightly so it doesn't toughen.

Ginger Thins

As delicate as fine glass, these elegant ginger biscuits (cookies) are ideal served with creamy desserts, syllabubs, sorbets and luxury ice creams.

Makes about 18
50g/2oz/¼ cup unsalted (sweet) butter, diced
40g/1½oz/3 tbsp liquid glucose (clear corn syrup)
90g/3½oz/½ cup caster (superfine) sugar
40g/1½oz/⅓ cup plain (all-purpose) flour
5ml/1 tsp ground ginger

1 Put the butter and liquid glucose in a heatproof bowl and place over a pan of simmering water. Stir until melted. Set aside.

2 Put the sugar in a bowl and sift over the flour and ginger. Stir into the butter mixture, then beat well until combined. Cover with clear film (plastic wrap) and chill for about 25 minutes, until firm. Meanwhile, preheat the oven to 180°C/350°F/Gas 4 and line two or three baking sheets with baking parchment.

3 Roll teaspoonfuls of the biscuit mixture into balls between your hands and place on the prepared baking sheets, spacing them well apart to allow room for spreading.

4 Place a second piece of baking parchment on top of the dough balls and roll them as thinly as possible. Peel off the top sheet, then stamp each rolled-out biscuit with a 7.5 or 9cm/ 3 or 3½in plain round cutter. Remove the trimmings.

5 Bake for 5–6 minutes, or until golden. Leave for a few seconds on the baking sheets to firm up slightly, then either leave flat or curl over in half. Leave to cool completely.

Cook's Tip
Use unlipped baking sheets, so that you can roll the biscuits (cookies) thinly.

Butterfly Pastries Energy 212Kcal/889kJ; Protein 3.4g; Carbohydrate 25.6g, of which sugars 10.6g; Fat 11.8g, of which saturates 0.2g; Cholesterol 16mg; Calcium 37mg; Fibre 0.2g; Sodium 136mg.
Ginger Thins Energy 55Kcal/229kJ; Protein 0.3g; Carbohydrate 8.7g, of which sugars 7g; Fat 2.3g, of which saturates 1.5g; Cholesterol 6mg; Calcium 7mg; Fibre 0.1g; Sodium 23mg.

Almond & Vanilla Biscuits with Praline Coating

These short-textured almond biscuits (cookies), filled with vanilla cream and coated in praline, are just the thing to serve with a light sorbet or fresh fruit salad. They're also great served alone, simply with a cup of strong coffee.

Makes 17–18

150g/5oz/1¼ cups plain
  (all-purpose) flour
75g/3oz/¾ cup ground almonds
75g/3oz/6 tbsp unsalted (sweet)
  butter, at room temperature,
  diced
1 egg yolk

5ml/1 tsp vanilla extract
icing (confectioners') sugar, sifted,
  for dusting

For the praline
oil, for greasing
25g/1oz/¼ cup whole blanched
  almonds
50g/2oz/¼ cup caster (superfine)
  sugar

For the filling
150g/5oz/1¼ cups icing
  (confectioners') sugar, sifted
75g/3oz/6 tbsp unsalted (sweet)
  butter, at room temperature,
  diced
5ml/1 tsp vanilla extract

1 Make the praline. Lightly oil a baking sheet and place the almonds on it, fairly close together. Melt the sugar in a small non-stick pan over a very low heat. Continue heating until it turns dark golden brown and pour immediately over the almonds. Set aside to cool. Crush the praline finely in a food processor.

2 Preheat the oven to 160°C/325°F/Gas 3. Line three baking sheets with baking parchment.

3 Put the flour, ground almonds and butter in a bowl. Rub together until the mixture starts to cling together. Add the egg and vanilla and work together using your hands to make a soft but not sticky dough. Roll out to a thickness of about 5mm/¼in on baking parchment. Using a 5cm/2in round biscuit (cookie) cutter, stamp out rounds and carefully transfer them to the prepared baking sheets.

4 Bake the biscuits for about 15–20 minutes, or until light golden brown. Leave on the baking sheets for 5 minutes to firm up slightly, then transfer to a wire rack to cool.

5 Make the filling. Beat together the icing sugar, butter and vanilla until light and creamy. Use this mixture to sandwich the biscuits in pairs. Be generous with the filling, spreading right to the edges. Press the biscuits gently so the filling oozes out of the sides and, using your finger, smooth around the sides of the biscuit.

6 Put the praline on a plate and roll the edges of each biscuit in the praline until thickly coated. Dust the tops of the biscuits with icing sugar and serve.

> **Cook's Tip**
> Serve these biscuits (cookies) on the day they are made. Left longer, the filling makes them soggy and unpleasant.

Tiramisu Biscuits

These sophisticated biscuits (cookies) taste like the famed Italian dessert, with its flavours of coffee, chocolate and rum. A perfect luxurious accompaniment to ices, fools or other light dishes.

Makes 14

50g/2oz/¼ cup butter, at room
  temperature, diced
90g/3½oz/½ cup caster
  (superfine) sugar
1 egg, beaten
50g/2oz/½ cup plain
  (all-purpose) flour

For the filling
150g/5oz/⅔ cup mascarpone
15ml/1 tbsp dark rum
2.5ml/½ tsp instant coffee
  powder
15ml/1 tbsp light muscovado
  (brown) sugar

For the topping
75g/3oz white chocolate
15ml/1 tbsp milk
30ml/2 tbsp crushed chocolate
  flake

1 Make the filling. Put the mascarpone in a bowl. Mix together the rum and coffee powder until the coffee has dissolved. Add to the cheese, with the sugar, and mix together well. Cover with clear film (plastic wrap) and chill until required.

2 Preheat the oven to 200°C/400°F/Gas 6. Line two or three baking sheets with baking parchment. Make the biscuits. Cream together the butter and sugar in a bowl until light and fluffy. Add the egg and mix well. Stir in the flour and mix thoroughly.

3 Put the mixture into a piping (pastry) bag fitted with a 1.5cm/½in plain nozzle and pipe 28 small blobs on to the baking sheets, spaced slightly apart. Cook for 6–8 minutes until firm in the centre and just beginning to brown on the edges. Remove from the oven and set aside to cool.

4 To assemble, spread a little of the filling on to half the biscuits and place the other halves on top. Put the chocolate and milk in a heatproof bowl and melt over a pan of hot water. When melted, stir vigorously until spreadable. Spread the chocolate evenly over the biscuits, then top with crushed chocolate flake.

Almond & Vanilla Biscuits Energy 172Kcal/717kJ; Protein 2.2g; Carbohydrate 18.5g, of which sugars 12g; Fat 10.4g, of which saturates 4.7g; Cholesterol 29mg; Calcium 34mg; Fibre 0.7g; Sodium 53mg.
Tiramisu Biscuits Energy 178Kcal/742kJ; Protein 2.4g; Carbohydrate 15.5g, of which sugars 12.8g; Fat 7.2g, of which saturates 4.3g; Cholesterol 26mg; Calcium 28mg; Fibre 0.2g; Sodium 34mg.

Mini Fudge Bites

These cute little treats have the flavour of butterscotch and fudge and are topped with chopped pecan nuts for a delicious crunch – ideal as a contrast to smooth, creamy desserts.

Makes 30
200g/7oz/1¾ cups self-raising (self-rising) flour
115g/4oz/½ cup butter, at room temperature, diced
115g/4oz/scant ½ cup dark muscovado (molasses) sugar
75g/3oz vanilla cream fudge, diced
I egg, beaten
25g/1oz/¼ cup pecan nut halves, sliced widthways

1 Preheat the oven to 190°C/375°F/Gas 5. Line two or three baking sheets with baking parchment. Put the flour in a bowl and rub in the diced butter, with your fingertips, until the mixture resembles fine breadcrumbs.

2 Add the sugar and diced vanilla cream fudge to the flour mixture and stir well until combined. Add the beaten egg and mix in well. Bring the dough together with your hands, then knead gently on a lightly floured surface. It will be soft yet firm.

3 Roll the dough into two cylinders, 23cm/9in long. Cut into 1cm/½in slices and place on the baking sheets. Sprinkle over the pecan nuts and press in lightly. Bake for about 12 minutes until browned at the edges. Transfer to a wire rack to cool.

Rosemary-Scented Citrus Tuiles

These elegant, crisp biscuits (cookies) are flavoured with tangy citrus rind, and made beautifully fragrant with fresh rosemary – an unusual but winning combination.

Makes 18–20
50g/2oz/¼ cup unsalted (sweet) butter, diced
2 egg whites
115g/4oz/generous ½ cup caster (superfine) sugar
finely grated rind of ½ lemon
finely grated rind of ½ orange
10ml/2 tsp finely chopped fresh rosemary
50g/2oz/½ cup plain (all-purpose) flour

1 Preheat the oven to 190°C/375°F/Gas 5. Line a baking sheet with baking parchment. Melt the butter in a pan over a low heat. Leave to cool. Whisk the egg whites until stiff, then gradually whisk in the sugar.

2 Fold in the lemon and orange rinds, rosemary and flour and then the melted butter. Place 2 large tablespoonfuls of the mixture on the baking sheet. Spread each to a thin disc about 9cm/3½in in diameter. Bake for 5–6 minutes until golden.

3 Remove from the oven and lift the tuiles using a palette knife (metal spatula) and drape over a rolling pin. Transfer to a wire rack when set in a curved shape. Continue baking the rest of the mixture in the same way.

Lace Biscuits

Very pretty, delicate and crisp, these lacy biscuits (cookies) are ideal for serving with elegant creamy or iced desserts at the end of a dinner party. Don't be tempted to bake more than four on a sheet.

Makes about 14
75g/3oz/6 tbsp butter, diced
75g/3oz/¾ cup rolled oats
115g/4oz/generous ½ cup golden caster (superfine) sugar
I egg, beaten
10ml/2 tsp plain (all-purpose) flour
5ml/1 tsp baking powder
2.5ml/½ tsp mixed spice (apple pie spice)

1 Preheat the oven to 180°C/350°F/Gas 4. Line three or four baking sheets with baking parchment. Put the butter in a pan and place over a low heat until just melted. Remove the pan from the heat.

2 Stir the rolled oats into the melted butter. Add the remaining ingredients and mix well.

3 Place only 3 or 4 heaped teaspoonfuls of the mixture, spaced well apart, on each of the lined baking sheets.

4 Bake for 5–7 minutes, or until they have turned a deepish golden brown all over. Leave the biscuits (cookies) on the baking sheets for a few minutes.

5 Carefully cut the baking parchment so that you can lift each biscuit singly. Invert on to a wire rack and carefully remove the parchment lining. Leave to cool before serving.

> **Cook's Tip**
> Do not try to prise the biscuits (cookies) off the baking parchment while they are still upright, as you will damage their shape. It is much easier and neater to gently peel off the parchment once the biscuits are upside down on the wire rack.

Mini Fudge Bites Energy 85Kcal/356kJ; Protein 1g; Carbohydrate 11.1g, of which sugars 6.2g; Fat 4.3g, of which saturates 2.3g; Cholesterol 15mg; Calcium 31mg; Fibre 0.2g; Sodium 53mg.
Citrus Tuiles Energy 51Kcal/214kJ; Protein 0.6g; Carbohydrate 8g, of which sugars 6.1g; Fat 2.1g, of which saturates 1.3g; Cholesterol 5mg; Calcium 7mg; Fibre 0.1g; Sodium 22mg.
Lace Biscuits Energy 94Kcal/391kJ; Protein 1.2g; Carbohydrate 11g, of which sugars 6.5g; Fat 5.3g, of which saturates 2.9g; Cholesterol 25mg; Calcium 8mg; Fibre 0.4g; Sodium 61mg.

Dark Chocolate Fingers

With their understated elegance and distinctly grown-up flavour, these deliciously decadent chocolate fingers add a touch of luxury to compotes and other fruity desserts.

Makes about 26
115g/4oz/1 cup plain (all-purpose) flour
2.5ml/½ tsp baking powder
30ml/2 tbsp (unsweetened) cocoa powder
50g/2oz/¼ cup unsalted (sweet) butter, softened
50g/2oz/¼ cup caster (superfine) sugar
20ml/4 tsp golden (light corn) syrup
150g/5oz dark (bittersweet) chocolate
chocolate flake, broken up, for sprinkling

1 Preheat the oven to 160°C/325°F/Gas 3. Line two baking sheets with baking parchment. Put the flour, baking powder, cocoa powder, butter, sugar and syrup in a large mixing bowl.

2 Work the ingredients together with your hands to combine and form into a dough.

3 Roll the dough out between sheets of baking parchment to an 18 x 24cm/7 x 9½in rectangle. Remove the top sheet. Cut in half lengthways, then into bars 2cm/¾in wide. Transfer to the baking sheets.

4 Bake for about 15 minutes, taking care not to allow the bars to brown or they will taste bitter. Transfer to a wire rack to cool.

5 Melt the chocolate in a heatproof bowl set over a pan of hot water. Half-dip the biscuits into the chocolate, then carefully place on a sheet of baking parchment. Sprinkle with chocolate flake, then leave to set.

> **Variation**
> *For an extra touch of sophistication, add a dash of orange-flavoured liqueur to the chocolate.*

Chocolate & Pistachio Wedges

These are rich and grainy in texture, with a delicious bitter chocolate flavour. They go extremely well with vanilla ice cream and are especially good with bananas and custard.

Makes 16
200g/7oz/scant 1 cup unsalted (sweet) butter, at room temperature, diced
90g/3½oz/½ cup golden caster (superfine) sugar
250g/9oz/2¼ cups plain (all-purpose) flour
50g/2oz/½ cup cocoa powder (unsweetened)
25g/1oz/¼ cup shelled pistachio nuts, finely chopped
cocoa powder (unsweetened), for dusting

1 Preheat the oven to 180°C/350°F/Gas 4 and line a 23cm/9in round sandwich tin (layer pan) with baking parchment.

2 Beat the butter and sugar until light and creamy. Sift the flour and cocoa powder, then add the flour mixture to the butter and work in with your hands until the mixture is smooth. Knead until soft and pliable then press into the prepared tin.

3 Using the back of a tablespoon, spread the mixture evenly in the tin. Sprinkle the pistachio nuts over the top and press in gently. Prick with a fork, then mark into 16 segments using a round-bladed knife.

4 Bake for 15–20 minutes. Do not allow to brown at all or the biscuits (cookies) will taste bitter.

5 Remove the tin from the oven and dust the biscuits with cocoa powder. Cut through the marked sections with a round-bladed knife and leave to cool completely before removing from the tin and serving.

> **Variation**
> *Try using almonds or hazelnuts instead of pistachio nuts.*

Choc. & Pistachio Wedges Energy 188Kcal/783kJ; Protein 2.4g; Carbohydrate 18.6g, of which sugars 6.3g; Fat 12g, of which saturates 7.1g; Cholesterol 27mg; Calcium 33mg; Fibre 1g; Sodium 115mg.
Dark Choc. Fingers Energy 72Kcal/303kJ; Protein 0.9g; Carbohydrate 9.9g, of which sugars 6.3g; Fat 3.5g, of which saturates 2.1g; Cholesterol 4mg; Calcium 11mg; Fibre 0.4g; Sodium 25mg.

Chocolate-Dipped Cinnamon & Orange Tuiles

These lightweight chocolate-dipped tuiles are a divine accompaniment to fruit or creamy desserts.

Makes 12–15
2 egg whites
90g/3½oz/½ cup caster
(superfine) sugar
7.5ml/1½ tsp ground cinnamon
finely grated rind of 1 orange

50g/2oz/½ cup plain
(all-purpose) flour
75g/3oz/6 tbsp butter, melted
15ml/1 tbsp recently boiled water

For the dipping chocolate
75g/3oz Belgian plain (semisweet)
chocolate
45ml/3 tbsp milk
75–90ml/5–6 tbsp double
(heavy) or whipping cream

1 Preheat the oven to 200°C/400°F/Gas 6. Line three large baking trays with baking parchment.

2 Whisk the egg whites until softly peaking, then whisk in the sugar until smooth and glossy. Add the cinnamon and orange rind, sift over the flour and fold in with the melted butter. When well blended, add water to thin the mixture.

3 Place 4–5 teaspoons of the mixture on each tray, well apart. Flatten out and bake, one tray at a time, for 7 minutes until just turning golden. Cool for a few seconds then remove from the tray with a metal spatula and immediately roll around the handle of a wooden spoon. Place on a rack to cool.

4 Melt the chocolate in the milk until smooth; stir in the cream. Dip one or both ends of the tuiles in the chocolate, then cool.

> **Cook's Tip**
> If you haven't made these before, cook only one or two at a time until you get the hang of it. If they harden too quickly to allow you time to roll them, return the baking sheet to the oven for a few seconds, then try rolling them again.

Chocolate Truffles

Gloriously rich chocolate truffles are given a really wicked twist in this recipe simply by the addition of a small quantity of cherry brandy – the perfect indulgent way to end a special dinner party. Instead of adding cherry brandy, experiment with using some other favourite alcoholic tipples.

Makes 18
50g/2oz/½ cup plain
(all-purpose) flour
25g/1oz/¼ cup cocoa powder
(unsweetened)
2.5ml/½ tsp baking powder
90g/3½oz/½ cup caster
(superfine) sugar
25g/1oz/2 tbsp butter, diced
1 egg, beaten
5ml/1 tsp cherry brandy
50g/2oz/½ cup icing
(confectioners') sugar

1 Preheat the oven to 200°C/400°F/Gas 6. Line two baking sheets with baking parchment.

2 Sift the flour, cocoa and baking powder into a bowl and stir in the sugar.

3 Rub the butter into the flour mixture with your fingertips until the mixture resembles coarse breadcrumbs.

4 Mix together the beaten egg and cherry brandy and stir thoroughly into the flour mixture. Cover with clear film (plastic wrap) and chill for approximately 30 minutes.

5 Put the icing sugar in a bowl. Shape walnut-size pieces of dough roughly into a ball and drop into the icing sugar. Toss until thickly coated then place on the baking sheets.

6 Bake for about 10 minutes, or until just set. Transfer to a wire rack to cool completely.

> **Variation**
> Try using fresh orange juice instead of cherry brandy.

Cinnamon & Orange Tuiles Energy 125Kcal/523kJ; Protein 1.2g; Carbohydrate 12.3g, of which sugars 9.7g; Fat 8.3g, of which saturates 5.2g; Cholesterol 18mg; Calcium 17mg; Fibre 0.2g; Sodium 42mg.
Choc. Truffles Energy 60Kcal/251kJ; Protein 0.9g; Carbohydrate 10.5g, of which sugars 8.2g; Fat 1.8g, of which saturates 1g; Cholesterol 14mg; Calcium 12mg; Fibre 0.3g; Sodium 26mg.

Florentine Bites

Extremely sweet and rich, these little mouthfuls – based on a classic Italian biscuit (cookie) – are really delicious when served with after-dinner coffee and liqueurs. Nicely wrapped, they would also make a very special gift for anyone – your dinner party host for example.

Makes 36
200g/7oz good quality plain (semisweet) chocolate (minimum 70 per cent cocoa solids)
50g/2oz/2½ cups cornflakes
50g/2oz/scant ½ cup sultanas (golden raisins)
115g/4oz/1 cup toasted flaked (sliced) almonds
115g/4oz/½ cup glacé (candied) cherries, halved
50g/2oz/⅓ cup mixed (candied) peel
200ml/7fl oz/scant 1 cup can sweetened condensed milk

1 Preheat the oven to 180°C/350°F/Gas 4. Line the base of a shallow 20cm/8in cake tin (pan) with baking parchment. Lightly grease the sides.

2 Melt the chocolate in a heatproof bowl over a pan of hot water. Spread over the base of the tin. Chill until set.

3 Meanwhile, put the cornflakes, sultanas, almonds, cherries and mixed peel in a large bowl.

4 Pour the condensed milk over the cornflake mixture and toss the mix gently, using a fork.

5 Spread the mixture evenly over the chocolate base and bake for 12–15 minutes or until golden brown.

6 Put the cooked Florentine mixture aside in the tin until completely cooled, then chill for 20 minutes.

7 Cut into tiny squares and serve.

Tunisian Almond Cigars

These delicate rolled pastries are a great favourite in North Africa. Wonderful with all manner of desserts, they are also excellent served on their own, with a small cup of fragrant mint tea or strong, dark coffee, at the end of a meal.

Makes 8–12
250g/9oz marzipan
1 egg, lightly beaten
15ml/1 tbsp rose water or orange flower water
5ml/1 tsp ground cinnamon
1.5ml/¼ tsp almond extract
8–12 sheets filo pastry
melted butter, for brushing
icing (confectioners') sugar and ground cinnamon, for dusting

1 Knead the marzipan until it is soft, then put in a bowl, and mix in the egg, rose water, cinnamon and almond extract. Chill for 1–2 hours.

2 Preheat the oven to 190°C/375°F/Gas 5. Lightly grease a baking sheet. Place a sheet of filo pastry on a piece of baking parchment, keeping the remaining pastry covered with a damp cloth, and brush with the melted butter.

3 Shape 30–45ml/2–3 tbsp of the filling mixture into a cylinder and place at one end of the pastry. Fold the pastry over to enclose the ends of the filling, then roll up to form a cigar shape. Place on the baking sheet and make 7–11 more cigars in the same way.

4 Bake the pastries for about 15 minutes, or until golden. Leave to cool, then serve, dusted with sugar and cinnamon.

Variation
Instead of dusting with sugar, drench the pastries in syrup. In a pan, dissolve 250g/9oz/1¼ cups sugar in 250ml/8fl oz/1 cup water and boil until thickened. Stir in a squeeze of lemon juice and a few drops of rose water and pour over the pastries. Allow the syrup to soak in before serving.

Florentine Bites Energy 87Kcal/364kJ; Protein 1.6g; Carbohydrate 12g, of which sugars 10.7g; Fat 3.9g, of which saturates 1.4g; Cholesterol 2mg; Calcium 30mg; Fibre 0.5g; Sodium 28mg.
Tunisian Almond Cigars Energy 101Kcal/428kJ; Protein 2g; Carbohydrate 17.3g, of which sugars 14.2g; Fat 3.2g, of which saturates 0.4g; Cholesterol 16mg; Calcium 22mg; Fibre 0.5g; Sodium 10mg.

Gazelles' Horns

These Moroccan pastries are a stylish accompaniment to light fruit dishes.

Makes about 16
200g/7oz/scant 2 cups ground almonds
115g/4oz/1 cup icing (confectioners') sugar, plus extra for dusting
30ml/2 tbsp orange flower water
25g/1oz/2 tbsp butter, melted

2 egg yolks, beaten
2.5ml/½ tsp ground cinnamon

For the pastry
200g/7oz/1¾ cups plain (all-purpose) flour
pinch of salt
25g/1oz/2 tbsp butter, melted
about 30ml/2 tbsp orange flower water
1 egg yolk, beaten
60–90ml/4–6 tbsp chilled water

1 Mix the almonds, icing sugar, orange flower water, butter, egg yolks and cinnamon in a mixing bowl to make a smooth paste.

2 Make the pastry. Sift the flour and salt into a large bowl, then stir in the melted butter, orange flower water and about three-quarters of the egg yolk. Stir in enough chilled water to make a fairly soft dough.

3 Quickly and lightly, knead the pastry until it is smooth and elastic, then place on a lightly floured surface and roll out as thinly as possible. With a sharp knife, cut the dough into long strips about 7.5cm/3in wide.

4 Preheat the oven to 180°C/350°F/Gas 4. Roll small pieces of the almond paste into thin sausages about 7.5cm/3in long with tapering ends. Place these in a line along one side of the strips of pastry, about 3cm/1¼in apart. Dampen the pastry edges with water, then fold the other half of the strip over the filling and press the edges together firmly.

5 Using a pastry wheel, cut around each pastry sausage to make a crescent shape. Pinch the edges firmly together. Prick the crescents with a fork and place on a buttered baking sheet. Brush with the remaining egg yolk and bake for 12–16 minutes until lightly coloured. Allow to cool, then dust with icing sugar.

Greek Fruit & Nut Pastries

Packed with candied citrus peel and walnuts, and soaked in a coffee syrup, these aromatic pastries make a different way to end a meal with coffee.

milk, to glaze
caster (superfine) sugar, for sprinkling

Makes 16
60ml/4 tbsp clear honey
60ml/4 tbsp strong brewed coffee
75g/3oz/½ cup mixed (candied) citrus peel, finely chopped
175g/6oz/1 cup walnuts, chopped
1.5ml/¼ tsp freshly grated nutmeg

For the pastry
450g/1lb/4 cups plain (all-purpose) flour
2.5ml/½ tsp ground cinnamon
2.5ml/½ tsp baking powder
pinch of salt
150g/5oz/10 tbsp butter
30ml/2 tbsp caster (superfine) sugar
1 egg
120ml/4fl oz/½ cup chilled milk

1 Preheat the oven to 180°C/350°F/Gas 4. Make the pastry. Sift the flour, cinnamon, baking powder and salt into a bowl. Rub or cut in the butter until the mixture resembles breadcrumbs. Stir in the sugar. Make a well.

2 Beat the egg and milk together and pour into the well. Mix to a soft dough. Divide the dough into two and wrap each piece in clear film (plastic wrap). Chill for 30 minutes.

3 Mix the honey and coffee in a mixing bowl. Stir in the mixed peel, walnuts and nutmeg. Cover and leave for 20 minutes.

4 Roll out one portion of the dough on a lightly floured surface to 3mm/⅛in thick. Stamp out rounds, using a 10cm/4in cutter.

5 Place a heaped teaspoonful of filling on one side of each round. Brush the edges with a little milk, then fold over and press together to seal. Repeat with the second piece of pastry.

6 Place the pastries on greased baking sheets, brush with a little milk and sprinkle with sugar. Make a steam hole in each with a skewer. Bake for 35 minutes until golden. Cool on a wire rack.

Fruit & Nut Pastries Energy 278Kcal/1162kJ; Protein 5g; Carbohydrate 30.2g, of which sugars 8.7g; Fat 16.1g, of which saturates 5.7g; Cholesterol 32mg; Calcium 69mg; Fibre 1.5g; Sodium 80mg.
Gazelles' Horns Energy 182Kcal/762kJ; Protein 4.4g; Carbohydrate 18.1g, of which sugars 8.2g; Fat 10.7g, of which saturates 2.5g; Cholesterol 44mg; Calcium 56mg; Fibre 1.3g; Sodium 23mg.

Rugelach

Thought to hail from Poland, these crisp, flaky pastries, with a sweet filling, resemble a snake or croissant. Memorable little bites to serve with coffee.

Makes 48–60

115g/4oz/½ cup unsalted (sweet) butter
115g/4oz/½ cup full-fat soft white (farmer's) cheese
15ml/1 tbsp sugar
1 egg
2.5ml/½ tsp salt

about 250g/9oz/2¼ cups plain (all-purpose) flour
about 250g/9oz/generous 1 cup butter, melted
250g/9oz/scant 2 cups sultanas (golden raisins)
130g/4½oz/generous 1 cup chopped walnuts or walnut pieces
about 225g/8oz/1 cup caster (superfine) sugar
10–15ml/1–2 tsp ground cinnamon

1 Make the pastry. Put the butter and soft cheese in a bowl and beat with an electric whisk until creamy. Beat in the sugar, egg and salt.

2 Fold the flour into the creamed mixture, a little at a time, until the dough can be worked with the hands. Continue adding the flour, kneading, until it is a consistency that can be rolled out. (Add only as much flour as needed.) Shape the dough into a ball, cover and chill for at least 2 hours or overnight. (The dough will be too soft if not chilled properly.)

3 Preheat the oven to 180°C/350°F/Gas 4. Divide the dough into six equal pieces. On a lightly floured surface, roll out each piece into a round about 3mm/⅛in thick, then brush with a little of the melted butter and sprinkle over the sultanas, chopped walnuts, a little sugar and the cinnamon.

4 Cut the rounds into eight to ten wedges and carefully roll the large side of each wedge towards the tip. (Some of the filling will fall out.) Arrange the rugelach on baking sheets, brush with a little butter and sprinkle with the sugar. Bake for 15–30 minutes until lightly browned. Leave to cool before serving.

Baklava

Serve wedges of this luxuriously sweet Greek treat with fresh fruit or lots of strong coffee to round off a meal with panache.

Makes 16

50g/2oz/½ cup blanched almonds, chopped
50g/2oz/½ cup pistachio nuts, chopped
75g/3oz/6 tbsp caster (superfine) sugar

75g/3oz/6 tbsp butter, melted
6 sheets of filo pastry, thawed if frozen

For the syrup
115g/4oz/generous ½ cup caster (superfine) sugar
7.5cm/3in piece cinnamon stick
1 whole clove
2 green cardamom pods, crushed
75ml/5 tbsp very strong brewed coffee

1 Preheat the oven to 180°C/350°F/Gas 4. Add the almonds, pistachio nuts and sugar to a small bowl and mix well, stirring to coat the nuts in sugar. Brush a shallow 18 × 28cm/7 × 11in baking tin (pan) with a little of the melted butter.

2 Using the tin as a guide, cut the six sheets of filo pastry with a very sharp knife so that they fit the tin exactly. It is easiest to cut through all the sheets in one go, rather than working through them singly. Lay a sheet of pastry in the tin and brush it all over with some of the melted butter.

3 Lay a second sheet of filo in the tin and brush with butter. Add a third sheet, brushing with a little butter. Sprinkle the filo with half of the nut mixture, making sure it is evenly distributed.

4 Layer three more sheets of filo pastry on top of the nut mixture, brushing each layer with butter as you go. Then spread the remaining nut mixture over the pastry, smoothing it evenly over the entire surface. Top with the remaining sheets of pastry, brushing with butter as before, and liberally brushing the top layer too. Gently press down all around the edges to seal.

5 Using a very sharp knife, mark the top of the baklava into diamonds. Place in the preheated oven and bake for 20–25 minutes, or until golden brown and crisp all over.

6 Meanwhile, make the syrup. Put the sugar, spices and coffee in a small pan and heat gently until the sugar has dissolved – be careful not to burn the sugar as there is a high proportion of it to the liquid. Cover the pan and set aside for 20 minutes, to give the spices time to flavour the syrup.

7 Remove the baklava from the oven. Reheat the syrup over a gentle heat, then strain it evenly over the pastry. Leave to cool in the tin. Set aside for 6 hours or preferably overnight to allow the flavours to mingle. To serve, cut the baklava into diamonds, following the lines scored prior to baking.

> **Variation**
> Try different nuts in the baklava filling if you prefer. Walnuts, pecan nuts and hazelnuts can all be used to great effect.

Rugelach Energy 111Kcal/463kJ; Protein 1g; Carbohydrate 10.4g, of which sugars 7.2g; Fat 7.6g, of which saturates 3.9g; Cholesterol 18mg; Calcium 15mg; Fibre 0.3g; Sodium 47mg.
Baklava Energy 130Kcal/545kJ; Protein 1.6g; Carbohydrate 15.3g, of which sugars 12.8g; Fat 7.4g, of which saturates 2.8g; Cholesterol 10mg; Calcium 22mg; Fibre 0.5g; Sodium 46mg.

Index

NOTES

NOTES

NOTES

NOTES

NOTES

Notes

NOTES

NOTES